IT Essentials: PC Hardware and Software Companion Guide

Fourth Edition

Cisco Networking Academy

Cisco Press

800 East 96th Street

Indianapolis, Indiana 46240 USA

IT Essentials: PC Hardware and Software Companion Guide, Fourth Edition

Cisco Networking Academy

Copyright© 2011 Cisco Systems, Inc.

Published by:
Cisco Press
800 East 96th Street
Indianapolis, IN 46240 USA

Printed in the United States of America

First Printing October 2010

Library of Congress Cataloging-in-Publication data is on file.

ISBN-13: 978-1-58713-263-6

ISBN-10: 1-58713-263-x

This book is part of the Cisco Networking Academy® series from Cisco Press. The products in this series support and complement the Cisco Networking Academy curriculum. If you are using this book outside the Networking Academy, then you are not preparing with a Cisco trained and authorized Networking Academy provider.

For more information on the Cisco Networking Academy or to locate a Networking Academy, Please visit www.cisco.com/edu.

ılıılı,
CISCO.

Warning and Disclaimer

This book is designed to provide information about the Cisco Networking Academy IT Essentials: PC Hardware and Software course. Every effort has been made to make this book as complete and as accurate as possible, but no warranty or fitness is implied.

The information is provided on an "as is" basis. The authors, Cisco Press, and Cisco Systems, Inc. shall have neither liability nor responsibility to any person or entity with respect to any loss or damages arising from the information contained in this book or from the use of the discs or programs that may accompany it.

The opinions expressed in this book belong to the author and are not necessarily those of Cisco Systems, Inc.

Publisher
Paul Boger

Associate Publisher
Dave Dusthimer

Manager, Global Certification
Erik Ullanderson

Business Operation Manager, Cisco Press
Anand Sundaram

Executive Editor
Mary Beth Ray

Managing Editor
Sandra Schroeder

Development Editor
Dayna Isley

Senior Project Editor
Tonya Simpson

Copy Editor
Bill McManus

Technical Editors
Rick McDonald,
William Shurbert

Editorial Assistant
Vanessa Evans

Book Designer
Louisa Adair

Cover Designer
Sandra Schroeder

Composition
Studio Galou, LLC

Indexer
Tim Wright

Proofreader
Sheri Cain

Trademark Acknowledgments

All terms mentioned in this book that are known to be trademarks or service marks have been appropriately cap-italized. Cisco Press or Cisco Systems, Inc., cannot attest to the accuracy of this information. Use of a term in this book should not be regarded as affecting the validity of any trademark or service mark.

Corporate and Government Sales

The publisher offers excellent discounts on this book when ordered in quantity for bulk purchases or special sales, which may include electronic versions and/or custom covers and content particular to your business, training goals, marketing focus, and branding interests. For more information, please contact: **U.S. Corporate and Government Sales**   1-800-382-3419   corpsales@pearsontechgroup.com

For sales outside the United States, please contact: **International Sales**   international@pearsoned.com

Feedback Information

At Cisco Press, our goal is to create in-depth technical books of the highest quality and value. Each book is crafted with care and precision, undergoing rigorous development that involves the unique expertise of members from the professional technical community.

Readers' feedback is a natural continuation of this process. If you have any comments regarding how we could improve the quality of this book, or otherwise alter it to better suit your needs, you can contact us through email at feedback@ciscopress.com. Please make sure to include the book title and ISBN in your message.

We greatly appreciate your assistance.

Americas Headquarters
Cisco Systems, Inc.
170 West Tasman Drive
San Jose, CA 95134-1706
USA
www.cisco.com
Tel: 408 526-4000
800 553-NETS (6387)
Fax: 408 527-0883

Asia Pacific Headquarters
Cisco Systems, Inc.
168 Robinson Road
#28-01 Capital Tower
Singapore 068912
www.cisco.com
Tel: +65 6317 7777
Fax: +65 6317 7799

Europe Headquarters
Cisco Systems International BV
Haarlerbergpark
Haarlerbergweg 13-19
1101 CH Amsterdam
The Netherlands
www-europe.cisco.com
Tel: +31 0 800 020 0791
Fax: +31 0 20 357 1100

Cisco has more than 200 offices worldwide. Addresses, phone numbers, and fax numbers are listed on the Cisco Website at **www.cisco.com/go/offices.**

©2007 Cisco Systems, Inc. All rights reserved. CCVP, the Cisco logo, and the Cisco Square Bridge logo are trademarks of Cisco Systems, Inc.; Changing the Way We Work, Live, Play, and Learn is a service mark of Cisco Systems, Inc.; and Access Registrar, Aironet, BPX, Catalyst, CCDA, CCDP, CCIE, CCIP, CCNA, CCNP, CCSP, Cisco, the Cisco Certified Internetwork Expert logo, Cisco IOS, Cisco Press, Cisco Systems, Cisco Systems Capital, the Cisco Systems logo, Cisco Unity, Enterprise/Solver, EtherChannel, EtherFast, EtherSwitch, Fast Step, Follow Me Browsing, FormShare, GigaDrive, GigaStack, HomeLink, Internet Quotient, IOS, IP/TV, iQ Expertise, the iQ logo, iQ Net Readiness Scorecard, iQuick Study, LightStream, Linksys, MeetingPlace, MGX, Networking Academy, Network Registrar, Packet, PIX, ProConnect, RateMUX, ScriptShare, SlideCast, SMARTnet, StackWise, The Fastest Way to Increase Your Internet Quotient, and TransPath are registered trademarks of Cisco Systems, Inc. and/or its affiliates in the United States and certain other countries.

All other trademarks mentioned in this document or Website are the property of their respective owners. The use of the word partner does not imply a partnership relationship between Cisco and any other company. (0609R)

About the Contributing Editor

Ben Conry (CCNA, CCAI, A+) is the lead instructor for Information Technology Essentials in the Baltimore County Public Schools. He teaches computer repair, networking, and cybersecurity at Sollers Point Technical High School. Conry has been honored for his commitment to educational excellence and for preparing students for college and the work force, and is recognized widely as an authority on the CompTIA A+ exam. He co-authored the Maryland State Department of Education core learning goals for Cisco Academy IT Essentials. Conry holds a master's degree in instructional technology from Johns Hopkins University. He lives in Lutherville, Maryland with his wife, Marisa, and their children, Daniel and Elijah.

About the Technical Reviewers

Rick McDonald teaches computer and networking courses via distance at the University of Alaska Southeast in Ketchikan, Alaska, where he is an associate professor. He holds a BA degree in English and an MA degree in educational technology from Gonzaga University in Spokane, Washington. After several years in the airline industry, he returned to full-time teaching. Rick started in the Cisco Academy in North Carolina and taught CCNA and CCNP courses and was a CCNA instructor trainer. Previous Academy projects include co-authoring *Network Fundamentals, CCNA Exploration Companion Guide*, and co-authoring *Routers and Routing Basics, CCNA 2 Companion Guide*. He also developed CCNP study guides and contributed as a technical editor on a previous edition of the CCNA 2 and 3 textbooks. His current project is developing methods for delivering hands-on training via distance in Alaska using web conferencing and NETLAB tools.

Bill Shurbert is a professor of information technology at NHTI, Concord's Community College, in Concord, New Hampshire. Bill holds a bachelor's degree in technical management from Southern New Hampshire University. He enjoys teaching Cisco CCNA and Wireless networking classes. In his off time, you can find Bill and Joanne, his wife of 28+ years, sailing the waters of Lake Winnipesaukee.

Contents at a Glance

Contents

Command Syntax Conventions

The conventions used to present command syntax in this book are the same conventions used in the IOS Command Reference. The Command Reference describes these conventions as follows:

- **Boldface** indicates commands and keywords that are entered literally as shown. In actual configuration examples and output (not general command syntax), boldface indicates commands that are manually input by the user (such as a **show** command).

- *Italic* indicates arguments for which you supply actual values.

- Vertical bars (|) separate alternative, mutually exclusive elements.

- Square brackets ([ ]) indicate an optional element.

- Braces ({ }) indicate a required choice.

- Braces within brackets ([{ }]) indicate a required choice within an optional element.

Introduction

IT Essentials: PC Hardware and Software Companion Guide, Fourth Edition, is a supplemental book to the Cisco Networking Academy IT Essentials: PC Hardware and Software version 4.1 course. The course teaches you how to build a computer and troubleshoot problems that occur in everyday use. The course is designed to prepare you to take and pass the CompTIA A+ exams (based on the 2009 objectives). By reading and completing this book, you have the opportunity to review all key concepts that the CompTIA A+ exams cover. If you use this book along with its companion *IT Essentials: PC Hardware and Software Lab Manual*, Fourth Edition (ISBN 1-58713-262-1), you can reinforce those concepts with hands-on exercises and test that knowledge with review questions and exercises.

The IT Essentials: PC Hardware and Software course is divided into two main units. The first unit, covered in Chapters 1 through 10, goes over the foundational knowledge that aligns with the CompTIA A+ Essentials exam (220-701). The second unit, covered in Chapters 11 through 16, explores more advanced concepts in greater depth to prepare you for the CompTIA A+ Practical Application exam (220-702). You must pass both exams to earn the CompTIA A+ certification.

The course and book also align with the objectives in the first three modules of the EUCIP IT Administrator certification (www.eucip.org): Module 1, PC Hardware; Module 2, Operating Systems; and Module 3, Local Area Network and Network Services.

Who Should Read This Book

This book is intended for students in the Cisco Networking Academy IT Essentials: PC Hardware and Software version 4.1 course. This student typically is pursuing a career in information technology (IT) or wants to have the knowledge of how a computer works, how to assemble a computer, and how to troubleshoot hardware and software issues.

Book Features

The features in this book facilitate an understanding of computer systems and troubleshooting system problems. The highlights of each chapter are as follows:

- **Objectives**: Each chapter starts with a list of objectives that should be mastered by the end of the chapter. The objectives are framed as focus questions addressing the concepts covered in the chapter.

- **Key terms**: Each chapter includes a list of the key terms identified in the chapter, listed in the order in which they appear in the chapter. These terms serve as a study aid and are defined in the book's glossary. The key terms reinforce the concepts introduced in the chapter and help you understand the chapter material before you move on to new concepts. You can find the key terms highlighted in blue throughout the chapter, in the context in which they are most important.

- **Explanatory text, lists, figures, and tables**: This book contains figures, procedures, and tables to accompany the thorough text explanations of the objective content and to help explain and visualize theories, concepts, commands, and setup sequences.

- **Chapter summaries**: At the end of each chapter is a summary of the concepts covered in the chapter. The summary provides a synopsis of the chapter and serves as a study aid.

- **Lab, Worksheet, and Class Discussion references**: There are references to the Labs, Worksheets, and Class Discussion exercises that can be found in the accompanying *IT Essentials: PC Hardware and Software Lab Manual*, Fourth Edition (ISBN 1-58713-262-1).

- **Virtual Desktop Activity and Virtual Laptop Activity references**: Designed and developed by the Cisco Networking Academy, these activities, found on the accompanying CD-ROM, are virtual learning tools to help you develop critical thinking and complex problem-solving skills.

- **Packet Tracer activities**: New for this edition, Cisco Packet Tracer simulation-based learning activity files on the accompanying CD-ROM promote the exploration of networking and network security concepts and enable you to experiment with network behavior. (Note: the Packet Tracer software is not included with this CD. Ask your instructor for access to Packet Tracer.)

- **"Check Your Understanding" review questions**: Review questions are presented at the end of each chapter to serve as an assessment. In addition, the questions reinforce the concepts introduced in the chapter and help test your understanding before you move on to subsequent chapters. Answers to the questions are available in the Appendix.

- **CD-ROM**: The CD-ROM that accompanies this book contains all the Virtual Desktop activities, Virtual Laptop activities, and Packet Tracer activities referenced throughout the book. These are standalone tools designed by Cisco to supplement classroom learning by providing a virtual "hands-on" experience where real equipment is limited.

How This Book Is Organized

This book corresponds closely to the Cisco IT Essentials Course and is divided into 16 chapters, one appendix, and a glossary of key terms:

- **Chapter 1, "Introduction to the Personal Computer"**: Information technology (IT) is the design, development, implementation, support, and management of computer hardware and software applications. An IT professional is knowledgeable about computer systems and operating systems. This chapter reviews IT certifications and the components of a basic personal computer system.

- **Chapter 2, "Safe Lab Procedures and Tool Use"**: This chapter covers basic safety practices for the workplace, hardware and software tools, and the disposal of hazardous materials. Safety guidelines help protect individuals from accidents and injury and protect equipment from damage. Some of these guidelines are designed to protect the environment from contamination by discarded materials. Stay alert to situations that could result in injury or damage to equipment. Warning signs are designed to alert you to danger. Always watch for these signs and take the appropriate action according to the warning given.

- **Chapter 3, "Computer Assembly—Step by Step"**: This chapter describes the assembly of a PC. The first step in the assembly process is gathering the components and completing the computer inventory. Preparing and installing the components are detailed in a step-by-step process. In the final steps, you review the checklist, assemble the case, and boot the system for the first time. Assembling computers is a large part of a technician's job. As a technician, you will need to work in a logical, methodical manner when working with computer components. As with any learned trade, computer assembly skills will improve dramatically with practice.

- **Chapter 4, "Basics of Preventive Maintenance and Troubleshooting"**: This chapter introduces preventive maintenance and the troubleshooting process. Preventive maintenance is a regular and systematic inspection, cleaning, and replacement of worn parts, materials, and systems. Preventive maintenance helps to prevent failure of parts, materials, and systems by ensuring that they are in good working order. Troubleshooting is a systematic approach to locating the cause of a fault in a computer system. A good preventive maintenance program helps minimize failures. With fewer failures, there is less troubleshooting to do, thus saving an organization time and money.

- **Chapter 5, "Fundamental Operating Systems"**: The operating system (OS) controls almost all functions on a computer. In this chapter, you learn about the components, functions, and terminology related to the Windows 2000, Windows XP, Windows Vista, and Widows 7 operating systems.

- **Chapter 6, "Fundamental Laptops and Portable Devices"**: Laptops, personal digital assistants (PDA), and smartphones are becoming more popular as their prices decrease and technology continues to progress. As a computer technician, you need to have knowledge of portable devices of all kinds. This chapter focuses on the differences between laptops and desktops and describes the features of PDAs and smartphones.

- **Chapter 7, "Fundamental Printers and Scanners"**: This chapter provides essential information about printers and scanners. You learn how printers operate, what to consider when purchasing a printer, and how to connect printers to an individual computer or to a network. You must understand the operation of various types of printers and scanners to be able to install and maintain them, as well as troubleshoot any problems that might arise.

- **Chapter 8, "Fundamental Networks"**: This chapter provides an overview of network principles, standards, and purposes. The different types of network topologies, protocols, and logical models, as well as the hardware needed to create a network, are also discussed in this chapter. Configuration, troubleshooting, and preventive maintenance are covered. You also learn about network software, communication methods, and hardware relationships.

- **Chapter 9, "Fundamental Security"**: Technicians need to understand computer and network security. Failure to implement proper security procedures can have an impact on users, computers, and the general public. Private information, company secrets, financial data, computer equipment, and items of national security are placed at risk if proper security procedures are not followed. This chapter covers why security is important, security threats, security procedures, and how to troubleshoot security issues.

- **Chapter 10, "Communication Skills"**: As a computer technician, you not only fix computers but also interact with people. In fact, troubleshooting is as much about communicating with the customer as it is about knowing how to fix a computer. In this chapter, you learn to use good communication skills as confidently as you use a screwdriver.

- **Chapter 11, "Advanced Personal Computers"**: In your career as a technician, you might have to determine whether a component for a customer's computer should be upgraded or replaced. It is important that you develop advanced skills in installation procedures, troubleshooting techniques, and diagnostic methods for computers. This chapter discusses the importance of component compatibility across hardware and software. It also covers the need for adequate system resources to efficiently run the customer's hardware and software.

- **Chapter 12, "Advanced Operating Systems"**: The installation, configuration, and optimization of operating systems are examined in greater detail in this chapter. There are various brands of operating systems on the market today, including Microsoft Windows, Apple Mac OS X, UNIX, and Linux. A technician must consider the current computer system when selecting an operating system. Each of these operating systems offers many of the same features with a similar interface. However, some functions necessary for specific customer needs might not be available in all of them. You must be able to compare and contrast operating systems to find the best one based on your customer's needs.

- **Chapter 13, "Advanced Laptops and Portable Devices"**: This chapter covers laptop and portable devices more in depth. With the increase in demand for mobility, the popularity of laptops and portable devices will continue to grow. During the course of your career, you will be expected to know how to configure, repair, and maintain these devices. The knowledge you acquire about desktop computers will help you service laptops and portable devices. However, there are important differences between the two technologies.

- **Chapter 14, "Advanced Printers and Scanners"**: This chapter explores the functionality of printers and scanners. You learn how to maintain, install, and repair these devices in both local and network configurations. The chapter discusses safety hazards, configuration procedures, preventive maintenance, and printer and scanner sharing.

- **Chapter 15, "Advanced Networks"**: This chapter focuses on advanced networking topics, including network design, network component upgrades, and email server installations. Basic networking topics such as safety, network components, and preventive maintenance are also discussed.

- **Chapter 16, "Advanced Security"**: This chapter reviews the types of attacks that threaten the security of computers and the data contained on them. A technician is responsible for the security of data and computer equipment in an organization. The chapter describes how you can work with customers to ensure that the best possible protection is in place.

- **Appendix, "Answers to Check Your Understanding Questions"**: This appendix lists the answers to the "Check Your Understanding" review questions that are included at the end of each chapter.

- **Glossary**: The glossary provides you with definitions for all the key terms identified in each chapter.

About the CompTIA A+ Certification

As a CompTIA Authorized Quality Curriculum, IT Essentials: PC Hardware and Software v4.1 will help prepare you for the new CompTIA A+ Essentials and Practical Applications certification exams. To become A+ certified, you need to pass two exams to become certified in your chosen career area:

- CompTIA A+ Essentials (220-701)

- CompTIA A+ Practical Application (220-702)

After becoming certified, you will be qualified to work as a computer support professional and technician in a variety of work environments and industries.

The CompTIA A+ exam is explained in detail, including a list of the objectives, at the following website:

www.comptia.org/certifications/listed/a.aspx

When you are ready to take the exam, you must purchase and schedule your two CompTIA A+ exams. The necessary information to accomplish this can be found at the following website:

http://certification.comptia.org/resources/registration.aspx

CHAPTER 1

Introduction to the Personal Computer

Objectives

Upon completion of this chapter, you should be able to answer the following questions:

- What are IT industry certifications?

- What is a computer system?

- How can I identify the names, purposes, and characteristics of cases and power supplies?

- What are the names, purposes, and characteristics of internal components?

- What are the names, purposes, and characteristics of ports and cables?

- How can I identify the names, purposes, and characteristics of input devices?

- How can I identify the names, purposes, and characteristics of output devices?

- What are system resources and their purposes?

Key Terms

This chapter uses the following key terms. You can find the definitions in the Glossary.

continues

Information technology (IT) is the design, development, implementation, support, and management of computer hardware and software applications. An IT professional is knowledgeable about computer systems and operating systems. This chapter will review IT certifications and the components of a basic personal computer system.

After completing this chapter, you will meet these objectives:

- Explain IT industry certifications.
- Describe a computer system.
- Identify the names, purposes, and characteristics of cases and power supplies.
- Identify the names, purposes, and characteristics of internal components.
- Identify the names, purposes, and characteristics of ports and cables.
- Identify the names, purposes, and characteristics of input devices.
- Identify the names, purposes, and characteristics of output devices.
- Explain system resources and their purposes.

Explain IT Industry Certifications

This course will focus on desktop and laptop computers. It will also discuss electronic devices, such as personal digital assistants and cell phones.

Training and experience will qualify a technician to service these computers and personal electronic devices. You will gain the specialized technical skills needed to install, maintain, and repair computers. Earning an industry-standard *certification* will give you confidence and increase your opportunities in IT.

This course is focused on the following two industry-standard certifications:

- CompTIA A+
- European Certification of Informatics Professionals (EUCIP) IT Administrator certification (Modules 1 and 2)

After completing this section, you will meet these objectives:

- Identify education and certifications.
- Describe the A+ certification.
- Describe the EUCIP certification.

Identify Education and Certifications

Information technology (IT) is a term that encompasses the relationship between hardware, software, networks, and technical assistance provided to users. The IT Essentials: PC Hardware and Software course covers the information that a technician needs to understand to be successful in IT. This course covers the following topics:

- Personal computers

- Safe lab procedures

- Troubleshooting

- Operating systems

- Laptop computers

- Printers and scanners

- Networks

- Security

- Communication skills

The IT Essentials course focuses on two hardware and software skills-based industry certifications: CompTIA A+ and EUCIP. This course is only an introduction into the world of IT. A technician may continue to study and earn the following certifications:

- CCENT: Cisco Certified Entry Network Technician

- CCNA: Cisco Certified Network Associate

- CCNP: Cisco Certified Network Professional

- CCIE: Cisco Certified Internetwork Expert

- CISSP: $(ISC)^2$ Certified Information Systems Security Professional

- MCP: Microsoft Certified Professional

- MCSA: Microsoft Certified Systems Administrator

- MCSE: Microsoft Certified Systems Engineer

- Network+: CompTIA Network certification

- Linux+: CompTIA Linux certification

- EUCIP: European Certification of Informatics Professionals

In some cases, IT certifications can be used as credits for university and college toward degrees in areas such as computer science and telecommunications.

Describe the A+ Certification

Computing Technology Industry Association (CompTIA) developed the A+ certification program. A CompTIA A+ certification signifies that a candidate is a qualified PC hardware and software technician. CompTIA certifications are known throughout the IT community as one of the best ways to enter the IT field and build a solid career.

The latest version of CompTIA A+ is CompTIA A+ 2009 Edition. Two exams are necessary to be certified: CompTIA A+ Essentials, exam code 220-701; and CompTIA A+ Practical Application, exam code 220-702.

CompTIA A+ Essentials measures the necessary competencies of an entry-level IT professional with at least 500 hours of hands-on experience in the lab or field. It tests for the fundamentals of computer technology, networking and security, and the communication skills and professionalism now required of all entry-level IT professionals.

CompTIA A+ Practical Application is an extension of the knowledge and skills identified in CompTIA A+ Essentials, with more of a hands-on orientation focused on scenarios in which troubleshooting and tools must be applied to resolve problems.

Describe the EUCIP Certification

The EUCIP IT Administrator program offers a recognized certification of competence in IT. The certification covers the standards prescribed by the Council of European Professional Informatics Societies (CEPIS). The EUCIP IT Administrator certification consists of five modules, with a corresponding exam for each module. This course will prepare you for Modules 1 and 2.

Module 1: PC Hardware

The PC Hardware module requires that the candidate understand the basic makeup of a personal computer and the functions of the components. The candidate should be able to effectively diagnose and repair hardware problems. The candidate should be able to advise customers of the appropriate hardware to buy.

Module 2: Operating Systems

The Operating Systems module requires that the candidate be familiar with the procedures for installing and updating most common operating systems and applications. The candidate should know how to use system tools for troubleshooting and repairing operating systems.

Module 3: Local Area Network and Network Services

This module is beyond the scope of the IT Essentials course, although some of the topics are covered. The Local Area Network and Network Services module requires that the candidate be familiar with the procedure of installing, using, and managing LANs. The candidate should be able to add and remove users and shared resources. The candidate should know how to use system tools for troubleshooting and repairing networks.

Module 4: Expert Network Use

This module is beyond the scope of the IT Essentials course, although some of the topics are covered. The Expert Network Use module requires that the candidate understand LAN communication.

Module 5: IT Security

This module is beyond the scope of the IT Essentials course, although some of the topics are covered. The IT Security module requires that the candidate be familiar with security methods and features that are available for a standalone or networked computer.

Worksheet 1.1.2: Job Opportunities

In this activity, you use the Internet, magazines, or a local newspaper to gather information on jobs in the computer service and repair field. Be prepared to discuss your research with the class. Refer to the worksheet in *IT Essentials: PC Hardware and Software Lab Manual, Fourth Edition*. You may complete this worksheet now or wait to do so until the end of the chapter.

Describe a Computer System

A computer system consists of hardware and software components. *Hardware* is the physical equipment such as the case, storage drives, keyboards, monitors, cables, speakers, and printers. The term *software* includes the operating system and programs. The operating system instructs the computer how to operate. These operations may include identifying, accessing, and processing information. Programs or applications perform different functions. Programs vary widely depending on the type of information that will be accessed or generated. For example, instructions for balancing a checkbook are very different from instructions for simulating a virtual-reality world on the Internet.

The rest of this chapter discusses the hardware components found in a computer system.

Identify the Names, Purposes, and Characteristics of Cases and Power Supplies

The computer case provides protection and support for the internal components of the computer. All computers need a power supply to convert alternating-current (AC) power from the wall socket into direct-current (DC) power. The size and shape of the computer case is usually determined by the motherboard and other internal components.

You can select a large computer case to accommodate additional components that may be required in the future. Other users may select a smaller case that requires minimal space. In general, the computer case should be durable, be easy to service, and have enough room for expansion.

The power supply must provide enough power for the components that are currently installed and allow for additional components that may be added at a later time. If you choose a power supply that powers only the current components, it may be necessary to replace the power supply when other components are upgraded.

After completing this section, you will meet these objectives:

- Describe cases.
- Describe power supplies.

Describe Cases

A computer case contains the framework to support the internal components of a computer while providing an enclosure for added protection. Computer cases are typically made of plastic, steel, and aluminum and are available in a variety of styles.

The size and layout of a case is called a form factor. There are many types of cases, but the basic form factors for computer cases include desktop and tower. Desktop cases may be slimline or full-sized, and tower cases may be mini or full-sized, as shown in Figure 1-1.

Figure 1-1   Tower Cases

Computer cases are referred to in a number of ways:

- Computer chassis
- Cabinet
- Tower
- Box
- Housing

In addition to providing protection and support, cases also provide an environment designed to keep the internal components cool. Case fans are used to move air through the computer case. As the air passes warm components, it absorbs heat and then exits the case. This process keeps the components of the computer from overheating.

You must consider many factors when choosing a case:

- The size of the motherboard
- The number of external or internal drive locations, called bays
- Available space

In addition to providing protection from the environment, cases help to prevent damage from static electricity. Internal components of the computer are grounded by attachment to the case.

Note

You should select a case that matches the physical dimensions of the power supply and motherboard.

Describe Power Supplies

The power supply, an example of which is shown in Figure 1-2, converts AC power coming from a wall outlet into DC power, which is a lower voltage. DC power is required for all of the components inside the computer.

Figure 1-2   Power Supply

Connectors

Most connectors today are keyed connectors. Keyed connectors are designed to be inserted in only one direction. Each part of the connector has a colored wire with a different voltage running through it, as described in Table 1-1.

Table 1-1   Power Color Codes

Voltage	Wire Color	Use
+12 V	Yellow	Disk drive motors, fans, cooling devices, and system bus slots
+5 V	Red	Motherboard, early processors, many motherboard components
+3.3 V	Orange	Modern CPU and AGP video cards
0 V	Black	Ground, the return loop for circuits
–5 V	White	ISA expansion slots and early PROMs
–12 V	Blue	Some serial ports and early PROMs

Note

AT power supplies did not have 3.3 volts and used a mechanical switch. The BIOS and OS could not control the power supply through the Advanced Configuration and Power Interface (ACPI).

Caution

The black wires in the PC are the electrical ground. They are essentially harmless. Do not assume the black wires in AC electrical systems (in the walls and ceilings) are ground. They are not. The black wires in an AC system are normally the "hot" or energized wire and if mishandled could kill you.

Different connectors are used to connect specific components to various ports on the motherboard:

- A Molex connector is a keyed connector used to connect to an optical drive or a hard drive.

- A Berg connector is a keyed connector used to connect to a floppy drive. A Berg connector is smaller than a Molex connector.

- A 20-pin or 24-pin slotted connector is used to connect to the motherboard. The 24-pin slotted connector has two rows of 12 pins each, and the 20-pin slotted connector has two rows of 10 pins each.

- A 4-pin to 8-pin auxiliary power connector has two rows of two to four pins and supplies power to all areas of the motherboard. The 4-pin to 8-pin auxiliary power connector is the same shape as the main power connector, but smaller.

- Older standard power supplies used two connectors called P8 and P9 to connect to the motherboard. P8 and P9 were unkeyed connectors. They could be installed backward, potentially damaging the motherboard or power supply. The installation required the connectors to be lined up with the black wires together in the middle.

Note

If you have a difficult time inserting a connector, try a different way, or check to make sure that there are no bent pins or foreign objects in the way. Remember, if it seems difficult to plug in any cable or other part, something is wrong. Cables, connectors, and components are designed to fit together snugly. Never force any connector or component. The connectors that are plugged in incorrectly will damage the plug and the connector. Take your time and make sure that you are handling the hardware correctly.

Electricity and Ohm's Law

These are the four basic units of electricity:

- **Voltage (V):** Voltage is a measure of the force required to push electrons through a circuit. Voltage is measured in volts (V). A computer power supply usually produces several different voltages.

- **Current (I):** Current is a measure of the amount of electrons going through a circuit. Current is measured in amperes, or amps (A). Computer power supplies deliver different amperages for each output voltage.

- **Power (P)**: Power is a measure of the pressure required to push electrons through a circuit, called voltage, multiplied by the number of electrons going through that circuit, called current. The measurement is called watts (W). Computer power supplies are rated in watts.

- **Resistance (R):** Resistance is the opposition to the flow of current in a circuit. Resistance is measured in ohms. Lower resistance allows more current, and therefore more power, to flow through a circuit. A good fuse will have low resistance or a measurement of almost 0 ohms.

A basic equation expresses how three of the terms relate to each other. It states that voltage is equal to the current multiplied by the resistance. This is known as *Ohm's Law*:

$$V = IR$$

In an electrical system, power (P) is equal to the voltage multiplied by the current:

$$P = VI$$

In an electrical circuit, increasing the current or the voltage will result in higher power.

As an example of how this works, imagine a simple circuit that has a 9-V light bulb hooked up to a 9-V battery. The power output of the light bulb is 100 W. Using the preceding equation, we can calculate how much current in amps would be required to get 100 W out of this 9-V light bulb.

To solve this equation, we know the following information:

$$P = 100 \text{ W}$$

$$V = 9 \text{ V}$$

$$I = 100 \text{ W} / 9 \text{ V} = 11.11 \text{ A}$$

What happens if a 12-V battery and a 12-V light bulb are used to get 100 W of power?

$$100 \text{ W} / 12 \text{ V} = 8.33 \text{ A}$$

This system produces the same power, but with less current.

Computers normally use power supplies ranging from 250-W to 650-W output capacity. However, some computers may need 850-W and higher-capacity power supplies. When building a computer, select a power supply with sufficient wattage to power all of the components. Each component inside the computer uses a certain amount of power. Obtain the wattage information for the components from the manufacturer's documentation. When deciding on a power supply, make sure to choose a power supply that has more than enough power for the current components. A power supply with a higher wattage rating has more capacity; therefore, it can handle more devices.

On the back of the power supply is a small switch called the voltage selector switch. This switch sets the input voltage to the power supply to either 110 V to 115 V or 220 V to 230 V. The correct voltage setting is determined by the country where the power supply will be used. Setting the voltage switch to the incorrect input voltage could damage the power supply and other parts of your computer. If a power supply does not have the voltage selector switch, your power supply will automatically detect and set the correct voltage.

Caution

Do not open a power supply. Electronic capacitors located inside of a power supply can hold a charge for extended periods of time even when unplugged from the wall. The power supply is considered to be a *field replaceable unit (FRU)*, which means that if it no longer works, don't fix it, but instead replace it.

Identify the Names, Purposes, and Characteristics of Internal Components

This section discusses the names, purposes, and characteristics of the internal components of a computer, as shown in Figure 1-3.

Figure 1-3   Computer Components

After completing this section, you will meet these objectives:

- Identify the names, purposes, and characteristics of motherboards.
- Explain the names, purposes, and characteristics of CPUs.
- Identify the names, purposes, and characteristics of cooling systems.
- Identify the names, purposes, and characteristics of ROM and RAM.
- Identify the names, purposes, and characteristics of adapter cards.

- Identify the names, purposes, and characteristics of storage drives.

- Identify the names, purposes, and characteristics of internal cables.

Identify the Names, Purposes, and Characteristics of Motherboards

The motherboard is the main printed circuit board and contains the buses, or electrical pathways, found in a computer. These buses allow data to travel between the various components that comprise a computer. Figure 1-4 shows a variety of motherboards. A motherboard is also known as the system board, the backplane, or the main board.

Figure 1-4   Motherboards

The motherboard accommodates the central processing unit (CPU), RAM, expansion slots, heat sink/fan assembly, BIOS chip, chipset, and the embedded wires that interconnect the motherboard components. Sockets, internal and external connectors, and various ports are also placed on the motherboard.

The form factor of motherboards pertains to the size and shape of the board. It also describes the physical layout of the different components and devices on the motherboard. The form factor determines how individual components attach to the motherboard and the shape of the computer case. Various form factors exist for motherboards, as shown in Figure 1-4.

The most common form factor in desktop computers was the AT, based on the IBM AT motherboard. The AT motherboard can be up to approximately one foot wide. This cumbersome size led to the development of smaller form factors. The placement of heat sinks and fans often interferes with the use of expansion slots in smaller form factors.

A newer motherboard form factor, ATX, improved on the AT design. The ATX case is designed to accommodate the integrated I/O ports on the ATX motherboard. The ATX power supply connects to the motherboard via a single 20-pin connector instead of the confusing P8 and P9 connectors used with some earlier form factors. Instead of using a physical toggle switch, the ATX power supply can be powered on and off using signaling from the motherboard.

Some manufacturers have proprietary form factors based on the ATX design. This causes some motherboards, power supplies, and other components to be incompatible with standard ATX cases.

An important set of components on the motherboard is the chipset. The chipset is composed of various integrated circuits attached to the motherboard that control how system hardware interacts with the CPU and motherboard. The CPU is installed into a slot or socket on the motherboard. The socket on the motherboard determines the type of CPU that can be installed.

The chipset of a motherboard allows the CPU to communicate and interact with the other components of the computer, and to exchange data with system memory, or RAM, hard disk drives, video cards, and other output devices. The chipset establishes how much memory can be added to a motherboard. The chipset also determines the type of connectors on the motherboard.

Most chipsets are divided into two distinct components: Northbridge and Southbridge. What each component does varies from manufacturer to manufacturer. In general, the Northbridge controls access to the RAM, video card, and the speeds at which the CPU can communicate with them. The video card is sometimes integrated into the Northbridge. AMD and Intel have chips that integrate the memory controller onto the CPU die, which improves performance and power consumption. The Southbridge, in most cases, allows the CPU to communicate with the hard drives, sound card, USB ports, and other I/O ports.

Identify the Names, Purposes, and Characteristics of CPUs

The *central processing unit (CPU)* is considered the brain of the computer. It is sometimes referred to as the processor. Most calculations take place in the CPU. In terms of computing power, the CPU is the most important element of a computer system. CPUs come in different form factors, each style requiring a particular slot or socket on the motherboard. Common CPU manufacturers include Intel and AMD.

The CPU socket or slot is the connector that interfaces between the motherboard and the processor. Most CPU sockets and processors in use today are built around the pin grid array (PGA) architecture, in which the pins on the underside of the processor are inserted into the socket, usually with Zero-Insertion Force (ZIF). ZIF refers to the amount of force needed to install a CPU into the motherboard socket or slot. Slot-based processors are cartridge-shaped and fit into a slot that looks similar to an expansion slot. Table 1-2 is a list of 486-class sockets and CPUs.

The arrangement of the CPU pins is called a pin grid array (PGA). There are many variations of PGAs. Staggered Pin Grid Array (SPGA) shifts alternating rows to create a zig-zag pattern. To conserve space a mobile socket called mPGA was developed. An older name for these CPU sockets was Plastic PGA or PPGA, although that term is seldom used today. Some newer sockets do not use pins. A Land Grid Array (LGA) uses contacts instead of pins. Other terms used to describe CPUs include DX, which introduced the floating-point decimal capability, and Overdrive (OD), a marketing term used to describe a slightly faster version of CPU.

Table 1-2   CPU Socket Specifications: Intel/AMD 486 Class

Socket	Pins	Layout	Supported CPUs
Socket 1	169	17x17 PGA	486 SX/SX2, DX/DX2, DX4 OD
Socket 2	238	19x19 PGA	486 SX/SX2, DX/DX2, DX4 OD, 486 Pentium OD
Socket 3	237	19x19 PGA	486 SX/SX2, DX/DX2, DX4, 486 Pentium OD, AMD 5x86
Socket 6	235	19x19 PGA	486 DX4, 486 Pentium OD

Note

Sockets 1–4 used 5-V DC. As CPUs became more efficient, 3.3-V DC was used in Sockets 3–5. All other CPUs since around 1995 use Auto VRM, which allows the BIOS to control the voltage to the CPU.

Table 1-3 outlines the Intel Pentium and AMD class sockets and CPUs.

Table 1-3   CPU Socket Specifications: Intel/AMD 586 (Pentium), and Cyrix M1/11 Classes

Socket	Pins	Layout	Supported CPUs
Socket 4	273	21x21 PGA	Pentium 60/66, OD
Socket 5	320	37x37 SPGA	Pentium 75–133, OD
Socket 7	321	37x37 SPGA	Pentium 75–233+, MMX, OD, AMD K5/K6, Cyrix M1/ll

Table 1-4 is a list of 686-class sockets and CPUs.

Table 1-4   CPU Socket Specifications: Intel/AMD 686 (Pentium II/III) Class

Socket	Pins	Layout	Supported CPUs
Socket 8	387	Dual-pattern SPGA	Pentium Pro, OD
Slot 1 (SC242)	242	Slot	Pentium II/III, Celeron SECC
Socket 370	370	37x37 SPGA	Celeron/Pentium III PPGA/FC-PGA

Table 1-5 is a list of Pentium 4–class sockets and CPUs.

Table 1-5   CPU Socket Specifications: Pentium 4 Class

Socket	Pins	Layout	Supported CPUs
Socket 423	423	39x39 SPGA	Pentium 4 FC-PGA
Socket 478	478	26x26m PGA	Pentium 4/Celeron FC-PGA2
Socket T (LGA775)	775	30x33 LGA	Pentium 4/Celeron LGA775

Table 1-6 is a list of AMD K7–class sockets and CPUs.

Table 1-6   CPU Socket Specifications: AMD K7 Class

Socket	Pins	Layout	Supported CPUs
Slot A	242	Slot	AMD Athlon SECC
Socket A (462)	462	37x37 SPGA	AMD Athlon/Athlon XP/Duron PGA/FC-PGA

Table 1-7 is a list of AMD K8 sockets and CPUs.

Table 1-7   CPU Socket Specifications: AMD K8

Socket	Pins	Layout	Supported CPUs
Socket 754	754	29x29 mPGA	AMD Athlon 64
Socket 939	939	31x31 mPGA	AMD Athlon 64 v.2
Socket 940	940	31x31 mPGA	AMD Athlon 64FX, Opteron

Table 1-8 is a list of Intel/AMD server- and workstation-class sockets and CPUs.

Table 1-8   CPU Socket Specifications: Intel/AMD Server and Workstation Class

Socket	Pins	Layout	Supported CPUs
Slot 2	330	Slot	Pentium II/III Xeon
Socket 603	603	31x25 mPGA	Xeon (P4)
PAC 418 Socket	611	25x28 mPGA	Itanium 2
PAC 611 Socket 940	940	31x31 mPGA	AMD Athlon 64FX, Opteron
LGA 771 Socket J	771	LGA Extreme	Dual- and Quad-Core Xeon, Core
LGA 775 Socket T	775	LGA	Pentium 4, D Extreme Edition, and Dual-Core, Celeron, Core2 Duo, Extreme, and Quad, Xeon
LGA 1156 Socket H	1156	LGA	Pentium, Core i3, i5, i7, Xeon
LGA 1366 Socket B	1366	LGA	I7 and Xeon
Socket F	1207	LGA	Athlon 64, FX, and Opteron
AM2	940	31x31 PGA	Athlon 64, X2, FX, Opteron, Sempron, and Phenom
AM2+	940	31x31 PGA	Athlon 64, X2, Opteron, and Phenom
AM3	941	31x31 PGA	Athlon II, Phenom II, Opteron, and Sempron

The CPU executes a program, which is a sequence of stored instructions. Each model of processor has an instruction set, which it executes. The CPU executes the program by processing each piece of data as directed by the program and the instruction set. While the CPU is executing one step of the program, the remaining instructions and the data are stored nearby in a special memory called *cache*. There are two major CPU architectures related to instruction sets:

- *Reduced Instruction Set Computer (RISC)*: Architectures use a relatively small set of instructions, and RISC chips are designed to execute these instructions very rapidly.

- *Complex Instruction Set Computer (CISC)*: Architectures use a broad set of instructions, resulting in fewer steps per operation.

Some CPUs incorporate *hyperthreading* to enhance the performance of the CPU. With hyperthreading, the CPU has multiple pieces of code being executed simultaneously on each pipeline. To an operating system, a single CPU with hyperthreading performs as though there are two CPUs.

The power of a CPU is measured by the speed and the amount of data that it can process. The speed of a CPU is rated in cycles per second. The speed of current CPUs is measured in millions of cycles per second, called megahertz (MHz), or billions of cycles per second, called gigahertz (GHz). The amount of data that a CPU can process at one time depends on the size of the processor data bus. This is also called the CPU bus or the front-side bus (FSB). The wider the processor data bus width, the more powerful the processor is. Current processors have a 32-bit or a 64-bit processor data bus. 32-bit processors as a group is often called x86. 64-bit processors are often called x64. The distinction is important because operating systems and applications are identified either x86 or x64.

Overclocking is a technique used to make a processor work at a faster speed than its original specification. Overclocking is not a reliable way to improve computer performance and can result in damage to the CPU. The opposite of overclocking is CPU throttling. CPU throttling is a technique used when the processor runs at less than the rated speed to conserve power or produce less heat. Throttling is commonly used on laptops and other mobile devices.

MMX is a set of multimedia instructions built into Intel processors. MMX-enabled microprocessors can handle many common multimedia operations that are normally handled by a separate sound or video card. However, only software specifically written to call MMX instructions can use the MMX instruction set. In Intel CPUs, MMX has been replaced by Streaming SIMD [single instruction, multiple data] Extensions (SSE), which is an enhancement to the instruction set. There are many versions of SSE, each of which includes additional instructions.

The latest processor technology has resulted in CPU manufacturers finding ways to incorporate more than one CPU core onto a single chip. These CPUs are capable of processing multiple instructions concurrently:

- *Single-core CPU*: One core inside a single CPU that handles all of the processing capability. A motherboard manufacturer may provide sockets for more than one single processor, providing the ability to build a powerful, multiprocessor computer.

- *Dual-core CPU*: Two cores inside a single CPU in which both cores can process information at the same time.

- **Triple-core CPU**: Three cores inside a single CPU that is actually a quad-core processor with one of the cores disabled.

- **Quad-core CPU**: Four cores inside a single CPU in which all cores can process information simultaneously for enhanced software applications.

Identify the Names, Purposes, and Characteristics of Cooling Systems

Electronic components generate heat. Heat is caused by the flow of current within the components. Computer components perform better when kept cool. If the heat is not removed, the computer may run slower. If too much heat builds up, computer components can be damaged.

Increasing the air flow in the computer case allows more heat to be removed. A case fan, shown in Figure 1-5, is installed in the computer case to make the cooling process more efficient.

Figure 1-5   Case Fan

In addition to case fans, a heat sink draws heat away from the core of the CPU. A fan on top of the heat sink, shown in Figure 1-6, moves the heat away from the CPU.

Figure 1-6   CPU Fans

Other components are also susceptible to heat damage and are sometimes equipped with fans. Video adapter cards also produce a great deal of heat. Fans are dedicated to cool the graphics-processing unit (GPU), as shown in Figure 1-7.

Figure 1-7   Graphics Card Cooling System

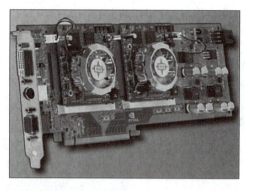

Computers with extremely fast CPUs and GPUs may use a water-cooling system. A metal plate is placed over the processor and water is pumped over the top to collect the heat that the CPU creates. The water is pumped to a radiator to be cooled by the air, and then recirculated.

Identify the Names, Purposes, and Characteristics of ROM and RAM

ROM and RAM provide memory for a vast amount of computer equipment. They come in different memory sizes and module sizes and have different features. RAM chips are stored on memory modules that can easily be installed and removed to expedite upgrades. Some RAM uses parity to increase data integrity and reliability. Another kind of specialized memory is called cache. It stores frequently used data and commands. The following sections cover ROM, RAM, modules, parity, and cache in greater detail.

ROM

Read-only memory (ROM) chips are located on the motherboard. ROM chips contain instructions that the CPU can access directly. ROM stores basic instructions for booting the computer and loading the operating system. ROM chips retain their contents even when the computer is powered down. The contents cannot be erased, changed, or rewritten by normal means. ROM types include the following:

- *Programmable read-only memory (PROM)*: Information is written to a PROM chip after it is manufactured. A PROM chip cannot be erased or rewritten.

- *Erasable programmable read-only memory (EPROM)*: Information is written to an EPROM chip after it is manufactured. An EPROM chip can be erased with exposure to UV light. Special equipment is required.

- *Electrically erasable programmable read-only memory (EEPROM)*: Information is written to an EEPROM chip after it is manufactured. EEPROM chips are also called flash ROMs. An EEPROM chip can be erased and rewritten without removing the chip from the computer.

Note

ROM is sometimes called firmware. This is misleading, because firmware is actually the software that is stored in a ROM chip.

RAM

Random-access memory (RAM) is the temporary storage for data and programs that are being accessed by the CPU. RAM is volatile memory, which means that the contents are erased when the computer is powered off. The more RAM in a computer, the more capacity the computer has to hold and process large programs and files. The different types of RAM are as follows:

- *Dynamic RAM (DRAM)* is a memory chip that is used as main memory. DRAM must be constantly refreshed with pulses of electricity to maintain the data stored in the chip.

- *Static RAM (SRAM)* is a memory chip that is used as cache memory. SRAM is much faster than DRAM and does not have to be refreshed as often.

- *Fast Page Mode (FPM)* DRAM is memory that supports paging. Paging enables faster access to the data than regular DRAM. Most 486 and Pentium systems from 1995 and earlier use FPM memory.

- *Extended Data Out (EDO)* RAM is memory that overlaps consecutive data accesses. This speeds up the access time to retrieve data from memory because the CPU does not have to wait for one data access cycle to end before another data access cycle begins.

- *Synchronous DRAM (SDRAM)* is DRAM that operates in synchronization with the memory bus. The memory bus is the data path between the CPU and the main memory.

- *Double Data Rate (DDR)* SDRAM is memory that transfers data twice as fast as SDRAM. DDR SDRAM increases performance by transferring data twice per cycle.

- *Double Data Rate 2 (DDR2)* SDRAM is faster than DDR-SDRAM memory. DDR2 SDRAM improves performance over DDR SDRAM by decreasing noise and crosstalk between the signal wires.

- *Rambus DRAM (RDRAM)* is a memory chip that was developed to communicate at very high rates of speed. RDRAM chips are not commonly used.

Memory Modules

Early computers had RAM installed on the motherboard as individual chips. These individual memory chips, called Dual Inline Package (DIP) chips, were difficult to install and often became loose on the motherboard. To solve this problem, designers soldered the memory chips on a special circuit board called a memory module. The different types of memory modules are as follows:

- *Dual in-line package (DIP)* is an individual memory chip. A DIP had dual rows of pins used to attach it to the motherboard.

- *Single in-line memory module (SIMM)* is a small circuit board that holds several memory chips. SIMMs have 30-pin and 72-pin configurations.

- *Dual in-line memory module (DIMM)* is a circuit board that holds SDRAM, DDR SDRAM, and DDR2 SDRAM chips. There are 168-pin SDRAM DIMMs, 184-pin DDR DIMMs, and 240-pin DDR2 DIMMs.

- *Rambus in-line memory module (RIMM)* is a circuit board that holds RDRAM chips. A typical RIMM has a 184-pin configuration.

Note

Memory modules can be single sided or double sided. Single-sided memory modules contain RAM on only one side of the module. Double-sided memory modules contain RAM on both sides of the module.

Cache Memory

SRAM is used as *cache memory* to store the most frequently used data. SRAM gives the processor faster access to the data than is possible by retrieving it from the slower DRAM, or main memory. The three types of cache memory are as follows:

- L1 is internal cache integrated into the CPU.

- L2 is external cache originally mounted on the motherboard near the CPU. L2 cache is now integrated into the CPU.

- L3 is used on some high-end workstations and server CPUs.

Error Checking

Memory errors occur when the data is stored incorrectly in the RAM chips. The computer uses different methods to detect and correct data errors in memory. Three different methods of memory error checking are as follows:

- *Nonparity* does not check for errors in memory.

■ *Parity* contains 8 bits for data and 1 bit for error checking. The error-checking bit is called a parity bit.

■ *Error-correcting code (ECC)* can detect multiple bit errors in memory and correct single bit errors in memory.

Identify the Names, Purposes, and Characteristics of Adapter Cards

Adapter cards increase the functionality of a computer by adding controllers for specific devices or by replacing malfunctioning ports. Figure 1-8 shows several types of adapter cards. Adapter cards are used to expand and customize the capability of the computer.

Figure 1-8   Adapter Cards

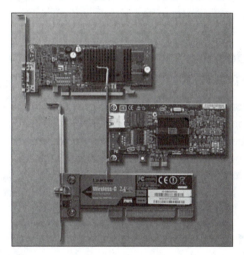

The following is a list of adapter cards and their uses:

■ *Network interface card (NIC)*: Connects a computer to a network using a network cable

■ **Wireless NIC**: Connects a computer to a network using radio frequencies

■ **Sound adapter**: Provides audio capability

■ **Video adapter**: Provides graphic capability

■ **Capture card**: Sends a video signal to a computer so that the signal can be recorded to the computer hard drive with video capture software

■ **TV tuner**: Provides the ability to watch and record TV signals on a PC by connecting a TV source, such as cable TV, satellite, or an antenna, to the installed tuner card

- **Modem adapter**: Connects a computer to the Internet using a phone line

- **Small Computer System Interface (SCSI) adapter**: Connects SCSI (pronounced "scuzzy") devices, such as hard drives or tape drives, to a computer

- *Redundant Array of Independent Disks (RAID)* **adapter**: Connects multiple hard drives to a computer to provide redundancy and to improve performance

- **Universal Serial Bus (USB) port**: Connects a computer to peripheral devices

- *Parallel port*: Connects a computer to peripheral devices

- *Serial port*: Connects a computer to peripheral devices

Computers have expansion slots on the motherboard in which to install adapter cards. The type of adapter card connector must match the expansion slot. A riser card allows adapter cards to be installed horizontally. The riser card was mainly used in slimline desktop computers.

Identify the Names, Purposes, and Characteristics of Storage Drives

Storage drives, as shown in Figure 1-9, read or write information to magnetic or optical storage media. The drive can be used to store data permanently or to retrieve information from a media disk. Storage drives can be installed inside the computer case, such as a hard drive. For portability, some storage drives can connect to the computer using a USB port, a FireWire port, or a SCSI port. These portable storage drives are sometimes referred to as removable drives and can be used on multiple computers. Common types of storage drives include the following:

- Floppy drive

- Hard drive

- Optical drive

- External Flash drive

The following sections describe each type of drive in greater detail.

Figure 1-9   Storage Drives

Floppy Drive

A floppy drive, or floppy disk drive, is a storage device that uses removable 3.5-inch floppy disks. These magnetic floppy disks can store 720 KB or 1.44 MB of data. In a computer, the floppy drive is usually configured as the A: drive. The floppy drive can be used to boot the computer if it contains a bootable floppy disk. A 5.25-inch floppy drive is older technology and is seldom used.

Hard Drive

A hard drive, or hard disk drive, is a magnetic storage device that is installed inside the computer. The hard drive is used as permanent storage for data. In a Windows computer, the hard drive is usually configured as the C: drive and contains the operating system and applications. The hard drive is often configured as the first drive in the boot sequence. The storage capacity of a hard drive is measured in billions of bytes, or gigabytes (GB). The speed of a hard drive is measured in revolutions per minute (rpm). Multiple hard drives can be added to increase storage capacity.

Traditional hard drives are magnetic. Magnetic hard drives have drive motors designed to spin magnetic platters and the drive heads. In contrast, the newer solid state drives (SSD) do not have moving parts. Because there are no drive motors and moving parts, the SSD uses far less energy than the magnetic hard drive. Nonvolatile flash memory chips manage all storage on an SSD, which results in faster access to data, higher reliability, and reduced power usage. SSDs have the same form factor as magnetic hard drives and use ATA or SATA interfaces. SSDs can be installed as a replacement for magnetic drives.

Optical Drive

An optical drive is a storage device that uses lasers to read data on the optical media. There are three types of optical drives:

- Compact disc (CD)
- Digital versatile disc (DVD)
- Blu-ray Disc (BD)

CD, DVD, and BD media can be prerecorded (read-only), recordable (write once), or re-recordable (read and write multiple times). CDs have a data storage capacity of approximately 700 MB. DVDs have a data storage capacity of approximately 4.3 GB on a single-layer disc, and approximately 8.5 GB on a dual-layer disc. BDs have a storage capacity of 25 GB on a single-layer disc, and 50 GB on a dual-layer disc.

There are several types of optical media:

- **CD-ROM**: CD read-only memory media that is prerecorded
- **CD-R**: CD recordable media that can be recorded one time
- **CD-RW**: CD rewritable media that can be recorded, erased, and re-recorded
- **DVD-ROM**: DVD read-only memory media that is prerecorded
- **DVD-RAM**: DVD random-access memory media that can be recorded, erased, and re-recorded
- **DVD+/-R**: DVD recordable media that can be recorded one time
- **DVD+/-RW**: DVD rewritable media that can be recorded, erased, and re-recorded
- **BD-ROM**: BD read-only media that is prerecorded with movies, games, or software
- **BD-R**: BD recordable media that can record HD video and PC data storage one time
- **BD-RE**: BD rewritable format for HD video recording and PC data storage

External Flash Drive

An external flash drive, also known as a thumb drive, is a removable storage device that connects to a USB port. An external flash drive uses the same type of nonvolatile memory chips as solid state drives and does not require power to maintain the data. These drives can be accessed by the operating system in the same way that other types of drives are accessed.

Types of Drive Interfaces

Hard drives and optical drives are manufactured with different interfaces that are used to connect the drive to the computer. To install a storage drive in a computer, the connection interface on the drive must be the same as the controller on the motherboard. Here are some common drive interfaces:

- **IDE**: Integrated Drive Electronics, also called Advanced Technology Attachment (ATA), is an early drive controller interface that connects computers and hard disk drives. An IDE interface uses a 40-pin connector.

- **EIDE**: Enhanced Integrated Drive Electronics, also called ATA-2, is an updated version of the IDE drive controller interface. EIDE supports hard drives larger than 512 MB, enables direct memory access (DMA) for speed, and uses the AT Attachment Packet Interface (ATAPI) to accommodate optical drives and tape drives on the EIDE bus. An EIDE interface uses a 40-pin connector.

- **PATA**: Parallel ATA refers to the parallel version of the ATA drive controller interface. This is just another name for IDE and EIDE.

- **SATA**: Serial ATA refers to the serial version of the ATA drive controller interface. A SATA interface uses a 7-pin data connector.

- **eSATA**: External Serial ATA provides a hot-swappable, external interface for SATA drives. The eSATA interface connects an external SATA drive using a 7-pin connector. The cable can be up to two meters (6.56 feet) in length.

- ***Small Computer System Interface (SCSI)***: A drive controller interface that can connect up to 15 drives. SCSI can connect both internal and external drives. A SCSI interface uses a 50-pin, 68-pin, or 80-pin connector.

RAID provides a way to store data across multiple hard disks for redundancy. To the operating system, RAID appears as one logical disk. Table 1-9 compares the different RAID levels. The following terms describe how RAID stores data on the various disks:

- **Parity**: A method used to detect data errors

- **Striping**: A method used to write data across multiple drives

- **Mirroring**: A method of storing duplicate data to a second drive

Table 1-9   Raid Levels

Raid	Min. No. of Drives	Description	Advantages	Disadvantages
0	2	Data striping without redundancy	Highest performance.	No data protection, and failure of one drive results in loss of all data.
1	2	Disk mirroring	High-performance data protection because all data is duplicated.	High cost of implementation because an additional drive of equal or larger capacity is required.

continues

Table 1-9   Raid Levels   *continued*

Raid	Min. No. of Drives	Description	Advantages	Disadvantages
2	2	Error-correcting code	This level is no longer used.	Same performance can be achieved at a lower cost using RAID 3.
3	3	Byte-level data striping with dedicated parity	For large sequential data requests.	Does not support multiple, simultaneous read and write requests.
4	3	Block-level data striping with dedicated parity	Supports multiple read requests, and if a disk fails, the dedicated parity is used to create a replacement disk.	Write requests are bottlenecked due to the dedicated parity.
5	3	Combination of data striping and parity	Supports multiple simultaneous reads and writes, data is written across all drives with parity, and data can be rebuilt from information found on the other drives.	Write performance is slower than RAID 0 and 1.
6	4	Independent data disks with double parity	Block-level striping with parity data distributed across all disks, and can handle two simultaneous drive failures.	Lower performance than RAID 5 and not supported on all RAID controllers.
1/0	4	Combination of data striping and disk mirroring	High performance and highest data protection.	High cost overhead because duplication of data requires twice the storage capacity.

Identify the Names, Purposes, and Characteristics of Internal Cables

Drives require both a power cable and a data cable. A power supply will have a SATA power connector for SATA drives, a Molex power connector for PATA drives, and a Berg 4-pin connector for floppy drives. The buttons and the light emitting diode (LED) lights on the front of the case connect to the motherboard with the front-panel cables. Figure 1-10 displays internal data cables.

Figure 1-10   Data Cables

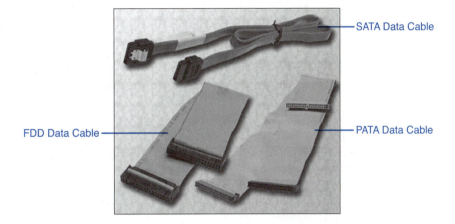

Data cables connect drives to the drive controller, which is located on an adapter card or on the motherboard. Here are some common types of data cables:

- **Floppy disk drive (FDD) data cable**: Data cable has up to two 34-pin drive connectors and one 34-pin connector for the drive controller.

- **PATA (IDE/EIDE) 40-conductor data cable**: Originally, the IDE interface supported two devices on a single controller. With the introduction of Enhanced IDE, two controllers capable of supporting two devices each were introduced. The 40-conductor ribbon cable uses 40-pin connectors. The cable has two connectors for the drives and one connector for the controller.

- **PATA (EIDE) 80-conductor data cable**: As the data rates available over the EIDE interface increased, the chance of data corruption during transmission increased. An 80-conductor cable was introduced for devices transmitting at 33.3 MBps and over, allowing for a more reliable balanced data transmission. The 80-conductor cable uses 40-pin connectors.

- **SATA data cable**: This cable has seven conductors, one keyed connector for the drive, and one keyed connector the drive controller.

- **eSATA data cable**: The eSATA external disk connects to the eSATA interface using a 7-pin data cable. This cable does not supply any power to the eSATA external disk. A separate power cable provides power to the disk.

- **SCSI data cable**: There are three types of SCSI data cable:

  — **Narrow SCSI data cable:** Has 50 conductors, up to seven 50-pin connectors for drives, and one 50-pin connector for the drive controller, also called the host adapter.

  — **Wide SCSI data cable:** Has 68 conductors, up to 15 68-pin connectors for drives, and one 68-pin connector for the host adapter.

  — **Alt-4 SCSI connector:** Has 80 conductors, up to 15 80-pin connectors for drives, and one 80-pin connector for the host adapter.

Note

A colored stripe on a cable identifies Pin 1 on the cable. When installing a data cable, always ensure that Pin 1 on the cable aligns with Pin 1 on the drive or drive controller. Some cables may be keyed and therefore they can only be connected one way to the drive and drive controller.

Worksheet 1.4.7: Research Computer Components

In this worksheet, you use the Internet, a newspaper, or a local store to gather information about the components you need to complete your customer's computer from the scenario provided. Be prepared to discuss your selections. Refer to the worksheet in *IT Essentials: PC Hardware and Software Lab Manual, Fourth Edition*. You may complete this worksheet now or wait to do so until the end of the chapter.

Identify the Names, Purposes, and Characteristics of Ports and Cables

Input/output (I/O) ports on a computer connect peripheral devices, such as printers, scanners, and portable drives. The following ports and cables are commonly used:

- Serial

- Modem

- USB

- FireWire
- Parallel
- SCSI
- Network
- PS/2
- Audio
- Video

Serial Ports and Cables

A serial port can be either a D-shaped plug called DB-9, as shown in Figure 1-11, or a longer DB-25 male connector. Serial ports transmit one bit of data at a time. To connect a serial device, such as a modem or printer, a serial cable must be used. A serial cable has a maximum length of 50 feet (15.2 m).

Figure 1-11   Serial Ports and Cables

Modem Ports and Cables

In addition to the serial cable used to connect an external modem to a computer, a telephone cable is used to connect a modem to a telephone outlet. This cable uses an RJ-11 connector,. A traditional setup of an external modem using a serial cable and a telephone cable.

USB Ports and Cables

The Universal Serial Bus (USB) is a standard interface that connects peripheral devices to a computer. It was originally designed to replace serial and parallel connections. USB devices are hot-swappable, which means that users can connect and disconnect the devices while the computer is powered on. USB connections can be found on computers, cameras, printers, scanners, storage devices, and many other electronic devices. A USB hub is used to connect multiple USB devices. A single USB port in a computer can support up to 127 separate devices with the use of multiple USB hubs. Some devices can also be powered through the USB port, eliminating the need for an external power source. Figure 1-12 shows USB cables with connectors.

Figure 1-12   USB Connectors

USB 1.1 allowed transmission rates of up to 12 Mbps in full-speed mode and 1.5 Mbps in low-speed mode. USB 2.0 allows transmission speeds up to 480 Mbps. USB devices can only transfer data up to the maximum speed allowed by the specific port.

FireWire Ports and Cables

FireWire is a high-speed, hot-swappable interface that connects peripheral devices to a computer. A single FireWire port in a computer can support up to 63 devices. Some devices can also be powered through the FireWire port, eliminating the need for an external power source. FireWire uses the IEEE 1394 standard and is also known as i.Link.

The IEEE 1394a standard supports data rates up to 400 Mbps and cable lengths up to 15 feet (4.5 m). This standard uses a 6-pin connector or a 4-pin connector. The IEEE 1394b standard allows for a greater range of connections, including Category 5 UTP and optical fiber. Depending on the media used, data rates are supported up to 3.2 Gbps over a 100-m distance. Figure 1-13 shows FireWire cables with connectors.

Figure 1-13   FireWire Connectors

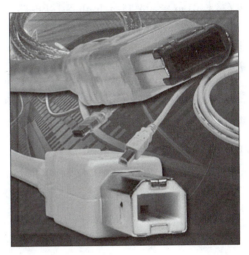

Parallel Ports and Cables

A parallel port on a computer is a standard Type A DB-25 female connector. The parallel connector on a printer is a standard Type B 36-pin Centronics connector. Some newer printers may use a Type C high-density 36-pin connector. Parallel ports can transmit 8 bits of data at one time and use the IEEE 1284 standard. To connect a parallel device, such as a printer, a parallel cable must be used. A parallel cable, as shown in Figure 1-14, has a maximum length of 15 feet (4.5 m).

Figure 1-14   Parallel Printer Cable

SCSI Ports and Cables

A SCSI port can transmit parallel data at rates in excess of 320 MBps and can support up to 15 devices. If a single SCSI device is connected to a SCSI port, the cable can be up to 80 feet (24.4 m) in length. If multiple SCSI devices are connected to a SCSI port, the cable can be up to 40 feet (12.2 m) in length. A SCSI port on a computer can be one of three different types, as shown in Figure 1-15:

- DB-25 female connector

- High-density 50-pin female connector

- High-density 68-pin female connector

Figure 1-15   SCSI Connectors

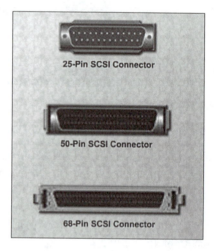

Note

SCSI devices must be terminated at the endpoints of the SCSI chain. Check the device manual for termination procedures.

Caution

Some SCSI connectors resemble parallel connectors. Be careful not to connect the cable to the wrong port. The voltage used in the SCSI format may damage the parallel interface. SCSI connectors should be clearly labeled.

Network Ports and Cables

A network port, also known as an RJ-45 port, connects a computer to a network. The connection speed depends on the type of network port. Standard Ethernet can transmit up to 10 Mbps, Fast Ethernet can transmit up to 100 Mbps, and Gigabit Ethernet can transmit up to 1000 Mbps. The maximum length of network cable is 328 feet (100 m). A network connector is shown in Figure 1-16.

Figure 1-16   Network Connector

PS/2 Ports

A *PS/2 port* connects a keyboard or a mouse to a computer. The PS/2 port is a 6-pin mini-DIN female connector. The connectors for the keyboard and mouse are often colored differently, as shown in Figure 1-17. If the ports are not color coded, look for a small figure of a mouse or keyboard next to each port.

Figure 1-17   PS/2 Ports

Audio Ports

An audio port connects audio devices to the computer. Some of the following audio ports are commonly used, as shown in Figure 1-18:

- **Line In**: Connects to an external source, such as a stereo system

- **Microphone**: Connects to a microphone

- **Line Out**: Connects to speakers or headphones

- **Sony/Philips Digital Interface Format (S/PDIF)**: Connects to fiber-optic cable to support digital audio

- **TosLink**: Connects to fiber-optic cable to support digital audio

- **Gameport/MIDI**: Connects to a joystick or MIDI-interfaced device

Figure 1-18   Audio Ports

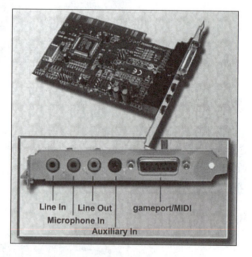

Video Ports and Connectors

A video port connects a monitor cable to a computer. Figure 1-19 shows three common video ports. There are several video port and connector types:

- *Video Graphics Array (VGA)*: VGA has a three-row, 15-pin female connector and provides analog output to a monitor.

- *Digital Visual Interface (DVI)*: DVI has a 24-pin female connector or a 29-pin female connector and provides an uncompressed digital output to a monitor. DVI-I provides both analog and digital signals. DVI-D provides digital signals only.

- *High-Definition Multimedia Interface (HDMI)*: HDMI has a 19-pin connector and provides digital video and digital audio signals.

- *S-Video*: S-Video has a 4-pin connector and provides analog video signals.

- *Component/RGB*: RGB has three shielded cables (red, green, blue) with RCA jacks and provides analog video signals.

Figure 1-19   Video Ports

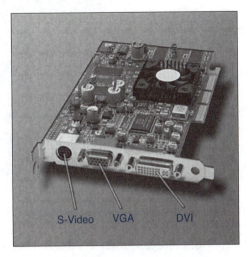

Identify the Names, Purposes, and Characteristics of Input Devices

An input device is used to enter data or instructions into a computer. Here are some examples of input devices:

- Mouse and keyboard

- Digital camera and digital video camera

- Biometric authentication device

- Touch screen

- Scanner

The mouse and keyboard are the two most commonly used input devices. The mouse is used to navigate the graphical user interface (GUI). The keyboard is used to enter text commands that control the computer.

Digital cameras and digital video cameras, shown in Figure 1-20, create images that can be stored on magnetic media. The image is stored as a file that can be displayed, printed, or altered.

Figure 1-20   Digital Camera

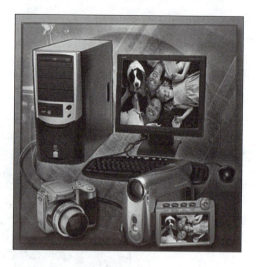

Biometric identification makes use of features that are unique to an individual user, such as fingerprints, voice recognition, or a retinal scan. When combined with ordinary usernames, biometric identification guarantees that the authorized person is accessing the data. Figure 1-21 shows a laptop that has a built-in fingerprint scanner. After measuring the physical characteristics of the fingerprint of the user, the scanner grants the user access if the fingerprint characteristics match the database and the user supplies the correct login information.

Figure 1-21   Fingerprint Scanner

A touch screen has a pressure-sensitive transparent panel. The computer receives instructions specific to the place on the screen that the user touches.

A scanner digitizes an image or document. The digitization of the image is stored as a file that can be displayed, printed, or altered. A bar code reader is a type of scanner that reads Universal Product Code (UPC) bar codes. It is widely used for pricing and inventory information.

Identify the Names, Purposes, and Characteristics of Output Devices

An output device is used to present information to the user from a computer. Here are some examples of output devices:

- Monitors and projectors
- All-in-one Printer
- Speakers and headphones

Monitors and Projectors

Monitors and projectors are primary output devices for a computer. There are different types of monitors, as shown in Figure 1-22. The most important difference between these monitor types is the technology used to create an image.

Figure 1-22   Types of Monitors

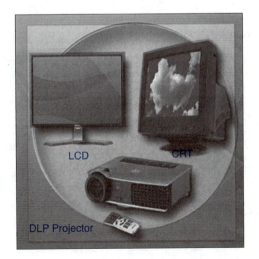

The following is an explanation of display technologies:

- **_CRT_**: The cathode-ray tube (CRT) has three electron beams. Each beam directs colored phosphor on the screen that glows either red, blue, or green. Areas not struck by an electron beam do not glow. The combination of glowing and nonglowing areas creates the image on the screen. This technology is also used by most televisions. CRTs usually have a degauss button on the front that the user can press to remove discoloration caused by magnetic interference. CRT technology has largely been replaced with LCD.

- **_LCD_**: Liquid crystal display is commonly used in flat panel monitors, laptops, and some projectors. It consists of two polarizing filters with a liquid crystal solution between them. An electronic current aligns the crystals so that light can either pass through or not pass through. The effect of light passing through in certain areas and not in others is what creates the image. LCD comes in two forms, active matrix and passive matrix. Active matrix is sometimes called thin film transistor (TFT). TFT allows each pixel to be controlled, which creates very sharp color images. Passive matrix is less expensive than active matrix but does not provide the same level of image control. Passive matrix is not commonly used in laptops.

- **_DLP_**: Digital light processing is another technology used in projectors. DLP projectors use a spinning color wheel with a microprocessor-controlled array of mirrors called a digital micromirror device (DMD). Each mirror corresponds to a specific pixel. Each mirror reflects light toward or away from the projector optics. This creates a monochromatic image of up to 1024 shades of gray in between white and black. The color wheel then adds the color data to complete the projected color image.

Monitor resolution refers to the level of image detail that can be reproduced. Table 1-10 is a chart of common monitor resolutions. Higher resolution settings produce better image quality.

Table 1-10   Display Resolutions

Display Standard	Linear Pixels (Height x Vertical)	Aspect Ratio
CGA	320x200	16:10
EGA	640x350	11:6
VGA	640x480	4:3
WVGA	854x480	16:9
SVGA	800x600	4:3
XGA	1024x768	4:3
WXGA	1280x800	16:10
SXGA	1280x1024	5:4

Display Standard	Linear Pixels (Height x Vertical)	Aspect Ratio
WSXGA	1600x1024	25:16
UXGA	1600x1200	4:3
HDTV	1920x1080	16:9
WUXGA	1920x1200	16:10
QXGA	2048x1536	4:3
QSXGA	2560x2048	5:4
WQUXGA	3840x2400	16:10

Several factors are involved in monitor resolution:

- *Pixel*: The term pixel is an abbreviation for picture element. Pixels are the tiny dots that comprise a screen. Each pixel consists of red, green, and blue.

- *Dot pitch*: Dot pitch is the distance between pixels on the screen. A lower dot pitch number produces a better image.

- *Contrast ratio*: The contrast ratio is a measurement of the difference in intensity of light between the brightest point (white) and the darkest point (black). A 10,000:1 contrast ratio shows dimmer whites and lighter blacks than a monitor with a contrast ratio of 1,000,000:1.

- *Refresh rate*: The refresh rate is how often per second the image is rebuilt. A higher refresh rate produces a better image and reduces the level of flicker.

- *Interlaced/noninterlaced*: Interlaced monitors create the image by scanning the screen two times. The first scan covers the odd lines, top to bottom, and the second scan covers the even lines. Noninterlaced monitors create the image by scanning the screen, one line at a time from top to bottom. Most CRT monitors today are noninterlaced.

- *Horizontal vertical colors (HVC)*: The number of pixels in a line is the horizontal resolution. The number of lines in a screen is the vertical resolution. The number of colors that can be reproduced is the color resolution.

- *Aspect ratio*: Aspect ratio is the horizontal to vertical measurement of the viewing area of a monitor. For example, a 4:3 aspect ratio would apply to a viewing area that is 16 inches wide by 12 inches high. A 4:3 aspect radio would also apply to a viewing area that is 24 inches wide by 18 inches high. A viewing area that is 22 inches wide by 12 inches high has an aspect ratio of 11:6.

- *Native resolution*: Native resolution is the number of pixels that a monitor has. A monitor with a resolution of 1280x1024 has 1280 horizontal pixels and 1024 vertical pixels. Native mode is when the image sent to the monitor matches the native resolution of the monitor.

Monitors have controls for adjusting the quality of the image. Here are some common monitor settings:

- **Brightness**: Intensity of the image
- **Contrast**: Ratio of light to dark
- **Position**: Vertical and horizontal location of image on the screen
- **Reset**: Returns the monitor settings to factory settings

Adding additional monitors increases the number of windows that are visible on the desktop. Many computers have built-in support for multiple monitors.

All-in-One Printer

Printers are output devices that create hard copies of computer files. Some printers specialize in particular applications, such as printing color photographs. Other, all-in-one type printers, like the one shown in Figure 1-23, are designed to provide multiple services such as printing, scanning, faxing, and copying.

Figure 1-23   All-in-One Printer

Speakers and Headphones

Speakers and headphones are output devices for audio signals. Most computers have audio support either integrated into the motherboard or on an adapter card. Audio support includes ports that allow input and output of audio signals. The audio card has an amplifier to power headphones and external speakers, which are shown in Figure 1-24.

Figure 1-24   Speakers and Headphones

Explain System Resources and Their Purposes

System resources are used for communication purposes between the CPU and other components in a computer. There are three common system resources:

- Interrupt requests (IRQ)

- Input/output (I/O) port addresses

- Direct memory access (DMA)

Interrupt Requests

Interrupt requests (IRQ) are used by computer components to request information from the CPU. The IRQ travels along a wire on the motherboard to the CPU. When the CPU receives an IRQ, the CPU determines how to fulfill this request. The priority of the request is determined by the IRQ number assigned to that computer component. Older computers only had eight IRQs to assign to devices. Newer computers have 16 IRQs, which are numbered 0 to 15, as shown in Table 1-11. As a general rule, each component in the computer must be assigned a unique IRQ. IRQ conflicts can cause components to stop functioning and even cause the computer to crash. Today, most IRQ numbers are assigned automatically with "plug-and-play" (PnP) operating systems and the implementation of PCI slots, USB ports, and FireWire ports. With the numerous components that can be installed in a computer, it is difficult to assign a unique IRQ to every component. PCI devices can now share IRQs without conflict.

Table 1-11   Interrupt Requests (IRQ)

IRQ	Description
0	System timer. Reserved for the system. The user cannot change it.
1	Keyboard. Reserved for the system. Cannot be altered, even if no keyboard is present or needed.
2	Second IRQ controller.
3	COM 2 (default), COM 4 (user).
4	COM 1 (default), COM 3 (user).
5	Sound card (Sound Blaster Pro or later) or LPT2 (user).
6	Floppy disk controller.
7	LPT1 (parallel port) or sound card (8-bit Sound Blaster and compatible).
8	Real-time clock.
9	ACPI SCSI or ISA MPU-401.
10	Free/open interrupt/available/SCSI.
11	Free/open interrupt/available/SCSI.
12	PS/2 connector mouse. If no PS/2 connector mouse is used, this can be used for other peripherals.
13	Math coprocessor. Cannot be changed.
14	Primary IDE. If no primary IDE exists, this can be changed.
15	Secondary IDE.

Input/Output (I/O) Port Addresses

Input/output (I/O) port addresses are used to communicate between devices and software. The I/O port address is used to send and receive data for a component. As with IRQs, each component will have a unique I/O port assigned. There are 65,535 I/O ports in a computer, and they are referenced by a hexadecimal address in the range of 0000h to FFFFh. Table 1-12 shows a chart of common I/O ports.

Table 1-12   I/O Addresses

I/O Port Addresses (in Hex)	Typical Device or Port Assignment	I/O Port Addresses (in Hex)	Typical or Device Port Assignment	I/O Port Addresses (in Hex)	Typical Device or Port Assignment
000–00f, 081–09F	DMA controller	1F0–1F7	Primary hard disk controller	3E8–3EF	COM 3 serial port
010–01F, 0A0–0A1	Programmable interrupt controller	200–207	Game port joystick	3F0–3F7	Floppy disk controller
040–043	System timer	220–22F	Sound card	3F6–3F6	PCI primary IDE controller
060–060, 064–064	Keyboard	294–297	PCI bus (data comm)	3F8–3FF	COM 1 serial port
061–061	PC speaker	278–27F	LPT 2 or LPT 3	E000–E01F	USB host controller
070–071	CMOS/real-time clock	2E8–2EF	COM 4 serial port	E800–E87F	Fast Ethernet adapter
0F0–0FF	Math coprocessor	2F8–2FF	COM 2 serial port	F000–F00F	IDE controller
130–14F	SCSI host adapter	376–376	PCI IDE controller		
170–177	Secondary hard disk controller	378–37F	LPT1		

Direct Memory Access

Direct memory access (DMA) channels are used by high-speed devices to communicate directly with main memory. These channels allow the device to bypass interaction with the CPU and directly store and retrieve information from memory. Only certain devices can be assigned a DMA channel, such as SCSI host adapters and sound cards. Older computers only had four DMA channels to assign to components. Newer computers have eight DMA channels that are numbered 0 to 7, as shown in Table 1-13.

Table 1-13   DMA Channels

DMA Channel	Default Device	Can Also Be Used For
0	Dynamic RAM memory refresh	
1	Sound card (low DMA setting)	Network cards, SCSI adapters, parallel printing port, and voice modems
2	Floppy disk controller	
3	Available	Network cards, SCSI adapters, parallel printing port, voice modems, and sound card (low DMA setting)
4	Cascade for DMA 0–3	
5	Sound card (high DMA setting)	Network cards, SCSI adapters
6	Available	Network cards, sound card (high DMA setting)
7	Available	Network cards, sound card (high DMA setting)

Summary

This chapter introduced the IT industry, options for training and employment, and some of the industry-standard certifications. This chapter also covered the components that comprise a PC system. Much of the content in this chapter will help you throughout this course:

- Information technology encompasses the use of computers, network hardware, and software to process, store, transmit, and retrieve information.

- A PC system consists of hardware components and software applications.

- You must carefully choose the computer case and power supply to support the hardware inside the case and allow for the addition of components.

- A computer's internal components are selected for specific features and functions. All internal components must be compatible with the motherboard.

- You should use the correct type of ports and cables when connecting devices.

- Typical input devices include the keyboard, mouse, touch screen, and digital cameras.

- Typical output devices include monitors, printers, and speakers.

- System resources must be assigned to computer components. System resources include IRQs, I/O port addresses, and DMAs.

Summary of Exercises

This is a summary of the Labs, Worksheets, Remote Technician exercises, Class Discussions, Virtual Desktop activities, and Virtual Laptop activities associated with this chapter.

Worksheets

The following worksheets cover material from this chapter. Refer to the labs in *IT Essentials: PC Hardware and Software Lab Manual, Fourth Edition*.

Worksheet 1.1.2: Job Opportunities

Worksheet 1.4.7: Research Computer Components

Check Your Understanding

You can find the answers to these questions in the appendix, "Answers to Check Your Understanding Questions."

1. How many FireWire devices can a single FireWire port support?

   A. 12

   B. 25

   C. 32

   D. 54

   E. 63

   F. 127

2. Which type of memory transfers data twice as fast as SDRAM and increases performance by transferring data twice per cycle?

   A. DDR-SDRAM

   B. DRAM2

   C. D-SDRAM

   D. ROM

3. Which type of video connector has a 24-pin or 29-pin female connector and provides compressed digital output to a monitor?

   A. AAV

   B. DVI

   C. HDMI

   D. RCA

   E. VGA

4. How many USB devices can be connected to a USB port?

   A. 256

   B. 127

   C. 64

   D. 128

5. What is the maximum data speed of high-speed USB 2.0?

    A. 1.5 Mbps

    B. 12 Mbps

    C. 380 Mbps

    D. 480 Mbps

    E. 480 Gbps

    F. 840 Gbps

6. Which IEEE standard defines the FireWire technology?

    A. 1284

    B. 1394

    C. 1451

    D. 1539

7. What is the maximum data rate supported by the IEEE 1394a standard?

    A. 200 Mbps

    B. 380 Mbps

    C. 400 Mbps

    D. 800 Mbps

    E. 900 Mbps

8. What is the purpose of a heat sink installed on a processor?

    A. To set the processor voltage

    B. To cool the processor

    C. To set the processor speed

    D. To ground the processor

CHAPTER 2

Safe Lab Procedures and Tool Use

Objectives

Upon completion of this chapter, you should be able to answer the following questions:

- What are the safe working conditions and procedures?

- What is proper tool use?

- What tools and software are used with personal computer components and what is their purpose?

Key Terms

This chapter uses the following key terms. You can find the definitions in the Glossary.

This chapter covers basic safety practices for the workplace, hardware and software tools, and the disposal of hazardous materials. Safety guidelines help protect individuals from accidents and injury and protect equipment from damage. Some of these guidelines are designed to protect the environment from contamination by discarded materials. Stay alert to situations that could result in injury or damage to equipment. Warning signs are designed to alert you to danger. Always watch for these signs and take the appropriate action according to the warning given.

After completing this chapter, you will meet these objectives:

- Explain the purpose of safe working conditions and procedures.
- Identify tools and software used with personal computer components and their purposes.
- Implement proper tool use.

Explain the Purpose of Safe Working Conditions and Procedures

Safe working conditions help to prevent injury to people and damage to computer equipment. A safe workspace is clean, organized, and properly lighted. Everyone must understand and follow safety procedures.

Follow proper procedures for handling computer equipment to reduce the risk of personal injury, damage to property, and loss of data. Any damage or loss may result in claims for damage from the owner of the property and data.

The proper disposal or recycling of hazardous computer components is a global issue. Make sure to follow regulations that govern how to dispose of specific items. Organizations that violate these regulations can be fined or face expensive legal battles.

After completing this section, you will meet these objectives:

- Identify safety procedures and potential hazards for users and technicians.
- Identify safety procedures to protect equipment from damage and data from loss.
- Identify safety procedures to protect the environment from contamination.

Identify Safety Procedures and Potential Hazards for Users and Technicians

Safety is very important both to the technician and to the equipment. Guidelines help to ensure that proper techniques and precautions are correctly and uniformly implemented.

General Safety Guidelines

Follow general safety guidelines to prevent cuts, burns, electrical shock, and damage to eyesight. General safety guidelines include the following:

- Manage cables properly to prevent tripping hazards and help protect the cables.
- Remove your watch or any other jewelry and secure loose clothing before handling equipment.
- Turn off the power and unplug equipment before performing service.
- Cover any sharp edges inside the case with tape.
- Never open a power supply or a monitor.
- Do not touch areas in a printer that are hot or that use high voltages.
- Know where the fire extinguisher and first-aid kit are located and how to use them.
- Keep food and drinks out of your workspace.
- Keep your workspace clean and free of clutter.
- Bend your knees when lifting objects to avoid injury to your back.

Electrical Safety Guidelines

Follow electrical safety guidelines to prevent electrical fires, injuries, and fatalities in the home and the workplace. Power supplies and monitors contain very high voltage. Only experienced technicians should attempt to repair power supplies and monitors. Most users should simply replace them when they stop working, because the cost of hiring a qualified technician typically is higher than the cost of replacement. Do not wear the antistatic wrist strap when repairing power supplies laser printers, or monitors.

Some printer parts may become very hot when in use, and other parts may contain very high voltages. Make sure that the printer has had time to cool before you make the repair. Check the printer manual for locations of various components that may contain high voltages. Some components may retain high voltages even after the printer is turned off.

Electrical devices have certain power requirements. For example, AC adapters are manufactured for specific laptops. Exchanging power cords with a different type of laptop or device may cause damage to both the AC adapter and the laptop.

Fire Safety Guidelines

Follow fire safety guidelines to protect lives, structures, and equipment. To avoid an electrical shock, and to prevent damage to the computer, turn off and unplug the computer before beginning a repair.

Fire can spread rapidly and be very costly. Proper use of a fire extinguisher can prevent a small fire from getting out of control. When working with computer components, always consider the possibility of an accidental fire and know how to react. You should be alert for odors emitting from computers and electronic devices. When electronic components overheat or short out, they will emit a burning odor. If there is a fire, you should follow these safety procedures:

- Never fight a fire that is out of control or not contained.

- Always have a planned fire escape route before beginning any work.

- Get out of the building quickly.

- Contact emergency services for help.

- Be sure to locate and read the instructions on the fire extinguishers in your workplace before you have to use them. Safety training may be available in your organization.

In the United States, there are four classifications for fire extinguishers. A different letter, color, and shape identify each fire extinguisher classification, as shown in Figure 2-1. Each type of fire extinguisher has specific chemicals to fight different types of fires:

- **Class A (green triangle)**: Paper, wood, plastics, cardboard

- **Class B (red square)**: Gasoline, kerosene, organic solvents

- **Class C (blue circle)**: Electrical equipment

- **Class D (yellow star)**: Combustible metals

Figure 2-1   Fire Extinguisher Classifications

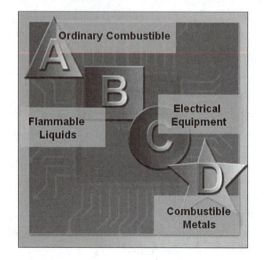

Fire extinguisher classifications might vary by country.

It is important to know how to use a fire extinguisher. Hold the canister in an upright/vertical position and use the memory aid P-A-S-S to help you remember the basic rules of fire extinguisher operation:

- **P**: Pull the pin.
- **A**: Aim at the base of the fire, not at the flames.
- **S**: Squeeze the lever.
- **S**: Sweep the nozzle from side to side.

Identify Safety Procedures to Protect Equipment from Damage and Data from Loss

Electrostatic discharge, harsh climates, and poor-quality sources of electricity can cause damage to computer equipment. Follow proper handling guidelines, be aware of environmental issues, and use equipment that stabilizes power to prevent equipment damage and data loss.

Electrostatic Discharge

Static electricity is the buildup of an electric charge resting on a surface. This buildup may jump to a component and cause damage. This is known as *electrostatic discharge (ESD)*. ESD can be destructive to the electronics in a computer system.

At least 3000 volts of static electricity must build up before a person can feel ESD. For example, static electricity can build up on you as you walk across a carpeted floor. When you touch another person, you both receive a shock. If the discharge causes pain or makes a noise, the charge was probably above 10,000 volts. By comparison, less than 30 volts of static electricity can damage a computer component.

ESD can cause permanent damage to electrical components. Follow these recommendations to help prevent ESD damage:

- Keep all components in antistatic bags until you are ready to install them.
- Use grounded mats on workbenches.
- Use grounded floor mats in work areas.
- Use *antistatic wrist straps* when working on computers.

Electromagnetic Interference

Electromagnetic interference (EMI) is the intrusion of outside electromagnetic signals in a transmission media, such as copper cabling. In a network environment, EMI distorts the signals so that the receiving devices have difficulty interpreting them.

EMI does not always come from expected sources such as cellular phones. Other types of electric equipment can emit a silent, invisible electromagnetic field that can extend for more than a mile.

There are many sources of EMI:

- Any source designed to generate electromagnetic energy
- Man-made sources, like power lines or motors
- Natural events, such as electrical storms or solar and other radiations from space

Wireless networks are affected by radio frequency interference (RFI). RFI is the interference caused by radio transmitters and other devices transmitting in the same frequency. For example, a cordless telephone can cause problems with a wireless network when both devices use the same frequency. Microwaves can also cause interference when positioned in close proximity to wireless networking devices.

Climate

Climate affects computer equipment in a variety of ways:

- If the environment temperature is too high, equipment can overheat.
- If the humidity level is too low, the chance of ESD increases.
- If the humidity level is too high, equipment can suffer from moisture damage.

Table 2-1 shows how environmental conditions increase or decrease the risk of ESD.

Table 2-1   ESD Probability

Conditions	ESD Probability
Cool and dry	High
Warm and humid	Low

Power Fluctuation Types

Voltage is the force that moves electrons through a circuit. The movement of electrons is called *current*. Computer circuits need voltage and current to operate electronic components. When the voltage in a computer is not accurate or steady, computer components may not operate correctly. Unsteady voltages are called *power fluctuations*.

The following types of AC power fluctuations can cause data loss or hardware failure:

- *Blackout*: Complete loss of AC power. A blown fuse, damaged transformer, or downed power line can cause a blackout.

- *Brownout*: Reduced voltage level of AC power that lasts for a period of time. Brownouts occur when the power line voltage drops below 80 percent of the normal voltage level. Overloading electrical circuits can cause a brownout.

- *Noise*: Interference from generators and lightning. Noise results in unclean power, which can cause errors in a computer system.

- *Spike*: Sudden increase in voltage that lasts for a very short period and exceeds 100 percent of the normal voltage on a line. Spikes can be caused by lightning strikes, but can also occur when the electrical system comes back on after a blackout.

- *Power surge*: Dramatic increase in voltage above the normal flow of electrical current. A power surge lasts for a few nanoseconds, or one-billionth of a second.

Power Protection Devices

To help shield against power fluctuation issues, use *power protection devices* to protect the data and computer equipment:

- *Surge suppressor*: Helps protect against damage from surges and spikes. A surge suppressor diverts extra electrical voltage on the line to the ground.

- *Uninterruptible power supply (UPS)*: Helps protect against potential electrical power problems by supplying electrical power to a computer or other device. The battery is constantly recharging while the UPS is in use. The UPS is able to supply a limited amount of power when brownouts and blackouts occur. A UPS can also act as a *line conditioner* if it uses the battery as a buffer from the minor but erratic fluctuations found in electrical lines. This form of UPS is called inline. Many UPS devices are able to communicate directly with the operating system on a computer. This communication allows the UPS to safely shut down the computer and save data prior to the UPS losing all electrical power.

- *Standby power supply (SPS)*: The most common type of UPS. It helps protect against potential electrical power problems by providing a backup battery to supply power when the incoming voltage drops below the normal level. The battery is on standby during the normal operation. When the voltage decreases, the battery provides DC power to a power inverter, which converts it to AC power for the computer. This device is not as reliable as a UPS because of the time it takes to switch over to the battery. If the switching device fails, the battery will not be able to supply power to the computer.

Figure 2-2 shows some examples of surge suppressors, UPSs, and SPS devices.

Figure 2-2   Surge Suppressors and UPS Devices

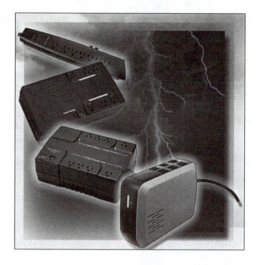

Caution

Never plug a printer into a UPS device. Doing so might overload the UPS device.

Identify Safety Procedures to Protect the Environment from Contamination

Computers and peripherals contain materials that can be harmful to the environment. Hazardous materials are sometimes called toxic waste. These materials can contain high concentrations of heavy metals such as cadmium, lead, or mercury. The regulations for the disposal of hazardous materials vary according to state or country. Contact the local recycling or waste removal authorities in your community for information about disposal procedures and services.

Material Safety Data Sheet

A *material safety data sheet (MSDS)* is a fact sheet that summarizes information about material identification, including hazardous ingredients that can affect personal health, fire hazards, and first aid requirements. In Figure 2-3, the MSDS contains chemical reactivity and incompatibility information that includes spill, leak, and disposal procedures. It also includes protective measures for the safe handling and storage of materials.

Figure 2-3   MSDS

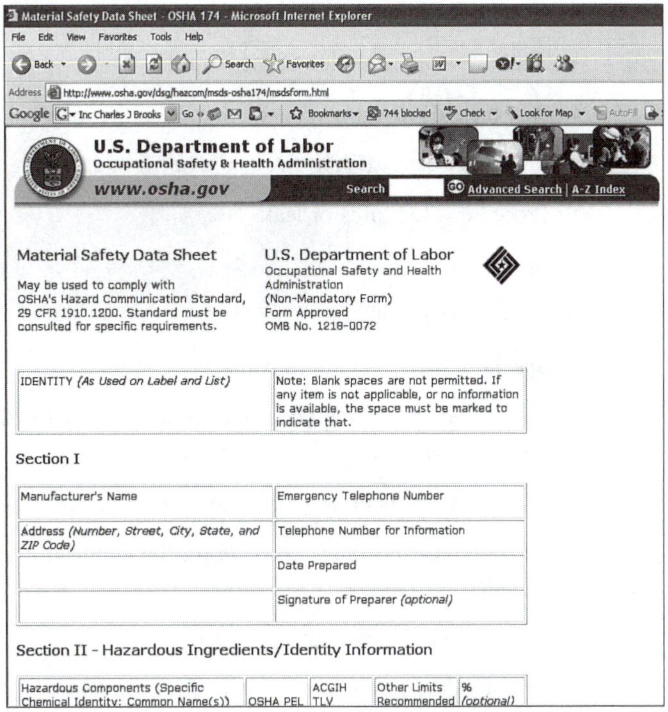

To determine whether a material is classified as hazardous, consult the manufacturer's MSDS. In the United States, the *Occupational Safety Health Administration (OSHA)* requires that all hazardous materials must be accompanied by an MSDS when transferred to a new owner. The MSDS information included with products purchased for computer repairs or maintenance can be relevant to computer technicians. OSHA also requires that employees be informed about the materials that they are working with and be provided with material safety information. In the United Kingdom, *Chemicals Hazard Information and Packaging for Supply Regulations 2002 (CHIP 3)* regulate the handling of hazardous materials. CHIP 3 requires chemical suppliers to safely package and transport dangerous chemicals and to include a data sheet with the product.

Note

The MSDS is valuable in determining how to dispose of any potentially hazardous materials in the safest manner. Always check local regulations concerning acceptable disposal methods before disposing of any electronic equipment.

Which organization governs the use of hazardous chemicals in your country? Are MSDSs mandatory?

The MSDS contains valuable information:

- The name of the material
- The physical properties of the material
- Any hazardous ingredients contained in the material
- Reactivity data, such as fire and explosion data
- Procedures for spills or leaks
- Special precautions
- Health hazards
- Special protection requirements

Computers and other computing devices are eventually discarded because of one of the following reasons:

- Parts or components begin to fail more frequently as the device ages.
- The computer becomes obsolete for the application for which it was originally intended.
- Newer models have improved features.

Before discarding a computer or any of its components, it is crucial to consider safe disposal of each separate component.

Proper Disposal of Batteries

Batteries often contain rare earth metals that can be harmful to the environment. Batteries from portable computer systems may contain lead, cadmium, lithium, alkaline manganese, and mercury. These metals do not decay and will remain in the environment for many years. Mercury is commonly used in the manufacturing of batteries and is extremely toxic and harmful to humans.

Recycling batteries should be a standard practice for a technician. All batteries, including lithium-ion, nickel-cadmium, nickel-metal hydride, and lead-acid, are subject to disposal procedures that comply with local environmental regulations.

Proper Disposal of Monitors or CRTs

Handle monitors and cathode ray tubes (CRT) with care. Extremely high voltage can be stored in monitors and CRTs, even after being disconnected from a power source. CRTs contain glass, metal, plastics, lead, barium, and rare earth metals. According to the U.S. Environmental Protection Agency (EPA), CRTs may contain approximately 4 lbs (1.8 kg) of lead. Monitors must be disposed of in compliance with environmental regulations.

Proper Disposal of Toner Kits, Cartridges, and Developers

Used printer toner kits and printer cartridges must be disposed of properly or recycled. Some toner cartridge suppliers and manufacturers will take empty cartridges for refilling. There are also companies that specialize in refilling empty cartridges. Kits to refill inkjet printer cartridges are available but are not recommended, because the ink may leak into the printer, causing irreversible damage. This can be especially costly because using refilled inkjet cartridges may also void the inkjet printer warranty.

Proper Disposal of Chemical Solvents and Aerosol Cans

Contact the local sanitation company to learn how and where to dispose of the chemicals and solvents used to clean computers. Never dump chemicals or solvents down a sink or dispose of them in any drain that connects to public sewers.

The cans or bottles that contain solvents and other cleaning supplies must be handled carefully. Make sure that they are identified and treated as special hazardous waste. For example, some aerosol cans may explode when exposed to heat if the contents are not completely used.

Identify Tools and Software Used with Personal Computer Components and Their Purposes

For every job, there is the right tool. Make sure that you are familiar with the correct use of each tool and that you use the right tool for the current task. Skilled use of tools and software makes the job less difficult and ensures that tasks are performed properly and safely. Figure 2-4 shows some common tools used in computer repair.

Figure 2-4   Computer Tools

Software tools are available that help diagnose problems. Use these tools to determine which computer device is not functioning correctly.

A technician must document all repairs and computer problems. The documentation can then be used as a reference for future problems or for other technicians who may not have encountered the problem before. The documents may be paper-based, but electronic forms are preferred because they can be easily searched for specific problems.

After completing this section, you will meet these objectives:

- Identify hardware tools and their purpose.
- Identify software tools and their purpose.
- Identify organizational tools and their purpose.

Identify Hardware Tools and Their Purpose

A toolkit should contain all of the tools necessary to complete hardware repairs. As you gain experience, you will learn which tools to have available for different types of jobs. Hardware tools are grouped into these four categories:

- ESD tools
- Hand tools
- Cleaning tools
- Diagnostic tools

ESD Tools

There are two ESD tools: the antistatic wrist strap and the *antistatic mat*. Both tools are designed to protect the PC from ESD. The antistatic wrist strap protects computer equipment when clipped to the computer chassis. The antistatic mat protects computer equipment by preventing static electricity from accumulating on the hardware or on the technician.

Hand Tools

Most tools used in the computer assembly process are small *hand tools*. They are available individually or as part of a computer repair toolkit. Toolkits range widely in size, quality, and price. Common hand tools include the following:

- *Flat-head screwdriver*: Used to tighten or loosen slotted screws
- *Phillips-head screwdriver*: Used to tighten or loosen cross-headed screws
- **Torx screwdriver**: Used to tighten or loosen screws that have a star-like depression on the top, a feature that is mainly found on laptops

- *Hex driver*: Used to tighten or loosen nuts in the same way that a screwdriver tightens or loosens screws (sometimes called a *nut driver*)

- *Needle-nose pliers*: Used to hold small parts

- **Wire cutters**: Used to strip and cut wires

- *Tweezers*: Used to manipulate small parts

- *Part retriever*: Used to retrieve parts from locations that are too small for your hand to fit

- **Flashlight**: Used to light up areas that you cannot see well

Cleaning Tools

Having the appropriate *cleaning tools* is essential when maintaining or repairing computers. Using these tools ensures that computer components are not damaged during cleaning. Cleaning tools include the following:

- **Soft cloth**: Used to clean different computer components without scratching or leaving debris

- **Compressed air**: Used to blow away dust and debris from different computer parts without touching the components

- **Cable ties**: Used to bundle cables neatly inside and outside of a computer

- **Parts organizer**: Used to hold screws, jumpers, fasteners, and other small parts and prevent them from getting mixed together

Diagnostic Tools

Diagnostic tools include the following:

- **Digital multimeter**: Used to test the integrity of circuits and the quality of electricity in computer components

- **Loopback adapter**: Used to test the basic functionality of computer ports

Identify Software Tools and Their Purpose

A technician must be able to use a range of software tools to help diagnose problems, maintain hardware, and protect the data stored on a computer.

Disk Management Tools

Disk management tools help detect and correct disk errors, prepare a disk for data storage, and remove unwanted files. The following are disk management tools:

- *Format*: Prepares a hard drive to store information

- *Scandisk* **or Chkdsk**: Checks the integrity of files and folders on a hard drive by scanning the file system; may also check the disk surface for physical errors

- *Defrag*: Optimizes space on a hard drive to allow faster access to programs and data

- *Disk Cleanup*: Clears space on a hard drive by searching for files that can be safely deleted

- *Disk Management*: Initializes disks, and creates, deletes, and formats partitions

- **System File Checker (SFC)**: Scans the operating system critical files and replaces any files that are corrupted

Use the Windows boot disk for troubleshooting and repairing corrupted files. The Windows boot disk is designed to repair Windows system files, restore damaged or lost files, and reinstall the operating system. Be sure to use the same OS boot disk as the OS installed on the PC. Use a Windows XP CD to troubleshoot a Windows XP PC, a Windows Vista CD or DVD on a Windows Vista PC, and so on. Third-party software tools are available to assist in troubleshooting problems.

Protection Software Tools

Each year, viruses, spyware, and other types of malicious attacks infect millions of computers. These attacks can damage an operating system, application, and data. Computers that have been infected may even have problems with hardware performance or component failure.

To protect data and the integrity of the operating system and hardware, use software designed to guard against attacks and to remove malicious programs.

Various types of software are used to protect hardware and data:

- **Windows XP Security Center**: Checks the status of essential security settings. The Security Center continuously checks to make sure that the software firewall and antivirus programs are running. It also ensures that automatic updates are set to download and install automatically.

- **Antivirus program**: Protects against virus attacks.

- **Spyware remover**: Protects against software that sends information about web surfing habits to an attacker. Spyware can be installed without the knowledge or consent of the user.

- **Firewall program**: Runs continuously to protect against unauthorized communications to and from your computer.

Worksheet 2.2.2: Diagnostic Software

In this worksheet, you will use the Internet, a newspaper, or a local store to gather information about a hard drive diagnostic program. Be prepared to discuss the diagnostic software you researched. Refer to the worksheet in *IT Essentials: PC Hardware and Software Lab Manual, Fourth Edition*. You can complete this worksheet now or wait to do so until the end of the chapter.

Identify Organizational Tools and Their Purpose

It is important that a technician document all services and repairs. These documents need to be stored centrally and made available to all other technicians. The documentation can then be used as reference material for similar problems that are encountered in the future. Good customer service includes providing the customer with a detailed description of the problem and the solution.

Personal Reference Tools

Personal reference tools include the following:

- **Notes**: Make notes as you go through the investigation and repair process. Refer to these notes to avoid repeating previous steps and to determine what steps to take next.

- **Journal**: Document the upgrades and repairs that you perform. The documentation should include descriptions of the problem, possible solutions that have been tried to correct the problem, and the steps taken to repair the problem. Be sure to note any configuration changes made to the equipment and any replacement parts used in the repair. Your journal, along with your notes, can be valuable when you encounter similar situations in the future.

- **History of repairs**: Make a detailed list of problems and repairs, including the date, replacement parts, and customer information. The history allows a technician to determine what work has been performed on a computer in the past.

Note

Keeping an electronic journal stored on a computer can be helpful for later troubleshooting because you can more easily search for possible solutions in electronic documents than in paper documents.

Internet Reference Tools

The Internet is an excellent source of information about specific hardware problems and possible solutions. You find this information through the following resources:

- Internet search engines
- Newsgroups

- Manufacturer FAQs

- Online computer manuals

- Online forums and chat

- Technical websites

Miscellaneous Tools

With experience, you will discover many additional items to add to the toolkit. Figure 2-5 shows case and drive mounting screws.

Figure 2-5   Labeled Computer Parts

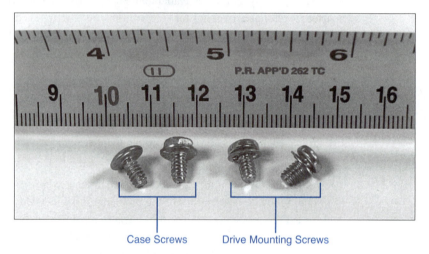

Case Screws   Drive Mounting Screws

A laptop is also a valuable resource to take with you on computer repairs in the field. Having your own working computer on a site visit can be used to research information, download tools or drivers, or communicate with other technicians.

Your toolkit should also include a variety of replacement parts. Figure 2-6 shows the types of replacement computer parts you might want to keep handy. Make sure that the parts are in good working order before you use them. Using known good components to replace possible bad ones in computers will help you quickly determine which component may not be working properly. You should store sensitive components, such as RAM, cards, and CPUs, in an antistatic bag prior to installation, as shown in Figure 2-7.

Figure 2-6   Replacement Computer Parts

Figure 2-7   Store Replacement Computer Parts in an Antistatic Bag

Lab 2.3.4: Computer Disassembly

In this lab, you will disassemble a computer using safe lab procedures and the proper tools. Use extreme care and follow all safety procedures. Familiarize yourself with the tools you will be using in this lab. Refer to the lab in *IT Essentials: PC Hardware and Software Lab Manual, Fourth Edition*. You can perform this lab now or wait until the end of the chapter.

Implement Proper Tool Use

Safety in the workplace is everyone's responsibility. You are much less likely to injure yourself or damage components when using the proper tool for the job.

Before cleaning or repairing equipment, check to make sure that your tools are in good condition. Clean, repair, or replace any items that are not functioning adequately.

After completing this section, you will meet these objectives:

- Demonstrate proper use of an antistatic wrist strap.

- Demonstrate proper use of an antistatic mat.

- Demonstrate proper use of various hand tools.

- Demonstrate proper use of cleaning materials.

Demonstrate Proper Use of an Antistatic Wrist Strap

As discussed previously, an example of ESD is the small shock that you receive when you walk across a room with carpet and touch a doorknob. Although the small shock is harmless to you, the same electrical charge passing from you to a computer can damage its components. Wearing an antistatic wrist strap can prevent ESD damage to computer components.

The purpose of an antistatic wrist strap is to equalize the electrical charge between you and the equipment. The antistatic wrist strap is a conductor that connects your body to the equipment that you are working on. When static electricity builds up in your body, the connection made by the wrist strap to the equipment, or ground, channels the electricity through the wire that connects the strap.

As shown in Figure 2-8, an antistatic wrist strap has two parts and is easy to wear. Following is the proper procedure for using an antistatic wrist strap:

How To

Step 1.   Wrap the strap around your wrist and secure it using the snap or Velcro. The metal on the back of the wrist strap must remain in contact with your skin at all times.

Step 2.   Snap the connector on the end of the wire to the wrist strap, and connect the other end either to the equipment or to the same grounding point that the antistatic mat is connected to. The metal skeleton of the case is a good place to connect the wire. When connecting the wire to equipment that you are working on, choose an unpainted metal surface. A painted surface does not conduct the electricity as well as unpainted metal.

Figure 2-8   Antistatic Wrist Strap

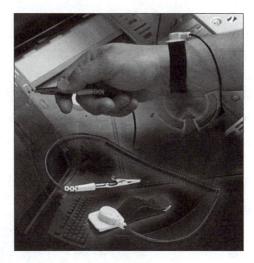

Note

Attach the wire on the same side of the equipment as the arm wearing the antistatic wrist strap. This will help to keep the wire out of the way while you are working.

Although wearing a wrist strap will help to prevent ESD, you can further reduce the risks by not wearing clothing made of silk, polyester, or wool. These fabrics are more likely to generate a static charge.

Note

Technicians should roll up their sleeves, remove scarves or ties, and tuck in their shirts to prevent interference from clothing. Ensure that earrings, necklaces, and other loose jewelry are properly secured or removed.

Caution

Never wear an antistatic wrist strap if you are repairing a monitor or a power supply unit.

Demonstrate Proper Use of an Antistatic Mat

You may not always have the option to work on a computer in a properly equipped workspace that includes workbenches and antistatic mats. If you can control the environment, try to set up your workspace away from carpeted areas. Carpets can cause the buildup of electrostatic charges. If you cannot avoid the carpeting, ground yourself to the unpainted portion of the case of the computer on which you are working before touching any components.

Antistatic Mat

An antistatic mat is slightly conductive. It works by drawing static electricity away from a component and transferring it safely from equipment to a grounding point, as shown in Figure 2-9. Following is the proper procedure for using an antistatic mat:

Step 1.   Lay the mat on the workspace next to or under the computer case.

Step 2.   Clip the mat to the case to provide a grounded surface on which you can place parts as you remove them from the system. Additional connections to the electrical earth ground is a best practice.

Figure 2-9   Antistatic Mat

Reducing the potential for ESD reduces the likelihood of damage to delicate circuits or components.

Note

Always handle components by the edges.

Workbench

When you are working at a *workbench*, ground the workbench and the antistatic floor mat. By standing on the floor mat and wearing the wrist strap, your body has the same charge as the equipment and reduces the probability of ESD. Either connect the table-top mat and the floor mat to each other or connect both to the electrical earth ground.

Demonstrate Proper Use of Various Hand Tools

A technician needs to be able to properly use each tool in the toolkit. This topic covers many of the various hand tools used when repairing computers.

Screws

Match each screw with the proper screwdriver. Place the tip of the screwdriver on the head of the screw. Turn the screwdriver clockwise to tighten the screw and counterclockwise to loosen the screw.

Screws can become stripped if you over-tighten them with a screwdriver. A stripped screw, shown in Figure 2-10, may get stuck in the screw hole or may not tighten firmly. Discard stripped screws.

Figure 2-10   Stripped Screw

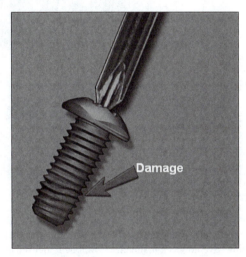

Flat-Head Screwdriver

Use a flat-head screwdriver when you are working with a slotted screw. Do not use a flat-head screwdriver to remove a Phillips-head screw. Never use a screwdriver as a pry bar.

Caution

If excessive force is needed to remove or add a component, something is probably wrong. Take a second look to make sure that you have not missed a screw or a locking clip that is holding the component in place. Refer to the device manual or diagram for additional information.

Phillips-Head Screwdriver

Use a Phillips-head screwdriver with crosshead screws. Do not use this type of screwdriver to puncture anything. This will damage the head of the screwdriver.

Hex Driver

Use a hex driver, shown in Figure 2-11, to loosen and tighten bolts that have a hexagonal (six-sided) head. Hex bolts should not be over-tightened because the threads of the bolts can be stripped. Do not use a hex driver that is too large for the bolt that you are using.

Figure 2-11   Hex Driver

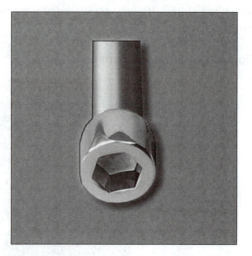

Caution

Some tools are magnetized. When working around electronic devices, be sure that the tools you are using have not been magnetized. Magnetic fields can be harmful to data stored on magnetic media. Test your tool by touching the tool with a metal screw. If the screw is attracted to the tool, do not use the tool.

Part Retriever, Needle-Nose Pliers, or Tweezers

The part retriever, needle-nose pliers, and tweezers, shown in Figure 2-12, can be used to place and retrieve parts that may be hard to reach with your fingers. Do not scratch or hit any components when using these tools.

Figure 2-12   Component-Retrieving Tools

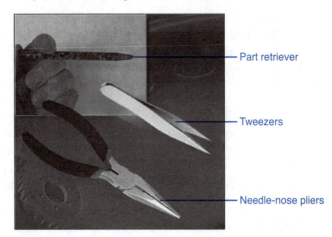

— Part retriever

— Tweezers

— Needle-nose pliers

Caution

Do not use a pencil inside the computer to change the setting of switches or to pry off jumpers. The pencil lead can act as a conductor and may damage the computer components.

Demonstrate Proper Use of Cleaning Materials

Keeping computers clean inside and out is a vital part of a maintenance program. Dirt can cause problems with the physical operation of fans, buttons, and other mechanical components. Severe dust can build up on computer components. On electrical components, an excessive buildup of dust will act like an insulator and trap the heat. This insulation will impair the ability of heat sinks and cooling fans to keep components cool, causing chips and circuits to overheat and fail.

Caution

When you use compressed air to clean inside the computer, blow air around the components with a minimum distance of four inches from the nozzle. Clean the power supply and the fan from the back of the case. Do not shake compressed air. The can must be held upright when in use.

Caution

Before cleaning any device, turn it off and unplug the device from the power source.

Computer Cases and Monitors

Clean computer cases and the outside of monitors with a mild cleaning solution on a damp, lint-free cloth. Mix one drop of dishwashing liquid with four ounces of water to create the cleaning solution. If any water drips inside the case, allow enough time for the liquid to dry before powering on the computer.

LCD Screens

Do not use ammoniated glass cleaners or any other solution on a liquid crystal display (LCD) screen, unless the cleaner is specifically designed for the purpose. Harsh chemicals will damage the coating on the screen. There is no glass protecting these screens, so be gentle when cleaning them and do not press firmly on the screen.

CRT Screens

To clean the screens of CRT monitors, dampen a soft, clean, lint-free cloth with distilled water and wipe the screen from top to bottom. Then use a soft, dry cloth to wipe the screen and remove any streaking after you have cleaned the monitor.

Clean dusty components with a can of compressed air. Compressed air does not cause electrostatic buildup on components. Make sure that you are in a well-ventilated area before blowing the dust out of the computer. A best practice is to wear a dust mask to make sure that you do not breathe in the dust particles.

Blow out the dust using short bursts from the can. Never tip the can or use the compressed air can upside down. Do not allow the fan blades to spin from the force of the compressed air. Hold the fan in place. Fan motors can be ruined from spinning when the motor is not turned on.

Component Contacts

Clean the contacts on components with isopropyl alcohol. Do not use rubbing alcohol. Rubbing alcohol contains impurities that can damage contacts. Make sure that the contacts do not collect any lint from the cloth or cotton swab. Blow any lint off the contacts with compressed air before reinstallation.

Keyboard

Clean a desktop keyboard with compressed air or a small, hand-held vacuum cleaner with a brush attachment.

Caution

Never use a standard vacuum cleaner inside a computer case. The plastic parts of the vacuum cleaner can build up static electricity and discharge to the components. Use only a vacuum approved for electronic components.

Mouse

Use glass cleaner and a soft cloth to clean the outside of the mouse. Do not spray glass cleaner directly on the mouse. If cleaning a ball mouse, you can remove the ball and clean it with glass cleaner and a soft cloth. Wipe the rollers clean inside the mouse with the same cloth. Do not spray any liquids inside the mouse.

The following list documents the computer items that you should clean and the cleaning materials you should use in each case:

- **Computer case and outside of monitor**: Mild cleaning solution of dishwashing liquid and water

- **LCD screen**: Mild cleaning solution of dishwashing liquid and water

- **CRT screen**: Glass cleaner and soft cloth (spray on the cloth, not on the screen)

- **Heat sink**: Compressed air

- **RAM stick**: Isopropyl alcohol and some Q-tips

- **Keyboard**: Handheld vacuum cleaner with a brush attachment

- **Mouse**: Glass cleaner and soft cloth (spray on the cloth, not on the mouse)

Summary

This chapter discussed safe lab procedures, correct tool usage, and the proper disposal of computer components and supplies. You have familiarized yourself in the lab with many of the tools used to build, service, and clean computer and electronic components. You have also learned the importance of organizational tools and found out how these tools help you work more efficiently.

The following are some of the important concepts to remember from this chapter:

- Work in a safe manner to protect both users and equipment.

- Follow all safety guidelines to prevent injuries to yourself and to others.

- Know how to protect equipment from ESD damage.

- Know about and be able to prevent power issues that can cause equipment damage or data loss.

- Know which products and supplies require special disposal procedures.

- Familiarize yourself with MSDSs for both safety issues and disposal restrictions to help protect the environment.

- Use the correct tool for the task.

- Know how to clean components safely.

- Use organizational tools during computer repairs.

Summary of Exercises

This is a summary of the Labs, Worksheets, Remote Technician exercises, Class Discussions, Virtual Desktop activities, and Virtual Laptop activities associated with this chapter.

Labs

The following lab covers material from this chapter. Refer to the lab in *IT Essentials: PC Hardware and Software Lab Manual, Fourth Edition*.

Lab 2.3.4: Computer Disassembly

Worksheets

The following worksheet covers material from this chapter. Refer to the worksheet in *IT Essentials: PC Hardware and Software Lab Manual, Fourth Edition*.

Worksheet 2.2.2: Diagnostic Software

Check Your Understanding

You can find the answers to these questions in the appendix, "Answers to Check Your Understanding Questions."

1. What class of fire extinguisher is used to extinguish electrical equipment fires?

   A. Class A

   B. Class B

   C. Class C

   D. Class D

2. Which of the following is a fact sheet that summarizes information about material identification, including hazardous ingredients that can affect personal health, fire hazards, and first aid requirements?

   A. ESD

   B. MSDS

   C. OSHA

   D. UPS

3. Which of the following can cause permanent damage to electrical components if you do not use proper tools and safety procedures?

   A. ESD

   B. UPS

   C. MSDS

   D. OSHA

4. What is the minimum level of electrostatic discharge that a person can normally feel?

   A. 5 volts

   B. 1000 volts

   C. 3000 volts

   D. 10,000 volts

5. Which recommendation should be followed first when a fire in the workplace is out of control?

   A. Try to use the elevators to get to the lowest floor faster.

   B. Get out of the room or building and contact emergency services for help.

   C. Use the company water system to stop the fire from extending to other areas.

   D. Try to control the fire with proper extinguishers.

6. Which of the following tools are recommended for cleaning a PC? (Choose two.)

    A. Antibacterial spray

    B. Compressed air

    C. Mild abrasive detergent

    D. Nylon brush

    E. Rubbing alcohol

    F. Soft cloth

7. How does a technician discharge static buildup?

    A. Touching the painted part of the computer case

    B. Touching an unpainted part of the computer case

    C. Touching an antistatic wrist strap before touching any computer equipment

    D. Touching an antistatic mat before touching any computer equipment

8. Which device is designed specifically to protect computers and electrical devices from excess electrical voltage?

    A. Power strip

    B. Standby power supply

    C. Surge protector

    D. Uninterruptible power supply

9. Which of the following effects can be observed on computer components as a result of climate? (Choose three.)

    A. Components overheat if the climate is too hot.

    B. Moisture damages computer parts if the climate is too humid.

    C. Components work too slowly if the climate is too cold.

    D. The risk of ESD increases if the humidity is too low.

    E. The risk of ESD increases if the temperature is too high.

    F. Components overheat if the humidity is too low.

10. Which condition refers to a sudden and dramatic increase in voltage, which is usually caused by lighting?

    A. Brownout

    B. Sag

    C. Spike

    D. Surge

CHAPTER 3

Computer Assembly—Step by Step

Objectives

Upon completion of this chapter, you should be able to answer the following questions:

- How do I open the case?

- What is the process to install the power supply?

- How do I attach the components to the motherboard and install the motherboard?

- How do I install internal drives?

- How do I install drives in external bays?

- How do I install adapter cards?

- What is the process to connect all internal cables?

- How do I reattach the side panels and connect external cables to the computer?

- What happens when I boot the computer for the first time?

Key Terms

This chapter uses the following key terms. You can find the definitions in the Glossary.

electrostatic discharge (ESD)   page 80

power supply   page 80

motherboard   page 81

central processing unit (CPU)   page 82

zero insertion force (ZIF) socket   page 83

thermal compound   page 83

isopropyl alcohol   page 83

heat sink/fan assembly   page 83

random-access memory (RAM)   page 84

volatile memory   page 85

hard disk drive (HDD)   page 86

optical drive   page 86

floppy disk drive (FDD)   page 86

Molex power connector   page 86

Berg power connector   page 87

adapter card   page 88

network interface card (NIC)   page 88

video adapter card   page 89

Advanced Technology Extended (ATX)   page 91

*serial advanced technology attachment (SATA)
  power connector   page 91*

*parallel advanced technology attachment (PATA)
  data cable   page 92*

SATA data cable   page 92

basic input/output system (BIOS)   page 96

beep code   page 97

*complementary metal-oxide semiconductor (CMOS)
  page 97*

Assembling computers is a large part of a technician's job. As a technician, you will need to work in a logical, methodical manner when working with computer components. As with any learned trade, your computer assembly skills will improve dramatically with practice.

Open the Case

Computer cases are produced in a variety of form factors. Form factors refer to the size and shape of the case.

Prepare the workspace before opening the computer case. There should be adequate lighting, good ventilation, and a comfortable room temperature. The workbench or table should be accessible from all sides. Avoid cluttering the surface of the workbench or table with tools and computer components. An antistatic mat on the table will help prevent physical and *electrostatic discharge (ESD)* damage to equipment. Small containers can be used to hold small screws and other parts as they are being removed.

There are different methods for opening cases. To learn how to open a particular computer case, consult the user manual or the manufacturer's website. Most computer cases are opened in one of the following ways:

- The computer case cover can be removed as one piece.

- The top and side panels of the case can be removed.

- The top of the case may need to be removed before the side panels can be removed.

- Tool-less entries allow technicians to enter a case without the use of tools.

Install the Power Supply

A technician may be required to replace or install a power supply, as shown in Figure 3-1. Most *power supplies* can fit into the computer case in only one way. There are usually three or four screws that attach the power supply to the case. Power supplies have fans that can vibrate and loosen screws that are not secured. When installing a power supply, make sure that all of the screws are used and that they are properly tightened.

These are the power supply installation steps:

Step 1. Insert the power supply into the case.

Step 2. Align the holes in the power supply with the holes in the case.

Step 3. Secure the power supply to the case using the proper screws.

Figure 3-1   Power Supply

Virtual Desktop Activity: Power Supply

Complete the power supply layer in the Virtual Desktop. Refer to the Virtual Desktop software on the CD that comes with this book.

Virtual Desktop Activity: Motherboard

System requirements for the Virtual Desktop include a minimum of 512 MB RAM and Windows 2000 or Windows XP operating system.

Lab 3.2.0: Install the Power Supply

In this lab, you install the power supply in the computer. Refer to the lab in *IT Essentials: PC Hardware and Software Lab Manual, Fourth Edition*. You may perform this lab now or wait until the end of the chapter.

Attach the Components to the Motherboard and Install the Motherboard

This section details the steps to install components on the *motherboard* and then install the motherboard into the computer case.

After completing this section, you will meet these objectives:

- Install a CPU and a heat sink/fan assembly.

- Install the RAM.

- Install the motherboard.

Install a CPU and a Heat Sink/Fan Assembly

The *central processing unit (CPU)* and the heat sink/fan assembly may be installed on the motherboard before the motherboard is placed in the computer case.

CPU

Figure 3-2 shows a close-up view of the CPU and the motherboard. The CPU and motherboard are sensitive to electrostatic discharge. When handling a CPU and motherboard, make sure that you place them on a grounded antistatic mat. You should wear an antistatic wrist strap while working with these components. Key electrostatic-sensitive components include the following:

- CPUs
- Motherboards
- RAM
- Expansion cards
- Hard disk drive electronics

Figure 3-2   CPU and Motherboard

The CPU is secured to the socket on the motherboard with a locking assembly. The CPU sockets today are *zero insertion force (ZIF) sockets*. You should be familiar with the locking assembly before attempting to install a CPU into the socket on the motherboard. Orient the missing pin in the corner of the CPU to the missing hole on the socket.

Thermal compound helps to conduct heat away from the CPU. Figure 3-3 shows thermal compound being applied to the CPU.

Figure 3-3   Thermal Compound on the CPU

When you are installing a used CPU, clean the CPU and the base of the heat sink with *isopropyl alcohol*. Doing this removes all traces of old thermal compound. The surfaces are now ready for a new layer of thermal compound. Follow all manufacturer recommendations about applying the thermal compound.

Heat Sink/Fan Assembly

Figure 3-4 shows the connector and the motherboard header for the *heat sink/fan assembly*. It is a two-part cooling device. The heat sink draws heat away from the CPU. The fan moves the heat away from the heat sink. The heat sink/fan assembly usually has a 3-pin power connector.

Figure 3-4   Heat Sink/Fan Assembly on the Motherboard

Follow these instructions for CPU and heat sink/fan assembly installation:

How To

Step 1.   Align the CPU so that the Connection 1 indicator is lined up with Pin 1 on the CPU socket. Doing this ensures that the orientation notches on the CPU are aligned with the orientation keys on the CPU socket.

Step 2.   Place the CPU gently into the socket.

Step 3.   Close the CPU load plate and secure it in place by closing the load lever and moving it under the load lever retention tab.

Step 4.   Apply a small amount of thermal compound to the CPU and spread it evenly. Follow the application instructions provided by the manufacturer.

Step 5.   Align the heat sink/fan assembly retainers with the holes on the motherboard.

Step 6.   Place the heat sink/fan assembly onto the CPU socket, being careful not to pinch the CPU fan wires.

Step 7.   Tighten the heat sink/fan assembly retainers to secure the assembly in place.

Step 8.   Connect the heat sink/fan assembly power cable to the header on the motherboard.

Install the RAM

Like the CPU and the heat sink/fan assembly, *random-access memory (RAM)* is installed in the motherboard before the motherboard is secured in the computer case. Before you install a memory module, consult the motherboard documentation or website of the manufacturer to ensure that the RAM is compatible with the motherboard.

RAM provides temporary data storage for the CPU while the computer is operating. RAM is *volatile memory*, which means that its contents are lost when the computer is shut down. Typically, more RAM will enhance the performance of your computer.

Follow these steps for RAM installation:

Step 1. Align the notches on the RAM module with the keys in the slot and press down until the side tabs click into place.

Step 2. Make sure that the side tabs have locked the RAM module. Visually check for exposed contacts.

Repeat these steps for additional RAM modules.

Install the Motherboard

The motherboard is now ready to install in the computer case. Plastic and metal standoffs are used to mount the motherboard and to prevent it from touching the metal portions of the case. You should install only the standoffs that align with the holes in the motherboard. Installing any additional standoffs may prevent the motherboard from being seated properly in the computer case.

Follow these steps for motherboard installation:

Step 1. Install standoffs in the computer case.

Step 2. Align the I/O connectors on the back of the motherboard with the openings in the back of the case.

Step 3. Align the screw holes of the motherboard with the standoffs.

Step 4. Insert all of the motherboard screws.

Step 5. Tighten all of the motherboard screws.

Virtual Desktop Activity: Motherboard

System requirements for the Virtual Desktop include a minimum of 512 MB RAM and Windows 2000 or Windows XP operating system.

Complete the motherboard assembly in the Virtual Desktop motherboard layer. Refer to the Virtual Desktop software on the CD that comes with this book.

Lab 3.3.3: Install the Motherboard

In this lab, you install the CPU, heat sink/fan assembly, RAM, and motherboard. Refer to the lab in *IT Essentials: PC Hardware and Software Lab Manual, Fourth Edition*. You may perform this lab now or wait until the end of the chapter.

Install Internal Drives

Drives that are installed in internal bays are called internal drives. A *hard disk drive (HDD)* is an example of an internal drive.

Follow these steps for HDD installation:

Step 1.   Position the HDD so that it aligns with the 3.5-inch drive bay.

Step 2.   Insert the HDD into the drive bay so that the screw holes in the drive line up with the screw holes in the case.

Step 3.   Secure the HDD to the case using the proper screws.

Virtual Desktop Activity: Internal Drives

System requirements for the Virtual Desktop include a minimum of 512 MB RAM and Windows 2000 or Windows XP operating system.

Complete the hard drive installation in the Virtual Desktop internal drive layer. Refer to the Virtual Desktop software on the CD that comes with this book.

Install Drives in External Bays

Drives, such as *optical drives* and *floppy disk drives (FDD)*, are installed in drive bays that are accessed from the front of the case. Optical drives and FDD store data on removable media. Drives in external bays allow access to the media without opening the case.

After completing this section, you will meet these objectives:

- Install the optical drive.
- Install the floppy drive.

Install the Optical Drive

An optical drive is a storage device that reads and writes information to CDs and DVDs. A *Molex power connector* provides the optical drive with power from the power supply. A PATA cable connects the optical drive to the motherboard. If you use a PATA data connector you might need a berg connector. To provides power to the (FDD), you will need the smaller berg power connector.

Follow these steps for optical drive installation:

Step 1.   Position the optical drive so that it aligns with the 5.25-inch drive bay.

Step 2.   Insert the optical drive into the drive bay so that the optical drive screw holes align with the screw holes in the case.

Step 3.   Secure the optical drive to the case using the proper screws.

Caution

If you use screws that are too long, you may damage the drive you are mounting.

Install the Floppy Drive

A floppy disk drive (FDD) is a storage device that reads and writes information to a floppy disk. A *Berg power connector* provides the FDD with power from the power supply. A floppy drive data cable connects the FDD to the motherboard.

A floppy disk drive fits into the 3.5-inch bay on the front of the computer case, as shown in Figure 3-5.

Follow these steps for FDD installation:

Step 1.   Position the FDD so that it aligns with the 3.5-inch drive bay.

Step 2.   Insert the FDD into the drive bay so that the FDD screw holes align with the screw holes in the case.

Step 3.   Secure the FDD to the case using the proper screws.

Figure 3-5   Floppy Disk Drive Installed

Virtual Desktop Activity: Drives in External Bays

System requirements for the Virtual Desktop include a minimum of 512 MB RAM and Windows 2000 or Windows XP operating system.

Complete the optical and floppy drive installation in the Virtual Desktop drives in the external bays layer. Refer to the Virtual Desktop software on the CD that comes with this book.

Lab 3.5.2: Install the Drives

In this lab, you install the hard drive, optical drive, and floppy drive. Refer to the lab in *IT Essentials: PC Hardware and Software Lab Manual, Fourth Edition*. You may perform this lab now or wait until the end of the chapter.

Install Adapter Cards

Adapter cards are installed to add functionality to a computer. Adapter cards must be compatible with the expansion slot. This section focuses on the installation of three types of adapter cards:

- PCIe x1 NIC
- PCI wireless NIC
- PCIe x16 video adapter card

After completing this section, you will meet these objectives:

- Install the NIC.
- Install the wireless NIC.
- Install the video adapter card.

Install the NIC

A *network interface card (NIC)* enables a computer to connect to a network. NICs use peripheral component interface (PCI) and PCIe expansion slots on the motherboard, as shown in Figure 3-6.

Figure 3-6   PCIe Network Interface Card

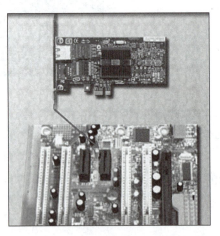

Follow these steps for NIC installation:

Step 1.   Remove the blank from the case where the new card will be installed so that the port can be accessed.

Step 2.   Align the NIC with the appropriate expansion slot on the motherboard.

Step 3.   Press down gently on the NIC until the card is fully seated.

Step 4.   Secure the NIC PC mounting bracket to the case with the appropriate screw.

Install the Wireless NIC

A wireless NIC, as shown in Figure 3-7, enables a computer to connect to a wireless network. Wireless NICs use PCI and PCIe expansion slots on the motherboard. Some wireless NICs are installed externally with a USB connector.

Follow these steps for wireless NIC installation:

Step 1.   Align the wireless NIC with the appropriate expansion slot on the motherboard.

Step 2.   Press down gently on the wireless NIC until the card is fully seated.

Step 3.   Secure the wireless NIC PC mounting bracket to the case with the appropriate screw.

Figure 3-7   Wireless NIC

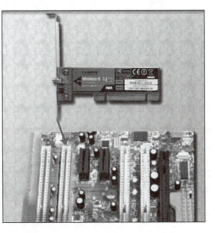

Install the Video Adapter Card

A *video adapter card*, as shown in Figure 3-8, is the interface between a computer and a display monitor. An upgraded video adapter card can provide better graphic capabilities for games and graphic programs. Video adapter cards use PCI, advance graphics port (AGP), and PCIe expansion slots on the motherboard. If the BIOS does not automatically sense the new video card and disable the integrated one, you may need to do that manually through BIOS settings.

Figure 3-8   Video Adapter Card

Follow these steps for video adapter card installation:

Step 1.   Remove the expansion slot case blank.

Step 2.   Align the video adapter card with the appropriate expansion slot on the mother-board.

Step 3.   Press down gently on the video adapter card until the card is fully seated.

Step 4.   Secure the video adapter card PC mounting bracket to the case with the appropriate screw.

Virtual Desktop Activity: Adapter Cards

System requirements for the Virtual Desktop include a minimum of 512 MB RAM and Windows 2000 or Windows XP operating system.

Complete the NIC, wireless NIC, and video adapter card installation in the Virtual Desktop adapter card layer. Refer to the Virtual Desktop software on the CD that comes with this book.

Lab 3.6.3: Install Adapter Cards

In this lab, you install the NIC, wireless NIC, and video adapter card. Refer to the lab in *IT Essentials: PC Hardware and Software Lab Manual, Fourth Edition.* You may perform this lab now or wait until the end of the chapter.

Connect All Internal Cables

Power cables are used to distribute electricity from the power supply to the motherboard and other components. Data cables transmit data between the motherboard and storage devices, such as hard drives. Additional cables connect the buttons and link lights on the front of the computer case to the motherboard.

After completing this section, you will meet these objectives:

- Connect the power cables.
- Connect the data cables.

Connect the Power Cables

Power cables are brightly colored bundles of wires that branch out from the power supply. As the name suggests, they provide internal devices with electricity. There are several kinds of power connectors.

Motherboard Power Connections

Just like other components, motherboards require power to operate. The *Advanced Technology Extended (ATX)* main power connector will have either 20 or 24 pins. The power supply may also have a 4-pin or 6-pin Auxiliary (AUX) power connector that connects to the motherboard. A 20-pin connector will work in a motherboard with a 24-pin socket.

Follow these steps for motherboard power cable installation:

How To

Step 1.   Align the 20-pin ATX power connector with the socket on the motherboard.

Step 2.   Gently press down on the connector until the clip clicks into place.

Step 3.   Align the 4-pin AUX power connector with the socket on the motherboard.

Step 4.   Gently press down on the connector until the clip clicks into place.

SATA Power Connectors

SATA power connectors use a 15-pin connector. *Serial advanced technology attachment (SATA) power connectors* are used to connect to hard disk drives, optical drives, or any devices that have a SATA power socket.

Molex Power Connectors

Hard disk drives and optical drives that do not have SATA power sockets use a Molex power connector.

Caution

Do not use a Molex connector and a SATA power connector on the same drive at the same time. It will prevent the drive from working properly.

Berg Power Connectors

The 4-pin Berg power connector supplies power to a floppy drive.

Follow these steps for Berg power connector installation:

How To

Step 1.   Plug the SATA power connector into the HDD.

Step 2.   Plug the Molex power connector into the optical drive.

Step 3.   Plug the 4-pin Berg power connector into the FDD.

Step 4.   Connect the 3-pin fan power connector into the appropriate fan header on the motherboard, according to the motherboard manual.

Step 5.   Plug the additional cables from the case into the appropriate connectors according to the motherboard manual.

Connect the Data Cables

Drives connect to the motherboard using data cables. The drive being connected determines the type of data cable used. The types of data cables are PATA, SATA, and floppy disk.

PATA Data Cables

The *parallel advanced technology attachment (PATA) data cable* is sometimes called a ribbon cable because it is wide and flat. The PATA cable can have either 40 or 80 conductors. A PATA cable usually has three 40-pin connectors. One connector at the end of the cable connects to the motherboard. The other two connectors connect to drives. If multiple hard drives are installed, the master drive connects to the end connector. The slave drive connects to the middle connector.

A stripe on the data cable denotes the location of Pin 1. Plug the PATA cable into the drive with the Pin 1 indicator on the cable aligned with the Pin 1 indicator on the drive connector. The Pin 1 indicator on the drive connector is usually closest to the power connector on the drive. Many motherboards have two PATA drive controllers, providing support for a maximum of four PATA drives.

SATA Data Cables

The *SATA data cable* has a 7-pin connector. One end of the cable is connected to the motherboard. The other end is connected to any drive that has a SATA data connector.

Reattach the Side Panels and Connect External Cables to the Computer

Now that all the internal components have been installed and connected to the motherboard and power supply, you need to reattach the side panels to the computer case. The next step is to connect the cables for all computer peripherals and the power cable.

After completing this section, you will meet these objectives:

- Reattach the side panels to the case.
- Connect external cables to the computer.

Reattach the Side Panels to the Case

Most computer cases have two panels, one on each side. Some computer cases have one three-sided cover that slides down over the case frame.

When the cover is in place, make sure that it is secured at all screw locations. Some computer cases use screws that are inserted with a screwdriver. Other cases have knob-type screws that can be tightened by hand. Tool-less cases simply "click" closed.

If you are unsure about how to remove or replace the computer case, refer to the documentation or website of the manufacturer for more information.

Caution

Handle case parts with care. Some computer case covers have sharp or jagged edges.

Connect External Cables to the Computer

After the case panels have been reattached, connect the cables to the back of the computer. Here are some common external cable connections:

- Monitor
- Keyboard
- Mouse
- USB
- Ethernet
- Power

When attaching cables, ensure that they are connected to the correct locations on the computer. For example, some mouse and keyboard cables use the same type of PS/2 connector.

Floppy Drive Data Cables

The floppy drive data cable has a 34-pin connector. Like the PATA data cable, the floppy drive data cable has a stripe to denote the location of Pin 1. A floppy drive cable usually has three 34-pin connectors. One connector at the end of the cable connects to the motherboard. The other two connectors connect to drives. If multiple floppy drives are installed, the A: drive connects to the end connector. The B: drive connects to the middle connector.

Plug the floppy drive data cable into the drive with the Pin 1 indicator on the cable aligned with the Pin 1 indicator on the drive connector. Motherboards have one floppy drive controller, providing support for a maximum of two floppy drives.

> **Note**
>
> If Pin 1 on the floppy drive data cable is not aligned with Pin 1 on the drive connector, the floppy drive does not function. This misalignment does not damage the drive, but the drive activity light displays continuously. To fix this problem, turn off the computer and reconnect the data cable so that Pin 1 on the cable and Pin 1 on the connector are aligned. Reboot the computer.

Follow these steps for data cable installation:

Step 1.   Plug the motherboard end of the PATA cable into the motherboard socket.

Step 2.   Plug the connector at the far end of the PATA cable into the optical drive.

Step 3.   Plug one end of the SATA cable into the motherboard socket.

Step 4.   Plug the other end of the SATA cable into the HDD.

Step 5.   Plug the motherboard end of the FDD cable into the motherboard socket.

Step 6.   Plug the connector at the far end of the FDD cable into the floppy drive.

Step 7.   Double check to make sure all cables are securely connected to the devices and to the motherboard.

Virtual Desktop Activity: Internal Cables

System requirements for the Virtual Desktop include a minimum of 512 MB RAM and Windows 2000 or Windows XP operating system.

Complete the internal cable installation in the Virtual Desktop internal cable layer. Refer to the Virtual Desktop software on the CD that comes with this book.

Lab 3.7.2: Install Internal Cables

In this lab, you install internal power and data cables in the computer. Refer to the lab in *IT Essentials: PC Hardware and Software Lab Manual, Fourth Edition*. You may perform this lab now or wait until the end of the chapter.

Caution

When attaching cables, never force a connection.

Note

Plug in the power cable after you have connected all other cables.

Follow these steps for external cable installation:

Step 1.   Attach the monitor cable to the video port.

Step 2.   Secure the cable by tightening the screws on the connector.

Step 3.   Plug the keyboard cable into the PS/2 keyboard port.

Step 4.   Plug the mouse cable into the PS/2 mouse port.

Step 5.   Plug the USB cable into a USB port.

Step 6.   Plug the network cable into the network port.

Step 7.   Connect the wireless antenna to the antenna connector.

Step 8.   Plug the power cable into the power supply.

Figure 3-9 shows all of the external cables plugged into the back of the computer.

Figure 3-9   All External Cables Plugged into the Back

Virtual Desktop Activity: External Cables

System requirements for the Virtual Desktop include a minimum of 512 MB RAM and Windows 2000 or Windows XP operating system.

Complete the external cable installation in the Virtual Desktop external cable layer. Refer to the Virtual Desktop software on the CD that comes with this book.

Lab 3.8.2: Complete the Computer Assembly

In this lab, you reattach the case and connect the external cables to complete the computer assembly. Refer to the lab in *IT Essentials: PC Hardware and Software Lab Manual, Fourth Edition*. You may perform this lab now or wait until the end of the chapter.

Boot the Computer for the First Time

When the computer is booted, the *basic input/output system (BIOS)* performs a check on all of the internal components, as shown in Figure 3-10. This check is called a power-on self test (POST).

After completing this section, you will meet these objectives:

- Identify beep codes.
- Describe BIOS setup.

Figure 3-10   BIOS Setup Screenshot

Identify Beep Codes

POST checks to see that all of the hardware in the computer is operating correctly. If a device is malfunctioning, an error or a beep code alerts the technician that there is a problem. Typically, a single beep denotes that the computer is functioning properly. If there is a hardware problem, the computer might emit a series of beeps. Each BIOS manufacturer uses different codes to indicate hardware problems. Table 3-1 shows a sample chart of *beep codes*. The beep codes for your computer might be different. Consult the motherboard documentation to view beep codes for your computer.

Table 3-1   Sample Beep Codes

Beep Code	Meaning	Cause
1 beep	Passed POST	Successfully passed POST
2 beeps	Memory parity error	Bad memory
3 beeps	Base 64K memory failure	Bad memory
4 beeps	Timer not operational	Bad motherboard
5 beeps	Processor error	Bad processor
6 beeps	8042 gate A20 failure	Bad CPU or motherboard
7 beeps	Processor exception	Bad processor
8 beeps	Video memory error	Bad video card or memory
9 beeps	ROM checksum error	Bad BIOS
10 beeps	CMOS checksum error	Bad motherboard
11 beeps	Cache memory bad	Bad CPU or motherboard

Describe BIOS Setup

The BIOS contains a setup program used to configure settings for hardware devices. The configuration data is saved to a special memory chip called a *complementary metal-oxide semiconductor (CMOS)*. CMOS is maintained by the battery in the computer. If this battery dies, all BIOS setup configuration data will be lost. If this occurs, replace the battery and reconfigure the BIOS settings.

To enter the BIOS setup program, you must press the proper key or key sequence during POST. Most computers use the Delete key. Your computer might use another key or combination of keys.

Figure 3-11 shows an example of a BIOS setup program.

Figure 3-11   BIOS Setup Program

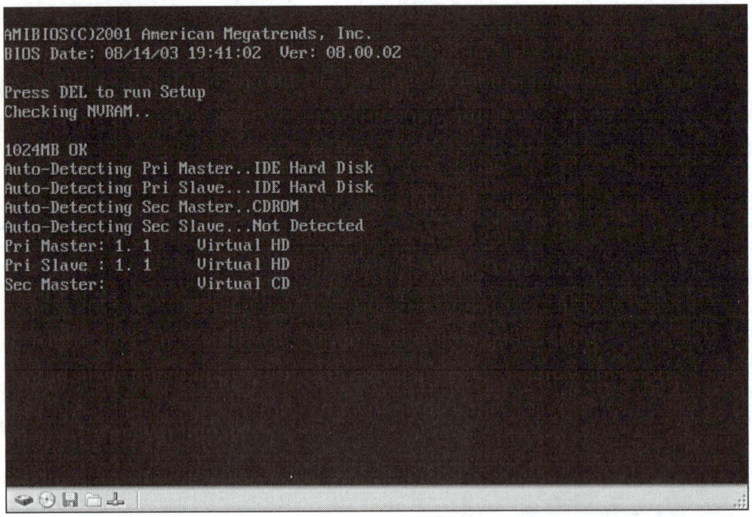

```
AMIBIOS(C)2001 American Megatrends, Inc.
BIOS Date: 08/14/03 19:41:02  Ver: 08.00.02

Press DEL to run Setup
Checking NVRAM..

1024MB OK
Auto-Detecting Pri Master..IDE Hard Disk
Auto-Detecting Pri Slave...IDE Hard Disk
Auto-Detecting Sec Master..CDROM
Auto-Detecting Sec Slave...Not Detected
Pri Master: 1. 1     Virtual HD
Pri Slave : 1. 1     Virtual HD
Sec Master:          Virtual CD
```

Here are some common BIOS setup menu options:

- **Main**: System time, date, HDD type, and so forth

- **Advanced**: Infrared port settings, parallel port settings, and so forth

- **Security**: Password settings to setup utility

- **Others**: Low battery alarm, system beep, and so on

- **Boot**: Boot order of the computer

- **Exit**: Setup utility exit

Lab 3.9.2: Boot the Computer

In this lab, you boot the computer and verify BIOS settings. Refer to the lab in *IT Essentials: PC Hardware and Software Lab Manual, Fourth Edition.* You may perform this lab now or wait until the end of the chapter.

Summary

This chapter detailed the steps used to assemble a computer and boot the system for the first time. These are some important points to remember:

- Computer cases come in a variety of sizes and configurations. Many of the computer's components must match the case's form factor.

- The CPU is installed on the motherboard with a heat sink/fan assembly.

- The power supply is installed in the PC.

- RAM is installed in RAM slots found on the motherboard.

- Adapter cards are installed in PCI and PCIe expansion slots found on the motherboard.

- Hard disk drives are installed in 3.5-inch drive bays located inside the case.

- Optical drives are installed in 5.25-inch drive bays that can be accessed from outside the case.

- Floppy drives are installed in 3.5-inch drive bays that can be accessed from outside the case.

- Power supply cables are connected to all drives and the motherboard.

- Internal data cables transfer data to all drives.

- External cables connect peripheral devices to the computer.

- Beep codes signify when hardware malfunctions.

- The BIOS setup program is used to display information about the computer components and allows the user to change system settings.

Summary of Exercises

This is a summary of the Labs, Worksheets, Remote Technician exercises, Class Discussions, Virtual Desktop activities, and Virtual Laptop activities associated with this chapter.

Labs

The following labs cover material from this chapter. Refer to the labs in *IT Essentials: PC Hardware and Software Lab Manual, Fourth Edition*.

Lab 3.2.0: Install the Power Supply

Lab 3.3.3: Install the Motherboard

Lab 3.5.2: Install the Drives

Lab 3.6.3: Install Adapter Cards

Lab 3.7.2: Install Internal Cables

Lab 3.8.2: Complete the Computer Assembly

Lab 3.9.2: Boot the Computer

Virtual Desktop Activities

The following Virtual Desktop activities cover material from this chapter. Refer to the Virtual Desktop software on the CD that comes with this book.

Virtual Desktop Activity: Power Supply

Virtual Desktop Activity: Motherboard

Virtual Desktop Activity: Internal Drives

Virtual Desktop Activity: Drives in External Bays

Virtual Desktop Activity: Adapter Cards

Virtual Desktop Activity: Internal Cables

Virtual Desktop Activity: External Cables

Check Your Understanding

You can find the answers to these questions in the appendix, "Answers to Check Your Understanding Questions."

1. A technician is installing a new power supply in a computer. Which type of power connector should be used to connect to a CD-ROM?

   A. Berg

   B. Mini-Molex

   C. Molex

   D. 20-pin ATX connector

2. A technician is installing a new power supply in a computer. Which type of power connector should be used to connect to an ATX motherboard?

   A. Berg

   B. Mini-Molex

   C. Molex

   D. 20-pin connector

3. When a technician installs a new CPU, what will help maintain even contact and heat distribution between the CPU and heat sink?

A. Silicon spray

B. Graphite paste

C. Glue

D. Thermal compound

4. When installing a CPU in a ZIF socket, how should the technician align the pins to avoid damage?

A. Pin 1 is always aligned with the corner opposite the base of the lever.

B. Pin 1 on the CPU is aligned with Pin 1 on the ZIF socket.

C. Pin 1 is aligned with the corner closest to the memory.

D. The removed corner of the CPU is always aligned with the corner opposite Pin 1.

5. A technician is installing additional memory in a computer. How can the technician guarantee that the memory is correctly aligned?

A. The label on the memory module should always face the CPU.

B. A notch in the memory module should be aligned with a notch in the slot on the motherboard.

C. The arrows on the memory module should be aligned with the arrows on the motherboard slot.

D. All memory and motherboard slots are color-coded, with one red end and one blue end.

6. When mounting a motherboard in a computer case, what does the technician use to prevent the motherboard from touching the bottom of the case?

A. Standoffs

B. Ground-fault isolators

C. Silicon spray

D. Grounding straps

7. When installing adapter cards in a computer, how should a technician properly secure the card?

A. Install the card, and attach it to the expansion slot using thermal paste.

B. Install the card, and attach it to the motherboard using thermal pads.

C. Install the card, and secure it using metal retaining clips located on the expansion slot.

D. Install the card, and secure it to the case with a screw. Or, if the case provides plastic or metal clips, use them.

8. Which two connectors are used to connect external peripherals?

A. EIDE

B. Molex

C. PATA

D. PS/2

E. USB

CHAPTER 4

Basics of Preventive Maintenance and Troubleshooting

Objectives

Upon completion of this chapter, you should be able to answer the following questions:

- What is the purpose of preventive maintenance?
- What are the elements of the troubleshooting process?

Key Terms

This chapter uses the following key terms. You can find the definitions in the Glossary.

This chapter introduces preventive maintenance and the troubleshooting process. This chapter discusses troubleshooting as a concept. Detailed troubleshooting techniques are outlined in subsequent chapters as they apply to specific software and devices.

Preventive maintenance is a regular and systematic inspection, cleaning, and replacement of worn parts, materials, and systems. Preventive maintenance helps to prevent failure of parts, materials, and systems by ensuring that they are in good working order.

Troubleshooting is a systematic approach to locating the cause of a fault in a computer system. A good preventive maintenance program helps minimize failures. With fewer failures, there is less troubleshooting to do, thus saving an organization time and money. Preventive maintenance can also include upgrading certain hardware or software such as a hard drive that is making noise, upgrading memory that is insufficient, or installing software updates for security or reliability.

Troubleshooting is a learned skill. Not all troubleshooting processes are the same, and technicians tend to refine their troubleshooting skills based on knowledge and personal experience. Use the guidelines in this chapter as a starting point to help develop your troubleshooting skills. Although each situation is different, the process described in this chapter will help you to determine your course of action when you are trying to solve a technical problem for a customer.

Explain the Purpose of Preventive Maintenance

Preventive maintenance reduces the probability of hardware or software problems by systematically and periodically checking hardware and software to ensure proper operation.

Hardware

Check the condition of cables, components, and peripherals. Clean components to reduce the likelihood of overheating. Repair or replace any components that show signs of damage or excessive wear.

Use the following tasks as a guide to create a hardware maintenance program:

- Remove dust from fan intakes.

- Remove dust from the power supply.

- Remove dust from components inside the computer.

- Clean the mouse and keyboard.

- Check and secure loose cables.

Software

Verify that installed software is current. Follow the policies of the organization when installing security updates, operating system updates, and program updates. Many organizations do not allow updates until extensive testing has been completed. This testing is done to confirm that the update will not cause problems with the operating system and software.

Use the tasks listed as a guide to create a software maintenance schedule that fits the needs of your computer equipment:

- Review security updates.
- Review software updates.
- Review driver updates.
- Update virus definition files.
- Scan for viruses and spyware.
- Remove unwanted programs
- Scan hard drives for errors.
- Defragment hard drives.

Benefits

Be proactive in computer equipment maintenance and data protection. By performing regular maintenance routines, you can reduce potential hardware and software problems. Regular maintenance routines reduce computer downtime and repair costs.

A preventive maintenance plan is developed based on the needs of the equipment. A computer exposed to a dusty environment, such as a construction site, needs more attention than equipment in an office environment. High-traffic networks, such as a school network, might require additional scanning and removal of malicious software or unwanted files. Document the routine maintenance tasks that must be performed on the computer equipment and the frequency of each task. This list of tasks can then be used to create a maintenance program. The following are the benefits of preventive maintenance:

- Increases data protection
- Extends the life of the components
- Increases equipment stability
- Reduces repair costs
- Reduces the number of equipment failures

Identify the Steps of the Troubleshooting Process

Troubleshooting requires an organized and logical approach to problems with computers and other components. A logical approach to troubleshooting allows you to eliminate variables in a systematic order. Asking the right questions, testing the right hardware, and examining the right data helps you understand the problem. This helps you form a proposed solution to try.

Troubleshooting is a skill that you will refine over time. Each time you solve another problem, you will increase your troubleshooting skills by gaining more experience. You will learn how and when to combine, as well as skip, steps to reach a solution quickly. The following troubleshooting process is a guideline that you can modify to fit your needs.

- Explain the purpose of data protection.

- Identify the problem.

- Establish a theory of probable causes.

- Test the theory to determine an exact cause.

- Establish a plan of action to resolve the problem and implement the solution.

- Verify full system functionality, and if applicable, implement preventive measures.

- Document findings, actions, and outcomes.

In this section, you will learn an approach to problem solving that can be applied to both hardware and software. You also can apply many of the steps to problem solving in other work-related areas.

Note

The term customer, as used in this book, is any user who requires technical computer assistance.

Explain the Purpose of Data Protection

Before you begin troubleshooting problems, always follow the necessary precautions to protect data on a computer. Some repairs, such as replacing a hard drive or reinstalling an operating system, might put the data on the computer at risk. Make sure that you do everything possible to prevent data loss while attempting repairs.

Caution

Although data protection is not one of the six troubleshooting steps, you must protect data before beginning any work on a customer's computer. If your work results in data loss for the customer, you or your company could be held liable.

Data Backup

A data *backup* is a copy of the data on a computer hard drive that is saved to media such as a CD, DVD, or tape drive. In an organization, backups are routinely done on a daily, weekly, and monthly basis.

If you are unsure that a backup has been done, do not attempt any troubleshooting activities until you check with the customer. Here is a list of items to verify with the customer about data backups:

- Date of the last backup
- Contents of the backup
- Data integrity of the backup
- Availability of all backup media for a data restore

If the customer does not have a current backup and you are not able to create one, you should ask the customer to sign a liability release form. A liability release form should contain at least the following information:

- Permission to work on the computer without a current backup available
- Release from liability if data is lost or corrupted
- Description of the work to be performed

Identify the Problem

During the troubleshooting process, gather as much information from the customer as possible. The customer should provide you with the basic facts about the problem. Here is a list of some of the important information to gather from the customer:

- Customer information
  - Company name
  - Contact name
  - Address
  - Phone number
- Computer configuration
  - Manufacturer and model
  - Operating system information
  - Network environment
  - Connection type

- Description of problem
  - Open-ended questions
  - Closed-ended questions

Conversation Etiquette

When you are talking to the customer, you should follow these guidelines:

- Ask direct questions to gather information.
- Do not use industry jargon when talking to customers.
- Do not talk down to the customer.
- Do not insult the customer.
- Do not accuse the customer of causing the problem.

By communicating effectively, you will be able to elicit the most relevant information about the problem from the customer.

Open-Ended Questions

When gathering information from customers, use both open-ended and closed-ended questions. Start with *open-ended questions* to obtain general information. Open-ended questions allow customers to explain the details of the problem in their own words. Some examples of open-ended questions are

- What problems are you experiencing with your computer or network?
- What software has been installed on your computer recently?
- What were you doing when the problem was identified?
- What hardware changes have recently been made to your computer?

Closed-Ended Questions

Based on the information from the customer, you can proceed with closed-ended questions. *Closed-ended questions* generally require a yes or no answer. These questions are intended to get the most relevant information in the shortest time possible. Some examples of closed-ended questions are

- Has anyone else used your computer recently?
- Can you reproduce the problem?
- Have you changed your password recently?

- Have you received any error messages on your computer?

- Are you currently logged in to the network?

Documenting Responses

Document the information obtained from the customer in the work order and in the repair journal. Write down anything that you think might be important for you or another technician. Often, the small details can lead to the solution of a difficult or complicated problem. It is now time to verify the customer's description of the problem by gathering data from the computer.

Event Viewer

When system, user, or software errors occur on a computer, *Event Viewer* is updated with information about the errors. The Event Viewer application shown in Figure 4-1 records the following information about the problem:

- What problem occurred

- Date and time of the problem

- Severity of the problem

- Source of the problem

- Event ID number

- Which user was logged in when the problem occurred

Figure 4-1   Event Viewer

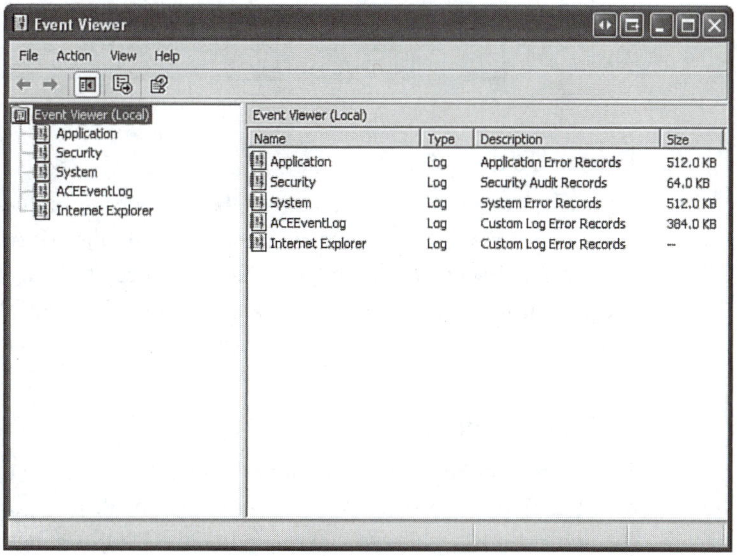

Although Event Viewer lists details about the error, you might need to further research the solution.

Device Manager

Device Manager, shown in Figure 4-2, displays all of the devices that are configured on a computer. Any device that the operating system determines to be acting incorrectly is flagged with an error icon. This type of error has a yellow circle with an exclamation point (!). If a device is disabled, it is flagged with a red circle and an ?. A yellow question mark (?) indicates that the hardware is not functioning properly because the system does not know which driver to install for the hardware.

Figure 4-2   Device Manager

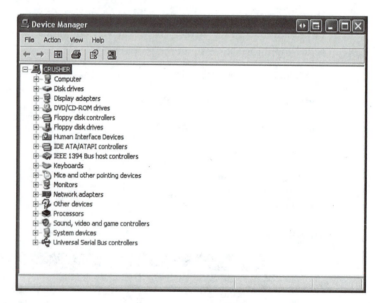

Beep Codes

Each BIOS manufacturer has a unique beep sequence for hardware failures. When troubleshooting, power on the computer and listen. As the system proceeds through the *power-on self test (POST)*, most computers emit one beep to indicate that the system is booting properly. If there is an error, you might hear multiple beeps. Document the beep code sequence, and research the code to determine the specific hardware failure.

BIOS Information

If the computer boots and stops after the POST, investigate the BIOS settings to determine where to find the problem. A device might not be detected or configured properly. Refer to the motherboard manual to make sure that the BIOS settings are accurate.

Diagnostic Tools

Conduct research to determine which software is available to help diagnose and solve problems. There are many programs available that can help you troubleshoot hardware. Often, manufacturers of system hardware provide diagnostic tools of their own. For instance, a hard drive manufacturer might provide a tool that you can use to boot the computer and diagnose why the hard drive does not boot Windows.

Establish a Theory of Probable Causes

First, create a list of the most common reasons why the error would occur. Even though the customer may think that there is a major problem, start with the obvious issues before moving to more complex diagnoses. List the easiest or most obvious causes at the top and the more complex causes at the bottom. You will test each of these causes in the next steps of the troubleshooting process.

Test the Theory to Determine an Exact Cause

The next step in the troubleshooting process is to determine an exact cause. You determine an exact cause by testing your theories of probable causes one at a time, starting with the quickest and easiest. After identifying an exact cause of the problem, determine the steps to resolve the problem. As you become more experienced at troubleshooting computers, you will work through the steps in the process faster. For now, practice each step to better understand the troubleshooting process.

If the exact cause of the problem has not been determined after you have tested all your theories, establish a new theory of probable causes and test it. If necessary, escalate the problem to a technician with more experience. Before you escalate, document each test that you try. Information about the tests is vital if the problem needs to be escalated to another technician. Many third-party tools are free to download.

Implement the Solution

After you have determined the exact cause of the problem, establish a plan of action to resolve the problem and implement the solution. Sometimes quick procedures can determine the exact cause of the problem or even correct the problem. If a quick procedure does correct the problem, you can go to step 5 to verify the solution and full system functionality. If a quick procedure does not correct the problem, you might need to research the problem further to establish the exact cause. When researching possible solutions for a problem, use the following sources of information:

- Your own problem-solving experience
- Other technicians

- Internet search
- Newsgroups
- Manufacturer FAQs
- Computer manuals
- Device manuals
- Online forums
- Technical websites

Evaluate the problem and research possible solutions. Divide larger problems into smaller problems that can be analyzed and solved individually. Prioritize solutions starting with the easiest and fastest to implement. Create a list of possible solutions and implement them one at a time. If you implement a possible solution and it does not work, reverse the solution and try another.

Verify Solution, Full System Functionality, and If Applicable, Implement Preventive Measures

After the repairs to the computer have been completed, continue the troubleshooting process by verifying full system functionality and implementing any preventive measures if needed. Verifying full system functionality confirms that you have solved the original problem and ensures that you have not created another problem while repairing the computer. Whenever possible, have the customer verify the solution and system functionality.

Document Findings, Actions, and Outcomes

Finish the troubleshooting process by closing with the customer. Communicate the problem and the solution to the customer verbally and in writing. If possible, demonstrate how your solution has solved the problem. Be sure to complete the documentation, which should include the following information:

- Description of the problem
- Steps to resolve the problem
- Components used in the repair

Summary

This chapter discussed the concepts of preventive maintenance and the troubleshooting process, including the following important points:

- Regular preventive maintenance reduces hardware and software problems.

- Before beginning any repair, back up the data on a computer.

- The troubleshooting process is a guideline to help you solve computer problems in an efficient manner.

- Document everything that you try, even if it fails. The documentation that you create will become a useful resource for you and other technicians.

Summary of Exercises

There are no Labs, Worksheets, Remote Technician exercises, Class Discussions, Virtual Desktop activities, or Virtual Laptop activities associated with this chapter.

Check Your Understanding

You can find the answers to these questions in the appendix, "Answers to Check Your Understanding Questions."

1. Which of the following common tasks are performed during preventive maintenance? (Choose three.)

    A. Check and secure loose cables.

    B. Update the RAM.

    C. Clean the mouse and keyboard.

    D. Update drivers.

    E. Reinstall the operating system.

    F. Install additional peripherals.

2. In which of the following situations is it recommended to ask the customer to sign a liability release form before attempting any kind of repair? (Choose two.)

    A. The technician needs to share the responsibility with the customer.

    B. The information on the computer is critical.

    C. The technician is unable to back up the customer information.

    D. The information in the backup is confidential.

    E. The customer is unable to provide a backup.

3. What is the first step in the troubleshooting process?

   A. Gather data from the computer.

   B. Gather data from the customer.

   C. Verify the obvious issues.

   D. Evaluate the problem and implement the solution.

   E. Close with the customer.

   F. Try quick solutions.

4. Which type of question allows the customer to completely describe the problem?

   A. Closed-ended

   B. Open-ended

   C. Specific

   D. Technical

5. What is the last step in the troubleshooting process?

   A. Gather data from the computer.

   B. Gather data from the customer.

   C. Verify the obvious issues.

   D. Evaluate the problem and implement the solution.

   E. Close with the customer.

   F. Try quick solutions.

CHAPTER 5

Fundamental Operating Systems

Objectives

Upon completion of this chapter, you should be able to answer the following questions:

- What is the purpose of an operating system?

- How do different operating systems compare with one another based on purpose, limitations, and compatibilities?

- How do you determine the appropriate operating system based on customer needs?

- How do you install an operating system?

- How do you navigate within an operating system GUI?

- What are some common preventive maintenance techniques for operating systems and how are they applied?

- What can be done to troubleshoot operating systems?

Key Terms

This chapter uses the following key terms. You can find the definitions in the Glossary.

operating system (OS)   page 117

command-line interface (CLI)   page 118

graphical user interface (GUI)   page 118

multiuser   page 120

multitasking   page 120

multiprocessing   page 120

multithreading   page 120

real mode   page 121

protected mode   page 121

virtual real mode   page 121

compatibility mode   page 122

Microsoft Windows   page 125

Novell NetWare   page 125

Linux   page 125

UNIX   page 125

hardware compatibility list (HCL)   page 128

primary partition   page 130

active partition   page 130

extended partition   page 130

logical drive   page 130

formatting   page 130

sector   page 130

cluster   page 130

track   page 131

cylinder   page 131

drive mapping   page 131

continues

The *operating system (OS)* controls almost all functions on a computer. In this chapter, you will learn about the components, functions, and terminology related to the Windows 2000, Windows XP, Windows Vista, and Windows 7 operating systems.

After completing this chapter, you will meet these objectives:

- Explain the purpose of an operating system.
- Describe and compare operating systems to include purpose, limitations, and compatibilities.
- Determine the operating system based on customer needs.
- Install an operating system.
- Navigate a graphical user interface (GUI).
- Identify and apply common preventive maintenance techniques for operating systems.
- Troubleshoot operating systems.

Explain the Purpose of an Operating System

All computers rely on an Operating System (OS) to provide the interface for interaction between users, applications, and hardware. The OS boots the computer and manages the file system. Almost all modern operating systems can support more than one user, task, or CPU.

Roles of an operating system include

- Control hardware access
- Manage files and folders
- Provide user interface
- Manage applications

Describe Characteristics of Modern Operating Systems

Regardless of the size and complexity of the computer and the operating system, all operating systems perform the same four basic functions. Operating systems control hardware access, manage files and folders, provide a user interface, and manage applications.

Control Hardware Access

The operating system manages the interaction between applications and the hardware. To access and communicate with the hardware, the operating system installs a device driver for each hardware component. A device driver is a small program written by the hardware manufacturer and supplied with the hardware component. When the hardware device is installed, the device driver is also installed, allowing the OS to communicate with the hardware component.

The process of assigning system resources and installing drivers can be performed with Plug and Play (PnP). The PnP process was introduced in Windows 95 to simplify the installation of new hardware. All modern operating systems are PnP-compatible. With PnP, the operating system automatically detects the PnP-compatible hardware and installs the driver for that component. The operating system then configures the device and updates the Registry, which is a database that contains all the information about the computer.

> **Note**
>
> The Registry contains information about applications, users, hardware, network settings, and file types.

File and Folder Management

The operating system creates a file structure on the hard disk drive to allow data to be stored. A file is a block of related data that is given a single name and treated as a single unit. Program and data files are grouped together in a directory. The files and directories are organized for easy retrieval and use. Directories can be kept inside other directories. These nested directories are referred to as subdirectories. Directories are called folders in Windows operating systems, and subdirectories are called subfolders.

User Interface

The operating system enables the user to interact with software and hardware. There are two types of user interfaces:

- *Command-line interface (CLI)*: The user types commands at a prompt, as shown in Figure 5-1.

- *Graphical user interface (GUI)*: The user interacts with menus and icons, as shown in Figure 5-2.

Most operating systems, such as Windows 2000, Windows XP, Windows Vista, and Windows 7, include both a GUI and a CLI.

Figure 5-1   Command-Line Interface

Figure 5-2   Graphical User Interface

Application Management

The operating system locates an application and loads it into the RAM of the computer. Applications are software programs, such as word processors, databases, spreadsheets, games, and many other applications. The operating system ensures that each application has adequate system resources.

An application programming interface (API) is a set of guidelines used by programmers to ensure that the application they are developing is compatible with an operating system. Here are two examples of APIs:

- **Open Graphics Library (OpenGL)**: Cross-platform standard specification for multimedia graphics

- **DirectX**: Collection of APIs related to multimedia tasks for Microsoft Windows

Explain Operating System Concepts

To understand the capabilities of an operating system, it is important to understand some basic terms. The following terms are often used when comparing operating systems:

- *Multiuser*: Two or more users can work with programs and share peripheral devices, such as printers, at the same time.

- *Multitasking*: The computer is capable of operating multiple applications at the same time.

- *Multiprocessing*: The computer can have two or more central processing units (CPU) that programs share.

- *Multithreading*: A program can be broken into smaller parts that can be loaded as needed by the operating system. Multithreading allows individual programs to be multitasked.

Almost all modern operating systems are multiuser and multitasking, and they support multiprocessing and multithreading.

Modes of Operation

All modern CPUs can run in different modes of operation. The mode of operation refers to the capability of the CPU and the operating environment. The mode of operation determines how the CPU manages applications and memory. Table 5-1 shows an example of the logical memory allocation. The four common modes of operation are real mode, protected mode, virtual real mode, and compatible mode.

Table 5-1   Memory Management

Memory Type	Logical Memory Allocation
Conventional	0 to 640 KB
Upper	640 KB to 1 MB
Extended	1 MB to the maximum amount of RAM installed

Real Mode

A CPU that operates in *real mode* can execute only one program at a time, and can address only 1 MB of system memory. Although all modern processors have real mode available, it is used only by DOS and DOS applications in old operating systems and by 16-bit operating environments, such as Windows 3.x.

Protected Mode

A CPU that operates in *protected mode* has access to all of the memory in the computer, including virtual memory. Virtual memory is hard disk space that is used to emulate RAM. Operating systems that use protected mode can manage multiple programs simultaneously. Protected mode provides 32-bit access to memory, drivers, and transfers between input and output (I/O) devices. Protected mode is used by 32-bit operating systems, such as Windows 2000 and Windows XP. In protected mode, applications are protected from using the memory reserved for another application that is currently running.

Virtual Real Mode

A CPU that operates in *virtual real mode* allows a real-mode application to run within a protected-mode operating system. This can be demonstrated when a DOS application runs in a 32-bit operating system, such as Windows XP. Table 5-2 is a chart of some common DOS commands that can still be used in modern operating systems, such as Windows XP.

Table 5-2   Common DOS Commands

Command	Function
help	Provides command-line help
dir	Displays the contents of a directory
attrib	Changes the attributes of a file to indicate a read-only, archive, system, or hidden file
edit	Opens a file for editing

continues

Table 5-2   Common DOS Commands   *continued*

Command	Function
copy	Copies a file
xcopy	Copies files and subdirectories
format	Formats a disk
md	Makes a new directory
cd	Changes to a specified directory
rd	Removes a directory

Compatibility Mode

Compatibility mode creates the environment of an earlier operating system for applications that are not compatible with the current operating system. As an example, an application that checks the version of the operating system might be written for Windows NT and require a particular service pack. Compatibility mode can create the proper environment or version of the operating system to allow the application to run as if it is in the intended environment.

Although Windows Vista is highly compatible with previous versions of Windows, two particularly useful features are available. The first feature is Windows XP Service Pack 2 (SP2) compatibility mode. This allows applications that are not compatible with Windows Vista to be executed as if the operating system were Windows XP SP2. The second feature is a method to override the User Account Control (UAC). This allows an application to be run even if the user does not have the required administrative privileges.

32-Bit Versus 64-Bit

There are three main differences between 32-bit and 64-bit operating systems. A 32-bit operating system, such as Windows XP Professional, is capable of addressing only 4 GB of RAM, while a 64-bit operating system can address more than 128 GB of RAM. Memory management is also different between these two types of operating systems, resulting in enhanced performance of 64-bit programs. A 64-bit operating system, such as Windows Vista 64-bit, has additional security features such as Kernel Patch Protection (KPP) and mandatory driver signing. With KPP, third-party drivers cannot modify the kernel. With mandatory driver signing, unsigned drivers cannot be used.

Processor Architecture

There are two common architectures used by CPUs to process data: x86 (32-bit architecture) and x64 (64-bit architecture). x86 uses a complex instruction set computing (CISC) architecture to process multiple instructions with a single request. Registers are storage areas used by the CPU when performing calculations. x86 processors use fewer registers than x64 processors. x64 architecture is backward compatible with x86 and adds additional registers specifically for instructions that use a 64-bit address space. The additional registers of the x64 architecture allow the computer to process much more complex instructions at a much higher rate.

Describe and Compare Operating Systems to Include Purpose, Limitations, and Compatibilities

A technician might be asked to choose and install an operating system for a customer. The type of OS selected depends on the customer's requirements for the computer. There are two distinct types of operating systems: desktop operating systems and network operating systems. A desktop operating system is intended for use in a small office/home office (SOHO) with a limited number of users. A network operating system (NOS) is designed for a corporate environment serving multiple users with a wide range of needs.

After completing this section, you will meet these objectives:

- Describe desktop operating systems.

- Describe network operating systems.

Describe Desktop Operating Systems

A desktop OS has the following characteristics:

- Supports a single user

- Runs single-user applications

- Shares files and folders on a small network with limited security

In the current software market, the most commonly used desktop operating systems fall into three groups: Microsoft Windows, Apple Mac OS, and UNIX/Linux.

Microsoft Windows

Windows is one of the most popular operating systems today. The following products are desktop versions of the Microsoft Windows operating systems:

- **Windows XP Professional**: Used on most computers that will connect to a Windows Server on a network

- **Windows XP Home Edition**: Used on home computers and has very limited security

- **Windows XP Media Center**: Used on entertainment computers for viewing movies and listening to music

- **Windows XP Tablet PC Edition**: Used for tablet PCs

- **Windows XP 64-bit Edition**: Used for computers with 64-bit processors

- **Windows 2000 Professional**: Older Windows operating system that has been replaced by Windows XP Professional

- **Windows Vista Home Basic**: Used on home computers for basic computing

- **Windows Vista Home Premium**: Used on home computers to expand personal productivity and digital entertainment beyond the basics

- **Windows Vista Business**: Used on small business computers for enhanced security and enhanced mobility technology

- **Windows Vista Ultimate**: Used on computers to combine all the needs of both home and business users

- **Windows 7 Home Premium**: Used on home computers to expand personal productivity and digital entertainment beyond the basics

- **Windows 7 Professional**: Used on small business computers for enhanced security and enhanced mobility technology

- **Windows 7 Ultimate**: Used on computers to combine all the needs of both home and business users

Apple Mac OS

Apple computers are proprietary and use an operating system called Mac OS. Mac OS is designed to be a user-friendly GUI operating system. Mac OS X is based on a customized version of UNIX.

UNIX/Linux

UNIX, which was introduced in the late 1960s, is one of the oldest operating systems. There are many different versions of UNIX today. One of the most recent is the extremely popular Linux. Linux was developed by Linus Torvalds in 1991, and it is designed as an open-source operating system. Open-source programs allow the source code to be distributed and changed by anyone as a free download or from developers at a much lower cost than other operating systems.

> **Note**
>
> In this course, all command paths refer to Windows XP unless otherwise noted.

Describe Network Operating Systems

A network OS has the following characteristics:

- Supports multiple users
- Runs multiuser applications
- Is robust and redundant
- Provides increased security compared to desktop operating systems

These are the most common network operating systems:

- *Microsoft Windows*: Network operating systems offered by Microsoft are Windows 2000 Server, Windows Server 2003, and Windows Server 2008. Windows Server operating systems use a central database called Active Directory to manage network resources.

- *Novell NetWare*: Novell NetWare was the first OS to meet network OS requirements and enjoy widespread deployment in PC-based local-area networks (LAN) back in the 1980s.

- *Linux*: Linux operating systems include Red Hat, Caldera, SUSE, Debian, Fedora, Ubuntu, and Slackware.

- *UNIX*: Various corporations offer proprietary operating systems based on UNIX.

Worksheet 5.2.2: NOS Certifications and Jobs

In this activity, you will use the Internet, a newspaper, or magazines to gather information about network operating system certifications and jobs that require these certifications. Refer to the worksheet in *IT Essentials: PC Hardware and Software Lab Manual, Fourth Edition*. You can complete this worksheet now or wait to do so until the end of the chapter.

Determine Operating System Based on Customer Needs

To select the proper operating system to meet the requirements of your customer, you need to understand how the customer wants to use the computer. The operating system that you recommend should be compatible with any applications that will be used and should support all hardware that is installed in the computer. If the computer will be attached to a network, the new operating system should also be compatible with other operating systems on the network.

After completing this section, you will meet these objectives:

- Identify applications and environments that are compatible with an operating system.

- Determine minimum hardware requirements and compatibility with the OS platform.

Identify Applications and Environments That Are Compatible with an Operating System

An operating system should be compatible with all applications that are installed on a computer. Before recommending an OS to your customer, investigate the types of applications that your customer will be using. If the computer will be part of a network, the operating system must also be compatible with the operating systems of the other computers in the network. The network type determines which operating systems are compatible. Microsoft Windows networks can have multiple computers using different versions of Microsoft operating systems. These are some guidelines that will help you determine the best operating system for your customer:

- Does the computer have "off-the-shelf" applications or customized applications that were programmed specifically for this customer? If the customer will be using a customized application, the programmer of that application will specify which operating system is compatible with it. Most off-the-shelf applications specify a list of compatible operating systems on the outside of the application package.

- Are the applications programmed for a single user or multiple users? This information helps you decide whether to recommend a desktop OS or a network OS. If the computer will be connected to a network, make sure to recommend the same OS platform that the other computers on the network use.

- Are any data files shared with other computers, such as a laptop or home computer? To ensure compatibility of file formats, recommend the same OS platform that the other data file–sharing computers use.

As an example, your customer has a Windows network installed and wants to add more computers to the network. In this case, you should recommend a Windows OS for the new computers. If the customer does not have any existing computer equipment, the choice of available OS platforms increases. To make an OS recommendation, you must review budget constraints, learn how the computer will be used, and determine which types of applications will be installed.

Determine Minimum Hardware Requirements and Compatibility with the OS Platform

Operating systems have minimum hardware requirements that must be met for the OS to install and function correctly. Table 5-3 provide a chart of the minimum hardware requirements and features for the various Windows operating systems.

Table 5-3   Minimum Hardware Requirements

	Windows 2000	Windows XP	Windows Vista	Windows 7
CPU	133 MHz	233 MHz	800 MHz	1 GHz
RAM	64 MB	64 MB	512 MB	1 GB
Hard drive	650 MB	1.5 GB	15 GB	16 GB
Other	CD drive or floppy drive	CD or DVD drive	CD or DVD drive WDDM video driver	CD or DVD drive DirectX9 graphics device with WDDM video driver

Identify the equipment that your customer has in place. If hardware upgrades are necessary to meet the minimum requirements for an OS, conduct a cost analysis to determine the best course of action. In some cases, it might be less expensive for the customer to purchase a new computer than to upgrade the current system. In other cases, it might be cost effective to upgrade one or more of the following components:

- RAM
- Hard disk drive
- CPU
- Video adapter card

Note

In some cases, the application requirements might exceed the hardware requirements of the operating system. For the application to function properly, it is necessary to satisfy the additional requirements.

After you have determined the minimum hardware requirements for an OS, ensure that all hardware in the computer is compatible with the OS that you have selected for your customer.

Hardware Compatibility List

Most operating systems have a ***hardware compatibility list (HCL)*** that can be found on the manufacturer's website, as shown in Figure 5-3. These lists provide a detailed inventory of hardware that has been tested and is known to work with the operating system. If any of your customer's existing hardware is not on the list, those components might need to be upgraded to match components on the HCL.

Figure 5-3   Hardware Compatibility List

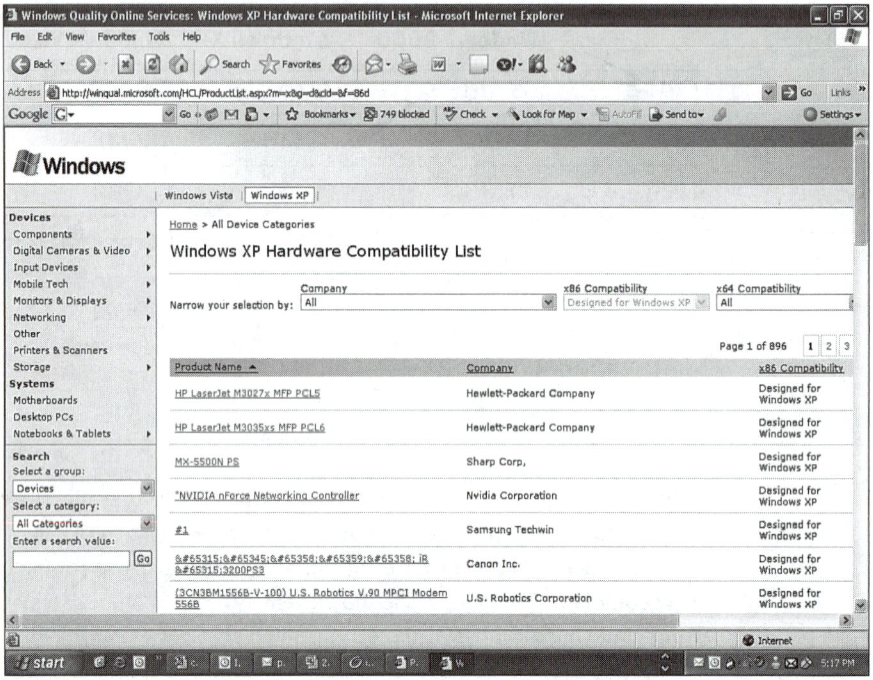

Note

An HCL might not be continuously maintained and therefore might not be a comprehensive reference.

Worksheet 5.3.2: Upgrade Hardware Components

In this worksheet, you will use the Internet, a newspaper, or a local store to gather information about hardware components. The scenario is that your customer's computer currently has one module of 256-MB RAM, a 40-GB hard disk drive, and an AGP video adapter card with 32 MB of RAM. Your customer wants to be able to play advanced video games. Refer to the worksheet in *IT Essentials: PC Hardware and Software Lab Manual, Fourth Edition*. You can complete this worksheet now or wait to do so until the end of the chapter.

Install an Operating System

As a technician, you might have to perform a clean installation of an operating system. Perform a clean install in the following situations:

- When a computer is passed from one employee to another
- When the operating system is corrupted
- When a new replacement hard drive is installed in a computer

Figure 5-4 shows an example of the Windows XP installation welcome screen.

Figure 5-4   Windows XP Installation

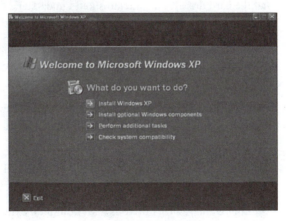

After completing this section, you will meet these objectives:

- Identify hard drive setup procedures.
- Prepare the hard drive.
- Install the operating system using default settings.
- Create user accounts.

- Complete the installation.

- Describe custom installation options.

- Identify the boot sequence files and Registry files.

- Describe how to manipulate operating system files.

- Describe directory structures.

Identify Hard Drive Setup Procedures

The installation and initial booting of the operating system is called the operating system setup. Although it is possible to install an operating system over a network from a server or from a local hard drive, the most common installation method is with CDs and DVDs. To install an OS from a CD or DVD, first configure the BIOS setup to boot the system from the CD or DVD.

Partitioning and Formatting

Before installing an operating system on a hard drive, the hard drive must be partitioned and formatted. When a hard drive is partitioned, it is logically divided into one or more areas. When a hard drive is formatted, the partitions are prepared to hold files and applications. During the installation phase, most operating systems automatically partition and format the hard drive. A technician should understand the process relating to hard drive setup. The following terms are used when referring to hard drive setup:

- *Primary partition*: This partition is usually the first partition. A primary partition cannot be subdivided into smaller sections. There can be up to four partitions per hard drive.

- *Active partition*: This partition is the partition used by the operating system to boot the computer. Only one primary partition can be marked active.

- *Extended partition*: This partition normally uses the remaining free space on a hard drive or takes the place of a primary partition. There can be only one extended partition per hard drive, and it can be subdivided into smaller sections called logical drives.

- *Logical drive*: This drive is a section of an extended partition that can be used to separate information for administrative purposes.

- *Formatting*: This process prepares a file system in a partition for files to be stored.

- *Sector*: A sector contains a fixed number of bytes, generally at least 512.

- *Cluster*: A cluster is also called a file allocation unit. It is the smallest unit of space used for storing data. It is made up of one or more sectors.

- *Track*: A track is one complete circle of data on one side of a hard drive platter. A track is broken into groups of sectors.

- *Cylinder*: A cylinder is a stack of tracks lined up one on top of another to form a cylinder shape.

- *Drive mapping*: Drive mapping is a letter assigned to a logical drive.

Figure 5-5 shows how the different parts of a hard drive correspond.

Figure 5-5   Hard Drive Access

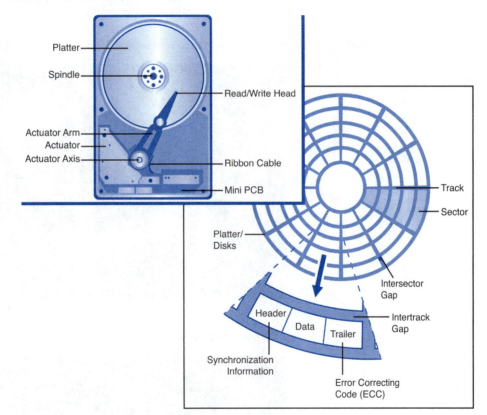

Prepare the Hard Drive

A clean installation of an operating system proceeds as if the disk were brand new; there is no attempt to preserve any information that is currently on the hard drive. The first phase of the installation process entails partitioning and formatting the hard drive. This process prepares the disk to accept the file system. The file system provides the directory structure that organizes the user's operating system, application, configuration, and data files.

The Windows XP operating system can use one of two file systems:

■ *File Allocation Table, 32-bit (FAT32)*: A file system that can support partition sizes up to 2 TB or 2048 GB. The FAT32 file system is supported by Windows 9.x, Windows Me, Windows 2000, and Windows XP.

■ *New Technology File System (NTFS)*: A file system that can support partition sizes up to 16 exabytes, in theory. NTFS incorporates more file system security features and extended attributes than the FAT file system.

Figure 5-6 through Figure 5-10 show the five steps required to partition and format a drive in Windows XP.

Figure 5-6   Hard Drive Preparation and Setup: Step 1

Figure 5-7   Hard Drive Preparation and Setup: Step 2

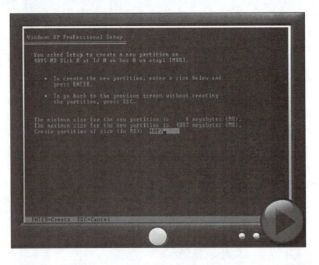

Figure 5-8   Hard Drive Preparation and Setup: Step 3

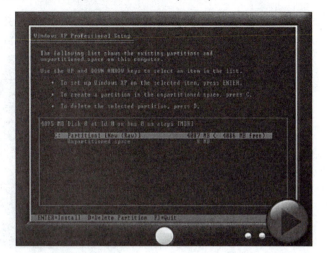

Figure 5-9   Hard Drive Preparation and Setup: Step 4

The Windows Vista operating system will automatically create a partition on the entire hard drive, format it for you, and begin installing Windows if you do not create your own partitions using the **New** option. If you decide to create and format your own partitions, the process is the same as Windows XP, except that Windows Vista does not provide a choice of file systems. NTFS formats the partition in which Windows Vista will be installed.

Figure 5-10   Hard Drive Preparation and Setup: Step 5

Lab 5.4.2: Install Windows XP

In this lab, you will install the Windows XP Professional operating system. Refer to the lab in *IT Essentials: PC Hardware and Software Lab Manual, Fourth Edition*. You can perform this lab now or wait until the end of the chapter.

Optional Lab 5.4.2: Install Windows Vista

In this optional lab, you will install the Windows Vista operating system. Refer to the lab in *IT Essentials: PC Hardware and Software Lab Manual, Fourth Edition*. You can perform this lab now or wait until the end of the chapter.

Install the Operating System Using Default Settings

When you're installing Windows XP, the installation wizard gives the option to install using typical (default) settings or custom settings. Using the typical settings increases the likelihood of a successful installation. However, the user must still provide the following information during the setup:

- Standards and formats that define currency and numerals
- Text input language
- Name of the user and company
- Product key
- Computer name

- Administrator password
- Date and time settings
- Network settings
- Domain or workgroup information

When a computer boots up with the Windows installation disc, the Windows XP installation starts with three options:

- **Setup XP**: To run the setup and install the XP operating system, press **Enter**.

- **Repair XP**: To repair an installation, press **R** to open the Recovery Console. The Recovery Console is a troubleshooting tool. It can be used to create and format partitions and repair the boot sector or Master Boot Record. It can also perform basic file operations on operating system files and folders. The Recovery Console configures services and devices to start or not start the next time the computer boots up.

- **Quit**: To quit Setup without installing Windows XP, press **F3**.

For this section, select the Setup XP option.

Figure 5-11 shows the installation window for Windows XP.

Figure 5-11   Installing Windows

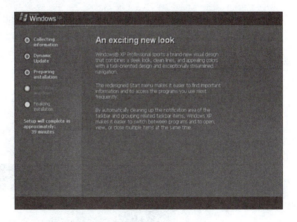

Windows setup searches for existing Windows installations. If no existing installation is found, you can perform a clean installation of Windows. If an existing installation is found, you have the option of performing a repair installation. A repair installation fixes the current installation using the original files from the Windows XP installation disc. Before performing a repair installation, back up any important files to a different physical location such as a second hard drive, CD, or USB storage device.

After a repair installation begins, Windows setup copies installation files to the hard drive and reboots. Following the reboot, a message to press any key to boot from CD appears. Do not press any keys at this time. Setup continues to install Windows as if it were a clean install, but any applications that you have installed and any settings that you have configured remain unchanged.

When a computer boots up with the Windows Vista installation disc, Windows Vista installation starts with three options:

- **Upgrade**: Keep your files, settings, and programs and upgrade Windows. Also use this option to repair an installation.

- **Custom (advanced)**: Install a clean copy of Windows, select where you want to install it, or make changes to disks and partitions.

- **Quit**: To quit Setup, click the x in the Close box.

Create User Accounts

An administrator account is automatically created when Windows XP is installed. The default administrator account is named "administrator." For security purposes, change this name as soon as possible. Use this privileged account to manage the computer only. Do not use it as a daily account. People have accidentally made drastic changes while using the administrator account instead of a regular user account. Attackers seek out the administrator account because it is so powerful.

Create a user account when prompted during the installation process. Unlike the administrator account, user accounts can be created at any time. A user account has fewer permissions than the computer administrator. For example, users may have the right to read, but not modify, a file.

Figure 5-12 shows the installation screen for setting the computer name and setting the initial administrator password.

Figure 5-12   Creating an Administrator Account

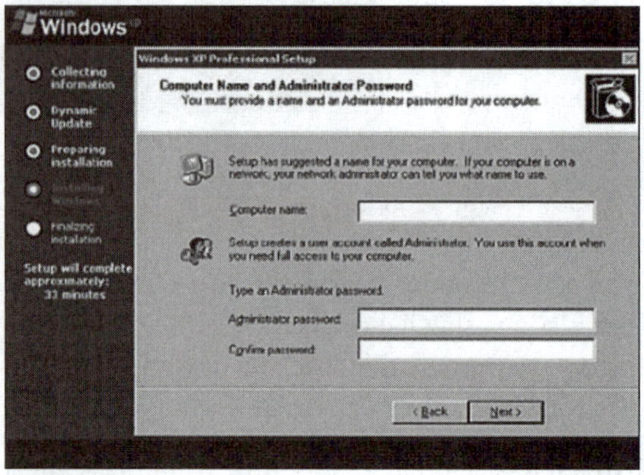

Complete the Installation

After the Windows installation copies all of the necessary operating system files to the hard drive, the computer reboots and prompts you to log in for the first time.

You must register Windows XP. As shown in Figure 5-13, you must also complete the verification that ensures that you are using a legal copy of the OS. Doing so enables you to download patches and service packs. Performing this step requires a connection to the Internet.

Figure 5-13   Activating Windows XP After Installation

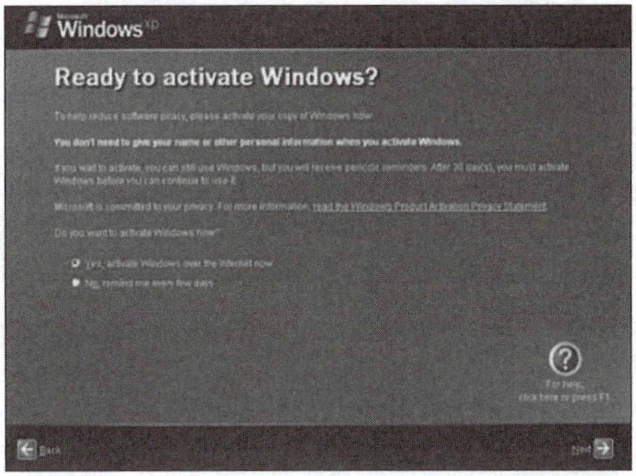

Depending on the age of the media at the time of your installation, there might be updates to install. As shown in Figure 5-14, you can use Microsoft Update Manager from the Start menu to scan for new software and to do the following:

- Install all service packs.
- Install all patches.

To start the update process navigate to Start > All Programs > Accessories > System Tools > Windows Update.

In Windows Vista, use the following path to access Windows Update: **Start > All Programs > Windows Update**.

You should also verify that all hardware is installed correctly. As shown in Figure 5-15, you can use Device Manager to locate problems and to install the correct or updated drivers using the following path:

Start > Control Panel > System > Hardware > Device Manager

Figure 5-14   Microsoft Update

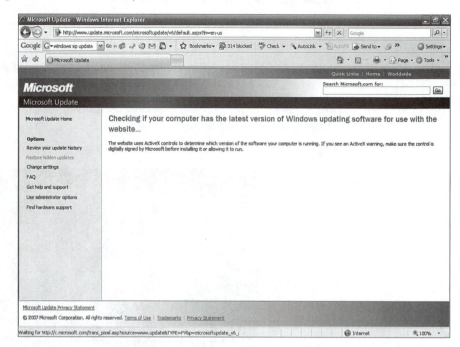

Figure 5-15   Device Manager Conflicts

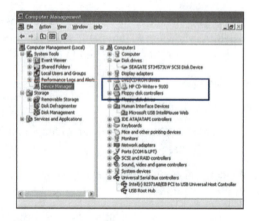

In Device Manager, warning icons are represented by a yellow exclamation point or a red X. A yellow exclamation point represents a problem with the device. To view the problem description, right-click the device and select **Properties**. A red X represents a device that has been disabled. To enable the device, right-click the disabled device and select **Enable**. To open a category that is not yet expanded, click the plus (+) sign.

> **Note**
>
> When Windows detects a system error, Windows reporting displays a dialog box. If you choose to send the report, Microsoft Windows Error Reporting (WER) collects information about the application and the module involved in the error and sends the information to Microsoft.

Lab 5.4.5: Create Accounts and Check for Updates in Windows XP

In this lab, you will create user accounts and configure the operating system for Automatic Updates after the Windows XP Professional installation process. Refer to the lab in *IT Essentials: PC Hardware and Software Lab Manual, Fourth Edition*. You can perform this lab now or wait until the end of the chapter.

Optional Lab 5.4.5: Create Accounts and Check for Updates in Windows Vista.

In this lab, you will create user accounts and configure the operating system for Automatic Updates after the Windows XP Professional installation process. Refer to the lab in *IT Essentials: PC Hardware and Software Lab Manual, Fourth Edition*. You can perform this lab now or wait until the end of the chapter.

Describe Custom Installation Options

Installing an operating system on a single computer takes time. Imagine the time it would take to install operating systems on multiple computers, one at a time, in a large organization. To simplify this activity, you can use the Microsoft System Preparation (Sysprep) tool to install and configure the same operating system on multiple computers. Sysprep prepares an operating system that will be used on computers with different hardware configurations. With Sysprep and a disk-cloning application, technicians are able to quickly install an operating system, complete the last configuration steps for the OS setup, and install applications.

Disk Cloning

There are many methods to copy an OS to speed and automate installation. A common *disk cloning* technique creates an image of a hard drive in a computer. Follow these steps for disk cloning:

How To

Step 1. Create a master installation on one computer. This master installation includes the operating system, software applications, and configuration settings that will be used by the other computers in the organization.

Step 2. Run **Sysprep** from the run dialog box.

Step 3.   Create a disk image of the configured computer using a third-party disk-cloning program like Norton Ghost by Symantec.

Step 4.   Copy the disk image onto a server. When the destination computer is booted, a shortened version of the Windows setup program runs. The setup creates a new system security identifier (SID), installs drivers for hardware, creates user accounts, and configures network settings to finish the OS install.

Network Installation

Windows can also be installed over a network:

How To

Step 1.   Prepare the computer by creating a FAT or FAT32 partition of at least 1.5 GB. You must also make the partition bootable and include a network client. You can also use a boot disk that contains a network client so that the computer can connect to a file server over the network.

Step 2.   Copy the Windows XP installation files (the I386 folder from the installation disc) to the network server and make sure to share the directory so that clients can connect and use the files.

Step 3.   Boot the computer and connect to the shared directory.

Step 4.   From the shared directory, run the setup program, WINNT.EXE. The setup program copies all of the installation files from the network share onto your hard drive. After the installation files have been copied, the installation continues much the same as if the installation were performed from a disc.

Recovery Disc

You can use a recovery disc when there has been a system failure and other recovery options have failed, such as booting in Safe Mode or booting a Last Known Good. An Automated System Recovery (ASR) set must be created before a recovery can be performed. Use the ASR Wizard in Backup to create the ASR set. The ASR Wizard creates a backup of the system state, services, and operating system components. The ASR Wizard also creates a file that contains information about your disks, the backup, and how to restore the backup.

To restore the ASR, press **F2** after booting the Windows XP installation disc. ASR reads the set and restores the disks that are needed to start the computer. After the basic disk information has been restored, ASR installs a basic version of Windows and begins restoring the backup created by the ASR Wizard.

Factory Recovery Partition

Some computers that have Windows XP preinstalled from the factory contain a section of disk that is inaccessible to the user. This partition on the disk contains an image of the bootable partition, created when the computer was built. This partition is called a factory recovery partition and can be used to restore the computer to its original configuration. Occasionally, the option to reach this partition for restoration is hidden and a special key or key combination must be used when the computer is being started. The option to restore from the factory recovery partition can also be found in the BIOS of some computers. Contact the manufacturer to find out how you can access the partition and restore the original configuration of the computer.

Identify the Boot Sequence Files and Registry Files

You should know the process that Windows XP uses when booting. Understanding these steps can help you to troubleshoot boot problems.

Windows XP Boot Process

To begin the boot process, you first turn on the computer, which is called a cold boot. The computer performs the Power On Self Test (POST). Because the video adapter has not yet been initialized, any errors that occur at this point in the boot process are reported by a series of audible tones, called beep codes.

After POST, the BIOS locates and reads the configuration settings that are stored in the CMOS. This configuration setting, called the boot device priority, is the order in which devices are checked to see if an operating system is located there. The boot device priority is set in the BIOS and can be arranged in any order. The BIOS boots the computer using the first drive that contains an operating system.

One common boot order is floppy drive, CD-ROM drive, and then the hard drive. This order allows you to use removable media to boot the computer. The BIOS checks the floppy drive, the CD-ROM, and finally the hard drive for an operating system to boot the computer. Network drives, USB drives, and even removable magnetic media, such as CompactFlash or Secure Digital (SD) cards, can also be used in the boot order, depending on the capabilities of the motherboard. Some BIOS also have a boot device priority menu that can be accessed using a special key combination while the computer is starting but before the boot sequence begins. You can use this menu to choose the device that you want to boot, which is useful if multiple drives can boot the computer.

When the drive with the operating system is located, the BIOS locates the Master Boot Record (MBR). The MBR locates the operating system boot loader. For Windows XP, the boot loader is called *NT Loader (NTLDR)*.

NTLDR and the Windows Boot Menu

At this point, NTLDR controls several installation steps. For instance, if more than one OS is present on the disk, BOOT.INI gives the user a chance to select which one to use. If there are no other operating systems, or if the user does not make a selection before the timer expires, the following steps occur:

- NTLDR runs NTDETECT.COM to get information about the installed hardware.

- NTLDR then uses the path specified in BOOT.INI to find the boot partition.

- NTLDR loads two files that make up the core of XP: NTOSKRNL.EXE and HAL.DLL.

- NTLDR reads the Registry files, chooses a hardware profile, and loads the device drivers.

Windows Registry

The Windows *Registry* files are an important part of the Windows XP boot process. These files are recognized by their distinctive names, which begin with HKEY_, as shown in Table 5-4, followed by the name of the portion of the operating system under their control. Every setting in Windows—from the background of the desktop and the color of the screen buttons to the licensing of applications—is stored in the Registry. When a user makes changes to the Control Panel settings, File Associations, System Policies, or installed software, the changes are stored in the Registry.

Table 5-4   Registry Keys

Key	Description
HKEY_CLASSES_ROOT	Information about which file extensions map to a particular application
HKEY_CURRENT_USER	Information, such as desktop settings and history, related to the current user of a PC
HKEY_USERS	Information about all users who have logged on to a system
HKEY_LOCAL_MACHINE	Information relating to the hardware and software
HKEY_CURRENT_CONFIG	Information relating to all active devices on a system

Each user has a unique section of the Registry. The Windows login process pulls system settings from the Registry to reconfigure the system to the state that it was in the last time that the user turned it on.

NT Kernel

At this point, the NT kernel, the heart of the Windows operating system, takes over. The name of this file is NTOSKRNL.EXE. It starts the login file called WINLOGON.EXE and displays the XP welcome screen.

Note

If a SCSI drive will boot the computer, Windows copies the NTBOOTDD.SYS file during installation. This file is not copied if SCSI drives are not being used.

Describe How to Manipulate Operating System Files

After you have installed Windows XP, you might want to make changes to the configuration. The following applications are used extensively for post-installation diagnostics and modifications and can be executed by entering their names in the run dialog box:

- *Msconfig*: This command starts the System configuration utility, as shown in Figure 5-16. It allows you to set the programs that run at startup and to edit configuration files. It also offers simplified control over Windows Services.

Figure 5-16   Msconfig

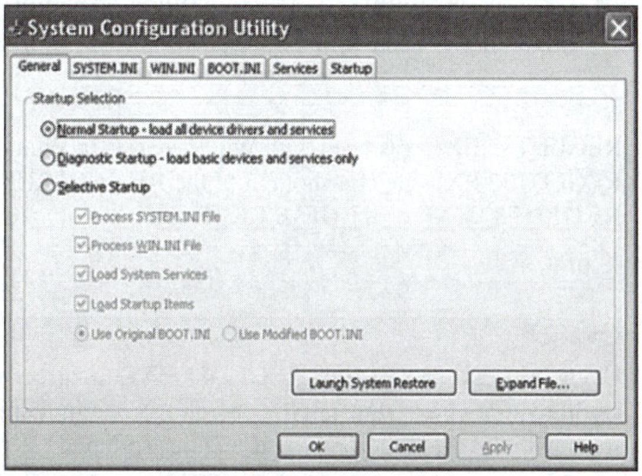

- *Regedit*: This application, named Registry Editor, as shown in Figure 5-17, allows you to edit the Registry. Make sure you back up the PC before making any changes using Regedit.

Figure 5-17   Regedit

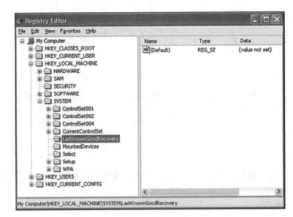

- *Msinfo32*: This utility displays a complete system summary of your computer, including hardware components and details and installed software and settings.

- *Dxdiag*: This utility shows details about all of the DirectX components and drivers that are installed in your computer. You can use this utility to ensure that DirectX is installed properly and configured correctly.

- *Cmd*: This command opens a command window when it is entered in the Run dialog box. This is used to execute command-line programs and utilities.

Note

REGEDT32.EXE was used with Windows NT. In Windows XP, and Windows Server 2003, the REGEDT32.EXE file is a shortcut to the **REGEDIT.EXE** command. In Windows XP, you can enter **REGEDT32.EXE** or **REGEDIT.EXE**; both commands run the same program.

Caution

Using **REGEDT32.EXE** or **REGEDIT.EXE** incorrectly might cause configuration problems that could require you to reinstall the operating system; therefore, make a backup copy of your Registry from within Regedit before you use either command.

Startup Modes

You can boot Windows in one of many different modes. Pressing the F8 key during the boot process opens the Windows Advanced Startup Options menu, which allows you to select how to boot Windows. The following startup options are commonly used:

- **Safe Mode**: Starts Windows but only loads drivers for basic components, such as the keyboard and display.

- **Safe Mode with Networking Support**: Starts Windows identically to Safe Mode and also loads the drivers for network components.

- **Safe Mode with Command Prompt**: Starts Windows and loads the command prompt instead of the GUI.

- **Last Known Good Configuration**: Enables a user to load the configuration settings of Windows that were used the last time that Windows started successfully. It does this by accessing a copy of the Registry that is created for this purpose.

- **Boot Normally**: Starts Windows and loads all the drivers and boots with no modifications.

Note

Last Known Good Configuration is not useful unless it is applied immediately after a failure occurs. If the machine is restarted and, despite its difficulties, manages to open Windows, the Registry key for Last Known Good Configuration will probably be updated with the faulty information.

Describe Directory Structures

Operating systems have organized locations for files and applications. The directory structures in Windows operating systems are quite similar among the versions. A path is a description of where a file is located within the directory structure.

File Extensions and Attributes

In Windows, the root level of the Windows partition is usually labeled drive C:\. Next, there is an initial set of standardized directories, called folders, for the operating system, applications, configuration information, and data files. Following the initial installation, users can install most applications and data in whichever directory they choose.

Files in the directory structure adhere to a Windows naming convention:

- Maximum of 255 characters can be used.

- Characters such as a slash or a backslash (/ \) are not allowed.

- An extension of three or four letters is added to the filename to identify the file type.

- Filenames are not case sensitive.

The following filename extensions are commonly used:

- **.doc**: Microsoft Word 2003 and earlier

- **.docx**: Microsoft Word 2007 and later

- **.txt**: ASCII text only

- **.jpg**: Graphics format

- **.ppt**: Microsoft PowerPoint

- **.zip**: Compression format

The directory structure maintains a set of attributes for each file that controls how the file can be viewed or altered. These are the most common file attributes:

- **R**: The file is read-only.

- **A**: The file will be archived the next time that the disk is backed up.

- **S**: The file is marked as a system file, and a warning is given if an attempt is made to delete or modify the file.

- **H**: The file is hidden in the directory display.

You can view the filenames, extensions, and attributes by entering the **ATTRIB** command in a DOS window, as shown in Figure 5-18. Choose **Start > Run**, type **cmd**, and press **Enter**.

In Windows Vista, choose **Start > Start Search**, type **cmd**, and press **Enter**.

Figure 5-18   File Attributes

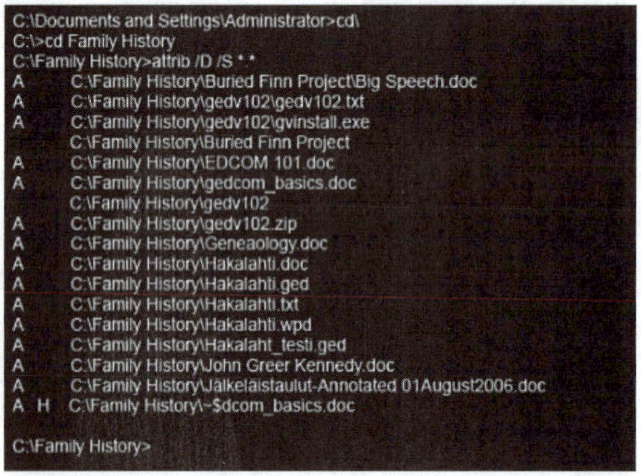

```
C:\Documents and Settings\Administrator>cd\
C:\>cd Family History
C:\Family History>attrib /D /S *.*
A          C:\Family History\Buried Finn Project\Big Speech.doc
A          C:\Family History\gedv102\gedv102.txt
A          C:\Family History\gedv102\gvinstall.exe
           C:\Family History\Buried Finn Project
A          C:\Family History\EDCOM 101.doc
A          C:\Family History\gedcom_basics.doc
           C:\Family History\gedv102
A          C:\Family History\gedv102.zip
A          C:\Family History\Geneaology.doc
A          C:\Family History\Hakalahti.doc
A          C:\Family History\Hakalahti.ged
A          C:\Family History\Hakalahti.txt
A          C:\Family History\Hakalahti.wpd
A          C:\Family History\Hakalaht_testi.ged
A          C:\Family History\John Greer Kennedy.doc
A          C:\Family History\Jälkeläistaulut-Annotated 01August2006.doc
A  H       C:\Family History\~$dcom_basics.doc

C:\Family History>
```

Navigate to the folder that contains the file that you are interested in. Type **ATTRIB** followed by the filename. Use a wildcard such as ***.*** to view many files at once. The attributes of each file appear in the left column of the screen. To get information about the **ATTRIB** command, type the following at the command prompt:

ATTRIB/?

You can access the Windows equivalent of **ATTRIB** by right-clicking a file in Windows Explorer and choosing **Properties**.

> **Note**
>
> To see the properties of a file in Windows Explorer, you must first set Windows Explorer to Show Hidden Files. Right-click **Start** and choose **Explore > Tools > Folder Options > View**. In Windows Vista, right-click **Start** and choose **Explore > Organize > Folder and Search Options > View**.

Describe NTFS and FAT32

Windows XP and Windows 2000 use FAT32 or NTFS, while Windows Vista uses NTFS. Security is one of the most important differences between these file systems. NTFS can support more and larger files than FAT32 and provides more flexible security features for files and folders. Figure 5-19 shows the file permission properties for FAT32 and NTFS.

Figure 5-19   NTFS Permissions

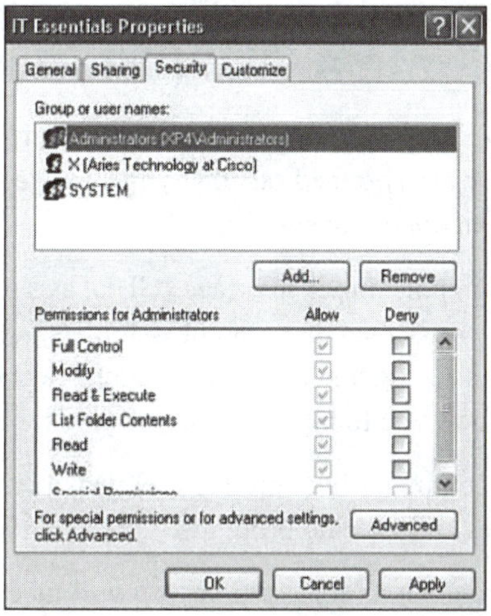

To use the extra security advantages of NTFS, you can convert partitions from FAT32 to NTFS using the CONVERT.EXE utility. To restore an NTFS partition back to a FAT32 partition, reformat the partition and restore the data from a backup.

> **Caution**
>
> Before converting a file system, remember to back up the data.

Lab 5.4.8: Managing System Files with Built-in Utilities in Windows XP

In this lab, you will manage system files with built-in utilities in Windows XP. Refer to the lab in *IT Essentials: PC Hardware and Software Lab Manual, Fourth Edition*. You can perform this lab now or wait until the end of the chapter.

Optional Lab 5.4.8: Managing System Files with Built-in Utilities in Windows Vista

In this lab, you will manage system files with built-in utilities in Windows Vista. Refer to the lab in *IT Essentials: PC Hardware and Software Lab Manual, Fourth Edition*. You can perform this lab now or wait until the end of the chapter.

Worksheet 5.4.9: Answer NTFS and FAT32 Questions

In this worksheet, you will answer questions about NTFS and FAT32, which are file systems used by the Windows XP operating system and provide different file system features. Refer to the worksheet in *IT Essentials: PC Hardware and Software Lab Manual, Fourth Edition*. You can complete this worksheet now or wait to do so until the end of the chapter.

Navigate a GUI (Windows)

The operating system provides a user interface that allows you to interact with the computer. There are two methods that you can use to navigate the file system and run applications within an operating system:

- A graphical user interface (GUI), as shown in Figure 5-20, provides graphical representations (icons) of all the files, folders, and programs on a computer. You manipulate these icons using a pointer that is controlled with a mouse or similar device. The pointer allows you to move icons by dragging and dropping, and execute programs by clicking.

- A command-line interface (CLI) is text based. You must type commands to manipulate files and execute programs.

After completing this section, you will meet these objectives:

- Manipulate items on the desktop.
- Explore Control Panel applets.
- Explore Administrative Tools.
- Install, navigate, and uninstall an application.
- Describe upgrading an operating system.

Figure 5-20   Operating System Navigation

Manipulate Items on the Desktop

After the operating system has been installed, the desktop can be customized to suit individual needs. A desktop on a computer is a graphical representation of a workspace. The desktop has icons, toolbars, and menus to manipulate files. The desktop can be customized with images, sounds, and colors to provide a more personalized look and feel. All of these customizable items together make up a theme. Windows Vista has a special theme called Aero. Aero is the default theme and has translucent window borders, numerous animations, and live icons that are thumbnail images of the contents of a file. Because of the advanced graphics needed, the Aero theme can only be used on computers that meet certain hardware requirements.

Note

Windows Vista Home Basic does not include the Aero theme.

In Windows Vista, a feature called the Sidebar can also be personalized. The Sidebar is a graphical pane on the desktop that keeps small programs called gadgets organized. Gadgets are small applications such as games, sticky notes, or a clock. Gadgets, like interfaces to web information such as weather maps or contacts on a social networking site, can also be added. Sidebar can be activated by navigating to **Start > All Programs > Accessories > Windows Sidebar**. It can be customized by right-clicking the Sidebar.

Display Properties

To customize the Windows XP GUI of your desktop, right-click the desktop and choose **Properties**, as shown in Figure 5-21. The Display Properties window has five tabs: Themes, Desktop, Screen Saver, Appearance, and Settings. Click any of these tabs to customize your display settings. In Windows Vista, right-click the desktop and choose Personalize. The Personalization window has seven links: Window Color and Appearance, Desktop Background, Screen Saver, Sounds, Mouse Pointers, Themes, and Display Settings. Click any of these links to customize your display settings.

Figure 5-21   Accessing Desktop Properties

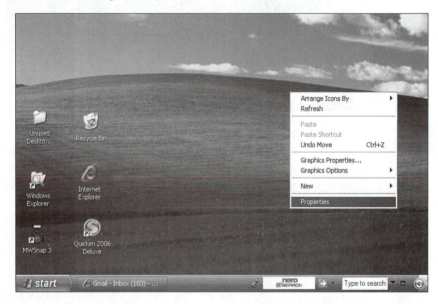

Desktop Items

There are several items on the desktop that can be customized, such as the taskbar and Recycle Bin. To customize any item, right-click the item and then choose **Properties**.

Start Menu

On the desktop, the Start menu is accessed by clicking the **Start** button. The Start menu, shown in Figure 5-22, displays all of the applications installed in the computer, a list of recently opened documents, and a list of other elements, such as a search feature, help center, and system settings. The Start menu can also be customized. There are two styles of Start menu: XP and Classic. The XP-style Start menu is used throughout this course for demonstrating command sequences.

Figure 5-22   Start Menu

My Computer

To access the various drives installed in the computer, double-click the **My Computer** icon that appears on the desktop. If it does not appear on the desktop, you can reinstate it by right-clicking the desktop, choosing **Properties**, and clicking **Customize Desktop** on the Desktop tab. Check **My Computer** under Desktop Icons. Click **OK** and **Apply**. To customize certain settings, right-click **My Computer** and choose **Properties**. Settings that can be customized include the following:

- Computer name
- Hardware settings
- Virtual memory

- Automatic Updates

- Remote access

> **Note**
>
> In Windows Vista, My Computer is called Computer. To customize certain settings, click the **Start** button, right-click **Computer**, and choose **Properties**. Access installed drives in Windows Vista with the following path: **Start > Computer**.

Launching Applications

You can launch applications in several ways:

- Click the application on the Start menu.

- Double-click the application shortcut icon on the desktop.

- Double-click the application executable file in My Computer.

- Launch the application from the Run dialog box or command line.

My Network Places

To view and configure network connections, right-click the **My Network Places** icon on the desktop. In My Network Places, you can connect to or disconnect from a network drive. Click **Properties** to configure existing network connections, such as a wired or wireless LAN connection.

> **Note**
>
> In Windows Vista, My Network Places is called Network.

Lab 5.5.1: Run Commands in Windows XP

In this lab, you will navigate Windows XP both by GUI and by the command line. Open programs by using either Windows Explorer and the Run command. Refer to the lab in *IT Essentials: PC Hardware and Software Lab Manual, Fourth Edition*. You can perform this lab now or wait until the end of the chapter.

Optional Lab 5.5.1: Run Commands in Windows Vista

In this lab, navigate Windows Vista both by GUI and CMD. Open the same program by using Windows Explorer and the Run command. Refer to the lab in *IT Essentials: PC Hardware and Software Lab Manual, Fourth Edition*. You can perform this lab now or wait until the end of the chapter.

Explore Control Panel Applets

Windows centralizes the settings for many features that control the behavior and appearance of the computer. These settings are categorized in *Control Panel applets*, or small programs, found in the Control Panel, as shown in Figure 5-23. Adding or removing programs, changing network settings, and changing the security settings are some of the configuration options available in the Control Panel.

Figure 5-23   Control Panel

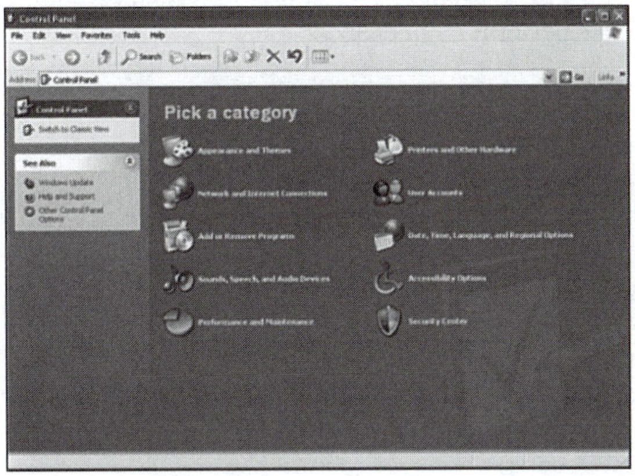

Control Panel Applets

The names of various applets in the Control Panel differ slightly depending on the version of Windows installed. In Windows XP, the icons are grouped into categories:

- **Appearance and Themes**: Applets that control the look of windows:
    - Display
    - Taskbar and Start Menu
    - Folder Options

- **Network and Internet Connections**: Applets that configure all of the connection types:
    - Internet Options
    - Network Connections
    - Internal NIC Configuration
    - Network Setup Wizard
    - Windows Firewall
    - Wireless Network Setup Wizard

- **Add or Remove Programs**: Applet to add or remove programs and windows components safely

- **Sounds, Speech, and Audio Devices**: Applets that control all of the settings for sound:

  — Sounds and Audio Devices

  — Speech

  — Portable Media Devices

- **Performance and Maintenance**: Applets to find information about your computer or perform maintenance:

  — Administrative Tools

  — Power Options

  — Scheduled Tasks

  — System

- **Printers and Other Hardware**: Applets to configure devices connected to your computer:

  — Game Controllers

  — Keyboard

  — Mouse

  — Phone and Modem Options

  — Printers and Faxes

  — Scanners and Cameras

- **User Accounts**: Applets to configure options for users and their email:

  — User Accounts

- **Date, Time, Language, and Regional Options**: Applets to change settings based on your location and language:

  — Date and Time

  — Regional and Language Options

- **Accessibility Options**: Wizard used to configure windows for vision, hearing, and mobility needs

- **Security Center**: Applet used to configure security settings for

    — Internet options

    — Automatic Updates

    — Windows Firewall

Display Settings

You can change the display settings by using the Display applet. Change the appearance of the desktop by modifying the resolution and color quality, as shown in Figure 5-24. You can change more advanced display settings, such as wallpaper, screen saver, power settings, and other options, with the following path:

Start > Control Panel > Appearances and Themes> Display > Settings > Advanced

Use the following path in Windows Vista:

Start > Control Panel > Personalization > Display Settings > Advanced Settings

Figure 5-24   Display Settings

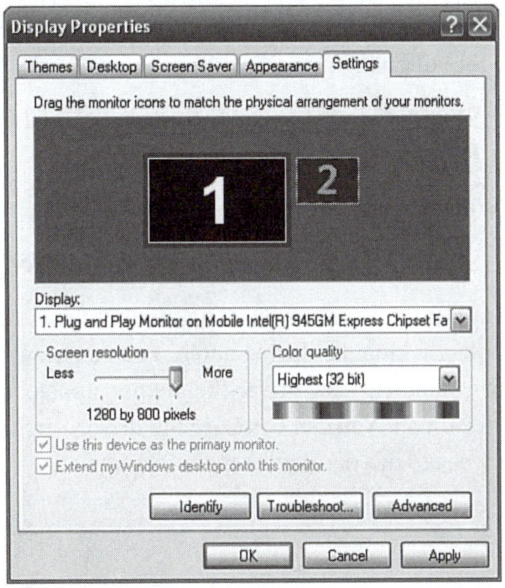

Explore Administrative Tools

Administrative Tools is a collection of very powerful tools that fundamentally change the OS. Unlike customizing the color of the desktop, these utilities create partitions, install drivers, enable services, and perform other significant modifications.

Computer Management

The Computer Management console allows you to manage many aspects of both your computer and remote computers. The Computer Management console addresses three main areas of administration: System Tools, Storage, and Services and Applications. You must have administrative privileges to access the Computer Management console. To view the Computer Management console, use the following path:

Start > Control Panel > Administrative Tools > Computer Management

To view the Computer Management console for a remote computer, right-click **Computer Management (Local)** in the console tree and click **Connect to Another Computer**. In the **Another Computer** dialog box, type the name of the computer or click **Browse** to find a computer you want to manage. This allows you to manage other computers on your network remotely.

Device Manager

Device Manager, shown in Figure 5-25, allows you to view all of the settings for devices in the computer. A common task for technicians is to view the values assigned for the IRQ, I/O address, and the DMA setting for all of the devices in the computer. Those settings control how the devices interact with the OS. To view the system resources in Device Manager, use the following path:

Start > Control Panel > System > Hardware > Device Manager > View > Resources

In Windows Vista, use the following path:

Start > Control Panel > System > Device Manager > Continue > View > Resources

From Device Manager, you can quickly view the properties of any device in the system by double-clicking the device name. You can view which version of the driver is installed in your computer, view driver file details, update a driver, or even roll back or uninstall a device driver. You can compare the driver version listed here with the version available from the website of your device manufacturer.

Figure 5-25   Device Manager

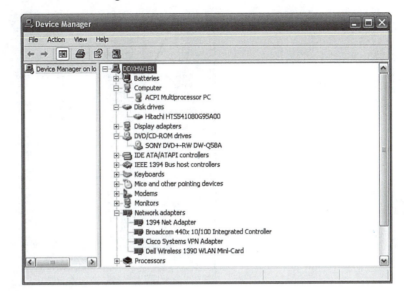

Task Manager

Task Manager, shown in Figure 5-26, allows you to view all applications that are currently running and to close any applications that have stopped responding. Task Manager allows you to monitor the performance of the CPU and virtual memory, view all processes that are currently running, and view information about the network connections. To view information in Task Manager, use the following path:

Ctrl-Alt-Delete > Task Manager

In Windows Vista, use the following path:

Ctrl-Alt-Delete > Start Task Manager

Figure 5-26   Task Manager

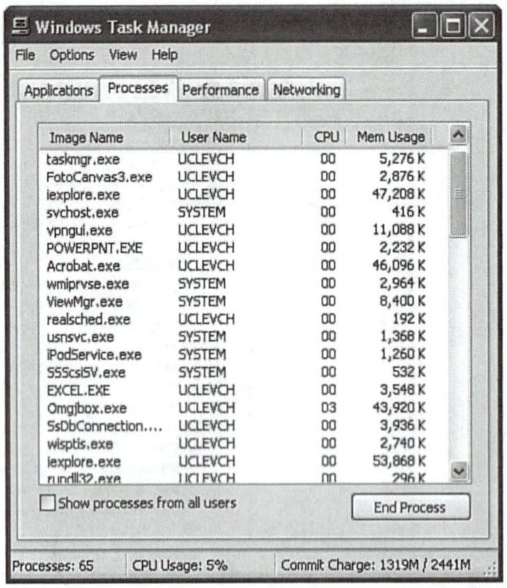

Services

Services are executable programs that require little or no user input. Services can be set to run automatically when Windows starts, or manually when required. The Services console allows you to manage all of the services on your computer and remote computers. You can start, stop, or disable services. You can also change how a service starts, or define actions for the computer to perform automatically when a service fails. You must have administrative privileges to access the Services console. To view the Services console, use the following path:

Start > Control Panel > Administrative Tools > Services

To view the Services console for a remote computer, right-click **Services (Local)** in the console tree and click **Connect to Another Computer** In the **Another Computer** dialog box, type the name of the computer or click **Browse** to find a computer you want to manage.

Performance Monitor

The Performance Monitor console has two distinct parts: System Monitor and Performance Logs and Alerts. System Monitor displays real-time information about the processors, disks, memory, and network usage for your computer. You can easily summarize these activities through histograms, graphs, and reports.

Performance Logs and Alerts allows you to record the performance data and configure alerts. The alerts will notify you when a specified usage falls below or rises above a specified threshold. You can set alerts to create entries in the event log, send a network message, begin a performance log, run a specific program, or any combination of these. You must have administrative privileges to access the Performance Monitor console. To view the Performance Monitor console in Windows XP, use the following path:

Start > Control Panel > Administrative Tools > Performance

In Windows Vista, use the following path:

Start > Control Panel > Administrative Tools > Reliability and Performance Monitor > Continue

Event Viewer

Event Viewer, as shown in Figure 5-27, logs a history of events regarding applications, security, and the system. These log files are a valuable troubleshooting tool. To access Event Viewer, use the following path:

Start > Control Panel > Administrative Tools > Event Viewer

In Windows Vista, use the following path:

Start > Control Panel > Administrative Tools > Event Viewer > Continue

Figure 5-27   Event Viewer

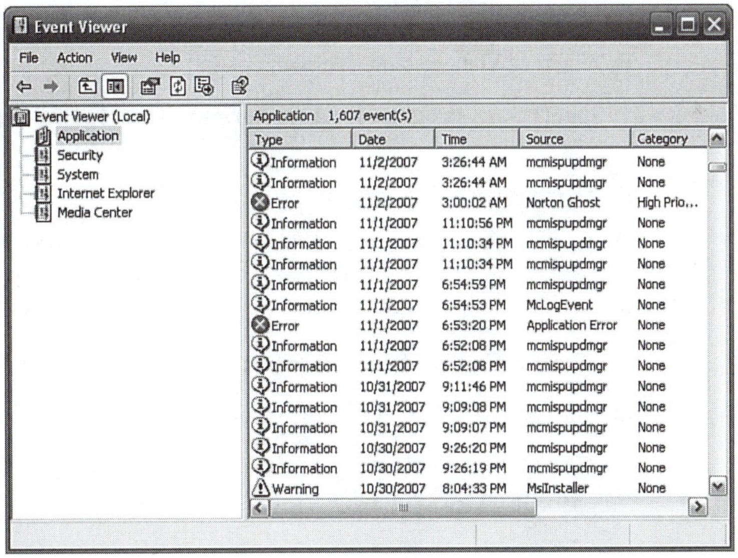

MMC

The Microsoft Management console (MMC) allows you to organize management tools, called snap-ins, in one location for easy administration. Web page links, tasks, ActiveX controls, and folders can also be added to the MMC. After you have configured an MMC, save it to keep all the tools and links in that MMC. You can create as many customized MMCs as needed, each with a different name. This is useful when multiple administrators manage different aspects of the same computer. Each administrator can have an individualized MMC for monitoring and configuring computer settings. You must have administrative privileges to access the MMC. For example, if one person's job is to monitor the performance of multiple servers but that person does not need privilege to make changes, a custom MMC can suit that network administrator. MMCs allow technicians to build a customized "toolbox." To view the MMC in Windows XP, use the following path:

Start > Run, type **mmc**, and press **Enter**

In Windows Vista, use the following path:

Start > Start Search, type **mmc**, and press **Enter**

Remote Desktop

Remote Desktop allows one computer to remotely take control of another computer. Remote technicians can use this troubleshooting feature to repair and upgrade computers. For Windows XP, Remote Desktop is available on Windows XP Professional only. To access Remote Desktop in Windows XP Professional, use the following path:

Start > All Programs > Accessories > Communications > Remote Desktop Connection

In Windows Vista, use the following path:

Start > All Programs > Accessories > Remote Desktop Connection

Performance Settings

To enhance the performance of the operating system, you can change some of the settings that your computer uses, such as virtual memory configuration settings, which are shown in Figure 5-28. To change the virtual memory settings in Windows XP, use the following path:

Start > Control Panel > System > Advanced > Performance > Settings button

In Windows Vista, use the following path:

Start > Control Panel > System > Advanced System Settings > Continue > Advanced > Performance > Settings > Advanced

Figure 5-28   Virtual Memory

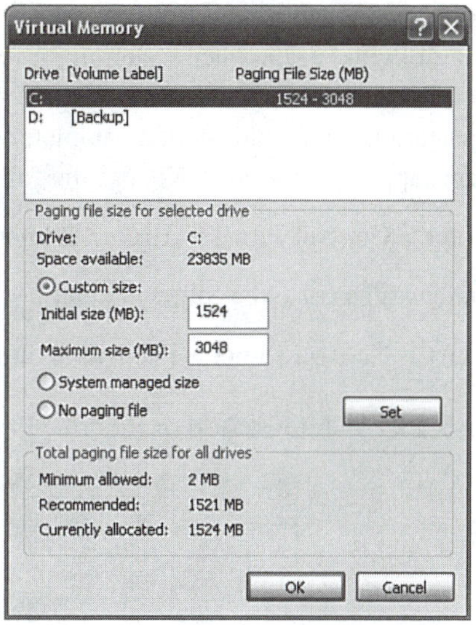

Lab 5.5.3: Managing Administrative Settings and Snap-ins in Windows XP

In this lab, you will manage administrative settings and snap-ins in Windows XP. Refer to the lab in *IT Essentials: PC Hardware and Software Lab Manual, Fourth Edition*. You can perform this lab now or wait until the end of the chapter.

Optional Lab 5.5.3: Managing Administrative Settings and Snap-ins in Windows Vista

In this lab, you will manage administrative settings and snap-ins in Windows Vista. Refer to the lab in *IT Essentials: PC Hardware and Software Lab Manual, Fourth Edition*. You can perform this lab now or wait until the end of the chapter.

Install, Navigate, and Uninstall an Application

As a technician, you will be responsible for adding and removing software from your customers' computers. Most applications use an automatic installation process when an application CD is inserted in the optical drive. The installation process updates the Add or Remove Programs utility. The user is required to click through the installation wizard and provide information when requested.

Add or Remove Programs Applet

Microsoft recommends that users always use the Add or Remove Programs utility, as shown selected in Figure 5-29, when installing or removing applications. When you use the Add or Remove Programs utility to install an application, the utility tracks installation files so that the application can be uninstalled completely, if desired. To open the Add or Remove Programs applet in Windows XP, use the following path:

Start > Control Panel > Add or Remove Programs

In Windows Vista, use the following path:

Start > Control Panel > Programs and Features

Figure 5-29   Windows Add or Remove Programs

Add an Application

If a program or application is not automatically installed when the CD is inserted, you can use the Add or Remove Programs applet to install the application in Windows XP, as shown in Figure 5-30. Click the **Add New Programs** button and navigate to where the application is located on the CD or the downloaded file. Windows installs the application for you. In Windows Vista, insert the CD or DVD, and the program installer should start. If the program does not start, browse the CD or DVD and run the "setup" or "install" file to begin installation.

After the application is installed, you can start the application from the Start menu or a shortcut icon that the application installs on the desktop. Check the application to ensure that it is functioning properly. If there are problems with the application, make the repair or uninstall the application. Some applications, such as Microsoft Office, provide a repair option in the install process. You can use this function to try to correct a program that is not working properly.

Figure 5-30   Add an Application

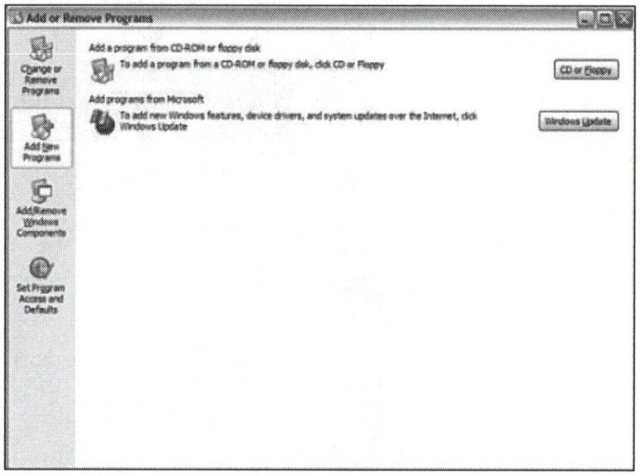

Uninstall an Application

If an application is not uninstalled properly, you may be leaving files on the hard drive and unnecessary settings in the Registry. This might not cause any problems, but it depletes available hard drive space, system resources, and the speed at which the Registry is read. Figure 5-31 shows the use of the Add or Remove Programs applet to uninstall programs in Windows XP. The wizard guides you through the software removal process and removes every file that was installed.

Lab 5.5.4: Install Third-Party Software in Windows XP

In this lab, you will install third-party software in Windows XP. Refer to the lab in *IT Essentials: PC Hardware and Software Lab Manual, Fourth Edition*. You can perform this lab now or wait until the end of the chapter.

Optional Lab 5.5.4: Install Third-Party Software in Windows Vista

In this lab, you will install third-party software in Windows Vista. Refer to the lab in *IT Essentials: PC Hardware and Software Lab Manual, Fourth Edition*. You can perform this lab now or wait until the end of the chapter.

Figure 5-31   Remove an Application

Describe Upgrading an Operating System

Sometimes it might be necessary to upgrade an operating system. Before upgrading the operating system, check the minimum requirements of the new operating system to ensure that the computer meets the minimum specifications. Check the HCL to ensure that the hardware is compatible with the new operating system. Back up all data before upgrading the operating system in case there is a problem with the installation.

Upgrading the Operating System to Windows XP

The following is how to upgrade an operating system to Windows XP:

Step 1.   Back up all data.

Step 2.   Insert the Windows XP disc into the optical drive to start the upgrade process. Choose **Start > Run**.

Step 3.   In the Run box, where D is the drive letter for the optical drive, type **D:\i386\winnt32** and press **Enter**. The Welcome to the Windows XP Setup Wizard displays.

Step 4.   Choose **Upgrade to Windows XP** and click **Next**. The License Agreement page displays.

Step 5.   Read the license agreement and click the button to accept this agreement.

Step 6.   Click **Next**. The Upgrading to the Windows XP NTFS File System page displays.

Step 7.   Follow the prompts and complete the upgrade. When the install is complete, the computer will restart.

> **Note**
>
> The Windows XP Setup Wizard might automatically start when the disc is inserted into the optical drive.

Upgrading the Operating System to Windows Vista

The following is how to upgrade an operating system to Windows Vista:

> **Note**
>
> Before you can upgrade from Windows XP to Windows Vista, you must install Windows XP Service Pack 2.

How To

Step 1.   Insert the Windows Vista disc into the optical drive. The Set Up window appears.

Step 2.   Select **Install Windows Vista**.

Step 3.   You are prompted to download any important updates for Windows Vista.

Step 4.   Enter your Product Key and then agree to the End User License Agreement (EULA).

Step 5.   You are presented with two choices, Custom or Upgrade.

Step 6.   Click **Upgrade** and setup will begin copying installation files.

Step 7.   Follow the prompts and complete the upgrade. When the install is complete, the computer will restart.

In some cases, you cannot upgrade to a newer operating system. If your operating system cannot be upgraded, you must perform a new installation.

When a new installation of Windows is needed, you can use the Windows User State Migration Tool (USMT) to migrate all of the current user files and settings to the new operating system. USMT allows users to restore the configurations and customizations from their current computer to the newly installed Windows operating system. Download and install USMT from Microsoft to create a store of user files and settings onto a separate drive or partition. After the new operating system is installed, download and install USMT again to restore the user files and settings to the new operating system.

Identify and Apply Common Preventive Maintenance Techniques for Operating Systems

Preventive maintenance for an operating system includes organizing the system, defragmenting the hard drive, keeping applications current, removing unused applications, and checking the system for errors.

After completing this section, you will meet these objectives:

- Create a preventive maintenance plan.
- Schedule a task.
- Back up the hard drive.

Create a Preventive Maintenance Plan

The goal of an operating system preventive maintenance plan is to avoid problems in the future. Perform preventive maintenance regularly, and record all actions taken and observations made. Some preventative maintenance should take place when it causes the least amount of disruption to the people who use the computers. This often means scheduling tasks at night, early in the morning, or over the weekend. There are also tools and techniques that can automate many preventive maintenance tasks.

Preventive Maintenance Planning

Preventive maintenance plans should include detailed information about the maintenance of all computers and network equipment, with emphasis on equipment that could impact the organization the most. Preventive maintenance includes the following important tasks:

- Hard drive backup
- Hard drive defragmentation
- Updates to the operating system and applications
- Updates to antivirus and other protective software
- Hard drive error checking

A preventive maintenance program that is designed to fix things before they break, and to solve small problems before they affect productivity, can provide the following benefits to users and organizations:

- Decreased downtime
- Improved performance

- Improved reliability

- Decreased repair costs

An additional part of preventive maintenance is documentation. A repair log helps you determine which equipment is the most or least reliable. It also provides a history of when a computer was last fixed, how it was fixed, and what the problem was.

Device Driver Updates

Manufacturers occasionally release new drivers to address issues with the current drivers. As a best practice, you should check for updated drivers regularly. Check for updated drivers when your hardware does not work properly or to prevent future problems. It is also important to update drivers that patch or correct security problems. Updating device drivers should be part of your preventive maintenance program to ensure that your drivers are always current. If a driver update does not work properly, use the Roll Back Driver feature to revert to the previously installed driver.

Firmware Updates

Manufacturers occasionally release new firmware updates to address issues that might not be fixed with driver updates. Firmware updates are less common than driver updates. They can increase the speed of certain types of hardware, enable new features, or increase the stability of a product. Follow the computer manufacturer's instructions carefully when performing a firmware update to avoid making the hardware unusable. Research the firmware updates completely because it might not be possible to revert to the original firmware. Checking for firmware updates should be part of your preventive maintenance program.

Operating System Updates

Microsoft releases updates to address security issues and other functionality problems. You can install individual updates manually from the Microsoft website or automatically using the Windows Automatic Update utility.

Downloads that contain multiple updates are known as service packs. A service pack usually contains all of the updates for an operating system. Installing a service pack is a good way to bring your operating system up to date quickly. Set a restore point and back up critical data prior to installing a service pack. Add operating system updates to your preventive maintenance program to ensure that your operating system has the latest functionality and security fixes.

Security

Security is an important aspect of your preventive maintenance program. Install virus and malware protection software and perform regular scans on your computer to help ensure that your computer remains free of malicious software. Use the Windows Malicious

Software Removal Tool to check a computer for specific, prevalent malicious software. If an infection is found, the tool removes it. Each time a new version of the tool is available from Microsoft, download it and scan your computer for new threats. This should be a standard item in your preventive maintenance program along with regular updates to your antivirus and spyware removal tools.

Startup Programs

Some programs, such as antivirus scanners and spyware removal tools, do not automatically start when the computer boots up. To ensure that these programs run each time the computer is booted, add the program to the Startup folder of the Start menu. Many programs have switches to allow the program to perform a specific action, start up without being displayed, or go to the Windows tray. Check the documentation to determine if your programs allow the use of special switches.

Schedule a Task

Some preventive maintenance consists of cleaning, inspecting, and doing minor repairs. Some preventive maintenance uses application tools that are either already in the operating system or can be loaded onto the user's hard drive. Most preventive maintenance applications can be set to run automatically according to a schedule.

Windows has the following utilities that launch tasks when you schedule them:

- The DOS **AT** command launches tasks at a specified time using the CLI.

- Windows Task Scheduler launches tasks at a specified time using a GUI.

Information about the **AT** command is available at this path in Windows XP:

> **Start > Run**, type **cmd**, and press **Enter**

Then type **AT /?** at the command line.

In Windows Vista, access the command line using the following path:

> **Start > Start Search**, type **cmd**, and press **Enter**

Then type **AT /?** at the command line.

Access Windows Task Scheduler by following this path in Windows XP:

> **Start > All Programs > Accessories > System Tools > Scheduled Tasks**

In Windows Vista, follow this path:

> **Start > All Programs > Accessories > System Tools > Task Scheduler**

Both of these tools allow you to run a command once at a specific time or schedule a command to run on selected days or times. Windows Task Scheduler, shown in Figure 5-32, is easier to learn and use than the **AT** command, especially when it comes to recurring tasks and deleting tasks already scheduled.

Figure 5-32 Windows Task Scheduler

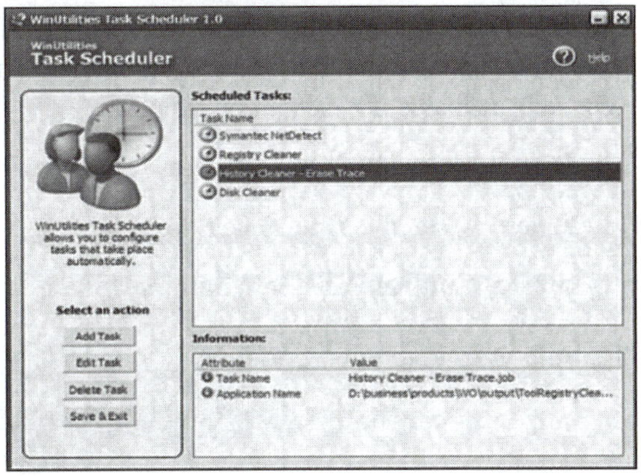

System Utilities

Several utilities included with DOS and Windows help maintain system integrity. Two *system utilities* that are useful tools for preventive maintenance are

- *ScanDisk* or *CHKDSK*: ScanDisk (Windows 2000) and CHKDSK (Windows XP and Vista) check the integrity of files and folders and scan the hard disk surface for physical errors. Consider using ScanDisk or CHKDSK at least once a month and also whenever a sudden loss of power causes the system to shut down.

- *Defrag*: As files increase in size, some data is written to the next available space on the disk. In time, data becomes fragmented, or spread all over the hard drive. It takes time to seek each section of the data. Defrag gathers the noncontiguous data into one place, making files run faster.

You can access both of these utilities by using this path in Windows XP:

Start > All Programs > Accessories > System Tools > Disk Defragmenter

In Windows Vista, use this path:

Start > Computer > right-click **Drive** *x* **> Properties > Tools**

Automatic Updates

If every maintenance task had to be scheduled every time it was run, repairing computers would be much harder than it is today. Fortunately, tools such as the Scheduled Task Wizard allow many functions to be automated. But how can you automate the update of software that has not been written?

Operating systems and applications are constantly being updated for security purposes and for added functionality. It is important that Microsoft and others provide an update service, as shown in Figure 5-33. The update service can scan the system for needed updates and then recommend what should be downloaded and installed. Enabling *Automatic Updates* can download and install updates as soon as they are available, or it can download updates as required and install them when the computer is next rebooted. The Microsoft Update Wizard is available at this path in Windows XP:

Start > Control Panel > System > Automatic Updates

In Windows Vista, it is available at this path:

Start > Control Panel > Windows Update

Figure 5-33 Automatic Updates

Most antivirus software contains its own update facility. It can update both its application software and its database files automatically. This feature allows it to provide immediate protection as new threats develop.

Restore Point

An update can sometimes cause serious problems. Perhaps an older program is in the system that is not compatible with the current operating system. An automatic update might install code that works for most users but does not work with your system.

You can solve this problem by creating a *restore point*, which is an image of the computer settings. If the computer crashes or an update causes system problems, the computer can roll back to a previous configuration. You can use the Windows System Restore utility, as shown in Figure 5-34, to create and revert to a restore point. Restore points are not the same as backups. Restore points monitor a limited number of critical files. A backup normally addresses all the files.

A technician should always create a restore point before updating or replacing the operating system. Restore points should also be created at the following times:

- When an application is installed

- When a driver is installed

Figure 5-34   Windows System Restore

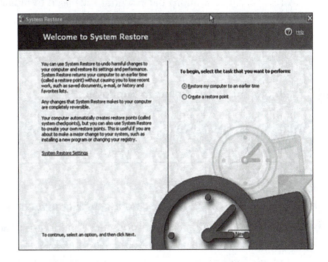

Note

A restore point backs up drivers, system files, and Registry settings but not application data.

To restore or create a restore point, use the following path:

Start > All Programs > Accessories > System Tools > System Restore

Backup Status and Configuration

Windows Vista has the Backup Status and Configuration tool for backing up photos, music, email, and other types of user data. Backups can be set to run automatically at regular intervals. Back up your data to a drive other than the drive that contains the operating system. The Backup Status and Configuration tool is not used to back up system settings. Windows

Vista Home Basic does not include the option to set automatic backups. To access the Backup Status and Configuration tool, use the following path:

Start > All Programs > Accessories > System Tools > Backup Status and Configuration

ERD and ASR

Windows 2000 offers the ability to create an *emergency repair disk (ERD)* that saves critical boot files and configuration information necessary to troubleshoot problems in Windows. Windows XP offers the same features with the *Automated System Recovery (ASR)* wizard. Although both ERD and ASR are powerful troubleshooting tools, they should never replace a good backup.

A recovery disc contains the essential files used to repair the system after a serious issue, such as a hard drive crash. The recovery disc can contain the original version of Windows, hardware drivers, and application software. When the recovery disc is used, the computer is restored to the original default configuration.

Lab 5.6.2: Restore Points in Windows XP

In this lab, you will create a restore point and return your computer back to that point in time in Windows XP. Refer to the lab in *IT Essentials: PC Hardware and Software Lab Manual, Fourth Edition*. You can perform this lab now or wait until the end of the chapter.

Optional Lab 5.6.2: Restore Points in Windows Vista

In this lab, you will create a restore point and return your computer back to that point in time in Windows Vista. Refer to the lab in *IT Essentials: PC Hardware and Software Lab Manual, Fourth Edition*. You can perform this lab now or wait until the end of the chapter.

Back Up the Hard Drive

Just as the system restore points allow the restoration of OS configuration files, backup tools allow the recovery of data. You can use the Microsoft Backup Utility, shown in Figure 5-35, to perform backups as required. It is important to establish a backup strategy that includes data recovery. The organization's requirements will determine how often the data must be backed up and the type of backup to perform.

Figure 5-35   Microsoft Backup Utility

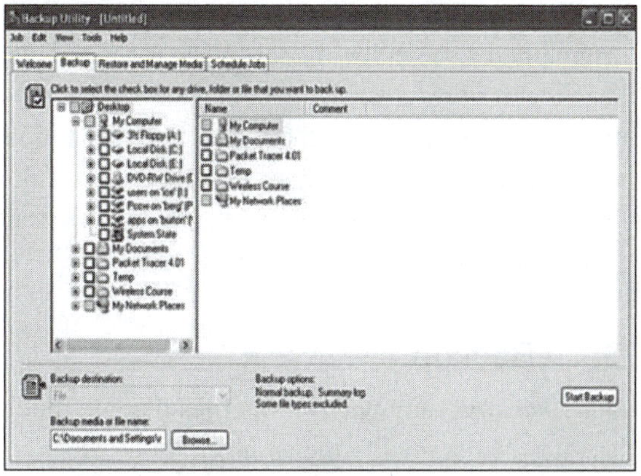

It can take a long time to run a backup. If the backup strategy is followed carefully, it will not be necessary to back up every file at every backup. It is only necessary to make copies of the files that have changed since the last backup. For this reason, there are several different types of backups.

Normal Backup

A *normal backup* is also called a *full backup*. During a normal backup, all selected files on the disk are archived to the backup medium. These files are marked as having been archived by clearing the archive bit. The archive bit flags files that have been modified and should be backed up.

Copy Backup

A *copy backup* copies all selected files. It does not mark the files as having been archived.

Differential Backup

A *differential backup* backs up all the files and folders that have been created or modified since either the last normal backup or the last incremental backup (see the next section). The differential backup does not mark the files as having been archived. Copies are made from the same starting point until the next incremental or full backup is performed. Making differential backups is important because only the last full and differential backups are needed to restore all the data.

Incremental Backup

An *incremental backup* procedure backs up all the files and folders that have been created or modified since either the last normal or incremental backup. It marks the files as having been archived by clearing the archive bit. This has the effect of advancing the starting point of differential backups without having to re-archive the entire contents of the drive. If you must perform a system restore, restore the last full backup first, then restore each incremental backup in order, and finally, restore the differential backups made since the last incremental backup.

Daily Backup

Daily backups only back up the files that are modified on the day of the backup. Daily backups do not modify the archive bit.

To access the daily backup utility on a Windows XP Professional system, use the following path:

Start > All Programs > Accessories > System Tools > Backup

To access the daily backup utility in Windows Vista, use the following path:

Start > All Programs > Accessories > System Tools > Backup Status and Configuration

Backup Media

Many types of backup media are available for computers:

- Tape drives are devices that are used for data backup on a network server drive. Tapes drives are an inexpensive way to store a lot of data.

- The Digital Audio Tape (DAT) standard uses 4-mm digital audiotapes to store data in the Digital Data Storage (DSS) format.

- Digital Linear Tape (DLT) technology offers high-capacity and relatively high-speed tape backup capabilities.

- USB flash memory can hold hundreds of times the data that a floppy disk can hold. USB flash memory devices are available in many capacities and offer better transfer rates than tape devices.

- Optical media, such as CDs, DVDs, and Blu-ray discs, are plastic discs used to store data. Many formats and capacities of optical media are available. A DVD holds much more data than a CD, and a Blu-ray disc holds much more data than a DVD.

- External hard disk drives (HDD) are hard drives that are connected to your computer using a USB, FireWire, or external Serial ATA (eSATA) connection. External HDDs can hold very large amounts of data and can transfer data very quickly.

- Network HDDs are frequently used as a backup media. There is a wide variety of network storage, ranging from simple network-attached storage (NAS) to highly complex and secure storage area networks (SAN).

Lab 5.6.3: Registry Backup and Recovery in Windows XP

In this lab, you will back up a computer Registry and perform a recovery of a computer Registry. Refer to the lab in *IT Essentials: PC Hardware and Software Lab Manual, Fourth Edition*. You can perform this lab now or wait until the end of the chapter.

Troubleshoot Operating Systems

Most operating systems contain utilities to assist in the troubleshooting process. These utilities help technicians determine why the computer crashes or does not boot properly. The utilities also help identify the problem and how to resolve it.

Follow the steps outlined in this section to accurately identify, repair, and document the problem.

After completing this section, you will meet these objectives:

- Review the troubleshooting process.
- Identify common problems and solutions.

Review the Troubleshooting Process

Operating system problems can result from a combination of hardware, application, and configuration issues. Computer technicians must be able to analyze the problem and determine the cause of the error to repair the operating system. This process is called troubleshooting.

Step 1: Identify the Problem

The first step in the troubleshooting process is to gather data from the customer. This can be done by asking the customer some open-ended and closed-ended questions. Table 5-5 provides a list of open-ended and closed-ended questions to ask the customer about operating system problems. (This list is *not* comprehensive.)

Table 5-5   Operating System Problems: Open-Ended and Closed-Ended Questions
to Ask

Open-Ended Questions	Closed-Ended Questions
What problems are you experiencing with your computer or network?	Has anyone else used your computer recently?
What software has been installed on your computer recently?	Does the computer boot up successfully?
What were you doing when the problem was identified?	Have you changed your password recently?
What operating system do you have installed on your computer?	Have you received any error messages on your computer?
What updates or patches have been installed on your computer?	Are you currently logged in to the network?

Step 2: Establish a Theory of Probable Causes

After you have talked to the customer, you should verify the obvious issues. Some issues
for operating systems include

- Incorrect settings are in the BIOS.

- The Caps Lock key is set to ON.

- Nonbootable media is in the floppy drive during computer bootup.

- The password has changed.

- The monitor does not have power.

- Monitor settings are incorrect.

Step 3: Determine an Exact Cause

After the obvious issues have been verified, try some quick solutions. A list of possible
quick solutions for operating systems include

- Press **F8** during bootup to use the Last Known Good Configuration settings.

- Press **F8** to enter Safe Mode to troubleshoot video problems.

- Uninstall an application that was recently added by using the Add or Remove Programs utility in the Control Panel.

- Roll back the system using a system restore point.

- Examine Device Manager for device conflicts.

- Run Cleanmgr to remove temporary files.

- Run ScanDisk to repair problems with the hard drive.

- Run Defrag to speed up the hard drive.

- Reboot the computer.

- Log in as a different user.

Step 4: Implement a Solution

If no solution is achieved in the previous step, further research is needed to implement the solution. Some different ways to gather information about the problem from the computer include the following:

- Helpdesk repair logs

- Other technicians

- Manufacture FAQs

- Technical websites

- News groups

- Computer manuals

- Device manuals

- Online forums

- Internet search

Step 5: Verify Solution and Full System Functionality

To ensure full system functionality, do the following tasks:

- Shut down the computer and restart it.

- Check event logs to make sure there are no new warnings or errors.

- Check Device Manager to see whether there are no warnings or errors.

- Run DxDiag to make sure DirectX is running correctly.

- Make sure the Internet can be accessed.

- Rerun system file checker to ensure that all files are correct.

- Rerun scandisk to make sure no problems remain on the hard drive.

- Check Task Manager to ensure that no programs are running incorrectly.

- Rerun any third-party diagnostic tools.

Step 6: Document Findings

After you have solved the problem, you will close with the customer. A list of the steps required to complete this task include the following:

- Discuss the solution implemented with the customer.

- Have the customer verify that the problem has been solved.

- Provide the customer with all paperwork.

- Document the steps taken to solve the problem in the work order and the technician's journal.

- Document any components used in the repair.

- Document the time spent to resolve the problem.

- Keep a copy of all paperwork generated during the troubleshooting process.

Identify Common Problems and Solutions

Operating system problems can be attributed to hardware, application, or configuration issues, or to some combination of the three. You will resolve some types of operating system problems more often than others. Table 5-6 is a chart of common operating system problems and solutions.

Table 5-6   Common Problems and Solutions

Identify the Problem	Probable Causes	Possible Solutions
The computer locks up and/or displays a blue screen.	The computer is overheating.	Reboot the computer. Check the event log for alerts and address them.
	Some of the operating system files may be corrupted.	Install or roll back updated drivers.
	The power supply, RAM, hard drive, or motherboard may be defective.	Test the power supply, RAM, hard drive or motherboard with third-party diagnostic software and replace as necessary.
	The BIOS settings may be incorrect.	Run the system file checker to replace corrupt operating system files.
	An incorrect driver has been installed.	

Identify the Problem	Probable Causes	Possible Solutions
		Examine and adjust the BIOS settings.
		Check the fan connections and ensure fans are operating properly.
The keyboard or mouse does not respond.	The computer has the wrong, incorrectly installed, not current, or incompatible driver.	Check the status light indicators on the keyboard.
		Reboot the computer.
	The input/output software in not installed properly.	Install or roll back updated drivers.
	The operating system is not up to date.	Reinstall the input/output device software.
	The cable has been damaged.	Update the operating system from the Windows Update website.
	The device is defective.	
	The computer has a virus.	Replace the device.
		Run a virus scan and obtain updates if necessary.
The application does not install.	The downloaded application installer contains a virus and has been prevented from installing by virus protection software.	Reboot the computer.
		Close applications before installing a new program.
	The installation disk or file is corrupt.	Scan the downloaded application installer of viruses.
	The application is not compatible with the operating system There are too many programs running and not enough memory remaining to install the application	Obtain a new installation disk or delete the file and download the installation file again.
		Run the installation application in compatibility mode.

continues

Table 5-6   Common Problems and Solutions   *continued*

Identify the Problem	Probable Causes	Possible Solutions
The operating system will not start.	There is a non-bootable disk in the boot drive.	Remove all non-bootable media from the drives.
	Dome of the operating system files may be corrupted.	Reboot the computer.
	The Master Boot Record is corrupt.	Use the Last Known Good Configuration option to start the operating system.
	The power supply, RAM, hard drive, or motherboard may be defective.	Boot the computer in Safe Mode.
		Use Recovery Console to fix the Master Boot Record.
		Disconnect any newly connected devices.
		Replace the power supply, RAM, hard drive, or motherboard with one that works.
		Perform a Repair Installation on the operating system.
A document will not print even though the printer is correctly installed and configured and the application is functioning properly.	The printer spooler has become overloaded and stopped responding.	Clear the print spooler of any print jobs.
	The printer software is outdated.	Restart the print spooler service.
	The operating system has been automatically updated with a bad driver.	Reboot the computer.
		Install or roll back updated drivers.
		Update the printer software.

Lab 5.7.2: Managing Device Drivers with Device Manager in Windows XP

In this lab, you will manage device drivers with Device Manager in Windows XP. Refer to the lab in *IT Essentials: PC Hardware and Software Lab Manual, Fourth Edition*. You can perform this lab now or wait until the end of the chapter.

Optional Lab 5.7.2: Managing Device Drivers with Device Manager in Windows Vista

In this lab, you will manage device drivers with Device Manager in Windows Vista. Refer to the lab in *IT Essentials: PC Hardware and Software Lab Manual, Fourth Edition*. You can perform this lab now or wait until the end of the chapter.

Summary

This chapter introduced computer operating systems. As a technician, you should be skilled at installing, configuring, and troubleshooting an operating system. The following concepts from this chapter are important to remember:

- There are several different operating systems available, and you must consider the customer's needs and environment when choosing an operating system.

- The main steps in setting up a customer's computer include preparing the hard drive, installing an operating system, creating user accounts, and configuring installation options.

- A GUI shows icons of all files, folders, and applications on the computer. A pointing device, such as a mouse, is used to navigate a GUI desktop.

- You should establish a backup strategy that allows the recovery of data. Normal, copy, differential, incremental, and daily backups are all optional backup tools available in Windows operating systems.

- Preventive maintenance techniques help to ensure optimal operation of the operating system.

- Some of the tools available for troubleshooting an operating system problem include the Windows Advanced Startup Options menu, event logs, Device Manager, and system files.

Summary of Exercises

This is a summary of the Labs and Worksheets associated with this chapter.

Labs

The following labs cover material from this chapter. Refer to the labs in *IT Essentials: PC Hardware and Software Lab Manual, Fourth Edition.*

Lab 5.4.2: Install Windows XP

Optional Lab 5.4.2: Install Windows Vista

Lab 5.4.5: Create Accounts and Check for Updates in Windows XP

Optional Lab 5.4.5: Create Accounts and Check for Updates in Windows Vista

Lab 5.4.8: Managing System Files with Built-in Utilities in Windows XP

Optional Lab 5.4.8: Managing System Files with Built-in Utilities in Windows Vista

Lab 5.5.1: Run Commands in Windows XP

Optional Lab 5.5.1: Run Commands in Windows Vista

Lab 5.5.3: Managing Administrative Settings and Snap-ins in Windows XP

Optional Lab 5.5.3: Managing Administrative Settings and Snap-ins in Windows Vista

Lab 5.5.4: Install Third-Party Software in Windows XP

Optional Lab 5.5.4: Install Third-Party Software in Windows Vista

Lab 5.6.2: Restore Points in Windows XP

Optional Lab 5.6.2: Restore Points in Windows Vista

Lab 5.6.3: Registry Backup and Recovery in Windows XP

Lab 5.7.2: Managing Device Drivers with Device Manager in Windows XP

Optional Lab 5.7.2: Managing Device Drivers with Device Manager in Windows Vista

Worksheets

The following worksheets cover material from this chapter. Refer to the labs in *IT Essentials: PC Hardware and Software Lab Manual, Fourth Edition*:

Worksheet 5.2.2: NOS Certifications and Jobs

Worksheet 5.3.2: Upgrade Hardware Components

Worksheet 5.4.9: Answer NTFS and FAT32 Questions

Check Your Understanding

You can find the answers to these questions in the appendix, "Answers to Check Your Understanding Questions."

1. Which open-source operating system is available on multiple hardware platforms?

    A. Linux

    B. Mac OS X

    C. Windows 2000

    D. Windows XP

2. Which Registry file contains information about the hardware and software in the computer system?

   A. HKEY_CLASSES_ROOT

   B. HKEY_CURRENT_USER

   C. HKEY_LOCAL_MACHINE

   D. HKEY_USERS

3. How can the command line be accessed in Windows XP?

   A. **Start > Run > Prompt**

   B. **Start > Run > cmd**

   C. **Start > Control Panel > Prompt**

   D. **Start > All programs > Accessories > Terminal**

   E. **Start > Run > Terminal**

4. Which file system is recommended for Windows XP for large file support and enhanced security?

   A. DirectX

   B. DOS

   C. FAT32

   D. HPFS

   E. NTFS

5. What does a red "X" on a device mean in the Device Manager?

   A. The device driver is unsigned.

   B. The device driver is missing or corrupt.

   C. The device has been disabled.

   D. The device is functioning properly.

6. What should be done before upgrading from Windows 2000 to Windows XP?

   A. Back up all the data files.

   B. Update all the device drivers.

   C. Detach all the peripheral devices.

   D. Download a legitimate Windows XP authentication key.

7. Which key or key sequence will enable a user to start Windows XP in Safe Mode?

    A. Alt-B

    B. Alt-X

    C. Alt-Z

    D. F1

    E. F8

    F. The Windows key

8. What is a good example of an open-ended question that a technician can ask the user to learn more about conditions before the failure?

    A. What software has been installed recently on the computer?

    B. Does the computer boot into the operating system?

    C. Are there any beeps when the computer boots?

    D. Has anybody else used the computer recently?

    E. How many users were logged on to the network when the failure occurred?

9. What is a common cause of the error message "Invalid system disk"?

    A. The Delete key was pressed during the system boot.

    B. There is a nonbootable floppy disk or CD in the drive.

    C. There is no floppy disk or CD in the drive.

    D. The BIOS has been changed to boot from the hard drive first.

CHAPTER 6

Fundamental Laptops and Portable Devices

Objectives

Upon completion of this chapter, you will be able to answer the following questions:

- What are laptops and other portable devices?
- What are the components of a laptop?
- How would you compare and contrast laptop and desktop components?
- What are different ways to configure laptops?
- What are the different mobile phone standards?
- What are some common preventive maintenance techniques used for laptops and portable devices?
- What are some ways to troubleshoot laptops and portable devices?

Key Terms

This chapter uses the following key terms. You can find the definitions in the Glossary.

personal digital assistant (PDA)   page 189

smartphone   page 189

battery   page 190

stylus   page 190

Universal Serial Bus (USB)   page 191

parallel port   page 193

AC power connector   page 193

battery bay   page 193

security keyhole   page 194

USB port pages 194, 200

S-Video connector   page 194

modem port   page 194

Ethernet port   page 194

network LEDs   page 194

stereo headphone jack   page 194

microphone jack   page 194

ventilation   page 194

PC combo expansion slot   page 194

infrared port   page 195

speaker   page 195

laptop latch   page 195

optical drive   page 195

optical drive status indicator   page 195

drive bay status indicator   page 195

Video Graphics Array (VGA)   page 195

hard drive access panel   page 196

battery latch   page 196

docking station connector   page 196

RAM access panel   page 196

input device   page 196

continues

One of the original laptops was the GRiD Compass 1101. Astronauts used it during space missions in the early 1980s. It weighed 11 lb (5 kg) and cost $8000 to $10,000! Laptops today often weigh less than one-half the weight and cost less than one-third the price of the GRiD Compass 1101. The compact design, convenience, and evolving technology of laptops have made them as popular as desktops.

Laptops, *personal digital assistants (PDA)*, and *smartphones* are becoming more popular as their prices decrease and technology continues to progress. As a computer technician, you need to have knowledge of portable devices of all kinds. This chapter focuses on the differences between laptops and desktops and describes the features of PDAs and smartphones.

After completing this chapter, you will meet these objectives:

- Describe laptops and other portable devices.

- Identify and describe the components of a laptop.

- Compare and contrast desktop and laptop components.

- Explain how to configure laptops.

- Compare the different mobile phone standards.

- Identify common preventive maintenance techniques for laptops and portable devices.

- Describe how to troubleshoot laptops and portable devices.

Describe Laptops and Other Portable Devices

Early laptops were heavy and expensive. Today, laptops are very popular because advances in technology have resulted in laptops that cost less, weigh less, and have improved capabilities. Many laptops can be configured with an additional video port, a FireWire port, an infrared port, or an integrated camera.

Note

Notebooks, laptops, and tablets are types of portable computers. For clarity and consistency in IT Essentials I, all portable computers will be called laptops.

PDAs and smartphones are examples of portable, handheld devices that are becoming more popular. PDAs offer features such as games, web surfing, email, instant messaging, and many other features offered by PCs. Smartphones are cell phones with many built-in PDA capabilities. PDAs and smartphones can run some of the same software as laptops.

After completing the following sections, you will meet these objectives:

- Identify some common uses of laptops.
- Identify some common uses of PDAs and smartphones.

Identify Common Uses of Laptops

The most significant feature of a laptop is the compact size. The design of the laptop places the keyboard, screen, and internal components into a small, portable case.

Another popular feature of the laptop is that it can be used almost anywhere. A rechargeable *battery* allows the laptop to function when it is disconnected from an AC power source.

The first laptops were used primarily by businesspeople who needed to access and enter data when they were away from the office. The use of laptops was limited because of expense, weight, and limited capabilities compared to less expensive desktops.

Today, laptops have lower prices and increased capabilities. A laptop is now a real alternative to a desktop computer.

Common uses for the laptop include the following:

- Taking notes in school or researching papers
- Presenting information in business meetings
- Accessing data away from home or the office
- Playing games or watching movies while traveling
- Accessing the Internet in a public place
- Sending and receiving email in a public place

Identify Common Uses of PDAs and Smartphones

The concept of the PDA has existed since the 1970s. The earliest models were computerized personal organizers designed to have a touch screen and a *stylus*. Today, some models have both a touch screen and a keyboard and use an operating system that is similar to operating systems used on desktop computers.

The PDA is an electronic personal organizer with the following tools:

- Address book
- Calculator
- Alarm clock
- Internet access

- Email

- Global positioning

The smartphone is a mobile phone with PDA capabilities. Smartphones combine cell phone and computer functions in a single, handheld device. The technology of the PDA and the technology of the smartphone continue to merge.

Smartphones can include these additional options:

- Built-in camera

- Document access

- Email

- Abbreviated note taking

- Television

Smartphone and PDA connectivity options include Bluetooth and regular *Universal Serial Bus (USB)* cable connections and through wireless networks.

Worksheet 6.1.2: Research Laptops, Smartphones, and PDAs

Research laptop, smartphone, and PDA specifications. Refer to the worksheet in *IT Essentials: PC Hardware and Software Lab Manual, Fourth Edition*. You can perform this worksheet now or wait until the end of the chapter.

Identify and Describe the Components of a Laptop

Common laptop features include the following:

- They are small and portable.

- They have an integrated display screen in the lid.

- They have an integrated keyboard in the base.

- They run on AC power or a rechargeable battery.

- They support hot-swappable drives and peripherals.

- Most laptops can use docking stations and port replicators to connect peripherals.

In the following sections, you look closely at the components of a laptop. You also examine a docking station. Remember, laptops and docking stations come in many models. Components can be located in different places on different models.

After completing these sections, you will meet these objectives:

- Describe the components found on the outside of the laptop.

- Describe the components found on the inside of the laptop.

- Describe the components found on the laptop docking station.

Describe the Components Found on the Outside of the Laptop

Laptop and desktop computers use the same types of ports so that peripherals can be interchangeable. These ports are specifically designed for connecting peripherals and providing network connectivity and audio access.

Ports, connections, and drives are located on the front, back, and sides of the laptop because of the compact design. Laptops contain PC Card or ExpressCard slots to add functionality such as more memory, a modem, or a network connection. You learn more about PC Card and ExpressCard slots in the section, "Compare and Contrast Desktop and Laptop Expansion Capabilities," later in this chapter.

Laptops require a port for external power. Laptops can operate using either a battery or an AC power adapter. This port can be used to power the computer or to charge the battery.

The exterior of the laptop also has status indicators (also called light-emitting diode [LED] displays), ports, slots, connectors, bays, jacks, vents, and a keyhole.

The top of the typical laptop has the following three LEDs, as shown in Figure 6-1:

- Bluetooth or Wi-Fi

- Battery

- Standby

Note

Exterior components and LED displays vary among different laptops. Technicians should consult the laptop manual for a list of specific components and status displays.

Figure 6-1   Laptop: Top View

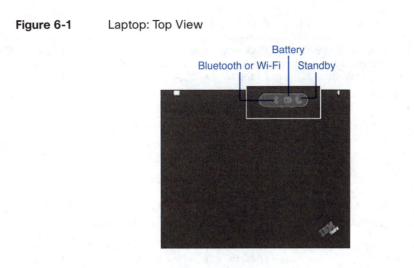

The back of some laptops has the following three components, as shown in Figure 6-2:

- *Parallel port:* Connects legacy devices, such as printers and scanners that do not have USB connectors.

- *AC power connector:* Supplies power and recharges the battery

- *Battery bay:* Securely holds the battery inside the laptop

Figure 6-2   Laptop: Rear View

A laptop operates using a battery or an AC power adapter. Laptop batteries are manufactured in various shapes and sizes. They use different types of chemicals and metals to store power.

Table 6-1 compares rechargeable batteries typically used in laptops.

Table 6-1   Laptop Battery Comparison

Type of Battery	Characteristics	Common Use	Disposal
Lithium-ion (Li-ion)	Lightweight for power, no memory effect, can easily overheat and sometimes explode. Keep cool, charge often, seek freshest batteries (most recently manufactured)	Cell phones, laptops	Check local rules, contents flammable
Lithium-polymer (Li-Poly or LiPo)	Costly, small, lightweight for power, moderate capacity, fast recharge, moderate life span, do not short-circuit, can explode but are not flammable	PDAs, laptop computers, portable MP3 players, portable gaming devices, radio controlled airplanes	Check local rules

The left side of the laptop, shown in Figure 6-3, has the following ten components:

- *Security keyhole*: A small slot designed to receive a specially shaped lock to reduce the risk of physical theft

- *USB port*: Connects the laptop to most peripheral devices

- *S-Video connector*: Connects the laptop to a external monitor or projector

- *Modem port*: Communicates on analog phone networks

- *Ethernet port*: Communicates on Ethernet networks

- *Network LEDs*: Indicate network traffic activity

- *Stereo headphone jack*: Allows the laptop to port audio to external speakers or head-phones

- *Microphone jack*: Allows a microphone to input sound

- *Ventilation*: Removes heat from the case

- *PC combo expansion slot*: Receives expansion cards like PCMCIA and PC Card/ExpressCard

Figure 6-3   Laptop: Left-Side View

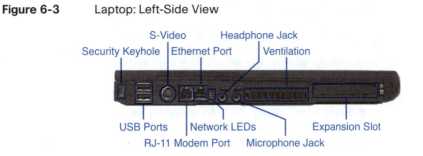

The front of the laptop, shown in Figure 6-4, has the following components:

- **Ventilation**: Removes heat from the case

- *Infrared port*: Allows the laptop to communicate with other infrared-enabled devices

- *Speakers*: Provide sound output

- *Laptop latch*: Keeps the lid closed

Figure 6-4   Laptop: Front View

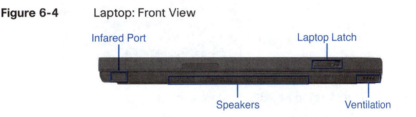

The right side of the laptop, shown in Figure 6-5, contains four components:

- *Optical drive*: Reads CDs, DVDs, and Blu-ray Discs

- *Optical drive status indicator*: Displays activity on the optical drive

- *Drive bay status indicator*: Displays activity on that drive bay

- *Video Graphics Array (VGA)* **port**: Allows for external monitor or projector

Figure 6-5   Laptop: Right-Side View

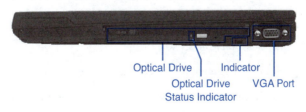

The bottom of the laptop, shown in Figure 6-6, has the following components:

- *Hard drive access panel*: Provides access to the hard drive

- *Battery latches* (**two areas**): Release the battery from the battery bay

- *Docking station connector*: Connects the laptop to a docking station or port replicator

- *RAM access panel*: Provides access to the RAM

Figure 6-6   Laptop: Bottom View

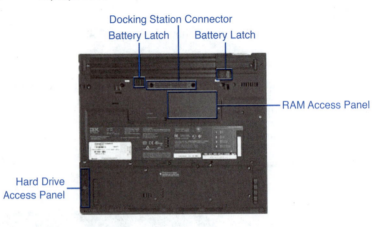

 Virtual Laptop Activity: Explore Laptop

Explore the different views of the Virtual Laptop. Refer to the Virtual Laptop software on the CD that accompanies this book.

Describe Input Devices Found on Laptops

Laptops use *input devices* to add functionality to the laptop. Installing input devices might require downloading drivers from the manufacturer's website. There are a variety of input devices:

- **Stylus or digitizer**: Inputs position more accurately than a touch pad

- **Barcode reader**: Reads bar codes

- **Scanner**: Inputs still images

- **Web camera**: Receives video input

- **Game controller**: Receives input to control games

Some input devices might need to be configured or optimized for speed, sensitivity, scrolling, or the number of taps needed. To gain access to these configuration utilities for input devices, use the following path in Category View:

Start > Control Panel > Printers and Other Hardware > Mouse

Not all devices can be configured through the Control Panel. When you install the software for some devices, programs might be installed in the All Programs section of the Start menu. These programs are used to configure more advanced settings.

Some input devices are built into the laptop. Typically, the laptop is closed when not in use. By opening the lid of the laptop, you can access a variety of input devices, LEDs, and a display screen. There are several input devices available when the laptop lid is open, as shown in Figure 6-7.

Figure 6-7   Open Laptop

A laptop receives and interprets data in many ways. As a result, the laptop is able to perform a variety of functions.

At the bottom of the screen in Figure 6-8, a row of LEDs shows the status of specific functions:

- Wireless
- Bluetooth
- Num Lock
- Caps Lock
- Hard drive activity
- Power on

- Battery status

- Hibernate/standby

Figure 6-8   Laptop Status LEDs

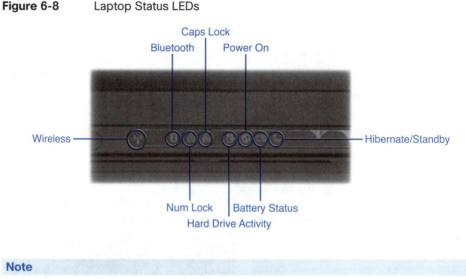

A laptop monitor is a built-in liquid crystal display (LCD). It is similar to a desktop LCD monitor, except that the resolution, brightness, and contrast settings can be adjusted using software or button controls. The laptop monitor cannot be adjusted for height and distance because it is integrated into the lid of the case.

The purpose of the *function (Fn) key* is to activate a second function on a dual-purpose key. The feature that is accessed by pressing and holding the Fn key is printed on another key in a smaller font or different color. There are several functions that can be accessed:

- Volume setting

- Display brightness

- Sleep states

- Wireless functionality

- Check battery status

The Fn key must not be confused with function keys F1 through F12. These keys are typically located in a horizontal row across the top of the keyboard. Their function depends on the operating system and application that is running when they are pressed. Each key can be made to perform up to seven separate operations. The key can be pressed alone or with one or more combinations of the Shift, Control, and Alt keys.

On many laptops, a small pin on the laptop cover contacts a switch when the case is closed, called an LCD cutoff switch. The LCD cutoff switch tells the CPU to conserve power by extinguishing the backlight and turning off the LCD. If this switch breaks or is dirty, the LCD remains dark while the laptop is open. Carefully clean this switch to restore normal operation.

Virtual Laptop Activity: Keyboard

Explore the Virtual Laptop keyboard. Refer to the Virtual Laptop software on the CD that accompanies this book.

Describe the Components Found on the Laptop Docking Station

A *base station* is a device that attaches to AC power and to desktop peripherals. When you plug the laptop into the base station, you have convenient access to power and the attached peripherals.

There are two types of base stations: *docking stations* and *port replicators*. Docking stations and port replicators are used for the same purpose. Port replicators are usually smaller than docking stations and do not have speakers or Personal Computer Memory Card International Association (PCMCIA) slots. Docking stations and port replicators use a variety of connection types:

- Manufacturer- and model-specific
- USB or FireWire
- PC Card or ExpressCard

The following are three typical areas on top of the docking station, as shown in Figure 6-9:

- Power button
- Eject button
- Laptop connector

Figure 6-9   Docking Station Top View

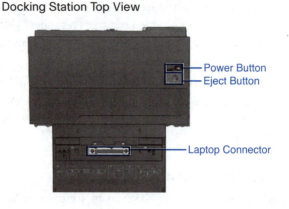

Some docking stations include drive bays and ports to provide additional functionality:

- Parallel
- USB
- Ethernet
- Video
- Audio

The back of the docking station contains ports and connectors used to attach to desktop peripherals such as a mouse, a monitor, or a printer. A vent is also necessary to expel hot air from the docking station.

The following components are typically located on the back of the docking station, as shown in Figure 6-10:

- *Exhaust vent*: Lets hot air out of the laptop
- **AC power connector**: Provides power to charge the battery
- *PC Card/ExpressCard slot*: Connects laptops to expansion cards
- **VGA port**: Allows for external monitor or projector
- *Digital Visual Interface (DVI) port*: Allows for external monitor or projector
- *Line In connector*: Allows audio input from pre-amplified sources like iPods
- *Headphone connector*: Allows audio output for headphones
- *USB port*: Connects the laptop to most peripheral devices
- *Mouse port*: Connects older mice to the laptop
- *Keyboard port*: Connects older keyboards to the laptop
- *External diskette drive connector*: Connects laptop to an external diskette drive

- **Parallel port**: Connects legacy devices such as printers and scanners that do not support USB

- *Serial port*: A legacy port that Connects devices like mice, keyboards and modems before widespread use of USB

- *RJ-11 (Modem port)*: Communicates on analog phone networks

- **Ethernet port**: Communicates on Ethernet networks

Figure 6-10   Docking Station Rear View

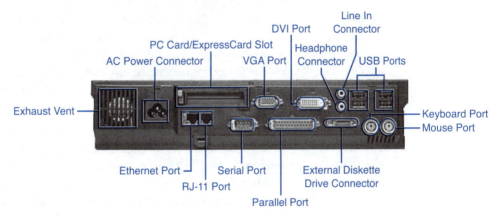

Secure the laptop to the docking station with a *key lock*, as shown in Figure 6-11.

Figure 6-11   Docking Station Key Lock

 Worksheet 6.2.3: Complete Docking Stations True or False Questions

Answer true or false for the statements about docking stations. Refer to the worksheet in *IT Essentials: PC Hardware and Software Lab Manual, Fourth Edition*. You can perform this worksheet now or wait until the end of the chapter.

Virtual Laptop Activity: Docking Station

Explore the different views of the docking station in the Virtual Laptop. Refer to the Virtual Laptop software on the CD that accompanies this book.

Compare and Contrast Desktop and Laptop Components

Most of the functions that a desktop can perform can also be performed by a laptop. However, these two kinds of computers are built very differently and the parts are not interchangeable. As an analogy, a airplane and a helicopter can each travel to the same destination, but they cannot be repaired with the same spare parts. This is also true for laptops and desktops. Few components can be shared between desktops and laptops.

Desktop components tend to be standardized. They usually meet universal *form factors*, meaning that desktops made by different manufacturers can often use the same components. A common desktop form factor is Advanced Technology Extended (ATX). When purchasing upgrade parts for this form factor, you will look for ATX motherboards and ATX power supplies. This standard should guarantee that the motherboard and power supply will work in the ATX case. A DVD/CD-RW drive is another example of a desktop component that has a standard form factor.

Laptop components are much more specialized than desktop components because laptop manufacturers focus on refining laptop components to make them more efficient and compact. As a result, manufacturers design laptop components to follow their own specific form factors. Laptop components are proprietary, so you might not be able to use components made by one laptop manufacturer to repair a laptop made by another manufacturer.

Note

Technicians might have to obtain certification for each laptop manufacturer they support.

After completing the following sections, you will meet these objectives:

- Compare and contrast desktop and laptop motherboards.
- Compare and contrast desktop and laptop processors.
- Compare and contrast desktop and laptop power management.
- Compare and contrast desktop and laptop expansion capabilities.

Compare and Contrast Desktop and Laptop Motherboards

Desktop motherboards have standard form factors. The standard size and shape allow motherboards from different manufacturers to be interchangeable.

Laptop motherboards vary by manufacturer and are proprietary. When you repair a laptop, it is strongly recommended that you obtain a replacement motherboard from the manufacturer of the laptop. Figure 6-12 shows a desktop motherboard and a laptop motherboard.

Figure 6-12   Laptop Motherboard and Desktop Motherboard

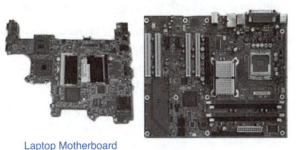

Laptop Motherboard

Desktop Motherboard

Laptop motherboards and desktop motherboards are designed differently. Components designed for a laptop generally cannot be used in a desktop. Laptops, some printers, and routers have space restrictions; therefore, they use small outline dual in-line memory modules (SODIMM).

Compare and Contrast Desktop and Laptop Processors

The central processing unit (CPU), or processor, is the brain of the computer. The CPU interprets and processes instructions that are used to manipulate data.

Laptop processors are designed to use less power and create less heat than desktop processors. As a result, laptop processors do not require cooling devices that are as large as those found in desktops. Laptop processors also use *CPU throttling* to modify the clock speed as needed to reduce power consumption and heat. This results in a slight decrease in performance. It also increases the life span of some components. These specially designed processors allow a laptop to operate for a longer period of time when using a battery power source.

Note

Technicians should refer to the laptop manual for processors that can be used as replacement processors and for processor replacement instructions.

Compare and Contrast Desktop and Laptop Power Management

Power management controls the flow of electricity to the components of a computer.

Desktops are usually set up in a location where they remain plugged into a power source. Desktop power management distributes electricity from the source to the components of the desktop. There is also a small battery in the desktop that provides electricity to maintain the internal clock and BIOS settings when the desktop is powered off.

Laptops are small and portable. This portability feature is achieved by combining the small size and weight of a laptop with the ability to operate from a battery. Unlike a desktop computer power supply, laptops can accept only DC power. AC adapters convert unregulated AC power to the regulated DC power required to run the laptop and charge the laptop battery.

When the laptop is plugged in, laptop power management converts the AC into DC and sends electricity to the laptop components. The laptop power management also recharges the battery. When the laptop is unplugged, laptop power management takes electricity from the battery and sends it to the laptop components.

There are two methods of power management:

- *Advanced Power Management (APM)*: APM is an earlier version of power management. With APM, the BIOS was used to control the settings for power management.

- *Advanced Configuration and Power Interface (ACPI)*: ACPI has replaced APM. ACPI offers additional power management features. With ACPI, the operating system controls power management.

You learn more about APM and ACPI in the section, "Describe How to Configure Power Settings," later in this chapter.

Compare and Contrast Desktop and Laptop Expansion Capabilities

Expansion capabilities add functionality to a computer. Many expansion devices can be used with both laptops and desktops:

- External drives
- Modems
- Network cards
- Wireless adapters
- Printers
- Other peripherals

Expansion devices are attached to laptops and desktops differently. A desktop attaches these devices with USB ports and parallel ports. A laptop attaches these devices with USB ports, parallel ports, and PC Cards.

The standardized use of USB and FireWire ports makes it possible to connect many types of external components to laptops, docking stations, port replicators, and desktops. The USB and FireWire standards make it possible to connect and remove external components without the need to power off the system. USB and FireWire ports are used to connect a range of external components:

- Printers

- Scanners

- Floppy disk drives

- Mice

- Cameras

- Keyboards

- Hard drives

- Flash drives

- Optical drives

- MP3 players

Laptops and desktops have similar expansion capabilities. The difference in form factor between the computers determines which type of expansion device is used. Desktops have internal bays that support 5.25-inch and 3.5-inch drives. Additionally, there is space to install other permanent expansion drives. Laptops have limited space, so the expansion bays on laptops are designed to allow different types of drives to fit into the same bay. Drives are *hot swappable* and are inserted or removed as needed.

Table 6-2 shows a comparison of desktop and laptop expansion components.

Table 6-2   Laptop and Desktop Expansion Components

Laptops			Desktops			
Component	PC Card	Integrated	External Ports (USB, Parallel, Video, FireWire, Serial)	Integrated	Adapter Card	External Ports (USB, Parallel, Video, FireWire, Serial)
External monitor			X			X
Printer			X			X
Keyboard		X	X			X
Mouse			X			X

continues

Table 6-2   Laptop and Desktop Expansion Components   *continued*

Laptops			Desktops			
Component	PC Card	Integrated	External Ports (USB, Parallel, Video, FireWire, Serial)	Integrated	Adapter Card	External Ports (USB, Parallel, Video, FireWire, Serial)
External drives			X			X
Ethernet NIC	X	X	X	X	X	X
Wireless NIC	X	X	X	X	X	X
CD/DVD drives			X			X
Drive controllers		X		X	X	

Expansion devices used for data storage use three types of storage methods:

- Magnetic
- Flash
- Optical

Traditional hard drives are magnetic. Magnetic hard drives have drive motors designed to spin magnetic platters and the drive heads.

A flash drive uses a special type of memory that requires no power to maintain the data. Flash memory chips manage all storage on a solid state drive (SSD), which results in faster access to data, higher reliability, and reduced power usage. SSDs do not have moving parts. Because there are no drive motors and moving parts, the SSD uses far less energy than the magnetic hard drive.

The optical drive is a storage device that uses lasers to read data on the optical medium. Optical drives have moving parts like hard drives. They have drive motors designed to spin a platter and move a drive head. There are three types of optical drives:

- Compact disc (CD)
- Digital versatile disc (DVD)
- Blu-ray Disc (BD)

CD, DVD, and BD media can be prerecorded (read-only), recordable (write once), or re-recordable (read and write multiple times). CDs have a data storage capacity of approximately 700 MB. The most common DVDs, single-sided, dual layer, have a data storage capacity of approximately 8.5 GB on one side of the disc. BDs have a storage capacity of 25 GB on a single-layer disc, and 50 GB on a dual-layer disc.

Laptops use the PC Card slot to add functionality. The PC Card slot uses an open standard interface to connect to peripheral devices using the CardBus standard. Examples of devices that connect using PC Cards include the following:

- Memory
- Modems
- Hard drives
- Network cards

PC Cards follow the PCMCIA standard. They come in three types: Type I, Type II, and Type III. Each type of PC Card is different in size and can attach to different devices. A newer type of PC Card is called the PC ExpressCard.

Table 6-3 shows a comparison of PC Cards.

Table 6-3   PC Card Specifications

PC Bus	Size (mm)	Thickness (mm)	Interface	Examples
Type I	85.6x54	3.3	Memory, I/O, CardBus	SRAM flash
Type II	85.6x54	5.5	Memory, I/O, CardBus	Modem LAN wireless
Type III	85.6x54	10.5	Memory, I/O, CardBus	Hard drive

Table 6-4 compares PC ExpressCards.

Table 6-4   PC ExpressCard Specifications

Express Bus	Size (mm)	Thickness (mm)	Interface	Examples
Express Card/34	75x34	5	PCI Express or USB 2.0	FireWire, TV tuner, wireless NIC
Express Card/54	75x54	5	PCI Express or USB 2.0	Smart card reader, CompactFlash reader, 1.8-inch disk drive

The PC ExpressCard has 34-pin and 54-pin configurations. Figure 6-13 shows an example of a PC Card and PC ExpressCards.

Figure 6-13   Laptop Expansion Cards

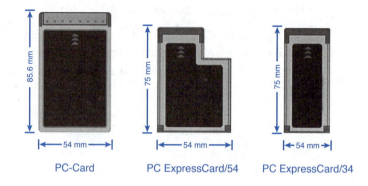

PC-Card   PC ExpressCard/54   PC ExpressCard/34

Worksheet 6.3.4: Answer Laptop Expansion Questions

Fill in the table and short-answer questions on laptop expansion specifications. Refer to the worksheet in *IT Essentials: PC Hardware and Software Lab Manual, Fourth Edition*. You can perform this worksheet now or wait until the end of the chapter.

Explain How to Configure Laptops

To allow applications and processes to run smoothly, you might need to configure and allocate system resources, install additional components and plug-ins, or change environmental settings to match software requirements. Adding external components is usually accomplished through the use of "plug and play," but occasionally driver installation and additional configuration might be required. Proper configuration of the power settings will help you get the maximum performance from a laptop, such as increasing the length of time the laptop can be used on battery power.

With laptops, you might need to exchange components occasionally to accomplish different tasks and respond to changing situations. You can customize a laptop for specific purposes by adding external components. For example, you can install a second hard drive in a laptop to provide additional storage capacity. Components need to be carefully inserted or connected to bays, connectors, and proprietary expansion areas to avoid damage to the equipment. It is important to follow safe removal procedures when disconnecting hot-swappable and non-hot-swappable devices.

After completing the following sections, you will meet these objectives:

- Describe how to configure power settings.
- Describe the safe installation and removal of laptop components.

Describe How to Configure Power Settings

One of the most popular features of a laptop is the ability to operate using batteries. This feature allows laptops to operate in locations where AC power is not available or is inconvenient. Advances in power management and battery technology are increasing the time laptop users can remain disconnected from AC power. Current batteries can last from 2 to 10 hours without recharging. Managing the power by configuring the power settings on a laptop is important to ensure that the battery charge is used efficiently.

The Advanced Configuration and Power Interface (ACPI) standards create a bridge between the hardware and OS and allow technicians to create power management schemes to get the best performance from the computer. The ACPI standards can be applicable to most computers, but they are particularly important when managing power in laptops. Table 6-5 shows information about each power state.

Table 6-5   Power Management States

ACPI Standard	Power Management State
S0	The computer is on and the CPU is running.
S1	The CPU is not running. However, the CPU and RAM are still receiving power.
S2	The CPU is off, but the RAM is refreshed. The system is in a lower power mode than S1.
S3	The CPU is off, and the RAM is set to slow refresh rate. This mode is often called "Save to RAM." In Windows XP, this state is known as the Standby mode.
S4	The CPU and RAM are off. The contents of RAM have been saved to a temporary file on the hard disk. This mode is also called "Saved to Disk." In Windows XP, this state is known as the Hibernate mode.
S5	The computer is off and nothing has been saved.

Technicians frequently are required to configure power settings by changing the settings found in BIOS. Configuring power settings in BIOS affects the following conditions:

- System states
- Battery and AC modes
- Thermal management
- CPU PCI bus power management
- Wake-On-LAN (WOL)

Note

WOL might require a cable connection inside the computer from the network adapter to the motherboard.

Figure 6-14 shows an example of power settings in BIOS.

Figure 6-14   BIOS Settings

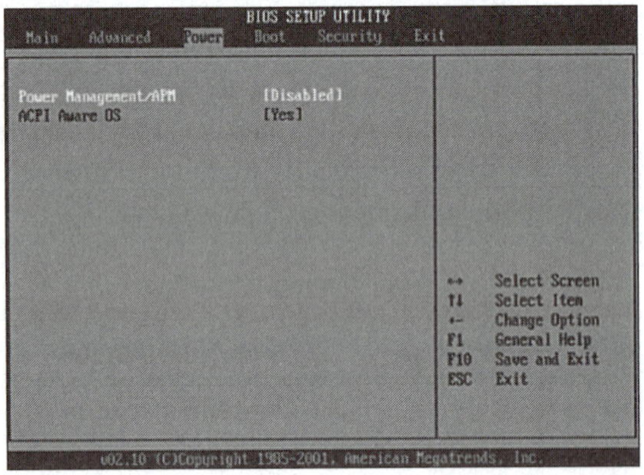

Note

When working in Windows XP, the ACPI power management mode must be enabled in BIOS to allow the OS to configure all the power management states. There is no standard name for each power management state. Manufacturers can use different names for the same state.

Here are the steps to check the ACPI settings in the BIOS:

How To

Step 1.   Enter BIOS setup by pressing the appropriate key or key combination while the computer is booting. Typically this is the Delete key or the F2 key, but there are several other options.

Step 2.   Locate and enter the Power Management Settings menu item.

Step 3.   Use the appropriate keys to enable ACPI mode.

Step 4.   Save and exit BIOS setup.

Note

These steps are common to most laptops and should be used only as a guideline. Be sure to check your laptop manual for specific configuration settings.

The *power options* in Windows XP allow you to reduce the power consumption of a number of devices or of the entire system. Power options allow you to control the power management features of the following:

- Hard drive

- Display

- Shut Down, Hibernate, and Standby modes

- Shut Down, Hibernate, and Sleep modes (Windows Vista)

- Low battery warnings

Configuring Power Settings in Windows XP and Vista

You can adjust power management by using Power Options in the Control Panel. The Power Options in the Control Panel display the only options that can be controlled.

Note

Power Options will automatically detect devices that might be unique to your computer. Therefore, the Power Options windows can vary by the hardware that is detected.

To configure your power settings, choose **Start > Control Panel > Power Options**.

Managing Power Usage

Power schemes in Windows XP and power plans in windows Vista allow the operating system to manage the power usage of the computer. These power settings can help you save energy, maximize system performance, or achieve a balance between the two. Both the hard drive and the display consume large amounts of power. They can be configured under the Power Schemes tab in Windows XP and the Change Plan settings in Windows Vista.

When you open Power Options, you will notice that Windows XP has preset power schemes and Windows Vista has preset power plans. These are the default settings and were created when the operating system was installed. You can use the default setting, or create customized schemes or plans that are based on specific work requirements. Sleep timers are user-defined periods of time that the computer waits before entering reduced power states like sleep and hibernate. Customized sleep timers are configured in the power scheme in Windows XP and in power plan in Windows Vista.

To configure sleep timers in Windows XP, click **Start > Control Panel > Power Options** and select how long the computer waits before entering sleep mode.

To configure sleep timers in Windows Vista, click **Start > Control Panel > Power Options,** click the link **Change When the Computer Sleeps,** and then select how long the computer waits before entering sleep mode.

Figure 6-15 shows the default power scheme set for a laptop.

Figure 6-15   Power Options Properties

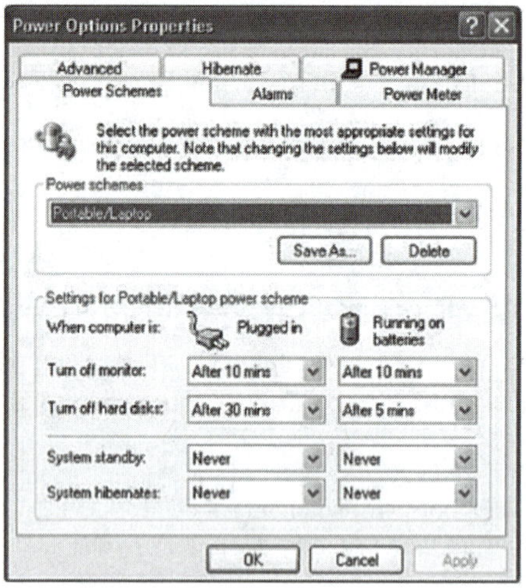

Power Management for the Hard Drive and the Display

One of the biggest power consumers on a laptop is the hard drive. If the hard drive is not accessed often. You might choose to set the Turn Off Hard Disks time for 1 hour when the laptop is plugged in, and 3 minutes when the laptop is "Running on batteries." You can also set the LCD to turn off after a specified period of time.

You decide that Windows XP default settings for the Standby and Hibernate modes are acceptable and no changes are made. In Windows Vista, these settings are Sleep, Hybrid Sleep, and Hibernate. Power schemes and power plans can be saved with a customized name. Saving the new setting with a custom name allows the user to easily switch back to the default settings. Figure 6-16 is an example of a customized power scheme that the user named Research.

Figure 6-16   Power Scheme: Research Settings

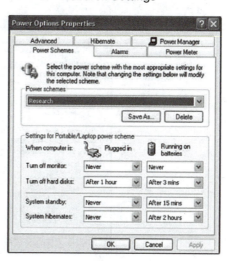

Setting the Laptop Power Options

If you do not want to completely shut down the laptop in Windows XP, you have two options:

- *Standby*: Documents and applications are saved in RAM, allowing the computer to power on quickly.

- *Hibernate*: Documents and applications are saved to a temporary file on the hard drive, and it takes a little longer than Standby to power on.

Figure 6-17 shows Hibernate enabled in the Power Options Properties dialog box.

Figure 6-17   Hibernate Options

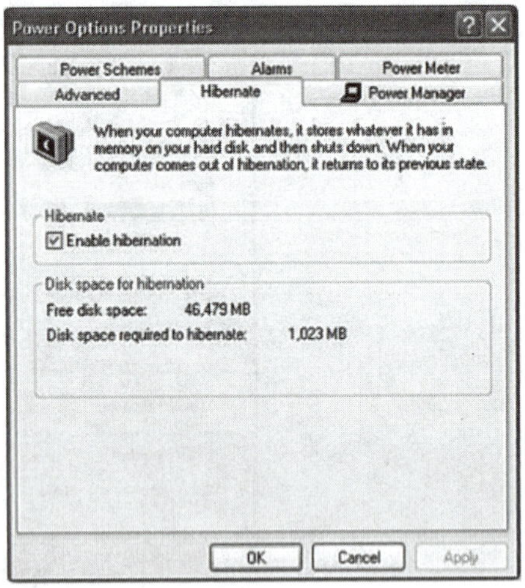

If you do not want to completely shut down the laptop, you have three options in Windows Vista: Sleep, Hybrid Sleep, and Hibernate. Hibernate is the same as in Windows XP, and the other two options are defined here:

- **Sleep**: Documents and applications are saved in RAM, allowing the computer to power on quickly.

- **Hybrid Sleep**: Documents and applications are saved in RAM and data is written to the hard disk, and it takes a little longer than Sleep to power on.

Adjusting Low Battery Warnings

In Windows XP, you can set the low battery warnings. There are two levels: *low battery alarm* and *critical battery alarm*. The low battery alarm will warn you that the battery is low. The critical battery alarm will initiate a forced Standby, Hibernate, or Shut Down mode, as shown in Figure 6-18.

Worksheet 6.4.1: Match ACPI Standards

Match the ACPI standard to the correct characteristic. Refer to the worksheet in *IT Essentials: PC Hardware and Software Lab Manual, Fourth Edition*. You can perform this worksheet now or wait until the end of the chapter.

Figure 6-18   Critical Battery Alarm Actions

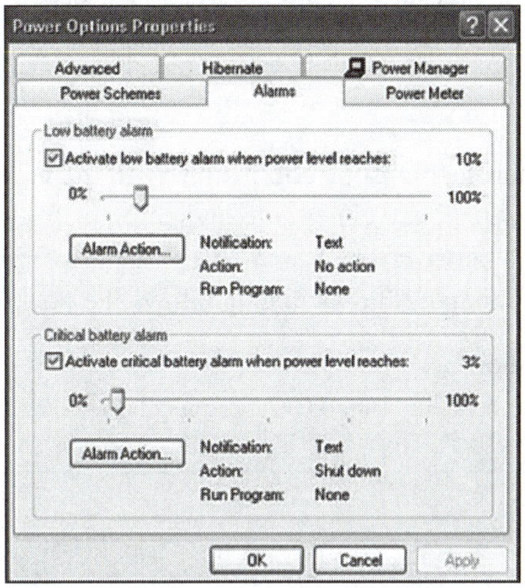

Describe the Safe Installation and Removal of Laptop Components

Some components of a laptop might need to be replaced. Remember always to make sure that you have the correct replacement component and tools as recommended by the manufacturer. Some components are hot swappable, which means that you can remove and replace them while the computer is on. Some components that you might need to replace include the following:

- AC adapter
- Battery
- Optical drive
- Hard drive
- Memory
- PC expansion cards

Note

Each laptop manufacturer uses unique hardware installation and removal procedures. Check the laptop manual for specific installation information, and follow safety installation and electrostatic discharge (ESD) precautions.

> **Caution**
>
> Always disconnect power and remove the battery before installing or removing laptop components that are not hot swappable. On some laptops, the PC Card, optical drive, and USB devices are hot swappable. However, the internal hard drive, RAM, and battery are *not* hot swappable.

AC adapters must be compatible with the manufacturer and model of laptop that you have. AC adapters are either auto-switching or fixed input. Auto-switching AC adapters can switch between 110 V and 220 V, while a fixed-input AC adapter only operates under a specific voltage. Auto-switching allows the power supply to be used in different countries.

> **Caution**
>
> On some laptops, the PC Card, optical drive, and USB devices are hot swappable. However, the internal hard drive, RAM, and battery are *not* hot swappable.

Battery Replacement Steps

Remove the battery from the battery bay by following these steps:

Step 1.   Move the battery latches to the unlocked position.

Step 2.   Hold the release lever in the unlock position and remove the battery.

Install the battery into the battery bay as follows:

Step 1.   Insert the battery.

Step 2.   Make sure that both battery latches are locked.

Optical Drive Replacement Steps

Remove the DVD/CD-RW drive by following these steps:

Step 1.   Press the button to open the drive and remove any media in the drive. Close the tray.

Step 2.   Slide the latch to release the lever that secures the drive.

Step 3.   Pull on the lever to expose the drive. Remove the drive.

Install the DVD/CD-RW drive by following these steps:

Step 1.   Insert the drive securely.

Step 2.   Push the lever inward.

Hard Drive Replacement Steps

Remove the hard drive by following these steps:

Step 1. On the bottom of the laptop, remove the screw that holds the hard drive in place.

Step 2. Slide the assembly outward. Remove the hard drive assembly.

Step 3. Remove the hard drive faceplate from the hard drive.

Install the hard drive by following these steps:

Step 1. Attach the hard drive faceplate to the hard drive.

Step 2. Slide the hard drive into the hard drive bay.

Step 3. On the bottom of the laptop, install the screw that holds the hard drive in place.

Expansion Memory Replacement Steps

Laptop expansion memory is also called *small outline dual in-line memory module (SODIMM)*. Remove the existing SODIMM if there are no available slots for the new SODIMM as follows:

Step 1. Remove the screw and cover to expose the SODIMM.

Step 2. Press outward on the clips that hold the sides of the SODIMM.

Step 3. Lift up to loosen the SODIMM from the slot and remove the SODIMM.

Install the SODIMM by following these steps:

Step 1. Align the notch at a 45-degree angle.

Step 2. Gently press down until the clips lock.

Step 3. Replace the cover and install the screw.

PC Expansion Card Replacement Steps

All PC expansion cards, including ExpressCards, are inserted and removed using similar steps.

To remove the PC expansion card, press the top eject button to release it.

Note

There are two buttons. The bottom blue button ejects the Type II PC Card.

Install the PC expansion card by following these steps:

Step 1. Press the blue button inward.

Step 2. Insert the PC expansion card into the expansion slot.

Hot-Swappable Device Removal Steps

Hot-swappable devices are designed to be removed while the laptop is running. When removing these devices, make sure to stop or unmount them first with the following steps:

Step 1.   Left-click the **Safely Remove Hardware** icon in the Windows system tray to ensure that the device is not in use.

Step 2.   Left-click the device that you want to remove. A message pops up to tell you that it is safe to remove the device.

Step 3.   Remove the hot-swappable device from the laptop.

Virtual Laptop Activity: Components and Devices

Replace components and devices in the Virtual Laptop. Refer to the Virtual Laptop software on the CD that accompanies this book.

Laptop Communication Hardware Installation and Configuration

Laptops use several different communication methods:

- Ethernet
- Wireless Ethernet
- Modem
- Bluetooth
- Infrared
- Cellular WAN

Ethernet Installation and Configuration Steps

Ethernet allows for a cabled network connection. Wired Ethernet is typically more reliable and faster than wireless but it comes at the cost of limited mobility. The following is a list of steps to connect a computer to a wired Ethernet network:

Step 1.   Plug the Ethernet cable into the NIC port.

Step 2.   Configure IP address, subnet mask, default gateway, and DNS server information or set the laptop's network interface card (NIC) to receive this information automatically via Dynamic Host Configuration Protocol (DHCP):

- In Windows XP, click **Start > Control Panel > Network Connections**. Right-click **Local Area Connection > Properties,** select **Internet Protocol (TCP/IP)**, click **Properties**, configure the IP settings, and click **OK > OK**.

- In Windows Vista, click **Start > Control Panel > Network and Sharing Center > Manage Network Connections**. Right-click the connection that you want to set up, click **Properties > TCP/IPv4 > Properties**, configure the IP settings, and click **OK > OK**.

Wireless Ethernet Installation and Configuration Steps

Wireless Ethernet NICs can be built into the laptop or attached to the laptop through one of the various laptop expansion ports. Wireless NIC IP address information is configured in much the same way as it is for wired NICs. The only difference is that you must use a utility called Wireless Network Connection in Windows to find a wireless network.

In Windows XP, click **Start > Control Panel > Network Connections**, right-click **Wireless Network Connection > View Available Wireless Connections**, select a wireless network, enter the correct encryption key, and then click **OK**.

In Windows Vista, click **Start > Control Panel > Network and Sharing Center > Manage Network Connections**, right-click **Wireless Network Connection > View Available Wireless Connections**, select a wireless network, enter the correct encryption key, and click **OK**.

Modem Installation and Configuration Steps

A modem allows a laptop to communicate on an analog phone system. It is slower than Ethernet but often is much less expensive and can travel greater distances.

> **Note**
>
> To configure an installed modem, open **Phone and Modem Options** in the Control Panel. On the Modems tab, click the modem you want to configure, and then click **Properties**. The following is a list of steps to connect a computer to a network using a modem.

How To

Step 1.   Make sure the modem is installed and turned on if an external modem is attached.

Step 2.   Attach a phone cable from the wall outlet to the appropriate RJ-11 modem port.

Step 3.   Use the Install New Modem Wizard to add the modem.

- In Windows XP, click **Start > Control Panel > Phone and Modem Options**. Specify the dialing information for your location and click **OK**. Start the **Add Hardware Wizard in the control panel** and then select **Modems > Add > Next**. After the Add Hardware Wizard installs the device, click **Finish**.

- In Windows Vista, click **Start > Control Panel > Phone and Modem Options**. Specify the dialing information for your location and click **OK**. Start the **Add Hardware Wizard** and select **Modems > Add**. If prompted for permission, click **Continue > Next**. After the Add Hardware Wizard installs the device, click **Finish**.

You can use the Phone and Modem Options tabs to configure settings:

- **Dialing Rules**: List, add, edit, and delete dialing locations.

- **Modems**: Add or remove a device or view the properties of a device.

- **Advanced**: List, add, remove, and configure telephony providers installed on the computer.

Bluetooth Installation and Configuration Steps

Windows activates Bluetooth connections by default. If the connection is not active, look for a switch on the front face or on the side of the laptop to enable the connection. The following is a list of steps to connect a Bluetooth device to a computer.

How To

Step 1.   Make sure Bluetooth is enabled in the BIOS before installing and configuring the device.

Step 2.   Turn on the device and make it discoverable to Windows. Check the device documentation to learn how to make your device discoverable.

Step 3.   Use the Bluetooth Wizard to search for and discover any Bluetooth devices that are in Discoverable mode.

- In Windows XP, click **Start > Control Panel > Bluetooth Devices > Device > Add**. Start the **Add Bluetooth Device Wizard**, select **My Device Is Set Up and Ready to Be Found**, and click **Next**. Select the discovered device and click **Next**. If prompted, enter a passkey and click **Next > Finish**.

- In Windows Vista, click **Start > Control Panel > Network and Internet > Set Up a Bluetooth Enabled Device > Device > Add**. If prompted, click **Continue**. Start the **Add Bluetooth Device Wizard**, select **My Device Is Set Up and Ready to Be Found**, and click **Next**. Select the discovered device and click **Next**. If prompted, enter a passkey and click **Finish**.

You can use the Bluetooth Devices tabs to configure the following Bluetooth settings:

- **Device**: Add or removes a device or view the properties of a device.

- **Options**: Control how devices discover and connect to your computer.

- **COM Ports**: Set up new incoming and outgoing serial ports.

- **Hardware**: Lists Bluetooth devices that are installed on your computer to which you can connect.

Infrared Installation and Configuration Steps

Infrared ports communicate with infrared-enabled devices such as remote controls and some printers. The main difference between infrared and Bluetooth wireless networking is that the infrared ports must be line-of-sight to each other. In other words, the ports must literally "see" one another. Range is also an issue. The usable signal strength is limited to about a meter and should be on the same horizontal plain. The following is a list of steps to connect an infrared device to a computer:

How To

Step 1. Make sure infrared is enabled in the BIOS before installing and configuring the device.

Step 2. Turn on the device to make it discoverable to Windows.

Step 3. Align your devices so that the infrared transceivers are within one meter of each other, and the transceivers are pointing at each other.

Step 4. When the devices are correctly aligned, an icon appears on the taskbar with a pop-up message.

Step 5. Click the pop-up message to display the Infrared dialog box.

Step 6. Select the device and click connect.

In both Windows XP and Windows Vista, the Infrared dialog box can be accessed in the Control Panel by double-clicking on the Wireless Link.

Laptops without an internal infrared device can connect a serial infrared transceiver to a serial port or a USB port.

You can use the Infrared dialog box tabs to configure infrared settings:

■ **Infrared**: Control how you are notified about an infrared connection, and control how files are transferred.

■ **Image Transfer**: Control how images are transferred from a digital camera.

■ **Hardware**: Lists infrared devices that are installed on your computer and let's you manage those devices.

Cellular WAN Installation and Configuration Steps

Laptops with integrated cellular WAN capabilities require no software installation and no additional antenna or accessories. When you turn on the laptop, the integrated WAN capabilities are ready to be used. If the connection is not active, look for a switch on the front face or on the side of the laptop to enable the connection. The following are steps to configure a cellular WAN connection:

How To

Step 1. Make sure cellular WAN is enabled in the BIOS before installing and configuring the device.

Step 2. Install the manufacturer's broadband card utility software.

Step 3. Use the utility software to manage the network connection.

The cellular WAN utility software can be located in the taskbar or in **Start > Programs**.

Compare the Different Mobile Phone Standards

When people began to use cell phones, there were few industry-wide standards that applied to cell phone technology. Without standards, it was difficult and expensive to make calls to people that were on another network. Today, cell phone providers use industry standards, which make it easier to use cell phones to make calls.

When the industry started, most cell phone standards were analog. Today, cell phone standards are mostly digital.

Note

Cell phone standards have not been adopted uniformly around the world. Some cell phones are capable of using multiple standards while others can use only one standard. As a result, some cell phones can operate in many countries while other cell phones can only be used locally.

The first generation (1G) of cell phones began service in the 1980s. First-generation phones primarily used analog standards, including Advanced Mobile Phone System (AMPS) and Nordic Mobile Telephone (NMT).

In an *analog transmission* system, the voice information is sent by varying the radio signals used by the phone in the same pattern as the speakers' voices. Unfortunately, this means that interference and noise, which also vary the signal, cannot easily be separated from the voice in the signal. This limits the usefulness of analog systems.

Digital signals convert the speakers' voices into a digital signal that uses a chain of 1s and 0s. This degrades the signal a little, because 1s and 0s are not a faithful representation of your voice. However, the digital signal is robust. It can be fixed using error-correction routines if there is interference. Also, digital signals can be compressed, making the systems much more efficient than analog systems.

In the 1990s, the second generation (2G) of cell phones was marked by a switch from analog to digital standards. Second-generation cell standards included Global System for Mobile (GSM), Integrated Digital Enhanced Network (iDEN), and Code Division Multiple Access (CDMA).

Third-generation (3G) standards enable cell phones to go beyond simple voice and data communications. It is now common for cell phones to send and receive text, photos, and video. It is also common for 3G cell phones to access the Internet and to use the Global Positioning System (GPS).

Note

As 3G cell phone standards were being developed, extensions to the existing 2G standards were added. These transitional standards are known as 2.5G standards.

Fourth-generation (4G) standards have been championed by many users because of the availability of increased data rates. Higher data rates allow users to download files, such as video and music, faster than what was available with standards of previous generations.

Table 6-6 shows more information about the different cell phone standards.

Table 6-6   Cell Phone Standards

Generation	Standard Name	Features	Used In
1G (Analog cell phone standards introduced in the 1980s)	Nordic Mobile Telephone (NMT)	Replaced wired telephones	Saudi Arabia, Scandinavia
	Advanced Mobile Phone System (AMPS)	Replaced wired telephones	United States, New Zealand
2G (Digital cellular)	GSM Communications	Digital-quality calls everywhere	Worldwide
	iDEN	Push-To-Talk service, international roaming	North and South America, Philippines, Singapore, Saudi Arabia
2.5G (Digital cellular + packet network for data)	General Packet Radio Service (GPRS)	Data layer for GSM	Worldwide
	Code Division Multiple Access (CDMA)	Unified digital data, voice service	North and South America, India, Indonesia, Japan, South Korea
	CDMA2000 1xRTT/IS-2000		
	EDGE (CDMA) Enhanced Data Rates for Global Evolution	Data upgrade to GPRS	Worldwide

continues

Table 6-6 Cell Phone Standards *continued*

Generation	Standard Name	Features	Used In
3G (Simultaneous voice and data, with email and instant messaging)	Universal Mobile Telecommunications System (UMTS, also called 3GSM)	Advanced GSM phone system	Europe, Africa, Asia, U.S.
	1xEV-DO/IS-856 (pronounced D-O)	Advanced CDMA telephone system	Worldwide
4G (Technologies that are "3G and beyond")	High Speed Downlink Packet Access (HSDPA)	Advanced UMTS system for voice, high-speed data	Worldwide

New technologies that add multimedia and networking functionality can be bundled with cell phone standards. Table 6-7 lists common technologies that can be added to the cell phone bundle of services. Most cell phone providers charge extra for adding these features.

Table 6-7 Internet Standards

Internet Standard	Purpose
Short Message Service (SMS)	Used for text messaging
Multimedia Message Service	Used for sending and receiving photos and videos
Packet switching	Used for accessing the Internet

Identify Common Preventive Maintenance Techniques for Laptops and Portable Devices

Because laptops are mobile, they are used in different types of environments. Some environments can be hazardous to a laptop. Even eating or drinking around a laptop creates a potentially hazardous condition.

Consider what would happen if a drink were spilled onto the keyboard of a laptop. Many components are placed in a very small area directly beneath the keyboard. Spilling liquid or dropping debris onto the keyboard can result in severe internal damage.

It is important to keep a laptop clean and to ensure that it is being used in the most optimal environment. The following sections cover preventive maintenance techniques for the laptop.

After completing these sections, you will meet these objectives:

- Identify appropriate cleaning procedures.
- Identify optimal operating environments.

Identify Appropriate Cleaning Procedures

Proper routine cleaning is the easiest, least expensive way to protect and to extend the life of a laptop. It is very important to use the right products and procedures when cleaning a laptop. Always read all warning labels on the cleaning products. The components are very sensitive and should be handled with care. Consult the laptop manual for additional information and cleaning suggestions. This section provides basic steps for cleaning the laptop keyboard, ventilation area, screen, touch pad, disk drives, and discs.

Laptop Keyboard Cleaning Procedures

Keyboards collect dirt and crumbs that can actually prevent keys from working properly. Maintain a clean laptop by following these steps:

Step 1. Turn off the laptop.

Step 2. Disconnect all attached devices.

Step 3. Disconnect the laptop from the electrical outlet.

Step 4. Remove all installed batteries.

Step 5. Clean the keys with compressed air or a nonelectrostatic vacuum.

Step 6. Wipe the laptop and keyboard with a soft, lint-free cloth that is lightly moistened with water or computer-screen cleaner.

Ventilation Cleaning Procedures

Ventilation is critical to the cooling system. To keep dust and lint from building up in the laptop follow these steps:

Step 1. Turn off the laptop.

Step 2. Disconnect all attached devices.

Step 3. Disconnect the laptop from the electrical outlet.

Step 4. Remove all installed batteries.

Step 5. Use compressed air or a nonelectrostatic vacuum to clean out the dust from the vents and the fan behind the vent.

Step 6. Use tweezers to remove any debris.

LCD Cleaning Procedures

Liquid crystal displays (LCD) are fragile and can easily be scratched when cleaning them. Follow these steps to clean LCDs correctly:

Step 1. Turn off the laptop.

Step 2. Disconnect all attached devices.

Step 3. Disconnect the laptop from the electrical outlet.

Step 4. Remove all installed batteries.

Step 5. Wipe the display with a soft, lint-free cloth that is lightly moistened with water or LCD cleaner.

Caution

Do not apply cleaning solution either directly or indirectly onto the LCD. Use products specifically designed for cleaning LCD screens.

Touch Pad Cleaning Procedures

Touch pads get dirty because of the frequent contact with customers' hands and fingers. Follow these steps to clean a touch pad.

Step 1. Turn off the laptop.

Step 2. Disconnect all attached devices.

Step 3. Disconnect the laptop from the electrical outlet.

Step 4. Remove all installed batteries.

Step 5. Wipe the surface of touch pad gently with a soft, lint-free cloth moistened with an approved cleaner. Never use a wet cloth.

Caution

Use a soft, lint-free cloth with an approved cleaning solution to avoid damaging laptop surfaces. Apply the cleaning solution to the lint-free cloth, not directly to the laptop.

Floppy Drive Cleaning Procedures

When cleaning a floppy drive, use a commercially available cleaning kit. Floppy drive cleaning kits include pretreated floppy disks that remove from the floppy drive heads contaminants that have accumulated through normal operation. Follow these steps:

Step 1. Remove all media from the floppy drive.

Step 2. Insert the cleaning disk and let it spin for the suggested amount of time.

Optical Drive Cleaning Procedures

Dirt, dust, and other contaminants can collect in your optical drives and on the discs. Contaminated drives and discs can cause malfunctions, missing data, error messages, and lost productivity. Follow these steps to clean your optical drive:

Step 1.   Use a commercially available CD or DVD drive cleaning disc. Many floppy disc cleaning kits include an optical disc cleaner. Like the floppy disc cleaner, optical disc cleaner kits contain a cleaning solution and a nonabrasive disc that is inserted into the optical drive.

Step 2.   Remove all media from the optical drive.

Step 3.   Insert the cleaning disc and let it spin for the suggested amount of time to clean all contact areas.

Cleaning a CD or DVD Disc

For a CD or DVD disc, inspect the disc for scratches. Replace discs that contain deep scratches because they can cause data errors. If you notice problems, such as skipping or degraded playback quality with your CDs or DVDs, clean the discs. Commercial products are available that clean discs and provide protection from dust, fingerprints, and scratches. Cleaning products for CDs are safe to use on DVDs. To clean a CD or DVD, follow these steps:

Step 1.   Hold the disc by its outer edge or by the inside edge of the center hole.

Step 2.   Gently wipe the disc with a lint-free cotton cloth. Never use paper or any material that can scratch the disc or leave streaks.

Step 3.   Wipe both sides from the center of the disc outward. Never use a circular motion.

Step 4.   Apply a commercial CD or DVD cleaning solution to the lint-free cotton cloth, and wipe again if any contaminates remain on the disc.

Step 5.   Allow the disc to dry before it is inserted into the drive.

Identify Optimal Operating Environments

An *optimal operating environment* for a laptop is clean, free of potential contaminants, and within the temperature and humidity range specified by the manufacturer. With most desktop computers, the operating environment can be controlled. However, because of the portable nature of laptops, it is not always possible to control the temperature, humidity, and working conditions. Laptops are built to resist adverse environments, but technicians should always take precautions to protect the equipment from damage and loss of data.

It is important to transport or ship laptops carefully. Use a padded laptop case to store your laptop. When you carry it, use an approved computer bag. If the laptop is shipped, use sufficient packing material to prevent damage during transport. Figure 6-19 shows examples of laptop carrying cases and packing boxes.

Figure 6-19   Shipping and Transporting a Laptop

Laptops are transported to many types of environments. Dust particles, temperature, and humidity can affect the performance of a laptop. Follow these guidelines to help ensure optimal operating performance from your laptop:

- Clean the laptop frequently to remove dust and potential contaminants.

- Do not obstruct vents or airflow to internal components. A laptop can overheat if air circulation is obstructed.

- Keep the room temperature between 45 and 90 degrees Fahrenheit (7 and 32 degrees Celsius).

- Keep the humidity level between 10 and 80 percent.

Temperature and humidity recommendations will vary by laptop manufacturer. You should research these recommended values, especially if you plan to use the laptop in extreme conditions.

Describe How to Troubleshoot Laptops and Portable Devices

When troubleshooting problems with laptops or portable devices, you should determine whether a repair is cost effective. To determine the best course of action, you should compare the cost of the repair to the replacement cost of the laptop or portable device, less the salvage value.

Because many portable devices change rapidly in design and functionality, portable devices are often more expensive to repair than to replace. For this reason, portable devices are usually replaced, whereas laptops can be replaced or repaired.

Follow the steps outlined in the following sections to accurately identify, repair, and document the problem. The troubleshooting process follows:

How To

Step 1.   Identify the problem.

Step 2.   Establish a theory of probable causes.

Step 3.   Determine n exact cause.

Step 4.   Implement a solution.

Step 5.   Verify solution and full system functionality.

Step 6.   Document findings.

After completing these sections, you will meet these objectives:

- Review the troubleshooting process.

- Identify common problems and solutions.

Review the Troubleshooting Process

The first step in the troubleshooting process is to Identify the problem. There are two types of questions you can ask the customer: open-ended and closed-ended.

Open-ended questions cannot be answered with yes or no answers. The purpose of open-ended questions is to allow the customer to describe the problem. Open-ended questions can include the following but this list is not exhaustive:

- What problems are you experiencing with your laptop?

- What software has been installed recently?

- What were you doing when the problem was identified?

- What error messages have you received?

Closed-ended questions can usually be answered with yes or no answers. This type of question can help a technician focus in on an error and locate the exact problem when a potential solution is being tested. Closed-ended questions can include the following but this list is not exhaustive:

- Is the laptop under warranty?

- Is the laptop currently using the battery?

- Can the laptop operate using the AC adapter?

- Can the laptop boot and show the operating system desktop?

After you have identified the problem , establish a theory of probable causes. Common causes of laptop problems include the following:

- Battery does not have a charge

- Battery will not charge

- Loose cable connections

- Keyboard does not work

- Num Lock key is on

- Loose RAM

After you have established a theory of probable causes, determine an exact cause. The following can help determine the cause:

- Use AC adapter with laptop.

- Replace battery.

- Reboot the laptop.

- Check BIOS settings.

- Disconnect and reconnect the cables.

- Disconnect peripherals.

- Toggle NUM Lock key.

- Remove and reinstall RAM.

- Check the Caps Lock key.

- Remove any non-bootable media in a boot device.

- Verify you are using correct passwords.

After you have determined an exact cause, implement the solution. Resources for possible solutions include the following:

- Helpdesk Repair Logs

- Other technicians

- Internet search

- Newsgroups

- Manufacturer FAQs

- Computer manuals

- Device manuals

- Online forums

- Technical websites

After you have implemented a solution, verify solution and full system functionality. Perform the following tasks to verify that the laptop is full working order:

- Reboot the laptop.

- Attach all peripherals.

- Operate laptop using only the battery.

- Print a document from an application.

- Type a sample document to the test the keyboard.

- Check Event Viewer for warnings or errors.

When you have verified the solution and full system functionality, document your findings:

- Discuss the solution implemented with the customer.

- Have the customer verify that the problem has been solved.

- Provide the customer with all paperwork.

- Document the steps taken to solve the problem in the work order and the technician's journal.

- Document any components used in the repair.

- Document the time spent to resolve the problem.

Identify Common Problems and Solutions

Laptop and portable device problems can be attributed to hardware, software, networks, or some combination of the three. You will resolve some types of Laptop and portable device problems more often than others. Table 6-8 addresses some common problems and solutions for laptops and portable devices.

Table 6-8   Common Problems and Solutions for Laptops and Portable Devices

Identify the Problem	Probable Causes	Possible Solutions
Laptop does not power on.	Laptop is not plugged in.	Plug laptop into AC power.
	Battery is not charged.	Remove and reinstall the battery.
	Battery will not hold a charge.	Replace battery if it will not charge.
Laptop battery supports the system but for a reduced time.	Proper battery charging and discharging practices have not been followed.	Follow the battery charging procedures described in your manual.
	Extra peripherals are draining the battery.	Remove unneeded peripherals and disable the wireless NIC if possible.
	Power scheme is not configured correctly.	Modify the power scheme to decrease battery usage.
	Battery is not holding a charge for very long.	Replace battery.
External display has power but no image on the screen.	Video cable is loose or damaged.	Reconnect or replace video cable.
	The laptop is not sending video to the external display.	Use the Fn key along with the multipurpose key to toggle to the external display.
Laptop is powered on but nothing is displayed on the LCD screen when the laptop lid is reopened.	LCD cutoff switch is dirty or damaged.	Check the laptop repair manual for instructions about cleaning or replacing the LCD cutoff switch.
	The laptop has gone into sleep mode.	Press a key on the keyboard to bring the computer out of sleep mode.
	The laptop is only sending video to the external display.	Use the Fn key along with the multipurpose key to toggle to the internal display.
The image on a laptop screen looks dull and pale.	The LCD backlight is not properly adjusted.	Check the laptop repair manual for instructions about calibrating the LCD backlight.

Identify the Problem	Probable Causes	Possible Solutions
The image on a laptop screen looks pixelated.	LCD display properties are incorrect.	Set the LCD screen to native resolution.
The network is fully functional and the wireless laptop connection is enabled, but the laptop cannot connect to the network.	Laptop wireless capability is turned off. External wireless antenna is misaligned.	Turn laptop wireless on using the wireless NIC properties or the Fn key along with the appropriate multipurpose key.
	The laptop is out of wireless range.	Realign antenna to pick up wireless signal. Move closer to the wireless access point.

Worksheet 6.7.2: Research Laptop Problems

Research laptop issues. Refer to the worksheet in *IT Essentials: PC Hardware and Software Lab Manual, Fourth Edition*. You can perform this worksheet now or wait until the end of the chapter.

Summary

This chapter discussed the features of laptops, PDAs, and smartphones. The following are some of the important concepts to remember from this chapter:

- Laptops, PDAs, and smartphones are becoming increasingly popular because of reduced costs, lighter weights, increased capabilities, and battery power for portability.

- Laptops and desktops have ports that are virtually the same, so peripherals are interchangeable. Laptops can use docking stations or port replicators to quickly connect to desktop peripherals and AC power.

- The laptop CPU is designed to use less power and create less heat than the desktop computer. It uses CPU throttling to reduce power consumption and heat.

- Functionality of the laptop can be expanded by adding components through PC Card or ExpressCard slots and USB, FireWire, and parallel ports.

- Cell phone standards were developed in the 1980s. The current, third-generation standards enable cell phones to share some laptop functions, such as email, Internet access, and calendar and address functions. Standards have not been adopted worldwide.

- Preventive maintenance will ensure optimal operation of the laptop. It is important to keep the laptop clean and in safe environments. It is critical to use the correct materials and techniques when cleaning the various components of a laptop. Procedures for cleaning the components were presented in the chapter.

- Dust, temperature, and humidity can affect laptop performance. Basic guidelines are to keep the laptop clean, with good ventilation and room temperature at 45 to 90 degrees Fahrenheit (7 to 32 degrees Celsius) and humidity levels in the range of 10 to 80 percent.

- Troubleshooting laptop problems requires the technician to identify, repair, and document the problem. Troubleshooting steps include gathering data from the customer, verifying the obvious, trying quick solutions first, gathering data from the computer, evaluating the problem, implementing the solution, and closing with the customer.

Chapter 13, "Advanced Laptops and Portable Devices," focuses on troubleshooting more difficult problems.

Summary of Exercises

This is a summary of the Labs, Worksheets, Remote Technician exercises, Class Discussions, Virtual Desktop activities, and Virtual Laptop activities associated with this chapter.

Worksheets

The following worksheets cover material from this chapter. Refer to the labs in *IT Essentials: PC Hardware and Software Lab Manual, Fourth Edition.*

Worksheet 6.1.2: Research Laptops, Smartphones, and PDAs

Worksheet 6.2.3: Complete Docking Stations True or False Questions

Worksheet 6.3.4: Answer Laptop Expansion Questions

Worksheet 6.4.1: Match ACPI Standards

Worksheet 6.7.2: Research Laptop Problems

Virtual Laptop Activities

The following Virtual Laptop activities cover material from this chapter. Refer to the Virtual Laptop software on the CD that accompanies this book.

Virtual Laptop Activity: Explore Laptop

Virtual Laptop Activity: Keyboard

Virtual Laptop Activity: Docking Station

Virtual Laptop Activity: Components and Devices

Check Your Understanding

You can find the answers to these questions in the appendix, "Answers to Check Your Understanding Questions."

1. A newer type of PC Card is called the _____.

   A. ExpressCard

   B. PC Card disk

   C. PC CardBus

   D. PCMCIA Card

2. The PC ExpressCard has _____ and _____ pin configurations.

   A. 64 and 128

   B. 34 and 54

   C. 28 and 40

   D. 9 and 15

3. Which power mode would you use on a laptop running Windows XP to minimize power consumption by reducing power to the hardware?

   A. Network

   B. Hibernate

   C. Active

   D. Conserving

4. When you are ready to clean a laptop's LCD, which of the following would you select?

   A. Trichloroethane solvent

   B. Ammonia-based solvent

   C. A window cleaning solvent

   D. LCD cleaning solution

5. Which of the following is similar to a port replicator, and adds more functionality with additional drives?

   A. USB hub

   B. Docking station

   C. Drive bay

   D. Storage area

6. Which of the following features make laptops a good alternative to desktop computers? (Choose two.)

   A. Compact design

   B. Lower costs

   C. Enhanced capabilities

   D. Portability

7. Which laptop device is commonly hot swappable?

   A. Display

   B. Internal hard drive

   C. PC Card

   D. RAM

8. Which type of memory is used in laptops?

   A. DIMM

   B. RIMM

   C. SIMM

   D. SODIMM

9. Which power management control was introduced prior to the Advanced Configuration and Power Interface?

    A. ACCI

    B. ACPI

    C. AMD

    D. APM

    E. APA

10. What do FireWire and USB devices have in common?

    A. Only one of these devices can be used at a time.

    B. They are considered hot-swappable devices.

    C. They cannot be used with desktop PCs.

    D. They are parallel communication devices.

11. What should a user do when operations on a USB memory device have been completed and it is necessary to remove it from the laptop computer?

    A. Reboot the computer.

    B. Choose **Start > Control Panel > System**. Select **USB Device** and then click the **Properties** tab. Click **Remove**.

    C. Click the **Safely Remove Hardware** icon in the Windows system tray.

    D. Just remove the USB device from the computer.

12. Which of the following steps are recommended when cleaning a laptop LCD screen? (Choose two.)

    A. Clean the display screen using tissue moistened with water.

    B. Disconnect all devices attached to the laptop prior to cleaning the display screen.

    C. Power off the laptop prior to cleaning the display screen.

    D. Remove all sources of power immediately after cleaning the display screen.

    E. Remove the LCD screen from the laptop.

13. What is the easiest, least expensive way to extend the life of a laptop and keep it in optimal working order?

    A. Replace parts regularly.

    B. Clean the laptop regularly.

    C. Do a clean reinstall of the OS.

    D. Back up important information monthly.

CHAPTER 7

Fundamental Printers and Scanners

Objectives

Upon completion of this chapter, you should be able to answer the following questions:

- What types of printers are currently available?

- What is the process of installation and configuration for printers?

- What types of scanners are currently available?

- What is the process of installation and configuration for scanners?

- How can I identify and apply common preventive maintenance techniques to printers and scanners?

- How can I troubleshoot printers and scanners?

Key Terms

This chapter uses the following key terms. You can find the definitions in the Glossary.

This chapter provides essential information about printers and scanners. You will learn how printers operate, what to consider when purchasing a printer, and how to connect printers to an individual computer or to a network.

Printers produce paper copies of electronic files. *Scanners* allow users to convert paper documents into electronic files. Many government regulations require physical records; therefore, hard copies of computer documents are often as important today as they were when the paperless revolution began several years ago.

You must understand the operation of various types of printers and scanners to be able to install and maintain them, as well as to troubleshoot any problems that may arise. After completing this chapter, you will meet these objectives:

- Describe the types of printers currently available.

- Describe the installation and configuration process for printers.

- Describe the types of scanners currently available.

- Describe the installation and configuration process for scanners.

- Identify and apply common preventive maintenance techniques for printers and scanners.

- Troubleshoot printers and scanners.

Describe the Types of Printers Currently Available

As a computer technician, you might be required to purchase, repair, or maintain a printer. The customer might request that you perform the following tasks:

- Select a printer.

- Install and configure a printer.

- Troubleshoot a printer.

After completing this section, you will meet these objectives:

- Describe the characteristics and capabilities of printers.

- Describe printer-to-computer interfaces.

- Describe laser printers.

- Describe impact printers.

- Describe inkjet printers.

- Describe solid-ink printers.

- Describe other printer types.

Describe the Characteristics and Capabilities of Printers

Printers available today are usually either laser printers using *electrophotographic technology* or *inkjet printers* using electrostatic spray technology. *Dot-matrix printers* using impact technology are used in applications that require carbon copies. When selecting a printer, consider the following criteria:

- Capacity
- Speed
- Color
- Quality
- Reliability
- Cost

Capacity and Speed

Printer capacity and speed are factors to consider when selecting a printer. Inkjet printers are usually slower, but they might be adequate for a home or small office. A printer's speed is measured in pages per minute (ppm). The speed of an inkjet printer is 2 to 6 ppm. The speed of a laser printer is 8 to 200 ppm. Capacity is a measure of how much paper, ink, or toner the printer can hold.

Color or Black and White

A computer monitor produces colors through the additive mixing of dots that are displayed on the screen. The eye picks up the colors directly. The dots produce the color range using red, green, and blue (RGB) dots.

A printer produces colors using subtractive mixing. The eye sees a color that reflects from the combination of colors on the paper.

The choice between a black-and-white printer and a color printer depends on your customer's needs. If your customer is primarily printing letters and does not need color capability, a black-and-white printer is sufficient. However, an elementary school teacher might need a color printer to add excitement to lessons.

Quality

The quality of printing is measured in *dots per inch (dpi)*. The more dpi, the higher the resolution. When the resolution is higher, text and images are usually clearer. To produce the best high-resolution images, you should use both high-quality ink or toner and high-quality paper.

Reliability

A printer should be reliable. Because there are so many types of printers on the market, you should research the specifications of several printers before selecting one. Here are some of the options available from the manufacturer:

- **Warranty**: Identify what is covered in the warranty.

- **Scheduled servicing**: Servicing is based on expected usage. Information is found in the manual or on the manufacturer's website.

- *Mean time between failures (MTBF)*: This is the average length of time that the printer will work without failing. You typically can find this information in the manual or on the manufacturer's website.

Total Cost of Ownership

Consider the cost when selecting hardware. When buying a printer, you must consider more than just the initial cost of the printer. The total cost of ownership (TCO) is how much the printer will cost to operate over its lifetime. TCO includes a number of factors:

- Initial purchase price

- Cost of supplies, such as paper and ink/toner

- Price per page

- Maintenance costs

- Warranty costs

- Data/communication cables

- The amount of material printed

- Lifetime of the printer

Describe Printer-to-Computer Interfaces

A computer must have a compatible interface with the printer to be able to print documents. Typically, printers connect to home computers using a parallel, USB, or NIC or wireless NIC interface.

The different types of printer ports are described in the following sections.

Serial Ports

Serial data transfer is the movement of single bits of information in a single cycle. A serial connection can be used for dot-matrix printers because they do not require high-speed data transfer. Serial printers are very rare today. Most commonly printers are connected via USB, network cable, or wireless Ethernet.

Parallel Ports

Parallel data transfer is faster than serial data transfer. Parallel data transfer is the movement of multiple bits of information in a single cycle. The path is wider for information to move to or from the printer.

IEEE 1284 is the current standard for parallel printer ports. Enhanced Parallel Port (EPP) and Enhanced Capabilities Port (ECP) are two modes of operation within the IEEE 1284 standard that allow bidirectional communication. Figure 7-1 shows a parallel port.

Figure 7-1   Printer Parallel, Ethernet, and Coaxial Ports

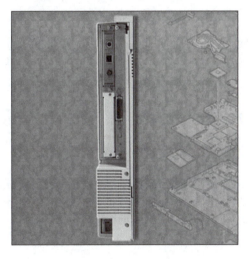

SCSI Interfaces

Small Computer System Interface (SCSI) is a type of interface that uses parallel communication technology to achieve high data-transfer rates.

USB Interfaces

Universal Serial Bus (USB) is a common interface for printers and other devices. The speed and simple setup have made USB very practical. Newer operating systems offer "plug-and-play" USB support. When a USB device is added to a computer system supporting plug-and-play, the device is automatically detected and starts the driver installation process.

USB 2.0 is the current USB standard. USB 2.0 can support up to 127 devices and has a transfer rate of as much as 480 Mbps.

FireWire Connections

FireWire, also known as i.LINK or IEEE 1394, is a high-speed communication bus that is platform independent. FireWire connects digital devices such as digital printers, scanners, digital cameras, and hard drives.

FireWire allows a peripheral device, such as a printer, to seamlessly plug into a computer. It also allows a device such as a printer to be hot-swappable. FireWire provides a single plug-and-socket connection that can attach up to 63 devices. FireWire has a data transfer rate of up to 400 Mbps.

Ethernet Connections

Printers can be shared over a network. Connecting a printer to the network requires cabling (such as *Ethernet*) that is compatible with both the existing network and the network port installed in the printer. Most network printers use an RJ-45 interface to connect to a network.

Wireless Connections

Wireless printing technology is available in infrared, Bluetooth, and wireless fidelity (Wi-Fi) technology.

For infrared communication to take place between a printer and a computer, transmitters and receivers are required on both devices. There must be a clear line of sight between the transmitter and receiver on both devices, with a maximum distance of 12 feet (3.7 m). Infrared uses a type of light that is invisible to the human eye.

Bluetooth technology uses an unlicensed radio frequency for short-range communication and is popular for wireless headsets and synching PDAs to laptops and desktop computers. A Bluetooth adapter allows a Bluetooth device to connect to a printer, usually by using a USB port.

Wi-Fi is the popular name for a relatively new technology that lets you connect computers to a network without using cables. Wi-Fi technology has four common standards, all of which begin with the number of the IEEE standard, 802.11:

- 802.11a transfers data at a rate of up to 54 Mbps at 5 GHz.
- 802.11b transfers data at a rate of up to 11 Mbps at 2.4 GHz.
- 802.11g transfers data at a rate of up to 54 Mbps at 2.4 GHz. 802.11g products are backward compatible with 802.11b.
- 802.11n is currently in the standardization process and is expected to be approved with a maximum data transfer rate of up to 248 Mbps.

Describe Laser Printers

A *laser printer*, such as the one shown in Figure 7-2, is a high-quality, fast printer that uses a laser beam to create an image. The central part of the laser printer is its electrophotographic drum. The drum is a metal cylinder that is coated with a light-sensitive insulating material. When a beam of laser light strikes the drum, it becomes a conductor at the point where the light hits it. As the drum rotates, the laser beam draws an electrostatic image on the drum, called the image. The undeveloped or latent image is passed by a supply of dry ink or toner that is attracted to it. The drum turns and brings this image into contact with the paper, which attracts the toner from the drum. The paper is passed through a fuser that is made up of hot rollers, which melts the toner into the paper.

Figure 7-2   Laser Printer

The laser printer process involves six steps to print information on a single sheet of paper:

How To

Step 1.   *Cleaning*: When an image has been deposited on the paper and fusion occurs, any remaining toner must be removed from the drum. A printer may have a blade that scrapes all excess toner from the drum. Some printers use AC voltage on a wire that removes the charge from the drum surface and allows the excess toner to fall away from the drum. The excess toner is stored in a used-toner container that may be emptied or discarded.

Step 2.   *Conditioning*: This step involves removing the old latent image from the drum and conditioning the drum for a new latent image. Conditioning is done by placing a special wire, grid, or roller that receives a negative charge of approximately –600 volts DC uniformly across the surface of the drum. The charged wire or grid is called the *primary corona wire*. The roller is called a conditioning roller.

Step 3.   *Writing*: The writing process involves scanning the photosensitive drum with the laser beam. Every portion of the drum that is exposed to the light has the surface charge reduced to about –100 volts DC. This electrical charge has a lower negative charge than the remainder of the drum. As the drum turns, an invisible latent image is created on the drum.

Step 4.   *Developing*: In the developing phase, the toner is applied to the latent image on the drum. The toner is a negatively charged combination of plastic and metal particles. A control blade holds the toner at a microscopic distance from the drum. The toner then moves from the control blade to the more positively charged latent image on the drum.

Step 5.   *Transferring*: In this step, the toner attached to the latent image is transferred to the paper. The transfer, or secondary corona, places a positive charge on the paper. Because the drum was charged negatively, the toner on the drum is attracted to the paper. The image is now on the paper and is held in place by the positive charge.

Step 6.   *Fusing*: In this step, the toner is permanently fused to the paper. The printing paper is rolled between a heated roller and a pressure roller. As the paper moves through the heated roller and the pressure roller, the loose toner is melted and fused with the fibers in the paper. The paper is then moved to the output tray as a printed page.

The following mnemonic will help you memorize the order of the steps of the laser printing process:

Continuous (cleaning)

Care (conditioning)

Will (writing)

Delay (developing)

Trouble (transferring)

Forever (fusing)

Caution

The primary corona wire or grid, or the conditioning roller, can be very dangerous. The voltage runs as high as –6000 volts. Only certified technicians should work on the unit. Before working inside a laser printer, you should make sure that the voltage is properly discharged.

Describe Impact Printers

Impact printers, such as the one shown in Figure 7-3, are basic. Impact printers have print heads that strike the inked ribbon, causing characters to be printed on the paper. Daisy-wheel and dot-matrix printers are examples of impact printers.

Figure 7-3   Impact Printer

In a daisy-wheel printer, the wheel contains the letters, numbers, and special characters. The wheel rotates until the required character is in place, and an electromechanical hammer pushes the character into the ink ribbon. The character then strikes the paper, printing the character on the paper.

A dot-matrix printer is similar to the daisy-wheel printer, except that instead of a wheel containing characters, a print head contains pins that are surrounded by electromagnets. When energized, the pins push forward onto the ink ribbon, creating a character on the paper.

The number of pins on a print head, 9 or 24, indicates the quality of the print.

Table 7-1 lists some advantages and disadvantages of an impact printer.

Table 7-1   Impact Printer Pros and Cons

Advantages	Disadvantages
Uses inexpensive consumables	Noisy
Uses continuous-feed paper	Low-resolution graphics
Has carbon copy printing capability	Limited color capability
	Slow printing, normally in the range of 32 to 76 characters per second (cps)

Describe Inkjet Printers

Inkjet printers produce high-quality prints. Inkjet printers are easy to use and inexpensive compared to laser printers. The low cost of the printer does not mean a low TCO. Usually the TCO of a inkjet printer is markedly higher than that of a laser printer. The print quality of an inkjet printer is measured in dpi. Higher dpi numbers provide greater image details. Figure 7-4 shows an all-in-one device that contains an inkjet printer. Figure 7-5 shows inkjet printer components.

Figure 7-4   Inkjet Printer

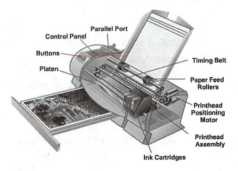

Figure 7-5   Inkjet Printer Components

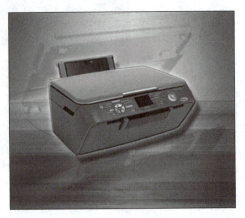

Inkjet printers use ink-filled cartridges that spray ink onto a page through tiny holes called nozzles. The ink is sprayed in a pattern on the page.

There are two types of inkjet nozzles:

- *Thermal*: A pulse of electrical current is applied to heating chambers around the nozzles. The heat creates a bubble of steam in the chamber. The steam forces ink out through the nozzle and onto the paper.

- *Piezoelectric*: Piezoelectric crystals are located in the ink reservoir at the back of each nozzle. A charge is applied to the crystal, causing it to vibrate. This vibration of the crystal controls the flow of ink onto the paper.

Inkjet printers use plain paper to make economical prints. Special-purpose paper may be used to create high-quality prints of photographs. When the inkjet print is complete and the paper leaves the printer, the ink is often wet. You should avoid touching printouts for 10 to 15 seconds to prevent the images from smearing.

Table 7-2 lists some advantages and disadvantages of an inkjet printer.

Table 7-2   Inkjet Printer Pros and Cons

Advantages	Disadvantages
Low cost.	Nozzles are prone to clogging.
High resolution.	Ink cartridges are expensive.
Quick to warm up.	Ink is wet after printing.

Describe Solid-Ink Printers

Solid-ink printers use solid sticks of ink rather than toner or ink cartridges, as shown in Figure 7-6. Solid-ink printers produce high-quality images. The ink sticks are nontoxic and can be handled safely.

Figure 7-6   Solid-Ink Printer

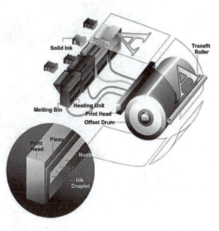

Solid-ink printers melt ink sticks and spray the ink through nozzles. The ink is sprayed onto a drum. The drum transfers the ink to paper.

Table 7-3 lists some advantages and disadvantages of a solid-ink printer.

Table 7-3 Solid-Ink Printer Pros and Cons

Advantages	Disadvantages
Produces vibrant color prints.	Printers are expensive.
Easy to use.	Ink is expensive.
Can use many different paper types.	Printers are slow to warm up.

Describe Other Printer Types

Two other printing technologies that you may work with are thermal and dye sublimation, as described in the following sections.

Thermal Printers

Some retail cash registers, most label makers, and older fax machines may contain *thermal printers*, as shown in Figure 7-7. The paper used in thermal printers is chemically treated and has a waxy quality. Thermal paper becomes black when heated. Most thermal printer print heads are the width of the paper. Areas of the print head are heated as required to make the pattern on the paper. The paper is supplied in the form of a roll.

Figure 7-7 Thermal Printer

Table 7-4 lists some advantages and disadvantages of a thermal printer.

Table 7-4   Thermal Printer Pros and Cons

Advantages	Disadvantages
Longer life because there are few moving parts.	Paper is expensive.
	Paper has a short shelf life.
	Images are poor quality.
	Paper must be stored at room temperature.

Dye-Sublimation Printers

Dye-sublimation printers, such as the one shown in Figure 7-8, produce photo-quality images for graphic printing. Dye-sublimation printers use solid sheets of ink that change directly from solid to gas in a process called sublimation. The print head passes over a sheet of cyan, magenta, yellow, and a clear overcoat (CMYO). There is a pass for each color. In photography, both dye-sublimation printers and small color inkjet printers provide quality prints.

Figure 7-8   Dye-Sublimation Printer

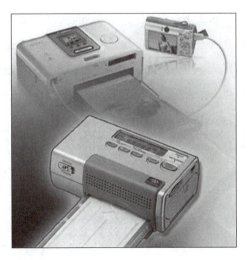

Table 7-5 lists some advantages and disadvantages of a dye-sublimation printer.

Table 7-5   Dye-Sublimation Printer Pros and Cons

Advantages	Disadvantages
Printers produce high-quality images.	Media can be expensive.
Overcoat layer reduces smearing and increases moisture resistance.	Printers are better for color than for grayscale (black and white).

Describe the Installation and Configuration Process for Printers

When you purchase a printer, the installation and configuration information is usually supplied by the manufacturer. An installation CD that includes drivers, manuals, and diagnostic software is included with the printer. The same tools may also be available as downloads from the manufacturer's website. Figure 7-9 show an example of what typically comes with a printer.

After completing this section, you will meet these objectives:

- Describe how to set up a printer.

- Explain how to power and connect the device using a local or network port.

- Describe how to install and update the device driver, firmware, and RAM.

- Identify configuration options and default settings.

- Describe how to optimize printer performance.

- Describe how to print a test page.

- Describe how to share a printer.

Figure 7-9   Printer Package Contents

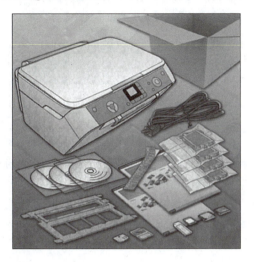

Describe How to Set Up a Printer

Although all types of printers are somewhat different to connect and configure, some procedures should be applied to all printers. After the printer has been unpacked and placed in position, connect it to the computer, network, or print server, and plug it into an electrical outlet. Print servers share a printer with other devices on a network. A print server can be a dedicated computer, a small network device, or integrated into the printer.

Follow these steps to set up a printer:

How To

Step 1.   Check the box to ensure that all required cables are provided.

Step 2.   Remove all packing materials from the printer.

Step 3.   Remove all plastic inserts from the consumables.

Step 4.   Ensure that the printer location will not cause overheating.

Step 5.   Install paper trays.

Step 6.   Install paper.

Step 7.   Read and follow the instruction manual.

Explain How to Power and Connect the Device Using a Local or Network Port

Now that the printer has been unpacked and placed in position, you must connect it to the computer, network, or print server and plug it into an electrical outlet by following these steps:

How To

Step 1.   Connect the appropriate data cable to the communication port on the back of the printer. If the printer has a USB, FireWire, or parallel port, connect the corresponding cable to the printer port.

Step 2.   Connect the other end of the data cable to the corresponding port on the back of the computer. If you are installing a network printer, connect the network cable to the network port.

Step 3.   After the data cable has been properly connected, attach the power cable to the printer, as shown in Figure 7-10.

Step 4.   Connect the other end of the power cable to an available electrical outlet.

Figure 7-10   Connecting the Data and Power Cables on a Printer

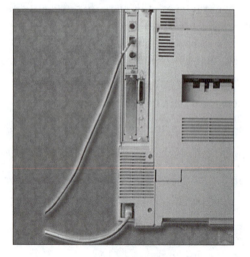

Caution

Never plug a printer into a UPS. The power surge that occurs when the printer is turned on will damage the UPS unit.

Describe How to Install and Update the Device Driver, Firmware, and RAM

After you have connected the power and data cables to the printer, the operating system may discover the printer and attempt to install a driver. If you have a driver disc from the manufacturer, use this driver. The driver that is included with the printer is usually more current than the drivers used by the operating system. Figure 7-11 shows the Add Printer Wizard, which can also be used to install the new printer.

Figure 7-11   Add Printer Wizard Screen

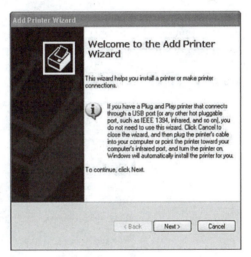

Printer Drivers

Printer drivers are software programs that enable the computer and the printer to communicate with each other. Drivers also provide an interface for the user to configure printer options. Every printer model has a unique driver. Printer manufacturers frequently update drivers to increase the printer's performance, to add options, or to fix problems. You can download new printer drivers from the manufacturer's website. To update and test a printer driver, follow these steps:

How To

Step 1.   Find out if a newer driver is available. Go to the printer manufacturer's website. Most manufacturer websites have a link from the main page to a page that offers drivers and support. Make sure that the driver is compatible with the computer that you are updating.

Step 2.   Download the driver. Download the printer driver files to your computer. Most driver files come in a compressed or "zipped" format. Download the file to a folder, and uncompress or "unzip" the contents. Save instructions or documentation to a separate folder on your computer.

Step 3.   Install the downloaded driver. Install the downloaded driver automatically or manually. Most printer drivers have a setup file that automatically searches the system for older drivers and replaces them with the new one. If no setup file is available, follow the directions supplied by the manufacturer.

Step 4.   Test the new printer driver. Run multiple tests to make sure that the printer works properly. Use a variety of applications to print different types of documents. Change and test each printer option.

Firmware

Firmware is a set of instructions stored on the printer. The firmware controls how the printer operates. Figure 7-12 shows a firmware upgrade utility. The procedure to upgrade firmware is very similar to the procedure for installing printer drivers.

Figure 7-12   Printer Firmware

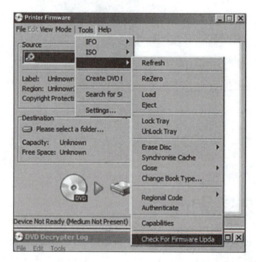

Printer Memory

Adding printer memory to a printer can improve printing speed by moving a print job off the printer's queue faster and allows the printer to handle more complex print jobs. All printers have at least some memory. Generally, the more memory a printer has, the more efficiently it operates. Here is a generic list of steps to follow to upgrade printer memory:

Step 1.   Turn off the printer.

Step 2.   Disconnect all cables.

Step 3.   Open the memory compartment.

Step 4.   Replace memory modules or add new modules.

Step 5.   Close the memory compartment.

Step 6.   Reconnect all cables.

Step 7.   Power on the printer.

Step 8.   Run a self-test.

Step 9.   Print a test page.

Consult the printer documentation for memory requirements:

- **Memory specifications**: Some printer manufacturers use standard types of memory, and other manufacturers use proprietary memory. Check the documentation for the type of memory, the speed of the memory, and the capacity of memory.

- **Memory population and availability**: Some printers have multiple memory slots. To find out how many memory slots are used and how many are available, you may need to open a compartment on the printer to check memory population.

Identify Configuration Options and Default Settings

Each printer may have different configurations and default options, as shown in Figure 7-13. Check the printer documentation for information about configurations and default settings.

Figure 7-13   Printer Settings

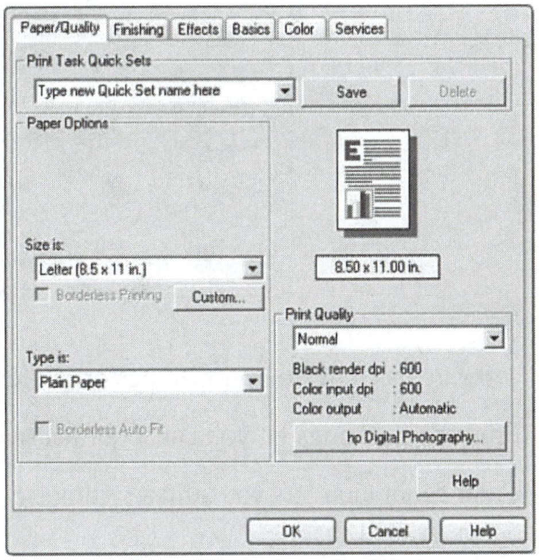

Here are some common configurations that are available for printers:

- **Paper type**: Standard, draft, gloss, or photo.

- **Print quality**: Draft, normal, photo, or automatic.

- **Color printing**: Multiple colors are used.

- **Black-and-white printing**: Only black ink is used.

- **Grayscale printing**: A color image is printed using only black ink in different shades.

- **Paper size**: Standard paper sizes or envelopes and business cards.

- **Paper orientation**: Landscape or portrait.

- **Print layout**: Normal, banner, booklet, or poster.

- **Duplex**: Normal or two-sided printing.

Describe How to Optimize Printer Performance

With printers, most optimization is completed through the software supplied with the drivers, as shown in Figure 7-14.

Figure 7-14   Color Calibration

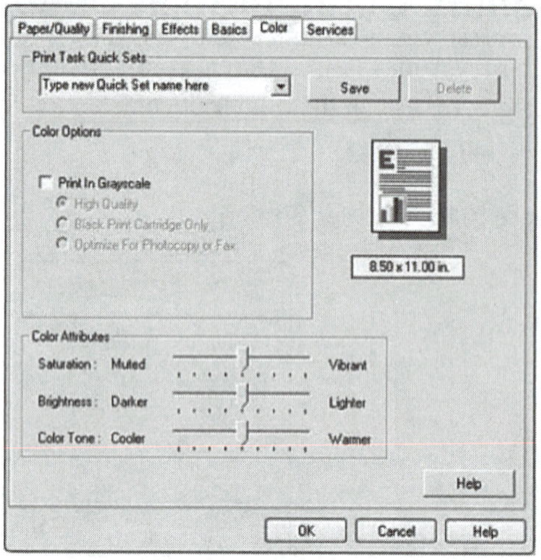

The software has tools to optimize performance:

- Print spool settings let you cancel or pause current print jobs in the printer queue.

- Color calibration lets you adjust settings to match the colors on the screen to the colors on the printed sheet.

- Paper orientation lets you select landscape or portrait image layout.

Describe How to Print a Test Page

After installing a printer, you should print a test page to verify that the printer is operating properly. The test page confirms that the driver software is installed and working correctly and that the printer and computer are communicating.

Printing a Test Page

To print a test page manually, choose **Start > Printers and Faxes** to display the Printers and Faxes menu.

Right-click the desired printer and choose **Properties**. Click the **General** tab and click **Print Test Page**, as shown in Figure 7-15.

A dialog box opens, asking you if the page printed correctly. If the page did not print, built-in help files will assist you in troubleshooting the problem.

Figure 7-15   Print Test Page

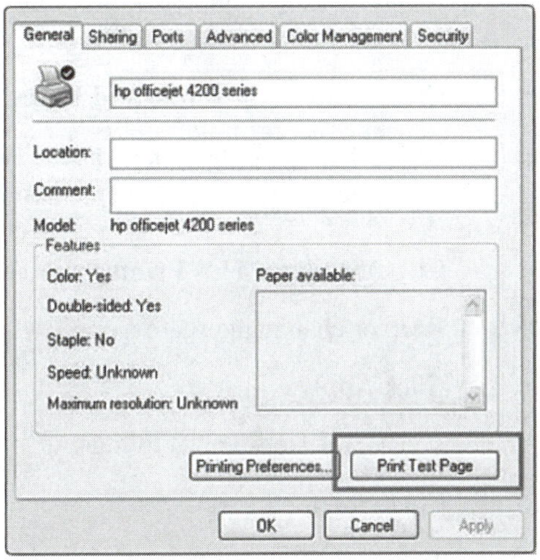

Printing from an Application

You can also test a printer by printing a test page from an application such as Notepad or WordPad. To access Notepad, choose **Start > Programs > Accessories > Notepad**.

A blank document opens. Enter some text in the document, and then print it by choosing **File > Print**.

Testing a Printer

You can also print from the command line to test the printer. Printing from the command line is limited to ASCII files, such as .txt and .bat files. Make a quick file named thefile.txt in Notepad. To send that file to the printer from the command line, choose **Start > Run**. The Run box appears. Enter **cmd** in the Run box, and then click **OK**. At the command-line prompt, enter the command **print thefile.txt**.

Testing the Printer from the Printer Panel

Most printers have a front panel with controls to allow you to generate test pages. This method of printing enables you to verify the printer operation separately from the network or computer. Consult the printer manufacturer's website or documentation to learn how to print a test page from the printer's front panel.

Describe How to Share a Printer

Printer sharing enables multiple users or clients to access a printer that they are not directly connected to. This arrangement reduces the expense on a network, because fewer printers are required.

Setting up printer sharing is simple with Windows XP. The following steps enable a computer to share a printer:

Step 1.   Choose **Start > Printers and Faxes**.

Step 2.   Right-click the printer, and choose **Properties**.

Step 3.   Click the **Sharing** tab.

Step 4.   Click the **Share This Printer** radio button, as shown in Figure 7-16.

Step 5.   Keep or change the share name.

Step 6.   Click **Apply**.

In Windows Vista, the steps are as follows:

Step 1.   Click **Start**.

Step 2.   Type **printer**.

Step 3.   Right-click **customize your printer**

Step 4.   Click the **Sharing** tab.

Step 5.   Keep or change the share name.

Step 6.   Click **Apply**.

In Windows 7, the steps are as follows:

Step 1.   Choose **Start > Printers**.

Step 2.   Double-click the printer.

Step 3.   Double-click **customize your printer**.

Step 4.   Click the **Sharing** tab.

Step 5.   Keep or change the share name.

Step 6.   Click **Apply**.

Figure 7-16   Printer Sharing

All the computers that use the shared printer must have the correct drivers installed. Drivers for other operating systems can be installed on the print server.

To connect to the printer from another computer on the network, choose **Start > Printers and Faxes > Add Printer**. The Add Printer Wizard appears. Follow the steps using the wizard.

Describe the Types of Scanners Currently Available

As a computer technician, you may be required to purchase, repair, or maintain a scanner. The customer may ask you to perform the following tasks:

- Select a scanner.

- Install and configure a scanner.

- Troubleshoot a scanner.

After completing this section, you will meet the following objectives:

- Describe scanner types, resolution, and interfaces.

- Describe all-in-one devices.

- Describe flatbed scanners.

- Describe handheld scanners.
- Describe drum scanners.

Describe Scanner Types, Resolution, and Interfaces

Scanners are used to convert printed data or images into an electronic data format that a computer can store or process as required. After an image has been scanned, it can be saved, modified, and even emailed, as you would with any other file. Although most scanners perform the same operation, different types of scanners are available, as shown in Figure 7-17 and described in the following list:

- *All-in-one*: Combination device that can scan, print, send faxes, and make copies
- *Flatbed*: Single-purpose device that converts hard-copy data to an electronic image
- *Drum*: High-quality scanner that spins film around a drum while a fixed laser or other beam of light captures the image as it spins
- *Handheld*: Portable scanner that is small enough to drag over text in books or other materials

Figure 7-17   Types of Scanners

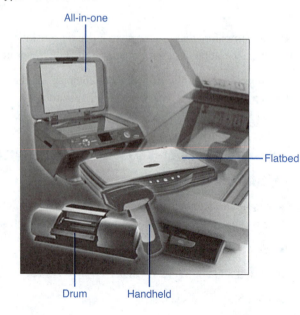

As with printers, the features, quality, and speed of the different types of scanners vary. Scanners typically create an RGB image that can be converted into common image formats such as JPEG, TIFF, BMP, and PNG. An RGB image has three channels: red, green, and blue. RGB channels generally follow the color receptors of the human eye and are used in computer displays and image scanners.

After the document is scanned, ***optical character recognition (OCR)*** software can create text documents. Once converted into text, the document can be edited with a word processor. A scanner's resolution is measured in dots per inch (dpi). As with printers, the higher the dpi, the better the image quality.

To allow communication of data, the scanner and computer must have compatible interfaces or a wireless network connection. The interfaces and cables used for printers typically are the same as the interfaces and cables used for scanners, as shown in Figure 7-18.

Figure 7-18   Scanner Interfaces and Cables

Describe All-in-One Devices

An all-in-one device combines the functionality of multiple devices into one physical piece of hardware. The devices may include media card readers and hard drives for storage. All-in-one devices generally include these functions:

- Scanner
- Printer
- Copier
- Fax

All-in-one devices typically are used in home-office environments or where space is limited. These devices often are used with a computer but can operate alone to copy and fax documents.

Table 7-6 lists some advantages and disadvantages of an all-in-one device.

Table 7-6   All-in-One Device Pros and Cons

Advantages	Disadvantages
All devices are built in: scanner, fax, and printer.	Not modular: if one device breaks, not all devices may be operational.
Low cost.	Not designed for heavy use.
	Upgrades are easier: software is designed for all devices.
	Connection and setup are easy: one port.

Describe Flatbed Scanners

A flatbed scanner, shown in Figure 7-19, is often used to scan books and photographs for archiving. An electronic image is acquired by placing the book or photograph facedown on the glass. The scanner head, consisting of an array of image sensors, lies beneath the glass and moves along the item, capturing the image.

Figure 7-19   Flatbed Scanner

Sheet feeders can be used with flatbed scanners to scan multiple images. A sheet feeder is a device that can be attached to some flatbed scanners to hold multiple sheets and feed them into the scanner one at a time. This feature allows for faster scanning; however, the image quality is usually not as good as that of a flatbed scanner that does not use a sheet feeder.

Table 7-7 lists some advantages and disadvantages of a flatbed scanner.

Table 7-7   Flatbed Scanner Pros and Cons

Advantages	Disadvantages
Most common type of desktop scanner.	Limited scanning size based on size of s canning bed.
Low cost.	
Connection and setup are easy: one port.	

Describe Handheld Scanners

A handheld scanner, as shown in Figure 7-20, is small and portable. It is difficult to smoothly scan an image using a handheld scanner. To scan an item, carefully pass the scanner head across the item that you want to scan. As with a flatbed scanner, digital images are made from the images collected by the handheld scanner.

Figure 7-20   Handheld Scanner

When you want to scan an item larger than the head of the handheld scanner, you must make more than one pass to capture the full image. It may be difficult to re-create the original image digitally when it is scanned in more than one pass. The images must be put back together to form a single image of the item that was scanned.

Table 7-8 lists some advantages and disadvantages of a handheld scanner.

Table 7-8   Handheld Scanner Pros and Cons

Advantages	Disadvantages
Small.	Multiple passes may need to be made to scan large items.
Portable.	Consistent image results vary, depending on the user experience.
Can scan images that cannot fit in or on any other type of scanner.	

Describe Drum Scanners

A drum scanner, shown in Figure 7-21, produces a high-quality transfer of an image. Drum scanners are usually used commercially but are being replaced by lower-priced, high-quality flatbed scanners. Many drum scanners are still in use for high-end reproductions, such as archiving photographs in museums.

Figure 7-21 Drum Scanner

To scan an image using a drum scanner, you attach the image to a revolving drum or load it into a supporting canister. The drum is rotated at high speed across optical scanners. The optical scanners move slowly across the drum surface until the entire image is captured. The captured image is then reproduced by the computer as a digital image file.

Table 7-9 lists some advantages and disadvantages of a drum scanner.

Table 7-9   Drum Scanner Pros and Cons

Advantages	Disadvantages
High-end image results	Expensive
	Difficult to operate

Describe the Installation and Configuration Process for Scanners

When you purchase a scanner, the installation and configuration information is usually supplied by the manufacturer. An installation CD that includes drivers, manuals, and diagnostic software is included with the scanner. The same tools may also be available as downloads from the manufacturer's website.

After completing this section, you will meet the following objectives:

- Explain how to power and connect a scanner.
- Describe how to install and update the device driver.
- Identify configuration options and default settings.

Explain How to Power and Connect a Scanner

Like printers, scanners can connect to a computer using the USB, FireWire, network, wireless network, or parallel port interface. Some scanners may connect using a SCSI interface.

Scanners that are built into an all-in-one device should be plugged directly into an AC wall outlet. This provides the AC current necessary to operate the all-in-one device. Other types of scanners may acquire power through the USB or FireWire connector.

After unpacking the scanner, connect the appropriate power and data cables. Use the scanner documentation as your guide, or check the manufacturer's website for instructions.

Describe How to Install and Update the Device Driver

As soon as you have connected and started the scanner, the computer operating system might be able to discover the scanner through the plug-and-play process. If the scanner is discovered, the operating system might automatically install a driver.

After you set up a scanner, install the driver software that the manufacturer includes with the scanner. This driver is usually more current than the drivers on your computer. It may also provide more functionality than the basic driver from Windows.

As with a printer, you might want to install drivers from the manufacturer's website to gain additional functionality, diagnostic tools, and troubleshooting utilities. Download software from the manufacturer's website, and follow any directions provided to install the software and utilities for your scanner. Some scanning software automatically downloads and installs updated software, drivers, or firmware. Follow the directions provided by the update utility to install these files.

Lab 7.4.2: Install All-in-One Device and Software

In this lab, you install an all-in-one device. You find, download, and update the driver and the software for the all-in-one device. Refer to the lab in *IT Essentials: PC Hardware and Software Lab Manual, Fourth Edition.* You may perform this lab now or wait until the end of the chapter.

Identify Configuration Options and Default Settings

Scanners have configuration options and default settings that differ between model types and manufacturers.

A scanner might come with a basic graphic editing software package for editing photographs and other images. Editing software packages may include optical character recognition (OCR) software that allows text in a scanned image to be manipulated.

Some of the configuration options that might be available on a scanner are as follows:

- Color, grayscale, or black-and-white scanning
- One-touch scanning into your choice of software

- Quality and resolution choices

- Sheet feeders

As shown in Figure 7-22, color calibration between devices is important so that you see true representations of color. To calibrate a scanner, scan a graphic that contains specific colors. A calibration application installed on the computer compares the scanner's output against the known colors of the sample graphic on the display. The software adjusts the scanner's color accordingly. When your scanner, monitor, and printer treat the same colors in the same way, the image you print matches the image you scan.

Figure 7-22   Scanner Calibration

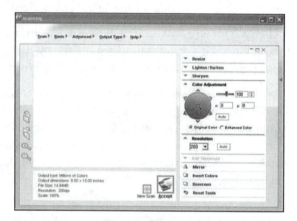

Identify and Apply Common Preventive Maintenance Techniques for Printers and Scanners

Printers and scanners have many moving parts that can wear out over time or through extended use. They must be maintained regularly to operate correctly.

Moving parts can be affected by dust and other air particles. Clean printers and scanners regularly to avoid downtime, loss of productivity, and high repair costs.

After completing this section, you will meet the following objectives:

- Describe printer maintenance.

- Describe scanner maintenance.

Describe Printer Maintenance

Printers have many moving parts and require a higher level of maintenance than most other electronic devices. Impurities produced by the printer collect on the internal components. Over time, if the impurities are not removed, the printer may malfunction. The maintenance schedule for a printer can be found in the manual or on the manufacturer's website.

Caution

Be sure to unplug the printer from the electrical source before beginning any type of maintenance.

Most printers come with printer monitoring and diagnostic software from the manufacturer that can help you maintain the printer. Observe the guidelines from the manufacturer for cleaning the following printer and scanner components:

- Printer roller surfaces
- Printer and scanner paper-handling mechanisms

The type and quality of paper and ink used can affect the printer's life:

- **Paper selection**: High-quality paper can help ensure that the printer operates efficiently and for a long time. Many types of printer paper are available, including inkjet and laser. The printer manufacturer may recommend the type of paper that should be used for best results. Some papers, especially photo paper and transparencies, have a right side and a wrong side. Load the paper according to the manufacturer's instructions.

- **Ink selection**: The manufacturer recommends the brand and type of ink that you should use. If the wrong type of ink is installed, the printer may not work, or the print quality may be reduced. You should avoid refilling the ink cartridges, because the ink may leak.

Describe Scanner Maintenance

The scanner surface should be kept clean. If the glass becomes dirty, consult the manufacturer's user manual for cleaning recommendations. To prevent liquid from leaking into the scanner case, do not spray glass cleaner directly on the device. Dampen a cloth with the cleaner, and then apply the cleaner gently to the glass.

If the inside of the glass becomes dirty, check the manual for instructions on how to open the unit or remove the glass from the scanner. If possible, thoroughly clean both sides of the glass and replace the glass as it was originally set in the scanner. When the scanner is not in use, keep the lid closed. Keep a handheld scanner in a safe place. Also, never lay anything heavy on a scanner, because you may damage the casing or internal parts.

Troubleshoot Printers and Scanners

With printer and scanner problems, a technician must be able to determine whether the problem exists with the device, the cable connection, or the computer that it is attached to. Follow the steps outlined in this section to accurately identify, repair, and document the problem.

After completing this section, you will meet these objectives:

- Review the troubleshooting process.
- Identify common problems and solutions.

Review the Troubleshooting Process

Printer problems can result from a combination of hardware, software, and network issues. Computer technicians must be able to analyze the problem and determine the cause of the error to repair the printer.

The first step in the troubleshooting process is to identify the problem. After you have talked to the customer, you can establish a theory of probable causes. After you have developed some theories about what is wrong, test your theories to determine the cause of the problem. If a quick procedure does correct the problem, you can verify full system functionality. If a quick procedure does not correct the problem, you might need to research the problem further to establish the exact cause.

After you have determined the exact cause of the problem, establish a plan of action to resolve the problem and implement the solution. After you have corrected the problem, verify full functionality and, if applicable, implement preventive measures.

In the final step of the troubleshooting process, you must document your findings, actions, and outcomes.

Identify Common Problems and Solutions

Printer or scanner problems can be attributed to hardware, software, networks, or some combination of the three. You will resolve some types of printer and scanner problems more often than others. Table 7-10 is a chart of common printer and scanner problems and solutions.

Table 7-10   Common Printer and Scanner Problems and Solutions

Identify the Problem	Probable Causes	Possible Solutions
An application document does not print.	There is a documentation error in the print queue.	Manage the print jobs by cancelling the documents from the print queue and pint again.
Printer cannot be added or there is a print spooler	The printer service is stopped or not working properly.	Start the print spooler and if necessary reboot the computer. error.
Printer jobs are sent to the print queue but are not printed.	The printer has been installed on the wrong port.	Use printer properties and settings to configure the printer port.
Print queue is functioning properly, but the printer does not print.	There is a bad cable connection.	Check for bent pins on the printer cable and check the printer cable connections to the printer and the computer.
Printer is printing unknown characters or does not print a test page.	Wrong or outdated printer driver is installed.	Uninstall incorrect print driver and install correct driver.
Printer prints unknown characters or does not print anything.	Printer may be plugged into a UPS.	Plug the printer directly into the wall outlet or surge protector.
	Incorrect print driver is installed.	Uninstall incorrect print driver and install correct driver.
	Printer cables are loose.	Secure printer cables.
	No paper in printer.	Add paper to the printer.
Paper jams when printing.	Printer is dirty.	The wrong paper type is being used.
	Humidity causes the paper to stick together.	Clean the printer.
		Replace paper with the manufacture's recommended paper type.
		Insert new paper in the paper tray.

Summary

This chapter discussed various types of printers and scanners. You learned that there are many different types and sizes of printers and scanners, each with different capabilities, speeds, and uses. You also learned that both printers and scanners can be connected directly to computers, as well as shared across a network. This chapter also introduced the different types of cables and interfaces available to connect a printer or scanner. Other facts about printers and scanners covered in this chapter include the following:

- Some printers and scanners have low output and are adequate for home use, whereas other printers and scanners have high output and are designed for commercial use.

- Printers may have different speeds and quality of print.

- Older printers and scanners use parallel cables and ports. Newer printers and scanners typically connect to computers through USB, FireWire, NIC, or wireless NICs.

- Larger printers and scanners may also have a network connection.

- Newer printers and scanners are plug-and-play. The computer automatically installs the necessary drivers.

- If the computer does not automatically install the device drivers, you have to supply the drivers on a CD or download them from the manufacturer's website.

- Most optimization is done through software drivers and utilities.

- After you have set up the printer or scanner, you can share the device with other users on the network. This arrangement is cost efficient because there is no need for every user to have a printer or scanner.

- A good preventive maintenance program will extend the life of printers and scanners and keep them performing well.

- Troubleshooting printer and laptop problems requires the technician to identify, repair, and document the problem. Troubleshooting steps include gathering data from the customer, verifying the obvious issues, trying quick solutions first, gathering data from the computer and printer, evaluating the problem, implementing the solution, and closing with the customer.

- Consulting previous documentation to see whether the problem has been identified and if a solution already exists.

Summary of Exercises

This is a summary of the Labs, Worksheets, Remote Technician exercises, Class Discussions, Virtual Desktop activities, and Virtual Laptop activities associated with this chapter.

Labs

The following lab covers material from this chapter. Refer to the lab in *IT Essentials: PC Hardware and Software Lab Manual, Fourth Edition*.

Lab 7.4.2: Install All-in-One Device and Software

Check Your Understanding

You can find the answers to these questions in the appendix, "Answers to Check Your Understanding Questions."

1. Which technology do dot-matrix printers use?

    A. Digital

    B. Drop electrostatic spray

    C. Electrophotographic

    D. Ink melting

    E. Impact

2. Which phase of the laser printing process includes applying toner to the latent image?

    A. Cleaning

    B. Conditioning

    C. Developing

    D. Fusing

    E. Transferring

    F. Writing

3. What are three disadvantages of impact printers?

    A. Expensive consumables

    B. High power consumption

    C. Limited color capability

    D. Noisy printing

    E. Slow printing

    F. Unable to use continuous-feed paper

4. Which type of printer melts ink and sprays it through a nozzle onto a drum to transfer an image onto paper?

A. Fusion ink

B. Impact

C. Inkjet

D. Laser

E. Solid-ink

F. Thermal

5. Which type of printing process uses solid sheets of ink that change directly to gas?

A. Dye sublimation

B. Impact

C. Inkjet

D. Laser

E. Solid-ink

F. Thermal

6. Which peripheral is used to convert paper documents into electronic files?

A. Digital reader

B. Printer

C. Projector

D. Scanner

7. Refer to Figure 7-23. A customer purchases the scanner shown and discovers that it is limited to converting hard-copy data into electronic images. Which type of scanner has the customer purchased?

Figure 7-23   Figure for Question 7

A. All-in-one

B. Flatbed

C. Handheld

D. Laser

8. How is the speed of a laser printer measured?

A. Dots per minute

B. Pages per minute

C. Pixels per second

D. Pages per second

E. Pages per week

CHAPTER 8

Fundamental Networks

Objectives

Upon completion of this chapter, you should be able to answer the following questions:

- What are the principles of networking?
- What are the different types of networks?
- What are the basic networking concepts and technologies?
- What makes up the physical components of a network?
- What are the LAN topologies and architectures?
- What are some of the standards organizations?
- What are the Ethernet standards?

- What are the OSI and TCP/IP data models?
- How do I configure a NIC and a modem?
- What are the names, purposes, and characteristics of other technologies used to establish connectivity?
- How do I identify and apply common preventive maintenance techniques used with networks?
- How do I troubleshoot a network?

Key Terms

This chapter uses the following key terms. You can find the definitions in the Glossary.

continues

This chapter provides an overview of network principles, standards, and purposes. The following types of networks are discussed in this chapter:

- Local-area network (LAN)

- Wide-area network (WAN)

- Wireless LAN (WLAN)

This chapter discusses the different types of network topologies, protocols, and logical models as well as the hardware needed to create a network. Configuration, troubleshooting, and preventive maintenance also are covered. In addition, you will learn about network software, communication methods, and hardware relationships.

After completing this chapter, you will meet these objectives:

- Explain the principles of networking.

- Describe types of networks.

- Describe basic networking concepts and technologies.

- Describe the physical components of a network.

- Describe LAN topologies and architectures.

- Identify standards organizations.

- Identify Ethernet standards.

- Explain OSI and TCP/IP data models.

- Describe how to configure a NIC and a modem.

- Identify names, purposes, and characteristics of other technologies used to establish connectivity.

- Identify and apply common preventive maintenance techniques used for networks.

- Troubleshoot a network.

Explain the Principles of Networking

Networks are systems that are formed by links. Websites that allow individuals to link to each other's pages are called social networking sites. A set of related ideas can be called a conceptual network. The connections you have with all your friends can be called your personal network.

People use the following networks every day:

- Mail delivery system

- Telephone system

- Public transportation system

- Corporate computer network

- The Internet

Computers can be linked by networks to share data and resources. A network can be as simple as two computers connected by a single cable or as complex as hundreds of computers connected to devices that control the flow of information. Networks can include general-purpose computers, such as PCs and servers, as well as devices with more specific functions, including printers, phones, televisions, and game consoles.

All data, voice, video, and converged networks share information and use various methods to direct how this information flows. The information on the network goes from one place to another, sometimes via different paths, to arrive at the appropriate destination.

The public transportation system is similar to a data network. The cars, trucks, and other vehicles are like the messages that travel within the network. Each driver defines a starting point (source) and an ending point (destination). Within this system are rules such as stop signs and traffic lights that control the flow from the source to the destination.

After completing this section, you will meet these objectives:

- Define computer networks.

- Explain the benefits of networking.

Define Computer Networks

A computer data network is a collection of hosts connected by *networking* devices. A host is any device that sends and receives information on the network. Peripherals are devices that are connected to hosts. Some devices can serve as either hosts or peripherals. For example, a printer connected to your laptop that is on a network is acting as a peripheral. If the printer is connected directly to a networking device, such as a hub, switch, or router, it is acting as a host.

Computer networks are used globally in businesses, homes, schools, and government agencies. Many of these networks are connected to each other through the Internet.

Many different types of devices can connect to a network:

- Desktop computers

- Laptop computers

- Printers

- Scanners

- PDAs

- Smartphones

- File/print servers

A network can share many different types of resources:

- Services, such as printing or scanning

- Storage space on removable devices, such as hard drives or optical drives

- Applications, such as databases

You can use networks to access information stored on other computers, print documents using shared printers, and synchronize the calendar between your computer and your smartphone.

Network devices are linked using a variety of connections:

- Copper cabling uses electrical signals to transmit data between devices.

- Fiber-optic cabling uses glass or plastic wire, also called fiber, to carry information as light pulses.

- Wireless connections use radio signals, infrared, or laser technologies.

Explain the Benefits of Networking

The benefits of networking computers and other devices include lower costs and increased productivity. With networks, resources can be shared, which results in less duplication and corruption of data. The following are some benefits of using networks:

- **Fewer peripherals are needed**: Figure 8-1 shows that many devices can be connected on a network. Each computer on the network does not need its own printer, scanner, or backup device. Multiple printers can be set up in a central location and can be shared among the network users. All network users send print jobs to a central print server that manages the print requests. The print server can distribute print jobs over multiple printers or can queue jobs that require a specific printer.

- **Increased communication capabilities**: Networks provide several different collaboration tools that can be used to communicate between network users. Online collaboration tools include email, forums and chats, voice and video, and instant messaging. With these tools, users can communicate with friends, family, and colleagues.

- **Avoid file duplication and corruption**: A server manages network resources. Servers store data and share it with users on a network. Confidential or sensitive data can be protected and shared with the users who have permission to access that data. Document-tracking software can be used to prevent users from overwriting files, or changing files that others are accessing at the same time.

- **Lower-cost licensing**: Application licensing can be expensive for individual computers. Many software vendors offer site licenses for networks, which can dramatically reduce the cost of software. The site license allows a group of people or an entire organization to use the application for a single fee.

- **Centralized administration**: Centralized administration reduces the number of people needed to manage the devices and data on the network, reducing time and cost to the company. Individual network users do not need to manage their own data and devices. One administrator can control the data, devices, and permissions of users on the network. Backing up data is easier because the data is stored in a central location.

- **Conserve resources**: Data processing can be distributed across many computers to prevent one computer from becoming overloaded with processing tasks.

Figure 8-1   Shared Resources

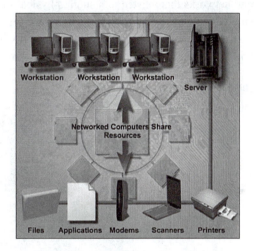

Describe Types of Networks

Data networks continue to evolve in complexity, use, and design. Different types of networks have different descriptive names. A computer network is identified by the following specific characteristics:

- The area it serves

- How the data is stored

- How the resources are managed

- How the network is organized

- The type of networking devices used

- The type of media used to connect the devices

After completing this section, you will meet these objectives:

- Describe a LAN.

- Describe a WAN.

- Describe a WLAN.

- Explain peer-to-peer networks.

- Explain client/server networks.

Describe a LAN

A *local-area network (LAN)* is a group of interconnected devices that is under the same administrative control, as shown in Figure 8-2. In the past, LANs were considered to be small networks that existed in a single physical location. Although LANs can be as small as a single local network installed in a home or small office, over time, the definition of LANs has evolved to include interconnected local networks consisting of many hundreds of devices, installed in multiple buildings and locations.

Figure 8-2   Local-Area Network

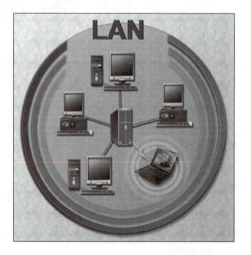

Remember that all the local networks within a LAN are under one administrative control group that governs the security and access control policies that are in force on the network. In this context, the word "local" in local-area network refers to local consistent control rather than being physically close to each other. Devices in a LAN may be physically close, but this is not a requirement.

Describe a WAN

Wide-area networks (WAN) are networks that connect LANs in geographically separated locations, as shown in Figure 8-3. The most common example of a WAN is the Internet. The Internet is a large WAN that is composed of millions of interconnected LANs. *Internet service providers (ISP)* are used to interconnect these LANs at different locations.

Figure 8-3   Wide-Area Network

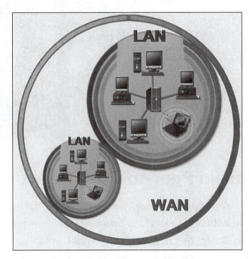

Describe a WLAN

In a traditional LAN, devices are interconnected using copper cabling. In some environments, installing copper cabling may not be practical, desirable, or even possible. In these situations, wireless devices are used to transmit and receive data using radio waves. These networks are called *wireless LANs (WLAN)*. Figure 8-4 shows a WLAN. As with LANs, on a WLAN you can share resources, such as files and printers, and access the Internet.

In a WLAN, wireless devices connect to access points within a specified area. Access points typically are connected to the network using copper cabling. Instead of providing copper cabling to every network host, only the *wireless access point (WAP)* is connected to the network with copper cabling. WLAN coverage can be small and limited to the area of a room or can have greater range.

Figure 8-4   Wireless Local-Area Network

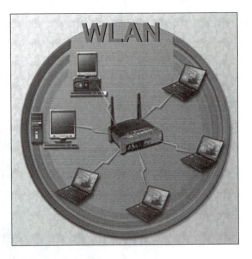

Explain Peer-to-Peer Networks

In a *peer-to-peer network*, devices are connected directly to each other without any addi-tional networking devices between them, as shown in Figure 8-5. If you needed a third computer on this network, you would need to use a hub or a switch. Peer-to-peer refers to how the network is managed. In this type of network, each device has equivalent capabilities and responsibilities. Individual users are responsible for their own resources and can decide which data and devices to share. Because individual users are responsible for the resources on their own computers, the network has no central point of control or administration.

Figure 8-5   Peer-to-Peer Network

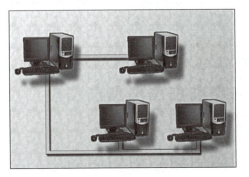

Peer-to-peer networks work best in environments with ten or fewer computers. Because individual users are in control of their own computers, there is no need to hire a dedicated network administrator.

Peer-to-peer networks have several disadvantages:

- They have no centralized network administration, which makes it difficult to determine who controls resources on the network.

- They have no centralized security. Each computer must use separate security measures for data protection.

- The network becomes more complex and difficult to manage as the number of computers on the network increases.

- There may be no centralized data storage. Separate data backups must be maintained. This responsibility falls on the individual users.

Peer-to-peer networks still exist inside larger networks today. Even on a large client network, users can still share resources directly with other users without using a network server. In your home, if you have more than one computer, you can set up a peer-to-peer network. You can share files with other computers, send messages between them, and print documents to a shared printer.

Explain Client/Server Networks

In a *client/server network*, shown in Figure 8-6, the client requests information or services from the server. The server provides the requested information or service to the client. Servers on a client/server network commonly perform some of the processing work for client machines, such as sorting through a database before delivering only the records requested by the client.

Figure 8-6   Client/Server Network

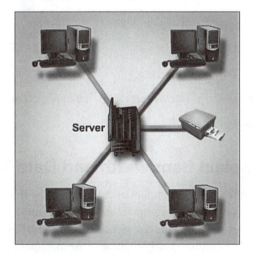

One example of a client/server network is a corporate environment in which employees use a company email server to send, receive, and store email. The email client on an employee computer issues a request to the email server for any unread email. The server responds by sending the requested email to the client.

In a client/server model, the servers are maintained by network administrators. Data backups and security measures are implemented by the network administrator. The network administrator also controls user access to the network resources. All the data on the network is stored on a centralized file server. Shared printers on the network are managed by a centralized print server. Network users with the proper permissions can access both the data and shared printers. Each user must provide an authorized username and password to gain access to network resources that he or she is permitted to use.

For data protection, an administrator performs a routine backup of all the files on the servers. If a computer crashes, or data is lost, the administrator can easily recover the data from a recent backup.

Describe Basic Networking Concepts and Technologies

As a computer technician, you will be required to configure and troubleshoot computers on a network. To effectively configure a computer on the network, you should understand *IP addressing*, *protocols*, and other network concepts.

After completing this section, you will meet these objectives:

- Explain bandwidth and data transmission.
- Describe IP addressing.
- Define DHCP.
- Define NAT.
- Describe Internet protocols and applications.
- Define ICMP.

Explain Bandwidth and Data Transmission

Bandwidth is the amount of data that can be transmitted within a fixed time period. When data is sent over a computer network, it is broken into small chunks called *packets*. Each packet contains *headers*. A *header* is information added to each packet that contains the packet's source and destination. A header also contains information that describes how to put all the packets back together again at the destination. The size of the bandwidth determines the amount of information that can be transmitted.

Bandwidth is measured in bits per second and usually is denoted by any of the following units of measure:

- *bps* is *bits per second*.

- *kbps* is *kilobits per second*.

- *Mbps* is *megabits per second*.

- *Gbps* is *gigabits per second*.

Note

1 byte is equal to 8 bits and is abbreviated with a capital *B*. 1 MBps is approximately 8 Mbps.

Figure 8-7 shows how bandwidth on a network can be compared to a highway. In this example, the cars and trucks represent the data. The number of lanes on the highway represents the number of cars that can travel on the highway at the same time. An eight-lane highway can handle four times the number of cars that a two-lane highway can.

Figure 8-7   Highway Analogy

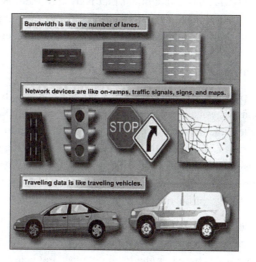

The data that is transmitted over the network can flow using one of the following three modes:

- *Simplex*: Simplex, also called unidirectional, is a single one-way transmission. An example of simplex transmission is the signal that is sent from a TV station to your TV.

- *Half duplex*: When data flows in one direction at a time, this is known as half duplex. With half duplex, the communications channel allows alternating transmission in two directions, but not in both directions simultaneously. Two-way radios, such as police and emergency communications mobile radios, work with half-duplex transmissions.

When you press the button on the microphone to transmit, you cannot hear the person on the other end. If people at both ends try to talk at the same time, neither transmission gets through.

- *Full duplex*: When data flows in both directions at the same time, this is known as full duplex. Although the data flows in both directions, the bandwidth is measured in only one direction. A network cable with 100 Mbps in full-duplex mode has a bandwidth of 100 Mbps. A telephone conversation is an example of full-duplex communication. Both people can talk and be heard at the same time.

Full-duplex networking technology increases network performance because data can be sent and received at the same time. Broadband technology allows multiple signals to travel on the same wire simultaneously. *Broadband* technologies, such as *digital subscriber line (DSL)* and cable, operate in full-duplex mode. With a DSL connection, for example, users can download data to their computer and talk on the telephone at the same time.

Describe IP Addressing

An *IP address* is a number that is used to identify a device on the network. Each device on a network must have a unique IP address to communicate with other network devices. As noted earlier, a host is a device that sends or receives information on the network. Network devices are devices that move data across the network, including hubs, switches, and routers.

A person's fingerprints usually do not change. They provide a label or address for the person's physical aspect—the body. A person's mailing address, on the other hand, relates to where the person lives or picks up mail. This address can change. On a host, the *Media Access Control (MAC) address* (explained in the section, "Manual Configuration") is assigned to the host NIC and is known as the physical address. The physical address remains the same regardless of where the host is placed on the network in the same way that fingerprints remain with someone regardless of where she goes.

The IP address is similar to someone's mailing address. It is known as a logical address because it is logically assigned based on the host location. The IP address, or network address, is based on the local network and is assigned to each host by a network administrator. This process is similar to the local government assigning a street address based on the logical description of the city or village and neighborhood.

Dotted Decimal

An IP address consists of a series of 32 binary bits (1s and 0s). It is very difficult for humans to read a binary IP address. For this reason, the 32 bits are grouped into four 8-bit bytes called octets. An IP address, even in this grouped format, is hard for humans to read, write, and remember. Therefore, each octet is presented as its decimal value, separated by a decimal point or period. This format is called dotted-decimal notation. When a host is configured with an IP address, it is entered as a dotted-decimal number, such as 192.168.1.5. Imagine if you had to enter the 32-bit binary equivalent of this: 11000000101010000000000100000101. If you mistyped just 1 bit, the address would be different, and the host may not be able to communicate on the network.

Classful Subnetting

The logical 32-bit IP address is *hierarchical* and is composed of two parts. The first part identifies the network, and the second part identifies a host on that network. Both parts are required in an IP address. For example, if a host has an IP address of 192.168.18.57, the first three octets, 192.168.18, identify the network portion of the address, and the last octet, 57, identifies the host. This is called hierarchical addressing, because the network portion indicates the network on which each unique host address is located. Routers only need to know how to reach each network, not the location of each individual host.

IP addresses are divided into the following five classes:

- Class A is for large networks, implemented by large companies and some countries.

- Class B is for medium-sized networks, implemented by universities.

- Class C is for small networks, implemented by ISPs for customer subscriptions.

- Class D is for special use for multicasting.

- Class E is used for experimental testing.

The point of subnetting is to create more networks. This is accomplished by defining which bits are used to name the network and which are used to name the host. That division is created by using a subnet mask.

Subnet Mask

The *subnet mask* indicates the network portion of an IP address. Like the IP address, the subnet mask is a dotted-decimal number. An IP address must work in tandem with a subnet mask because network devices compare the two numbers to determine the network bits or the host bits. The "255" is equal to 8 bits "turned on" indicated by the number 1. The "0" represents 8 bits in the "off" state indicated by the number 0. When the IP address is compared to the subnet mask, the 1s indicate the network portion and the 0s indicate the host portion. Usually all hosts within a LAN use the same subnet mask. Figure 8-8 shows default subnet masks for usable IP addresses that are mapped to the first three classes of IP addresses:

- **255.0.0.0**: Class A, which indicates that the first octet of the IP address is the network portion

- **255.255.0.0**: Class B, which indicates that the first two octets of the IP address are the network portion

- **255.255.255.0**: Class C, which indicates that the first three octets of the IP address are the network portion

The number in the first octet determines the class of the address. If the first octet is between 0 and 126, it is a Class A address. If the first octet is between 128 and 191, it is a Class B address. If the first octet is a number between 192 and 223, then it is a Class C address.

Figure 8-8   IP Address Classes

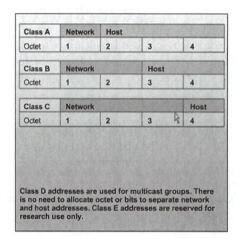

If an organization owns one Class B network but needs to provide IP addresses for four LANs, the organization would have to subdivide the Class B address into four smaller parts. Subnetting is a logical division of a network. It provides the means to divide a network, and the subnet mask specifies how it is subdivided. An experienced network administrator typically performs subnetting. After the subnetting scheme has been created, the proper IP addresses and subnet masks can be configured on the hosts in the four LANs. These skills are taught in the Cisco Networking Academy courses related to CCNA-level networking skills.

Manual Configuration

To manually enter an IP address on a host, go to the TCP/IP settings in the Properties window for the network interface card (NIC). The NIC is the hardware that enables a computer to connect to a network. It has an address called the MAC address. Whereas the IP address is a logical address that is defined by the network administrator, a MAC address is "burned in," or permanently programmed into the NIC when it is manufactured. The IP address of a NIC can be changed, but the MAC address never changes.

If more than a few computers comprise the LAN, manually configuring IP addresses for every host on the network can be time consuming and prone to errors. In this case, using a Dynamic Host Configuration Protocol (DHCP) server would automatically assign IP addresses and greatly simplify the addressing process.

Worksheet 8.3.2: Identify IP Address Classes

In this worksheet, you identify the IP address class for an IP address. Refer to the worksheet in *IT Essentials: PC Hardware and Software Lab Manual, Fourth Edition.* You may perform this worksheet now or wait until the end of the chapter.

Define DHCP

Dynamic Host Configuration Protocol (DHCP) is a software utility used to dynamically assign IP addresses to network devices. This dynamic process eliminates the need to manually assign IP addresses. A DHCP server can be set up and the hosts can be configured to automatically obtain an IP address. When a computer is set to obtain an IP address automatically, all the other IP addressing configuration boxes are dimmed, as shown in Figure 8-9. The server maintains a list of IP addresses to assign, and it manages the process so that every device on the network receives a unique IP address. Each address is held for a predetermined amount of time. When the time expires, the DHCP server can use this address for any computer that joins the network.

Figure 8-9   TCP/IP Properties

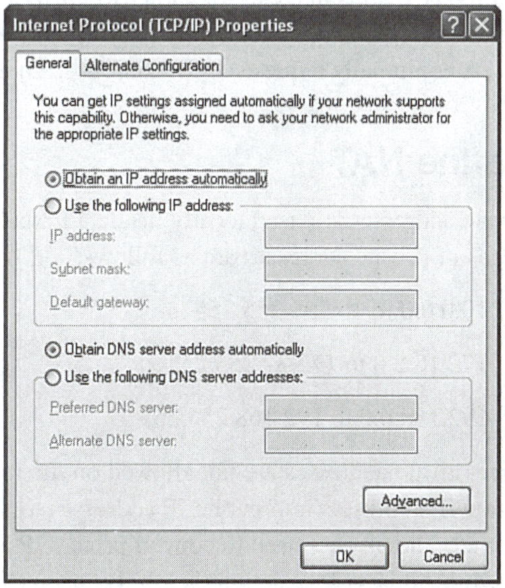

This is the IP address information that a DHCP server can assign to hosts:

- IP address

- Subnet mask

- Default gateway

- Optional values, such as a *Domain Name System (DNS)* server address

The DHCP server receives a request from a host. The server then selects IP address information from a set of predefined addresses that is stored in a database. After the IP address information is selected, the DHCP server offers these values to the requesting host on the network. If the host accepts the offer, the DHCP server leases the IP address for a specific period of time.

Using a DHCP server simplifies the administration of a network because the software keeps track of IP addresses. Automatically configuring TCP/IP also reduces the possibility of assigning duplicate or invalid IP addresses. Before a computer on the network can take advantage of the DHCP server services, the computer must be able to identify the server on the local network. You can configure a computer to accept an IP address from a DHCP server by clicking the **Obtain an IP Address Automatically** option in the NIC configuration window, as shown in Figure 8-9.

If your computer cannot communicate with the DHCP server to obtain an IP address, the Windows operating system automatically assigns a private IP address. If your computer is assigned an IP address in the range of 169.254.0.0 to 169.254.255.255, it can communicate with only other computers in the same range. An example of when these private addresses would be useful is in a classroom lab where you want to prevent access outside to your network. This operating system feature is called Automatic Private IP Addressing (APIPA). APIPA continually requests an IP address from a DHCP server for your computer.

Define NAT

Private addresses are used locally inside a LAN but cannot be used on the Internet. The ranges of private addresses are as follows:

- 10.0.0.0 to 10.255.255.255

- 172.16.0.0 to 172.31.255.255

- 192.168.0.0 to 192.168.255.255

Since private addresses are not allowed on the Internet, a process is needed for translating private IP addresses into public IP addresses to allow local clients to communicate over the Internet. The process used to convert private IP addresses to public IP addresses is called Network Address Translation (NAT). By using NAT, a router is able to translate many internal IP addresses to the same public address.

Describe Internet Protocols and Applications

A protocol is a set of rules. Internet protocols are sets of rules governing communication within and between computers on a network. Protocol specifications define the format of the messages that are exchanged. A letter sent through the postal system also uses protocols. Part of the protocol specifies where on the envelope the delivery address needs to be written. If the delivery address is written in the wrong place, the letter cannot be delivered. If the letter is traveling between cities, the street address is unimportant for that step of the journey; similarly, when a packet travels between networks, the host part of the address is unimportant and thus is masked. And when a letter is delivered to a specific mailbox, the relevant information is the street address, not the city, state, and ZIP information; similarly, local packet delivery focuses on the host portion of the address.

These are the main functions of protocols:

- Identifying errors

- Compressing the data

- Deciding how the data is to be sent

- Addressing the data

- Deciding how to announce sent and received data

To understand how networks and the Internet work, you must be familiar with the commonly used protocols. These protocols are used to browse the web, send and receive email, and transfer data files. You will encounter other protocols as your experience in IT grows, but they are not used as often as the common protocols described here:

- *TCP/IP*: The TCP/IP suite of protocols has become the dominant standard for internetworking. TCP/IP represents a set of public standards that specifies how packets of information are exchanged between computers over one or more networks.

- **Internetwork Packet Exchange/Sequenced Packet Exchange (IPX/SPX)**: IPX/SPX is the protocol suite originally employed by Novell Corporation's network operating system, NetWare. It delivers functions similar to those included in TCP/IP. Novell in its current releases supports the TCP/IP suite. A large installed base of NetWare networks continues to use IPX/SPX.

- **NetBIOS Extended User Interface (NetBEUI)**: NetBEUI is a protocol used primarily on small Windows NT networks. NetBEUI cannot be routed or used by routers to talk to each other on a large network. NetBEUI is suitable for small peer-to-peer networks, involving a few computers directly connected to each other. It can be used in conjunction with another routable protocol such as TCP/IP. This gives the network administrator the advantages of the high performance of NetBEUI within the local network and the ability to communicate beyond the LAN over TCP/IP.

- **AppleTalk**: AppleTalk is a protocol suite to network Macintosh computers. It is composed of a comprehensive set of protocols that spans the seven layers of the Open Systems Interconnection (OSI) reference model. The AppleTalk protocol was designed to run over LocalTalk, which is the Apple LAN physical topology. This protocol is also designed to run over major LAN types, notably Ethernet and Token Ring.

- *Hypertext Transfer Protocol (HTTP)*: HTTP governs how files such as text, graphics, sound, and video are exchanged on the World Wide Web. The Internet Engineering Task Force (IETF) developed the standards for HTTP.

- *File Transfer Protocol (FTP)*: FTP provides services for file transfer and manipulation. FTP allows multiple simultaneous connections to remote file systems.

- **Secure Shell (SSH):** SSH is used to securely connect to a remote computer.

- *Telnet*: Telnet is an application used to connect to a remote computer that lacks security features.

- **Post Office Protocol 3 (POP3)**: POP3 is used to download email from a remote mail server.

- **Internet Message Access Protocol (IMAP)**: IMAP is also used to download email from a remote mail server.

- *Simple Mail Transfer Protocol (SMTP)*: SMTP is used to send email to a remote email server.

The more you understand about each of these protocols, the more you will understand how networks and the Internet work.

Define ICMP

Devices on a network use the *Internet Control Message Protocol (ICMP)* to send control and error messages to computers and servers. ICMP has several different uses, such as announcing network errors, announcing network congestion, and troubleshooting.

ping is commonly used to test connections between computers. **ping** is a simple but highly useful command-line utility that determines whether a specific IP address is accessible. You can ping the IP address to test IP connectivity. **ping** works by sending an ICMP echo request to a destination computer or other network device. The receiving device then sends back an ICMP echo reply message to confirm connectivity.

ping is a troubleshooting tool used to determine basic connectivity. Example 8-1 shows the command-line switches that can be used with the **ping** command. Four ICMP echo requests (pings) are sent to the destination computer. If it can be reached, the destination computer responds with four ICMP echo replies. The percentage of successful replies can help you determine the reliability and accessibility of the destination computer.

Example 8-1 ping Command Switches

```
C:\> ping /?

Usage: ping [-t] [-a] [-n count] [-l size] [-f] [-i TTL] [-v TOS]
            [-r count] [-s count] [[-j host-list] | [-k host-list]]
            [-w timeout] target_name

Options:
    -t              Ping the specified host until stopped.
                    To see statistics and continue - type Control-Break;
                    To stop - type Control-C.
    -a              Resolve addresses to hostnames.
    -n count        Number of echo requests to send.
    -l size         Send buffer size.
    -f              Set Don't Fragment flag in packet.
    -i TTL          Time To Live.
    -v TOS          Type Of Service.
    -r count        Record route for count hops.
    -s count        Timestamp for count hops.
    -j host-list    Loose source route along host-list.
    -k host-list    Strict source route along host-list.
    -w timeout      Timeout in milliseconds to wait for each reply.
```

You can also use ping to find a host's IP address when you know the name. If you ping the name of a website, such as www.cisco.com, as shown in Example 8-2, the server's IP address appears.

Example 8-2 Using the **ping** Command to Find an IP Address

```
C:\> ping cisco.com

Pinging cisco.com [198.133.219.25] with 32 bytes of data:

Request timed out.
Request timed out.
Request timed out.
Request timed out.

Ping statistics for 198.133.219.25:
    Packets: Sent = 4, Received = 0, Lost = 4 (100% loss),
```

Other ICMP messages are used to report undelivered packets, data on an IP network that includes source and destination IP addresses, and whether a device is too busy to handle the packet. Data, in the form of a packet, arrives at a router, which is a networking device that forwards data packets across networks toward their destinations. If the router does not know where to send the packet, the router deletes it. The router then sends an ICMP message back to the sending computer, informing it that the data was deleted. When a router becomes very busy, it may send a different ICMP message to the sending computer, indicating that it should slow down because the network is congested.

Describe the Physical Components of a Network

Many devices can be used in a network to provide connectivity, as shown in Figure 8-10. Which device you use depends on how many devices you are connecting, the type of connections they use, and the speed at which the devices operate. These are the most common devices on a network:

- Computers
- Hubs
- Switches
- Routers
- Wireless access points

Figure 8-10   Physical Network Components

The physical components of a network are needed to move data between these devices. The characteristics of the media determine where and how the components are used. These are the most common media used on networks:

■ Twisted pair

■ Fiber-optic cabling

■ Radio waves

After completing this section, you will meet these objectives:

■ Identify the names, purposes, and characteristics of network devices.

■ Identify the names, purposes, and characteristics of common network cables.

Identify the Names, Purposes, and Characteristics of Network Devices

To make data transmission more extensible and efficient than a simple peer-to-peer network, network designers use specialized network devices such as hubs, switches, routers, and wireless access points to send data between devices.

Hubs

A *hub*, shown in Figure 8-11, is a device that extends a network's range by receiving data on one port and then regenerating the data and sending it out to all other ports. This process means that all traffic from a device connected to the hub is sent to all the other devices connected to the hub every time the hub transmits data. This causes a large amount of network traffic. Hubs are also called *concentrators* because they serve as a central connection point for a LAN. They are also sometimes called multiport repeaters because they send data out all the ports.

Figure 8-11   Hub

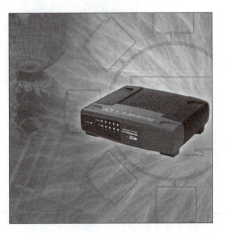

Bridges and Switches

Files are broken into small pieces of data, called packets, before they are transmitted over a network. This process allows for error checking and easier retransmission if the packet is lost or corrupted. Address information is added to the beginning and end of packets before they are transmitted. The packet, along with the address information, is called a frame.

LANs are often divided into sections called segments, similar to how a company is divided into departments. The boundaries of segments can be defined using a bridge. A *bridge* is a device used to filter network traffic between LAN segments. Bridges keep a record of all the devices on each segment to which the bridge is connected. When the bridge receives a frame, it examines the destination address to determine if the frame is to be sent to a different segment, or dropped. The bridge also helps improve the flow of data by keeping frames confined to only the segment to which the frame belongs.

A *switch*, shown in Figure 8-12, is sometimes called a *multiport bridge*. A typical bridge has just two ports, linking two segments of the same network. A switch has several ports, depending on how many network segments are to be linked. A switch is a more sophisticated device than a bridge. A switch maintains a table of the MAC addresses for computers that are connected to each port. When a frame arrives at a port, the switch compares the address information in the frame to its MAC address table. The switch then determines which port to use to forward the frame.

Figure 8-12   Switch

Routers

Whereas a switch connects segments of a network, *routers*, shown in Figure 8-13, are devices that connect entire networks to each other. Switches use MAC addresses to forward a frame within a single network. Routers use IP addresses to forward frames to other networks. A router can be a computer with special network software installed, or it can be a device built by network equipment manufacturers. Routers contain tables of IP addresses along with optimal destination routes to other networks.

Figure 8-13   Routers

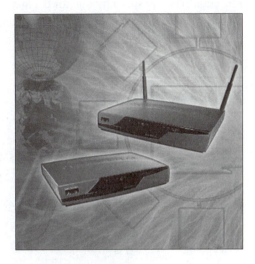

Wireless Access Points

A *wireless access point (WAP)*, shown in Figure 8-14, provides network access to wireless devices such as laptops and PDAs. The WAP uses radio waves to communicate with radios in computers, PDAs, and other WAPs. A WAP has a limited range of coverage. Large networks require several WAPs to provide adequate wireless coverage. A *basic service set (BSS)* is one WAP that supports multiple devices. An *extended service set (ESS)* has more than one WAP with the same SSID so that users can roam among the WAPs.

Figure 8-14   Wireless Access Point

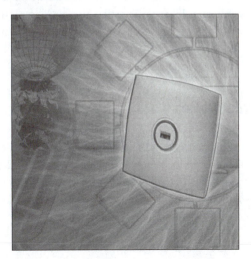

Multipurpose Devices

Some network devices perform more than one function. It is more convenient to purchase and configure one device that serves all your needs than to purchase a separate device for each function. This is especially true for the home user. In your home, you would purchase a multipurpose device instead of a switch, a router, and a wireless access point. The Linksys 300N, shown in Figure 8-15, is an example of a multipurpose device.

Figure 8-15   Multipurpose Device

Identify the Names, Purposes, and Characteristics of Common Network Cables

Until recently, cables were the only medium used to connect devices on networks. A wide variety of networking cables are available. Coaxial and twisted-pair cables use copper to transmit data. Fiber-optic cables use glass or plastic to transmit data. These cables differ in bandwidth, size, and cost. You need to know what type of cable to use in different situations so that you install the correct cables for the job. You also need to be able to troubleshoot and repair problems you encounter.

Twisted Pair

Twisted pair is a type of copper cabling that is used for telephone communications and most Ethernet networks. A pair of wires forms a circuit that can transmit data. The pair is twisted to provide protection against crosstalk, which is the noise generated by adjacent pairs of wires in the cable. Pairs of copper wires are encased in color-coded plastic insulation and are twisted together. An outer jacket protects the bundles of twisted pairs. Figure 8-16 shows a twisted-pair cable.

Figure 8-16   Twisted-Pair Cabling

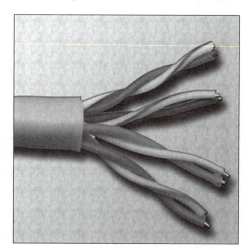

When electricity flows through a copper wire, a magnetic field is created around the wire. A circuit has two wires, which have oppositely charged magnetic fields. When the two wires of the circuit are next to each other, the magnetic fields cancel each other out. This is called the cancellation effect. Without the cancellation effect, your network communications become slow because of the interference caused by the magnetic fields.

The two basic types of twisted-pair cables are as follows:

- *Unshielded twisted pair (UTP)* is cable that has two or four pairs of wires. This type of cable relies solely on the cancellation effect produced by the twisted-wire pairs that limits signal degradation caused by electromagnetic interface (EMI) and radio frequency interference (RFI). UTP is the most commonly used cabling in networks. UTP cables have a range of 328 feet (100 m).

- With *shielded twisted pair (STP)*, each pair of wires is wrapped in metallic foil to better shield the wires from noise. Four pairs of wires are then wrapped in an overall metallic braid or foil. STP reduces electrical noise from within the cable. It also reduces EMI and RFI from outside the cable.

Although STP prevents interference better than UTP, STP is more expensive because of its extra shielding. It also is more difficult to install because of the thickness. In addition, the metallic shielding must be grounded at both ends. If it's improperly grounded, the shield acts like an antenna, picking up unwanted signals. STP is primarily used outside North America. STP cables also have a range of 328 feet (100 m).

Category Rating

UTP comes in several categories that are based on two factors:

- The number of wires in the cable

- The number of twists in those wires

Category 3 is the wiring used for telephone systems and Ethernet LAN at 10 Mbps. Category 3 has four pairs of wires.

Category 5 and Category 5e have four pairs of wires with a transmission rate of 100 Mbps. Category 5 and Category 5e are the most common network cables used. Category 5e has more twists per foot than Category 5 wiring. These extra twists further prevent interference from outside sources and the other wires within the cable.

Some Category 6 cables use a plastic divider to separate the pairs of wires, which prevents interference. The pairs also have more twists than Category 5e cable.

Coaxial Cable

Coaxial cable is a copper-cored cable surrounded by a heavy shielding, as shown in Figure 8-17. Coaxial cable is used to connect the computers to the rest of the network. Coaxial cable uses BNC connectors (sometimes called British Naval Connectors or Bayonet Neill-Concelman connectors) at the ends of the cables to make the connection. Several types of coaxial cable exist:

- *Thicknet (10BASE5)* is coaxial cable that was used in networks and operated at 10 Mbps, with a maximum length of 500 meters.

- *Thinnet (10BASE2)* is coaxial cable that was used in networks and operated at 10 Mbps, with a maximum length of 185 meters.

- *RG-59* is most commonly used for cable television in the United States.

- *RG-6* is higher-quality cable than RG-59, with more bandwidth and less susceptibility to interference.

Figure 8-17   Coaxial Cabling

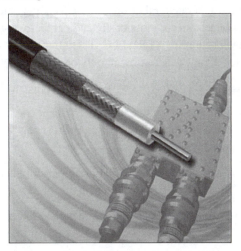

Fiber-Optic Cable

An optical fiber is a glass or plastic conductor that transmits information using light. *Fiber-optic cable*, shown in Figure 8-18, has one or more optical fibers enclosed in a sheath or jacket. Because it is made of glass, fiber-optic cable is not affected by EMI or RFI. All signals are converted to light pulses to enter the cable and are converted back into electrical signals when they leave it. This means that fiber-optic cable can deliver signals that are clearer, that can go farther, and that have greater bandwidth than cable made of copper or other metals.

Figure 8-18   Fiber-Optic Cabling

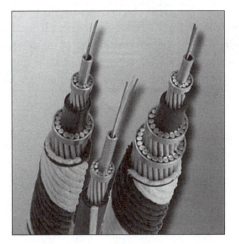

Fiber-optic cable can reach distances of several miles or kilometers before the signal needs to be regenerated. Fiber-optic cable usually is more expensive to use than copper cable, and the connectors are more costly and harder to assemble. Common connectors for fiber-optic networks are SC, ST, and LC. These three types of fiber-optic connectors are half duplex, which allows data to flow in only one direction. Therefore, two cables are needed.

These are the two types of glass fiber-optic cable:

- *Multimode* is cable that has a thicker core than single-mode cable. It is easier to make, can use simpler light sources (LEDs), and works well over distances of a few kilometers or less.

- *Single-mode* is cable that has a very thin core. It is harder to make, uses lasers as a light source, and can transmit signals dozens of kilometers with ease.

A fiber-optic cable is one or more optical fibers enclosed together in a sheath or jacket.

Packet Tracer Activity: 8.4.2 Cabling a Simple Network

In this Packet Tracer activity, you will cable a simple network. Refer to the CD in this book to find the activity. You may perform this activity now or wait until the end of the chapter.

Describe LAN Topologies and Architectures

Most of the computers that you work on will be part of a network. Topologies and architectures are building blocks for designing a computer network. Although you may not build a computer network, you need to understand how they are designed so that you can work on computers that are part of a network.

The two types of LAN topologies are physical and logical. A physical topology, shown in Figure 8-19, is the physical layout of the components on the network. A *logical topology*, shown in Figure 8-20, determines how the hosts communicate across a medium, such as a cable or the airwaves. Topologies commonly are represented as network diagrams.

Figure 8-19 Physical Topology

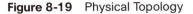

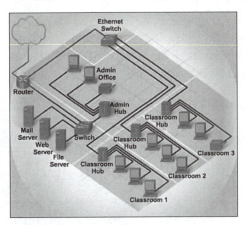

Figure 8-20 Logical Topology

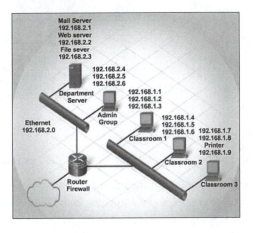

A LAN architecture is built around a topology. A LAN architecture comprises all the components that make up the structure of a communications system. These components include the hardware, software, protocols, and sequence of operations.

After completing this section, you will meet these objectives:

- Describe LAN topologies.
- Describe LAN architectures.

Describe LAN Topologies

A physical topology defines the way in which computers, printers, and other devices are connected to a network. A logical topology describes how the hosts access the medium and communicate on the network. The type of topology, as shown in Figure 8-21, determines the network's capabilities, such as ease of setup, speed, and cable lengths.

Figure 8-21   LAN Physical Topologies

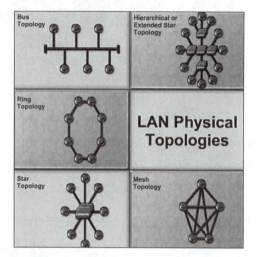

Physical Topologies

The common LAN physical topologies are as follows:

- **Bus topology**: In the bus topology, each computer connects to a common cable. The cable connects one computer to the next, like a bus line going through a city. The cable has a small cap installed at the end, called a terminator. The terminator prevents signals from bouncing back and causing network errors.

- **Ring topology**: In a ring topology, hosts are connected in a physical ring or circle. Because the ring topology has no beginning or end, the cable does not need to be terminated. A specially formatted frame, called a token, travels around the ring, stopping at each host. If a host wants to transmit data, it adds the data and the destination address to the frame. The frame then continues around the ring until it stops at the host with the destination address. The destination host takes the data out of the frame.

- **Star topology**: The star topology has a central connection point, which normally is a device such as a hub, switch, or router. Each host on a network has a cable segment that attaches the host directly to the central connection point. The advantage of a star topology is that it is easy to troubleshoot. Each host is connected to the central device with its own wire. If there is a problem with that cable, only that host is affected. The rest of the network remains operational.

- *Extended star topology*: The extended star topology is a star network with an additional networking device connected to the main networking device. Typically, a network cable connects to one hub, and then several other hubs connect to the first hub. Larger networks, such as those of corporations or universities, use the hierarchical star topology.

- *Mesh topology*: The mesh topology connects all devices to each other. When every device is connected to every other device, a failure of any cable does not affect the network. The mesh topology is used in WANs that interconnect LANs.

Logical Topologies

The two most common types of logical topologies are broadcast and token passing.

In a broadcast topology, each host addresses data either to a particular host or to all hosts connected on a network. There is no order that the hosts must follow to use the network. It is first come, first served for transmitting data on the network.

Token passing controls network access by passing an electronic token sequentially to each host. When a host receives the token, it can send data on the network. If the host has no data to send, it passes the token to the next host, and the process repeats.

Describe LAN Architectures

A *LAN architecture* describes both the physical and logical topologies used in a network. Table 8-1 lists the most common LAN architectures.

Table 8-1   LAN Architectures

Architecture	Physical Topology	Logical Topology
Ethernet	Bus	
Star		
Extended star	Bus	
Token Ring	Star	Ring
Fiber Distributed Data Interface (FDDI)	Double ring	Ring

Ethernet

The *Ethernet* architecture is based on the Institute of Electrical and Electronic Engineers (IEEE) 802.3 standard. The IEEE 802.3 standard specifies that a network must use the carrier sense multiple access collision detect (CSMA/CD) access control method. In CSMA/CD, hosts access the network using the first-come, first-served broadcast topology method to transmit data.

Ethernet uses a logical bus or broadcast topology and either a bus or star physical topology. As networks expand, most Ethernet networks are implemented using an extended star or hierarchical star topology. Standard transfer rates are 10 Mbps and 100 Mbps, but new standards outline Gigabit Ethernet, which can attain speeds of up to 1000 Mbps (1 Gbps).

Token Ring

IBM originally developed *Token Ring* as a reliable network architecture based on the token-passing access control method. Token Ring is used with computers and mainframes.

Token Ring is an example of an architecture in which the physical topology is different from its logical topology. The Token Ring topology is called a star-wired ring because the outer appearance of the network design is a star. The computers connect to a central hub, called a multistation access unit (MSAU). Inside the device, however, the wiring forms a circular data path, creating a logical ring. The logical ring is created by the token traveling out of an MSAU port to a computer. If the computer does not have any data to send, the token is sent back to the MSAU port and then out the next port to the next computer. This process continues for all computers and therefore resembles a physical ring.

FDDI

Fiber Distributed Data Interface (FDDI) is a type of Token Ring network. The implementation and topology of FDDI differs from the IBM Token Ring LAN architecture. FDDI is often used to connect several buildings in an office complex or on a university campus.

FDDI runs on fiber-optic cable. FDDI combines high-speed performance with the advantages of the token-passing ring topology. FDDI runs at 100 Mbps on a dual-ring topology. The outer ring is called the primary ring, and the inner ring is called the secondary ring.

Normally, traffic flows on only the primary ring. If the primary ring fails, the data automatically flows onto the secondary ring in the opposite direction.

An FDDI dual ring supports a maximum of 500 computers per ring. The total distance of each length of the cable ring is 62 miles (100 km). A repeater, which is a device that regenerates signals, is required every 1.2 miles (2 km). In recent years, many Token Ring networks have been replaced by faster Ethernet networks.

Identify Standards Organizations

Several worldwide standards organizations are responsible for setting networking standards. Manufacturers use standards as a basis for developing technology, especially communications and networking technologies. Standardizing technology ensures that the devices you use are compatible with other devices using the same technology. Standards groups create, examine, and update standards. These standards are applied to the development of technology to meet the demands for higher bandwidth, efficient communication, and reliable service.

Here is a list of standards organizations:

- **Institute of Electrical and Electronic Engineers (IEEE):** The IEEE is a nonprofit technical professional association of more than 395,000 members in 160 countries. The organization is composed of engineers, scientists, and students. Through its members, the IEEE is a leading authority in technical areas ranging from computer engineering, biomedical technology, and telecommunications to electric power, aerospace, and consumer electronics.

- **International Organization for Standardization (ISO):** ISO is an international organization composed of national standards bodies from more than 163 countries. The American National Standards Institute (ANSI), for example, is a member of ISO. ISO is a nongovernmental organization established to promote the development of standardization and related activities. ISO's work results in international agreements, which are published as International Standards.

  ISO has defined a number of important computer standards, the most significant of which is perhaps the OSI model, a standardized architecture for designing networks.

  ISO together with the International Electrotechnical Commission (IEC) and the International Telecommunication Union (ITU) have built a strategic partnership with the World Trade Organization (WTO).

- **Internet Architecture Board (IAB):** The IAB is the committee that oversees the technical and engineering development of the Internet by the Internet Society (ISOC). The committee oversees the Internet Engineering Task Force (IETF) and the Internet Research Task Force (IRTF). When the Internet transitioned to a public entity in 1992, the name was changed to what it is today, the Internet Architecture Board, originally formed by the U.S. Department of Defense.

- **International Electrotechnical Commission (IEC):** Founded in 1906, the IEC is the global organization that prepares and publishes international standards for all electrical, electronic, and related technologies. The IEC was founded because of a resolution passed at the International Electrical Congress held in St. Louis (U.S.) in 1904. The membership consists of more than 80 participating countries, including all the world's major trading nations and a growing number of industrialized countries. The IEC's mission is to promote, through its members, international cooperation on all questions related to electrotechnologies, electroacoustics, multimedia, telecommunications, and energy production and distribution, as well as associated general disciplines such as terminology and symbols, electromagnetic compatibility, design and development, safety, and the environment.

  The IEC is one of the bodies recognized by the WTO and entrusted by it to monitor the national and regional organizations agreeing to use the IEC's international standards as the basis of national or regional standards as part of the WTO's Technical Barriers to Trade Agreement.

- **American National Standards Institute (ANSI)**: ANSI is a private, nonprofit organization that administers and coordinates the U.S. voluntary standardization and conformity assessment system. ANSI identifies industrial and public requirements for national consensus standards and coordinates and manages their development, resolves national standards problems, and ensures effective participation in international standardization. Since 1918, the institute's mission has been to enhance both the global competitiveness of U.S. business and quality of life by promoting and facilitating voluntary consensus standards and conformity assessment systems and safeguarding their integrity.

   ANSI does not develop standards itself. Rather, it facilitates development by establishing consensus processes among qualified groups. This is why its acronym is seen on many standards.

- *Telecommunications Industry Association and Electronic Industries Alliance (TIA/EIA)*: TIA and EIA are trade associations that jointly develop and publish a series of standards covering structured voice and data wiring for LANs. These industry standards evolved after the U.S. telephone industry deregulation in 1984, which transferred responsibility for on-premises cabling to the building owner. Before that, AT&T used proprietary cables and systems.

Identify Ethernet Standards

Ethernet protocols describe the rules that control how communication occurs on an Ethernet network. To ensure that all Ethernet devices are compatible with each other, the IEEE developed standards for manufacturers and programmers to follow when developing Ethernet devices. Figure 8-22 shows an example of how different devices can communicate using these standards.

After completing this section, you will meet these objectives:

- Explain cabled Ethernet standards.
- Explain wireless Ethernet standards.

Figure 8-22   Interoperability Between Standards

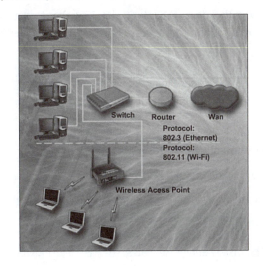

Explain Cabled Ethernet Standards

The Ethernet architecture is based on the ***Institute of Electrical and Electronic Engineers (IEEE) 802.3*** standard, which specifies that a network must implement the CSMA/CD access control method.

In ***carrier sense multiple access collision detect (CSMA/CD)***, all end stations "listen" to the network wire for clearance to send data. This process is similar to waiting to hear a dial tone on a phone before dialing a number. When the end station detects that no other host is transmitting, it attempts to send data. If no other station sends data at the same time, the transmission arrives at the destination computer with no problems. If another end station observes the same clear signal and transmits at the same time, a collision occurs on the network medium.

The first station that detects the collision, or the doubling of voltage, sends out a jam signal that tells all stations to stop transmitting and to run a backoff algorithm. A backoff algorithm calculates random times at which the end station retries the network transmission. This random time typically is one or two milliseconds (ms), or thousandths of a second. This sequence occurs every time a collision occurs on the network and can reduce Ethernet transmission by up to 40 percent.

Ethernet Technologies

The IEEE 802.3 standard defines several physical implementations that support Ethernet. Some of the common implementations are described here.

Ethernet

10BASE-T is an Ethernet technology that uses a star topology. 10BASE-T is a popular Ethernet architecture whose features are indicated in its name:

- The 10 represents a speed of 10 Mbps.
- BASE represents baseband transmission. In baseband transmission, the entire bandwidth of a cable is used for one type of signal.
- The T represents twisted-pair copper cabling.

The advantages of 10BASE-T are as follows:

- Installation of cable is inexpensive compared to fiber-optic installation.
- Cables are thin, flexible, and easier to install than coaxial cabling.
- Equipment and cables are easy to upgrade.

The disadvantages of 10BASE-T are as follows:

- The maximum length of a 10BASE-T segment is only 328 feet (100 m).
- Cables are susceptible to EMI.

Fast Ethernet

The high-bandwidth demands of many modern applications, such as videoconferencing and streaming audio, have created a need for higher data-transfer speeds. Many networks require more bandwidth than 10 Mbps Ethernet.

100BASE-TX is much faster than 10BASE-T and has a theoretical bandwidth of 100 Mbps.

The advantages of 100BASE-TX are as follows:

- At 100 Mbps, transfer rates of 100BASE-TX are ten times that of 10BASE-T.
- 100BASE-X uses twisted-pair cabling, which is inexpensive and easy to install.

The disadvantages of 100BASE-TX are as follows:

- The maximum length of a 100BASE-TX segment is only 328 feet (100 m).
- Cables are susceptible to EMI.

Gigabit Ethernet

1000BASE-T is commonly known as Gigabit Ethernet. Gigabit Ethernet is a LAN architecture.

The advantages of 1000BASE-T are as follows:

- The 1000BASE-T architecture supports data-transfer rates of 1 Gbps. At 1 Gbps, it is ten times faster than Fast Ethernet and 100 times faster than Ethernet. This increased speed makes it possible to implement bandwidth-intensive applications, such as live video.

- The 1000BASE-T architecture is interoperable with 10BASE-T and 100BASE-TX.

The disadvantages of 1000BASE-T are as follows:

- The maximum length of a 1000BASE-T segment is only 328 feet (100 m).

- It is susceptible to interference.

- Gigabit NICs and switches are expensive.

- Additional equipment is required.

Summary of Ethernet Technologies

Table 8-2 summarizes the Ethernet standards.

Table 8-2   Cabled Ethernet Standards

	10BASE-T	**100BASE-TX**	**1000BASE-T**
Media	EIA/TIA Category 3, 4, 5 UTP, two pair	EIA/TIA Category 5, 5e UTP, two pair	EIA/TIA Category 5, 5e UTP, four pair
Maximum Segment Length	100 m (328 feet)	100 m (328 feet)	100 m (328 feet)
Topology	Star	Star	Star
Connector	ISO 8877 (RJ-45)	ISO 8877 (RJ-45)	ISO 8877 (RJ-45)

10BASE-FL, 100BASE-FX, 1000BASE-SX, and LX are fiber-optic Ethernet technologies.

Explain Wireless Ethernet Standards

IEEE 802.11 is the standard that specifies connectivity for wireless networks. IEEE 802.11, or Wi-Fi, refers to the collective group of standards, 802.11a, 802.11b, 802.11g, and 802.11n. These protocols specify the frequencies, speeds, and other capabilities of the different Wi-Fi standards:

- *IEEE 802.11a*: Devices conforming to the 802.11a standard allow WLANs to achieve data rates as high as 54 Mbps. IEEE 802.11a devices operate in the 5-GHz radio frequency range and within a maximum range of 150 feet (45.7 m).

- **_IEEE 802.11b_**: 802.11b operates in the 2.4-GHz frequency range, with a maximum theoretical data rate of 11 Mbps. These devices operate within a maximum range of 300 feet (91.4 m).

- **_IEEE 802.11g_**: IEEE 802.11g provides the same theoretical maximum speed as 802.11a, which is 54 Mbps, but operates in the same 2.4-GHz spectrum as 802.11b. Unlike 802.11a, 802.11g is backward-compatible with 802.11b. 802.11g also has a maximum range of 300 feet (91.4 m).

- **_IEEE 802.11n_**: 802.11n is a newer wireless standard that has a theoretical bandwidth of 540 Mbps and operates in either the 2.4-GHz or 5-GHz frequency range with a maximum range of 820 feet (250 m).

Table 8-3 summarizes Wireless Ethernet standards.

Table 8-3   Wireless Ethernet Standards

Standard	Bandwidth	Frequency	Range	Interoperability
IEEE 802.11a	Up to 54 Mbps	5-GHz band	150 ft (45.7 m)	Not interoperable with 802.11b, 802.11g, and 802.11n
IEEE 802.11b	Up to 11 Mbps	2.4-GHz band	300 ft (91 m)	Interoperable with 802.11g
IEEE 802.11g	Up to 54 Mbps	2.4-GHz band	300 ft (91 m)	Interoperable with 802.11b
IEEE 802.11n (prestandard)	Up to 540 Mbps	2.4-GHz or 5-GHz band	820 ft (250 m)	Interoperable with 802.11b and 802.11g

Explain the OSI and TCP/IP Data Models

An architectural model is a common frame of reference for explaining Internet communications and developing communication protocols. It separates the functions of protocols into manageable layers. Each layer performs a specific function in the process of communicating over a network.

The TCP/IP model was created by researchers in the U.S. Department of Defense (DoD). The TCP/IP model is a tool used to help explain the TCP/IP suite of protocols, which is the dominant standard for transporting data across networks. This model has four layers, as shown in Table 8-4.

Table 8-4   TCP/IP Model Versus the OSI Model

TCP/IP Model	OSI Model
Application	Application
	Presentation
	Session
Transport	Transport
Internet	Network
Network Access	Data link
	Physical

In the early 1980s, the ISO developed the Open Systems Interconnection (OSI) model, which was defined in ISO standard 7498-1, to standardize how devices communicate on a network. This model has seven layers, as shown in Table 8-4. This model was a major step toward ensuring that network devices could interoperate.

After completing this section, you will meet these objectives:

- Define the TCP/IP model.
- Define the OSI model.
- Compare the OSI and TCP/IP models.

Define the TCP/IP Model

The TCP/IP reference model provides a common frame of reference for developing the protocols used on the Internet. It consists of layers that perform functions necessary to prepare data for transmission over a network. Table 8-5 describes the four layers of the TCP/IP model.

Table 8-5   TCP/IP Model

TCP/IP Model	Layer	Description
Application	4	Where high-level protocols such as SMTP and FTP operate
Transport	3	Where flow-control and connection protocols exist
Internet	2	Where IP addressing and routing take place
Network Access	1	Where MAC addressing and physical network components exist

A message begins at the top layer, the application layer, and moves down the TCP/IP layers to the bottom layer, the network access layer. Header information is added to the message as it moves down through each layer and then is transmitted. After reaching the destination, the message travels back up through each layer of the TCP/IP model. The header information that was added to the message is stripped away as the message moves up through the layers toward its destination.

Application Layer Protocols

Application layer protocols provide network services to user applications such as web browsers and email programs. Here are some of the *application layer protocols* that operate at the TCP/IP application layer:

- **Hypertext Transfer Protocol (HTTP)**: HTTP governs how files such as text, graphics, sound, and video are exchanged on the Internet or World Wide Web. A web server runs an HTTP service or daemon. A daemon is a program that services HTTP requests. These requests are transmitted by HTTP client software, which is another name for a web browser.

- **Telnet**: Telnet is an application that you can use to access, control, and troubleshoot remote computers and network devices.

- **File Transfer Protocol (FTP)**: FTP is a set of rules governing how files are transferred. FTP allows multiple simultaneous connections to remote file systems.

- **Simple Mail Transport Protocol (SMTP)**: SMTP provides messaging services over TCP/IP and supports most Internet email programs.

- **Domain Name System (DNS)**: DNS translates domain names, such as www.cisco.com, to IP addresses.

- *Hypertext Markup Language (HTML)*: HTML is a page-description language. Web designers use HTML to indicate to web browser software how the page should look. HTML includes tags to indicate boldface and italic type, line breaks, paragraph breaks, hyperlinks, and insertion of tables, among other instructions.

Transport Layer Protocols

Transport layer protocols provide end-to-end management of the data. One of the functions of these protocols is to divide the data into manageable segments for easier transport across the network. Here are the two *transport layer protocols* that operate at the TCP/IP transport layer:

- *Transmission Control Protocol (TCP)*: TCP is the primary Internet protocol for the reliable delivery of data. TCP includes facilities for end-to-end connection establishment, error detection and retransmission, and metering the rate of data flow into the network. Many standard applications, such as email, web browser, file transfer, and Telnet, depend on the services of TCP.

- *User Datagram Protocol (UDP)*: UDP offers a connectionless service for delivery of data. UDP uses lower overhead than TCP and doesn't handle issues of reliability. Network management applications, network file systems, and simple file transport use UDP.

Internet Layer Protocols

Internet layer protocols operate at the third layer from the top in the TCP/IP model. Internet protocols are used to provide connectivity between hosts in the network. Here are some of the protocols that operate at the TCP/IP Internet layer:

- *Internet Protocol (IP)*: IP provides source and destination addressing, much like the address and return address on a postal envelope. In conjunction with routing protocols, IP provides packet-forwarding information from one network to another.

- **Internet Control Message Protocol (ICMP)**: ICMP is used for network testing and troubleshooting. It enables diagnostic and error messages. The ping application uses ICMP echo messages to test if a remote device can be reached.

- *Routing Information Protocol (RIP)*: RIP operates between router devices to discover paths between networks. In an intranet, routers depend on a routing protocol to build and maintain information about how to forward packets toward the destination. RIP chooses routes based on the distance or hop count to the destination.

- *Address Resolution Protocol (ARP)*: ARP is used to map the MAC address of a node on the network when its IP address is known. End stations and routers use ARP to discover MAC addresses.

Network Access Layer Protocols

Network access layer protocols describe the standards that hosts use to access the physical media. The IEEE 802.3 Ethernet standards and technologies, such as CSMA/CD and 10BASE-T, are defined at this layer.

Define the OSI Model

The OSI model is an industry-standard framework that is used to divide network communications into seven distinct layers. Although other models exist, most network vendors today build their products using this framework.

A system that implements protocol behavior consisting of a series of these layers is known as a protocol stack. Protocol stacks can be implemented in either hardware or software, or a combination of both. Typically, only the lower layers are implemented in hardware, and the higher layers are implemented in software.

Each layer is responsible for part of the processing to prepare data for transmission on the network. Table 8-6 describes each layer of the OSI model.

Table 8-6   OSI Model

OSI Model	Layer	Description
Application	7	Responsible for network services to applications
Presentation	6	Transforms data formats to provide a standard interface for the application layer
Session	5	Establishes, manages, and terminates the connections between the local and remote applications
Transport	4	Provides reliable transport and flow control across a network
Network	3	Responsible for logical addressing and the domain of routing
Data link	2	Provides physical addressing and media access procedures
Physical	1	Defines all the electrical and physical specifications for devices

In the OSI model, when data is transferred, it is said to virtually travel down the OSI model layers of the sending computer and up the OSI model layers of the receiving computer.

When a user wants to send data, such as an email, the encapsulation process starts at the application layer. The application layer provides network access to applications. Information flows through the top three layers and is considered to be data when it gets down to the transport layer.

At the transport layer, the data is broken into more manageable segments, or transport layer protocol data units (PDU), for orderly transport across the network. A PDU describes data as it moves from one layer of the OSI model to another. The transport layer PDU also contains information such as port numbers, sequence numbers, and acknowledgment numbers, which is used for reliable data transport.

At the network layer, each segment from the transport layer becomes a packet. The packet contains logical addressing and other Layer 3 control information.

At the data link layer, each packet from the network layer becomes a frame. The frame contains physical address and error-correction information.

At the physical layer, the frame becomes bits. These bits are transmitted one at a time across the network medium.

At the receiving computer, the de-encapsulation process reverses the process of encapsulation. The bits arrive at the physical layer of the OSI model of the receiving computer. The process of virtually traveling up the OSI model of the receiving computer brings the data to the application layer, where an email program displays the email.

Note

Mnemonics can help you remember the seven layers of the OSI. Two examples are "**A**ll **P**eople **S**eem **T**o **N**eed **D**ata **P**rocessing" and "**P**lease **D**o **N**ot **T**hrow **S**am's **P**aper **A**irplane."

Compare the OSI and TCP/IP Models

The OSI model and the TCP/IP model are both reference models used to describe the data communication process. The TCP/IP model is used specifically for the TCP/IP suite of protocols. The OSI model is used to develop standard communication for equipment and applications from different vendors.

The TCP/IP model performs the same process as the OSI model, but it uses four layers instead of seven. Figure 8-23 shows how the layers of the two models compare.

Figure 8-23   OSI Model and TCP/IP Model Compared

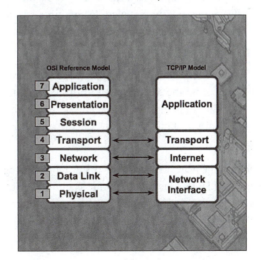

Describe How to Configure a NIC and a Modem

A NIC is required to connect to the Internet. The NIC may come preinstalled, or you may have to purchase one. In rare cases, you may need to update the NIC driver. You can use the driver disc that comes with the motherboard or adapter card, or you can supply a driver that you downloaded from the manufacturer.

After the NIC and the driver have been installed, you can connect the computer to the network.

In addition to installing a NIC, you may need to install a modem to connect to the Internet.

After completing this section, you will meet these objectives:

- Install or update a NIC driver.
- Uninstall a NIC driver.
- Attach the computer to an existing network.
- Describe the installation of a modem.

Install or Update a NIC Driver

Sometimes a manufacturer publishes new driver software for a NIC. A new driver may enhance the functionality of the NIC, or it may be needed for operating system compatibility.

When installing a new driver, be sure to disable virus protection software so that none of the files is incorrectly installed. Some virus scanners detect a driver update as a possible virus attack. Also, only one driver should be installed at a time; otherwise, some updating processes may conflict.

A best practice is to close all applications that are running so that they do not use any files associated with the driver update. Before updating a driver, you should visit the manufacturer's website. In many cases, you can download a self-extracting executable driver file that automatically installs or updates the driver. Alternatively, you can click the Update Driver button in the Device Manager toolbar.

Clicking the + next to the Network Adapters category expands the category and shows the network adapters installed in your system. To view and change the adapter's properties, or update the driver, double-click the adapter. In the adapter Properties dialog box, click the **Driver** tab, and then click the **Update Driver** button. Figure 8-24 shows an example of a network card adapter Properties dialog box in Device Manager.

When the update is complete, it is a good idea to reboot the computer, even if you do not receive a message telling you to do so. Rebooting the computer ensures that the installation has gone as planned and that the new driver is working properly. When installing multiple drivers, reboot the computer between each update to make sure that no conflicts exist. This step takes extra time but ensures a clean installation of the driver.

Figure 8-24   Adapter Properties in Device Manager

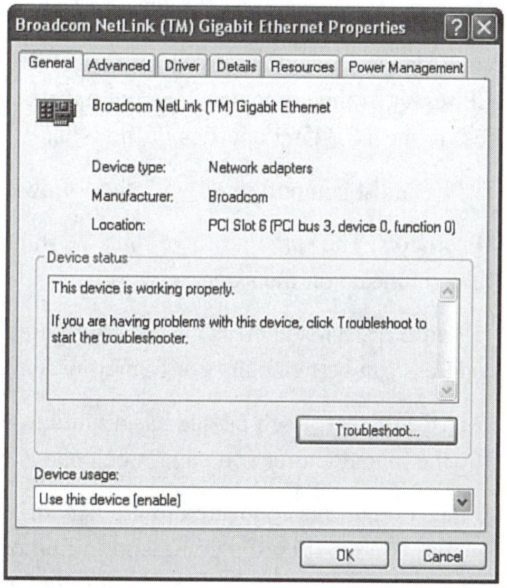

Uninstall a NIC Driver

If a new NIC driver does not perform as expected after it has been installed, the driver can be uninstalled, or rolled back, to the previous driver. Double-click the adapter in Device Manager. In the adapter Properties dialog box, click the **Driver** tab, and click **Roll Back Driver**. If no driver was installed before the update, this option is unavailable. In that case, you need to find a driver for the device and install it manually if the operating system cannot find a suitable driver for the NIC.

Worksheet 8.9.1: Internet Search for NIC Drivers

In this worksheet, you research NIC drivers. Refer to the worksheet in *IT Essentials: PC Hardware and Software Lab Manual, Fourth Edition*. You may perform this worksheet now or wait until the end of the chapter.

Attach the Computer to an Existing Network

Now that the NIC drivers are installed, you are ready to connect to the network. Plug a network cable, also called an Ethernet patch or straight-through cable, into the network port on the computer. Plug the other end into the network device or wall jack.

After connecting the network cable, look at the LEDs, or link lights, next to the Ethernet port on the NIC to see if any activity is occurring. If no activity is going on, this may indicate a faulty cable, a faulty hub port, or even a faulty NIC. You may have to replace one or more of these devices to correct the problem.

After you have confirmed that the computer is connected to the network and that the link lights on the NIC indicate a working connection, the computer needs an IP address. Most networks are set up so that the computer receives an IP address automatically from a local DHCP server. If the computer does not have an IP address, you need to enter a unique IP address in the TCP/IP properties of the NIC.

Every NIC must be configured with the following information:

- **Protocols**: The same protocol must be implemented between any two computers that communicate on the same network.

- **IP address**: This address can be configured and must be unique to each device. The IP address can be manually configured or automatically assigned by DHCP.

- **MAC address**: Each device has a unique MAC address. The MAC address is assigned by the manufacturer and cannot be changed.

After the computer is connected to the network, you should test connectivity with the **ping** command. Use the **ipconfig** command to find out what your IP address is. Example 8-3 shows sample output from the **ipconfig /all** command.

Example 8-3 ipconfig /all Command

```
C:\> ipconfig /all

Windows IP Configuration

        Host Name . . . . . . . . . . . . : computer
        Primary Dns Suffix  . . . . . . . :
        Node Type . . . . . . . . . . . . : Hybrid
        IP Routing Enabled. . . . . . . . : No
        WINS Proxy Enabled. . . . . . . . : No

Ethernet adapter Local Area Connection:

        Connection-specific DNS Suffix  . :        Description . . . . . . . . :
    Broadcom 440x 10/100 Integrated Controller
        Physical Address. . . . . . . . . : 00-12-3F-E0-59-3D
        Dhcp Enabled. . . . . . . . . . . : Yes
        Autoconfiguration Enabled . . . . : Yes
        IP Address. . . . . . . . . . . . : 192.168.1.112
        Subnet Mask . . . . . . . . . . . : 255.255.255.0
        Default Gateway . . . . . . . . . : 192.168.1.1
```

```
DHCP Server . . . . . . . . . . . : 192.168.1.1
DNS Servers . . . . . . . . . . . : 192.168.1.1
Lease Obtained. . . . . . . . . . : Monday, November 05, 2007 5:05:13 PM
Lease Expires . . . . . . . . . . : Monday, November 12, 2007 5:05:13 PM
```

Ping your own IP address to make sure that your NIC is working properly. After you have determined that your NIC is working, **ping** your default gateway or another computer on your network, as shown in Example 8-4. A *default gateway* allows a host to communicate outside your network. If you have an Internet connection, ping a popular website, such as www.cisco.com. If you can successfully ping an Internet site or another computer on your network, everything is working properly with your connection. If you cannot ping one of these, you need to troubleshoot the connection.

Example 8-4 ping Command

```
C:\> ping 192.168.1.112

Pinging 192.168.1.112 with 32 bytes of data:

Reply from 192.168.1.112: bytes=32 time<1ms TTL=128
Reply from 192.168.1.112: bytes=32 time<1ms TTL=128
Reply from 192.168.1.112: bytes=32 time<1ms TTL=128
Reply from 192.168.1.112: bytes=32 time<1ms TTL=128

Ping statistics for 192.168.1.112:
    Packets: Sent = 4, Received = 4, Lost = 0 (0% loss),
Approximate round trip times in milli-seconds:
    Minimum = 0ms, Maximum = 0ms, Average = 0ms
```

Lab 8.9.2: Configure an Ethernet NIC to Use DHCP in Windows XP

In this lab, you configure a NIC to use DHCP from a 300N router. Refer to the lab in *IT Essentials: PC Hardware and Software Lab Manual, Fourth Edition.* You may perform this lab now or wait until the end of the chapter.

Optional Lab 8.9.2: Configure an Ethernet NIC to Use DHCP in Windows Vista

In this lab, you configure a NIC to use DHCP from a 300N router. Refer to the lab in *IT Essentials: PC Hardware and Software Lab Manual, Fourth Edition.* You may perform this lab now or wait until the end of the chapter.

Packet Tracer Activity: 8.9.2 Adding Computers to an Existing Network

In this Packet Tracer activity, you will add computers to an existing network, configure the computers to use DHCP, and observe the use of DHCP on the network. Refer to the CD in this book to find the activity. You may perform this activity now or wait until the end of the chapter.

Describe the Installation of a Modem

A modem, several examples of which are shown in Figure 8-25, is an electronic device that transfers data between one computer and another using analog signals over a telephone line. The modem converts digital data to analog signals for transmission. The modem at the receiving end reconverts the analog signals to digital data to be interpreted by the computer. The process of converting analog signals to digital and back again is called *mo*dulation/ *dem*odulation, hence the name modem. Modem-based transmission is very accurate, despite the fact that telephone lines can be noisy because of clicks, static, and other problems.

Figure 8-25   Modems

An internal modem plugs into an expansion slot on the motherboard. To configure a modem, you might have to set jumpers to select the IRQ and I/O addresses. No configuration is needed for a "plug-and-play" modem, which can only be installed on a motherboard that supports plug and play. A modem using a serial port that is not yet in use must be configured. Additionally, the software drivers that come with the modem must be installed for the modem to work properly. Drivers for modems are installed the same way drivers are installed for NICs.

External modems connect to a computer through the serial and USB ports.

When computers use the public telephone system to communicate, this is called dialup networking (DUN). Modems communicate with each other using audio tone signals. This means that modems can duplicate the dialing characteristics of a telephone. DUN creates a Point-to-Point Protocol (PPP) connection between two computers over a phone line.

After the line connection has been established, a "handshaking sequence" takes place between the two modems and the computers. The handshaking sequence is a series of short communications that occur between the two systems. This is done to establish the readiness of the two modems and computers to engage in data exchange. Dialup modems send data over the serial telephone line in the form of an analog signal. Because the analog signals change gradually and continuously, they can be drawn as waves. In this system, the digital signals are represented by 1s and 0s. The digital signals must be converted to a waveform to travel across telephone lines. The receiving modem converts them back to digital form, 1s and 0s, so that the receiving computer can process the data.

AT Commands

All modems require software to control the communication session. Most modem software uses the Hayes-compatible command set. The Hayes-compatible command set is based on a group of instructions that always begins with a set of attention (AT) characters, followed by the command characters. These are known as AT commands. Table 8-7 shows the AT command set.

Table 8-7   AT Commands

AT Command	Function
AT	The attention code that precedes all modem action commands
ATP *xxxxxx*	Dials the phone number, *xxxxxx*, using pulse dialing
ATDT *xxxxxx*	Dials the phone number, *xxxxxx*, using tone dialing
ATA	Answers the phone immediately
ATHO	Hangs up the phone immediately
ATZ	Resets the modem to its power-up settings
ATF	Resets modem parameters and settings to the factory defaults
AT+++	Breaks the signal, changing from data mode to command mode
P	Signifies pulse dialing
T	Signifies tone dialing
W	Indicates that the modem will wait

The AT commands are modem control commands. The AT command set is used to issue dial, hang-up, reset, and other instructions to the modem. Most user manuals that come with a modem contain a complete listing of the AT command set.

The standard Hayes-compatible code to dial is ATD*xxxxxxx*. An AT string usually has no spaces. If a space is inserted, most modems ignore it. The *x* signifies the number dialed. A local call has seven digits, and a long-distance call has 11 digits. A W indicates that the modem will wait for an outside line, if necessary, to establish a tone before proceeding. Sometimes, a T is added to signify tone dialing, or a P is added to signify pulse dialing.

Identify the Names, Purposes, and Characteristics of Other Technologies Used to Establish Connectivity

There are many ways to connect to the Internet. Phone, cable, satellite, and private telecommunications companies offer Internet connections for businesses and home use.

In the 1990s, the Internet typically was used for data transfer. Transmission speeds were slow compared to the high-speed connections that are available today. Most Internet connections were analog modems that used the plain old telephone system (POTS) to send and receive data. In recent years, many businesses and home users have switched to high-speed Internet connections. The additional bandwidth allows for transmission of voice and video as well as data.

You should understand how users connect to the Internet and the advantages and disadvantages of different connection types.

After completing this section, you will meet these objectives:

- Describe telephone technologies.
- Define power line communication.
- Define broadband.
- Define VoIP.
- Define VPN.

Describe Telephone Technologies

Several WAN solutions are available for connecting between sites or to the Internet. WAN connection services provide different speeds and levels of service. Before committing to any type of Internet connection, research all the available services to determine the best solution to meet the customer's needs.

Analog Telephone

Analog telephone technology uses standard voice telephone lines. This type of service uses a modem to place a telephone call to another modem at a remote site, such as an Internet service provider (ISP). Using the phone line with an analog modem has two major disadvantages. The first is that the telephone line cannot be used for voice calls while the modem is in use. The second is the limited bandwidth provided by analog phone service. The maximum bandwidth using an analog modem is 56 Kbps, but in reality, it usually is much lower than that. An analog modem is not a good solution for the demands of busy networks.

Integrated Services Digital Network (ISDN)

The next advancement in WAN service is *Integrated Services Digital Network (ISDN)*. ISDN is a standard for sending voice, video, and data over normal telephone wires. ISDN technology uses the telephone wires as an analog telephone service. However, ISDN uses digital technology to carry the data. Because it uses digital technology, ISDN provides higher-quality voice and higher-speed data transfer than traditional analog telephone service.

ISDN digital connections offer three services: Basic Rate Interface (BRI), Primary Rate Interface (PRI), and Broadband ISDN (BISDN). ISDN uses two different types of communication channels. The B channel is used to carry the information—data, voice, or video. The D channel usually is used for controlling and signaling, but it can be used for data.

Here are the types of ISDN:

- **BRI**: ISDN Basic Rate Interface offers a dedicated 128-Kbps connection using two 64-Kbps B channels. ISDN BRI also uses one 16-Kbps D channel for call setup, control, and teardown.

- **PRI**: ISDN Primary Rate Interface offers up to 1.544 Mbps over 23 B channels in North America and Japan or 2.048 Mbps over 30 B channels in Europe and Australia. ISDN PRI also uses one 64-Kbps D channel for call maintenance.

- **BISDN**: Broadband ISDN manages different types of service all at the same time. BISDN is mostly used only in network backbones.

Digital Subscriber Line (DSL)

DSL is an "always-on" technology. This means that you don't need to dial up each time to connect to the Internet. DSL uses the existing copper telephone lines to provide high-speed digital data communication between end users and telephone companies. Unlike ISDN, in which digital data communication replaces analog voice communication, DSL shares the telephone wire with analog signals.

The telephone company limits the bandwidth of the analog voice on the lines. This limit allows the DSL to place digital data on the phone wire in the unused portion of the bandwidth. This sharing of the phone wire allows voice calls to be placed while DSL is connecting to the Internet.

You must consider two major points when selecting DSL. DSL has distance limitations. The phone lines used with DSL were designed to carry analog information. Therefore, the length that the digital signal can be sent is limited, and the signal cannot pass through any form of multiplexer used with analog phone lines. The other consideration is that the voice information and the data carried by DSL must be separated at the customer site. A device called a splitter separates the connection to the phones and the connection to the local network devices.

Asymmetric digital subscriber line (ADSL) is currently the most commonly used DSL technology. ADSL has different bandwidth capabilities in each direction. ADSL has a fast downstream speed, typically 1.5 Mbps. Downstream is the process of transferring data from the server to the end user. This is beneficial to users who download large amounts of data. The high-speed upload rate of ADSL is slower. ADSL does not perform well when hosting a web server or FTP server, both of which involve upload-intensive Internet activities.

The following are some of the most common DSL types:

- *Asymmetric DSL (ADSL)*: ADSL currently is the most common implementation. It has speeds that vary from 384 Kbps to more than 6 Mbps downstream. The upstream speed typically is lower.

- *High data rate DSL (HDSL)*: HDSL provides equal bandwidth in both directions. It is 1.544 Mbps in North America and 2.048 Mbps in Europe.

- **Symmetric DSL (SDSL)**: SDSL provides the same speed, up to 3 Mbps, for uploads and downloads.

- **Very high data rate DSL (VDSL)**: VDSL is capable of bandwidths between 13 and 52 Mbps downstream and 16 Mbps upstream.

- *Integrated Services Digital Network DSL (IDSL)*: ISDN DSL is actually DSL over ISDN lines. It is a set of CCIT/ITU standards for digital transmission over ordinary telephone copper wire, as well as over other media, with a top speed of 144 Kbps. ISDN is available in areas that do not qualify for other DSL implementations. An ISDN adapter at both the user side and service provider side is required. ISDN generally is available in urban areas in the United States and Europe from the local phone company.

Define Power Line Communication

Power line communication (PLC) is a communication method that uses power distribution wires (the local electric grid) to send and receive data, as shown in Figure 8-26.

Figure 8-26   Power Line Communication

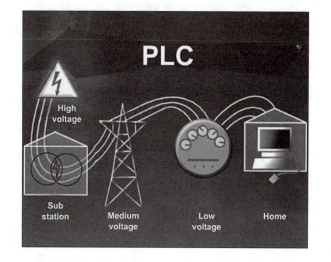

PLC is known by other names:

- Power line networking (PLN)

- Mains communication

- Power line telecom (PLT)

With PLC, an electric company can superimpose an analog signal over the standard 50- or 60-Hz AC that travels in power lines. The analog signal can carry voice and data signals.

PLC may be available in areas where other high-speed connections are not. PLC is faster than an analog modem and may cost much less than other high-speed connection types. As this technology matures, it will become more common to find and may increase in speed.

You can use PLC to network computers within your home instead of installing network cabling or wireless technology. PLC connections can be used anywhere there is an electrical outlet. You can control lighting and appliances using PLC without installing control wiring.

Define Broadband

Broadband is a technique used to transmit and receive multiple signals using multiple frequencies over one cable. For example, the cable used to bring cable television to your home can carry computer network transmissions at the same time. Because the two transmission types use different frequencies, they do not interfere with each other.

Broadband is a signaling method that uses a wide range of frequencies that can be further divided into channels. In networking, the term broadband describes communication methods that transmit two or more signals at the same time. Sending two or more signals simultaneously increases the rate of transmission. Some common broadband network connections include cellular, cable, DSL, and satellite.

Cellular

Cellular technology enables the transfer of voice, video, and data. With a cellular WAN adapter installed, a laptop user can access the Internet over the cellular network.

Although slower than DSL and cable connections, cellular WANs are still fast enough to be classified as a high-speed connection. Cellular networks use one or more of the following technologies:

- *Global System for Mobile Communications (GSM)*: Standard used by the worldwide cellular network

- *General Packet Radio Service (GPRS)*: Data service for users of GSM

- *Quad-band*: Allows a cellular phone to operate on all four GSM frequencies: 850 MHz, 900 MHz, 1800 MHz, and 1900 MHz

- *Short Message Service (SMS)*: Data service used to send and receive text messages

- *Multimedia Messaging Service (MMS)*: Data service used to send and receive text messages and can include multimedia content

- *Enhanced Data Rates for GSM Evolution (EDGE)*: Provides increased data rates and improved data reliability

- *Evolution-Data Optimized (EV-DO)*: Provides fast download rates

- *High Speed Downlink Packet Access (HSDPA)*: Provides enhanced G3 access speed

Cable

A *cable modem* connects your computer to the cable company using the same coaxial cable that connects to your cable television. You can plug your computer directly into the cable modem, or you can connect a router, switch, hub, or multipurpose network device so that multiple computers can share the connection to the Internet.

DSL

With DSL, the voice and data signals are carried on different frequencies on the copper telephone wires. A filter is used to prevent DSL signals from interfering with phone signals. Plug the filter into a phone jack, and plug the phone into the filter.

The DSL modem does not require a filter. The DSL modem is unaffected by the telephone frequencies. Like a cable modem, a DSL modem can connect directly to your computer, or it can be connected to a networking device to share the Internet connection with multiple computers.

Satellite

Broadband satellite is an alternative for customers who cannot get cable or DSL connections. A satellite connection does not require a phone line or cable; it uses a satellite dish for two-way communication. Download speeds typically are up to 500 Kbps; uploads are closer to 56 Kbps. It takes time for the signal from the satellite dish to be relayed to your ISP through the satellite orbiting the Earth.

People who live in rural areas often use satellite broadband because they need a faster connection than dialup, and no other broadband connection is available.

Fiber Broadband

Fiber broadband provides faster connection speeds and bandwidth than cable modems, DSL, or ISDN. Fiber broadband can deliver a multitude of digital information such as telephone, video, data, and advanced features like video conferencing. A single fiber pair can carry millions of phone calls, as compared to a single copper pair, which can carry six phone calls.

Worksheet 8.10.3: Answer Broadband Questions

In this worksheet, you identify the different types of broadband. Refer to the worksheet in *IT Essentials: PC Hardware and Software Lab Manual, Fourth Edition*. You may perform this worksheet now or wait until the end of the chapter.

Define VoIP

Voice over IP (VoIP) is a method to carry telephone calls over the data networks and Internet. VoIP converts the analog signals of our voices into digital information that is transported in IP packets. VoIP can also use an existing IP network to provide access to the public switched telephone network (PSTN).

When using VoIP, you are dependent on an Internet connection. This can be a disadvantage if the Internet connection experiences an interruption in service. When a service interruption occurs, the user cannot make phone calls.

Note

If your area does not use enhanced E911, reaching emergency services may require unique or additional numbers rather than simply dialing 911.

Figure 8-27 shows some examples of VoIP phones.

Figure 8-27   VoIP Phones

Define VPN

A Virtual Private Network (VPN) is a private network that uses a public network, like the Internet, to connect remote sites or users together. A VPN uses dedicated secure connections routed through the Internet from the company private network to the remote user. When connected to the company private network, users become part of that network and have access to all services and resources as if they were physically connected to the LAN.

Remote-access users must install the VPN client on their computers to form a secure connection with the company private network. The VPN client software encrypts data before sending it over the Internet to the VPN gateway at the company private network. VPN gateways establish, manage, and control VPN connections, also known as VPN tunnels.

Identify and Apply Common Preventive Maintenance Techniques Used for Networks

Certain common preventive maintenance techniques should continually be performed for a network to operate properly. If an organization has one malfunctioning computer, generally only one user is affected. But if the network is malfunctioning, many or all users will be unable to work.

One of the biggest problems with network devices, especially in the server room, is heat. Network devices, such as computers, hubs, and switches, do not perform well when they overheat. Often, excess heat is generated by accumulated dust and dirty air filters. When dust gathers in and on network devices, it impedes the flow of cool air and sometimes even clogs fans. It is important to keep network rooms clean and to change air filters often. It is also a good idea to have replacement filters available for prompt maintenance.

Preventive maintenance involves checking a network's various components for wear. Check the condition of network cables, because they are often moved, unplugged, and kicked. Many network problems can be traced to a faulty cable. You should replace any cables that have exposed wires, that are badly twisted, or that are bent.

Label your cables. This practice will save troubleshooting time later. Refer to wiring diagrams, and always follow your company's cable-labeling guidelines.

Counterfeiting and the IT Industry

A critical aspect of preventive maintenance that is sometimes overlooked is the issue of counterfeiting. Counterfeit products are often called fakes. They can be hardware, software, and documentation that bear a trademark or logo without the trademark owner's knowledge or consent. These include products that do not originate from authorized manufacturers or are produced without the approval of a trademark owner.

Counterfeit products are often made with cheaper materials and with little or no quality control, and can cause problems in your network. These products might also have invalid warranty and software licenses, no support entitlement, or incorrect initial settings. In addition, counterfeit equipment often fails health and safety compliance testing. The counterfeit product might be cheaper to buy initially, but might be more expensive to maintain. A counterfeit product can create risk to a network and can even be a potential health and safety hazard.

To minimize the risk of purchasing counterfeit products, it is recommended that customers purchase only from the manufacturer's authorized partners or directly from the manufacturer. When products are not purchased through authorized channels, the manufacturer cannot guarantee the source, quality, or authenticity of those products. When the equipment you are buying is mission critical, quality and authenticity should always be your most important consideration.

Troubleshoot a Network

Network issues can be simple or complex. To assess how complicated the problem is, you should determine how many computers on the network are experiencing the problem.

If there is a problem with one computer on the network, start the troubleshooting process at that computer. If there is a problem with all computers on the network, start the troubleshooting process in the network room where all computers are connected. As a technician, you should develop a logical and consistent method for diagnosing network problems by eliminating one problem at a time.

Follow the steps outlined in this section to accurately identify, repair, and document the problem. The troubleshooting process is as follows:

How To

Step 1.   Identify the problem.

Step 2.   Establish a theory of probable causes.

Step 3.   Determine an exact cause.

Step 4.   Implement a solution.

Step 5.   Verify solution and full system functionality.

Step 6.   Document findings.

After completing this section, you will meet these objectives:

- Review the troubleshooting process.
- Identify common network problems and solutions.

Review the Troubleshooting Process

Network problems can result from a combination of hardware, software, and connectivity issues. Computer technicians must be able to analyze the problem and determine the cause of the error to repair the network issue. This process is called troubleshooting.

The first step in the troubleshooting process to identify the problem. Start by gathering data from the customer. Here are some open-ended questions to ask the customer:

- What problems are you experiencing with your computer or network?
- What software has been installed on your computer recently?
- What were you doing when the problem was identified?
- What error messages have you received on your computer?
- What type of network connection is the computer using?

Here are some closed-ended questions to ask the customer:

- Has anyone else used your computer recently?
- Can you see any shared files or printers?
- Have you changed your password recently?
- Can you access the Internet?
- Are you currently logged into the network?

After you have talked to the customer, you should establish a theory of possible causes:

- Loose cable connections
- Improperly installed NIC
- Check to make sure NIC link lights are blinking
- Low wireless signal strength
- Invalid IP address

Next, determine the exact cause:

- Check that all cables are connected to the proper locations.
- Unseat and then reconnect cables and connectors.
- Reboot the computer or network device.
- Log in as a different user.
- Repair or reenable the network connection.
- Contact the network administrator.

Implement a solution. The following are helpful places to find solutions:

- Problem-solving experience
- Other technicians
- Internet search
- Newsgroups
- Manufacturer FAQs
- Computer manuals
- Device manuals
- Online forums
- Technical websites

Before giving the computer back to the customer, verify your solution and make sure the entire system is functional. The following commands help verify that the networking is functional:

- Use **ping** to check network connectivity. It sends a packet to the specified address and waits for a reply.
- Use **nslookup** to query Internet domain name servers. It returns a list of hosts in a domain or the information for one host.

- Use **tracert** to determine the route taken by packets when they travel across the network. It shows where communications between your computer and another computer are having difficulty.

- Use **net view** to display a list of computers in a workgroup. It shows the available shared resources on a network. To find out what services a computer is providing on a network, use the command **net view** *hostname*, where *hostname* is the name of the target computer.

After you have solved the network problem, document your findings. Here are some of the tasks required to complete this step:

- Discuss the solution implemented with the customer.

- Have the customer verify that the problem has been solved.

- Provide the customer with all the paperwork.

- Document the steps taken to solve the problem in the work order and the technician's journal.

- Document any components used in the repair.

- Document the time spent to resolve the problem.

Identify Common Network Problems and Solutions

Network problems can be attributed to hardware, software, connectivity issues, or some combination of the three. You will resolve some types of network problems more often than others. Table 8-8 is a chart of common network problems and solutions.

Table 8-8   Common Problems and Solutions

Identify the Problem	Probable Causes	Possible Solutions
NIC LED lights are not lit.	The network cable is unplugged, wrong type, or damaged.	Reconnect or replace network cable connected to the computer.
User cannot telnet into remote device.	The firewall is blocking port 23.	Set the firewall to allow port 23 connectivity.
	The remote device is not configured for Telnet access.	Configure the remote device for telnet access.
	Telnet is not allowed from the user or a particular network.	Allow telnet access from the user or the network.

Identify the Problem	Probable Causes	Possible Solutions
Older laptop cannot detect the wireless router.	The wireless router/wireless access point is configured with an incompatible 802.11 protocol.	Configure the wireless router so it is compatible with the laptop.
	The router/wireless access point is not broadcasting an SSID.	Use a newer USB wireless NIC that is compatible with the existing router and protocol.
	The wireless NIC in the laptop is disabled.	Configure the wireless router to broadcast an SSID.
		Enable the wireless NIC in the laptop in the BIOS, the device manager, and the button on the side of the laptop or, in some cases, a fn key.
Computer has an IP address of 169.254.x.x.	The network cable is unplugged.	Reconnect the network cable.
	The router is powered off or the connection is bad.	Ensure the router is on and is properly connected to the network.
	The NIC is bad.	Replace the NIC.
		Release and renew the IP address on the computer.

continues

Table 8-8   Common Problems and Solutions   *continued*

Identify the Problem	Probable Causes	Possible Solutions
Remote device does not respond to a ping request.	Windows firewall disables ping by default.	Set the firewall to enable ping protocol.
	The remote device is configured to not respond to ping requests.	Configure the remote device to respond to ping requests.
One user can log on to the local network but cannot access the Internet.	The gateway address is incorrect.	
	The browser might be configured incorrectly.	Ensure the correct gateway address is assigned to the NIC.
		Reconfigure or reinstall the browser.
The network is fully functional and the wireless laptop connection is enabled, but the laptop cannot connect to the network.	The laptop wireless capability is turned off.	Enable the wireless NIC in the laptop in the BIOS, the device manager, and the button on the side of the laptop or, in some cases, a fn key.
	The external wireless antenna is misaligned.	
	The laptop is out of wireless range.	Move within range of the wireless signal.

Worksheet 8.12.2: Diagnose a Network Problem

In this worksheet, you diagnose a network problem. Refer to the worksheet in *IT Essentials: PC Hardware and Software Lab Manual, Fourth Edition*. You may perform this worksheet now or wait until the end of the chapter.

Summary

This chapter introduced you to the fundamentals of networking, the benefits of having a network, and the ways to connect computers to a network. The different aspects of troubleshooting a network were discussed, with examples of how to analyze and implement simple solutions. The following concepts from this chapter are important to remember:

- A computer network is composed of two or more computers that share data and resources.

- A local-area network (LAN) is a group of interconnected computers that is under the same administrative control.

- A wide-area network (WAN) connects LANs in geographically separated locations.

- In a peer-to-peer network, devices are connected directly to each other or to additional hosts through the use of a hub or a switch. A peer-to-peer network is easy to install, and no additional equipment or dedicated administrator is required.

- The network topology defines how computers, printers, and other devices are connected. The physical topology describes the layout of the wire and devices, as well as the paths used by data transmissions. The logical topology is the path that signals travel from one point to another. Topologies include bus, star, ring, and mesh.

- Networking media can be defined as the means by which signals, or data, are sent from one computer to another. Signals can be transmitted by either cable or wireless means. The media types discussed were coaxial cable, twisted-pair cable, fiber-optic cable, and radio frequencies.

- Ethernet architecture is currently the most popular type of LAN architecture.

- The OSI reference model is an industry-standard framework that is used to divide networking functions into seven distinct layers: application, presentation, session, transport, network, data link, and physical. It is important to understand the purpose of each layer.

- The TCP/IP suite of protocols has become the dominant standard for the Internet.

- A NIC is a device that plugs into a motherboard and provides ports for the network cable connections. It is the computer interface with the LAN.

- The three transmission methods for sending signals over data channels are simplex, half duplex, and full duplex. Full-duplex networking technology increases performance because data can be sent and received at the same time. DSL, two-way cable modem, and other broadband technologies operate in full-duplex mode.

- It is important to clean equipment regularly and to use a proactive approach to prevent problems.

- When troubleshooting network problems, listen to what your customer tells you so that you can formulate open-ended and closed-ended questions that will help you determine where to begin fixing the problem. Verify obvious issues, and try quick solutions before escalating the troubleshooting process.

Summary of Exercises

This is a summary of the Labs, Worksheets, Remote Technician exercises, Class Discussions, Virtual Desktop activities, and Virtual Laptop activities associated with this chapter.

Labs

The following labs cover material from this chapter. Refer to the lab in *IT Essentials: PC Hardware and Software Lab Manual, Fourth Edition.*

Lab 8.9.2: Configure an Ethernet NIC to Use DHCP in Windows XP

Optional Lab 8.9.2: Configure an Ethernet NIC to Use DHCP in Windows Vista

Worksheets

The following worksheets cover material from this chapter. Refer to the worksheets in *IT Essentials: PC Hardware and Software Lab Manual, Fourth Edition.*

Worksheet 8.3.2: Identify IP Address Classes

Worksheet 8.9.1: Internet Search for NIC Drivers

Worksheet 8.10.3: Answer Broadband Questions

Worksheet 8.12.2: Diagnose a Network Problem

Packet Tracer Activities

The following Packet Tracer activities cover material from this chapter. Refer to the Packet Tracer software on the CD that accompanies this book.

Packet Tracer Activity 8.4.2: Cabling a Simple Network

Packet Tracer Activity 8.9.2: Adding Computers to an Existing Network

Check Your Understanding

You can find the answers to these questions in the appendix, "Answers to Check Your Understanding Questions."

1. The Internet is an example of which type of network?

    A. LAN

    B. SAN

    C. WAN

    D. WLAN

2. What is the suggested maximum number of PCs in a peer-to-peer network?

    A. 10

    B. 25

    C. 50

    D. 100

3. Which method of data transfer allows information to be sent and received at the same time?

    A. Full duplex

    B. Half duplex

    C. Multiplex

    D. Simplex

4. Which dotted-decimal number is used to distinguish the network portion of the IP address from the host portion?

    A. Default gateway

    B. MAC address

    C. Physical address

    D. Subnet mask

5. Which suite of protocols is used to transmit data across the Internet?

    A. AppleTalk

    B. ARP

    C. DNS

    D. IPX/SPX

    E. TCP/IP

6. Which cable type is a common choice for use on Ethernet networks?

   A. Thick coaxial

   B. Thin coaxial

   C. STP

   D. UTP

7. Which networking protocol translates a network name such as www.cisco.com into a unique IP address?

   A. APIPA

   B. ARP

   C. DHCP

   D. DNS

   E. Proxy ARP

8. Which protocol maps known IP addresses to MAC addresses on a local network?

   A. ARP

   B. DHCP

   C. FTP

   D. RARP

9. A technician wants to update the NIC driver for a computer. What is the best way to find new drivers for the NIC?

   A. Installation media that came with the NIC

   B. Windows Update

   C. The website for the manufacturer of the NIC

   D. The Microsoft website

10. What is the most commonly used DSL technology?

    A. ADSL

    B. HDSL

    C. IDSL

    D. SDSL

    E. VDSL

CHAPTER 9

Fundamental Security

Objectives

Upon completion of this chapter, you should be able to answer the following questions:

- Why is security important?
- What are security threats?
- What are some security procedures?
- What are the preventive maintenance techniques for security?
- What can be done to troubleshoot security?

Key Terms

This chapter uses the following key terms. You can find the definitions in the Glossary.

malicious threat   page 348

accidental threat   page 348

virus   page 349

worm   page 349

Trojan horse   page 349

virus protection software   page 349

antivirus software   page 349

ActiveX   page 350

Java   page 350

JavaScript   page 350

adware   page 350

grayware   page 351

malware   page 351

spyware   page 351

social engineering   page 351

denial of service (DoS)   page 351

ping of death   page 351

email bomb   page 351

distributed DoS (DDoS)   page 351

spam   page 351

popup   page 352

SYN flood   page 353

spoofing   page 353

replay   page 353

DNS poisoning   page 353

card key   page 356

biometric devices   page 356

password protection   page 358

data encryption   page 359

port protection   page 359

data backup   page 360

file system security   page 361

continues

Technicians need to understand computer and network security. Failure to implement proper security procedures can affect users, computers, and the general public. Private information, company secrets, financial data, computer equipment, and items of national security are placed at risk if proper security procedures are not followed.

After completing this chapter, you will meet these objectives:

- Explain why security is important.
- Describe security threats.
- Identify security procedures.
- Identify common preventive maintenance techniques for security.
- Troubleshoot security.

Explain Why Security Is Important

Computer and network security help keep data and equipment safe by giving only the appropriate people access. Everyone in an organization should give high priority to security, because everyone can be affected by a lapse in security.

Theft, loss, network intrusion, and physical damage are some of the ways a network or computer can be harmed. Damage or loss of equipment can mean a loss of productivity. Repairing and replacing equipment can cost the company time and money. Unauthorized use of a network can expose confidential information and reduce network resources.

An attack that intentionally degrades the performance of a computer or network can also harm an organization's production. Poorly implemented security measures that allow unauthorized access to wireless network devices demonstrate that physical connectivity is not necessary for security breaches by intruders.

A technician's primary responsibilities include data and network security. A customer or an organization may depend on you to ensure that their data and computer equipment are secure. You will perform tasks that are more sensitive than those assigned to the average employee. You may have to repair, adjust, and install equipment. You need to know how to configure settings to keep the network secure, but still keep it available to those who need to access it. You will ensure that software patches and updates are applied, antivirus software is installed, and antispyware software is used. You may also be asked to instruct users on how to maintain good security practices with computer equipment.

Worksheet 9.1: Security Attacks

In this worksheet, you use the Internet, a newspaper, or magazines to gather information to help you become familiar with computer crime and security attacks in your area. Be prepared to discuss your research with the class. Refer to the worksheet in *IT Essentials: PC Hardware and Software Lab Manual, Fourth Edition*. You may complete this worksheet now or wait until the end of the chapter.

Describe Security Threats

To successfully protect computers and the network, a technician must understand both of the following types of threats to computer security:

- **Physical**: Events or attacks that steal, damage, or destroy such equipment as servers, switches, and wiring

- **Data**: Events or attacks that remove, corrupt, deny access to, allow access to, or steal information

Threats to security can come from inside or outside an organization, and the level of potential damage can vary greatly. Potential threats include the following:

- **Internal**: Employees who have access to data, equipment, and the network. Internal attacks can be characterized as follows:

   — *Malicious threat*: An employee intends to cause damage

   — *Accidental threat*: An employee damages data or equipment unintentionally

- **External**: Users outside an organization who do not have authorized access to the network or resources. External attacks can be characterized as follows:

   — **Unstructured attacks**: Use available resources, such as passwords or scripts, to gain access to and run programs designed to vandalize

   — **Structured attacks**: Use code to access operating systems and software

Physical loss or damage to equipment can be expensive, and data loss can be detrimental to your business and reputation. Threats against data are constantly changing as attackers find new ways to gain entry and commit their crimes.

After completing this section, you will meet these objectives:

- Define viruses, worms, and Trojans.

- Explain web security.

- Define adware, spyware, and grayware.

- Explain denial of service.

- Describe spam and popup windows.

- Explain social engineering.

- Explain TCP/IP attacks.

- Explain hardware deconstruction and recycling.

Define Viruses, Worms, and Trojans

Computer viruses are created with malicious intent and sent by attackers. A *virus* is attached to small pieces of computer code, software, or documents. The virus executes when the software is run on a computer. If the virus spreads to other computers, those computers could continue to spread the virus.

A virus is transferred to another computer through email, file transfers, and instant messaging. The virus hides by attaching itself to a file on the computer. When the file is accessed, the virus executes and infects the computer. A virus has the potential to corrupt or even delete files on your computer, use your email to spread itself to other computers, or even erase your hard drive.

Some viruses can be exceptionally dangerous. The most damaging type of virus is used to record keystrokes. Attackers can use these viruses to harvest sensitive information, such as passwords and credit card numbers. Viruses may even alter or destroy information on a computer. Stealth viruses can infect a computer and lay dormant until summoned by the attacker.

A *worm* is a self-replicating program that is harmful to networks. A worm uses the network to duplicate its code to the hosts on a network, often without any user intervention. It is different from a virus because a worm does not need to attach to a program to infect a host. Even if the worm does not damage data or applications on the hosts it infects, it harms networks because it consumes bandwidth.

A *Trojan horse* does not need to be attached to other software. Instead, a Trojan threat is hidden in software that appears to do one thing, and yet behind the scenes it does another. Trojans often are disguised as useful software. The Trojan program can reproduce like a virus and spread to other computers. Computer data damage and production loss could be significant. A technician may be needed to perform the repairs, and employees may lose or have to replace data. An infected computer could be sending critical data to competitors while at the same time infecting other computers on the network.

Virus protection software, known as *antivirus software*, is software designed to detect, disable, and remove viruses, worms, and Trojans before they infect a computer. Antivirus software becomes outdated quickly, however. The technician is responsible for applying the most recent updates, patches, and virus definitions as part of a regular maintenance schedule. Many organizations establish a written security policy stating that employees are not permitted to install any software that is not provided by the company. Organizations also make employees aware of the dangers of opening email attachments that may contain a virus or worm.

Worksheet 9.2.1: Third-Party Antivirus Software

In this worksheet, you use the Internet, a newspaper, or a local store to gather information about third-party antivirus software. Refer to the worksheet in *IT Essentials: PC Hardware and Software Lab Manual, Fourth Edition*. You may complete this worksheet now or wait until the end of the chapter.

Explain Web Security

Web security is important because so many people visit the World Wide Web every day. Some of the features that make the web useful and entertaining can also make it harmful to a computer.

Tools that are used to make web pages more powerful and versatile can also make computers more vulnerable to attacks. Here are some examples of web tools:

- *ActiveX* is technology created by Microsoft to control interactivity on web pages. If ActiveX is on a page, the user must download an applet or small program to gain access to the full functionality.

- *Java* is a programming language that allows applets to run within a web browser. Examples of applets include a calculator and a counter.

- *JavaScript* is a programming language developed to interact with HTML source code to allow interactive websites. Examples include a rotating banner and a popup window.

Attackers can use any of these tools to install a program on a computer. To protect against these attacks, most browsers have settings that force the computer user to authorize the downloading or use of ActiveX, Java, and JavaScript.

Define Adware, Spyware, and Grayware

Adware, spyware, and grayware are usually installed on a computer without the user's knowledge. These programs collect information stored on the computer, change the computer configuration, or open extra windows on the computer without the user's consent.

Adware is a software program that displays advertising on your computer. Adware is usually distributed with downloaded software. Most often, adware is displayed in a popup window. Adware popup windows are sometimes difficult to control; they open new windows faster than users can close them.

Grayware and *malware* are files or programs other than a virus that are potentially harmful. Many grayware attacks are phishing attacks, which try to persuade the user to unknowingly give attackers access to personal information. As you fill out an online form, the data is sent to the attacker. Grayware can be removed using spyware and adware removal tools.

Spyware, a type of grayware, is similar to adware. It is distributed without any user intervention or knowledge. After it is installed, the spyware monitors activity on the computer. The spyware then sends this information to the organization responsible for launching the spyware.

Phishing is a form of *social engineering*, in which the attacker pretends to represent a legitimate outside organization, such as a bank. A potential victim is contacted via email. The attacker might ask for verification of information, such as a password or username, to supposedly prevent some terrible consequence from occurring.

Note

There is rarely a need to give out sensitive personal or financial information online. Be suspicious. Use the postal service to share sensitive information.

Explain Denial of Service

Denial of service (DoS) is a form of attack that prevents users from accessing normal services, such as email or a web server. DoS works by sending so many requests for a system resource that the requested service is overloaded and ceases to operate.

DoS attacks can affect servers and computers in the following ways:

- *Ping of death* is a series of repeated, larger-than-normal pings that are intended to crash the receiving computer.

- An *email bomb* is a large quantity of bulk email sent to individuals, lists, or domains, intending to prevent users from accessing email.

Distributed DoS (DDoS) is another form of attack that uses many infected computers, called zombies, to launch an attack. With DDoS, the intent is to obstruct or overwhelm access to the targeted server. Zombie computers located at different geographic locations make it difficult to trace the origin of the attack.

Describe Spam and Popup Windows

Spam, also known as junk mail, is unsolicited email. In most cases, spam is used for advertising. However, spam can be used to send harmful links or deceptive content.

When used as an attack method, spam might include links to an infected website or an attachment that could infect a computer. These links or attachments might generate lots of windows (called *popups*) designed to capture your attention and lead you to advertising sites. Uncontrolled popup windows can quickly cover your screen and prevent you from getting any work done.

Many antivirus and email software programs automatically detect and remove spam from an email inbox. Some spam still may get through, so you should look for some of the more common indications:

- No subject line
- An incomplete return address
- Return emails not sent by the user

Explain Social Engineering

A social engineer is a person who gains access to equipment or a network by tricking people into providing the necessary information. Often, the social engineer gains the confidence of an employee and convinces that person to divulge username and password information.

A social engineer may pose as a technician to try to gain entry into a facility. When he is inside, he may look over employees' shoulders to gather information, seek out papers on desks with passwords and phone extensions, or obtain a company directory with email addresses.

The following are some basic precautions to help protect against social engineering:

- Never give out your password.
- Always ask for the ID of unknown persons.
- Restrict the access of unexpected visitors.
- Escort all visitors.
- Never post your password in your work area.
- Log off or lock your computer when you leave your desk.
- Do not let anyone follow you through a door that requires an access card.

Note

These practices should be officially outlined in a security policy. It is important to remember that technical solutions to security problems cannot replace human common sense.

Explain TCP/IP Attacks

TCP/IP is the protocol suite that is used to control all the communications on the Internet. Unfortunately, TCP/IP can also make a network available to attackers through the use of the following common types of attacks:

- A *SYN flood* randomly opens TCP ports, tying up network equipment or a computer with a large number of false requests, causing sessions to be denied to others.

- *DoS* attempts to make a computer resource unavailable to its intended users.

- *DDoS* is a DoS attack that uses "zombies" to make tracing the origin of the attack difficult.

- *Spoofing* is a method of gaining access to resources on devices by pretending to be a trusted computer.

- *Man-in-the-middle* intercepts or inserts false information in traffic between two hosts.

- *Replay* uses network sniffers to extract usernames and passwords to be used later to gain access.

- *DNS poisoning* changes the DNS records on a system to point to false servers where the data is recorded.

Explain Data Wiping, Hard Drive Destruction, and Recycling

Hardware destruction is the process of removing sensitive data from hardware and software before recycling or discarding it. Hard drives should be fully erased to prevent the possibility of recovery using specialized software. Three methods are commonly used to either destroy or recycle data and hard drives:

- Data wiping
- Hard drive destruction
- Hard drive recycling

Data Wiping

Data wiping, also known as secure erase, is a procedure performed to permanently delete data from a hard drive. Data wiping is often performed on hard drives containing sensitive data such as financial information. It is not enough to delete files or even format the drive. Use a third-party tool to overwrite data multiple times, rendering the data unusable. It is important to remember that data wiping is irreversible, and the data can never be recovered.

Hard Drive Destruction

Companies with sensitive data should always establish clear policies for hard drive disposal. It is important to be aware that formatting and reinstalling an operating system on a computer does not ensure that information cannot be recovered. Destroying the hard drive is the best option for companies with sensitive data. To fully ensure that data cannot be recovered from a hard drive, you should carefully shatter the platters with a hammer and safely dispose of the pieces.

Other storage media, such as CDs and floppy disks, must also be destroyed. Use a shredding machine that is designed to destroy this type of media.

Note

Hard drives are found in some unusual places, most notably in printers, where they can keep copies of images scanned and or printed. Hard drives can exist inside of network devices, especially if that device functions as a server. Some projectors also act as network servers and store movies, presentations, photos, and so on.

Hard Drive Recycling

Hard drives that do not contain sensitive data should be reused in other computers. The drive can be reformatted, and a new operating system can be installed. If the drive is not needed, it can be sold or donated.

Identify Security Procedures

You should use a security plan to determine what will be done in a critical situation. Security plan policies should be constantly updated to reflect the latest threats to a network. A security plan with clear security procedures is the basis for a technician to follow. Security plans should be reviewed each year.

Part of the process of ensuring security is conducting tests to determine areas where security is weak. Testing should be done on a regular basis. New threats are released daily. Regular testing provides details of any possible weaknesses in the current security plan that should be addressed. The technician needs to understand how to implement security procedures to protect equipment and data.

After completing this section, you will meet these objectives:

- Explain what is required in a basic local security policy.
- Explain the tasks required to protect physical equipment.
- Describe ways to protect data.
- Describe wireless security techniques.

Explain What Is Required in a Basic Local Security Policy

Although local security policies may vary between organizations, all organizations should ask the following questions:

- What assets require protection?
- What are the possible threats?
- What should be done in the event of a security breach?

The scope of the policy and the consequences of noncompliance should be clearly described. Security policies should be reviewed regularly and updated as necessary. You should keep a revision history to track all policy changes. Security is the responsibility of every person within the company. All employees, including those who don't use computers, must be trained to understand the security policy and notified of any security policy updates.

Password guidelines are an important component of a security policy. Passwords should be required to have a minimum length and include uppercase and lowercase letters combined with numbers and symbols. It is common for a security policy to require users to change their passwords on a regular basis, and to govern the number of password attempts before an account is temporarily locked out.

You should also define employee access to data in a security policy. The policy should protect highly sensitive data from public access, while ensuring employees can still perform their job tasks. Data can be classified from public to top secret, and can have several different levels between them. Public information can be seen by anyone and has no security requirements. Public information cannot be used maliciously to hurt a company or an individual. However, top secret information needs the most security, because the data exposure can be extremely detrimental to a government, a company, or an individual.

A company's security policy should describe the following:

- A process for handling network security incidents
- A process for auditing existing network security
- A general security framework for implementing network security
- Behaviors that are allowed
- Behaviors that are prohibited
- What to log and how to store the logs: Event Viewer, system log files, or security log files
- Which account permissions are required to access specific network resources
- Which authentication technologies (such as usernames, passwords, biometrics, and smart cards) must be provided to access network data

Explain the Tasks Required to Protect Physical Equipment

Physical security is as important as data security. When a computer is stolen, the data is also stolen.

There are several ways to physically protect computer equipment:

- Control access to facilities.
- Use cable locks with equipment, as shown in Figure 9-1.
- Keep telecommunication rooms locked.
- Fit equipment with security screws, as shown in Figure 9-2.
- Use security cages around equipment, as shown in Figure 9-2.
- Label and install sensors, such as radio frequency identification (RFID) tags, on equipment.

Figure 9-1   Physical Security

- Install physical alarms triggered by motion-detection sensors.
- Use webcams with motion-detection and surveillance software.

For access to facilities, there are several means of protection:

- *Card keys* that store user data, including level of access
- *Biometric devices* that identify the user's physical characteristics, such as fingerprints or retinas

- Posted security guard

- Sensors, such as RFID tags, to monitor equipment

Figure 9-2   Locking Devices

One form of hardware security is the Trusted Platform Module (TPM). The TPM is a specialized chip installed on the motherboard of a computer to be used for hardware and software authentication. The TPM stores information specific to the host system, such as encryption keys, digital certificates, and passwords. Applications that use encryption can make use of the TPM chip to secure things like user authentication information, software license protection, and encrypted files, folders, and disks. An added benefit of using TPM is that if the hard drive is stolen, it cannot be accessed because it can no longer communicate with the TPM chip. Integrating hardware security, such as TPM, with software security results in a much safer computer system than using software security alone.

Describe Ways to Protect Data

The value of physical equipment is often far less than the value of the data it contains. The loss of sensitive data to a company's competitors or to criminals may be costly. Such losses may result in a lack of confidence in the company and the dismissal of computer technicians in charge of computer security. To protect data, you can implement several methods of security protection, as described in the following sections.

Password Protection

Password protection can prevent unauthorized access to content, as shown in Figure 9-3. To keep attackers from gaining access to data, all computers should be password-protected. Two levels of password protection are recommended:

- **BIOS**: Prevents BIOS settings from being changed without the appropriate password

- **Login**: Prevents unauthorized access to the network

Figure 9-3   Secured Connection

Network logins provide a means of logging activity on the network and either preventing or allowing access to resources. This makes it possible to determine what resources are being accessed. Usually, the system administrator defines a naming convention for the usernames when creating network logins. A common example of a username is the person's first initial and last name. You should keep the username naming convention simple so that people do not have a hard time remembering it. Usernames, like passwords, are an important piece of information and should not be revealed. Default usernames should be changed so that hackers do not know either part of the username and password combination.

When passwords are assigned, the level of password control should match the level of protection required. A good security policy should be strictly enforced and should include, but not be limited to, the following rules:

- Passwords should expire after a specific period of time.

- Passwords should contain a mixture of numbers, special characters, and uppercase and lowercase letters so that they cannot easily be broken. They should have a minimum of eight characters.

- Users should not write down passwords and leave them where anyone can find them.

- Rules about password expiration and lockout should be defined. Lockout rules apply when an unsuccessful attempt has been made to access the system or when a specific change has been detected in the system configuration.

To simplify the process of administering security, it is common to assign users to groups and then assign groups to resources. This allows you to easily change the access level of users on a network by assigning the users to or removing them from various groups. This is useful when setting up temporary accounts for visiting workers or consultants, giving you the ability to limit access to resources.

To prevent unauthorized users from accessing local computers and network resources, lock your workstation, laptop, or server before you leave it unattended.

Data Encryption

Encrypting data involves using codes and ciphers. *Data encryption* can help prevent attackers from monitoring or recording traffic between resources and computers. It may not be possible to decipher captured data in time to make any use of it. A security alert may inform you that you are using an encrypted connection.

A Virtual Private Network (VPN) is an encryption system that protects data as though it resides on a private network. The data actually travels over the Internet or another unsecured public network.

Software Firewall

Data being transported on a network is called *traffic*. A software firewall is a program that runs on a computer to allow or deny traffic between the computer and the network to which it is connected. Every communication using TCP/IP is associated with a port number. HTTPS, for instance, by default uses port 443. A firewall, as illustrated in Figure 9-4, is a way of protecting a computer from intrusion through the ports. The user can control the type of data sent to a computer by selecting which ports will be open and which will be secured. You must create exceptions to allow certain traffic or applications to connect to the computer. Firewalls can block incoming and outgoing network connections unless exceptions are defined to open and close the ports required by a program.

With *port protection*, the user can control the type of data sent to a computer by selecting which ports will be open and which will be secured. Data being transported on a network is called *traffic*. Table 9-1 shows the ports and protocols associated with the more common types of traffic.

Figure 9-4   Firewall

Table 9-1   Ports and Protocols

Port	Protocol
20	File Transfer Protocol (FTP) data
21	FTP
25	Simple Mail Transfer Protocol (SMTP)
53	Domain Name System (DNS)
80	Hypertext Transfer Protocol (HTTP)

Data Backups

You should include data backup procedures in a security plan. Data can be lost or damaged in circumstances such as theft or equipment failure, or in a disaster, such as a fire or flood. Backing up data is one of the most effective ways of protecting against data loss. Here are some considerations for *data backups*:

- **Frequency of backups**: Backups can take a long time. Sometimes it is easier to make a full backup monthly or weekly and then do frequent partial backups of any data that has changed since the last full backup. However, spreading the backups over many recordings increases the amount of time needed to restore the data.

- **Storing backups**: Backups should be transported to an approved offsite storage location for extra security. The current backup medium is transported to the offsite location on a daily, weekly, or monthly rotation, as required by the local organization.

- **Security of backups:** Backups can be protected with passwords. These passwords have to be entered before the data on the backup media can be restored.

Smart Card Security

A smart card is a small plastic card, about the size of a credit card, with a small chip embedded in it. The chip is an intelligent data carrier, capable of processing, storing, and safeguarding thousands of bytes of data. Smart cards store private information such as bank account numbers, personal identification, medical records, and digital signatures. Smart cards provide authentication and encryption to keep data safe. The weakness of smart cards is that, like all highly portable computer technology, it can get lost, stolen, or broken.

Biometric Security

Biometric security compares physical characteristics against stored profiles to authenticate people. A profile is a data file containing known characteristics of an individual such as a fingerprint or a handprint. In theory, biometric security is more secure than security measures such as passwords or smart cards, because passwords can be discovered and smart cards can be stolen. Common biometric devices available include fingerprint readers, handprint readers, iris scanners, and face recognition devices. There are three weaknesses of biometric security:

- The device itself can brake accidentally or be broken maliciously.

- The application that manages the biometric data can get compromised.

- A user might suffer a physical injury that changes his biometric signature to the point that it is unrecognizable to the application.

File System Security

All file systems keep track of resources, but only file systems with journals can log access by user, date, and time. FAT32, which is used in some versions of the Windows file system, lacks both journaling and encryption capabilities. As a result, situations that require good security are usually deployed using a file system such as NTFS, which is part of Windows 2000 and Windows XP. When increased *file system security* is needed, it is possible to run certain utilities, such as CONVERT, to upgrade a FAT32 file system to NTFS. The conversion process is not reversible. It is important to define your goals clearly before making the transition. Table 9-2 compares the FAT32 and NTFS file systems.

Table 9-2   FAT32 and NTFS Comparison

	FAT32	**NTFS**
Security	Little security.	File- and folder-level permissions, encryption.
Compatibility	Compatible with Windows 95/98/Me. Can be read/ written to by Linux users as well.	Compatible only with Windows (NT, XP, Vista). Linux/UNIX read-only.
File Size	Limit of 4-GB files/32-GB volumes.	Limit of 16-terabyte files/256-terabyte volumes.
Files Per Volume	4.17 million.	4.29 billion (4,294,967,295).
File Size Efficiency	Large clusters waste some space.	Smaller clusters use more of the available space. Built-in compression maximizes space.
Reliability	File allocation tables are nonjournaling (do not record file transfer history for use in reconstruction after errors).	Includes journaling to rebuild after errors.

Describe Wireless Security Techniques

Because traffic flows through radio waves in wireless networks, it is easy for attackers to monitor and attack data without having to physically connect to a network. Attackers gain access to a network by being within range of an unprotected wireless network. A technician needs to know how to configure access points and wireless NICs to an appropriate level of security.

When installing wireless services, you should apply wireless security techniques immediately to prevent unwanted access to the network. Wireless access points should be configured with basic security settings that are compatible with the existing network security. The following items are basic security settings that can be configured on a wireless router or access point:

- **Service set identifier (SSID)**: The name of the wireless network. A wireless router or access point broadcasts the SSID by default so that wireless devices can detect the wireless network. Manually enter the SSID on wireless devices to connect to the wireless network when the SSID broadcast has been disabled on the wireless router or access point.

- **MAC address filtering**: A technique used to deploy device-level security on a wireless LAN. Because every wireless device has a unique MAC address, wireless routers and access points can prevent wireless devices from connecting to the wireless network if the devices do not have authorized MAC addresses. Enable MAC address filtering, and list each wireless device MAC address to enforce MAC address filtering.

An attacker can access data as it travels over the radio signal. A wireless encryption system can be used to prevent unwanted capture and use of data by encoding the information that is sent. Both ends of every link must use the same encryption standard. The following items are wireless encryption and authentication technologies:

- *Wired Equivalent Privacy (WEP)*: The first-generation security standard for wireless. Attackers quickly discovered that WEP encryption was easy to break. The encryption keys used to encode the messages could be detected by monitoring programs. Once the keys were obtained, messages could be easily decoded.

- *Wi-Fi Protected Access (WPA)*: An improved version of WEP. It was created as a temporary solution until the 802.11i standard (a security layer for wireless systems) was fully implemented. Now that 802.11i has been ratified, WPA2 has been released. It covers the entire 802.11i standard. WPA uses much stronger encryption than WEP encryption.

- *Wi-Fi Protected Access 2 (WPA2)*: An improved version of WPA. This protocol was released to introduce higher levels of security than WPA. WPA2 supports robust encryption providing government grade security. WPA2 can be enabled in two versions: Personal (password authentication) and Enterprise (server authentication).

- *Lightweight Extensible Authentication Protocol (LEAP)*: A wireless security protocol created by Cisco to address the weaknesses in WEP and WPA. LEAP (also called EAP-Cisco) is a good choice when using Cisco equipment in conjunction with operating systems like Windows and Linux.

Wireless Transport Layer Security (WTLS) is a security layer used in mobile devices that employ the Wireless Applications Protocol (WAP). Mobile devices do not have a great deal of spare bandwidth to devote to security protocols. WTLS was designed to provide security for WAP devices in a bandwidth-efficient manner.

Packet Tracer Activity 9.3.4: Connecting Wireless PCs to a Linksys WRT300N

In this Packet Tracer activity you will configure basic wireless settings on a PC, configure basic security on the Linksys WRT300N, and verify full connectivity. Refer to the CD in this book to find the activity. You may perform this activity now or wait until the end of the chapter.

Identify Common Preventive Maintenance Techniques for Security

Regular security updates are essential to meet the threat from attackers constantly searching for new ways of breaching security. Software manufacturers have to regularly create and issue new patches to fix flaws and vulnerabilities in products. If a technician leaves a computer unprotected, an attacker can easily gain access. Unprotected computers on the Internet may become infected within a few minutes.

Because of the constantly changing security threats, a technician should understand how to install patches and updates, as shown in Figure 9-5. They should also be able to recognize when new updates and patches are available. Some manufacturers release updates on the same day every month and also send out critical updates when necessary. Other manufacturers provide automatic update services that patch the software every time a computer is turned on. Manufacturers also often send email notifications when a new patch or update is released.

Figure 9-5   Security Updates

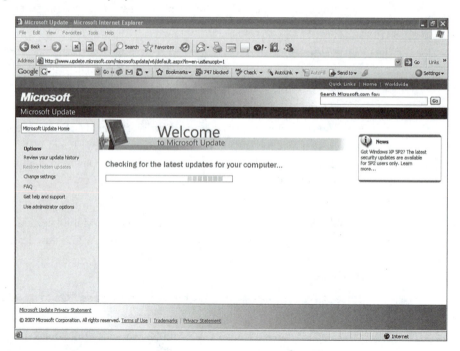

At the end of this section, you will meet these objectives:

- Explain how to update signature files for antivirus and antispyware software.

- Explain how to install operating system service packs and security patches.

Explain How to Update Signature Files for Antivirus and Antispyware Software

Threats to security from viruses and worms are always present. Attackers constantly look for new ways to infiltrate computers and networks. Because new viruses are always being developed, security software must be continually updated. This process can be performed automatically, but a technician should know how to manually update any type of protection software and all customer application programs.

Virus, spyware, and adware detection programs look for patterns in the programming code of the software in a computer. These patterns are determined by analyzing viruses that are intercepted on the Internet and on local-area networks (LAN). These code patterns are called *signatures*. The publishers of protection software compile the signatures into virus definition tables. To update *signature files* for antivirus and antispyware software, first check to see if the signature files are the most recent ones. You can do this by navigating to the About option of the protection software or by launching the update tool for the protection software. If the signature files are out of date, update them manually with the Update Now option available on most protection software.

You should always retrieve the signature files from the manufacturer's website. However, to avoid creating too much traffic at a single site, some manufacturers distribute the signature files for download to multiple download sites. These download sites are called *mirrors*.

To update a signature file, follow these steps:

How To

Step 1. Set the Windows restore point.

Step 2. Open the antivirus or antispyware program.

Step 3. Locate the update control button, and click it.

Step 4. After the program is updated, use it to scan your computer.

Step 5. When the scan is complete, check the report for viruses or other problems that could not be treated, and delete them yourself.

Step 6. Set the antivirus or antispyware program to automatically update and to run on a scheduled basis.

Caution

When downloading the signature files from a mirror, ensure that the mirror site is legitimate. Always link to the mirror site from the manufacturer's website.

Explain How to Install Operating System Service Packs and Security Patches

Viruses and worms can be difficult to remove from a computer. Software tools are required to remove viruses and repair the computer code that the virus has modified. These software tools are provided by operating system manufacturers and security software companies. Make sure that you download these tools from a legitimate site.

Manufacturers of operating systems and software applications may provide code updates called *patches* that prevent a newly discovered virus or worm from making a successful attack. From time to time, manufacturers combine patches and upgrades into a comprehensive update application called a *service pack*. Many infamous and devastating virus attacks could have been much less severe if more users had downloaded and installed the latest service pack.

The Windows operating system routinely checks the Windows Update website for high-priority updates that can help protect a computer from the latest security threat. These updates can include security updates, critical updates, and service packs. Depending on the setting you choose, Windows automatically downloads and installs any high-priority updates that your computer needs, or notifies you as these updates become available.

Updates must be installed, not just downloaded. If you use the Automatic setting, you can schedule the time and day. Otherwise, new updates are installed at 3 a.m. by default. If your computer is turned off during a scheduled update, updates are installed the next time you start your computer. You can also choose to have Windows notify you when a new update is available and install the update yourself.

To update the operating system with a service pack or security patch, follow these steps:

How To

Step 1.   Create a restore point in case of a problem with the update.

Step 2.   Check the updates to ensure that you have the latest ones.

Step 3.   Download the updates using Automatic Updates or from the operating system manufacturer's website.

Step 4.   Install the update.

Step 5.   Restart the computer if required.

Step 6.   Test all aspects to ensure that the update has not caused any issues.

Worksheet 9.4.2: Operating System Updates

In this worksheet, you use the Internet to research operating system updates. Be prepared to discuss your research with the class. Refer to the worksheet in *IT Essentials: PC Hardware and Software Lab Manual, Fourth Edition*. You may complete this worksheet now or wait until the end of the chapter.

Troubleshoot Security

The troubleshooting process is used to help resolve security issues. These problems range from simple, such as preventing someone from watching over your shoulder, to more complex problems, such as manually removing infected files. Use the troubleshooting steps as a guideline to help diagnose and repair problems.

After completing this section, you will meet these objectives:

- Review the troubleshooting process.
- Identify common problems and solutions.

Review the Troubleshooting Process

Computer technicians must be able to analyze a security threat and determine the appropriate method to protect assets and repair damage. This process is called *troubleshooting*.

Step 1: Identify the Problem

The first step in the troubleshooting process is identify the problem. Table 9-3 lists open-ended and closed-ended questions to ask the customer about security issues. (This list is *not* comprehensive.)

Table 9-3   Security Issues: Open-Ended and Closed-Ended Questions to Ask

Open-Ended Questions	Closed-Ended Questions
When did the problem start?	Has anyone else used your computer?
What problems are you experiencing?	Is your security software up to date?
Can you tell me anything else about the problem?	Have you scanned your computer recently for viruses?
What websites have you visited recently?	Did you open any attachments from a suspicious email?
What security software is installed on your computer?	Have you ever had any problems like this before?
How are you connected to the Internet?	Have you changed your password recently?
Have any unexpected visitors been in your work area?	Have you received any error messages on your computer?
	Have you told anyone your password?

Step 2: Establish a Theory of Probably Causes

After you have talked to the customer, you should establish a theory of probable causes. Here are some issues that apply to security:

- Virus
- Trojan Horse
- Worm
- Spyware
- Adware
- Grayware or Malware
- Phishing scheme
- Compromised password
- Unprotected equipment rooms
- Unsecure work environment

Step 3: Determine an Exact Cause

After you have established a theory of possible causes, determine an exact cause:

- Secure equipment rooms.
- Enforce security policy.
- Secure work environment.
- Update anti-virus and spyware signatures.
- Scan the computer with antivirus and other protection programs.
- Update the OS with the latest patches and updates.

Step 4: Implement the Solution

At this point, you have enough information to evaluate the problem and to research and implement possible solutions. Here are some resources for possible solutions:

- Help Desk logs
- Problem-solving experience
- Other technicians

- Internet search

- Newsgroups

- Manufacturer FAQs

- Computer manuals

- Device manuals

- Online forums

- Technical websites

Step 5: Verify Solution and Full System Functionality

After you have identified and solved the problem, perform the following tasks to verify the solution and verify full system functionality:

- Rescan the computer to ensure no viruses remain.

- Rescan the computer to ensure no spyware remains.

- Check the security logs to ensure no problems remain.

- Test network and Internet connectivity.

- Ensure all applications are working.

- Verify access to authorized resources such as shared printer and databases.

- Make sure doors, windows, and cabinets are secured.

- Ensure security policy is enforced.

Step 6: Document Findings

After you have solved the problem, you close with the customer. Here are the steps required to complete this task:

How To

Step 1.   Discuss the solution implemented with the customer.

Step 2.   Have the customer verify that the problem has been solved.

Step 3.   Provide the customer with all the paperwork.

Step 4.   Document the steps taken to solve the problem in the work order and the technician's journal.

Step 5.   Document any components used in the repair.

Step 6.   Document the time spent to resolve the problem.

Identify Common Problems and Solutions

Maintaining a computer can be a challenge. One of the biggest challenges is making sure that your computer software is updated and secure. Table 9-4 is a chart of common security issues and solutions.

Table 9-4   Common Security-Related Issues and Solutions

Problem Symptom	Probable Causes	Possible Solutions
A wireless network is compromised even though 128-bit WEP encryption is in use.	A hacker is using commonly available wireless hacking tools to crack the encryption.	Upgrade to WPA or EAP-Cisco security.
A user is receiving hundreds or thousands of junk emails each day.	The network is not providing detection or protection for the email server from spammers.	At the email server, filter out email from the sender(s).
An unknown printer repair person is observed looking under keyboards and on desktops.	Visitors are not being monitored or user credentials have been stolen to enter the building.	Contact security or police. Advise users never to hide passwords near their work area.
An unauthorized wireless access point is discovered on the network.	A user has added a wireless access point to increase the wireless range of the company network.	Immediately report the unauthorized device to a supervisor. Enforce security policy by taking action against the person responsible for the security breach.
Users with flash drives are infecting computers on the network with viruses.	The flash drive is infected with a virus and is not scanned by virus protection software when a network computer accesses it.	Prevent the use of removable media on network computers, or set virus protection software to scan removable media when data is accessed.

Worksheet 9.5.2: Gather Information from the Customer

In this worksheet, you gather data from the customer to begin the troubleshooting process and document the customer's problem in the work order provided in the worksheet. Refer to the worksheet in *IT Essentials: PC Hardware and Software Lab Manual, Fourth Edition*. You may perform this worksheet now or wait until the end of the chapter.

Summary

This chapter discussed computer security and why it is important to protect computer equipment, networks, and data. Threats, procedures, and preventive maintenance relating to data and physical security were described to help you keep computer equipment and data safe. Security protects computers, network equipment, and data from loss and physical danger. The following are some of the important concepts to remember from this chapter:

- Security threats can come from inside or outside an organization.

- Viruses and worms are common threats that attack data.

- Develop and maintain a security plan to protect both data and physical equipment from loss.

- Keep operating systems and applications up to date and secure with patches and service packs.

Summary of Exercises

This is a summary of the Worksheets and Packet Tracer activities associated with this chapter.

Worksheets

The following worksheets cover material from this chapter. Refer to the labs in *IT Essentials: PC Hardware and Software Lab Manual, Fourth Edition.*

Worksheet 9.1: Security Attacks

Worksheet 9.2.1: Third-Party Antivirus Software

Worksheet 9.4.2: Operating System Updates

Worksheet 9.5.2: Gather Information from the Customer

Packet Tracer Activities

Refer to the CD-ROM in the back of this book to access the following Packet Tracer activity:

Packet Tracer Activity 9.3.4: Connecting Wireless PCs to a Linksys WRT300N

Check Your Understanding

You can find the answers to these questions in the appendix, "Answers to Check Your Understanding Questions."

1. Which of the following is a software program that displays advertising on your computer?

   A. Adware

   B. Spyware

   C. Grayware

   D. Virus

2. Which of the following uses the network to duplicate its code to the hosts on a network, often without any user intervention?

   A. Adware

   B. Spyware

   C. Virus

   D. Worm

3. Which of the following is a threat that is hidden in software that appears to do one thing, but does another?

   A. Virus

   B. Spyware

   C. Adware

   D. Trojan

4. Which of the following is a form of attack that prevents users from accessing normal services, such as email or the web server?

   A. Ping of death

   B. Denial of service

   C. Email bomb

   D. Distributed denial of service

5. Which of the following is an encryption system that protects data as if it is on a private network, even though the data is actually traveling over the Internet or other unsecured public networks?

   A. Data encryption

   B. Port protection

   C. Virtual Private Network

   D. File system security

6. What characterizes a DDoS attack?

   A. Many hosts participate in a coordinated attack.

   B. It takes only a short time to set up.

   C. Home computers with Internet connections are not susceptible.

   D. It is easy to determine a packet's intent.

7. Which two of the following threats are physical threats?

   A. Laptops are stored in an unlocked cabinet.

   B. Antivirus software has outdated virus definitions.

   C. All users use the same generic username and password to connect to the network.

   D. The network server and network equipment are kept in the corner of the office for easy access.

   E. The computers are secured to the desks of each user.

8. Which type of security threat installs to a computer without the user's knowledge and then monitors all computer activity but does not attempt to persuade the user to unknowingly give attackers access to personal information?

   A. Adware

   B. Grayware

   C. Malware

   D. Spyware

9. Which type of security threat uses email that appears to be from a legitimate sender and asks the email recipient to visit a website to enter confidential information?

   A. Badware

   B. Phishing

   C. Stealth virus

   D. Worm

10. A technician is attempting to secure a wireless network. Which two options should be performed to secure access to the network?

   A. Change the default administrator password for all access points.

   B. Install a security appliance to stop all wireless traffic.

   C. Enable the broadcasting of the SSID for only one access point.

   D. Use MAC filtering.

   E. Use the default SSID values for the access points.

11. A technician has configured a wireless network with WEP encryption. Several users who were able to use the wireless network are now unable to connect to the access point. What is the probable cause of the connection problem?

   A. WEP is a strong encryption technique that requires a successful handshake to establish connectivity.

   B. The access point cannot broadcast SSIDs when WEP is enabled.

   C. The users have not configured their computers for WEP encryption.

   D. The access point uses 64-bit encryption, which is obsolete with newer wireless NICs.

12. Which step should a technician perform first when troubleshooting security issues?

   A. Gather data from the computer.

   B. Gather data from the customer.

   C. Evaluate the problem.

   D. Verify the obvious issues.

CHAPTER 10

Communication Skills

Objectives

Upon completion of this chapter, you should be able to answer the following questions:

- What is the relationship between communication and troubleshooting?

- Why are good communication skills and professional behavior important?

- Does working with computer technology have ethical and legal aspects?

- What is a call center environment, and what are the technician's responsibilities?

Key Terms

This chapter uses the following key terms. You can find the definitions in the Glossary.

troubleshooting   *page 378*

communication skills   *page 378*

professionalism   *page 379*

level-one technician   *page 385*

level-two technician   *page 385*

Netiquette   *page 386*

workstation ergonomics   *page 386*

time management   *page 387*

stress management   *page 388*

service level agreement (SLA)   *page 389*

customer call rules   *page 390*

call center employee rules   *page 390*

call center   *page 392*

What is the relationship between communication skills and troubleshooting? As a computer technician, you will not only fix computers; you also will interact with people. In fact, ***troubleshooting*** is as much about communicating with the customer as it is about knowing how to fix a computer. In this chapter, you will learn how to use good communication skills as confidently as you use a screwdriver. After completing this chapter, you will meet these objectives:

- Explain the relationship between communication and troubleshooting.

- Describe good communication skills and professional behavior.

- Explain ethics and legal aspects of working with computer technology.

- Describe the call center environment and technician responsibilities.

Explain the Relationship Between Communication and Troubleshooting

Think of a time when you had to call a repair person to get something fixed. Did it feel like an emergency to you? Did you appreciate it when the repair person was sympathetic and responsive? Perhaps you had a bad experience with a repair person. Are you likely to call that same person to fix a problem again?

Good *communication skills* enhance a technician's troubleshooting skills. Both of these skill sets take time and experience to develop. As your hardware, software, and operating system knowledge increases, your ability to quickly determine a problem and find a solution will improve. The same principle applies to developing communication skills. The more you practice good communication skills, the more effective you will become when working with customers. A knowledgeable technician who uses good communication skills will always be in demand in the job market.

To troubleshoot a computer, you need to learn the details of the problem from the customer. Most people who need a computer problem fixed are probably feeling some stress. If you establish a good rapport with the customer, he or she may relax a bit. A relaxed customer is more likely to provide the information you need to determine the source of the problem and then fix it.

Speaking directly with the customer is usually the first step in resolving the computer problem. As a technician, you will have access to several communication and research tools. You can use all these resources to gather information for the troubleshooting process. Some examples of technician resources are

- Personal experience

- Scripts

- Websites

- Search engines

- Online FAQs

- Coworkers

- Support vendors

- Diagnostic repair tools

- Manufacturer manuals

- Email

Worksheet 10.1.0: Technician Resources

In this worksheet, you use the Internet to find online resources for a specific computer component and then search online for resources that can help you troubleshoot the component. Refer to the worksheet in *IT Essentials: PC Hardware and Software Lab Manual, Fourth Edition*. You may complete this worksheet now or wait until the end of the chapter.

Describe Good Communication Skills and Professional Behavior

Whether you are talking with a customer on the phone or in person, it is important to communicate well and to represent yourself professionally. Your *professionalism* and good communication skills will enhance your creditability with the customer.

A customer can "see" your body language. A customer can hear your sighs and sense that you are sneering, even over the phone. Conversely, customers can also sense that you are smiling when you speak with them on the phone. Many call center technicians have a mirror at their desk to monitor their facial expressions.

Successful technicians control their reactions and emotions from one customer call to the next. A good rule for all technicians to follow is that a new customer call means a fresh start. Never carry your frustration from one call to the next.

After completing this section, you will meet these objectives:

- Determine the computer problem of the customer.

- Display professional behavior with the customer.

- Focus the customer on the problem during the call.

- Use proper Netiquette.

- Implement time and stressmanagement techniques.

- Observe service level agreements (SLA).

- Follow business policies.

Determine the Computer Problem of the Customer

One of the technician's first tasks is to determine the type of computer problem that the customer is experiencing.

Remember these three rules at the beginning of your conversation:

- **Know**: Call your customer by name.

- **Relate**: Use brief communication to create a one-to-one connection between you and your customer.

- **Understand**: Determine the customer's level of knowledge about her computer to know how to effectively communicate with her.

To accomplish these tasks, you should practice active listening skills. Allow the customer to tell the whole story. As the customer is explaining the problem, occasionally interject a small word or phrase, such as "I understand," "Yes," "I see," or "Okay." This behavior lets the customer know that you are there and listening.

However, occasionally interjecting is not the same as interrupting the customer to ask a question or make a statement. A technician should not interrupt the customer to ask a question or make a statement. This is rude and disrespectful and creates tension. Many times in a conversation, you might find yourself thinking about what to say before the other person finishes talking. When you do this, you are not really listening. As practice, try listening carefully when other people speak, and let them finish their thoughts.

After you have listened to the customer explain the whole problem, clarify what the person has said. This helps convince the customer that you have heard and understand the situation. A good practice for clarification is to paraphrase the customer's explanation by beginning with "Let me see if I understand what you have told me...." This is a very effective tool that shows the customer that you have listened and that you are concerned about the issues.

After you have assured the customer that you understand the problem, you will probably have to ask some follow-up questions. Make sure that these questions are pertinent. Do not ask questions that the customer has already answered while describing the problem. Doing this only irritates the customer and shows that you were not listening.

Follow-up questions should be targeted, closed-ended questions based on the information you have already gathered. Closed-ended questions should focus on obtaining specific information. The customer should be able to answer with a simple "yes" or "no" or with a factual response such as "Windows XP Pro." Use all the information you have gathered from the customer to continue filling out the work order.

Display Professional Behavior with the Customer

When dealing with customers, it is necessary to be professional in all aspects of your role. You must handle customers with respect and prompt attention. When on the phone, make sure that you know how to put a customer on hold, as well as how to transfer a customer without losing the call. How you conduct the call is important. Your job is to help the customer focus on and communicate the problem so that you can solve it.

Be positive when communicating with the customer. Tell him what you can do. Do not focus on what you cannot do. Be prepared to explain alternative ways in which you can help him, such as emailing information, faxing step-by-step instructions, or using remote-control software to solve the problem. Customers will quickly sense whether you are interested in helping them.

Here are some recommendations to follow before you put a customer on hold. First, let the customer finish speaking. Then, explain that you have to put him on hold, and ask him for permission to do so. When the customer agrees to be put on hold, thank him. Tell him that you will be away only a few minutes, and explain what you will be doing during that time.

Table 10-1 lists dos and don'ts for conversing with a customer.

Table 10-1   Customer Communication Dos and Don'ts

Do	Don't
Let the customer finish talking.	Interrupt.
Tell the customer that you must put him on hold, and explain why.	Abruptly put the customer on hold.
Ask if it is all right to put the customer on hold. After you are given consent, tell the customer you will be just a minute.	Put the customer on hold without an explanation and the customer's consent.

Follow the same process for a call transfer as you do when placing a customer on hold. Let the customer finish talking, and then explain that you have to transfer the call. When the customer agrees to be transferred, tell her the phone number that you are transferring her to. You should also tell the new technician your name, the name of the customer you are transferring, and the related ticket number.

Table 10-2 lists dos and don'ts for transferring a call from the customer.

Table 10-2   Customer Call Transfer Dos and Don'ts

Do	Don't
Let the customer finish talking.	Interrupt.
Explain that you have to transfer the call, and tell the customer to whom and why.	Abruptly transfer the call.
Tell the customer the number you are transferring her to (for example, 142).	Transfer without an explanation and the customer's consent.
Ask if it is all right to transfer the call now.	Transfer without informing the new tech.
After you are given consent, begin the transfer.	Tell the new tech who you are, the ticket number, and the customer's name.

When dealing with customers, it is sometimes easier to explain what you should *not* do. When communicating with a customer, avoid the following:

- Minimizing customer problems

- Using jargon, abbreviations, and acronyms

- Displaying a negative attitude or using a negative tone of voice

- Arguing with customers or becoming defensive

- Being judgmental or insulting or calling the customer names

- Distractions and interruptions when talking with customers

- Unnecessary and abrupt holds

- Transferring a call without explaining the purpose of the transfer and getting the customer's consent

- Making negative remarks about other technicians to the customer

Class Discussion 10.2.2: Controlling the Call

In this activity, the class discusses positive ways to tell customers negative things through the use of four scenarios. Refer to the relevant topics in *IT Essentials: PC Hardware and Software Lab Manual, Fourth Edition* to help you prepare for this discussion.

Focus the Customer on the Problem During the Call

Part of your job is to focus the customer during the phone call. Keeping the customer focused on the problem allows you to control the call. This makes the best use of your time and the customer's time on troubleshooting the problem. Do not take any comments personally, and do not retaliate with comments or criticism. If you stay calm, finding a solution to the problem remains the focal point of the call.

Just as there are many different computer problems, there are many different types of customers. The list of problem-customer types described in the following sections is not comprehensive; often a customer can display a combination of traits. You need to recognize which traits your customer exhibits. Recognizing these traits will help you manage the call accordingly.

Talkative Customer

A talkative customer discusses everything except the problem. This kind of customer often uses the call as an opportunity to socialize. It can be difficult to get a talkative customer to focus on the problem. Table 10-3 lists dos and don'ts for dealing with a talkative customer.

Table 10-3   Dealing with a Talkative Customer Dos and Don'ts

Do	Don't
Allow the customer to talk for one minute.	Encourage non-problem-related conversation by asking social questions, such as "How are you today?"
Gather as much information about the problem as possible.	
Politely step in to refocus the customer. This is the exception to the rule of never interrupting a customer.	
Ask as many closed-ended questions as you need to after you have regained control of the call.	

Rude Customer

A rude customer complains during the call and often makes negative comments about the product, the service, and the technician. This type of customer is sometimes abusive and uncooperative and is easily aggravated. Table 10-4 lists dos and don'ts for dealing with a rude customer.

Table 10-4   Dealing with a Rude Customer Dos and Don'ts

Do	Don't
Listen carefully, because you do not want to ask the customer to repeat any information.	Ask the customer to follow any obvious steps if there is any way you can determine the problem without the customer.
Follow a step-by-step approach to determining and solving the problem.	Be rude to the customer.
If the customer has a favorite technician, try to contact that technician to see if he or she can take the call. For example, tell the customer, "I can either help you right now or see if (the preferred technician) is available. He will be available in two hours. Is that acceptable?" If the customer wants to wait for the other technician, record this in the ticket.	
Apologize for the wait time and the inconvenience, even if there has been no wait time.	
Reiterate that you want to solve the customer's problem as quickly as possible.	

Angry Customer

An angry customer talks loudly during the call and often tries to speak when the technician is talking. Angry customers are usually frustrated that they have a problem and upset that they have to call somebody to fix it. Table 10-5 lists dos and don'ts for dealing with an angry customer.

Table 10-5   Dealing with an Angry Customer Dos and Don'ts

Do	Don't
Let the customer explain his problem without interrupting, even if he is angry. This allows the customer to release some of his anger before you proceed.	If at all possible, try not to put this customer on hold or transfer the call.
Sympathize with the customer's problem.	Spend call time talking about what caused the problem. Instead, redirect the conversation to solving the problem.
Apologize for the wait time or inconvenience.	

Knowledgeable Customer

A knowledgeable customer wants to speak with a technician who is equally experienced in computers. This type of customer usually tries to control the call and does not want to speak with a *level-one technician*. Table 10-6 lists dos and don'ts for dealing with a knowledgeable customer.

Table 10-6   Dealing with a Knowledgeable Customer Dos and Don'ts

Do	Don't
If you are a level-one technician, you might try to set up a conference call with a *level-two technician*.	Follow a step-by-step process with the customer.
Explain your overall approach to what you are trying to verify.	Ask the customer to check the obvious, such as the power cord or the power switch. For example, you could suggest a reboot instead.

Inexperienced Customer

An inexperienced customer has difficulty describing the problem. These customers usually can't follow directions or communicate the errors they encounter. Table 10-7 lists dos and don'ts for dealing with an inexperienced customer.

Table 10-7   Dealing with an Inexperienced Customer Dos and Don'ts

Do	Don't
Use a simple step-by-step process of instructions.	Use industry jargon.
Speak in plain terms.	Condescend to your customer or belittle him or her.

Class Discussion 10.2.3: Identifying Difficult Customer Types

In this activity, the class identifies difficult customer types through the use of five scenarios. Refer to the relevant topics in *IT Essentials: PC Hardware and Software Lab Manual, Fourth Edition* to help you prepare for this discussion.

Use Proper Netiquette

Have you read a blog where two or three members have stopped discussing the issue and are simply insulting each other? These are called "flame wars," and they occur in blogs and email threads. Have you ever wondered if they would say those things to each other in person? Perhaps you have received an email that had no greeting or was written entirely in capital letters. How did this make you feel?

As a technician, you should be professional in all communications with customers. Email and text communications have a set of personal and business etiquette rules called *Netiquette*.

In addition to email and text Netiquette, general rules apply to all your online interactions with customers and coworkers:

- Remember that you are dealing with people.
- Adhere to the same standards of behavior that you follow in real life.
- Respect people's time and bandwidth.
- Share expert knowledge.
- Do not engage in "flame wars" online.
- Respect people's privacy.
- Be forgiving of people's mistakes.

The preceding list is not comprehensive. When dealing with a customer, consider all the rules about online communication that you can think of.

Implement Time and Stress Management Techniques

As a technician, you are a very busy person. It is important for your well-being to ensure that your work area is as comfortable as possible and that you use proper time- and stress-management techniques. The following sections describe these considerations and techniques in greater detail.

Workstation Ergonomics

Workstation ergonomics can help you do your job or make it more difficult. Because you may spend the major portion of your day at your workstation, make sure that the desk layout works well, as shown in Figure 10-1. Good workstation ergonomics allows for safe and efficient productivity by customizing the design and arrangement to suit your needs. Have your headset and phone in a position that is both easy to reach and easy to use. Your chair should be adjusted to a height that is comfortable. Adjust your computer screen to a comfortable angle so that you do not have to tilt your head to see it. Make sure your keyboard and mouse are also in a comfortable position. You should not have to bend your wrists to type. If possible, try to minimize external distractions, such as noise.

Figure 10-1   Workstation Ergonomics

Time Management

For *time management*, it isimportant to prioritize your activities. Make sure that you carefully follow your company's business policy. The company policy may state that you must take "down" calls first, even though they may be harder to solve. A "down" call usually means that a server is not working and the entire office or company is waiting for the problem to be resolved before they can resume business.

If you have to call a customer back, make sure that you do so as close to the callback time as possible. Keep a list of callback customers, and check them off one at a time as you complete these calls. Doing this ensures that you do not forget a customer.

When working with many customers, do not give your favorite customers faster or better service. When reviewing the call boards (as shown in Figure 10-2), do not take only the easy calls. Do not take the call of another technician unless you have permission to do so.

Figure 10-2   Call Board

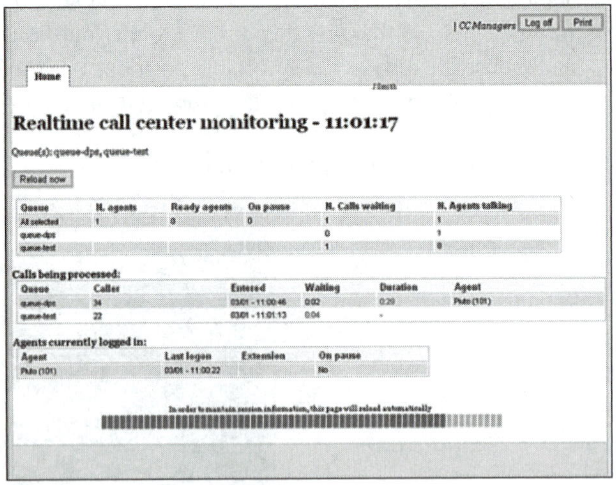

Stress Management

For *stress management*, take a moment to compose yourself between customer calls. Every call should be independent of the others. Do not carry any frustrations from one call to the next.

You might have to do some physical activity to relieve stress. Stand up and take a short walk. Do a few simple stretch movements or squeeze a tension ball. Take a break if you can, and try to relax. You then will be ready to answer the next customer call effectively.

Here are some ways to relax:

- Practice relaxed breathing: inhale-hold-exhale-repeat.

- Stand (or if more appropriate remain seated) and stretch.

- Listen to soothing sounds.

- Massage your temples.

- Take a break. Go for a quick walk, or climb a flight of stairs.

- Eat something small (a snack with protein is best).

- Plan your weekend.

- Avoid stimulants such as coffee, carbonated drinks, and chocolate. All contain caffeine and can add to stress.

Think of other appropriate activities that might relieve stress for you at work.

Observe Service Level Agreements

When dealing with customers, it is important to adhere to that customer's *service level agreement (SLA)*. This is a contract that defines expectations between an organization and the service vendor to provide an agreed-upon level of support. As an employee of the service company, your job is to honor the SLA that you have with the customer. Figure 10-3 shows a sample SLA with some of the standard sections highlighted:

- Service monitoring
- Contingency
- Maintenance windows
- Response time guarantee

Figure 10-3 Service Level Agreement

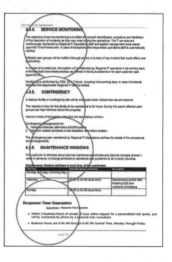

An SLA typically is a legal agreement that describes the responsibilities and liabilities of all parties involved. Some of the contents of an SLA usually include the following:

- Response-time guarantees (often based on the type of call and the SLA)
- Equipment and/or software that will be supported
- Where service will be provided
- Preventive maintenance
- Diagnostics
- Part availability (equivalent parts)

- Cost and penalties

- Time of service availability (for example, 24/7; Monday through Friday, 8 a.m. to 5 p.m. EST; and so on)

There may be exceptions to the SLA. Be sure to follow your company business rules in detail. Some of the exceptions may include the customer's ability to upgrade the service level and the ability to escalate to management for review. Escalation to management should be reserved for special situations. For example, a long-standing customer or a customer from a very large company might have a problem that falls outside the parameters stated in his or her SLA with your service company. In these cases, your management may choose to support the customer for customer-relations reasons.

Consider other circumstances in which it might be a good idea to escalate a call to management.

Follow Business Policies

As a technician, you should be aware of all business policies related to customer calls. Don't make a promise to a customer that you cannot keep. You should also have a good understanding of all rules governing employees. Table 10-8 lists typical *customer call rules* as well as *call center employee rules*.

Table 10-8 Customer Call and Call Center Employee Rules

Customer Call Rules	Call Center Employee Rules
Maximum time on call (example: 15 minutes)	Arrive at your workstation early enough to be prepared, usually about 15 to 20 minutes before the first call.
Maximum call time in queue (example: three minutes)	Do not exceed the allowed number and length of breaks.
Number of calls per day (example: minimum of 30)	Do not take a break or go to lunch if a call is on the board.
Rules about passing calls to other technicians (example: only when absolutely necessary, and not without that technician's permission)	Do not take a break or go to lunch at the same time as other technicians. Stagger breaks among technicians.
Rules about what you can and cannot promise to the customer (see that customer's SLA for details)	Do not leave an ongoing call to take a break or go to lunch.

Customer Call Rules	Call Center Employee Rules
When to follow the SLA and when to escalate to management	Make sure that another technician is available if you have to leave.
	If no other technician is available, check with the customer to see if you can call back later, possibly in the morning.
	Do not show favoritism to certain customers.
	Do not take another technician's calls without permission.
	Do not talk negatively about the capabilities of another technician.

Explain Ethics and Legal Aspects of Working with Computer Technology

When you are working with customers and their equipment, you should observe some general ethical customs and legal rules. Often, these customs and rules overlap.

Ethical Customs

You should always respect your customers, as well as their property. Property includes any information or data that may be accessible. Information or data that is subject to ethical customs includes the following items:

- Emails
- Phone lists
- Records or data on the computer
- Hard copies of files, information, or data left on the desk

Before accessing a computer account, including the administrator account, you should get the customer's permission. From the troubleshooting process, you may have gathered some private information, such as usernames and passwords. If you document this type of private information, you must keep it confidential. Divulging any customer information to anyone else is not only unethical, but it might be illegal. Legal details of customer information are usually covered under the SLA.

Do not send unsolicited messages to a customer. Do not send unsolicited mass mailings or chain letters to customers. Never send forged or anonymous emails. All these activities are considered unethical and, in certain circumstances, may be illegal. In either case, these activities could result in job termination.

Legal Rules

Several computer-related activities are not only unethical, but illegal. Be aware that this is not an exhaustive list of legal rules:

- Do not make any changes to system software or hardware configurations without the customer's permission.

- Do not access a customer's or coworker's accounts, private files, or email messages without permission.

- Do not install, copy, or share digital content (including software, music, text, images, and video) in violation of copyright or software agreements or applicable federal and state laws.

- Do not use a customer's company IT resources for commercial purposes.

- Do not make a customer's IT resources available to unauthorized users.

- Keep sensitive customer information confidential.

- Do not knowingly use a customer's company resources for illegal activities. Criminal or illegal use may include child pornography, threats, harassment, copyright infringement, university trademark infringement, defamation, theft, identity theft, and unauthorized access.

Make sure you know the copyright and trademark laws in your state or country.

Class Discussion 10.3.0: Customer Privacy

In this activity, the class discusses the importance of respecting customer privacy through the use of three scenarios. Refer to the relevant topics in *IT Essentials: PC Hardware and Software Lab Manual, Fourth Edition* to help you prepare for this discussion.

Describe the Call Center Environment and Technician Responsibilities

A *call center* environment is professional and fast-paced. A call center is a help desk system where customers call in and are placed on a call board. Available technicians take the customer calls. A technician must supply the level of support that is outlined in the customer's SLA.

After completing this section, you will meet these objectives:

- Describe the call center environment.
- Describe level-one technician responsibilities.
- Describe level-two technician responsibilities.

Describe the Call Center Environment

A call center may exist within a company and offer service to the employees of that company as well as to the customers of that company's products. Alternatively, a call center may be an independent business that sells computer support as a service to outside customers. In either case, a call center is a busy, fast-paced work environment, often operating 24 hours a day.

Call centers tend to have a large number of cubicles. Each cubicle has a chair, at least one computer, and a phone with a headset. The technicians working at these cubicles have varied levels of experience in computers. Some have specialties in certain types of computers, software, or operating systems.

All the computers in a call center have help-desk software. The technicians use this software to manage many of their job functions. Although it is not a complete list of most features of help-desk software, the following list provides more detail:

- **Log and track incidents**: The software may manage call queues, set call priorities, assign calls, and escalate calls.
- **Record contact information**: The software may store, edit, and recall customer names, email addresses, phone numbers, locations, websites, fax numbers, and other information in a database.
- **Research product information**: The software may provide to technicians information on the products they support, including features, limitations, new versions, configuration constraints, known bugs, product availability, links to online help files, and other information.
- **Run diagnostic utilities**: The software may have several diagnostic utilities, including remote diagnostic software, in which the technician can "take over" a customer's computer while sitting at a desk in the call center.
- **Research a knowledge base**: The software may contain a knowledge database that is preprogrammed with common problems and their solutions. This database may grow as technicians add their own records of problems and solutions.
- **Collect customer feedback**: The software may collect customer feedback on satisfaction with the call center's products and services.

Your call center will have its own business policies for call priority. Table 10-9 is a sample chart of how calls may be named, defined, and prioritized.

Table 10-9   Call Prioritization

Name	Definition	Priority
Down	The company cannot operate any computer equipment.	1 (most urgent)
Hardware	One or more computers are not functioning correctly.	2 (urgent)
Software	One or more computers have software or operating system errors.	2 (urgent)
Network	One or more computers cannot access the network.	2 (urgent)
Enhancement	Request for additional functionality.	3 (important)

Describe Level-One Technician Responsibilities

Call centers sometimes have different names for level-one technicians. These technicians may be known as level-one analysts, dispatchers, or incident screeners. Regardless of the title, the level-one technician's responsibilities are fairly similar from one call center to the next.

The primary responsibility of a level-one technician is to gather pertinent information from the customer. The technician has to document all the information in the ticket or work order. Here is some of the information a level-one technician must obtain:

- Contact information
- Description of the problem
- Priority of the problem
- The computer's manufacturer and model
- The computer's operating system
- Whether the computer uses AC or DC power
- Whether the computer is on a network and, if so, whether it is a wired or wireless connection
- If a specific application was being used when the problem occurred
- If any new drivers or updates have been installed recently and, if so, what they are

Some problems are very simple to resolve, and a level-one technician usually can take care of these without escalating the work order to a level-two technician.

Often, a problem requires the expertise of a level-two technician. In these cases, the level-one technician must be able to translate the customer's problem description into a succinct sentence or two that are entered into the work order. This translation is important so that other technicians can quickly understand the situation without having to ask the customer the same questions again. Table 10-10 shows how a customer might describe some of the most common problems and how a technician should document those problems.

Table 10-10 Customer and Technician Problems

Customer Problem Description	Technician Documentation
Printer does not print.	The printer prints a test page but does not print from a specified application.
Mouse does not work.	The mouse is dirty, and the user is unable to control the cursor.
Cannot get onto the network.	The user is unable to log in to the network.
Monitor does not work.	The monitor settings have been altered. No images can be seen on the screen.
Computer does not turn on.	The computer does not boot to the Windows desktop.

Describe Level-Two Technician Responsibilities

As with level-one technicians, call centers sometimes have different names for level-two technicians. These technicians may be known as product specialists or technical-support personnel. The level-two technician's responsibilities generally are the same from one call center to the next.

The level-two technician is usually more knowledgeable than the level-one technician about technology, or has been working for the company for a longer period of time. When a problem cannot be resolved within ten minutes, the level-one technician prepares an escalated work order. The level-two technician receives the escalated work order with the description of the problem. That person then calls the customer back to ask additional questions and resolve the problem.

The following list of guidelines details when to escalate a problem to a more experienced technician. These are generic guidelines; you should follow your company's business policy for problem escalation.

- Escalate problems that require opening the computer case.
- Escalate problems that require installing applications, operating systems, or drivers.

- Escalate problems that will take a long time to walk a customer through, such as Configuration Memory Operating System (CMOS) changes.

- Escalate "down" calls. The entire network is down, and a more experienced tech may be able to resolve the issue faster.

Problems that require opening the computer case need a level-two technician. Level-two technicians can also use remote diagnostic software to connect to the customer's computer to update drivers and software, access the operating system, check the BIOS, and gather other diagnostic information to solve the problem.

Summary

In this chapter, you learned about the relationship between communication skills and troubleshooting skills. You have learned that these two skills need to be combined to make you a successful technician. You also learned about the legal aspects and ethics of dealing with computer technology and the customer's property.

The following concepts from this chapter are important to remember:

- To be a successful technician, you need to practice good communication skills with customers and coworkers. These skills are as important as technical expertise.

- You should always conduct yourself in a professional manner with your customers and coworkers. Professional behavior increases customer confidence and enhances your credibility. You should also learn to recognize the classic signs of a difficult customer and learn what to do and what not to do when you are on a call with this customer.

- You can use a few techniques to keep a difficult customer focused on the problem during a call. Primarily, you must remain calm and ask pertinent questions in an appropriate fashion. These techniques keep you in control of the call.

- There is a right way and a wrong way to put a customer on hold, or transfer a customer to another technician. Learn and use the right way every time. Performing either of these operations incorrectly can seriously damage your company's relationship with its customers.

- Netiquette is a list of rules to use whenever you communicate through email, text messaging, instant messaging, or blogs. This is another area where doing things the wrong way can damage your company's relationship with its customers.

- You must understand and comply with your customer's service level agreement (SLA). If the problem falls outside the SLA, you need to find positive ways of telling the customer what you can do to help, not what you cannot do. In special circumstances, you may decide to escalate the work order to management.

- In addition to the SLA, you must follow the company's business policies. These policies include how your company prioritizes calls, how and when to escalate a call to management, and when you are allowed to take breaks and lunch.

- A computer technician's job is stressful. You will rarely talk to a customer who is having a good day. You can alleviate some of the stress by setting up your workstation in the most ergonomic way possible. You should practice time- and stress-management techniques every day.

- There are ethical and legal aspects to working in computer technology. You should be aware of your company's policies and practices. In addition, you may need to become familiar with your state's or country's trademark and copyright laws.

- The call center is a fast-paced environment. Level-one technicians and level-two technicians each have specific responsibilities. These responsibilities may vary slightly from one call center to another.

Summary of Exercises

This is a summary of the Labs, Worksheets, Remote Technician exercises, Class Discussions, Virtual Desktop activities, and Virtual Laptop activities associated with this chapter.

Worksheets

The following worksheet covers material from this chapter. Refer to the worksheet in *IT Essentials: PC Hardware and Software Lab Manual, Fourth Edition.*

Worksheet 10.1.0: Technician Resources

Class Discussions

The following Class Discussions cover material from this chapter. Refer to these topics in *IT Essentials: PC Hardware and Software Lab Manual, Fourth Edition.*

Class Discussion 10.2.2: Controlling the Call

Class Discussion 10.2.3: Identifying Difficult Customer Types

Class Discussion 10.3.0: Customer Privacy

Check Your Understanding

You can find the answers to these questions in the appendix, "Answers to Check Your Understanding Questions."

1. What is a good rule for a call center technician to follow?

   A. Be proactive by avoiding speaking with upset or angry customers.

   B. Consider each new customer call a fresh start.

   C. Go with your first impression of the customer, and use Netiquette.

   D. Focus on how to repair the problem while the customer is speaking.

2. Which two actions are examples of good Netiquette?

   A. Avoid beginning an email with a formal greeting when it is a reply.

   B. Check grammar and spelling before sending an email.

   C. Use both uppercase and lowercase letters in emails instead of all uppercase or all lowercase.

   D. Engage in flame wars.

3. What is an SLA?

   A. An itemized record detailing all levels of service performed on equipment covered by a manufacturer warranty

   B. A legal agreement between a customer and a service technician confirming specific services performed on equipment not covered by any warranty

   C. A legal agreement between a customer and the service vendor confirming a specific level of support

   D. A legal record of customer invoices showing that all expenses were approved before the repair of equipment

4. What is the primary responsibility of a level-one technician?

   A. Determining the cause of complex computer problems

   B. Gathering information from the customer

   C. Using remote diagnostic software to connect to the customer's computer

   D. Resolving computer problems that require opening the computer case

5. Which task is the responsibility of a level-two technician?

   A. Resolving computer problems that are limited to software errors

   B. Gathering information from the customer

   C. Directing the customer to the appropriate computer vendor for help

   D. Resolving computer problems that require opening the computer case

6. Which two skills are the most important for a successful computer technician to possess?

   A. Communication

   B. Computer repair

   C. Task maintenance

   D. Work escalation

   E. Computer prioritization

7. What is the proper way to conduct a telephone call to troubleshoot a computer problem?

    A. Always gather information from the customer and escalate the problem.

    B. Maintain professional behavior at all times.

    C. Ask personal questions to get better acquainted with the customer.

    D. Explain each step to help the customer understand the troubleshooting process.

8. A user calls to report that his new computer is broken. The technician determines that the user is inexperienced and possesses a limited understanding of computer technology. How should the technician handle this call?

    A. Write up a brief trouble ticket and send a technician to the customer to resolve the computer problem.

    B. Attempt to gather information using a simple step-by-step process to determine the problem.

    C. Explain technical terms to the customer to educate him so that he can describe the problem.

    D. Direct the user to several websites to help him identify the problem.

9. A customer calls, asking for help with an error code displayed on a computer running Linux. The technician has limited experience with Linux. What should she do?

    A. Attempt the repair anyway.

    B. Apologize, and tell the customer that she hopes to receive training for Linux in the future.

    C. Gather information about the problem and escalate the call to a level-two technician.

    D. Direct the customer to the manufacturer's website.

10. Your office informs you that a customer will be contacting you by cell phone within the next ten minutes about an emergency. The customer does not contact you before your next appointment with another customer. What should you do if the previous customer calls you while you are with the next customer?

    A. Call your supervisor.

    B. Let the call go to voice mail.

    C. Excuse yourself and take the call.

    D. Send the customer a text message.

11. A customer who just contacted you is very angry about your company's service. During the call, you discover that another technician responded to the customer's issue. What should you do?

   A. Stay calm.

   B. Do not ask for clarification.

   C. Ask the customer why he or she is so angry.

   D. Transfer the customer to the technician who initially handled the issue.

12. A customer calls you and explains in great detail a problem she is having with her computer. What should you do?

   A. Interrupt her and obtain only the relevant information.

   B. Interrupt her and obtain only the basic information.

   C. Allow her to finish explaining the problem, and record all the details she gives you.

   D. Allow her to finish explaining the problem, but record only the information you feel is relevant.

CHAPTER 11

Advanced Personal Computers

Objectives

Upon completion of this chapter, you will able to answer the following questions:

- What are the differences between field, remote, and bench technician jobs?

- What are safe lab procedures and tool use?

- What situations require replacement of computer components?

- How do I upgrade and configure personal computer components and peripherals?

- What are common preventive maintenance techniques for personal computer components and how do I identify and apply them?

- How can I troubleshoot computer components and peripherals?

Key Terms

This chapter uses the following key terms. You can find the definitions in the Glossary.

electrostatic discharge (ESD)   page 406

antistatic wrist strap   page 409

antistatic mat   page 409

power supply   page 410

motherboard   page 413

random-access memory (RAM)   page 417

adapter card   page 419

central processing unit (CPU)   page 434

heat sink/fan   page 436

basic input/output system (BIOS)   page 438

In your career as a technician, you might have to determine whether a component for a customer's computer should be upgraded or replaced. It is important that you develop advanced skills in installation procedures, troubleshooting techniques, and diagnostic methods for computers. This chapter discusses the importance of component compatibility across hardware and software. It also covers the need for adequate system resources to efficiently run the customer's hardware and software.

After completing this chapter, you will meet these objectives:

- Give an overview of field, remote, and bench technician jobs.
- Explain safe lab procedures and tool use.
- Describe situations requiring replacement of computer components.
- Upgrade and configure personal computer components and peripherals.
- Identify and apply common preventive maintenance techniques for personal computer components.
- Troubleshoot computer components and peripherals.

Give an Overview of Field, Remote, and Bench Technician Jobs

Your experience working with computers and earning a technical certification can help you become qualified for employment as any of the following:

- Field technician
- Remote technician
- Bench technician

Technicians in different computer careers work in different environments. The skills required by each career can be very similar. The degree to which different skills are needed vary from one job to the next. When you train to become a computer technician, you are expected to develop the following skills:

- Building and upgrading computers
- Performing installations
- Installing, configuring, and optimizing software
- Performing preventive maintenance
- Troubleshooting and repairing computers

- Communicating clearly with the customer

- Documenting customer feedback and the steps involved in finding the solution to a problem

Field technicians work in various conditions and businesses. You might work for one company and only repair that company's assets. Alternatively, you might work for a company that provides onsite computer equipment repair for a variety of companies and customers. In either of these situations, you need both excellent troubleshooting skills and customer service skills, because you are in regular contact with customers and work on a wide variety of hardware and software.

If you are a remote technician, you might work at a help desk answering calls or emails from customers who have computer problems. You create work orders and communicate with the customer to try to diagnose and repair the problem.

Good communication skills are valuable because the customer must clearly understand your questions and instructions. Some help desks use software to connect directly to a customer's computer to fix the problem. As a remote technician, you can work on a team of help desk technicians at a corporate site or from home.

As a bench technician, you typically would not work directly with customers. Bench technicians are often hired to perform computer warranty service in a central depot or work facility.

Worksheet 11.1.0: Job Opportunities

In this worksheet, you research computer-related jobs. Refer to the worksheet in *IT Essentials: PC Hardware and Software Lab Manual, Fourth Edition*. You can perform this worksheet now or wait until the end of the chapter.

Explain Safe Lab Procedures and Tool Use

Safety should always be your priority on a job or in the lab. As a computer technician, you should be aware of the many workplace hazards, and you should take the necessary precautions to avoid them.

You should try to practice safety in the lab so that it becomes part of your regular routine. Follow all safety procedures and use the correct tools for the job. This policy will help prevent personal injury and damage to equipment.

To accomplish a safe working environment, it is easier to prevent problems than to fix them. Here is a list of safety rules to help you maintain a safe working environment:

- Keep the work area clean and free of clutter.

- Keep food and drinks out of the work area.

- Never open a computer monitor unless you have been properly trained.

- Remove all your jewelry and watches.

- Make sure that the power is off and that the power plug has been removed.

Note

In the absence of a properly grounded workstation, such as on a site job, some technicians use the power cord to ground the chassis. In that case, the power cord is connected to the wall outlet and the PC. Regardless, the equipment should be unpowered while it is serviced.

- Do not look into the laser beams located in the computer equipment.

- Make sure that a fire extinguisher and first aid kit are available.

- Cover sharp edges with tape when working inside the computer case.

After completing this section, you will meet these objectives:

- Review safe working environments and procedures.

- Review names, purposes, characteristics, and safe and appropriate use of tools.

- Identify potential safety hazards and implement proper safety procedures for computer components.

- Describe environmental issues.

Review Safe Working Environments and Procedures

Workplace safety is necessary to ensure that you, and everyone near you, stay unharmed. In any situation, you should always follow these basic rules:

- Use antistatic mats and pads to reduce the chance of *electrostatic discharge (ESD)* damaging your equipment.

- Store hazardous or toxic materials in a secured cabinet.

- Keep the floor clear of anything that might trip someone.

- Clean work areas on a regular basis.

Figure 11-1 shows examples of safety equipment.

Figure 11-1   Safety Equipment

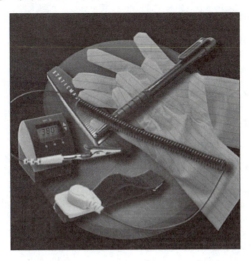

You should use caution when you move computer equipment from one place to another. Turn off the PC before moving it to prevent hard drive damage. Make sure that customers follow the safety rules in your work area. You might need to explain these rules and assure customers that the rules are there to protect them.

Follow local codes and government rules whenever you dispose of such things as batteries, solvents, computers, and monitors. Failing to do so can result in a fine. Many countries have agencies to enforce safety standards and ensure safe working conditions for employees.

Review Names, Purposes, Characteristics, and Safe and Appropriate Use of Tools

A computer technician needs proper tools to work safely and to prevent damage to the computer equipment. There are many tools, as shown in Figure 11-2, that a technician uses to diagnose and repair computer problems:

- Flat head screwdriver, large and small

- Phillips head screwdriver, large and small

- Tweezers or part retriever

- Needle-nose pliers

- Wire cutters

- Chip extractor

- Hex wrench set

- Torx screwdriver

- Nut driver, large and small

- Three-claw component holder

- Digital multimeter

- Wrap plugs

- Small mirror

- Small dust brush

- Soft, lint-free cloth

- Cable ties

- Scissors

- Small flashlight

- Electrical tape

- Pencil or pen

- Compressed air

Various specialty tools, such as Torx bits, antistatic bags and gloves, and integrated circuit pullers, can be used to repair and maintain computers. Always avoid magnetized tools, such as screwdrivers with magnetic heads, or tools that use extension magnets to retrieve small metal objects that are out of reach. Using magnetic tools can cause loss of data on hard drives and floppy disks. Magnetic tools can also induce current, which can damage internal computer components. Additionally, there are specialized testing devices used to diagnose computer and cable problems:

- **Multimeter**: A device that measures AC/DC voltage, electric current, and other cable and electrical characteristics.

- **Power supply tester**: A device that checks whether the computer power supply is working properly. A simple power supply tester might just have indicator lights, while more advanced versions show the amount of voltage and amperage.

- **Cable tester**: A device that checks for wiring shorts or faults, such as wires connected to the wrong pin.

- **Loopback plug**: A device that connects to a computer, hub, switch, or router port to perform a diagnostic procedure called a *loopback test*. In a loopback test, a signal is transmitted through a circuit and then returned to the sending device to test the integrity of the data transmission.

Figure 11-2   Organized Tool Storage

Static electricity is one of the biggest concerns for computer technicians when working in many environments. The tools you use and even your own body can store or conduct thousands of volts of electricity. Walking across carpet or a rug and touching a computer component before grounding yourself can severely damage the component. It only takes a few volts to damage electronics, but humans don't feel voltage until it is thousands of volts. Careless handling of equipment and parts can destroy them even if you did not feel the shock.

Antistatic devices help control static electricity. Use antistatic devices to prevent damage to sensitive components. Before you touch a computer component, be sure to ground yourself by touching a grounded computer chassis or mat. These are some antistatic devices:

- *Antistatic wrist strap*: Conducts static electricity from your body to the ground

- *Antistatic mat*: Grounds the computer frame

- **Antistatic bag**: Keeps sensitive computer components safe when not installed inside a computer

- **Cleaning products**: Maintain components without creating a buildup of static electricity

Caution

To help prevent electric shock, do not wear an antistatic wrist strap when working with high-voltage circuits, such as those found in monitors and printers. Do not open monitors or power supplies unless you are properly trained.

Lab 11.2.2: Use a Multimeter and a Power Supply Tester

In this lab, you learn how to use and handle a multimeter and a power supply tester. Refer to the lab in *IT Essentials: PC Hardware and Software Lab Manual, Fourth Edition.* You can perform this lab now or wait until the end of the chapter.

Lab 11.2.2: Testing UTP Cables Using a Loopback Plug and a Cable Meter

In this lab, you use a loopback plug and a cable meter to test an Ethernet cable. Refer to the lab in *IT Essentials: PC Hardware and Software Lab Manual, Fourth Edition.* You can perform this lab now or wait until the end of the chapter.

Identify Potential Safety Hazards and Implement Proper Safety Procedures for Computer Components

Most internal computer components use low-voltage electricity. Some components, however, operate with high voltage and can be dangerous if you do not follow safety precautions. The following dangerous, high-voltage computer components should only be serviced by authorized personnel:

- *Power supplies*: The cost to repair a power supply can sometimes equal the cost of a new power supply, so most broken or used power supplies are replaced. Only experienced certified technicians should service power supplies.

- **Display monitors**: The internal electronic parts of a display monitor cannot be repaired, but they can be replaced. Monitors, especially CRT monitors, operate using high voltages. Only a certified electronics technician should service them.

- **Laser printers**: Laser printers can be very expensive. It is more cost effective to fix broken printers by repairing or replacing broken parts. Laser printers use high voltages and can have very hot surfaces inside. Use caution when servicing laser printers.

Figure 11-3 shows an example of a high-voltage warning sign.

Figure 11-3   High-Voltage Warning

Describe Environmental Issues

Earth's environment is delicately balanced. The hazardous materials found in computer components must be disposed of in specific ways to help maintain this balance. A computer recycling warehouse is a place where discarded computer equipment can be taken apart. Computer parts that are still usable can be recycled for repairing other equipment.

Recycling warehouses must obey the codes and regulations for the disposal of each type of computer part. Before parts are recycled, they are separated into groups. CRT monitors contain as much as 4 to 5 lbs (1.6 to 2.3 kg) of lead, a dangerous element. Much of the lead is inside cathode ray tubes. Other materials inside computer equipment are also dangerous:

- Mercury
- Cadmium
- Hexavalent chromium

Batteries are used to power laptop computers, digital cameras, camcorders, and remote-control toys. Batteries can contain some of these toxic materials:

- Nickel cadmium (Ni-Cd)
- Nickel metal hydride (Ni-MH)
- Lithium ion (Li-ion)
- Lead (Pb)

Many organizations have policies that define disposal methods for the hazardous components found in electronic equipment. These methods typically include programs to reuse, recycle, or exchange.

You might need to dispose of computer components because they have become outdated, or you might need additional functionality. In addition to recycling parts, you can donate them to other people or organizations. Some businesses exchange used computer equipment for partial payment of new equipment.

Describe Situations Requiring Replacement of Computer Components

Situations that require the replacement of computer components include the repair of broken parts or an upgrade for functionality.

After completing this section, you will meet these objectives:

- Select a case and power supply.
- Select a motherboard.

- Select a CPU and cooling system.

- Select RAM.

- Select adapter cards.

- Select storage devices and hard drives.

- Select input and output devices.

Select a Case and Power Supply

You should determine the customer's needs before making any purchases or performing upgrades. Ask your customer what devices will be connected to the computer and what applications will be used.

The computer case holds the power supply, motherboard, memory, and other components, as shown in Figure 11-4. When purchasing a new computer case and power supply separately, you should ensure that all the components will fit into the new case and that the power supply is powerful enough to operate all the components. Many times, a case comes with a power supply inside. You still need to verify that the power supply provides enough power to operate all the components that will be installed in the case.

Power supplies convert AC input to DC output voltages. Power supplies typically provide voltages of 3.3, 5, and 12 V, and are measured in wattage. It is recommended that the power supply has approximately 25 percent more wattage than all the attached components require. Determine the total wattage required by adding together the wattage for each component in the computer. If the wattage is not listed on a component, calculate it by multiplying the voltage and amperage of the component. If the component requires different levels of wattage, use the higher required wattage. After determining the wattage required for the power supply, ensure that the power supply has the required connectors for all of the components.

Underperforming power supplies are tricky to diagnosis. Symptoms range from lost data to random shutdowns. Be sure to purchase one with more than enough watts. Make sure your power supply has additional connectors so you can add devices in the future.

Figure 11-4   Computer Case and Power Supply

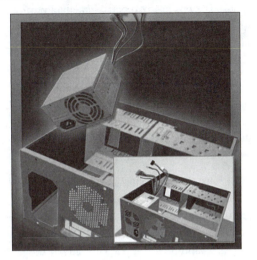

Select a Motherboard

New motherboards, as shown in Figure 11-5, often have new features or standards that can be incompatible with older components. When you select a replacement ***motherboard***, make sure that it supports the CPU, RAM, video adapter, and other adapter cards. The socket and chipset on the motherboard must be compatible with the CPU. The motherboard must also accommodate the existing heat sink/fan assembly.

Pay particular attention to the number and type of expansion slots. Do they match the existing adapter cards? The existing power supply must have connections that fit the new motherboard. Finally, the new motherboard must physically fit into the current computer case.

Different motherboards use different chipsets. A chipset consists of integrated circuits, which allows the CPU to communicate and interact with the other components of the computer. The chipset establishes how much memory can be added to a motherboard and the type of connectors on the motherboard. When building a computer, choose a chipset that provides the capabilities that you need. For example, you can purchase a motherboard with a chipset that enables multiple USB ports, eSATA connections, surround sound, or basic video.

Motherboards have different types of CPU sockets and CPU slots that are determined by the chipset. This socket or slot provides the connection point and the electrical interface for the CPU. The CPU package must match the motherboard socket type or CPU slot type. A CPU package contains the CPU, connection points, and materials that surround the CPU and dissipate heat.

Data travels from one part of a computer to another through a collection of wires known as the bus. The bus has two parts. The data portion of the bus, known as the data bus, carries data between components of a computer. The address portion of the bus, known as the address bus, carries the memory addresses of the locations where data is read or written by the CPU.

The bus size refers to the width of the bus. The bus size determines how much data can be transmitted at one time. A 32-bit bus transmits 32 bits of data at one time from the processor to RAM or to other motherboard components, while a 64-bit bus transmits 64 bits of data at one time. The speed at which data travels through the bus is determined by the clock speed, measured in megahertz (MHz).

PCI expansion slots connect to a parallel bus, which sends multiple bits over multiple wires simultaneously. PCI expansion slots are being replaced with PCIe expansion slots that connect to a serial bus, which sends one bit at a time at a faster rate. When building a computer, choose a motherboard that has slots to meet your current and future needs. For example, if you are building a computer for advanced gaming that needs dual graphics cards, you might choose a motherboard with dual PCIe slots.

Motherboards have expansion slots, which provide a connection point on the motherboard where a circuit board can be attached to add new capabilities to the computer. Expansion slots are used to add a variety of capabilities, such as video adapters, TV tuner cards, video capture cards, and NICs. Figure 11-5 shows a motherboard.

Figure 11-5   Motherboard

Select the CPU and Heat Sink/Fan Assembly

Replace the CPU when it fails or is no longer adequate for the current applications. For example, you might have a customer who has purchased an advanced graphics application. The application might run poorly because it requires a faster processor than the current CPU.

Before you buy a CPU, make sure that it is compatible with the existing motherboard:

- The new CPU must use the same socket type and chipset.

- The BIOS must support the new CPU.

- The new CPU might require a different heat sink/fan assembly.

Manufacturers' websites are a good resource to investigate the compatibility between CPUs and other devices. When upgrading the CPU, make sure that the correct voltage is maintained. A voltage regulator module (VRM) is integrated into the motherboard. The voltage setting for the CPU can be configured with jumpers or switches located on the motherboard or settings in the BIOS.

Multicore processors have two or more processors on the same integrated circuit. By integrating the processors on the same chip, a very fast connection is created between them. Multicore processors execute instructions more quickly than single-core processors and have increased data throughput. Instructions can be distributed to all of the processors at the same time. With multicore processors, RAM is shared between the processors because the cores reside on the same chip. A multicore processor is recommended for applications such as video editing, gaming, and photo manipulation.

High power consumption creates more heat in the computer case. Multicore processors conserve power and produce less heat than multiple single-core processors, thus increasing performance and efficiency.

Processors have areas of fast memory designed to increase the speed and performance of the processor. When this area of memory is located inside the processor, it is the primary, or Level 1 (L1), cache. Cache memory external to the processor is Level 2 (L2) cache. Starting with the Pentium Pro and later processors, the L2 cache was included in the processor architecture. After the L2 cache was added to the processor, the extra cache installed on the motherboard was named Level 3 (L3). These CPU caches are much faster than the main memory. With multicore processors, the L3 cache contains duplicate instructions found in the L1 and L2 caches.

The speed of a processor is measured in gigahertz (GHz). A maximum speed rating refers to the maximum speed at which a processor can function without errors. Two primary factors can limit the speed of a processor:

- The processor chip is a collection of transistors interconnected by wires. There are delays created by the transmission of data flowing through the transistors and wires.

- As the transistors change state, from on to off or off to on, small amounts of electricity are released. The amount of heat generated increases as the speed of the processor increases. When the processor becomes too hot, it will begin to produce errors.

The front-side bus (FSB) is the path between the CPU and the various components, such as the chip set, expansion cards, and RAM. Data can travel in both directions across the FSB. The frequency of the bus is measured in megahertz (MHz). The frequency at which a CPU operates is determined by applying a clock multiplier to the FSB speed. For example, a processor running at 3200 MHz might be using a 400-MHz FSB. 3200 MHz divided by 400 MHz is 8. In this example, the CPU is eight times faster than the FSB.

Processors are further classified as 32 bit and 64 bit. The primary difference is the number of instructions that can be handled by the processor at one time. A 64-bit processor processes more instructions per clock cycle than a 32-bit processor. A 64-bit processor can also support much more memory than a 32-bit processor. To utilize the 64-bit processor capabilities, ensure that the operating system installed supports a 64-bit processor and applications are compatible.

One of the most expensive and sensitive components in the computer case is the CPU. The CPU can become very hot. Many CPUs require a heat sink, combined with a fan for cooling. A heat sink is a piece of copper or aluminum that sits between the processor and the CPU fan. The heat sink absorbs the heat from the processor and then the fan disperses the heat. When choosing a heat sink or fan, there are several factors to consider:

- **Socket type**: The heat sink or fan type must match the socket type of the motherboard.

- **Motherboard physical specifications**: The heat sink or fan must not interfere with any components attached to the motherboard.

- **Case size**: The heat sink or fan must fit within the case.

- **Physical environment**: The heat sink or fan must be able to disperse enough heat to keep the CPU cool in warm environments.

The CPU is not the only component in a computer case that can be adversely affected by heat. A computer has many internal components that generate heat while the computer is running. Case fans should be installed to move cooler air into the computer case while moving heat out of the case. When choosing case fans, there are several factors to consider:

- **Case size**: Larger cases often require larger fans because smaller fans cannot create enough air flow.

- **Fan speed**: Larger fans spin more slowly than smaller fans, which reduces fan noise.

- **Number of components in the case**: Multiple components in a computer create additional heat, which requires more fans, larger fans, or faster fans.

- **Physical environment**: The case fans must be able to disperse enough heat to keep the interior of the case cool.

- **Number of mounting places available**: Different cases have different numbers of mounting places for fans.

- **Location of mounting places available**: Different cases have different locations for mounting fans.

- **Electrical connections**: Some case fans are connected directly to the motherboard while others are connected directly to the power supply.

The direction of air flow created by all the fans in the case must work together to bring the cooler air in while moving the hotter air out. Installing a fan backward or using fans with the incorrect size or speed for the case can cause the air flows to work against each other.

Figure 11-6 shows two similar CPUs that use different sockets.

Figure 11-6   Incompatible CPUs with Similar Capabilities

Select RAM

New *random-access memory (RAM)* might be needed when an application locks up or if the computer displays frequent error messages. To determine whether the problem is the RAM, replace the old RAM module, as shown in Figure 11-7. Restart the computer to see whether the application runs properly.

To close a stalled application, press Ctrl-Alt-Delete to open Windows Task Manager. In the window, select the application. Click **End Task** to close it, as shown in Figure 11-8.

Figure 11-7   RAM Module

Figure 11-8   Task Manager

When selecting new RAM, you must ensure that it is compatible with the current mother-board. It must also be the same type of RAM as installed in the computer. The speed of the new RAM must be the same or faster than the existing RAM. It can help to take the original memory module with you or note serial and model numbers when you shop in person or online for the replacement RAM.

The OS controls the primary memory (RAM). Bad RAM will show up in the power-on self test (POST) as not being counted. RAM will need to be replaced only when it is too slow or insufficiently large enough to accommodate the application. The OS will accommodate the application by increasing the virtual memory requirement, and hard disk thrashing will occur. *Disk thrashing* is a term that describes failure from overuse due to not enough RAM.

Select Adapter Cards

Adapter cards, also called expansion cards, add extra functionality to a computer. Figure 11-9 shows some of the adapter cards available.

Figure 11-9   Adapter Cards

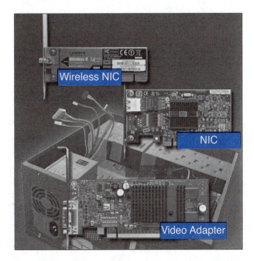

Before you purchase an adapter card, do some research:

- Is there an open expansion slot?
- Is the adapter card compatible with the open slot?

If the motherboard does not have compatible expansion slots, external devices can be an option:

- Are USB or FireWire versions of the external device available?
- Does the computer have an open USB or FireWire port?

Consider the upgrade situation in which a customer requires a wireless adapter card to connect to the network. The new wireless adapter card must be compatible with the existing wireless network and with the computer.

Investigate wireless network interface cards (NIC) before you purchase one. You should ensure that the new wireless NIC is compatible with the 802.11 wireless standard being used on the wireless network.

Examine the computer for an available expansion slot or an open USB port. Purchase either an adapter card that will fit an available expansion slot or a USB wireless NIC. Cost, warranty, brand name, and availability are the last factors for you to consider.

Graphics Cards

The type of graphics card installed has a big impact on the overall performance of a computer. The programs and tasks that the graphics card may need to support could be RAM intensive, CPU intensive, or both. There are several factors to consider when purchasing a new graphics card:

- Slot type

- Port types

- Amount and speed of video RAM (VRAM)

- Graphics-processing unit (GPU)

- Maximum resolution

- Frames per second

A computer system must have the slots, RAM, and CPU to support the full functionality of an upgraded graphics card to receive all of the benefits of the card. Choose the correct graphics card based on your customer's current and future needs. For example, if a customer wants to play 3D games, the graphics card must meet or exceed the minimum requirements for any game they wish to play.

Sound Cards

The type of sound card installed will determine the sound quality of your computer. There are several factors to consider when purchasing a new sound card:

- Slot type

- Digital signal processor (DSP)

- Sample rate

- Port and connection types

- Hardware decoders

- Signal-to-noise ratio

A computer system must have quality speakers and a subwoofer to support the full functionality of an upgraded sound card to receive all of the benefits of the card. Choose the correct sound card based on your customer's current and future needs. For example, if a customer wants to hear a specific type of surround sound, the sound card must have the correct hardware decoder to reproduce it. Also, the customer can get improved sound accuracy with a sound card that has a higher sample rate.

Storage Controllers

A storage controller is a chip that can be integrated into the motherboard or on an expansion card. Storage controllers allow for the expansion of internal and external drives for a computer system. The drives can be connected internally using IDE, SCSI, or SATA connectors. External drives can be connected using SCSI or eSATA connectors. Storage controllers, such as RAID controllers, can also provide fault tolerance or increased speed. There are several factors to consider when purchasing a new storage controller card:

- Slot type
- Drive type
- Connector quantity
- Connector location
- Card size
- Controller card RAM
- Controller card processor
- RAID types

The amount of data and the level of data protection needed for the customer will influence the type of storage controller required. Choose the correct storage controller based on your customer's current and future needs. For example, if a customer wants to implement RAID 5, a RAID storage controller with at least three drives is needed.

Input/Output Cards

Installing an input/output (I/O) card in a computer is a fast and easy way to add I/O ports. There are several factors to consider when purchasing an I/O card:

- Slot type
- I/O port type
- I/O port quantity
- Additional power requirements

FireWire, USB, parallel, and serial ports are some of the most common ports to install on a computer. Choose the correct I/O card based on your customer's current and future needs. For example, if a customer wants to add an internal card reader, a USB I/O card with an internal USB connection is needed.

Network Interface Cards

Customers upgrade their NICs to get faster speeds, more bandwidth, and better access. There are several factors to consider when purchasing a NIC:

- Slot type
- Speed
- Connector type
- Connection type
- Standards compatibility
- Wake on LAN

Wired and wireless NICs should be selected based on your customer's current and future needs. For example, if a customer wants to connect to a wireless N network, a wireless NIC that is compatible with the 802.11n standard is needed to operate at the full speed provided by 802.11n.

Capture Cards

A capture card imports video into a computer and records it on a hard drive. The addition of a capture card with a TV tuner allows you to view and record television programming. There are several factors to consider when purchasing a capture card:

- Slot type
- Resolution and frame rate
- I/O ports
- Format standards

The computer system must have enough CPU processing power, adequate RAM, and a high-speed storage system to support the capture, recording, and editing demands of the customer. Choose the correct capture card based on your customer's current and future needs. For example, if a customer wants to record one program while watching another, either multiple capture cards or a capture card with dual TV tuners must be installed.

Select Storage Devices and Hard Drives

You might need to replace a hard drive when it no longer meets your customer's needs for data storage or fails. The signs that a hard drive is failing include the following:

- Unusual noises

- Error messages

- Corrupt data or applications

If your hard drive exhibits any of these symptoms, you should replace it as soon as possible. Figure 11-10 shows Parallel Advanced Technology Attachment (PATA), Serial Advanced Technology Attachment (SATA), and Small Computer System Interface (SCSI) connectors.

Figure 11-10 Hard Drive Connectors

ATA was renamed Parallel ATA, or PATA, with the introduction of Serial ATA (SATA). PATA hard drives can use a 40-pin, 80-conductor cable or a 40-pin, 40-conductor cable.

SATA hard drives connect to the motherboard using a serial interface. SATA hard drives have a higher data-transfer rate than PATA drives. The smaller data cable allows improved airflow through the computer case. Early versions of SATA offered a speed of 1.5 Gbps. Current versions offer a speed of 3.0 Gbps.

PATA hard drives use a 40-pin, 80-conductor cable or a 40-pin, 40-conductor cable. Choose the PATA hard drive if your customer's system is a legacy system or does not support SATA.

SATA and eSATA hard drives use a 7-pin, 4-conductor cable. Although SATA and eSATA cables are similar, they are not interchangeable. SATA drives are internal. eSATA drives are external. Choose a SATA or eSATA hard drive if your customer needs a much higher data-transfer rate than PATA and the system supports SATA or eSATA.

The SCSI standard is typically used for hard drives and for tape storage. However, printers, scanners, and optical drives can also use SCSI. Today, SCSI devices are used mostly on servers or computers that require high transfer speeds and reliability.

SCSI is a more advanced interface controller than PATA or SATA. It is ideal for high-end computers, including network servers. Devices can include hard drives, Optical drives, tape drives, scanners, and removable drives. SCSI devices are typically connected in a series, forming a chain that is commonly called a daisy chain, as shown in Figure 11-11. Each end of the daisy chain must be terminated to prevent signals from bouncing off the ends of cables and causing interference. Generally, the SCSI controller on one end of the SCSI bus has onboard termination. The other end of the SCSI cable is either terminated by a resistor on the last drive on the chain or a physical terminator on the end of the SCSI bus.

Figure 11-11   SCSI Daisy Chain

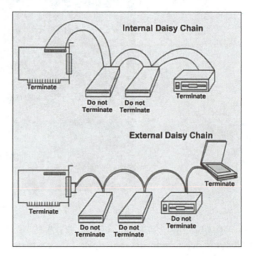

Most SCSI buses can handle a total of seven devices and a SCSI controller. The channels are numbered from 0 through 7. Some versions of SCSI support a total of 15 devices plus the SCSI controller. These channels are numbered 0 through 15. Each device on a SCSI channel must have a unique SCSI ID. For example, the primary drive would be 0 and the controller card is usually 7. The SCSI ID is generally set by jumpers on a SCSI drive.

The SCSI bus was originally 8 bits wide and operated at a transfer rate of 5 MBps. Later SCSI technologies used a 16-bit bus and operated at 320–640 MBps. Table 11-1 shows the different types of SCSI. Current and future SCSI technologies use a serial interface for increased speed.

Table 11-1   SCSI Types

SCSI Type	Also Called	Connector	Maximum Throughput (MBps)
SCSI-1	—	50-pin	
Centronics 50-pin	5		
Fast SCSI	Plain SCSI	50-pin	
Centronics 50-pin	10		
Fast Wide SCSI	—	50-pin	
68-pin	20		
Ultra SCSI	Fast-20	50-pin	20
Ultra Wide SCSI	—	68-pin	40
Ultra2 SCSI	Fast-40	50-pin	40
Ultra2 Wide SCSI	—	68-pin	
80-pin	80		
Ultra3 SCSI	Ultra160	68-pin	
80-pin	160		
Ultra320 SCSI	—	68-pin	
80-pin	320		

SCSI is 8 bits wide and Wide SCSI is 16 bits wide. SCSI uses 50-pin connectors and Wide SCSI uses 68-pin connectors. Internal connections use 80-pin connectors.

Floppy Disk Drive

While floppy disk drives (FDD) still have some limited uses, they have been largely super-seded by USB flash drives, external hard drives, CDs, DVDs, and memory cards. If an existing FDD fails, replace it with one of the newer storage devices.

Media Readers

A media reader is a device that reads and writes to different types of media cards—for example, those found in a digital camera, smartphone, or MP3 player. When replacing a media reader, ensure that it supports the type of cards used and the storage capacity of the cards to be read. There are several factors to consider when purchasing a new media reader:

- Internal or external

- Type of connector used

- Type of media cards supported

Choose the correct media reader based on your customer's current and future needs. For example, if a customer needs to use multiple types of media cards, a multiple-format media reader is needed.

Hard Drives

A hard drive stores data on magnetic platters. There are several different types and sizes of hard drives. Hard drives use different connection types. There are several factors to consider when purchasing a hard drive:

- Adding or replacing

- Internal or external

- Case location

- System compatibility

- Heat generation

- Noise generation

- Power requirements

Solid State Drives

A solid state drive (SSD) uses static RAM instead of magnetic platters to store data. SSDs are considered to be reliable because they have no moving parts. This is a relatively new technology and is still more expensive compared to platter-based HDDs. There are several factors to consider when purchasing an SSD:

- Cost

- Adding or replacing

- Internal or external

- Case location

- System compatibility

- Power requirements

- Speed

- Capacity

Choose an SSD if your customer needs to do any of the following:

- Connect to any interface used by traditional hard drives
- Operate in extreme environments
- Use less power
- Produce less heat
- Reduce startup time

Optical Drives

An optical drive uses a laser to read and write data to and from optical media. There are several factors to consider when purchasing an optical drive:

- Interface type
- Reading capabilities
- Writing capabilities
- Formats

A CD-ROM drive can only read CDs. A CD-RW drive can read and write to CDs. Choose a CD-RW drive if your customer needs to read and write to CDs.

A DVD-ROM drive can only read DVDs and CDs. A DVD-RW drive can read and write to DVDs and CDs. DVDs hold significantly more data than CDs. Choose a DVD-RW drive if your customer needs to read and write to DVDs and CDs.

A Blu-ray Disc reader (BD-R) can only read Blu-ray Discs, DVDs, and CDs. A Blu-ray Disc writer (BD-RE) can read and write to Blu-ray Discs and DVDs. Blu-ray Discs hold significantly more data than DVDs. Choose a BD-RE drive if your customer needs to read and write to Blu-ray Discs.

External Storage

This type of storage connects to an external port such as a USB, IEEE 1394, SCSI, or eSATA port. External flash drives, sometimes called thumb drives, that connect to a USB port are a type of removable storage. There are several factors to consider when purchasing external storage:

- Port type
- Storage capacity
- Speed
- Portability
- Power requirements

External storage offers portability and convenience when working with multiple computers. Choose the correct type of external storage for your customer's needs. For example, if your customer needs to transfer a small amount of data, such as a single presentation, an external flash drive is a good choice. If your customer needs to back up or transfer large amounts of data, choose an external hard drive.

Select Input and Output Devices

An input device can be any piece of equipment that transfers information into a computer:

- Mouse
- Keyboard
- Scanner
- Camera
- Process-control sensor
- MIDI interface
- Microphone

An output device transfers information to the outside of the computer:

- Display monitor
- Projector
- Printer
- Process-control equipment
- Speaker

To select input and output devices, you should first find out what the customer wants. Next, you should select the hardware and software by researching the Internet for possible solutions. After you determine which input or output device the customer needs, you must determine how to connect it to the computer. Figure 11-12 shows common input and output port symbols.

Technicians should have a good understanding of several types of interfaces:

- **USB 1.1**: Transfers data at a maximum speed of 12 Mbps.
- **USB 2.0**: Transfers data at a maximum speed of 480 Mbps.
- **IEEE 1394 (FireWire)**: Transfers data at 100, 200, or 400 Mbps.
- **Parallel (IEEE 1284)**: Transfers data at a maximum speed of 3 Mbps.

- **Serial (RS-232)**: Early versions were limited to 20 kbps, but newer versions can reach transfer rates of 1.5 Mbps.

- **SCSI (Ultra320 SCSI)**: Connects as many as 15 devices with a transfer rate of 320 Mbps.

Figure 11-12   Common Input and Output Port Symbols

Worksheet 11.3.7: Research Computer Components

In this worksheet, you research computer components. Refer to the worksheet in *IT Essentials: PC Hardware and Software Lab Manual, Fourth Edition*. You can perform this worksheet now or wait until the end of the chapter.

Upgrade and Configure Personal Computer Components and Peripherals

Computer systems need periodic upgrades for various reasons:

- User requirements change.

- Upgraded software packages require new hardware.

- New hardware offers enhanced performance.

Changes to the computer can cause you to upgrade or replace components and peripherals. You should research the effectiveness and cost for both options: upgrading and replacing.

After completing this section, you will meet these objectives:

- Upgrade and configure a motherboard.

- Upgrade and configure a CPU and a heat sink/fan assembly.

- Upgrade and configure RAM.

- Upgrade and configure BIOS.

- Upgrade and configure storage devices and hard drives.

- Upgrade and configure input and output devices.

Figure 11-13 shows some of the different components and peripherals to upgrade or replace.

Figure 11-13   Upgrade or Replace

Upgrade and Configure a Motherboard

To upgrade or replace a motherboard, you might have to replace several other components, such as the CPU, heat sink/fan assembly, and RAM. Figure 11-14 shows an example of an old motherboard and a replacement/new motherboard.

A new motherboard must fit into the old computer case. The power supply must also be compatible with the new motherboard and be able to support all new computer components.

You should begin the upgrade by moving the CPU and heat sink/fan assembly to the new motherboard. These are much easier to work with when they are outside of the case. You should work on an antistatic mat and wear an antistatic wrist strap to avoid damaging the CPU. Remember to use thermal compound between the CPU and the heat sink. If the new motherboard requires different RAM, install it at this time.

Figure 11-14   Motherboards

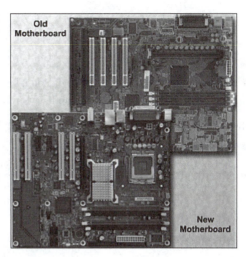

CPU Installation

Different CPU architectures are installed in four common socket connection designs:

- Single-Edge Connector (SEC)
- Low-Insertion Force (LIF)
- Zero-Insertion Force (ZIF)
- Land Grid Array (LGA) socket

SEC and LIF sockets are no longer commonly used. Consult the motherboard manual for instructions on how to install the CPU.

Jumper Settings

Jumpers are upright gold pins on the motherboard. Each grouping of two or more pins is called a *jumper block*. A motherboard might use a dual in-line package (DIP) switch instead of jumpers. Both methods are used to complete electrical circuits which provide a variety of options supported by the motherboard. The motherboard manual indicates which pins should be connected or not connected to accommodate the various options:

- CPU voltage
- CPU speed
- Bus speed
- Cache size and type
- Flash BIOS enabled

- Clear CMOS
- Size of system memory

CMOS Battery Installation

A CMOS battery might need to be replaced after a few years. Make sure the new battery matches the model required by the motherboard.

Follow these instructions for CMOS battery installation:

How To

Step 1.   Gently slide aside, or raise, the thin metal clips to remove the old battery.

Step 2.   Line up positive and negative poles to the correct orientation.

Step 3.   Gently slide aside, or raise, the thin metal clips to insert the new battery.

Motherboard Installation

When it is time to remove and replace the old motherboard, remove the cables from the motherboard that attach to the case LEDs and buttons. They can have the same labels, but there might be minor differences. Make the appropriate notes in your journal to know where and how everything is connected before you start the upgrade.

Note how the motherboard secures to the case. Some mounting screws provide support, and some can provide an important grounding connection between the motherboard and chassis. In particular, you should pay attention to screws and standoffs that are nonmetallic. These can be insulators. Replacing insulating screws and supports with metal hardware that conducts electricity can have disastrous results.

Make sure that you use the correct screws. Do not swap threaded screws with self-tapping metal screws; they will damage the threaded screw holes and might not be secure. Make sure that threaded screws are the correct length and have the same number of threads per inch. If the thread is correct, they will fit easily. You can make a screw fit by using force, but you will damage the threaded hole and the screw will not hold the motherboard securely. Using the wrong screw can also produce metal shavings that can cause short circuits.

Note

It does not matter whether you replace a flat head screw with a Phillips head screw as long as the threaded part of the screw is the same length and has the same number of threads.

Next, you should connect the power supply cables. If the Advanced Technology eXtended (ATX) power connectors are not the same size (some have more pins), you might need to use an adapter. Connect the cables for the case LEDs and buttons.

Refer to the motherboard manual for the layout of these connections. The connectors are not keyed, so it is possible to connect the wire backward. Polarized connectors usually have a small arrow or plus sign adjacent to indicate which conductor should attach to the positive pin. The polarized connectors include the power and reset switch, the hard disk drive LED, and the power LED.

Follow these instructions for front panel connections:

How To

Step 1.   Align the connector with the correct pins on the motherboard.

Step 2.   Press down gently until the connector is fully seated.

Note

If an LED or button does not work, the wire to the motherboard is probably connected improperly.

After the new motherboard is in place and cabled, you should install and secure all expansion cards.

It is now time to check your work. Make sure there are no loose parts or leftover wires. Connect a keyboard, mouse, monitor, and power. If any problem is detected, shut the power supply off immediately.

An expansion card can have the same functionality that is integrated into the motherboard. In this case, you may need to disable the onboard functions in the system BIOS. Use the documentation that came with the motherboard to learn what BIOS adjustments may be required.

BIOS Updates

The firmware encoded in the motherboard EEPROM chip may need to be updated so that the motherboard can support added hardware. Updating the firmware can be risky. Before updating motherboard firmware, record the manufacturer of the BIOS, the motherboard, and the motherboard model. You will need this information when you go to the motherboard manufacturer's site to get the correct software. Only update the firmware if there are problems with system hardware or to add functionality to the system.

Advanced BIOS Settings

Some computer manufacturers limit the advanced options in the BIOS to reduce errors resulting from incorrectly configuring BIOS settings. The advanced chipset features in the BIOS may allow overclocking the processor. *Overclocking* is changing the settings of a component so that it runs at a higher speed than its original specification. Overclocking should be done with caution because it will void the CPU warranty and might damage the system. The default settings found in the advanced BIOS settings menu usually do not need to be changed.

After the new motherboard is in place and cabled, you should install and secure all expansion cards. Check your work. Make sure that there are no loose parts or leftover wires. Connect a keyboard, mouse, monitor, and power. If there is any sign of trouble, you should shut the power supply off immediately.

Do not forget that an expansion card can have the same functionality that is integrated into the motherboard. In this case, you might need to disable the onboard functions in the system BIOS. Use the documentation that came with the motherboard to learn what BIOS adjustments might be required.

Lab 11.4.1: Install a NIC in Windows XP

In this lab, you install a NIC and disable an integrated motherboard network adapter on a PC with Windows XP. Refer to the lab in *IT Essentials: PC Hardware and Software Lab Manual, Fourth Edition*. You can perform this lab now or wait until the end of the chapter.

Optional Lab 11.4.1: Install a NIC in Windows Vista

In this optional lab, you install a NIC and disable an integrated motherboard network adapter on a PC with Windows Vista. Refer to the lab in *IT Essentials: PC Hardware and Software Lab Manual, Fourth Edition*. You can perform this lab now or wait until the end of the chapter.

Upgrade and Configure a CPU and a Heat Sink/Fan Assembly

One way to increase the apparent power of a computer is to increase the processing speed. You can often do this by upgrading the *central processing unit (CPU)*. However, there are some requirements that you must meet:

- The new CPU must fit into the existing CPU socket.
- The new CPU must be compatible with the motherboard chipset.
- The new CPU must operate with the existing motherboard and power supply.
- The new CPU must operate with the existing RAM. The RAM might need to be upgraded or expanded to take advantage of the faster CPU.

If the motherboard is older, you might not be able to find a compatible CPU. In that case, you would replace the motherboard.

To change the CPU, you should remove the existing CPU by releasing it from the socket using the zero insertion force (ZIF) lever. Different sockets have slightly different mechanisms, but all serve to lock the CPU in place after it is correctly oriented in the socket.

Insert the new CPU into place. Do not force the CPU into its socket, or use excessive force to close the locking bars. Excessive force can damage the CPU or its socket. If you encounter resistance, make sure that you have aligned the CPU properly. Most have a pattern of pins that will fit only one way. If there is a question, examine the new CPU to ensure that it is physically similar to the old one.

- **SEC socket**: Align the notches on the CPU to the keys in the SEC socket.

- **LIF or ZIF socket**: Align the CPU so that the connection 1 indicator is lined up with pin 1 on the CPU socket.

- **LGA socket**: Align the CPU so that the two notches on the CPU will fit into the two socket extensions.

If there is a question, examine the new CPU to ensure it is physically similar to the old one. The new CPU may require a different heat sink/fan assembly. The heat sink/fan assembly must physically fit the CPU and be compatible with the CPU socket. The heat sink/fan assembly must also be adequate to remove the heat of the faster CPU.

The following steps outline how to install the heat sink/fan assembly:

How To

Step 1.   Align the heat sink/fan assembly retainers with the holes on the motherboard.

Step 2.   Place the heat sink/fan assembly onto the CPU socket, being careful not to pinch the CPU fan wires.

Step 3.   Tighten the heat sink/fan assembly retainers to secure the assembly in place.

Step 4.   Connect the heat sink/fan assembly power cable to the header on the motherboard.

The new CPU might require a different heat sink/fan assembly. The heat sink/fan assembly, as shown in Figure 11-15, must physically fit the CPU and be compatible with the CPU socket. The heat sink/fan assembly must also be adequate to remove the heat of the faster CPU.

Figure 11-15   CPU and Heat Sink/Fan Assembly

> **Note**
>
> You must apply thermal compound between the new CPU and the *heat sink/fan* assembly. This is because the surface of the heat sink and CPU is not entirely flat, and if you place the heat sink directly on the CPU, there might be gaps that you cannot see. Air conducts heat poorly, and the gaps have a negative effect on heat transfer. By applying a thermal compound that has a high thermal conductivity, you improve the heat conductivity between the heat sink and CPU.

With some types of BIOS, you can view thermal settings to determine whether there are any problems with the CPU and the heat sink/fan assembly. Third-party software applications can report CPU temperature information in an easy-to-read format. Refer to the motherboard or CPU user documentation to determine whether the chip is operating in the correct temperature range. Some CPU and case fans turn on and off automatically depending on the CPU temperature and the internal case temperature. The temperatures are measured through thermal probes built into the fan assembly, or internal circuitry in the CPU.

The following steps outline how to install extra case fans:

How To

Step 1.   Align the fan so that it faces the correct direction to either draw air in or blow air out.

Step 2.   Mount the fan using the predrilled holes in the case. Mount the fan at the bottom of the case to draw air into the case or at the top of the case to direct hot air out of the case.

Step 3.   Connect the fan to the power supply or the motherboard, depending on the case fan plug type.

Upgrade and Configure RAM

Increasing the amount of system RAM almost always improves overall system perform-ance. Prior to upgrading or replacing the RAM, there are some questions you must answer:

- What type of RAM does the motherboard currently use?

- Can the RAM be installed one module at a time, or should it be grouped into matching banks?

- Are there any available RAM slots?

- Does the new RAM chip match the speed, latency, type, and voltage of the existing RAM?

Caution

When working with system RAM, work on an antistatic mat and wear an antistatic wrist strap. Place the RAM on the mat until you are ready to install it. Store RAM in antistatic packaging.

Remove the existing RAM by freeing the retaining clips that secure it. Pull it from the socket. Current dual in-line memory modules (DIMM) pull straight out and insert straight down. Earlier single in-line memory modules (SIMM) were inserted at an angle to lock into place.

Insert the new RAM, as shown in Figure 11-16, and lock it into place with the retaining clips.

Figure 11-16   Installing RAM

Caution

Make sure to insert the memory module completely into the socket. RAM can cause serious damage to the motherboard if it is incorrectly aligned and shorts the main system bus.

The system discovers the newly installed RAM if it is compatible and installed correctly. If the BIOS does not indicate the presence of the correct amount of RAM, check to make sure that the RAM is compatible with the motherboard and is correctly installed.

Lab 11.4.3: Install Additional RAM in Windows XP

In this lab, you install additional RAM in the computer with Windows XP. Refer to the lab in *IT Essentials: PC Hardware and Software Lab Manual, Fourth Edition.* You can perform this lab now or wait until the end of the chapter.

Optional Lab 11.4.3: Install Additional RAM in Windows Vista

In this optional lab, you install additional RAM in the computer with Windows Vista. Refer to the lab in *IT Essentials: PC Hardware and Software Lab Manual, Fourth Edition.* You can perform this lab now or wait until the end of the chapter.

Upgrade and Configure BIOS

Motherboard manufacturers periodically release updates for their *basic input/output system (BIOS)*. The release notes describe the upgrade to the product, compatibility improvements, and the known bugs that have been addressed. Some newer devices only operate properly with an updated BIOS.

Early computer BIOS information was contained in ROM chips. To upgrade the BIOS information, the ROM chip had to be replaced, which was not always possible. Modern BIOS chips are electrically erasable programmable ROM (EEPROM), or flash memory, which can be upgraded by the user without opening the computer case. This process is called *flashing the BIOS*.

To view the current BIOS settings on your computer, you must enter the BIOS setup program, as shown in Figure 11-17. Press the setup sequence keys while the computer is performing the POST. Depending on the computer, the setup key might be F1, F2, or Delete. Watch the text on the screen or consult the motherboard manual to find the setup key or combination of keys.

Figure 11-17   BIOS Version

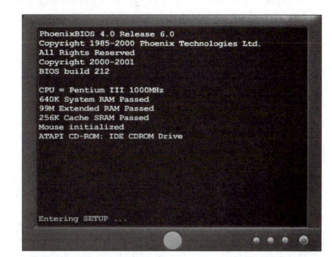

```
PhoenixBIOS 4.0 Release 6.0
Copyright 1985-2000 Phoenix Technologies Ltd.
All Rights Reserved
Copyright 2000-2001
BIOS build 212

CPU = Pentium III 1000MHz
640K System RAM Passed
99M Extended RAM Passed
256K Cache SRAM Passed
Mouse initialized
ATAPI CD-ROM: IDE CDROM Drive




Entering SETUP ...
```

The first part of the boot process displays a message that tells you which key to press to enter the setup, or BIOS, mode. There are a variety of settings in the BIOS that should not be altered by anyone unfamiliar with this procedure. If you are unsure, it is best not to change any BIOS setting unless you research the problem in depth.

To download a new BIOS, consult the manufacturer's website and follow the recommended installation procedures. Installing BIOS software online can involve downloading a new BIOS file, copying or extracting files to a floppy disk, and then booting from the floppy. An installation program prompts the user for information to complete the process. Some newer programs will do a BIOS update without the need to create a floppy disk. The BIOS will be updated after you reboot your computer.

Although it is still common to flash the BIOS through a command prompt, several mother-board manufacturers provide software on their websites that allow a user to flash the BIOS from within Windows. The procedure varies from manufacturer to manufacturer.

Caution

An improperly installed or aborted BIOS update can cause the computer to become unusable.

Lab 11.4.4: BIOS File Search

In this lab, you search for newer BIOS versions. Refer to the lab in *IT Essentials: PC Hardware and Software Lab Manual, Fourth Edition*. You can perform this lab now or wait until the end of the chapter.

Upgrade and Configure Storage Devices and Hard Drives

Instead of purchasing a new computer to get increased access speed and storage space, you can consider adding another hard drive. There are several reasons for installing an additional drive:

- To install a second operating system
- To provide additional storage space
- To provide a faster hard drive
- To hold the system swap file
- To provide a backup for the original hard drive
- To increase fault tolerance

If the new drive is PATA and is on the same data cable, one of the drives must be set as the master drive and the other must be set as the slave drive. Figure 11-18 shows jumper settings on the back of a PATA hard drive. Also, any new partitions or drive letter assignments should be well planned. The boot order in the BIOS might need to be adjusted.

Some drives can be jumpered to auto-detect. Refer to the hard drive diagram or manual for correct jumper settings. If the new drive is PATA and is on the same data cable, one of the drives must be set as the master drive and the other must be set as the slave drive. Each SATA hard drive has its own data cable; therefore, there is no master-slave relationship between drives. Any new partitions or drive letter assignments should be well planned. The boot order in BIOS may need to be adjusted. Be aware of the additional power load caused by adding hard drives. Make sure your power supply can handle the load. Figure 11-18 shows jumper settings.

Figure 11-18 Hard Drive Jumper Settings

Redundant Array of Independent Disks (RAID) can improve fault tolerance when connecting multiple hard drives, as shown in Figure 11-19. Some types of RAID require two or more hard drives. You can install RAID using hardware or software. Hardware installations are usually more dependable but are more expensive. Software installations are created and managed by an operating system, such as Windows Server 2003.

Figure 11-19   Types of RAID

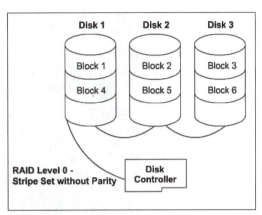

Lab 11.4.5: Install, Configure, and Partition a Second Hard Drive in Windows XP

In this lab, you install and configure a second hard drive on a computer with Windows XP. Refer to the lab in *IT Essentials: PC Hardware and Software Lab Manual, Fourth Edition*. You can perform this lab now or wait until the end of the chapter.

Optional Lab 11.4.5: Install, Configure, and Partition a Second Hard Drive in Windows Vista

In this optional lab, you install and configure a second hard drive on a computer with Windows Vista. Refer to the lab in *IT Essentials: PC Hardware and Software Lab Manual, Fourth Edition*. You can perform this lab now or wait until the end of the chapter.

Upgrade and Configure Input and Output Devices

If an input or output device stops operating, you might have to replace the device. Some customers might want to upgrade their input or output devices to increase performance and productivity.

An ergonomic keyboard, shown in Figure 11-20, can be more comfortable to use. Sometimes a reconfiguration is necessary to enable a user to perform special tasks, such as typing in a second language with additional characters. Finally, replacing or reconfiguring an input or output device can make it easier to accommodate users with disabilities.

Sometimes it is not possible to perform an upgrade using the existing expansion slots or sockets. In this case, you might be able to accomplish the upgrade using a USB connection. If the computer does not have an extra USB connection, you must install a USB adapter card or purchase a USB hub, as shown in Figure 11-21.

Figure 11-20   Ergonomic Wireless Keyboard and Mouse

Figure 11-21   USB Hub

After obtaining new hardware, you might have to install new drivers. You can usually do this by using the installation CD. If you do not have the CD, you can obtain updated drivers from the website of the manufacturer.

Note

A signed driver is a driver that has passed the Windows Hardware Quality Lab (WHQL) test and has been given a driver signature by Microsoft. Installing an unsigned driver can cause system instability, error messages, and boot problems. During hardware installation, if an unsigned driver is detected, you will be asked whether you want to continue installation of this driver.

Identify and Apply Common Preventive Maintenance Techniques for Personal Computer Components

To keep computers working properly, you must maintain them by performing preventive maintenance. Preventive maintenance can extend the life of the components, protect data, and improve computer performance.

After completing this section, you will meet these objectives:

- Clean internal components.
- Clean the case.
- Inspect computer components.

Clean Internal Components

One important part of computer preventive maintenance is to keep the system clean. The amount of dust in the environment and the habits of the user determine how often to clean the computer components. Most of your cleaning is to prevent the accumulation of dust.

To remove dust, do not use a vacuum cleaner. Vacuum cleaners can generate static and can damage or loosen components and jumpers. Instead, you should use compressed air to blow the dust away. If you use compressed air from a can, keep the can upright to prevent the fluid from leaking onto computer components. Always follow the instructions and warnings on the compressed-air can. Once the dust is removed from the PC, dispose of it so it does not get sucked back into the case by fans.

Regular cleaning also gives you a chance to inspect components for loose screws and connectors. There are several parts inside the computer case that you should keep as clean as possible:

- Heat sink/fan assembly
- RAM
- Adapter cards
- Motherboard
- Case fan
- Power supply
- Internal drives

Caution

When you clean a fan with compressed air, hold the fan blades in place. This prevents overspinning the rotor or moving the fan in the wrong direction.

Clean the Case

Dust or dirt on the outside of a computer can travel through cooling fans and loose computer case covers. Dirt can also enter a computer through missing expansion slot covers, as shown in Figure 11-22. If dust accumulates inside the computer, it can prevent the flow of air and affect cooling.

Figure 11-22   Cleaning the Computer Case

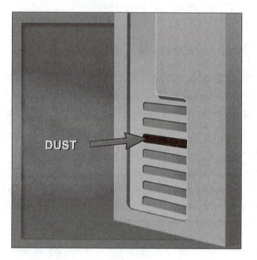

Use a cloth or duster to clean the outside of the computer case. If you use a cleaning product, do not spray it directly on the case. Instead, put a small amount onto a cleaning cloth or duster and wipe the outside of the case.

While cleaning the case, you should look for and correct things that might cause a problem later:

- Missing expansion slot covers that let dust, dirt, or living pests into the computer as well as disrupt the air flow

- Loose or missing screws that secure adapter cards

- Missing or tangled cables that can pull free from the case

Note

Airflow in the case is critical to heat removal. Missing expansion slot covers, unorganized cables, dust, and pests all work against the case's designed airflow. When installing fans, make sure they work together, not opposing one another.

Inspect Computer Components

The best method of keeping a computer in good condition is to examine the computer on a regular schedule. Cleaning provides a good opportunity to make this inspection. You should have a checklist of components to inspect, as described in the following sections.

CPU and Cooling System

Examine the CPU and cooling system for dust buildup. Make sure that the fan can spin freely. Check that the fan power cable is secure, as shown in Figure 11-23. Check the fan while the power is on to see the fan turn. Inspect the CPU to be sure that it is seated securely in the socket. Make sure that the heat sink is well attached. To avoid damage, do not remove the CPU for cleaning.

Figure 11-23   Loose Heat Sink/Fan Assembly Connector

RAM Connections

The RAM chips, as shown in Figure 11-24, should be seated securely in the RAM slots. Sometimes the retaining clips can loosen. Reseat them, if necessary. Use compressed air to remove any dust.

Figure 11-24   RAM Chips

Storage Devices

Inspect all storage devices, including the hard drives, floppy drive, optical drives, and tape drive. All cables should be firmly connected. Check for loose, missing, or incorrectly set jumpers, as shown in Figure 11-25. A drive should not produce rattling, knocking, or grinding sounds. Read the manufacturer's manual to learn how to clean optical drive and tape heads by using cotton swabs and compressed air. Clean floppy drives with a drive cleaning kit.

Figure 11-25   Hard Drive Jumpers

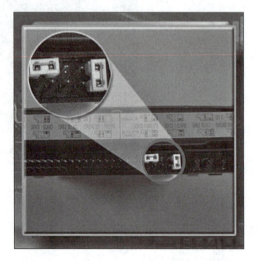

Adapter Cards

Adapter cards should be seated properly in their expansion slots. Loose cards, as shown in Figure 11-26, can cause short circuits. Secure adapter cards with the retaining screw to avoid the cards coming loose in their expansion slots. Use compressed air to remove any dirt or dust on the adapter cards or the expansion slots.

Figure 11-26   Loose Adapter Card

Note

The video adapter can sometimes become unseated because the large monitor cable can put pressure on it, or it might be mishandled when someone is tightening the retainer screws. If a video adapter is used in an expansion slot, the integrated video adapter from the motherboard is likely to be disabled. If you connect a monitor to it in error, the computer appears not to work.

Power Devices

Inspect power strips, surge suppressors (surge protectors), and uninterruptible power supply (UPS) devices. Make sure that there is proper and unobstructed ventilation. Replace the power strip if there have been electrical problems or excessive thunderstorms in the area.

Loose Screws

Loose screws can cause problems if they are not immediately fixed or removed. A loose screw in the case can later cause a short circuit or can roll into a position where the screw is hard to remove.

Keyboard and Mouse

Use compressed air or a small nonelectrostatic vacuum cleaner to clean the keyboard and mouse. If the mouse is the mechanical type, remove the ball and clean off any dirt.

Cables

Examine all cable connections. Look for broken and bent pins. Ensure that all connector retaining screws are finger tight. Make sure cables are not crimped, pinched, or severely bent.

Troubleshoot Computer Components and Peripherals

The troubleshooting process helps resolve problems with the computer or peripherals. These problems range from simple, such as updating a drive, to more complex problems, such as installing a CPU. Use the troubleshooting steps as a guideline to help you diagnose and repair problems.

After completing the following sections, you will meet these objectives:

- Review the troubleshooting process.
- Identify common problems and solutions.
- Apply troubleshooting skills.

Review the Troubleshooting Process

Computer technicians must be able to analyze the problem and determine the cause of the error to repair the computer. This process is called *troubleshooting*.

The first step in the troubleshooting process is to identify the problem.

Ask the customer open-ended questions about computer errors. Examples are shown in the following list. (This list is *not* comprehensive.)

- What type of computer do you have?
- What is the brand and modle of the computer?
- Can you describe what happens when the computer boots?
- How often does the computer fail to start?
- What is the first screen you see when you turn on the computer?
- What sound does the computer make as it starts?

Also ask the customer closed-ended questions about computer errors. (This list is *not* comprehensive.)

- Has anyone done any repair work on the computer recently?
- Has anyone else used the computer?
- Has the computer been moved recently?
- Does this computer have a floppy drive?
- Does this computer have a USB drive installed?
- Is there a wireless NIC in this computer?
- Is the computer secured in a locked room at night?
- Do you have a Windows XP installation CD-ROM on hand?

After you have talked to the customer, establish a theory of probable causes. Issues that apply to computer hardware include the following:

- Are all the cables to this computer tightly in their sockets?
- Is the power cord firmly seated at both ends?
- Is the cable that connects the computer to the monitor squarely seated in its socket with the thumbscrews finger tight?
- Are any of the rear-panel expansion slot covers loose so that the adapter cards could have loosened?
- Was the computer recently dropped or jarred?
- Are there any missing screws or signs that the computer has been tampered with?

After you have verified the obvious issues, try some quick solutions to computer hardware problems:

- Check the external cables for loose connections that could cause a restart.
- Check the internal data and power cables for loose connections.
- Ensure that adapter cards and RAM are properly secured.
- Verify that all cooling fans are operating properly.

Next, determine the exact cause. Common methods to determine exact cause include the following:

- Restart the computer.
- Disconnect and reconnect the external cables.
- Disconnect and reconnect the internal cables.

- Secure the adapter cards.

- Secure the RAM.

- Roll back or reinstall the device driver.

- Replace the RAM.

- Clean the fans.

- Reset the jumpers.

- Secure or replace the CMOS battery.

- Update the firmware.

At this point, you have enough information to evaluate the problem and research and implement a solution. When researching possible solutions for a problem, use the following sources of information:

- Helpdesk repair logs

- Problem-solving experience

- Other technicians

- Internet search

- Newsgroups

- Manufacturer FAQs

- Computer manuals

- Device manuals

- Online forums

- Technical websites

Next, verify solutions and full system functionality.

- Reboot the computer.

- Restart external devices.

- Access all drives and shared resources.

- Print a document.

- Read and write to all storage devices.

- Validate the amount of RAM, the CPU speed, and the data and time.

After you have solved the problem, document your findings. Tasks required to complete this step include the following:

- Discuss the solution implemented with customer.

- Have the customer verify that the problem has been solved.

- Provide the customer with all paperwork.

- Document steps taken to solve the problem in the work order and the technician's journal.

- Document any components used in the repair.

- Document the time spent to resolve the problem.

Identify Common Problems and Solutions

Computer problems can be attributed to hardware, software, networks, or some combination of the three. You will resolve some types of computer problems more often than others. Table 11-2 through Table 11-5 outline common hardware problems and solutions.

Storage Device Problems

Storage device problems are often related to loose or incorrect cable connections, incorrect drive and media formats, and incorrect jumper and CMOS settings, as shown in Table 11-2.

Table 11-2   Common Storage Device Problems and Solutions

Identify the Problem	Probable Causes	Possible Solutions
The computer does not recognize a storage device.	The power cable is loose.	Secure the power cable.
	The data cable is loose.	Secure the data cable.
	The jumpers are set incorrectly	Reset the jumpers.
	The storage device has failed.	Replace the storage device.
	The storage device settings in the CMOS are incorrect.	Reset the storage device settings in the CMOS.

continues

Table 11-2   Common Storage Device Problems and Solutions   *continued*

Identify the Problem	Probable Causes	Possible Solutions
The floppy disk drive will not read media or the drive light stays on constantly.	The power or the data cable connection is loose.	Secure the power cable or the data cable to the drive and the motherboard.
	Pin 1 on the data cable is not connected to pin 1 on the drive.	Correctly connect the data cable. Reset the FDD settings in CMOS.
	The FDD settings in the CMOS are incorrect.	Try another disc.
	The disc is damaged or not formatted.	Reinsert the disc correctly.
	The disc is inserted upside down.	
The computer fails to recognize an optical disc.	The optical drive is faulty.	Replace the optical drive.
	The disc is inserted upside down.	Insert the disc correctly.
	More than one disc is inserted in the drive.	Ensure that only one disc is inserted in the drive.
	The disc is damaged.	Replace the disc.
	The disc is the wrong format.	Use the correct type disc.
The computer will not eject the optical disc.	The optical drive is jammed.	Insert a pin in the small hole next to the eject button on the drive to open the tray.
	The optical drive has been locked by software.	Reboot the computer.
	The optical drive is faulty.	Replace the optical drive.

Identify the Problem	Probable Causes	Possible Solutions
The computer does not recognize a SCSI drive.	The SCSI drive has an incorrect SCSI ID.	Reconfigure the SCSI ID. Ensure that the SCSI chain is terminated at the correct end points.
	The SCSI termination is not set correctly.	Turn on the external drive before turning on the computer.
	The external drive was not powered on prior to booting the computer.	
The computer does not recognize a removable external drive.	The removable external drive is faulty.	Replace the external removable drive.
	The removable external drive connection is not seated properly.	Remove and reinsert the drive connection to the computer.
	The OS does not have the correct drivers for the removable external drive.	Download and install the correct drivers for the external removable drive.
	The external ports are disabled in the CMOS.	Enable the ports in the CMOS.
	The external ports could be disabled in the Device Manager.	Enable the ports in the Device Manager.
	The external ports might not have drivers or might have incorrect drivers installed.	Download and install the correct drivers for the ports.
	The removable external drive requires a power supply of its own.	Make sure the removable external drive is powered.
	The removable external drive might not be turned off.	Make sure it is turned on.

continues

Table 11-2   Common Storage Device Problems and Solutions   *continued*

Identify the Problem	Probable Causes	Possible Solutions
A media reader cannot read an SD card that works fine in the camera.	The media reader does not support the SD card type.	Use a different SD card type.
	The media reader is not connected correctly.	Ensure the media reader is connected in the computer.
	The media reader is not configured properly in the CMOS settings.	Reconfigure the media reader in the CMOS settings.
	The media reader is damaged.	Install a known good media reader.

Motherboard and Internal Component Problems

Often, these problems are caused by incorrect or loose cables, failed components, incorrect drivers, and corrupted updates, as shown in Table 11-3.

Table 11-3   Common Motherboard and Internal Component Problems and Solutions

Identify the Problem	Probable Causes	Possible Solutions
The clock on the computer is no longer keeping the correct time or the CMOS settings are changing when the computer is rebooted.	The CMOS battery might be loose.	Secure the battery.
	The CMOS battery might be failing.	Replace the battery.
Retrieving or saving from a USB flash drive is slow.	The motherboard does not support USB 2.0.	Update the motherboard or USB flash drive to support USB 2.0.
	The USB flash drive does not support USB 2.0. The port is set to full speed in the CMOS.	Set the port speed in the CMOS setting to high speed.
After updating the BIOS firmware, the computer will not start.	The BIOS firmware did not install correctly.	Contact the motherboard manufacture.

Identify the Problem	Probable Causes	Possible Solutions
The computer displays the incorrect CPU information when the computer boots.	The motherboard has the incorrect jumper settings.	Set the appropriate CPU jumper settings on the motherboard.
	The CPU settings are not correct in the CMOS.	Set the CMOS settings correctly for the CPU
	The BIOS does not properly recognize the CPU.	Update the BIOS.
The hard drive LED on the front of the computer does not light.	The hard drive LED cable is not connected or is loose.	Reconnect the hard drive LED cable to motherboard.
	The hard drive LED is incorrectly oriented to the front case panel connections.	Correctly orient the hard drive LED cable to the front of the case panel connection and reconnect.
The integrated NIC has stopped working on a computer.	The NIC drivers are corrupted.	Update the NIC drivers.
	The NIC is damaged.	Add a new NIC.
	The NIC could be disabled in the BIOS.	Enable the NIC in the BIOS.
	An additional NIC could be installed and the integrated NIC automatically disabled by the BIOS.	Remove additional NIC or enable the integrated NIC in the BIOS.

continues

Table 11-3   Common Motherboard and Internal Component Problems and Solutions
continued

Identify the Problem	Probable Causes	Possible Solutions
The computer does not have any video after installing a new PCIe video card.	CMOS settings are set to use the built-in video.	Disable the built-in video in the CMOS settings.
	The cable is still connected to the built-in video.	Connect the cable to the new video card.
	Drivers for the new video card are not installed or are incorrect.	Install a known good video card.
	The new video card is not working.	
The new sound card does not work.	An incorrect device driver is installed.	Install the correct device driver.
	The speakers are not connected to the correct jack.	Connect the speakers to the correct jack.
	The audio is muted.	Unmute the audio.
	The sound card is malfunctioning.	Install a known good sound card.
	CMOS settings are set to use on-board sound device.	Disable the onboard audio device in the CMOS settings.

Power Supply Problems

Power problems often are caused by a faulty power supply, loose connections, and inadequate wattage, as shown in Table 11-4.

Table 11-4   Common Power Supply Problems and Solutions

Identify the Problem	Probable Causes	Possible Solutions
The computer will not turn on.	The computer is not plugged in to an AC power outlet.	Correctly plug in the computer to a known good AC outlet.
	The AC outlet is not providing power.	Use a known good power cord.
	The power supply switch is not turned on.	Turn on a power supply switch.
	The power supply switch is incorrect voltage.	Set theh power supply switch to the correct voltage.
	The power button is not connected to the front panel corently.	Correctly orient the power button to the face of the computer and reconnect.
	The power supply has malfunctioned.	Install a known-good power supply.
The computer reboots, turns off unexpectedly, or has a burning smell.	The power supply is starting to fail.	Replace the power supply.
	The thermocouple is misplaced.	Place the thermocouple correctly.

CPU Problems and Memory Problems

Processor and memory problems often are caused by incorrect installations, bad CMOS settings, inadequate cooling and ventilation, and compatibility issues, as shown in Table 11-5.

Table 11-5   Common CPU and Memory Problems and Solutions

Identify the Problem	Probable Causes	Possible Solutions
The computer will not boot, it locks up, or the CPU fan is making an unusual noise.	The CPU has failed.	Reinstall the CPU.
	The CPU has overheated.	Replace the CPU.
	The CPU fan is failing.	Ensure that the CPU has a good bond with the heat sink and that the thermal compound is correctly applied.
		Increase the circulation in the case by adding fans to the case.
		Replace the CPU cooling device.
The computer reboots without warning, locks up, or displays error messages to the BSOD.	The front-side bus is set too high.	Reset to the factory default settings for the motherboard.
	The CPU multiplier is set too high.	Lower the FSB settings.
	The CPU voltage is set too high.	Lower the multiplier settings.
		Lower the CPU voltage settings.
After upgrading from a single-core CPU to a dual-core CPU, the computer runs slower and shows only one CPU graph in the Task Manager.	The BIOS does not recognize the dual-core CPU.	Update the BIOS firmware to support the dual-core CPU.
Some external devices from a 32-bit computer do not work on a new 64-bit computer.	Incorrect device drivers are installed.	Update the device drivers to 64-bit drivers.
A new CPU will not install onto the motherboard.	The CPU is the incorrect type.	Replace the CPU with a CPU that matches the motherboard socket type.

Identify the Problem	Probable Causes	Possible Solutions
The computer does not recognize the new RAM that was added.	The new RAM is damaged.	Install the correct type of RAM.
	The incorrect RAM type was installed.	Replace the RAM.
	The new RAM is loose in the memory slot.	Secure the RAM in the memory slot.
		Ensure that the RAM is installed in the correct memory slots.
After updating a computer to Windows Vista, the computer runs very slowly.	The computer does not have enough RAM.	Install additional RAM.
	The video card does not have enough memory.	Install a video card that has more memory.
		Turn off Aero in Windows Vista.
A computer with both DDR and DDR2 RAM installed recognizes only the DDR2 RAM.	The motherboard does not support the installation of both DDR and DDR2 RAM.	Check the motherboard manual to see whether the computer will support both types of RAM.

Apply Troubleshooting Skills

Now that you understand the troubleshooting process, it is time to apply your listening and diagnostic skills.

Lab 11.6.3 is designed to reinforce your skills with PC hardware problems. You will troubleshoot and repair a computer that does not boot.

Remote Technician 11.6.3 is designed to reinforce your communication and troubleshooting skills with PC hardware problems. In this lab, you perform the following steps:

- Receive the work order.
- Take the customer through various steps to try and resolve the problem.
- Document the problem and the resolution.

Lab 11.6.3: Repair Boot Problem

In this lab, you repair a computer boot problem. Refer to the lab in *IT Essentials: PC Hardware and Software Lab Manual, Fourth Edition*. You can perform this lab now or wait until the end of the chapter.

Lab 11.6.3: Remote Technician: Repair Boot Problem

In this lab, you instruct a customer on how to repair a computer boot problem. Refer to the activity in *IT Essentials: PC Hardware and Software Lab Manual, Fourth Edition*. You can perform this lab now or wait until the end of the chapter.

Lab 11.6.3: Troubleshooting Hardware Problems in Windows XP

In this lab, you troubleshoot hardware problems in Windows XP. Refer to the activity in *IT Essentials: PC Hardware and Software Lab Manual, Fourth Edition*. You can perform this lab now or wait until the end of the chapter.

Optional Lab 11.6.3: Troubleshooting Hardware Problems in Windows Vista

In this optional lab, you troubleshoot hardware problems in Windows Vista. Refer to the activity in *IT Essentials: PC Hardware and Software Lab Manual, Fourth Edition*. You can perform this lab now or wait until the end of the chapter.

Summary

In this chapter, you learned about advanced computer diagnosis and repair and found out how to consider upgrades and select components. This chapter also presented some detailed troubleshooting techniques to help you locate and resolve problems, and present your findings to the customer. A summary of the topics is as follows:

- You learned about the roles of the field, remote, and bench technicians and the job possibilities that are available to those who enter the workforce with some knowledge of advanced troubleshooting skills.

- You can explain and perform safe lab procedures and tool use. You can describe basic electrical safety, especially as it applies to monitors and laser printers. You understand the purpose and enforcement of worker safety standards.

- You can describe situations requiring replacement of computer components like power supplies, motherboards, CPU and heat sinks, RAM, adapter cards, storage devices, and input and output devices.

- You can upgrade and configure personal computer components and peripherals, power supplies, motherboards, CPU and heat sinks, RAM, adapter cards, and storage devices.

- You can identify and apply common preventive maintenance techniques for personal computer components.

- You can troubleshoot computer components and peripherals.

Summary of Exercises

This is a summary of the Labs and Worksheets associated with this chapter.

Labs

The following labs cover material from this chapter. Refer to the labs in *IT Essentials: PC Hardware and Software Lab Manual, Fourth Edition*.

Lab 11.2.2: Using a Multimeter and a Power Supply Tester

Lab 11.2.2: Testing UTP Cables Using a Loopback Plug and a Cable Meter

Lab 11.4.1: Install a NIC in Windows XP

Optional Lab 11.4.1: Install a NIC in Windows Vista

Lab 11.4.3: Install Additional RAM in Windows XP

Optional Lab 11.4.3: Install Additional RAM in Windows Vista

Lab 11.4.4: BIOS File Search

Lab 11.4.5: Install, Configure, and Partition a Second Hard Drive in Windows XP

Optional Lab 11.4.5: Install, Configure, and Partition a Second Hard Drive in Windows Vista

Lab 11.6.3: Repair Boot Problem

Lab 11.6.3: Remote Technician: Repair Boot Problem

Lab 11.6.3: Troubleshooting Hardware Problems in Windows XP

Optional Lab 11.6.3: Troubleshooting Hardware Problems in Windows Vista

Worksheets

The following worksheets cover material from this chapter. Refer to the labs in *IT Essentials: PC Hardware and Software Lab Manual, Fourth Edition.*

Worksheet 11.1: Job Opportunities

Worksheet 11.3.7: Research Computer Components

Check Your Understanding

You can find the answers to these questions in the appendix, "Answers to Check Your Understanding Questions."

1. Computer components should be disposed of properly to meet state and federal standards. Which of the following dangerous materials can be found in computer components? (Choose three.)

   A. Cadmium

   B. Carbon

   C. Hydrogen

   D. Lead

   E. Mercury

   F. Nitrogen

2. A technician has been called to troubleshoot a computer. The user reports that the computer has become louder during use and programs are slow to load. Which component is most likely beginning to fail?

   A. CPU

   B. Hard drive

   C. Memory

   D. Floppy drive

3. Which of the following devices should not be repaired while using antistatic devices? (Choose two.)

   A. Hard drive

   B. Memory

   C. Modem

   D. Monitor

   E. Power supply

4. Which of the following peripherals would be considered output devices? (Choose three.)

   A. Camera

   B. Display monitor

   C. Keyboard

   D. Microphone

   E. Projector

   F. Speaker

5. What is a safety concern that technicians need to remember when working on a CRT?

   A. Risk of chemical burns

   B. Risk of electrical shock

   C. Risk of phosphor contamination

   D. Risk of radiation

6. A user has moved to a different location on the same campus. The network media is different at the new location. Which of the following considerations will affect the choice of the replacement NIC? (Choose two.)

   A. Availability of expansion slot

   B. Type of memory

   C. Network protocols used in the new location

   D. Type of hard drive

   E. Type of lighting

7. While performing regular maintenance on a computer, a technician notices that the NIC is loose in an expansion slot. What is the proper course of action?

   A. Replace the NIC with a new card.

   B. Use thermal paste to secure the card in the expansion slot.

   C. Secure the adapter card in the expansion slot and tighten the retaining screw.

   D. The slot is most likely damaged. Use a new slot if one is available.

8. Which activity increases the chance of computer components becoming damaged from ESD?

    A. Touching the metal case before working on a computer

    B. Walking across a carpet or a rug and touching components

    C. Using antistatic mats when working with components

    D. Using nonmagnetic tools when working on a computer

9. Which of the following causes can affect the correct flow of air and lead to a computer overheating? (Choose two.)

    A. Two case fans: one pulling and one pushing

    B. Missing expansion slot cover

    C. Dust buildup around fans and air vents

    D. Heat sink added to the Northbridge chipset

    E. Missing slot coolers

10. As an onsite technician, you have been given the assignment of replacing a damaged motherboard on a customer's computer. You will need to transport the motherboard to the residence. Which is the best method to carry the motherboard?

    A. Wrap the motherboard in a piece of lint-free cloth.

    B. Carry the motherboard in an antistatic bag.

    C. Carry the motherboard in a metal-lined plastic box.

    D. Carry the motherboard in a paper bag.

11. Which of the following actions should you not perform if you want to prevent your computer from any type of ESD while servicing the computer? (Choose two.)

    A. Wear an antistatic wrist strap.

    B. Keep one hand in contact with the bare metal frame of the computer at all times.

    C. Make sure that the room in which the computer is serviced is carpeted.

    D. Make sure that the room in which the computer is serviced is cool and dry.

    E. Do not wear cotton clothes.

CHAPTER 12

Advanced Operating Systems

Objectives

Upon completion of this chapter, you should be able to answer the following questions:

- How can I select the appropriate operating system based on customer needs?

- What is the best way to install, configure, and optimize an operating system?

- How do I upgrade operating systems?

- What are the preventive maintenance procedures for operating systems?

- How do I troubleshoot operating systems?

Key Terms

This chapter uses the following key terms. You can find the definitions in the Glossary.

The installation, configuration, and optimization of operating systems are examined in greater detail in this chapter.

There are various brands of operating systems available on the market today, including Microsoft Windows, Apple Mac OS X, UNIX, and Linux. A technician must consider the current computer system when selecting an operating system. Additionally, there are several versions or distributions of an operating system. Some versions of Microsoft Windows include Windows 2000 Professional, Windows XP Home Edition, Windows XP Professional, Windows Media Center, Windows Vista Home Basic, Windows Vista Business, Windows Vista Premium, Windows 7 Home Premium, Windows 7 Professional, Windows 7 Enterprise, and Windows 7 Ultimate.

Each of these operating systems offers many of the same features with a similar interface. However, some functions necessary for specific customer needs might not be available in all of them. You must be able to compare and contrast operating systems to find the best one based on your customer's needs.

After completing this chapter, you will meet these objectives:

- Select the appropriate operating system based on customer needs.
- Install, configure, and optimize an operating system.
- Describe how to upgrade operating systems.
- Describe preventive maintenance procedures for operating systems.
- Troubleshoot operating systems.

Select the Appropriate Operating System Based on Customer Needs

There are many operating systems to choose from, each with features that should be considered when consulting with a customer. When selecting an operating system for a customer, you should select hardware that meets or exceeds the minimum requirements for equipment called for by the operating system.

In this chapter, Windows XP Professional is used to describe the functions of an operating system. At some point during your career, you will most likely upgrade or repair a computer with a Windows operating system.

Table 12-1 shows a comparison of Windows operating systems.

Table 12-1   Windows OS Features

Microsoft OS	Remote Desktop?	Network Sharing?	Scalable CPU Support?	Encrypted File System (EFS) Support?	Enhanced Security?
Windows 7 Ultimate	Yes	Yes	Yes	Yes	Yes
Windows 7 Enterprise	Yes	Yes	Yes	Yes	Yes
Windows 7 Professional	Yes	Yes	Yes	Yes	Yes
Windows 7 Home Premium	Yes	Yes	Yes	Yes	No
Windows Vista Premium	Yes	Yes	Yes	Yes	Yes
Windows Vista Professional	Yes	Yes	Yes	Yes	Yes
Windows Vista Home Premium	Client only	Yes	Yes	Yes	No
Windows XP Professional	Yes	Yes	Yes	Yes	Yes
Windows XP Home Edition	No	Yes	No	No	No
Windows XP Media Center Edition	Yes	Yes	Yes	Yes	Yes
Windows 2000	Add-on	Yes	Yes	Yes	Yes

After completing this section, you will meet these objectives:

- Describe operating systems.
- Describe network operating systems.

Describe Operating Systems

An *operating system* is the interface between the user and the computer. Without an operating system, the user would not be able to interact with the hardware or software on the computer. An operating system provides the following operational and organizational capabilities:

- Provides a bridge between the hardware and applications

- Creates a file system to store data

- Manages applications

- Interprets user commands

Operating systems have minimum requirements for hardware. Table 12-2 shows the minimum hardware requirements for several operating systems.

Table 12-2   OS Hardware Requirements

	Windows 7	Windows Vista	Windows XP	Mac OS X	Linux (Ubuntu Desktop)	UNIX (BSD)
CPU	1 GHz	1 GHz	223 MHz	867 MHz	100 MHz	233 MHz
Minimum RAM	1 GB (x86) 2 GB (x64)	1 GB	64 MB	1 GB	128 MB	64 MB
Minimum Hard Disk Space	16 GB (x86) 20 GB (x64)	40 GB (at least 25 GB free space)	1.5 GB	5 GB	2 GB	1 GB
Display	DirectX 9 with WDDM 1.0	DirectX 9 with WDDM 128 MB graphics memory	Video output at SVGA (800x600) resolution	—	—	—
Other	—	DVD-ROM Internet access	CD-ROM or DVD-ROM	DVD-ROM Internet access	—	—

Describe Network Operating Systems

A *network operating system (NOS)* is an operating system that contains additional features to increase functionality and manageability in a networked environment. The following are examples of network operating systems:

- Windows 2000 Server

- Windows 2003 Server

- UNIX

- Linux

- Novell NetWare

- Mac OS X

The NOS is designed to provide network resources to clients:

- Server applications, such as shared databases

- Centralized data storage

- Directory services that provide a centralized repository of user accounts and resources on the network, such as Lightweight Directory Access Protocol (LDAP) or Active Directory

- Network print queue

- Network access and security

- *Redundant storage systems*, such as Redundant Array of Independent Disks (RAID) and backups

Network operating systems provide several protocols designed to perform network functions. These protocols are controlled by code on the network servers. Protocols used by network operating systems provide services such as web browsing, file transfer, email, name resolution, and automatic IP addressing. Network protocols include the following:

- **HTTP (Hypertext Transport Protocol)**: Defines how files are exchanged on the web

- **FTP (File Transfer Protocol)**: Provides services for file transfer and manipulation

- **POP3 (Post Office Protocol)**: Retrieves email messages from an email server

- **DNS (Domain Name System)**: Resolves URLs for websites with their IP addresses

- **DHCP (Dynamic Host Control Protocol)**: Automates assignment of IP addresses

Windows OS Directory Structures

There are many different versions of each Windows OS. During installation, the Windows setup program creates directories that have specific purposes. There are directories designed to store the system files, user files, and program files, among others. When files of the same type are saved to a certain location, it is easy for users to find needed data.

User File Locations

By default, Windows stores most of the files created by the user in the folder C:\Documents and Settings*User_name*\My Documents\.

The My Documents folder contains folders for music, videos, websites, and pictures, among others. Many programs also store specific user data here. All users of a single computer have their own My Documents folder containing each user's favorites, cookies, and desktop items.

System File Locations

When the Windows operating system is installed, all of the files that are used to run the computer are located in the folder C:\WINNT\system32 for Windows 2000 and C:\Windows\system32 for Windows XP and Windows Vista.

Fonts

The Fonts folder contains all of the fonts that have been installed in the computer. Fonts come in several formats, including TrueType, OpenType, Composite, and PostScript. Font typefaces are the fonts that you can choose from within programs. Some examples of font typefaces are Arial, Times New Roman, and Courier.

The Fonts folder can be accessed through the Control Panel. Fonts can be installed using the File > Install New Font menu. All of the installed fonts are located in C:\Windows\Fonts.

Temporary Files

The Temporary Files folder contains files created by the operating system and programs that are needed for a short period of time. For example, temporary files might be created while an application is being installed to make more RAM available for other applications.

Temporary files are found in the folder C:\Documents and Settings*User_name*\Local Settings\Temp.

Program Files

The Program Files folder is used by most application installation programs to install software. Programs are usually installed in the folder C:\Program Files.

Offline Files and Folders

With Windows 2000, a new feature to help mobile users be more productive was introduced. Offline Files and Folders allows you to select shared files and folders from the network to be stored on your computer. These files are available after the computer is disconnected from the network. When you reconnect to the network, the changes that you have made offline are automatically applied to the original files on the network.

To set up your computer to use offline files and folders, follow these steps:

How To Q

Step 1.   Select **Start > My Computer > C: drive**.

Step 2.   Select **Tools > Folder Options > Offline Files**.

Step 3.   Check the **Enable Offline Files** check box.

To make a file or folder available to you offline, follow these steps:

How To Q

Step 1.   Select **Start > My Computer**.

Step 2.   Open a network drive.

Step 3.   Select the shared network files or folders to make available offline.

Step 4.   Select **File > Make Available Offline**.

To view a list of all of the shared, offline network files, follow these steps:

How To Q

Step 1.   Select **Tools > Folder Options**.

Step 2.   Select **Offline Files > View Files**.

Install, Configure, and Optimize an Operating System

Most operating systems are easy to install. After the computer starts, the Windows XP Professional installation CD-ROM displays a wizard, as shown in Figure 12-1, to guide you through the installation process with a series of questions. After the answers to the questions are provided, the installation wizard completes the installation automatically. In the following sections, you will perform a custom installation of Windows XP Professional.

Figure 12-1   Windows XP Installation

After completing this section, you will meet these objectives:

- Compare and contrast a default installation and a custom installation.

- Install Windows XP Professional using a custom installation.

- Create, view, and manage disks, directories, and files.

- Identify procedures and utilities used to optimize the performance of operating systems.

- Identify procedures and utilities used to optimize the performance of browsers.

- Describe the installation, use, and configuration of email software.

- Set screen resolution and update the video driver.

- Describe the installation of a second operating system.

Compare and Contrast a Default Installation and a Custom Installation

The default installation of Windows XP Professional is sufficient for most computers used in a home or small office network. A custom installation of Windows XP Professional is typically used in a larger network.

Default installation requires minimal user interaction. You are prompted to provide information for the specific computer and the owner/user.

In Windows XP, the *custom installation* is similar to the default installation. There are only two screens that offer a custom selection during setup. The first screen allows you to customize the regional settings, and the second screen (shown in Figure 12-2) allows you to customize the network settings.

Figure 12-2   Windows Installations Types

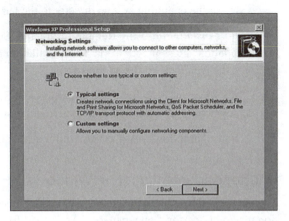

A technician or a user with technical experience often performs the custom installation. In a custom installation, the wizard prompts the user for detailed performance information to ensure that the operating system is customized to meet the preferences or requirements of the individual user or the network administrator of a company. You can perform a custom Windows XP Professional installation on more than one computer on a network by using an answer file that contains predefined settings and answers to the questions that are asked by the wizard during setup.

The technician can automate and customize a Windows XP Professional installation to include the following features:

- Productivity applications, such as Microsoft Office

- Custom applications

- Support for multiple languages

- Operating System Deployment Feature Pack using Microsoft Systems Management Server (SMS)

- Hardware device drivers

Install Windows XP Professional Using a Custom Installation

A custom installation of Windows XP Professional can save time and provide a consistent configuration of the operating system across computers on a large network.

The most common types of custom installations are as follows:

- *Unattended installation* from a network distribution point using an answer file.

- *Image-based installation* using Sysprep and a disk-imaging program, which copies an image of the operating system directly to the hard drive with no user intervention.

- *Remote installation* using Remote Installation Services (RIS), which can download the installation across the network. This installation can be requested by the user or forced onto the computer by the administrator.

- OS Deployment Feature Pack using Microsoft SMS, which can dramatically simplify deployment of an operating system across the organization.

The sections that follow describe these different custom installation methods in more detail.

Unattended Installation in Windows XP

The unattended installation using an unattend.txt answer file is the easiest custom installation method to perform on a network. An answer file can be created using an application called setupmgr.exe, which is located within the deploy.cab file on the Windows XP Professional CD-ROM.

Figure 12-3 shows an example of an answer file.

Figure 12-3   Sample Answer File

```
<unattend xmlns="urn:schemas-microsoft-com:unattend"
xmlns:wcm="http://schemas.microsoft.com/WMIConfig/2002/State">
   <settings pass="specialize">
   <component name="Microsoft-Windows-Shell-Setup"
publicKeyToken="31bf3856ad364e35"
      language="neutral" versionScope="nonSxS"
processorArchitecture="x86">
      <ComputerName>JohnWayne</ComputerName>
      <ProductKey>AAAAA-AAAAA-AAAAA-AAAAA-AAAAA</ProductKey>
      <TimeZone>Central European Standard Time</TimeZone>
   </component>
   </settings>
   <settings pass="oobeSystem">
   <component name="Microsoft-Windows-Shell-Setup"
processorArchitecture="x86" publicKeyToken="31bf3856ad364e35"
      language="neutral" versionScope="nonSxS"
processorArchitecture="x86">
      <FirstLogonCommands>
       <SynchronousCommand wcm:action="add">
       <Order>1</Order>
       <CommandLine>C:\runonce.cmd</CommandLine>
       <Description>RunOnce Command</Description>
       </SynchronousCommand>
      </FirstLogonCommands>
   </component>
   </settings>
```

After you have answered all the questions, the unattend.txt file is copied to the distribution shared folder on a server. At this point, you can do one of two things:

- Run the unattended.bat file on the client machine. This prepares the hard drive and automatically installs the operating system from the server over the network.

- Create a boot disk that boots up the computer and connects to the distribution share on the server. Run the batch file to install the operating system over the network.

Unattended Installation in Windows Vista

To customize a standard Windows Vista installation, Windows System Image Manager (SIM) is used to create the setup answer file. Windows SIM allows you to perform the following operations:

- Create an unattended answer file.

- Update an unattended answer file.

- Add packages such as applications or drivers to an unattended answer file.

- Validate an unattended answer file.

Windows SIM is part of the Windows Automated Installation Kit (AIK) and can be downloaded from the Microsoft website.

Image-Based Installation

When performing image-based installations, you should begin by completely configuring one computer to an operational state. Next, run Sysprep to prepare the system for imaging. A third-party disk-imaging application prepares an image of the completed computer that can be burned onto a CD or DVD. This image can then be copied onto computers with compatible hardware abstraction layers (HAL) to complete the installation of multiple computers. After the image has been copied, you can boot up the computer, but you might have to configure some settings, such as computer name and domain membership.

Remote Installation

With Remote Installation Service (RIS), the process is very much like an image-based installation, except you would not use a disk-imaging utility. You can use RIS to remotely set up new Microsoft Windows computers by using an RIS network shared folder as the source of the Windows operating system files. You can install operating systems on remote boot-enabled client computers. User computers that are connected to the network can be started by using a Preboot eXecution Environment (PXE)–capable network adapter or remote boot disk. The client then logs on with valid user account credentials.

RIS is designed to be used in a relatively small network and should not be used over low-speed links of a wide-area network (WAN). Microsoft SMS allows a network administrator to manage large numbers of computers on a network. SMS can be used to manage updates, provide remote control, and perform inventory management. An optional feature is operating system deployment, which requires the installation of the SMS OS Deployment Feature Pack on Windows 2003 Server. SMS allows the concurrent installation of a large number of client computers across the entire network, such as a LAN or WAN.

Lab 12.2.2: Advanced Installation of Windows XP

In this lab, you install a Windows XP Professional operating system by using an answer file for automation. You customize partition settings and create an administrative user and limited users. Refer to the lab in *IT Essentials: PC Hardware and Software Lab Manual, Fourth Edition*. You can perform this lab now or wait until the end of the chapter.

Optional Lab 12.2.2: Advanced Installation of Windows Vista

In this lab, you install a Windows Vista Professional operating system by using an answer file for automation. You customize partition settings and create an administrative user and limited users. Refer to the lab in *IT Essentials: PC Hardware and Software Lab Manual, Fourth Edition*. You can perform this lab now or wait until the end of the chapter.

Create, View, and Manage Disks, Directories, and Files

Within the operating system, disks and directories are locations where data is stored and organized. The file system used by the operating system determines additional factors that affect storage such as partition size, cluster size, and security features.

Disk Structure

The *Disk Management* utility displays information and performs services such as partitioning and formatting disks in Windows. Figure 12-4 shows the Disk Management utility used in Windows XP.

You can access the Disk Management utility in the following ways:

- From the Start menu, right-click **My Computer** and then choose **Manage > Disk Management**.

- From the Start menu, choose **Settings > Control Panel > Administrative Tools > Computer Management**. Double-click **Storage** and then double-click **Disk Management**.

Figure 12-4   Disk Management

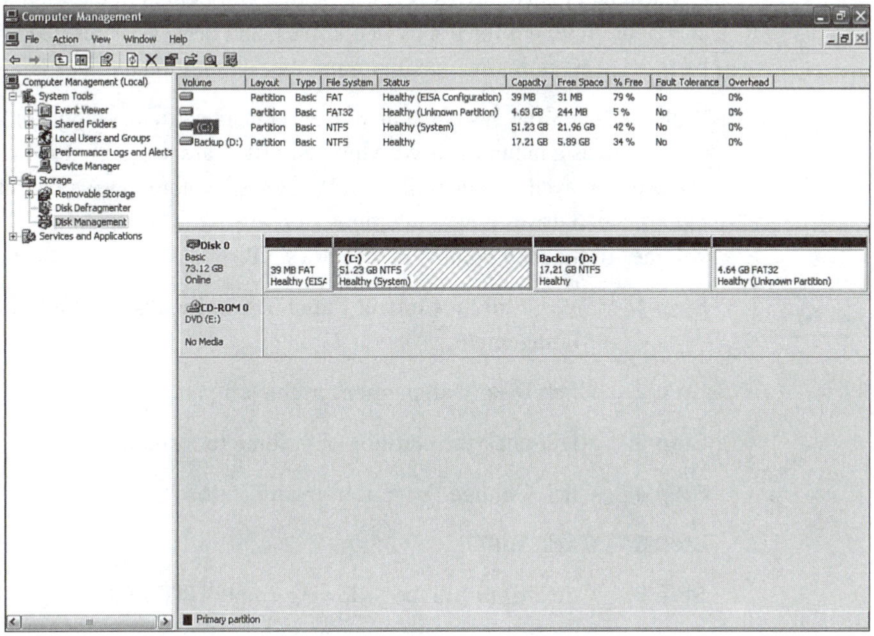

There are several types of partitions on a hard drive:

- **Primary partition**: This is usually the first partition. A primary partition cannot be subdivided into smaller sections. There can be up to four partitions per hard drive.

- **Extended partition**: This partition is used by the operating system to boot the computer. Only one primary partition can be marked active.

- **Logical drive**: This partition normally uses the remaining free space on a hard drive or takes the place of a primary partition. There can be only one extended partition per hard drive, and it can be subdivided into smaller sections called logical drives.

Note

At any given time, you can designate only one partition as the active partition. The operating system uses the active partition to boot up the system. The active partition must be a primary partition.

In most cases, the C: drive is the active partition and contains the boot and system files. Some users create additional partitions to organize files or to be able to dual-boot the computer.

In Windows, letters are used to name the drives. A Windows computer can have up to 26 physical and logical drives because there are 26 letters in the English alphabet. Drives A: and B: are reserved for floppy disk drives, and drive C: is reserved for the primary, active partition. Therefore, the maximum number of additional drives is 23.

With the NTFS file system, a drive can be mapped to an empty folder on a volume and is referred to as a mounted drive. Mounted drives are assigned drive paths instead of letters and are displayed as a drive icon in Windows Explorer. Use a mounted drive to configure more than 26 drives on your computer or when you need additional storage space on a volume. To mount a volume in Windows XP:

How To

Step 1. Select **Start > Control Panel > Administrative Tools > Computer Management**.

Step 2. Click **Disk Management** in the left pane.

Step 3. Right-click the partition or volume to be mounted.

Step 4. Click **Change Drive Letter and Paths**.

Step 5. Click **Add**.

Step 6. Click **Mount** in the following empty NTFS folder.

Step 7. Create an empty folder, type the path to an empty folder, or browse to an empty folder on an NTFS volume and click **OK**.

Step 8. Close Computer Management.

Drive Status

The Disk Management utility displays the status of each disk. The hard drives in the computer display one of the following conditions:

- **Foreign**: A dynamic disk that has been moved to a computer from another computer running Windows 2000 or Windows XP
- **Healthy**: A volume that is functioning properly
- **Initializing**: A basic disk that is being converted into a dynamic disk
- **Missing**: A dynamic disk that is corrupted, turned off, or disconnected
- **Not Initialized**: A disk that does not contain a valid signature
- **Online**: A basic or dynamic disk that is accessible and shows no problems
- **Online (Errors)**: I/O errors that are detected on a dynamic disk
- **Offline**: A dynamic disk that is corrupted or unavailable
- **Unreadable**: A basic or dynamic disk that has experienced hardware failure, corruption, or I/O errors

Other drive status indicators might be displayed when using drives other than hard drives:

- **Audio CD**: An audio CD that is in the optical drive

- **No Media**: An optical or removable drive that is empty

File System

Partitions are formatted with a file system. The two file systems available in Windows XP are FAT32 and NTFS. NTFS has greater stability and security features.

For example, Windows does not display the file extension, but this practice can cause security problems. Virus writers are able to distribute executable files disguised as nonexecutable files. To avoid this security breach, you should always show file extensions. To do so, choose **Start > Control Panel > Folder Options > View** and deselect the **Hide Extensions for Known File Types** check box, as shown in Figure 12-5.

Figure 12-5   Showing File Extensions

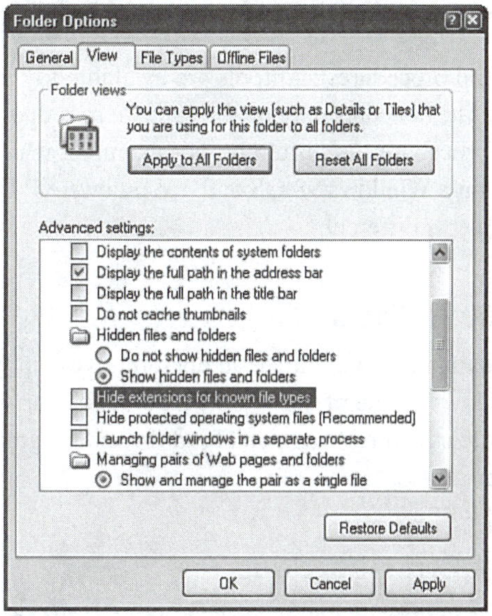

Note

Saving files to the root directory of the C: drive can cause organizational problems with data. It is a best practice to store data in folders created on the C: drive.

Lab 12.2.3: Create a Partition in Windows XP

In this lab, you create a FAT32-formatted partition on a disk using Windows XP. You convert the partition to NTFS. You identify the differences between the FAT32 format and the NTFS format. Refer to the lab in *IT Essentials: PC Hardware and Software Lab Manual, Fourth Edition*. You can perform this lab now or wait until the end of the chapter.

Optional Lab 12.2.3: Create a Partition in Windows Vista

In this lab, you create a FAT32-formatted partition on a disk using Windows Vista. You convert the partition to NTFS. You identify the differences between the FAT32 format and the NTFS format. Refer to the lab in *IT Essentials: PC Hardware and Software Lab Manual, Fourth Edition*. You can perform this lab now or wait until the end of the chapter.

Identify Procedures and Utilities Used to Optimize the Performance of Operating Systems

Several procedures and tools are available to optimize the performance of an operating system. The concepts may be the same across operating systems, but the optimization methods and procedures are different. For example, while virtual memory performs the same function on a Windows 98 OS and a Windows XP OS, the path to find and set virtual memory settings is different.

System Tools

To maintain and optimize an operating system, you can access various tools within Windows. Some of these tools include disk error checking, which can scan the hard drive for file structure errors, and hard drive defragmentation, which can consolidate files for faster access.

Disk Error-Checking Tool

The Windows operating system uses *CHKDSK* from within the GUI or at the command line to detect and repair disk errors.

To check a drive for errors using the GUI, follow these steps:

Step 1.   Double-click **My Computer** on the desktop.

Step 2.   Right-click the drive that you want to check and click **Properties**.

Step 3.   On the Tools tab, under Error-checking, click **Check Now.**

Step 4.   Under Check Disk Options, select the **Scan for and Attempt Recovery of Bad Sectors** check box and click **Start**.

Note

The Scan for and Attempt Recovery of Bad Sectors option automatically fixes file system errors and checks the disk for bad sectors and recovers any data from sectors that are found to be bad. Any data that is recovered is saved to files in the root directory of the disk.

The CLI version of the utility has four options to check a drive for errors:

- **chkdsk**: Displays a status report of the drive

- **chkdsk /f**: Fixes errors on the disk

- **chkdsk /r**: Recovers readable information from bad sectors

- **chkdsk /x**: Dismounts the volume if necessary

CHKDSK makes multiple passes over the disk, checking for specific criteria:

- **Phase 1: Checking Files**: CHKDSK examines each file record in the Master File Table (MFT) for consistency. By the end of this phase, used and available space on the volume have been identified.

- **Phase 2: Checking Indexes**: CHKDSK examines the MFT to ensure that every file and directory is referenced by at least one entry. Finally, CHKDSK checks that the time stamps and file sizes are correct in the directory listings.

- **Phase 3: Checking Security Descriptors**: CHKDSK examines the security descriptors for file or directory ownership information and NTFS permissions.

- **Phases 4 and 5: Checking Sectors**: If the **/r** option is used, CHKDSK makes two more passes looking for sectors that have physical damage.

Disk Defragmenter

To help optimize the files on the hard drive, Windows operating systems provide a defragmentation utility. As files are accessed and stored on a hard drive, the files change from being contiguous on the disk to being scattered across the disk. This can cause the operating system to slow down. The hard drive has to search several areas on the hard drive platter to find the entire file. For one file, the effect of the process is minimal. When this occurs for thousands of files, however, the process physically slows down the reading and writing of a file to a hard drive.

To defragment a drive in Windows XP or Windows Vista, double-click **My Computer** on the desktop. Right-click the drive that you want to optimize, and choose **Properties**. On the Tools tab, click **Defragment Now**.

System Information

Administrators can use the System Information tool to collect and display information about local and remote computers. The System Information tool quickly finds information about software, drivers, hardware configurations, and computer components. The information can be used by support personnel to diagnose and troubleshoot a computer.

To access the System Information tool, use the following path:

Start > All Programs > Accessories > System Tools > System Information

It might be necessary to send a file containing all of the information about a computer to another technician or help desk. To export a System Information file, click **File > Export**, type the name of the file, choose a location, and click **Save**.

The System Information tool in Windows XP also provides quick access to many other tools via its Tools menu:

- **Network Diagnostics**: This tool runs a variety of network tests to troubleshoot network-related problems.

- **System Restore**: rstsui.exe creates or loads a restore point for restoring the computer's system files and settings.

- **File Signature Verification Utility**: sigverif.exe checks for system files that are not digitally signed.

- **DirectX Diagnostic Tool**: dxdiag.exe reports detailed information about the DirectX components that are installed on your computer.

- **Dr Watson**: This tool debugs Windows to help diagnose program errors.

To view the information from a remote computer, follow these steps:

How To

Step 1.   Choose **View > Remote Computer**.

Step 2.   Choose **Remote Computer on the Network**.

Step 3.   Type the name of the computer that you want to view and click **OK**.

Remote Desktop Protocol

The Remote Desktop Protocol (RDP) allows you to use an application such as Remote Desktop or Remote Assistance to connect to another computer. These applications allow you to view the screen and control the computer's mouse and keyboard as though you were local to that computer. RDP is also used to operate computers that are connected to the network but do not have a monitor, mouse, or keyboard.

To access the Remote Desktop program, use the following path:

Start > All Programs > Accessories > Remote Desktop Connection

Remote Assistance uses RDP to allow another user to connect to your computer, see your computer screen, and chat over a network. With your permission, the remote user can control your computer.

To access the Remote Assistance program in Windows XP, use the following path:

> **Start > Help and Support > Invite a Friend to Connect to Your Computer with Remote Assistance > Invite Someone to Help You**

In Windows Vista, use the following path:

> **Start > Help and Support > Use Windows Remote Assistance to Get Help from a Friend or Offer Help > Invite Someone You Trust to Help You**

An email invitation must be sent to another user to allow them to connect and control your computer. After the recipient has received the invitation, the recipient can see your desktop and help you.

Virtual Memory

Virtual memory allows the CPU to address more memory than is installed in the computer. This is done so that every application can address the same amount of memory. Virtual memory is a swap file or *page file* that is constantly read in and out of RAM. Typically, you should let Windows manage the size of the swap file. The only setting that you should change is the location of the swap file. You must be a member of the administrator group to make this change.

To access virtual memory settings in Windows XP, use the following path:

> **Start > Control Panel > System > Advanced** tab, click **Settings** under Performance, and click the **Advanced** tab

To access virtual memory settings in Windows Vista, use the following path:

> **Start > Control Panel > System > Advanced System Settings > Continue > Advanced** tab, click **Settings** under Performance, and click the **Advanced** tab

Administrative Tools

Windows contains many tools that are used to manage permissions and users or configure computer components and services. You must possess administrator rights to access administrative tools. These are some of the most common administrative tools:

- *Event Viewer*: Logs a history of events regarding applications, security, and the system

- *Computer Management*: Allows you to access administrative areas such as System Tools, Storage, and Services and Applications

- *Services*: Allows you to manage all of the services on local and remote computers

- *Performance Monitor*: Displays and logs real-time information about the processors, disks, memory, and network usage for the computer

Services

Services are a type of application that runs in the background to achieve a specific goal or wait for a request. Only necessary services should be started, to reduce unnecessary security risks. Four settings, or states, can be used to control the services:

- Automatic

- Manual

- Disabled

- Stopped

If a service, such as DHCP or Automatic Updates, is set to automatic, it will start up when the PC starts. Manual services, such as the support of a UPS, need to be manually configured to work. Some services may be stopped or disabled for troubleshooting purposes, such as turning off the print spooler when there are printer problems.

Device Manager

Device Manager allows you to view all of the settings for devices in a computer, such as the IRQ, I/O address, and the DMA settings. It can also be used to diagnose and resolve device conflicts. From Device Manager, you can view details about the installed driver version. You can also perform the following functions:

- Update a driver.

- Roll back a driver.

- Uninstall a driver.

- Disable a device.

Device Manager uses special icons to indicate a problem with a specific device:

- A red X appears on the icon of devices that have been disabled.

- An exclamation point inside a yellow triangle appears on the icon of devices that do not have properly installed drivers or do not respond.

Task Manager

Task Manager allows you to view information about applications that are currently running. From Task Manager, you can perform many functions:

- Close any applications that have stopped responding.
- Start a new task.
- Monitor the performance of the CPU.
- Monitor the performance of the virtual memory.
- View all processes that are currently running.
- View information about network connections.

There are five tabs within Task Manager:

- **Applications**: Shows all of the applications that are running. From this tab, you can create, switch to, or end tasks using the buttons at the bottom of the tab.
- **Processes**: Shows all of the processes that are running. A process is any set of instructions running on the computer that was started by a user, a program, or the operating system. From this tab, you can end processes or set process priorities.
- **Performance**: Shows the CPU and page file usage of the computer.
- **Networking**: Shows the usage of all network adapters in the computer.
- **Users**: Shows all users that are logged on the computer. From this tab, you can disconnect remote users or log off local users.

Be careful when ending processes. Ending a process will cause the program to end immediately without saving any information. Ending a process that Windows has initiated may prevent the system from running correctly. Be careful when changing the priority of processes. If you change the priority of a process, the change might adversely affect the performance of the computer.

System Monitor

System Monitor is part of the Performance Monitor Console and displays real-time information about the processors, disks, memory, and network usage of the computer. You can easily summarize these activities through histograms, graphs, and reports.

You must have administrative privileges to access the Performance Monitor console. To view the Performance Monitor console in Windows XP, use the following path:

Start > Control Panel > Administrative Tools > Performance

To view the Performance Monitor console in Windows Vista, use the following path:

Start > Control Panel > Administrative Tools > Reliability and Performance Monitor > Continue

The data that System Monitor displays is used to help you understand how the workload of the computer affects system resources such as the CPU, memory, and network. Use System Monitor to display detailed data about the resources that you are using when performing specific tasks or multiple tasks. The data that you collect helps you to determine when an upgrade might be necessary. System Monitor shows how configuration changes or system tuning affects the computer. For example, use System Monitor to determine whether a newly installed program needs more RAM in the computer.

Regional and Language Options

You can change many of the standards and formats for numbers, currencies, dates, and time by using the Regional and Language Options settings. These settings also allow you to change the primary language or install an additional language. To access the Regional and Language Options settings, use the following path:

Start > Control Panel > Regional and Language Options

Temporary Files

Almost every program uses temporary files, which are usually automatically deleted when the application or the operating system is finished using them. However, some of the temporary files must be deleted manually. Because temporary files take up hard drive space that could be used for other files, it is a good idea to check for and delete temporary files as necessary every two or three months. Temporary files are usually located in the following locations in Windows XP:

- C:\Temp
- C:\Tmp
- C:\Windows\Temp
- C:\Windows\Tmp
- C:\Documents and Settings\%USERPROFILE%\Local Settings\Temp

Temporary files are usually located in the following locations in Windows Vista:

- C:\Windows\Temp
- C:\Users\%USERPROFILE%\AppData\Local\Temp

Note

In the preceding paths, %USERPROFILE% is an environment variable set by the operating system with the name of the user that is currently logged on to the computer. Environment variables are used by the operating system, applications, and software installation programs. To see the environment variables that are configured on your Windows XP computer, use the following path:

Start > Control Panel > System > Advanced > Environment Variables

Lab 12.2.4: Customize Settings in Windows XP

This lab is composed of five parts:

Part 1: Customize Virtual Memory settings, customize the Startup Folder and RunOnce Key in the Registry, and change the default Windows Update option.

Part 2: Examine the results after using Disk Check and Disk Defragmenter on a hard drive.

Part 3: Examine Regional and Language Optional settings and explore how to manage processes in Task Manager.

Part 4: Manage and monitor Windows XP system performance.

Part 5: Remotely connect to a computer, examine device drivers, and provide remote assistance.

Refer to the lab in *IT Essentials: PC Hardware and Software Lab Manual, Fourth Edition.* You can perform this lab now or wait until the end of the chapter.

Optional Lab 12.2.4: Customize Settings in Windows Vista

This lab is composed of five parts:

Part 1: Customize Virtual Memory settings, customize the Startup Folder and RunOnce Key in the Registry, and change the default Windows Update option.

Part 2: Examine the results after using Disk Check and Disk Defragmenter on a hard drive.

Part 3: Examine Regional and Language Settings and explore how to manage processes in Task Manager.

Part 4: Manage and monitor Windows Vista system performance.

Part 5: Remotely connect to a computer, examine device drivers, and provide remote assistance.

Refer to the lab in *IT Essentials: PC Hardware and Software Lab Manual, Fourth Edition.* You can perform this lab now or wait until the end of the chapter.

Identify Procedures and Utilities Used to Optimize the Performance of Browsers

Web browsers and email applications are typically the applications used the most on a computer. Optimizing the web browsers and the email application should increase the performance of the computer.

The Microsoft browser, *Internet Explorer (IE)*, has general settings for changing the home page and browser appearance settings. Additional settings allow you to view or delete the information saved by the browser:

- History
- Temporary files
- Cookies
- Passwords
- Web-form information

Note

Cookies hold information transmitted between a web browser and a web server with the purpose of tracking user information to customize the page delivered to the user.

To access the settings in IE, open an IE browser window and choose **Tools > Internet Options**, which opens the window shown in Figure 12-6.

Figure 12-6   Internet Explorer Options

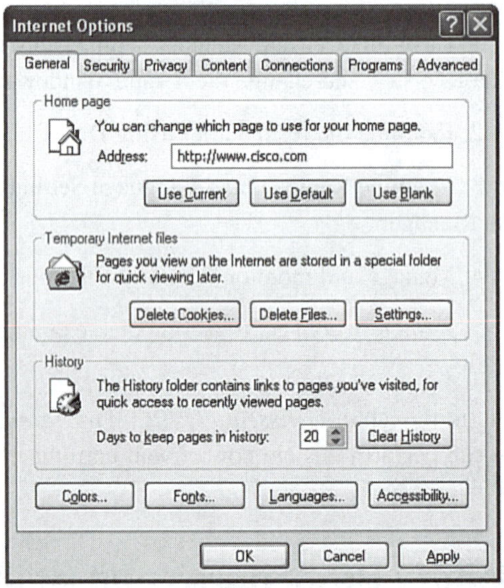

The following list describes the settings you can access from the tabs in this window:

- **General**: Used to set the home page, view and delete temporary Internet files, and change the browser appearance settings
- **Security**: Used to select Internet zones and trusted sites

- **Privacy**: Used for privacy settings to block third-party cookies and popup windows

- **Content**: Used to block unwanted website content and set identification and personal information

- **Connections**: Used to set up the Internet Connection settings for the browser

- **Programs**: Used to set up which programs Windows automatically uses for each Internet service

- **Advanced**: Used to enable and disable operation settings of the browser

Caching, or storing, Internet files is a feature of the web browser that is used to speed the process of accessing previously visited websites. The file-storing tool in IE downloads to the hard disk copies of the images or the HTML files of sites you have visited. When you revisit the website, the site opens more quickly because the files are in the local disk cache and do not need to be downloaded again.

Cached files in the web browser can become outdated or can be very large. These IE settings allow you to control the size of the cache and indicate when the cache should be refreshed:

- Every visit to the page

- Every time you start IE

- Automatically

- Never

To access the cache settings, click **Settings** in the Temporary Internet Files section of the General tab of the Internet Options window, shown in Figure 12-6.

Optional Lab 12.2.5: Install an Alternate Browser

In this lab, you install the *Mozilla Firefox* web browser. Refer to the lab in *IT Essentials: PC Hardware and Software Lab Manual, Fourth Edition*. You can perform this lab now or wait until the end of the chapter.

Describe Installation, Use, and Configuration of Email Software

Email software can be installed as part of a web browser or as a standalone application. *Outlook Express* is an email tool that is a component of the Microsoft Windows operating system. To configure Outlook Express, you must provide information about your email account, as shown in Figure 12-7.

Figure 12-7   Email Account Information

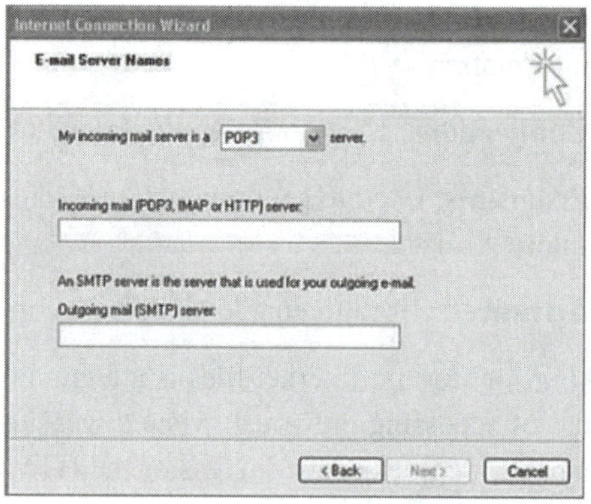

You should have the following information available when installing email accounts into the email client software:

- Display name

- Email address

- Type of incoming mail server, such as POP3 or IMAP

- Incoming mail server name

- Outgoing mail server name

- Username

- Account password

The protocols used in email include the following:

- **Post Office Protocol version 3 (POP3)**: Retrieves emails from a remote server over TCP/IP. It does not leave a copy of the email on the server; however, some implementations allow users to specify that mail be saved for some period of time.

- **Internet Message Access Protocol (IMAP)**: Allows local email clients to retrieve email from a server. Typically leaves a copy of the email on the server until you move the email to a personal folder in your email application. IMAP synchronizes email folders between the server and client.

- **Simple Mail Transfer Protocol (SMTP)**: Transmits emails across a TCP/IP network. It is the email format for text that only uses ASCII encoding.

- **Multipurpose Internet Mail Extensions (MIME)**: Extends the email format to include text in ASCII standard, as well as other formats, such as pictures and word processor documents. Normally used in conjunction with SMTP.

Additional features are available with email software:

- Automatic-handling rules for email messages

- Different email coding, such as HTML, plain text, or rich text

- Newsgroups

Set Screen Resolution and Update the Video Driver

After the operating system is installed, you can set the screen resolution to meet the requirements of your customer. If the screen resolution is not set properly, you can get unexpected display results from different video cards and monitors. The unexpected results could include a Windows desktop that does not take up the full area of the screen, or a blank screen if the resolution is set too high.

When using an LCD screen, the resolution should be set to native mode, or native resolution. Native mode is the screen resolution that is the same as the number of pixels that the monitor has. If you change from native mode, the monitor does not produce the best picture. To set resolution, right-click the desktop and choose Properties. Figure 12-8 shows the screen resolution settings on a Windows XP Professional computer.

Figure 12-8   Display Properties

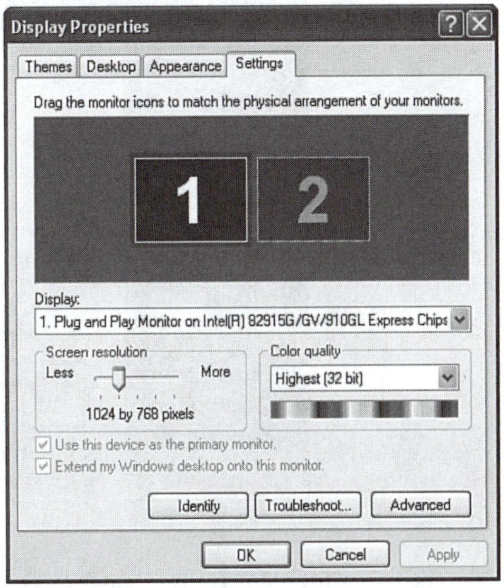

You can change the following screen resolution settings on the Settings tab of the Display Properties Control Panel applet:

- **Screen Resolution**: Determines the number of pixels. A higher number of pixels displays a better resolution and picture.

- **Refresh rate**: Determines how often the image on the screen is redrawn. Refresh rate is expressed in hertz (Hz). The higher the refresh rate, the more steady the screen image. To modify the refresh rate settings from the screen in Figure 12-8, click Advanced and then the tab called Monitor.

- **Color Qualities**: Determines the number of colors visible on the screen at once. Colors are created by varying the intensity of the three basic colors (red, green, and blue). The more bits, the greater the number of colors. The following is a list of color depths:

  — **256 colors**: 8-bit color

  — **65,536 colors**: 16-bit color (High Color)

  — **16 million colors**: 24-bit color (True Color)

  — **16 million colors**: 24-bit color (True Color with 8-bit padding to allow 32-bit processing)

When troubleshooting a display problem, check that the driver is fully compatible with the graphics card. Windows might install a default driver that works, but might not provide all the available options for best viewing and performance. See Figure 12-9 for the Hardware Update Wizard in Windows XP Professional.

Figure 12-9   Video Driver Update

Perform the following steps for the best graphical performance:

How To

Step 1. Download the most recent driver from the manufacturer's website.

Step 2. Remove the current driver.

Step 3. Disable antivirus software.

Step 4.   Install the new driver.

Step 5.   Restart the computer.

Step 6.   Reenable your antivirus software.

Caution

Disabling the antivirus software leaves your computer vulnerable to viruses and should not be done if you are connected to the Internet.

You might encounter problems when you install or reinstall a video driver. For example, after performing the graphical performance steps, you are unable to view the screen when you restart the computer. To investigate the problem and restore the settings, reboot the computer. During the boot phase, press **F8**. Enter the boot options when prompted and select **Enable VGA Mode** to use a 640x480 resolution. When the operating system is loaded, you can then select **Roll Back Driver** from the Properties menu of the graphics card. You should then do some research to determine the possible issues with the driver that you tried to install.

Describe Installation of a Second Operating System

You can have multiple operating systems on a single computer. Some software applications might require the most recent version of an operating system, while other applications require an older version. There is a dual-boot process for multiple operating systems on a computer. When the boot.ini file determines that more than one operating system is present during the boot process, you are prompted to choose the operating system that you want to load. Figure 12-10 shows a sample boot.ini file.

Figure 12-10   The boot.ini File

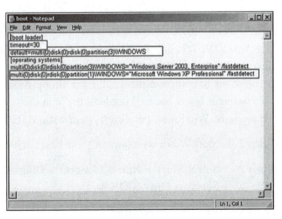

To create a dual-boot system in Microsoft Windows, you typically must have more than one hard drive or the hard drive must contain more than one partition.

For a *dual-boot setup*, you should install first the *oldest* operating system on the primary partition or the hard drive marked as the active partition. You should then install the second operating system on the second partition or hard drive. The boot files are automatically installed in the active partition.

The Boot.ini File

During the installation, the *boot.ini* file is created on the active partition to allow the selection of the operating system to boot on startup. The boot.ini file can be edited to change the order of the operating systems. You can also edit the file for the length of time an operating system selection can be made during the boot phase. Typically, the default time to select an operating system is 30 seconds. This always delays the boot time of the computer by 30 seconds, unless the user intervenes to select a particular operating system. In the boot.ini file, the boot time should be changed to 5 or 10 seconds to boot up the computer faster.

To edit the boot.ini file in Windows XP, right-click **My Computer > Properties > Advanced** tab. In the Startup and Recovery area, select **Settings**. Click **Edit**.

To edit the boot configuration data in Windows Vista, use the bcdedit.exe command-line tool. To access the bcdedit.exe tool, select **Start > All Programs > Accessories** and then right-click **Command Prompt > Run as Administrator > Continue** and type **bcdedit.exe**.

Windows CLI Commands

When troubleshooting problems with the operating system, you may need to use command-line interface (CLI) commands and options to perform tasks. This may be necessary when Windows will not start from the command prompt.

MSCONFIG

The *MSCONFIG* command brings up the System Configuration Utility that performs diagnostic procedures on the Windows startup files. You must be logged on with Administrator permissions to complete the troubleshooting procedure. MSCONFIG should be used when the computer boots but will not load the Windows operating system correctly. To troubleshoot the Windows operating system with MSCONFIG, follow these steps:

How To

Step 1.   Start Windows using only the basic drivers and services by booting in safe mode.

Step 2.   Select **Start > Run > General > Diagnostic Startup – Load Basic Devices and Services Only > OK**.

Step 3.   Restart the computer.

If the problem still exists after restarting, you will need to investigate other possible causes such as a missing or corrupted file, a corrupted registry, or a virus infection.

If the computer restarted successfully with basic drivers and services, open the System Configuration Utility and follow these steps:

Step 1.   Select **General > Selective Startup**.

Step 2.   Uncheck all items under Selective Startup.

Step 3.   Check only the first item under Selective Startup.

Step 4.   Restart the computer.

Step 5.   If the computer starts successfully, select one more item under Selective Startup.

Step 6.   Restart the computer.

Step 7.   Repeat steps 5 and 6 until the problem is identified.

Step 8.   After the problem has been identified, click the tab of the last item you selected under Selective Startup.

Use the same process of elimination to determine which item is causing the problem. You must research the problem and implement fixes until the problem is solved.

SFC

The *System File Checker (SFC)* allows you to check all of the protected system files, such as krnl386.exe, and replace them with known good versions if they have become corrupted or deleted. If you receive a notice from Windows or suspect that a file has been altered, replaced, or corrupted, use the command **sfc /scannow** at the command line to initiate the SFC. The SFC replaces any bad files with known good versions. You might be asked for the original installation media if Windows is unable to retrieve a copy from its cache of original files.

Describe How to Upgrade Operating Systems

An operating system must be upgraded periodically to remain compatible with the latest hardware and software. When newer versions of an operating system are released, support for older operating systems is eventually withdrawn.

Hardware products are continually coming on the market. The new design of the products often requires that the latest operating system be installed to operate correctly. While this might be expensive, you gain advanced functionality through new features and support for newer hardware.

A Windows XP upgrade can be performed from a CD or over a network. You should ensure that the new operating system is compatible with the computer. Microsoft provides a utility called *Upgrade Advisor*, as shown in Figure 12-11, to scan the system for incompatibility issues before upgrading to newer Windows operating systems. You can download Upgrade Advisor from the Microsoft Windows website free of charge. After Upgrade Advisor is finished, it produces a report to inform you of any problems. Incompatibility in hardware is the most common reason for failure in the upgrade process.

Figure 12-11   Windows Upgrade Advisor

Note

Windows 7 can only be upgraded from Vista. If you install Windows 7 on an XP or earlier computer, you will need to back up the users' data to a remote media and perform a clean install of Windows 7.

Not all older Windows operating systems are upgradeable to the newer versions, as described in the following list:

- Windows 98, Windows 98 SE, and Windows Me can be upgraded to Windows XP Home or Windows XP Professional.

- Windows NT Workstation 4.0 with Service Pack 6 and Windows 2000 Professional can be upgraded only to Windows XP Professional.

- Windows 3.1 and Windows 95 cannot be upgraded to Windows XP.

Note

Remember to back up all data prior to beginning the upgrade.

Describe Preventive Maintenance Procedures for Operating Systems

Preventive maintenance for an operating system includes automating tasks to perform scheduled updates. It also includes installing service packs that help keep the system up to date and compatible with new software and hardware.

If a driver or system becomes corrupted, you can use *restore points* to restore the system to a previous state. However, restore points cannot recover lost data.

After completing this section, you will meet these objectives:

- Schedule automatic tasks and updates.
- Set restore points.

Schedule Automatic Tasks and Updates

You can automate tasks in Windows XP using the Scheduled Tasks utility. The *Scheduled Tasks utility* monitors selected, user-defined criteria and then executes the tasks when the criteria have been met.

GUI Scheduled Tasks

Some of the common tasks that are automated using the Scheduled Tasks utility include the following:

- Disk cleanup
- Backup
- Disk defragmentation
- Starting other applications

To open the Scheduled Tasks wizard, choose **Start > All Programs > Accessories > System Tools > Scheduled Tasks**. Double-click **Add Scheduled Task**, as shown in Figure 12-12.

Figure 12-12   Scheduling Automated Tasks

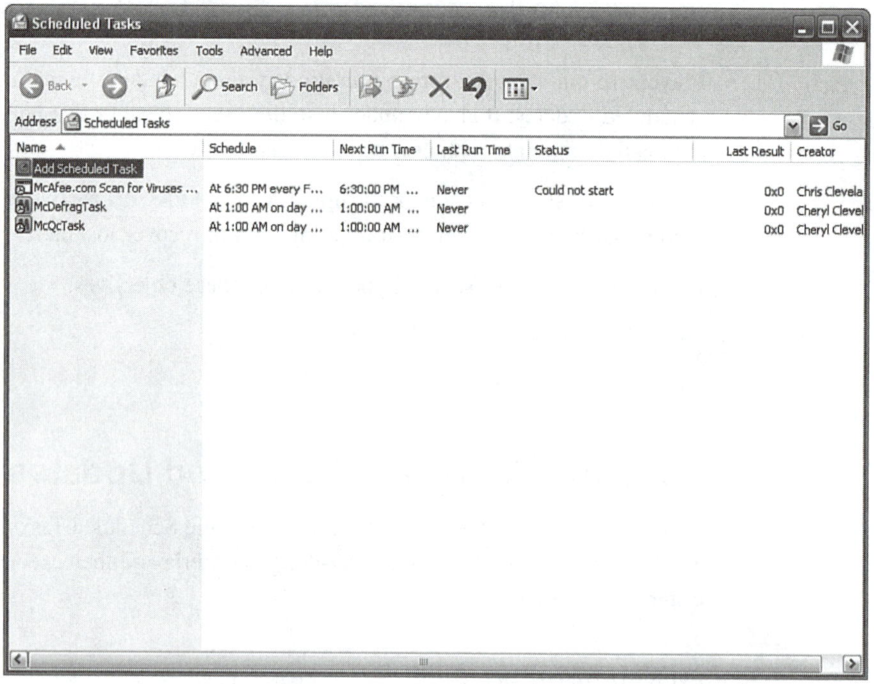

CLI Scheduled Tasks

The Scheduled Tasks utility is a Windows-based GUI utility. You can also use the **at** command in the command-line utility to automatically schedule a command, a script file, or an application to run at a specific date and time. To use the **at** command, you must be logged in as a member of the administrator group.

To learn more about the **at** command, choose **Start > Run**. At the CLI prompt, type **cmd** and then press **Enter**. At the command prompt, type **at/?**.

Windows Automatic Updates

You should use one of the following options in Automatic Updates, shown in Figure 12-13, to configure updates for the Windows XP operating system:

- Automatic (need to specify a date and time)

- Download Updates for Me, but Let Me Choose When to Install Them

- Notify Me but Don't Automatically Download or Install Them

- Turn Off Automatic Updates

You can access the Automatic Updates screen from the Control Panel.

Figure 12-13   Automatic Updates

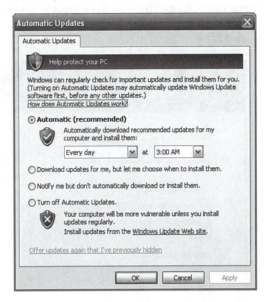

Lab 12.4.1: Schedule Task Using GUI and "at" Command in Windows XP

In this lab, you schedule a task using the Windows XP GUI and schedule a task in a command window using the **at** command. Refer to the lab in *IT Essentials: PC Hardware and Software Lab Manual, Fourth Edition*. You can perform this lab now or wait until the end of the chapter.

Lab 12.4.1: Schedule Task Using GUI and "at" Command in Vista

In this lab, you schedule a task using the Windows Vista GUI and schedule a task in a command window using the **at** command. Refer to the lab in *IT Essentials: PC Hardware and Software Lab Manual, Fourth Edition*. You can perform this lab now or wait until the end of the chapter.

Set Restore Points

Restore points return the operating system to a predefined point in time. In some cases, the installation of an application or a hardware driver can cause instability or create unexpected changes to the computer. Uninstalling the application or hardware driver normally corrects the problem. If uninstalling does not solve the problem, you should try to restore the computer to an earlier time when the system worked properly.

To open the System Restore utility, as shown in Figure 12-14, choose **Start > All Programs > Accessories > System Tools > System Restore**.

Figure 12-14 System Restore

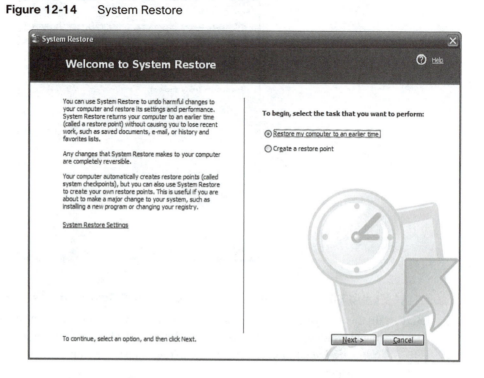

Windows XP can create restore points in the following scenarios:

- When an install or upgrade takes place

- Every 24 hours, if the computer is running

- Manually, at any time

The restore points contain information about the system and registry settings that are used by Windows operating systems. System Restore does not back up personal data files nor recover personal files that have been corrupted or deleted. To back up data, you should use a dedicated backup system, such as a tape drive, CDs, or even a USB storage device.

Lab 12.4.2: Restore Points in Windows XP

In this lab, you create a restore point in Windows XP and return your computer back to that point in time. Refer to the lab in *IT Essentials: PC Hardware and Software Lab Manual, Fourth Edition*. You can perform this lab now or wait until the end of the chapter.

Optional Lab 12.4.2: Restore Points in Windows Vista

In this lab, you create a restore point in Windows Vista and return your computer back to that point in time. Refer to the lab in *IT Essentials: PC Hardware and Software Lab Manual, Fourth Edition*. You can perform this lab now or wait until the end of the chapter.

Troubleshoot Operating Systems

The troubleshooting process helps resolve problems with the operating system. These problems range from simple, such as a driver that does not operate properly, to complex, such as a system that locks up. Use the following troubleshooting steps as a guideline to help you diagnose and repair problems:

Step 1.   Identify the problem.

Step 2.   Establish a theory of probable causes.

Step 3.   Determine an exact cause.

Step 4.   Implement a solution.

Step 5.   Verify solution and full system functionality.

Step 6.   Document your findings.

After completing this section, you will meet these objectives:

- Review the troubleshooting process.
- Identify common problems and solutions.
- Apply troubleshooting skills.

Review the Troubleshooting Process

Computer technicians must be able to analyze the problem and determine the cause of the error to repair the computer. This process is called *troubleshooting*.

Step 1: Identify the Problem

The first step in the troubleshooting process is to identify the problem. Table 12-3 provides a list of open-ended and closed-ended questions to ask the customer about operating system errors. (This list is *not* comprehensive.)

Table 12-3   OS Errors: Open-Ended and Closed-Ended Questions to Ask

Open-Ended Questions	Closed-Ended Questions
Have you made any changes to your system?	Can you access the Internet?
Have you been on the Internet?	Does anyone else have this problem?
Has anyone else had access to your password recently?	Have you changed your computer?
Does the system look different?	Have you received any error messages on your computer?

Step 2: Establish a Theory of Probable Causes

After you have talked to the customer to help identify the problem, you should establish a theory of probable causes:

- Do you have the current service pack installed?
- Do you have the current drivers installed?
- Do you run a virus spyware scanner?
- Have you changed any system defaults?
- Have you noticed problems with the screen resolution?
- Have you noticed problems when running certain applications?
- Has any software been added or upgraded?
- Has any hardware been added or removed?
- Have any cables been added or disconnected?

Step 3: Determine an Exact Cause

After you have established a theory of probable causes, determine an exact cause:

- Reboot the computer (warm boot)
- Turn the computer off and then on (cold boot)
- Driver roll back
- System restore
- Last known good configuration
- Virus scan
- Spyware scan

Step 4: Implement a Solution

After you have established a theory of probable causes, it is time to implement a solution:

- System files
- Event logs
- Device Manager
- Configuration files
- Restore points
- Diagnostic software

Step 5: Verify Solution and Full System Functionality

Next, verify solutions and full system functionality.

- Problem-solving experience
- Other technicians
- Internet search
- Newsgroups
- Manufacturer FAQs
- Computer manuals
- Device manuals
- Online forums
- Technical websites

Step 6: Document Your Findings

After you have verified full system functionality, document your findings, which requires completing the following tasks:

How To

Step 1. Discuss the solution implemented with customer.

Step 2. Have the customer verify that the problem has been solved.

Step 3. Provide the customer with all paperwork.

Step 4. Document the steps taken to solve the problem in the work order and the technician's journal.

Step 5. Document any components used in the repair.

Step 6. Document the time spent to resolve the problem.

Identify Common Problems and Solutions

Computer problems can be attributed to hardware, software, networks, or some combination of the three. You will resolve some types of computer problems more often than others. A stop error is a hardware or software malfunction that causes the system to lock up. This type of error is known as the *blue screen of death (BSoD)* and appears when the system is unable to recover from an error. The BSoD is usually caused by device driver errors. The Event Log and other diagnostic utilities are available to research a stop error or BSoD error. To prevent these types of errors, verify that the hardware and software drivers are compatible. In addition, install the latest patches and updates for Windows.

When the system locks up during startup, the computer can automatically reboot. The reboot is caused by the auto-restart function in Windows and makes it difficult to see the error message. The auto-restart function can be disabled in the Advanced Startup Options menu. Table 12-4 is a chart of common Windows XP problems and solutions.

Table 12-4   Common Windows XP Problems and Solutions

Identify the Problem	Probable Causes	Possible Solutions
The computer displays an "invalid Boot Disk" error after POST.	Media that does not have an operating system is in a drive.	Remove all media from the drives.
	The boot order is not set correctly in the CMOS.	Change the boot order in CMOS to start with the boot drive.
	The hard drive is not detected or the jumpers are not set correctly.	Reconnect the hard drive cables or reset the jumpers.
	The hard drive does not have an operating system installed.	Install an operating system, run **fdisk /mbr** from the CLI.
	The MBR is corrupted.	Run virus removal software.
	The computer has a boot-sector virus.	Replace the hard drive.
	The hard drive is failing.	

Identify the Problem	Probable Causes	Possible Solutions
The computer displays an "inaccessible Boot Device" error after POST.	A recently installed device driver is incompatible with the boot controller.	Use the Last Known Good Configuration to boot the computer.
	The NTLDR is corrupted.	Boot the computer in safe mode and load a restore point from before the installation of the new hardware.
		Restore NTLDR from installation media.
The computer displays a "Missing NTLDR" error after POST.	NTLDR is missing or damaged.	The jumpers are not set correctly.
	ntdetect.com is missing or damaged.	Restore NTLDR from installation media.
	boot.ini is missing or damaged.	Restore ntdetect.com from installation media.
	The boot order is not set correctly in the CMOS.	Restore boot.ini from installation media.
	The MBR is corrupted.	Change the boot order in CMOS to start with the boot drive.
	The hard drive is failing.	Run **fdisk /mbr** from the command prompt.
		Run **chkdsk /f /r** from the recovery console.
		Reset the hard drive jumpers.

continues

Table 12-4   Common Windows XP Problems and Solutions   *continued*

Identify the Problem	Probable Causes	Possible Solutions
A service failed to start when the computer booted.	The service is not enabled.	Enable the service.
	The service is set to manual.	Set the service to automatic.
	The failed service requires another service to be enabled.	Reenable or reinstall the required services.
	A driver is corrupt.	Reinstall the driver for the device.
A device did not start properly when the computer booted.	The data cable or power cable is not connected to the device.	Secure the data cable and power cable to the device.
	The device has been disabled in the Device Manager or the CMOS.	Enable the device in CMOS.
	The device has malfunctioned.	Replace the device.
	The device has a conflict with a newly installed device.	Remove the newly installed device.
A program listed in the Registry is not found.	One or more program files have been deleted.	Reinstall the program.
	The uninstall program did not work correctly.	Reinstall the program and run the uninstall program again.
	The installation directory has been removed.	Run **chkdsk /f /r** to fix the hard drive file entries.
	The hard drive has become corrupted.	Scan for and remove the virus.
	The computer has a virus.	

Identify the Problem	Probable Causes	Possible Solutions
The computer continually restarts without displaying the desktop.	The computer is set to restart when there is a failure.	Press F8 to open the Advanced Options menu and choose Disable Automatic Restart on System Failure.
	A startup file has become corrupted.	Run **chkdsk /f /r** from the recovery console.
The computer displays a BSOD.	A driver is not compatible with the hardware.	Research the STOP error and the name of the module that produced the error
	The RAM is failing.	Replace any failing devices with known-good devices.
	The power supply is failing.	
	The CPU is failing.	
	The motherboard is failing.	
The computer locks up without any errors.	The CPU or FSB settings are incorrect on the motherboard or in the CMOS.	Check and reset the CPU and FSB settings.
	The computer is overheating.	Check and replace any cooling as necessary.
	An update has corrupted the operating system.	Uninstall the software update or perform a system restore.
	The hard drive is failing.	Run **chkdsk /f /r** from the recovery console.
	The power supply is failing.	Replace any failing devices with known-good devices.

continues

Table 12-4   Common Windows XP Problems and Solutions   *continued*

Identify the Problem	Probable Causes	Possible Solutions
An application fails to install, start, or load.	The installation files are corrupted.	The hard drive is failing.
	The hardware does not meet the minimum requirements.	Install the application using known-good installation media.
	The application is incompatible with the OS.	Update the hardware required by the application.
		Run the application in Windows XP compatibility mode.
		Run **chkdsk /f /r** from the recovery console.
		Replace the hard drive.

Table 12-5 is a chart of common Windows Vista problems and solutions.

Table 12-5   Common Windows Vista Problems and Solutions

Identify the Problem	Probable Causes	Possible Solutions
A computer with Windows Vista installed does not run Aero.	The computer does not meet the minimum hardware requirements for running Aero.	Upgrade the processor, RAM, and video card to meet the minimum Microsoft requirements for Aero.
The search feature takes a long time to find results.	The index service is not running.	Start the index services using services.msc.
	The index service is not indexing the correct locations.	Change the settings of the index service in the Advanced Options panel.
The UAC no longer prompts the user for permission.	The UAC has been turned off.	Turn on the UAC in the User Account applet in the Control Panel.
No gadgets appear in the sidebar.	The XML necessary to render the gadget is broken, corrupted, or not installed.	Register the file msxml3.dll by entering **regsrv32 msxml3.dll > Enter** at the command prompt.

Identify the Problem	Probable Causes	Possible Solutions
The computer is running closely and has delayed response to user input.	A process is using most of the CPU resources.	Restart the process with services.msc.
		If the process is not needed, end the process with the Task Manager.
		Restart the computer.

Apply Troubleshooting Skills

Now that you understand the troubleshooting process, it is time to apply your listening and diagnostic skills.

The first lab is designed to reinforce your skills with the operating system. You will check restore points before and after using Windows Update.

The second lab is designed to reinforce your communication and troubleshooting skills. In this lab, you will perform the following steps:

How To

Step 1.   Receive the work order.

Step 2.   Take the customer through various steps to try and resolve the problem.

Step 3.   Document the problem and the resolution.

The third lab is designed to reinforce your skills with operating system problems. You will troubleshoot and repair a computer that has more than one problem.

Lab 12.5.3: Fix Operating System Problem

In this lab, you troubleshoot and fix a computer that does not connect to the network. Refer to the lab in *IT Essentials: PC Hardware and Software Lab Manual, Fourth Edition*. You can perform this lab now or wait until the end of the chapter.

Lab 12.5.3: Remote Technician: Fix an Operating System Problem

In this lab, you gather data from the customer and then instruct the customer on how to fix a computer that does not connect to the network. You then document the customer's problem in the work order provided in the activity. Refer to the lab in *IT Essentials: PC Hardware and Software Lab Manual, Fourth Edition*. You can perform this activity now or wait until the end of the chapter.

Lab 12.5.3: Troubleshooting Operating System Problems in Windows XP

In this lab, the instructor introduces various operating system problems. You diagnose the causes and solve the problems. Refer to the lab in *IT Essentials: PC Hardware and Software Lab Manual, Fourth Edition*. You can perform this activity now or wait until the end of the chapter.

Optional Lab 12.5.3: Troubleshooting Operating System Problems in Windows Vista

In this lab, the instructor introduces various operating system problems. You diagnose the causes and solve the problems. Refer to the lab in *IT Essentials: PC Hardware and Software Lab Manual, Fourth Edition*. You can perform this activity now or wait until the end of the chapter.

Summary

This chapter discussed how to select an operating system based on the needs of the customer. You have learned the differences between operating systems and network operating systems. The labs have helped you become familiar with using Windows XP, creating partitions, customizing virtual memory, and scheduling tasks. You have also learned some optimization tips for operating systems, as well as how to troubleshoot a computer problem from the perspective of a level-two technician. The following concepts discussed in this chapter will be useful to you when selecting and installing an operating system:

- Ensure that you fully understand the technology needs of the customer.
- Know the differences between common operating systems.
- Carefully match the customer needs to the proper technologies.
- Know the different methods to install an operating system.
- Know how to upgrade different operating systems.
- Understand how preventive maintenance can stop problems before they start.
- Know which preventive maintenance procedures are appropriate for the customer.
- Know how to troubleshoot operating system problems.

Summary of Exercises

This is a summary of the Labs, Worksheets, Remote Technician exercises, Class Discussions, Virtual Desktop activities, and Virtual Laptop activities associated with this chapter.

Labs

The following labs cover material from this chapter. Refer to the labs in *IT Essentials: PC Hardware and Software Lab Manual, Fourth Edition.*

Lab 12.2.2: Advanced Installation of Windows XP

Optional Lab 12.2.2: Advanced Installation of Windows Vista

Lab 12.2.3: Create a Partition in Windows XP

Optional Lab 12:2.3: Create a Partition in Windows Vista

Lab 12.2.4: Customize Settings in Windows XP

Optional Lab 12.2.4: Customize Settings in Windows Vista

Optional Lab 12.2.5: Install an Alternate Browser

Lab 12.4.1: Schedule Task Using GUI and "at" Command in Windows XP

Lab 12.4.1: Schedule Task Using GUI and "at" Command in Windows Vista

Lab 12.4.2: Restore Points in Windows XP

Optional Lab 12.4.2: Restore Points in Windows Vista

Lab 12.5.3: Fix Operating System Problem

Lab 12.5.3: Remote Technician: Fix an Operating System Problem

Lab 12.5.3: Troubleshoot Operating System Problems in Windows XP

Optional Lab 12.5.3: Troubleshoot Operating System Problems in Windows Vista

Check Your Understanding

You can find the answers to these questions in the appendix, "Answers to Check Your Understanding Questions."

1. How many active partitions can a hard drive have?

   A. 1

   B. 2

   C. 3

   D. 4

2. Which of the following file systems can be used by Windows XP? (Choose two.)

   A. DOS

   B. EXT3

   C. FAT32

   D. HPFS

   E. NTFS

   F. Vista

3. Which system tool consolidates files to enable faster access?

   A. File attributes

   B. Computer management

   C. Defragmentation

   D. Disk format

4. How can the Last Known Good Configuration option be accessed?

   A. Press **F8** to access the advanced boot options.

   B. Choose **Start > All Programs > System Tools > Restore**.

   C. Choose **Start > All Programs > Accessories > System Tools > Backup**.

   D. Press **Delete** to access the Recovery Console.

5. A new graphics card is installed in a computer. When the computer is powered on, the default drivers are loaded but some of the applications do not work properly. What should the user do to improve the graphics card performance?

   A. Check the Microsoft website to find the latest drivers.

   B. Check the website of the manufacturer for the latest drivers.

   C. Configure the application to run correctly with the new graphics card.

   D. Configure the graphics card settings correctly in the Start menu.

6. Which is the recommended Windows Update setting?

   A. Automatically Download Recommended Updates for My Computer and Install Them.

   B. Download Updates for Me, but Let Me Choose When to Install Them.

   C. Notify Me but Don't Automatically Download or Install Them.

   D. Turn off Automatic Updates.

7. Which Windows XP function allows a system to roll back to a previous state?

   A. Automatic Update

   B. ntbackup

   C. Restore point

   D. scanreg

CHAPTER 13

Advanced Laptops and Portable Devices

Objectives

Upon completion of this chapter, you should be able to answer the following questions:

- What are wireless communication methods for laptops and portable devices?

- How can I repair laptops and portable devices?

- What is the best way to select laptop components?

- What are the preventive maintenance procedures for laptops?

- How do I troubleshoot a laptop?

Key Terms

This chapter uses the following key terms. You can find the definitions in the Glossary.

With the increase in demand for mobility, the popularity of *laptops*, *notebooks*, *netbooks*, *tablets* and other *portable devices* will continue to grow. During the course of your career, you will be expected to know how to configure, repair, and maintain these devices. The knowledge you acquire about desktop computers will help you service laptops and portable devices. However, there are important differences between the two technologies.

To facilitate mobility, laptops and portable devices use wireless technologies more than desktops. All laptops use batteries when they are disconnected from a power source. *Docking stations* are commonly used to connect a laptop to peripheral devices. As a computer technician, you will be required to configure, optimize, and troubleshoot these docking stations and accessories, as well as the laptop or portable device that they accompany. Many laptop components are proprietary, so some manufacturers require that you complete specialized certification training to perform laptop repairs.

Servicing laptops can be very challenging. Mastering the skills necessary to work on laptops is important to your career advancement.

After completing this chapter, you will meet these objectives:

- Describe wireless communication methods for laptops and portable devices.
- Describe repairs for laptops and portable devices.
- Select laptop components.
- Describe preventive maintenance procedures for laptops.
- Describe how to troubleshoot a laptop.

Describe Wireless Communication Methods for Laptops and Portable Devices

Wireless devices give people the freedom to work, learn, play, and communicate wherever they want. People using wireless-capable devices do not need to be tied to a physical location to send and receive voice, video, and data communications. As a result, wireless facilities, such as Internet cafes, are opening in many countries. College campuses use wireless networks to allow students to sign up for classes, watch lectures, and submit assignments in areas where physical connections to the network are unavailable. This trend toward wireless communications will continue to grow as more people use wireless devices.

After completing this section, you will meet these objectives:

- Describe Bluetooth technology.
- Describe infrared technology.
- Describe cellular WAN technology.

- Describe Wi-Fi technology.

- Describe satellite technology.

Describe Bluetooth Technology

Bluetooth is a wireless technology that enables devices to communicate over short distances. A Bluetooth device can connect up to seven other Bluetooth devices to create a wireless personal-area network (WPAN). This technical specification is described by the Institute of Electrical and Electronics Engineers (IEEE) 802.15.1 standard. Bluetooth devices can handle voice and data and are ideally suited for connecting the following devices:

- Laptops

- Printers

- Cameras

- PDAs

- Cell phones

- *Hands-free headsets*

Common Bluetooth characteristics include the following:

- It is a short-range wireless technology designed to eliminate the need for cables between portable and fixed-configuration devices.

- It operates at 2.4 to 2.485 GHz in the unlicensed Industrial, Scientific, and Medical (ISM) band.

- It uses little power and has a low cost and a small size.

- It uses adaptive frequency hopping (AFH).

The distance of a Bluetooth WPAN is limited by the amount of power used by the devices in the PAN. Bluetooth devices are broken into three classifications, as shown in Table 13-1. The most common Bluetooth network is Class 2, which has a range of approximately 33 feet (10 m).

Table 13-1   Bluetooth Classifications

Class	Maximum Permitted Power	Approximate Distance
Class 1	100 mW	~330 feet (100 m)
Class 2	2.5 mW	~33 feet (10 m)
Class 3	1 mW	~3 feet (1 m)

Bluetooth devices operate in the 2.4- to 2.485-GHz radio frequency range, which is in the ISM band. This band often does not require a license if approved equipment is used. The Bluetooth standard incorporates AFH. AFH allows signals to "hop around" using different frequencies within the Bluetooth range, thereby reducing the chance of interference when multiple Bluetooth devices are present. AFH also allows the device to learn frequencies that are already in use and to choose a different subset of frequencies.

Security measures are included in the Bluetooth standard. The first time that a Bluetooth device connects, the device is authenticated using a personal identification number (PIN). Bluetooth supports both 128-bit encryption and PIN authentication.

Describe Infrared Technology

Infrared (IR) wireless technology is a low-power, short-range wireless technology. IR transmits data using light emitting diodes (LED) and receives data using photodiodes.

IR wireless networks are globally unregulated. However, the Infrared Data Association (IrDA) defines the specifications for IR wireless communication. Common IR characteristics include the following:

- It is low-power, short-range, wireless technology that uses LEDs.
- Infrared light signals operate in the lowest light frequency, and transmission distances are limited to a few feet or meters.
- Infrared light cannot penetrate ceilings or walls.

Four types of IR networks exist:

- **Line of sight**: The signal is transmitted only if there is a clear, unobstructed view between devices.
- **Scatter**: The signal bounces off ceilings and walls.
- **Reflective**: The signal is sent to an optical transceiver and is redirected to the receiving device.
- **Broadband optical telepoint**: Transmission can handle high-quality multimedia requirements.

Infrared networks are ideal for connecting laptops to the following types of devices that are in close proximity:

- Multimedia projector
- PDA
- Printer
- Remote control

- Wireless mouse

- Wireless keyboard

Setting up and configuring IR devices is quite simple. Many IR devices connect to the USB port on a laptop or desktop computer. As soon as the computer detects the new device, Windows XP installs the appropriate drivers, as shown in Figure 13-1.

Figure 13-1   Installing an Infrared Driver

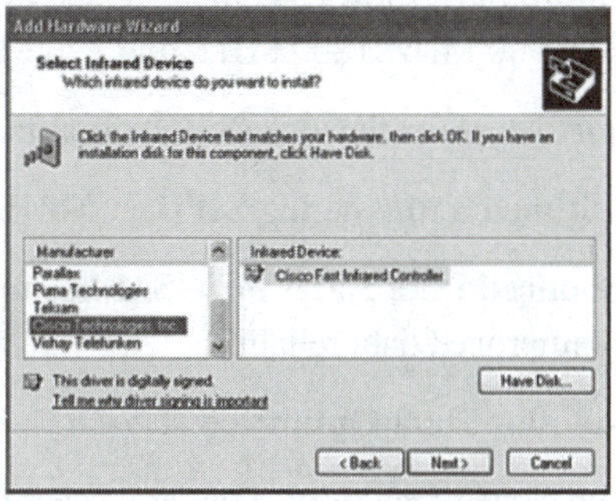

The installation is similar to setting up a LAN connection.

IR is a practical, short-range connection solution, but it has some limitations:

- IR light cannot penetrate ceilings or walls.

- IR signals are susceptible to interference and dilution by strong light sources, such as fluorescent lighting.

- Scatter IR devices can connect without line of sight, but data transfer rates are lower, and distances are shorter.

- IR distances should be 3 feet (1 m) or less when used for computer communications.

Describe Cellular WAN Technology

Originally, cellular networks were designed for voice communication only. Cellular technology has been evolving and now enables the transfer of voice, video, and data simultaneously. It also enables the use of laptops and portable devices remotely. With a *cellular WAN* adapter installed, a laptop user can access the Internet without interruption while traveling. Common cellular WAN characteristics include the following:

- Cellular WAN connections are powerful two-way wireless networks that have been around since the late 1970s.

- Cellular networks operate in one of two ranges: approximately 800 MHz and approximately 1900 MHz.

- Three generations of cellular WAN include voice-only analog, digital, and high-speed data and voice.

Although they are slower than DSL and cable connections, cellular WANs are still fast enough to be classified as a high-speed connection. To connect a laptop to a cellular WAN, you should install an adapter that is designed to work with cellular networks. A cellular adapter needs to support some or all of the following:

- **Global System for Mobile Communications (GSM)**: Worldwide cellular network

- **General Packet Radio Service (GPRS)**: Data service for users of GSM

- **Quad-band**: Allows a cellular phone to operate on all four GSM frequencies: 850 MHz, 900 MHz, 1800 MHz, and 1900 MHz

- **Short Message Service (SMS)**: Text messages

- **Multimedia Messaging Service (MMS)**: Multimedia messages

- **Enhanced Data Rates for GSM Evolution (EDGE)**: Provides increased data rates and improved data reliability

- **Evolution Data Optimized (EV-DO)**: Faster download rates

- **High Speed Downlink Packet Access (HSDPA)**: Provides enhanced G3 access speed

Connecting to a cellular WAN is a simple process. Cellular WAN cards, as shown in Figure 13-2, are "plug and play." These cards plug into the PC Card slot or are built into the laptop.

Figure 13-2   Cellular WAN Card

Describe Wi-Fi Technology

The wireless technology *Wi-Fi* is based on IEEE 802.11 networking standards and specifications. The number 802.11 denotes a set of standards that is specified in the IEEE 802.11

documentation. Hence, the terms 802.11 and Wi-Fi are interchangeable. Here are some characteristics of Wi-Fi:

- It is a wireless technology that provides a simple connection from anywhere within range of a base station.

- Connection distances are 300 feet (91 m) or more, depending on the environment.

- Ease of access makes Wi-Fi a simple solution for network connectivity.

Currently, four major Wi-Fi 802.11 standards exist:

- 802.11a

- 802.11b

- 802.11g

- 802.11n

Technicians often refer to Wi-Fi standards by just the final letter. For example, a technician may refer to an 802.11b wireless router as simply a "b" router.

The 802.11g standard was released in 2003 and currently is the most common Wi-Fi standard. The 802.11n standard was released in draft form in 2006 and ratified in 2009 to become an official *IEEE standard*.

The 802.11b, 802.11g, and 802.11n standards use the 2.4-GHz frequency band. The 2.4-GHz frequency band is unregulated and heavily used. The large amount of traffic can cause wireless signals in the 2.4-GHz range to be interfered with by other 2.4-GHz wireless devices, such as cordless phones. For this reason, the 802.11a standard was designed to use the 5.0-GHz frequency band. As a result, 802.11a is incompatible with other 802.11x standards. Table 13-2 provides data rate and range information for the four major Wi-Fi standards.

Table 13-2   Wi-Fi Standards

Standard	Release Date	Maximum Data Rate	Range
802.11a	1999	54 Mbps	~100 feet (30.5 m)
802.11b	1999	11 Mbps	~100 feet (30.5 m)
802.11g	2003	54 Mbps	~100 feet (30.5 m)
802.11n	2006 (draft)	540 Mbps	~165 feet (50.3 m)

Security is a major concern for wireless networks. Anyone within the coverage area of a wireless router can potentially gain access to the network. The following precautions should be taken for security purposes:

- Never send login or password information using clear, unencrypted text.

- Use a VPN connection when possible.

- Enable security on home networks.

- Use *Wi-Fi Protected Access (WPA)* security.

Wi-Fi Protected Access standards (WPA, WPA2) are used to secure Wi-Fi networks. WPA uses a sophisticated encryption and authentication technology to protect data flow between Wi-Fi devices. WPA uses a 128-bit encryption key and should be enabled on all wireless devices. WPA was introduced to replace Wired Equivalent Privacy (WEP), which had known security issues. *Wi-Fi Protected Access 2 (WPA2)* offers stronger 256 bit encryption.

Describe Satellite Technology

Satellite technology service is ideal for rural or remote users who require high-speed broadband access in areas where no other high-speed services are available. However, because of the higher initial cost and relatively slower speeds, high-speed satellite network connections are recommended only if a cable or digital subscriber line (DSL) connection is unavailable. Common satellite characteristics include the following:

- Satellite networks are faster than dialup connections but are slower than cable and DSL connections.

- Satellite service is ideal for rural or remote Internet users.

- Downloading files is faster than uploading files.

- Adverse weather conditions can interfere with satellite reception.

Satellite Internet connections use two-way data channels. One channel is used for uploading and another for downloading. Both download and upload can be accomplished using a satellite connection. In some cases, a telephone line and modem are used for the upload. Download speeds typically are in the 500-kbps range, and uploads are about 50 kbps, making this an asymmetrical connection similar to DSL. Satellite connections are slower than cable or DSL connections but are faster than telephone modem connections. Some advantages of connecting by satellite are as follows:

- It makes two-way, high-speed Internet access available in rural and remote areas.

- File downloads are quick.

- The satellite dish may also be used for TV access.

Proper placement, installation, and configuration of a satellite system are important for the system to work effectively. Even if you point the satellite dish toward the equator, where most satellites orbit Earth, obstructions and adverse weather can still interfere with signal reception.

Specific equipment is needed to set up a satellite connection:

- 24-inch (610-mm) satellite dish

- Modem for uplink and downlink

- Coaxial cable and connectors

Describe Repairs for Laptops and Portable Devices

When a laptop or portable device begins to malfunction, what should you do? The customer can replace some parts of a laptop, typically called *customer-replaceable units (CRU)*. CRUs include such components as the laptop battery and additional RAM. Parts that the customer should not replace are called *field-replaceable units (FRU)*. FRUs include such components as the laptop motherboard, LCD display, and keyboard. In many cases, the device may need to be returned to the place of purchase, a certified service center, or even the manufacturer.

Figure 13-3 shows an example of a CRU and FRU.

Figure 13-3   Repair Methods for Laptops and Portable Devices

A repair center can provide service on laptops made by different manufacturers, or a repair center may specialize in a specific brand and be considered an authorized dealer for warranty work and repair. The following are common repairs performed at local repair centers:

- Replacing a hard drive

- Hardware and software diagnostics

- Data transfer and recovery

- Hard drive installation and upgrades

- RAM installation and upgrades

- Keyboard and fan replacement

- Internal laptop cleaning

- LCD screen repair

- LCD inverter and backlight repair

Most repairs to LCD displays must be performed in a repair center. These repairs include replacing the LCD screen, the backlight that shines through the screen to illuminate the display, and the inverter that produces the high voltage required by the backlight. If the backlight has failed, the screen is visible only when you look at it from an angle.

If no local services are available, you might be required to send the laptop to a regional repair center or to the manufacturer. If the laptop damage is severe or requires specialized software and tools, the manufacturer might decide to replace the laptop instead of attempting a repair.

Caution

Before attempting to repair a laptop or portable device, check the warranty to see if repairs during the warranty period must be done at an authorized service center to avoid invalidating the warranty. If you repair a laptop yourself, you should always back up the data and disconnect the device from the power source.

Worksheet 13.2.0: Investigating Repair Centers

For this worksheet, you investigate the services provided by a computer repair center. Use the Internet or a local phone directory to locate one. After you have found a repair center, use its website to obtain information, and answer the questions in the worksheet. If a website is not available, contact the local repair center. Refer to the worksheet in *IT Essentials: PC Hardware and Software Lab Manual, Fourth Edition*. You may complete this worksheet now or wait to do so until the end of the chapter.

Select Laptop Components

Laptop components need to be replaced for a variety of reasons:

- The original part might be worn, damaged, or faulty.

- You might want additional functionality, such as a wireless PC card that supports new standards.

- You might want to improve performance by adding memory.

When implementing any of these changes, make sure that all new components are physically and electrically compatible with the existing components and operating system.

It is always a good idea to purchase components from a reputable source and research the warranty information. Components generally fall into two categories:

- **Retail packaged**: These components usually come with documentation, a full warranty, cables, mounting hardware, drivers, and software.

- *Original equipment manufacturer (OEM)*: OEM components are usually sold without packaging and require the user to locate documentation, software, drivers, and any additional hardware that might be needed. OEM components are usually less expensive and offer a shorter warranty period than similar retail packaged components. Using OEM components can result in substantial savings when upgrades are performed in bulk on many laptops and additional support is not needed.

After completing this section, you will meet these objectives:

- Select batteries.

- Select a docking station or port replicator.

- Select storage devices.

- Select additional RAM.

Select Batteries

How do you know when you need a new laptop battery? The signs might not always be apparent, but some are obvious:

- The laptop shuts off immediately when AC power is removed.

- The battery is leaking.

- The battery overheats.

- The battery does not hold a charge.

If you experience problems that you suspect are battery related, exchange the battery with a known good battery that is compatible with the laptop. If a replacement battery cannot be located, take the battery to an authorized repair center for testing.

A replacement battery, as shown in Figure 13-4, must meet or exceed the specifications of the laptop manufacturer. New batteries must use the same form factor as the original battery. Voltages, power ratings, and AC adapters must also meet manufacturer specifications.

Figure 13-4   Laptop Batteries

Note

Always follow the instructions provided by the manufacturer when charging a new battery. The laptop can be used during an initial charge, but do not unplug the AC adapter. Ni-Cad and NiMH
rechargeable batteries should occasionally be discharged completely to remove the memory. When
the battery is completely discharged, it should then be charged to maximum capacity.

Caution

Always be careful when handling batteries. Batteries can explode if improperly charged, shorted, or
mishandled. Be sure that the battery charger is designed for the chemistry, size, and voltage of your
battery. Batteries are considered toxic waste and must be disposed of according to local laws.

Worksheet 13.3.1: Laptop Batteries

For this worksheet, you use the Internet, a newspaper, or a local store to gather information
and then enter the specifications for a laptop battery onto this worksheet. Refer to the worksheet in *IT Essentials: PC Hardware and Software Lab Manual, Fourth Edition*. You may
complete this worksheet now or wait to do so until the end of the chapter.

Select a Docking Station or Port Replicator

Docking stations and port replicators increase the number of ports available to a laptop. A
port replicator may contain a SCSI port, a networking port, PS/2 ports, USB ports, and a
game port. A docking station has the same ports as a port replicator, but it adds the capability to connect to PCI cards, additional hard drives, optical drives, and floppy disk drives.

Docking stations make it convenient to connect a laptop to an office network and peripherals. A laptop connected to a docking station has the same capabilities as a desktop computer. Figure 13-5 shows several docking stations and port replicators that support the same laptop.

Figure 13-5   Docking Stations and Port Replicators

Docking stations and port replicators offer several connection options:

- Ethernet (RJ-45)
- Modem (RJ-11)
- *S-Video,* TV out
- USB 2.0 port
- External monitor
- Parallel port
- High-speed serial port
- IEEE 1394 port
- Stereo headphone output
- Stereo microphone input
- Docking port

Some docking stations connect to a laptop using a docking station port that is located on the bottom of the laptop, as shown in Figure 13-6. Other docking stations are designed to plug directly into a USB port of the laptop. Most laptops can be docked when in use or while shut off. You can add new devices when docking by using plug-and-play technology that recognizes and configures the newly added components, or by having a separate hardware profile for the docked and undocked state.

Figure 13-6   Docking Station Connector

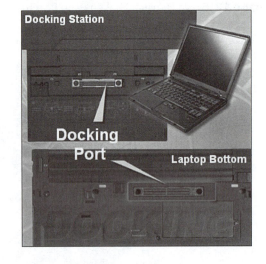

Many docking stations and port replicators are proprietary and work only with particular laptops. Before buying a docking station or port replicator, check the laptop documentation or the manufacturer's website to determine the laptop's make and model.

Worksheet 13.3.2: Docking Station

For this worksheet, you use the Internet, a newspaper, or a local store to gather information and then enter the specifications for a laptop docking station onto this worksheet. Be prepared to discuss your decisions about the docking station you select. Refer to the worksheet in *IT Essentials: PC Hardware and Software Lab Manual, Fourth Edition*. You may complete this worksheet now or wait to do so until the end of the chapter.

Select Storage Devices

Storage devices are CRUs, unless a warranty requires technical assistance. You have several options when adding, replacing, or upgrading a storage device for a laptop:

- *External USB hard drive*: An external USB hard drive connects to a laptop using the USB port. A laptop automatically detects when an external hard drive is plugged into a USB port.

- *FireWire hard drive*: An IEEE 1394 external hard drive that connects to the FireWire port. A laptop automatically detects when an external hard drive is plugged into a FireWire port.

- *DVD/CD burner*: A DVD/CD RW burner is an optical drive that reads and writes data to and from a CD and reads data from a DVD. This is a convenient method of creating backups and archiving data. The two most common types of writable CDs and DVDs are writable (R) and rewritable (RW).

The form factor of an internal hard drive storage device is smaller for a laptop than for a desktop computer. However, the smaller drive may have a greater storage capacity.

Before purchasing a new internal or external hard drive, check the laptop documentation or the manufacturer's website for compatibility requirements. Documentation often contains Frequently Asked Questions (FAQ) that may be helpful. It is also important to research known laptop component issues on the Internet.

On most laptops, the internal hard drive and the internal optical drive are connected behind a cover on the underside of the case. However, on some laptops, the keyboard must be removed to access these drives. It is important to note that Blu-ray, DVD, and CD drives may not be interchangeable in the laptop.

To confirm the currently installed storage device, check the POST screen or BIOS. If installing a second hard drive or an optical drive to the laptop, confirm proper installation in the Device Manager window:

Use the following path in Windows XP:

> **Start > Control Panel > System > Hardware** tab **> Device Manager**

Use the following path in Windows Vista:

> **Start > Control Panel > System > Device Manager**

Worksheet 13.3.3: Research DVD Drives

For this worksheet, you use the Internet, a newspaper, or a local store to gather information about a DVD rewritable (DVD-RW) drive for a specified laptop. Refer to the worksheet in *IT Essentials: PC Hardware and Software Lab Manual, Fourth Edition*. You may complete this worksheet now or wait to do so until the end of the chapter.

Select Additional RAM

Adding RAM can optimize laptop performance. Additional RAM speeds up the process by decreasing the number of times the operating system reads and writes data to the hard drive swap file. Reading and writing data directly from RAM is faster than using swap files. Also, RAM helps the operating system run multiple applications more efficiently.

Graphic processing in laptops usually is performed by the CPU and often requires extra RAM to store the video while the CPU decodes it for viewing. New applications, such as video sharing and video editing, demand increased performance from laptops. Installing expansion RAM can help increase laptop performance.

The laptop's make and model determine the type of RAM chip needed. It is important to select the correct memory type that is physically compatible with the laptop. Most desktop computers use memory that fits into a dual in-line memory module (DIMM) slot. Most laptops use a smaller-profile memory chip that is called a *small outline dual in-line memory module (SODIMM)* (see Figure 13-7). SODIMMs are smaller than DIMMs, so they are ideal for use in laptops, printers, and other devices where conserving space is desirable. When replacing or adding memory, determine whether the laptop has available slots to add memory and whether the laptop supports the quantity and type of memory to be added.

Figure 13-7   SODIMM RAM

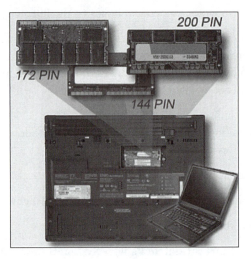

It is important to purchase the correct RAM for your computer. Before purchasing and installing additional RAM, consult the laptop documentation or the manufacturer's website for form-factor specifications. RAM manufactures' websites usually offer tools to help choose the correct RAM for a computer. Use the documentation to find where to install RAM on the laptop. On most laptops, RAM is inserted into slots behind a cover on the underside of the case, as shown in Figure 13-8. However, on some laptops, you must remove the keyboard to access the RAM slots.

Caution

Before installing RAM, remove the battery and unplug the computer from the electrical outlet to avoid damage related to electrostatic discharge (ESD) when you are installing memory modules.

To confirm the currently installed amount of RAM, check the POST screen, BIOS, or System Properties window by choosing **Start > Control Panel > System** and then clicking the **General** tab. Figure 13-9 shows where the amount of RAM can be found in the System Properties window.

Figure 13-8   Laptop SODIMM Installation

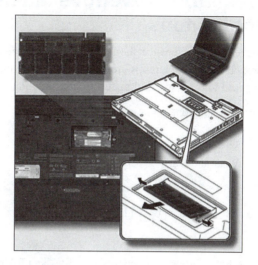

Figure 13-9   System Properties

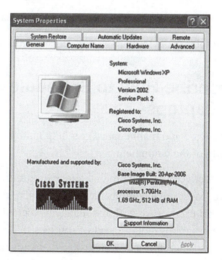

Worksheet 13.3.4: Laptop RAM

For this worksheet, you use the Internet, a newspaper, or a local store to gather information about expansion memory for a specified laptop. Refer to the worksheet in *IT Essentials: PC Hardware and Software Lab Manual, Fourth Edition*. You may complete this worksheet now or wait to do so until the end of the chapter.

Describe Preventive Maintenance Procedures for Laptops

Preventive maintenance should be scheduled at regular intervals to keep laptops running properly. Because laptops are portable, they are more likely than desktop computers to be exposed to these harmful materials and situations:

- Dirt and contamination
- Spills
- Wear and tear
- Drops
- Excessive heat or cold
- Excessive moisture

In addition, properly managing data files and folders can ensure data integrity.

After completing this section, you will meet these objectives:

- Describe how to schedule and perform maintenance on laptops.
- Explain how to manage data version control between desktops and laptops.

Describe How to Schedule and Perform Maintenance on Laptops

Proper care and maintenance can help laptop components run more efficiently and extend the life of the equipment.

An effective preventive maintenance program must include a routine schedule for maintenance. Most organizations have a preventive maintenance schedule in place. If a schedule does not exist, work with the manager to create one. The most effective preventive maintenance programs require a set of routines to be conducted monthly but still allow maintenance to be performed when usage demands it.

The preventive maintenance schedule for a laptop may include practices that are unique to a particular organization, but they should also include these standard procedures:

- Cleaning
- Hard-drive maintenance
- Software updates

To keep a laptop clean, be proactive, not reactive. Keep fluids away from the laptop. Do not eat when you are working on it, and close it when it is not in use. When cleaning a laptop, never use harsh cleaners or solutions that contain ammonia. Nonabrasive materials are recommended for cleaning a laptop:

- Compressed air
- A mild cleaning solution
- Cotton swabs
- A soft, lint-free cleaning cloth

Caution

Before you clean a laptop, disconnect it from all power sources, including the battery.

Routine maintenance includes the monthly cleaning of these laptop components:

- Exterior case
- Cooling vents
- I/O ports
- Display
- Keyboard

Note

At any time, if it is obvious that the laptop needs to be cleaned, clean it. Do not wait for the next scheduled maintenance.

The operating system should also be maintained. The hard drive can become disorganized as files are opened, saved, and deleted. The computer can slow down if the operating system must search through fragmented files. Fortunately, Windows XP, Windows Vista, and Windows 7 have two programs that help clean up the hard drive:

- Disk Cleanup
- Disk Defragmenter

To run Disk Cleanup in Windows XP, follow these steps:

How To

Step 1.   Click the **Start** button.

Step 2.   Select **All Programs > Accessories > System Tools > Disk Cleanup**.

Step 3.   As shown in Figure 13-10, the files available for deletion are listed. Check the check box next to files to mark them for deletion, and then click **OK**.

Figure 13-10   Disk Cleanup

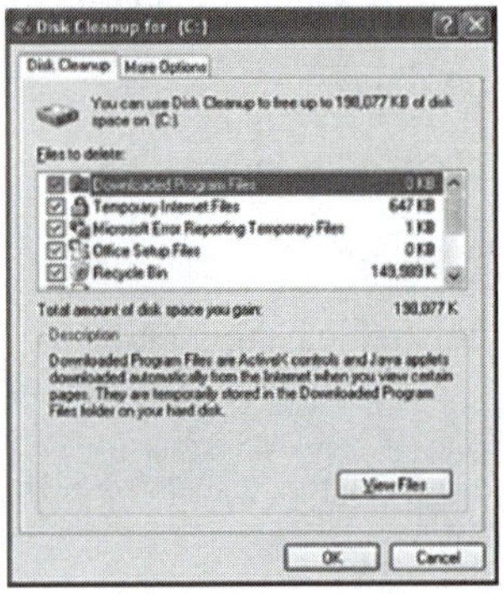

To run Disk Cleanup in Windows Vista, follow these steps:

Step 1.   Select the hard drive from **My Computer** that you want to clean.

Step 2.   Right-click and choose **Properties**.

Step 3.   On the General tab, click **Disk Cleanup**.

Step 4.   Choose which files to clean up, **My Files Only** or **Files from All Users on This Computer.**

Step 5.   The files available for deletion are listed. Check the check box next to files to mark them for deletion, and then click **OK**.

To navigate to Disk Cleanup in Windows 7, follow these steps:

Step 1.   Click the **Windows** button.

Step 2.   Type **Disk Cleanup**.

Step 3.   Click **Disk Cleanup** in the results.

Step 4.   Check the check box next to files to mark them for deletion, and then click **OK**.

To run Disk Defragmenter in Windows XP and Windows Vista, follow these steps:

Step 1.   Select the hard drive that you want to clean.

Step 2.   Right-click and choose **Properties**.

Step 3.   On the Tools tab, click **Defragment Now**. In Windows Vista, you must click **Continue**. The length of time to complete the defragmentation varies according to the amount of hard drive fragmentation.

To run Disk Defragmenter in Windows 7, follow these steps:

Step 1.   From My Computer, select the hard drive you want to clean.

Step 2.   Right-click and choose **Properties**.

Step 3.   On the Tools tab, click **Defragment Now**. The length of time it takes to complete the defragmentation varies according to how fragmented the hard drive is.

Figure 13-11   Disk Defragmenter

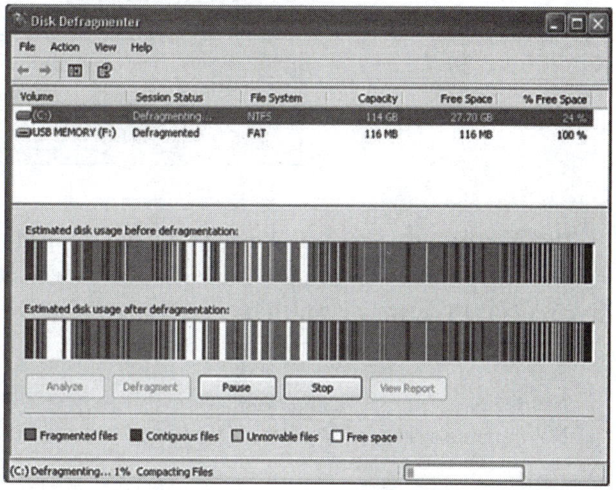

It might be necessary to close all programs running in the background before you run Disk Defragmenter.

Explain How to Manage Data Version Control Between Desktops and Laptops

It is important to manage your data files and folders properly. Restore and recover procedures, as well as backups, are more successful if the data is organized.

Windows XP has a default location, sometimes available as an icon on the desktop, called My Documents. You can use My Documents to create a folder structure and store files.

When moving files from a laptop to a desktop computer, start by creating a similar folder structure in both locations. Files can be transferred over a network, with an optical disc, or with a portable drive.

You should be careful that data copied from one computer does not inadvertently overwrite data on the other computer. When you are copying a file to a destination folder, you might encounter a "Confirm File Replace" message, as shown in Figure 13-12.

Figure 13-12   File Replacement Confirmation

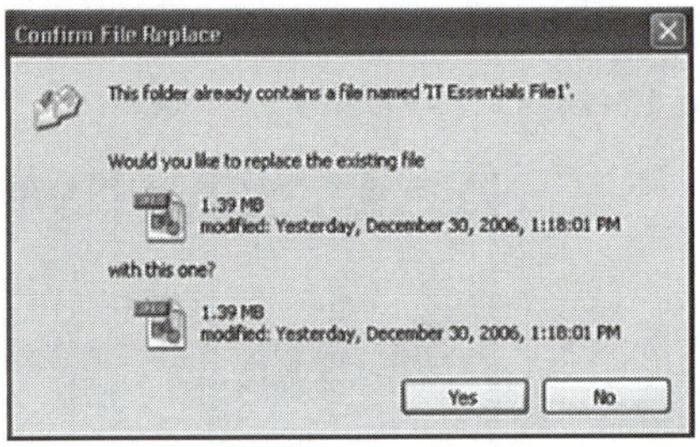

This message indicates that Windows XP has stopped the copying process until you choose whether to replace the original file with the file that is being transferred. If you are unsure, click **No**. To determine which file to keep, compare the dates and file sizes. You may also open the files to view their content.

Note

No operating system allows files with the same name to exist in the same folder.

Caution

Be careful not to unintentionally "cut" a file from its original location when you only meant to "copy" it.

Describe How to Troubleshoot a Laptop

The troubleshooting process helps resolve problems with the laptop or peripherals. These problems range from simple ones, such as updating a drive, to more complex problems, such as installing a CPU. Use the following basic troubleshooting steps as a guideline to help diagnose and repair problems:

How To

Step 1.   Identify the problem.

Step 2.   Establish a theory of probably causes.

Step 3.   Determine an exact cause.

Step 4.   Implement a solution.

Step 5.   Verify solution and full system functionality.

Step 6.   Document findings.

After completing this section, you will meet these objectives:

- Review the troubleshooting process.

- Identify common problems and solutions.

- Apply troubleshooting skills.

Review the Troubleshooting Process

Computer technicians must be able to analyze the problem and determine the cause of the error to repair a laptop. This process is called troubleshooting.

Step 1: Identify the Problem

The first step in the troubleshooting process is Identify the problem. Table 13-3 lists open-ended and closed-ended questions to ask the customer about laptop errors. (This list is *not* comprehensive.)

Table 13-3　Laptop Errors: Open-Ended and Closed-Ended Questions to Ask

Open-Ended Questions	Closed-Ended Questions
In what environment are you using your laptop?	Has anyone done any repair work on the laptop recently?
When did the problem start?	Has anyone else used the laptop?
What problems are you experiencing?	How does your laptop connect to the Internet?
Can you describe precisely what happens when the laptop boots?	Does your laptop have a wireless NIC?
Can you tell me anything else?	Have you ever had any problems like this before? about the problem?

Step 2: Establish a Theory of Probable Causes

After you have identified the problem, you should establish a theory of probable causes. The following is a list of common laptop problems:

- Laptop battery does not have a charge.

- Laptop battery will not charge.

- Loose cable connections.

- External keyboard does not work.

- Num Lock key is on.

- Loose RAM.

Step 3: Determine an Exact Cause

After you have established a theory of probable causes, determine an exact cause. (This list is *not* comprehensive.)

- Use AC power instead of battery.

- Replace AC adapter.

- Remove and reinsert the battery.

- Replace the battery.

- Check BIOS settings.

- Disconnect and reconnect cables one at a time.

- Disconnect and reconnect peripherals one at a time.

- Verify Num Lock key is off.

- Reinstall RAM.

- Reboot the laptop.

Step 4: Implement a Solution

If no solution is achieved in the previous step, further research is needed to implement the solution. The following resources contain possible solutions to the problem:

- Help desk repair logs

- Other technicians

- Manufacture FAQs

- Technical websites

- News groups

- Computer manuals

- Device manuals

- Online forums

- Internet search

Step 5: Verify Solution and Full System Functionality

At this point, verify your solution and full system functionality:

Step 1. Reboot the laptop.

Step 2. Attach all peripherals.

Step 3. Operate laptop using only battery.

Step 4. Print a document from an application.

Step 5. Type a sample document to test the keyboard.

Step 6. Check Event Viewer for warnings or errors.

Step 6: Document Findings

After you have solved the problem, you close with the customer, which requires the following tasks:

Step 1. Discuss the solution implemented with the customer.

Step 2. Have the customer verify that the problem has been solved.

Step 3. Provide the customer with all paperwork.

Step 4. Document the steps taken to solve the problem in the work order and the technician's journal.

Step 5. Document any components used in the repair.

Identify Common Problems and Solutions

Laptop problems can be attributed to hardware, software, networks, or some combination of the three. You will resolve some types of laptop problems more often than others. Table 13-4 describes common laptop problems and solutions.

Table 13-4   Common Laptop LCD Problems and Solutions

Identify the Problem	Probable Causes	Possible Solutions
Laptop screen appears black or very dim. A buzzing noise may also be heard.	LCD screen inverter or back light failure.	Replace the LCD inverter. Replace the backlight lamp.
Laptop screen displays only vertical lines that can change color.	LCD screen failure.	Replace the laptop LCD screen.

continues

Table 13-4   Common Laptop LCD Problems and Solutions   *continued*

Identify the Problem	Probable Causes	Possible Solutions
External LCD connected to the laptop shows content but the laptop screen is blank.	The laptop screen is not set to display output.	Press the Fn key with the appropriate multifunction key to display output on the laptop screen.
The display is rotated or inverted.	The display settings in the operating system have been set to rotate or invert the image.	Rotate the displayed images using the display control panel.
	Keyboard key combinations have rotated or inverted the image.	Rotate the displayed images using a keyboard combination such as CTrl-Alt plus up-arrow or side-arrow.
LCD screen and external monitor will not display images, while the laptop hard drive and fans operate normally.	The laptop motherboard or the video card has failed.	Replace the laptop motherboard if it has onboard video. Replace the video card.
Laptop does not return from Standby or Hibernate mode.	The laptop has a conflict between the BIOS and the Windows power management settings.	Reconfigure the laptop BIOS and the Windows power management settings.

Table 13-5 describes common laptop storage and RAM problems and solutions.

Table 13-5   Common Laptop Storage Device and RAM Problems and Solutions

Identify the Problem	Probable Causes	Possible Solutions
Laptop hard drive has access errors and makes noises.	Hard drive failure.	Replace the hard drive.
Laptop will not boot or access a newly installed hard drive.	The hard drive is not connected properly.	Reconnect the hard drive.
	The BIOS does not recognize the new hard drive.	Update the laptop BIOS.

Identify the Problem	Probable Causes	Possible Solutions
Laptop accesses the hard drive excessively.	The virtual memory is set incorrectly.	Change the virtual settings.
	Additional RAM is needed.	Install additional RAM.
	Free space is limited.	Delete or remove unneeded files and applications.
Laptop makes long beeping noise after installing new RAM.	The wrong type of RAM is installed.	Install the correct type of RAM.
		Remove the RAM.
	The RAM is installed incorrectly.	Replace the damaged RAM modules.
	A damaged RAM module is installed.	

Table 13-6 describes common power and input device problems and solutions.

Table 13-6   Common Laptop Power and Input Device Problems and Solutions

Identify the Problem	Probable Causes	Possible Solutions
Laptop LED power light is on when laptop is plugged into AC outlet.	The AC power source is not working.	Plug the laptop into a known-good AC power source.
	The power cable is not securely connected to the laptop.	Unplug and securely reconnect the power supply to the laptop. Replace the AC adapter.
	The AC adapter is defective.	
The laptop operational time while using the battery is very short.	The battery is old.	Replace the battery.

continues

Table 13-6 Common Laptop Power and Input Device Problems and Solutions
continued

Identify the Problem	Probable Causes	Possible Solutions
The date and time are incorrect when laptop is powered on.	The CMOS battery has failed.	Replace CMOS battery.
	The CMOS battery is loose.	Remove and install the laptop keyboard.
		Remove and reinstall of the battery.
The laptop touch pad or pointer device is not responsive	The touch pad or pointer device is disabled.	Enable the pointer device from the Device Manager.
	The touch pad or pointer device is defective.	Replace the pointer device.
		Use a mouse as a new pointer device.
The laptop touch pad responds erratically.	The touch pad is not calibrated.	Reboot the laptop.
		Use the control panel to calibrate.
		Update the device driver.
The laptop keyboard does not work or individual keys do not work.	The keyboard has been damaged by liquid.	Clean the keyboard.
		Reconnect the laptop keyboard.
	The laptop keyboard has a loose connection.	Replace the laptop keyboard.
	The keyboard is worn or old.	Use an external keyboard.

Table 13-7 describes additional common laptop problems and solutions.

Table 13-7   More Common Laptop Problems and Solutions

Identify the Problem	Probable Causes	Possible Solutions
Laptop shuts off randomly or is excessively hot.	The laptop has poor ventilation.	Clean all the vents. Replace any faulty fans.
	The laptop has a faulty fan.	Clean and reset the heat sink.
	The CPU heat sink is dirty or loose.	
Laptop will not start up and only the fans and LEDs are working.	The CPU has failed.	Replace the CPU.
Laptop built-in speakers are not producing any sound.	The audio is disabled in BIOS.	Enable the audio in the BIOS.
	The sound is muted.	Unmute the sound.
	The laptop built-in speakers are damaged.	Replace the speakers. Use external speakers.
Cannot insert a PC card into laptop.	The PC card is not supported by the laptop.	Replace the PC card with an ExpressCard.
	The plastic protector is installed in the card slot.	Remove the plastic protector from the card slot. Purchase a PC card to ExpressCard Adapter.

Note

Each laptop manufacturer uses unique hardware installation and removal procedures. Check the laptop manual for specific installation information and follow safe installation and ESD precautions.

Caution

Always disconnect power and remove the battery before installing or removing laptop components that are not hot-swappable.

For proper reassembly, remember these disassembly recommendations:

- Document screw locations.
- Organize parts.
- Refer to manufacturer documentation.
- Use appropriate hand tools.

Hard Drive Replacement Steps

Follow these steps to replace your hard drive:

How To

Step 1.   On the bottom of the laptop, remove the screw that holds the hard drive in place.

Step 2.   Slide the assembly outward. Remove the hard drive assembly.

Step 3.   Remove the hard drive faceplate from the hard drive.

Step 4.   Attach the hard drive faceplate to the new hard drive.

Step 5.   Slide the hard drive into the hard drive bay.

Step 6.   On the bottom of the laptop, install the screw that holds the hard drive in place.

Expansion Memory Replacement Steps

Laptop expansion memory is also called SODIMM. Remove the existing SODIMM if there are no available slots for the new SODIMM:

How To

Step 1.   Remove the screw to expose the SODIMM.

Step 2.   Press outward on the clips that hold the sides of the SODIMM.

Step 3.   Lift up to loosen the SODIMM from the slot and remove the SODIMM.

Step 4.   Align the notch at a 45-degree angle.

Step 5.   Gently press down until the clips lock.

Step 6.   Replace the cover and install the screw.

Optical Drive Replacement Steps

Follow these steps to replace an optical drive:

How To

Step 1.   Press the button to open the drive and remove any media in the drive. Close the tray.

Step 2.   Slide the latch to release the lever that secures the drive.

Step 3.   Pull on the lever to expose the drive. Remove the drive.

Step 4.   Insert the drive securely.

Step 5.   Push the lever inward.

Battery Replacement Steps

Follow these steps to replace a battery:

Step 1.   Move the battery lock to the unlocked position.

Step 2.   Hold the release lever in the unlock position and remove the battery.

Step 3.   Insert the new battery.

Step 4.   Make sure that both battery levers are locked.

PC Expansion Card Replacement Steps

Follow these steps to replace a PC expansion card:

Step 1.   Press the top eject button to release the PC expansion card.

Step 2.   Press the blue button inward.

Step 3.   Insert the PC expansion card into the express slot.

Hot-Swappable Device Removal Steps

Follow these steps to remove a hot-swappable device:

Step 1.   Click the **Safely Remove Hardware** icon in the Windows system tray to ensure that the device is not in use.

Step 2.   Click the device that you want to remove. A message window appears when it is safe to remove the device.

Step 3.   Remove the hot-swappable device from the laptop.

Note

On some laptops, the PC Card, optical drive, and USB devices are hot-swappable. However, the internal hard drive, RAM, and battery are not hot-swappable.

Apply Troubleshooting Skills

Now that you understand the troubleshooting process, it is time to apply your listening and diagnostic skills.

The worksheets are designed to reinforce your troubleshooting and communication skills to verify information from the customer.

The optional lab is designed to test your troubleshooting skills with laptop hardware and software problems. You will troubleshoot and repair a laptop that has more than one problem.

Worksheet 13.5.3: Verify Work Order Information

For this worksheet, a level-two call center technician finds creative ways to verify information that the level-one tech has documented in the work order. Refer to the worksheet in *IT Essentials: PC Hardware and Software Lab Manual, Fourth Edition*. You may complete this worksheet now or wait until the end of the chapter.

Worksheet 13.5.3: Investigating Support Websites and Repair Companies

For this worksheet, you investigate support websites and repair companies. Refer to the worksheet in *IT Essentials: PC Hardware and Software Lab Manual, Fourth Edition*. You may complete this worksheet now or wait until the end of the chapter.

Lab 13.5.3: Troubleshooting Laptop Problems in Windows XP

In this lab, you troubleshoot laptop problems in Windows XP. Refer to the lab in *IT Essentials: PC Hardware and Software Lab Manual, Fourth Edition*. You may complete this lab now or wait until the end of the chapter.

Optional Lab 13.5.3: Troubleshooting Laptop Problems in Windows Vista

In this lab, you troubleshoot laptop problems in Windows Vista. Refer to the lab in *IT Essentials: PC Hardware and Software Lab Manual, Fourth Edition*. You may complete this lab now or wait until the end of the chapter.

Summary

This chapter has described components of laptops and portable devices. Here are some important concepts contained in this chapter:

- Bluetooth creates a small, wireless PAN for connected cell phones, printers, and laptops.

- An IR network uses infrared light to create short-range networks that are primarily used to control input devices and mobile devices.

- A cellular WAN allows you to use your cell phone and laptop for voice and data communications.

- The most popular wireless technology is Wi-Fi. The four major Wi-Fi releases, each with different speed and bandwidth ratings, are IEEE 802.11 a, b, g, and n.

- Satellite networks are faster than modems but slower than DSL and cable networks. Satellite networks are primarily used in remote locations.

- A CRU is a component that a user can easily install without technical training.

- A FRU is a component that a trained service technician may install at a remote location.

- Most repairs can be done at customers' sites or at any local repair center. However, on some occasions a laptop must be sent to the manufacturer for repairs.

- Professional technicians follow preventive maintenance schedules to keep their equipment at optimal performance levels.

- Laptops are more susceptible to contamination and damage. A well-maintained laptop reduces repair costs.

- A docking station allows a laptop to easily connect to peripheral devices similar to those found on desktop computers. A port replicator can be added to a laptop if the user needs more I/O ports.

- A well-trained technician must possess good customer communication skills.

Summary of Exercises

This is a summary of the Labs, Worksheets, Remote Technician exercises, Class Discussions, Virtual Desktop activities, and Virtual Laptop activities associated with this chapter.

Worksheets

The following worksheets cover material from this chapter. Refer to the worksheets in *IT Essentials: PC Hardware and Software Lab Manual, Fourth Edition.*

Worksheet 13.2.0: Investigating Repair Centers

Worksheet 13.3.1: Laptop Batteries

Worksheet 13.3.2: Docking Station

Worksheet 13.3.3: Research DVD Drive

Worksheet 13.3.4: Laptop RAM

Worksheet 13.5.3: Verify Work Order Information

Worksheet 13.5.3: Investigating Support Websites and Repair Companies

Labs

Optional Lab 13.5.3: Troubleshooting Laptop Problems in Windows XP

Optional Lab 13.5.3: Troubleshooting Laptop Problems in Windows Vista

Check Your Understanding

You can find the answers to these questions in the appendix, "Answers to Check Your Understanding Questions."

1. Which IEEE specification defines Bluetooth WPAN technology?

    A. 802.3.1

    B. 802.5.1

    C. 802.7.5

    D. 802.11.1

    E. 802.13.5

    F. 802.15.1

2. Which IEEE specification defines Wi-Fi technology?

    A. 802.3

    B. 802.5

    C. 802.7

    D. 802.11

    E. 802.13

    F. 802.15

3. Which two battery characteristics must you consider when choosing a replacement for a laptop?

    A. Brand

    B. Charging time

    C. Color

    D. Form

    E. Voltage

4. Which IEEE specification defines the FireWire standard?

    A. 1284

    B. 1294

    C. 1384

    D. 1394

5. After you resolve a computer problem, what is the next step in the troubleshooting process?

    A. Inform the supervisor.

    B. Test other components randomly.

    C. Cancel the work order.

    D. Reevaluate the problem.

    E. Close with the customer.

6. Which two Windows utilities can be used to help maintain hard disks on computers that have had long periods of normal use?

    A. Disk Cleanup

    B. Disk Maintenance

    C. Disk Defragmenter

    D. Disk Partition

    E. Disk Format

7. What acronym refers to the name given to laptop parts that can be easily replaced by end users?

    A. CRU

    B. FRU

    C. NRU

    D. SRU

8. Which two materials are recommended for use when you clean a laptop?

   A. Diluted ammonia

   B. Compressed air

   C. Cotton balls

   D. Detergent

   E. Silver oxide

   F. Mild cleaning solutions

CHAPTER 14

Advanced Printers and Scanners

Objectives

Upon completion of this chapter, you should be able to answer the following questions:

- What are the potential safety hazards and safety procedures associated with printers and scanners?

- How do I install and configure a local printer and scanner?

- How do I share a printer and a scanner on a network?

- What does it take to upgrade and configure printers and scanners?

- What are some good printer and scanner preventive maintenance techniques?

- How can I troubleshoot printers and scanners?

Key Terms

This chapter uses the following key terms. You can find the definitions in the Glossary.

This chapter explores the functionality of printers and scanners. You will learn how to maintain, install, and repair these devices in both local and network configurations. The chapter discusses safety hazards, configuration procedures, preventive maintenance, and printer and scanner sharing.

After completing this chapter, you will meet these objectives:

- Describe potential safety hazards and safety procedures associated with printers and scanners.

- Install and configure a local printer and scanner.

- Describe how to share a printer and a scanner on a network.

- Upgrade and configure printers and scanners.

- Describe printer and scanner preventive maintenance techniques.

- Troubleshoot printers and scanners.

Describe Potential Safety Hazards and Safety Procedures Associated with Printers and Scanners

You must always follow safety procedures when working on any computer. There are also rules that you must follow as you work with printers and scanners. These rules keep you and the equipment safe.

The first rule of safety concerns moving large pieces of equipment. Always lift equipment by using the strength in your legs and knees, not your back. Wear appropriate work clothes and shoes. Do not wear loose jewelry or baggy clothes when servicing computer equipment.

Printers, scanners, and all-in-one devices that connect to AC outlets can become hot while in use. If you plan to perform any services on equipment, you should turn it off and allow it to cool before beginning any repairs on internal components. Print heads on dot-matrix printers can become very hot when in use. The *fuser assembly* on a laser printer can also become hot.

Some printers retain a large amount of voltage even after you disconnect them from a power source. Only qualified technicians should perform advanced repairs on laser printers, particularly if the repair involves the corona wire or transfer roller assembly, as shown in Figure 14-1. These areas can retain high voltage, even after the printer has been turned off. Check the service manuals or contact the manufacturer to be sure that you know where these areas are inside the devices.

Before you get rid of a printer, be sure to format any hard drives and any other memory devices. The toner must be disposed of by following local governmental guidelines and laws.

Printers and scanners can be expensive. If you do not service printers correctly, or if you install the wrong part, you can damage them beyond repair.

Figure 14-1   Laser Printer Hazards

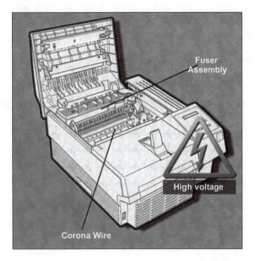

Install and Configure a Local Printer and Scanner

A local device is one that connects directly to the computer. Before you install a local device, such as a printer or scanner, be sure that you remove all packing material. Take out anything that prevents moving parts from shifting around during shipping. Keep the original packing material in case you need to return the equipment to the manufacturer for warranty repairs.

General printer and scanner installation is as follows:

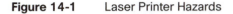

Step 1.   Connect the device (USB, FireWire [IEEE 1394], LPT [IEEE 1284], Serial [RS232], Print Server).

Step 2.   Use Windows XP's "plug-and-play driver.

Step 3.   Add software from the manufacturer.

Step 4.   Check for driver updates on the Internet.

Step 5.   Change default settings.

Step 6.   Make a test print.

Step 7.   Scan a picture.

Step 8.   Print the scanned picture.

After completing this section, you will meet the following objectives:

- Connect the device to a local port.

- Install and configure the driver and software.

- Configure options and default settings.

- Verify functionality.

Connect the Device to a Local Port

Depending on the manufacturer, local printers can communicate with computers using serial, parallel, USB, FireWire, or SCSI ports and cables. Wireless technologies, such as Bluetooth and infrared, are also used to connect these devices. Review the characteristics of these ports:

- *Serial*: Serial data transfer is the movement of single bits of information in a single cycle. A serial connection can be used for dot-matrix printers because the printers do not require high-speed data transfer.

- *Parallel*: Parallel data transfer is faster than serial data transfer. Parallel data transfer is the movement of multiple bits of information in a single cycle. The path is wider for information to move to or from the printer. IEEE 1284 is the current standard for parallel printer ports. Enhanced Parallel Port (EPP) and Enhanced Capabilities Port (ECP) are two modes of operation that allow bidirectional communication.

- *SCSI*: There are several types of SCSI, including the following common types:

    — **SCSI 1**: 50-pin connector

    — **SCSI 2 (fast SCSI)**: 50-pin connector

    — **SCSI 2 (wide SCSI)**: 68-pin connector

    — **SCSI 3 (fast/wide SCSI)**: 68-pin connector

    SCSI printers and computers require the proper cabling for the ports. These ports can be DB 50, Mini DB 50, and DB 68. All of these ports can be male or female.

- *USB*: USB is a common interface for printers and other devices. The speed and simple setup have made USB very practical. Newer operating systems offer plug-and-play (PnP) USB support. When a USB device is added to a computer system supporting PnP, the device is automatically detected, and the computer starts the driver installation process.

- *FireWire*: FireWire, also known as i.LINK or IEEE 1394, is a high-speed communication bus that interconnects digital devices such as printers, scanners, cameras, and hard drives, among others. FireWire provides a single plug-and-socket connection on which up to 63 devices can be attached with data transfer speeds up to 400 Mbps.

- *Ethernet*: Printers can be shared over a network. Connecting a printer to the network requires cabling that is compatible with both the existing network and the network port installed in the printer. Most network printers use an RJ-45 interface to connect to a network.

To connect a printer, attach the appropriate cable to the communication port on the back of the printer. Connect the other end of the cable to the corresponding port on the back of the computer.

After the data cable has been properly connected, attach the power cable to the printer. Connect the other end of the power cable to an available electrical outlet. When you turn on the power to the device, the computer tries to determine the correct device driver to install.

Tip

Always check the packaging for cables when you buy a printer or scanner. Many manufacturers keep production costs down by not including a cable with the printer. If you have to buy a cable, be sure that you buy the correct type.

Install and Configure the Driver and Software

Printer drivers are software programs that make it possible for computers and printers to communicate with each other. Configuration software provides an interface that enables users to set and change printer options. Every printer model has its own type of driver and configuration software.

When you connect a new printer device to a computer, Windows XP tries to locate and install a default driver by using the PnP utility. If Windows cannot find the necessary driver on the computer, it tries to connect to the Internet to find one. Printer manufacturers frequently update drivers to increase the performance of the printer, to add new and improved printer options, and to address general compatibility issues.

Printer Driver Installation

The *printer driver installation* and updating process usually involves the following five steps:

How To

Step 1.   Determine the current version of the installed printer driver. Remember to select a newer version to increase functionality.

Step 2.   Search the Internet to locate the most recent version of the driver.

Step 3.   Download the driver. Follow the instructions on the website.

Step 4. Install the driver. When activated, most driver installation programs automatically install the new driver.

Step 5. Test the driver. To test the driver in Windows XP, choose **Start > Settings > Printers and Faxes**. In Windows Vista the location is **Start > Control Panel > Devices and Printers**. Right-click the printer and choose **Properties**. Then choose **Print Test Page**. If the printer does not work, restart the computer and then try again.

The printed test page should contain text that you can read. If the text is unreadable, the problem could be a bad driver or that the wrong page description language has been used.

Page Description Language

A *page description language (PDL)* is a type of code that describes the appearance of a document in a language that a printer can understand. The PDL for a page includes the text, graphics, and formatting information. Software applications use PDLs to send What You See Is What You Get (WYSIWYG) images to the printer. The printer translates the PDL file so that whatever is on the computer screen is what is printed. PDLs speed the printing process by sending large amounts of data at one time. PDLs also manage the computer fonts.

There are three common PDLs:

- *Printer Command Language (PCL)*: Hewlett-Packard developed PCL for communication with early inkjet printers. PCL is now an industry standard for nearly all printer types.

- *PostScript (PS)*: Adobe Systems developed PS to allow fonts or text types to share the same characteristics on the screen as on paper.

- *Graphics Device Interface (GDI)*: GDI is a Windows component that manages how graphical images are transmitted to output devices. GDI works by converting images to a bitmap that uses the computer instead of the printer to transfer the images.

Table 14-1 compares PostScript to PCL.

Table 14-1   PostScript Versus PCL

PostScript	PCL
Page is rendered by the printer.	Page is rendered on the local workstation.
Better quality output.	Faster print jobs.
Handles more complex print jobs.	Requires less printer memory.
Used on Mac OS.	Not supported by Mac OS.
Output is identical on different printers.	Output varies slightly on different printers.

Configure Options and Default Settings

Common printer options that can be configured by the user include media control and printer output.

The following media control options set the way a printer manages media:

- Input paper tray selection
- Output path selection
- Media size and orientation
- Paper weight selection

The following printer output options manage how the ink or toner goes on the media:

- Color management
- Print speed

Some printers have control switches for users to select options. Other printers use the printer driver options. Two methods of selecting options are the global and per-document methods, as described in the sections that follow.

Global Method

The global method refers to printer options that are set to affect all documents. Each time a document is printed, the global options are used, unless overridden by per-document selections.

To change the configuration of a global printer in Windows XP, choose **Start > Control Panel > Printers and Faxes** and right-click the printer. In Windows Vista, go to **Start > Control Panel > Devices and Printers** and right-click the printer. From there, you can change how the printer prints and handles paper as well as change the drivers and ports.

To designate a default printer, choose **Start > Control Panel > Printers and Faxes**. In Windows Vista, the location is **Start > Control Panel > Devices and Printers**. Right-click the printer, and then choose **Set as Default Printer**, as shown in Figure 14-2.

Note

Depending on the driver installed, Set as Default Printer might not appear on the menu. If this happens, double-click the printer to open the Document Status window and then choose **Printer > Set as Default Printer**.

To limit printing to only black and white in Windows XP, choose **Start > Control Panel > Printer and Faxes**. In Windows Vista, navigate to **Start > Control Panel > Devices and Printers**. Right-click the printer, and then choose **Printing Preferences**. Choose the **Color** tab. Select the **Print In Grayscale** check box and choose the **Black Print Cartridge Only** radio button in the window shown in Figure 14-3. Click **OK**.

Figure 14-2   Selecting a Default Printer

Figure 14-3   Set Color Options

Per-Document Method

Letters, spreadsheets, and digital images are some of the document types that can require special printer settings. You can change the settings for each document sent to the printer by changing the document printer settings.

To change the printer settings, keep the document open and choose **File > Print > Properties**. The default settings are displayed, as shown in Figure 14-4. You can alter the colors, print quality, paper direction, and margin size for the document that you are printing without changing the default settings.

Figure 14-4   Changing the Printer Settings on a Per-Document Basis

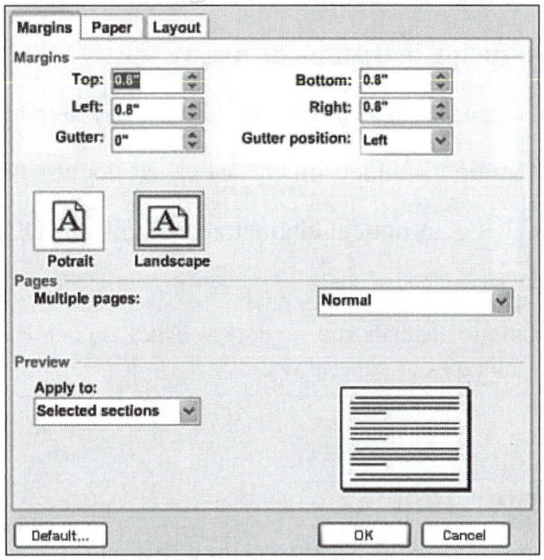

Scanner Calibrations

Calibrating a device is one of the first tasks after installing a driver. Use the bundled software that came with the device to perform this procedure. The default settings can be altered later to meet customer requirements.

Scanner calibrations can include positioning the sensor and using an IT8 target to adjust the color. An IT8 target is a color calibration chart that you use to create profiles for specific devices. A scanner analyzes the target for comparison, while a printer reproduces the target for comparison.

To ensure calibration, compare the printed output of the device to the IT8 target. Adjust the printer color settings to match. The next time you print or scan an image, the color will be as accurate as the target.

Printer Calibrations

The calibration of the printer is performed using the print driver software. This process makes sure that the print heads are aligned and can print on special paper. Inkjet print heads are usually fitted to the ink cartridge, which means that you might have to recalibrate the printer each time you change a cartridge.

Verify Functionality

The installation of any device is not complete until you have successfully tested all the device functions. This includes special tasks such as the following:

- Printing double-sided documents to save paper
- Using different types of paper trays for special paper sizes

- Changing the settings of a color printer so that it prints in black and white or grayscale to print draft copies of documents

- Printing in draft mode to save ink

- Changing a scanner's resolution to make an image easier to view

- Editing scanned images of saved documents

- Using an optical character recognition (OCR) application

Note

Electronic manuals and support websites explain how to clear paper jams, install ink cartridges, and load all types of paper trays.

Printer Test

There are several ways to print a test page:

- Using the Print Test Page option from the printer

- Using the Print Test Page option from Windows, as shown in Figure 14-5

- Using the print function of an application

- Sending a file directly to a parallel port printer using the command line

Figure 14-5   Print Test Page

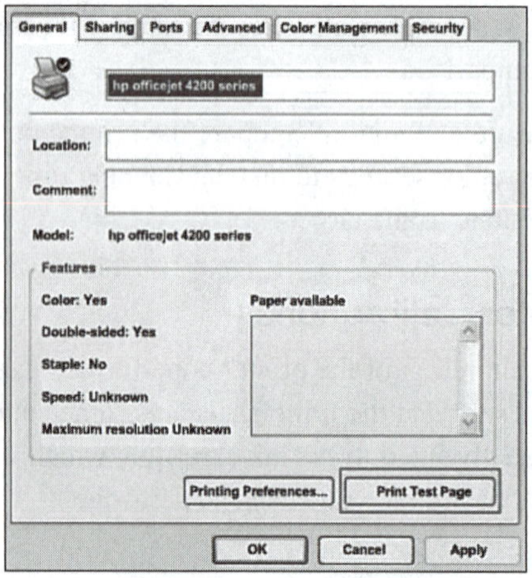

To test a printer, first print a test page from the printer and then print from the Printer Properties function or from an application. To get to the printer properties and print a test page, choose **Start > Printer and Faxes >** (*select your printer*) **> Print > Properties > Print Test Page**. This ensures that the printer is working properly, that the driver software is installed and working, and that the printer and computer are communicating.

Scanner Test

Test the scanner by scanning a document. Use the buttons on the device for automatic scanning. Next, initiate scans from the scanner software and make sure that the software opens automatic scan. If the scanned images appear to be the same as the image on the screen, you have successfully completed the installation.

For an all-in-one device, you should test all the functions:

- **Fax**: Fax to another known working fax machine

- **Copy**: Create a copy of a document

- **Scan**: Scan a document

- **Print**: Print a document

Lab 14.2.4: Install an All-in-One Printer/Scanner

In this lab, you check the Windows XP Hardware Compatibility List (HCL) for the Epson Stylus CX7800, install the all-in-one printer/scanner, upgrade the driver and any associated software, and test the printer and scanner. Refer to the lab in *IT Essentials: PC Hardware and Software Lab Manual, Fourth Edition*. You can perform this lab now or wait until the end of the chapter.

Describe How to Share a Printer and a Scanner on a Network

One of the primary reasons that networks were developed was to allow groups of computer users to share peripheral devices. The most common shared device is the printer. Sharing a single printer among a group of users costs much less than buying a printer for each computer.

Low-cost printers usually require a separate print server to allow network connectivity because these printers do not have built-in network interfaces. The computer that is connected to the printer can serve as the print server. Most personal computer operating systems have built-in printer-sharing capability.

After you confirm that the printer-sharing software is installed, the server must know which printer it is going to share. From the Control Panel, choose **Printers and Faxes**, right-click the printer to share, and choose **Sharing**. Choose the **Share This Printer** option, as shown in Figure 14-6, and assign the printer a name.

Figure 14-6   Shared Printer

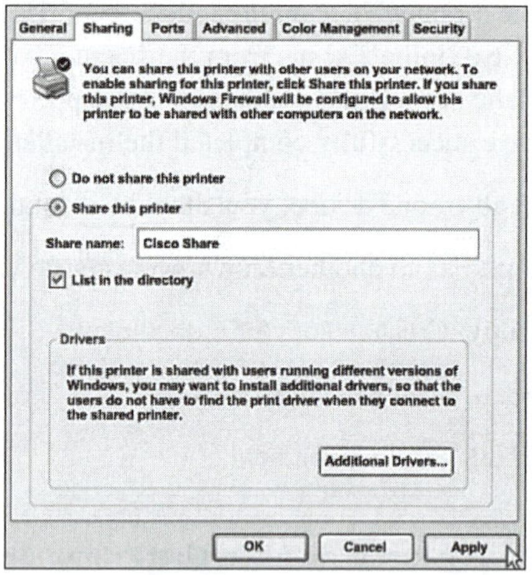

After completing this section, you will meet these objectives:

- Describe the types of print servers.
- Describe how to install network printer software and drivers on a computer.

Describe the Types of Print Servers

Print servers enable multiple computer users to access a single printer. A print server has three functions:

- To provide client access to print resources
- To administrate print jobs, storing them in a queue until the print device is ready for them, and then feeding or spooling the print information to the printer
- To provide feedback to the users, including providing notification that a print job is finished, or error messages that something has gone wrong

As a technician, you must choose one of the three types of print server that best suits the customer's needs:

- Network print server devices
- Dedicated PC print servers
- Computer-shared printers

Network Print Server Devices

Network print server devices allow many users on a network to access a single printer. A network print server device can manage network printing through either wired or wireless connections. Figure 14-7 shows a wired print server. You should consider the advantages and disadvantages of a dedicated PC print server before you install one:

- An advantage of using a network print server is that the server accepts incoming print jobs from computers, and then frees the computers for other tasks. The print server is always available to the users, unlike a printer shared from a user's computer.

- A disadvantage of a network print server is that it might not be able to use all the functions of an all-in-one device.

Figure 14-7   Network Print Server Device

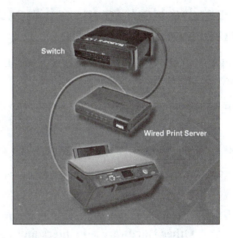

Dedicated PC Print Servers

A *dedicated PC print server* is a computer dedicated to handling client print jobs in the most efficient manner. Because it handles requests from multiple clients, a print server is usually one of the most powerful computers on the network. Dedicated PC print servers can manage more than one printer at a time. A print server needs to have resources available to meet the requests of print clients:

- **Powerful processor**: Because the PC print server uses its processor to manage and route printing information, it needs to be fast enough to handle all incoming requests.

- **Adequate hard disk space**: A PC print server captures print jobs from clients, places them in a print queue, and sends them to the printer in a timely way. This requires the computer to have enough storage space to hold these jobs until completed.

- **Adequate memory**: The server processor and RAM handle sending print jobs to a printer. If server memory is not large enough to handle an entire print job, the hard drive must send the job, which is much slower.

Computer-Shared Printers

A user's computer that has a printer attached can share that printer with other users on the network. Windows XP makes the process of enabling *shared printers* fast and easy. In a home network, it means that users can print documents from wherever they are in the house by using a wireless laptop. In a small office network, sharing a printer means one printer can serve many users.

Sharing a printer from a computer also has disadvantages. The computer sharing the printer uses its own resources to manage the print jobs coming to the printer. If a user on the desktop is working at the same time that a user on the network is printing, the desktop user might notice a performance slowdown. In addition, the printer is not available if the user reboots or powers down the computer with a shared printer.

Describe How to Install Network Printer Software and Drivers on a Computer

Windows XP allows computer users to share their printers with other users on the network. There are two steps:

How To

Step 1.   Configure the computer attached to the printer to share the printer with other network users.

Step 2.   Configure a user's computer to recognize the shared printer and print to it.

To configure the computer with the printer attached to accept print jobs from other network users, follow these steps:

How To

Step 1.   If you are using Windows XP, choose **Start > Control Panel > Printers and Other Hardware > Printers and Faxes**. In Windows Vista, the location is **Start > Control Panel > Devices and Printers**.

Step 2.   Select the printer you want to share.

Step 3.   The Printer Tasks dialog box will appear on the left. Select **Share This Printer**.

Step 4.   The Printer Properties dialog box for that printer will display. Select the **Sharing** tab. Select **Share This Printer** and enter the desired share name. This is the name that the printer will appear as to other users.

Step 5.   Verify that sharing has been successful. Return to the Printers and Faxes folder and notice that the printer icon now has a hand under it, as shown in Figure 14-8. This shows that the printer is now a shared resource.

Figure 14-8   Shared Printer Icon

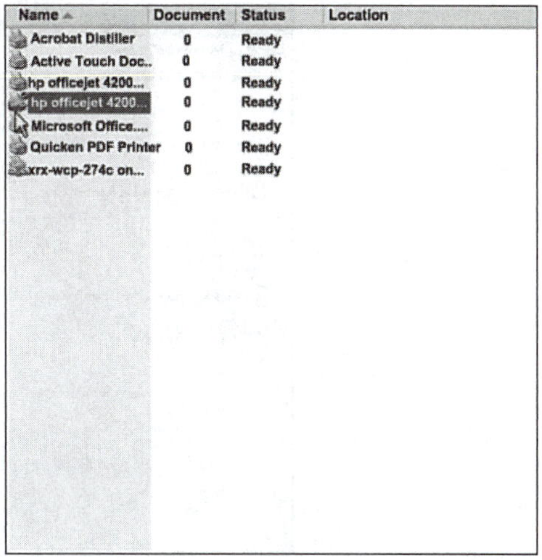

Name ▲	Document	Status	Location
Acrobat Distiller	0	Ready	
Active Touch Doc..	0	Ready	
hp officejet 4200...	0	Ready	
hp officejet 4200...	0	Ready	
Microsoft Office....	0	Ready	
Quicken PDF Printer	0	Ready	
xrx-wcp-274c on...	0	Ready	

Other users who can now connect to the shared printer might not have the required drivers installed. These other users might also be using different operating systems from the OS used by the computer that is hosting the shared printer. Windows XP can automatically upload the correct drivers to these other users. Click the **Additional Drivers** button to select operating systems that the other users might be using. When you close that dialog box by clicking **OK**, Windows XP asks whether you want to obtain those additional drivers. If all the other users are also operating Windows XP, you do not need to click the Additional Drivers button. To find the Additional Drivers button, choose **Start > Printers and Faxes**, right-click the printer you are sharing, and choose **Properties > Sharing > Additional Drivers** button.

Other users on the network can now connect to this printer by following these steps:

How To

Step 1. Choose **Start > Control Panel > Printers and other Hardware > Add a Printer**.

Step 2. The Add Printer Wizard appears. Click **Next**.

Step 3. Select a network printer, or a printer attached to another computer, as shown in Figure 14-9. Click **Next**.

Step 4. Type in the name of the printer, or browse for it on the network using the Next button. A list of shared printers will appear.

Step 5. After you select the printer, a virtual printer port is created and displayed in the Add a Printer window. The required print drivers are downloaded from the print server and installed on the computer. The wizard then finishes the installation.

Figure 14-9   Connecting to a Shared Printer

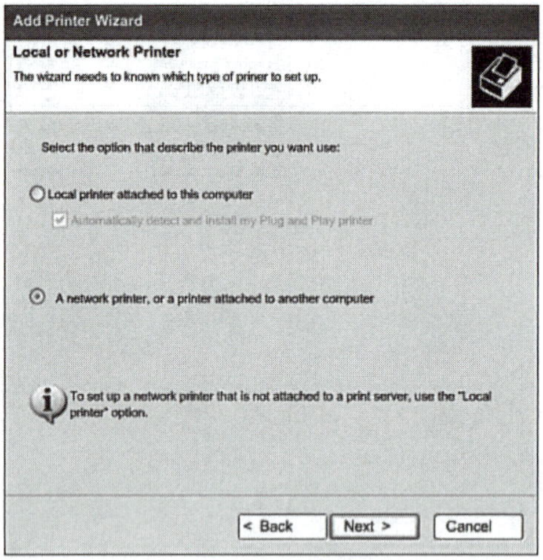

Lab 14.3.2: Share the All-in-One Printer/Scanner in Windows XP

In this lab, you share the Epson printer/scanner, configure the printer on a networked computer, and print a test page from the remote computer. Refer to the lab in *IT Essentials: PC Hardware and Software Lab Manual, Fourth Edition*. You can perform this lab now or wait until the end of the chapter.

Optional Lab 14.3.2: Share the All-in-One Printer/Scanner in Windows Vista

In this lab, you share the Epson printer/scanner, configure the printer on a networked computer, and print a test page from the remote computer. Refer to the lab in *IT Essentials: PC Hardware and Software Lab Manual, Fourth Edition*. You can perform this lab now or wait until the end of the chapter.

Upgrade and Configure Printers and Scanners

Some printers can be expanded by adding hardware to them, enabling them to print faster and to accommodate more print jobs. The hardware can include additional paper trays, sheet feeders, network cards, and expansion memory.

Scanners can also be configured to do more to meet customer needs. Examples for scanner optimization include color correction and resizing. These tasks cannot be completed with the default settings.

After completing this section, you will meet these objectives:

- Describe printer upgrades.
- Describe scanner optimization.

Describe Printer Upgrades

Upgrading the printer memory improves the printing speed and enhances the ability to perform complex print jobs. All printers today have at least a small amount of RAM. The more memory a printer has, the more efficiently it works. The added memory helps with tasks such as print job buffering, page creation, improved photo and graphics printing.

Print job buffering refers to capturing a print job into the internal printer memory. Buffering allows the computer to continue with other work instead of waiting for the printer to finish. Buffering is a common feature in laser printers and plotters, as well as in advanced inkjet and dot-matrix printers.

Printers usually arrive from the factory with enough memory to handle jobs that involve text. However, print jobs involving graphics, and especially photographs, run more efficiently if the printer memory is adequate to store the entire job before it starts. If you receive errors that indicate the printer is "out of memory" or that there has been a "memory overload," you might need more memory.

Installing Printer Memory

The first step in installing additional printer memory is to read the printer manual to determine the following:

- **Memory type**: Physical type of memory, speed, and capacity; some are standard types of memory, whereas others require special or proprietary memory.

- **Memory population and availability**: Number of memory upgrade slots in use, and how many are available; this can require opening a compartment to check RAM.

Printer manufacturers have set procedures for upgrading memory, including the following tasks:

- Removing covers to access the memory area
- Installing or removing memory
- Initializing the printer to recognize the new memory
- Installing updated drivers if needed

Additional Printer Upgrades

Some additional printer upgrades include the following:

- Duplex printing to enable dual-sided printing
- Extra trays to hold more paper
- Specialized tray types for different media
- Network cards to access a wired or wireless network
- Firmware upgrades to add functionality or to fix bugs

Follow the instructions included with the printer when you install or upgrade components. Memory manufactures have tools on their home pages to help customers determine proper memory for a device. Contact the manufacturer or an authorized service technician for additional information if you have any problems when installing upgrades. Follow all safety procedures outlined by the manufacturer.

Describe Scanner Optimization

Scanners work well for most users without any changes to the default settings. There are, however, features that can improve document or image scans depending on user requirements. The most common types of scanner options are as follows:

- Resizing
- Sharpening
- Brightening or darkening
- Color correction
- Resolution changes
- Output file format
- Color inversion

Scanning resolution affects the size of the output file. The end use of the image determines the required resolution. If the image is for use in a web publication, you only need low resolution and a small file size. This makes it possible for browsers to load the image quickly. Medium-resolution images are normally used for laser prints. In commercial printing, where the quality of the image is very important, a higher resolution is the best setting. Low resolution means a small file size; high resolution means a large file size. Figure 14-10 shows the settings for resolution and output type.

Figure 14-10   Resolution Settings

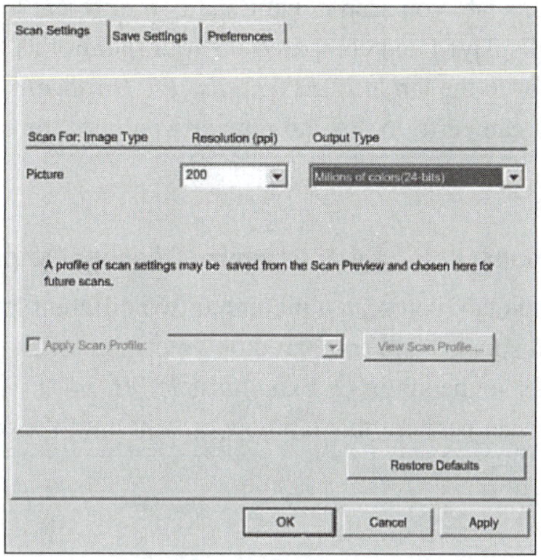

Scanners allow you to choose different file formats for the scanned output, as shown in Figure 14-11.

Figure 14-11   Output Options

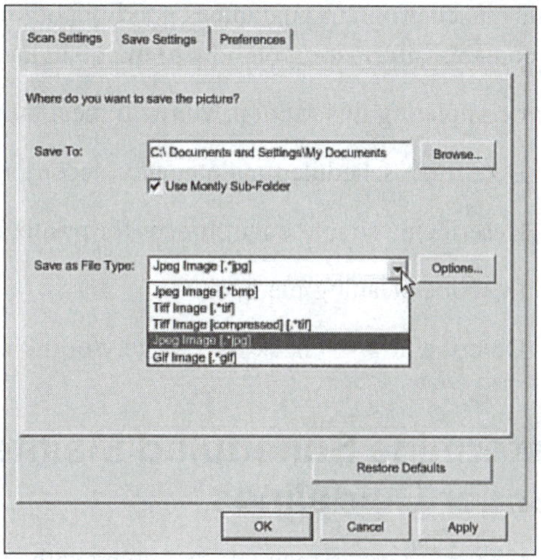

If a scanner does not produce output in a file format required by the customer, the format can be converted later using software tools. After changing device settings, you should test the changes by making some sample printouts.

Lab 14.4.2: Optimize Scanner Output in Windows XP

In this lab, you scan a picture at two different levels of dots per inch (dpi). The results will be displayed and compared on your monitor as two saved files and as two printed images. Refer to the lab in *IT Essentials: PC Hardware and Software Lab Manual, Fourth Edition.* You can perform this lab now or wait until the end of the chapter.

Optional Lab 14.4.2: Optimize Scanner Output in Windows Vista

In this lab, you scan a picture at two different levels of dots per inch (dpi). The results will be displayed and compared on your monitor as two saved files and as two printed images. Refer to the lab in *IT Essentials: PC Hardware and Software Lab Manual, Fourth Edition.* You can perform this lab now or wait until the end of the chapter.

Describe Printer and Scanner Preventive Maintenance Techniques

Preventive maintenance decreases downtime and increases the service life of the components. You should maintain printers and scanners to keep them working properly. A good maintenance program guarantees good-quality prints and scans. The printer or scanner manual contains information on how to maintain and clean the equipment.

After completing this section, you will meet these objectives:

- Determine scheduled maintenance according to vendor guidelines.
- Describe a suitable environment for printers and scanners.
- Describe cleaning methods.
- Describe how to check the capacity of ink cartridges and toners.

Determine Scheduled Maintenance According to Vendor Guidelines

Read the information manuals that come with every new piece of equipment. Follow the recommended maintenance instructions. Also, use the supplies listed by the manufacturer. Less-expensive supplies can save money but might produce poor results, damage the equipment, or void the warranty.

When maintenance is completed, reset the counters to allow the next maintenance to be completed at the correct time. On many types of printers, the page count is viewed through the LCD or a counter located inside the main cover.

Most manufacturers sell maintenance kits for their printers. Figure 14-12 shows items that are commonly included in a maintenance kit. The kit has instructions that any technician can follow. For laser printers, the kit may contain replacement parts that often break or wear out:

- Fuser assembly

- *Transfer rollers*

- *Separation pads*

- *Pickup rollers*

Figure 14-12   Maintenance Kit

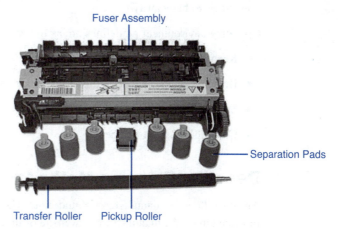

Each time you install new parts or replace toners and cartridges, do a visual inspection of all the internal components:

- Remove bits of paper and dust.

- Clean spilled ink.

- Look for any worn gears, cracked plastic, or broken parts.

Users that do not know how to maintain printing equipment should call a manufacturer-certified technician.

 Worksheet 14.5.1: Search for Certified Printer Technician Jobs

For this worksheet, you use the Internet to gather information about becoming a certified printer technician. Be prepared to discuss your answers with the class. Refer to the worksheet in *IT Essentials: PC Hardware and Software Lab Manual, Fourth Edition*. You can complete this worksheet now or wait until the end of the chapter.

Describe a Suitable Environment for Printers and Scanners

Printers and scanners, like all other electrical devices, are affected by temperature, humidity, and electrical interference. For example, laser printers produce heat. Operate them in well-ventilated areas to prevent overheating. If possible, store all printers, scanners, and supplies in a cool and dry place, away from dust. This ensures that they will work properly and for a long time.

Keep paper and toner cartridges in their original wrappers and in a cool, dry environment. High humidity causes paper to absorb moisture from the air. This makes it difficult for the toner to attach to the paper correctly. If the paper and printer are dusty, you can use compressed air to blow away the dust.

Operating environment guidelines are as follows:

- Keep paper dry.
- Keep the printer in a cool, dust-free environment.
- Store toner in a clean, dry environment.
- Clean the glass on scanners.

Describe Cleaning Methods

Always follow the manufacturer's guidelines when cleaning printers and scanners. Information on the manufacturer's website or in the user manual explains the proper cleaning methods.

Caution

Remember to unplug scanners and printers before cleaning to prevent danger from high voltage.

Printer Maintenance

Make sure that you turn off and unplug any printer before performing *printer maintenance*. Use a damp cloth to wipe off any dirt, paper dust, and spilled ink on the exterior of the device.

Print heads in an inkjet printer are replaced when the cartridges are replaced. However, sometimes print heads become clogged and require cleaning. Use the utility supplied by the manufacturer to clean the print heads. After you clean them, you should test them. Repeat this process until the test shows a clean and uniform print.

Printers have many moving parts. Over time, the parts collect dust, dirt, and other debris. If not cleaned regularly, the printer might not work well, or could stop working. When working with dot-matrix printers, clean the roller surfaces with a damp cloth. On inkjet printers, clean the paper-handling machinery with a damp cloth.

Caution

Do not touch the drum of a laser printer while cleaning. You can damage the surface of the drum.

Laser printers do not usually require much maintenance unless they are in a dusty area or they are very old. When cleaning a laser printer, use a specially designed vacuum cleaner to pick up toner particles. Figure 14-13 shows a vacuum designed for electronic equipment. A standard vacuum cleaner cannot hold the tiny particles of toner and can scatter them about. Use only a vacuum cleaner with *HEPA filtration*. HEPA filtration catches microscopic particles within the filters.

Choosing the correct paper type for a printer helps the printer last longer and print more efficiently. Several types of paper are available. Each type of paper is clearly labeled with the type of printer for which it is intended. The manufacturer of the printer might also recommend the best type of paper. Check the printer manual.

Information about the brands and types of ink recommended by the manufacturer is also found in the manual. Using the wrong type of ink can cause the printer not to work or can reduce the print quality. To prevent ink leaks, do not refill ink cartridges.

Figure 14-13   Printer Vacuum

Scanner Maintenance

For proper *scanner maintenance*, you should clean scanners regularly to prevent dirt, fingerprints, and other smudges from showing in scanned images. On flatbed scanners, keep the lid closed when the scanner is not in use. This will help to prevent dust buildup and accidental fingertip smudges. If the glass becomes dirty, consult the user guide for the manufacturer's cleaning recommendations. If the manual does not list any recommendations, use a glass cleaner and a soft cloth to protect the glass from scratching. Even very small scratches can be visible on high-resolution scans. If dirt becomes lodged in the scratches, the scratches will become more visible.

If the inside of the glass becomes dirty, check the manual for instructions on how to open the unit or remove the glass from the scanner. If possible, thoroughly clean both sides and replace the glass as it was originally installed in the scanner.

Describe Checking Capacity of Ink Cartridges and Toners

When an inkjet printer produces blank pages, the ink cartridges might be empty. Laser printers do not produce blank pages, but they do begin to print very poor-quality printouts. Most inkjet printers provide a utility that shows ink levels in each cartridge, as shown in Figure 14-14. Some printers have LCD message screens or LED lights that warn users when ink supplies are low.

Figure 14-14   Estimated Ink Level

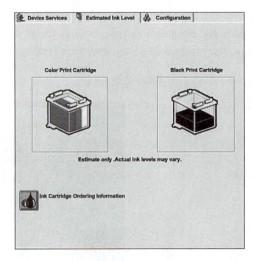

A method for checking ink levels is to look at the page counter inside the printer or the printer software to determine how many pages have been printed. Then look at the cartridge label information. The label should show how many pages the cartridge can print. You can then easily estimate how many more pages you can print. For this method to be accurate, each time you replace the cartridge, you must remember to reset the counter. In addition, some printouts use more ink than others do. For example, a letter uses less ink than a photograph.

You can set the printer software to reduce the amount of ink or toner that the printer uses. This setting might be called "toner save" or "draft quality." This setting reduces the print quality of laser and inkjet products and reduces the time it takes to print a document on an inkjet printer.

Troubleshoot Printers and Scanners

With printer and scanner problems, a technician must be able to determine whether the problem exists with the device, cable connection, or the computer that it is attached to. Follow the steps outlined in the following sections to accurately identify, repair, and document the problem.

How To

Step 1. Identify the problem.

Step 2. Establish a theory or probable causes.

Step 3. Determine an exact cause.

Step 4. Implement a solution.

Step 5. Verify solution and full system functionality.

Step 6. Document your findings.

After completing this section, you will meet these objectives:

- Review the troubleshooting process.
- Identify common problems and solutions.
- Apply troubleshooting skills.

Review the Troubleshooting Process

Printer and scanner problems can result from a combination of hardware, software, and connectivity issues. Computer technicians must be able to analyze the problem and determine the cause of the error to address the printer and scanner issues.

Step 1: Identify the Problem

The first step in the troubleshooting process is to identify the problem. Table 14-2 provides a list of open-ended and closed-ended questions to ask the customer about printer/scanner errors to help identify the problem. (This list is *not* comprehensive.)

Table 14-2   Printer/Scanner Errors: Open-Ended and Closed-Ended Questions
to Ask

Open-Ended Questions	Closed-Ended Questions
What type of printer/scanner do you have?	Does the problem appear on every page?
What type of paper are you using?	Has the paper been changed recently?
What problems are you experiencing with this printer/scanner?	How old is the printer/scanner?

continues

Table 14-2   Printer/Scanner Errors: Open-Ended and Closed-Ended Questions
to Ask   *continued*

Open-Ended Questions	Closed-Ended Questions
What error messages have you received?	Is the problem only with this printer/scanner?
What changes, including changes to the operating system and software, have been made recently?	What application were you using?
What steps do you take to maintain your printer/scanner?	Does the problem occur when you use other applications?
	What make and model of printer/scanner is it?
	Is the printer/scanner local or networked?
	What is the location of the printer/scanner?

Step 2: Establish a Theory of Probable Causes

After you have identified the problem, you should establish a theory of probable that apply to printers and scanners:

- Is the data cable the correct cable and installed correctly?
- Is the printer plugged into an uninterruptible power source (UPS)?
- Is the glass surfaces clean on the printer or scanner?
- Is the toner cartridge full?
- Is the toner cartridge old?
- Is the ink cartridge full?
- Are the wiper bar and the inside of the printer clean?
- Is the scanner arm not taped or blocked in place?

Step 3: Determine an Exact Cause

After the obvious issues have been verified, try some quick solutions. Some quick solutions to printer and scanner problems include

- Restart the equipment.
- Disconnect and reconnect the cables.
- Check the printer or paper jams.
- Reseat the paper and in the paper trays.

- Open and close the paper trays.

- Ensure the printer doors are closed.

- Clear the jobs in the printer queue.

- Restart the printer spooler service.

- Remove and reinsert data cables.

- Remove and shake the toner cartridge.

- Reinstall printer software.

- Reinsert paper.

- Remove packing tape from inkjet cartridge nozzles or the scanner arm.

Step 4: Implement a Solution

At this point, you will have enough information implement possible solutions. Some resources for possible solutions include the following:

- Problem-solving experience

- Other technicians

- Internet search

- Newsgroups

- Manufacturer FAQs

- Computer manuals

- Device manuals

- Online forums

- Technical websites

Step 5: Verify Solution and Full System Functionality

After you have implemented a solution, verify it and verify that the entire system is functional. The following helps ensure that everything works before you send the printer or scanner back to the customer:

- Reboot the computer.

- Reboot the printer/scanner.

- Print a document from the printer control panel.

- Print a document from an application.

- Reprint the customer's problem document.

Step 6: Document Findings

After you have solved the problem, you will close with the customer, which requires completing the following tasks:

Step 1. Discuss the solution implemented with the customer.

Step 2. Have the customer verify that the problem has been solved.

Step 3. Provide the customer with all paperwork.

Step 4. Document the steps taken to solve the problem in the work order and the technician's journal.

Step 5. Document any components used in the repair.

Step 6. Document the time spent to resolve the problem.

Identify Common Problems and Solutions

Printer and scanner problems can be attributed to hardware, software, networks, or some combination of the three. You will resolve some types of problems more often than others. Table 14-3 provides a chart of common problems and solutions.

Table 14-3   Common Printer and Scanner Problems and Solutions

Identify the Problem	Probable Causes	Possible Solutions
Printer prints unknown characters or does not print anything.	The printer may be plugged into a UPS.	Plug the printer directly into the wall outlet.
	An incorrect print driver is installed.	Uninstall the incorrect print driver and install the correct driver.
	The printer cables are loose.	Secure the printer cables.
	There is no paper in the printer.	Add paper to the printer.
	The printer has been set to Pause Printing.	Set the printer to Resume Printing.
	The printer has been set to Offline.	Set the printer to Printer Online.

Identify the Problem	Probable Causes	Possible Solutions
Paper jams when printing.	The printer is dirty.	Clean the printer.
	The printer is using the wrong kind of paper.	Replace the paper with the manufacture's recommended paper type.
	Humidity caused the paper to stick together.	Insert new paper in the paper tray.
Printer outputs only blank paper for print jobs.	The toner or ink cartridge is empty or locked in place with packaging tape.	Remove the packaging tape from the toner or ink cartridge.
	The drum is not holding a charge.	Replace the ink cartridge.
	The nozzles in the ink cartridge are clogged with dust or dried ink.	Replace the drum or replace the toner cartridge when it contains the drum.
		Use the cleaning utility to clean the ink cartridge.
Printer will not print large or complex images.	The printer does not have enough memory.	Add more memory to the printer.
Laser printer prints lines or streaks on every page.	The drum is damaged.	Replace the drum or replace the toner cartridge if it contains the drum.
		Remove and shake the toner cartridge.
Printed pages show ghost images.	The drum is scratched or dirty.	Replace the drum or replace the toner cartridge if it contains the drum.
	The drum wiper blade is worn.	

Apply Troubleshooting Skills

Now that you understand the troubleshooting process, it is time to apply your listening and diagnostic skills.

The first lab is designed to reinforce your skill with printers. You troubleshoot and fix a printer problem. The second lab is designed to reinforce your communication and troubleshooting skills with printers. In this lab, you perform the following steps:

How To Q

Step 1. Receive the work order.

Step 2. Take the customer through various steps and resolve the problem.

Step 3. Document the problem and the solution.

The third and fourth labs are designed to reinforce your skills with printer and scanner problems. You troubleshoot and repair multiple printing problems.

Lab 14.6.3: Fix a Printer Problem

In this lab, you troubleshoot and fix a printer that does not print documents for a user. Refer to the lab in *IT Essentials: PC Hardware and Software Lab Manual, Fourth Edition*. You can perform this lab now or wait until the end of the chapter.

Lab 14.6.3: Remote Technician: Fix a Printer Problem

In this lab, you gather data from the customer and then instruct the customer on how to fix a printer that does not print documents. You then document the customer's problem in the work order provided in the lab. Refer to the Remote Technician Lab in *IT Essentials: PC Hardware and Software Lab Manual, Fourth Edition*. You can perform this lab now or wait until the end of the chapter.

Lab 14.6.3: Troubleshooting Printer Problems in Windows XP

In this lab, you diagnose and solve various printer problems while using Windows XP. Refer to the Remote Technician Lab in *IT Essentials: PC Hardware and Software Lab Manual, Fourth Edition*. You can perform this lab now or wait until the end of the chapter.

Optional Lab 14.6.3: Troubleshooting Printer Problems in Windows Vista

In this lab, you diagnose and solve various printer problems while using Windows Vista. Refer to the Remote Technician Lab in *IT Essentials: PC Hardware and Software Lab Manual, Fourth Edition*. You can perform this lab now or wait until the end of the chapter.

Summary

This chapter reviewed and discussed information about printers and scanners. The chapter explored hazards and safety procedures associated with printers and scanners. You have learned preventive maintenance methods, and you have installed, configured, and upgraded a printer or scanner, both locally and on a network. Here are some other important facts covered in this chapter:

- Always follow safety procedures when working with printers and scanners. There are many parts inside printers that contain high voltage or become very hot with use.

- Use the device manual and software to install a printer or scanner. After the installation, update the drivers and firmware to fix problems and increase functionality.

- Use the Windows interface to share printers and scanners across the network.

- Consult with the customers to determine how best to upgrade and configure printers and scanners to meet their needs.

- Keep printers, scanners, and supplies clean and dry. Keep supplies in their original packaging to prevent breakdowns and downtime. Develop a maintenance schedule to clean and check devices on a regular basis.

- Use a sequence of steps to fix a problem. Start with simple tasks before you decide on a course of action. Call a qualified or certified printer technician when a problem is too difficult for you to fix.

Summary of Exercises

This is a summary of the Labs, Worksheets, Remote Technician exercises, Class Discussions, Virtual Desktop activities, and Virtual Laptop activities associated with this chapter.

Labs

The following labs cover material from this chapter. Refer to the labs in *IT Essentials: PC Hardware and Software Lab Manual, Fourth Edition*.

Lab 14.2.4: Install an All-in-One Printer/Scanner

Lab 14.3.2: Share the All-in-One Printer/Scanner in Windows XP

Optional Lab 14.3.2: Share the All-in-One Printer/Scanner in Windows Vista

Lab 14.4.2: Optimize Scanner Output

Lab 14.6.3: Fix a Printer Problem

Lab 14.6.3: Remote Technician: Fix a Printer Problem

Lab 14.6.3: Troubleshooting Printer Problems in Windows XP

Optional Lab 14.6.3: Troubleshooting Printer Problems in Windows Vista

Worksheets

The following worksheet covers material from this chapter. Refer to the labs in *IT Essentials: PC Hardware and Software Lab Manual, Fourth Edition.*

Worksheet 14.5.1: Search for Certified Printer Technician Jobs

Check Your Understanding

You can find the answers to these questions in the appendix, "Answers to Check Your Understanding Questions."

1. Which of the following connectors are SCSI types? (Choose two.)

   A. Fast/wide: 68-pin connector

   B. Fast SCSI: 68-pin connector

   C. SCSI 1: 50-pin connector

   D. Wide SCSI: 50-pin connector

   E. Wide SCSI: 80-pin connector

2. What is the name given to the code that describes the layout and contents of a printed page?

   A. Page Layout Language

   B. Preview description language

   C. Page description language

   D. Page preview language

   E. Page preview description

3. Which of the following functions are provided by a print server? (Choose two.)

   A. Drop damaged files.

   B. Provide client access to print resources.

   C. Automatically reformat print requests to reduce network bandwidth consumed.

   D. Provide feedback to the users.

   E. Automatically reload paper.

4. What is an advantage of using network print servers?

  A. Print servers offer specialized operating system support to PCs on the network.

  B. Print servers offer more functions than all-in-one devices.

  C. Print servers are always accessible because they are always powered on.

  D. Print servers keep a communication link to the computer that sent the print job until the document is printed.

5. Which of the following scanner options are used to improve document or image scans? (Choose two.)

  A. Resolution changes

  B. Output file format

  C. Printing capacity

  D. Source image size

  E. Input file format

6. When closing with a customer, which of the following actions are expected to be performed by a technician? (Choose three.)

  A. Evaluate the user efficiency in the troubleshooting process.

  B. Document any components used and the time spent to resolve the problem.

  C. Evaluate the information gathered from the user against the solution.

  D. Document steps taken to solve the problem in the work order.

  E. Educate the user by making the user follow the steps to repair the reported problem.

  F. Discuss the solution implemented.

7. Which of the following resources ensure that dedicated print servers can meet the demands of print clients? (Choose two.)

  A. Adequate storage space

  B. Adequate backup capacity

  C. Adequate RAM

  D. Wireless network support

  E. Firewall support

8. How many peripherals can be attached to a USB port?

   A. 24

   B. 50

   C. 127

   D. 80

   E. 63

   F. 255

CHAPTER 15

Advanced Networks

Objectives

Upon completion of this chapter, you will be able to answer the following questions:

- What are the potential safety hazards, and how do I implement proper safety procedures related to networks?

- How do I design a network based on the customer's needs?

- How do I determine the components for the customer's network?

- What does it take to implement the customer's network?

- How do I upgrade the customer's network?

- How do I install, configure, and manage a simple mail server?

- What are preventive maintenance procedures for a network?

- How do I troubleshoot the network?

Key Terms

This chapter uses the following key terms. You can find the definitions in the Glossary.

Secure Shell (SSH)   *page 591*

Post Office Protocol (POP)   *page 591*

Simple Mail Transfer Protocol (SMTP)   *page 591*

plain old telephone service (POTS)   *page 595*

digital subscriber line (DSL)   *page 596*

To meet the expectations and needs of your customers and network users, you must be familiar with networking technologies. You must understand the basics of how a network is designed and why some components affect the flow of data on a network.

This chapter focuses on advanced networking topics, including network design, network component upgrades, and email server installations. Basic networking topics such as safety, network components, and preventive maintenance are also discussed. This chapter also describes troubleshooting advanced network situations.

After completing this chapter, you will meet these objectives:

- Identify potential safety hazards and implement proper safety procedures related to networks.

- Design a network based on the customer's needs.

- Determine the components for your customer's network.

- Implement the customer's network.

- Upgrade the customer's network.

- Describe installation, configuration, and management of a simple mail server.

- Describe preventive maintenance procedures for networks.

- Troubleshoot the network.

Identify Potential Safety Hazards and Implement Proper Safety Procedures Related to Networks

Installing network cables, whether copper or fiber-optic, can be dangerous. Often, cables must be pulled through ceilings and walls where there are obstacles and unexpected or toxic materials. You should wear clothing that protects you from these materials. For example, wear long pants, a long-sleeved shirt, sturdy shoes that cover your feet, and gloves. Most importantly, wear safety glasses. If possible, ask building management, or someone responsible for the building, if there are any dangerous materials, obstacles, or building safety codes that you need to be aware of before entering the ceiling area.

Be aware of these safety issues when using a ladder:

- Read the labels on the ladder, and follow any safety instructions written on it.

- Never stand on the top rung of the ladder. You could easily lose your balance and fall.

- Make sure that people in the area know you will be working there.

- Cordon off the area with caution tape or safety cones.

- When you are using a ladder that leans up against a wall, follow the instructions written on the ladder, and have someone hold the ladder to help keep it steady.

The tools required to install copper and fiber-optic cable may be dangerous to use. When working with cables, follow these rules:

- Make sure that the tools you are using are in good working order.

- Watch what you are doing, and take your time. Make sure that you do not cut yourself or place anyone in danger.

- Always wear safety glasses when cutting, stripping, or splicing cables of any kind. Tiny fragments can injure your eyes.

- Wear gloves whenever possible, and dispose of any waste properly.

Use common sense when installing cables and fixing network problems. Call another person to help you if you need assistance.

After completing this section, you will meet these objectives:

- Explain fiber-optic safety.

- Explain cable, cable cutters, and cable-cutting safety hazards.

Explain Fiber-Optic Safety

Fiber-optic cables are useful for communications, but they have certain hazards:

- Dangerous chemicals

- Tools with sharp edges

- Light that you cannot see that can burn your eyes

- Glass shards produced by cutting fiber-optic cable that can cause bodily harm

Specific types of tools and chemicals are used when working with fiber-optic cable. These materials must be handled safely. Fiber optics are a specialty field within computer repair and networking. Technicians who work in this field have special training and additional certifications.

Chemicals

The solvents and glues used with fiber optics are dangerous. You should handle them with extreme care. Read any instructions, and follow them carefully. Also, read the material safety data sheet (MSDS) that accompanies the chemicals to know how to treat someone in an emergency.

Tools

When working with any tool, safety should always be your first priority. Any compromise in safety could result in serious injury or even death. The tools used for working with fiber optics have sharp cutting surfaces that are used to scribe glass. Other tools pinch cables with high pressure to fasten connectors to them. These tools can produce shards of glass that can splinter and fly into the air. You must avoid getting them on your skin and in your mouth or eyes.

Harmful Light

Protect your eyes from the harmful light that may be in the fiber-optic strands. The light is a color that humans cannot see. It can damage your eyes before you can feel it. When you use a magnifier to inspect fiber-optic cable and connectors, the light emitted from the fiber could be directed into your eyes. When working with fiber, be sure to disconnect the light source. Special detectors can tell you if a fiber is energized.

Glass Shards

The process of cutting and trimming the strands of fiber-optic cables can produce tiny fragments of glass or plastic that can penetrate your eyes or skin and cause severe irritation. The fibers can be extremely difficult to see on your skin because they are clear and small. When you work with fiber-optic cabling, the working surface should be a dark mat so that you can see the tiny glass or plastic fragments. The mat should also be resistant to chemical spills.

You should keep the work area clean and neat. Never pick up fiber-optic fragments with your fingers. Use tape to pick up small fragments, and dispose of them properly. Use a disposable container, such as a plastic bottle with a screw-on lid, to store fiber fragments. Close the lid tightly before disposing of the container.

Caution

Obtain proper training before you attempt to cut, strip, or splice fiber-optic cable. An experienced technician should supervise you until you become adequately skilled.

Explain Cable, Cable Cutters, and Cable-Cutting Safety Hazards

All levels of technicians should know the hazards before working with network cables and equipment. This section describes the safety hazards of working with copper cables, which, like fiber-optic cables, can be dangerous to handle.

Caution

When handling cable, always wear eye protection. Never touch the ends of any type of cable to bare skin.

When you cut copper cable, the small copper strands can puncture your skin or cut you. The small pieces that come off after cables are cut often fly into the air. Remember to always wear safety glasses when cutting any type of cable.

The cutting and crimping tools used to repair or terminate copper cables can be dangerous if not used properly. Read the documentation that comes with the tool. Practice using the tool on scrap cable, and ask an experienced installer for help if you need it.

Remember that copper cable conducts electricity. An equipment fault, static electricity, or lightning can energize even a disconnected cable. If in doubt, test the cable you are working on with a simple voltage detector before touching it.

Design a Network Based on the Customer's Needs

A network is most effective if it is designed to meet the customer's needs. Building a network requires analyzing the environment and understanding networking options. You should interview the customer, as well as any other people involved in the project. It is important to have a general idea about the hardware and software that will be used on the network. You should inquire about future growth of the company and the network.

After completing this section, you will meet these objectives:

- Determine a topology.
- Determine protocols and network applications.

Determine a Topology

You must understand the customer's needs and determine the general layout of the new network to properly determine the network topology. You need to discuss these important issues with the customer:

- Cable and wireless types
- Scalability
- Number and location of users

The number of users and the estimated amount of future growth determine the network's initial physical and logical topology. You should create a checklist to record the customer's needs.

You should do an inspection, called a site survey, early in the project. A site survey is a physical inspection of the building that helps determine a basic logical topology, which is the flow of data and protocols. The number of users and the estimated amount of future growth determine the network's initial physical and logical topology. You should consider the following factors:

- The location of the users' computers

- The location of network equipment such as switches and routers

- The location of servers

A floor plan or blueprint is helpful to determine the physical layout of equipment and cables. This may be in the same room as the network equipment, or it could be elsewhere. The decision is often based on available space, power, security, and air conditioning. Figure 15-1 shows a comparison of network topologies, including bus, ring, star, extended star, hierarchical, and mesh.

Figure 15-1   Types of Topologies

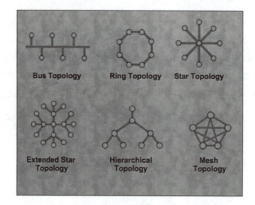

If a floor plan or blueprint is not available, you should make a drawing of where the network devices will be located, including the location of the server room, the printers, the end stations, and cable runs. This drawing can be used for discussions when the customer makes the final layout decisions.

Determine Protocols and Network Applications

When designing a network, you must determine which protocols will be used. Some protocols are proprietary and work on only specific equipment, and others are open standards and work on a variety of equipment. Here are the details of the various network protocols:

- **Transmission Control Protocol/Internet Protocol (TCP/IP)**: TCP/IP represents a set of public standards that specifies how packets of information are exchanged between computers over one or more networks. The TCP/IP suite of protocols has become the dominant standard for internetworking.

- **Internetwork Packet Exchange/Sequenced Packet Exchange (IPX/SPX)**: IPX/SPX is the protocol suite employed originally by Novell Corporation's network operating system, NetWare. It delivers functions similar to those included in TCP/IP. Novell in its current releases supports the TCP/IP suite. A large installed base of NetWare networks continues to use IPX/SPX.

- **NetBIOS Extended User Interface (NetBEUI)**: NetBEUI is a protocol used primarily on small Windows NT networks. NetBEUI cannot be routed or used by routers to talk to each other on a large network. NetBEUI is suitable for small, peer-to-peer, Microsoft Windows–based networks involving a few computers directly connected to each other. It can be used in conjunction with another routable protocol such as TCP/IP. This gives the network administrator the advantages of the high performance of NetBEUI within the local network and the capability to communicate beyond the LAN over TCP/IP.

- **AppleTalk**: AppleTalk is a protocol suite to network Macintosh computers. It consists of a comprehensive set of protocols that spans the seven layers of the OSI reference model. The AppleTalk protocol was designed to run over LocalTalk, which is the Apple LAN physical topology. It is also designed to run over major LAN types, notably Ethernet and Token Ring.

- **Hypertext Transfer Protocol (HTTP)**: HTTP governs how files such as text, graphics, sound, and video are exchanged on the World Wide Web. The Internet Engineering Task Force (IETF) developed the standards for HTTP.

- **File Transfer Protocol (FTP)**: FTP provides services for transferring files. FTP allows multiple simultaneous connections to remote file systems.

- *Secure Shell (SSH)*: SSH is used to securely connect to a remote computer.

- **Telnet**: Telnet is an application used to connect to a remote computer, but it lacks security features.

- *Post Office Protocol (POP)*: POP is used to download email from a remote mail server.

- **Internet Message Access Protocol (IMAP)**: IMAP is also used to download email from a remote mail server.

- *Simple Mail Transfer Protocol (SMTP)*: SMTP is used to send email to a remote email server.

Consider the following when selecting protocols:

- The TCP/IP suite of protocols is required for every device to connect to the Internet. This makes it a preferred protocol for networking.

- NetBEUI is a small, fast protocol that is useful in low-security networks. NetBEUI performs well in a small network that is not connected to the Internet. It is easy to install and requires no configuration. However, NetBEUI can cause unnecessary traffic on a large network, so it is not a good choice if the network will grow.

- IPX/SPX is a protocol that belongs to older versions of Novell Netware. Because of the growth of the Internet, newer versions of Novell Netware use TCP/IP instead of IPX/SPX.

- Apple Macintosh networks have abandoned the AppleTalk protocol for the TCP/IP suite of protocols to ensure connectivity with other TCP/IP networks, most notably the Internet.

When the TCP/IP protocol stack is enabled, other protocols become available on specific ports, as shown in Table 15-1.

Table 15-1   Protocol Ports

Protocol	Port	Description
HTTP	Port 80	Transports web pages over a TCP/IP network
HTTPS	Port 443 network	Securely transports web pages over a TCP/IP
SMTP	Port 25	Sends email over a TCP/IP network
Telnet/SSH	Ports 23/22	Provides connections to computers over a TCP/IP network
FTP	Port 20 or 21	Transports files over a TCP/IP network
DNS	Port 53	Translates URLs to IP addresses
DHCP	Ports 67 and 68	Automates the assignment of IP addresses on a network
TFTP	Port 69	Used to transfer files over a network

Network software applications use these protocols and ports to perform functions over the Internet or over a network.

Some network software applications include services to host a web page, send email, and transfer files. These services may be provided by a single server or by several servers. Clients use well-known ports for each service. Client requests can be identified by using a specific destination port.

VoIP is a popular example of a network software application. VoIP is a method to carry telephone calls over the data networks and Internet. VoIP converts the analog signals of our voices into digital information that is transported in IP packets. VoIP can also use an existing IP network to provide access to the public switched telephone network (PSTN).

There are several ways to use VoIP:

- **IP phone**: A device that connects to an IP network using an RJ-45 Ethernet connector or a wireless connection

- **Analog Telephone Adapter (ATA)**: A device that connects standard analog devices, such as telephones, fax machines, or answering machines, to an IP network

- **IP phone software**: An application that connects by using a microphone, speakers, and a sound card to emulate the IP phone functionality

Worksheet 15.2.2: Protocols

In this worksheet, you identify the proper protocol to use in different network configurations. Refer to the worksheet in *IT Essentials: PC Hardware and Software Lab Manual, Fourth Edition*. You may complete this worksheet now or wait until the end of the chapter.

Determine the Components for the Customer's Network

The choice of network topology determines the type of devices, cables, and network interfaces that will be required to construct the network. In addition, an outside connection to an Internet service provider (ISP) must be set up. One of the steps in building a network is to determine suitable network components that work with user devices and the network cabling.

After completing this section, you will meet these objectives:

- Select cable types.
- Select the ISP connection type.
- Select network cards.
- Select the network device.

Select Cable Types

Select the cable type that is the most beneficial and cost effective for the users and services that will connect to the network.

The size of the network determines the type of network cable that will be used. Most networks today are wired using one or more types of twisted-pair copper cable:

- Category 5 (Cat5)
- Category 5e (Cat5e)

- Category 6 (Cat6)

- Category 6a (Cat6a)

Cat5 and Cat5e cables look the same, but Cat5e cable is manufactured with a higher standard to allow for higher data transfer rates. Cat6 cable is constructed with even higher standards than Cat5e. Cat6 cable may have a center divider to separate the pairs inside the cable.

The most common type of cable used in a network is Cat5e. Cat5e cable is an enhanced version of Cat 5 that adds specifications for far-end crosstalk. It was formally defined in 2001 in the TIA/EIA-568-B standard, which no longer recognizes the original Cat5. Cat5e is suitable for Fast Ethernet up to 330 feet (100 m).

Some businesses and homes have installed Cat6 cable so that they are prepared for additional bandwidth requirements in the future. Applications such as video, videoconferencing, and gaming use a large amount of bandwidth. Cat6 features more stringent specifications for crosstalk and system noise. The cable standard is suitable for 10BASE-T/100BASE-TX and 1000BASE-T (Gigabit Ethernet) connections. It provides performance of up to 250 MHz.

The most recent type of twisted-pair cable available is Cat6a. Cat6a cable carries Ethernet signals at a rate of 10 Gbps. The abbreviation for 10 Gigabit Ethernet over twisted-pair cable is 10GBASE-T, as defined in the IEEE 802.3an-2006 standard. Customers who need high-bandwidth networks can benefit from installing cable that can support Gigabit Ethernet or 10 Gigabit Ethernet.

New or renovated office buildings often have some type of UTP cabling that connects every office to a central point called the main distribution facility (MDF). The distance limitation of UTP cabling used for data is 330 feet (100 m). Network devices that are farther away than this distance limitation need a repeater or hub to extend the connection to the MDF.

When designing a network and selecting cable types, you also need to consider cost, security, future needs, and wireless options.

Wireless

A wireless solution may be possible in places where cables cannot be installed. Consider an older, historic building where local building codes do not permit structural modifications. In this case, installing cable is not possible and therefore a wireless connection is the only solution.

Cost

When designing a network, cost is a consideration. Installing cables is expensive, but after a one-time expense, a wired network normally is inexpensive to maintain. Most of the devices on a wired network cost much less than the devices on a wireless network.

Security

A wired network usually is more secure than a wireless network. The cables in a wired network usually are installed in walls and ceilings and therefore are not easily accessible. Wireless is easier to eavesdrop. The signals are available to anyone who has a receiver. Making a wireless network as secure as a wired network requires the use of encryption.

Design for the Future

Many organizations install the highest-grade cable available to ensure that their networks can handle the network speeds that will be available in the future. These organizations want to avoid expensive reinstallation of cable later. You and your customer must decide if the cost of installing a higher grade of cable is necessary.

Select the ISP Connection Type

The ISP that you choose can have a noticeable effect on network service. Some private resellers that connect to a phone company may sell more connections than allowed, which slows the overall speed of the service to customers.

An Internet connection has three main considerations:

- Speed
- Reliability
- Availability

This section describes ISP connection types and the advantages and disadvantages of each.

Plain Old Telephone Service

A *plain old telephone service (POTS)* connection is extremely slow, but it is available wherever there is a telephone. The modem uses the telephone line to transmit and receive data.

Integrated Services Digital Network

Integrated Services Digital Network (ISDN) offers faster connection times and has faster speeds than dialup. It also allows multiple devices to share a single telephone line. ISDN is very reliable because it uses POTS lines. ISDN is available in most places where the telephone company supports digital signaling. Newer and better broadband technologies are rapidly replacing ISDN.

Digital Subscriber Line

Digital subscriber line (DSL), like ISDN, allows multiple devices to share a single telephone line. DSL speeds generally are faster than ISDN. DSL allows the use of high-bandwidth applications and lets multiple users share the same connection to the Internet. In most cases, the copper wires already in your home or business can carry the signals needed for DSL communication.

DSL technology has some limitations. DSL service is not available everywhere. It works better and faster the closer the installation is to the telephone provider's central office (CO). Also, DSL is much faster when receiving data over the Internet than when sending it. In some cases, the lines that are in place to carry telephone signals do not technically qualify to carry DSL signals.

Cable

Cable Internet connection does not use telephone lines. Cable uses coaxial cable lines originally designed to carry cable television. Like DSL, cable offers high speeds and an "always-on" connection, which means that even when the connection is not in use, the connection to the Internet is still available. Many cable companies offer telephone service as well.

Because cable television reaches many homes, it is an alternative for people unable to receive DSL service. Theoretically, the bandwidth of cable is higher than DSL, but it can be affected by limitations of the cable provider. Most homes that have cable television have the option to install high-speed Internet service.

Satellite

For people who live in rural areas, broadband satellite Internet connections provide a high-speed connection that is always on. A satellite dish is used to transmit and receive signals to and from a satellite that relays these signals back to a service provider.

The cost of installation and the monthly service fees are much higher than those for DSL and cable subscribers. Heavy storm conditions can degrade the quality of the connection between the user and the satellite, or between the satellite and the provider, slowing down or even disconnecting the connection. In most cases, the service provider provides a dialup connection as a backup.

Cellular

Many types of wireless Internet services are available. The same companies that offer cellular service may offer Internet service. PCMCIA and PCI cards are used to connect a computer to the Internet. The service is not available in all areas.

Service providers may offer wireless Internet service using microwave technology in limited areas. Signals are transmitted directly to an antenna on the roof of the house or building.

Research the connection types that the ISPs offer before selecting an ISP. Check the services available in your area. Compare connection speeds, reliability, and cost before committing to a service agreement.

Wireless

Many types of wireless Internet service are available. The same companies that offer cellular service may offer Internet service. PCMCIA and PCI cards are used to connect a computer to the Internet. This service is not available in all areas.

Service providers may offer wireless Internet service using microwave technology in limited areas. Signals are transmitted directly to an antenna on the roof of the house or building.

Compare ISP Connection Types

Research the connection types that the ISPs offer before selecting an ISP. Check the services available in your area. Compare connection speeds, reliability, and cost before committing to a service agreement.

Table 15-2 describes some of the protocol details.

Table 15-2   Protocol Details

Type	Advantages	Disadvantages	Speed
POTS	Very common	Very slow speeds Cannot receive phone calls while connected	Maximum of 56 kbps
ISDN	Higher speeds than POTS	Still much slower than other broadband technologies	BRI: up to 128 kbps PRI: up to 2.048 Mbps
DSL	Low cost	Must be close to the carrier	256 kbps to 24 Mbps
Cable	Very high download speed	Slow upload speeds	384 kbps to 24 Mbps
Satellite	Available when DSL and cable are not	Significant time lag More expensive than other broadband technologies	9 kbps to 24 Mbps

continues

Table 15-2   Protocol Details   *continued*

Type	Advantages	Disadvantages	Speed
Wireless	Scalable to customer needs	Very expensive	Up to 450 Mbps
		Limited market availability	

Worksheet 15.3.2: ISP Connection Types

In this worksheet, you identify the best ISP based on a given scenario. Refer to the worksheet in *IT Essentials: PC Hardware and Software Lab Manual, Fourth Edition*. You may complete this worksheet now or wait until the end of the chapter.

Select Network Cards

Every device on a network requires a network interface. Many types of network interfaces exist:

- Most network interfaces for desktop computers are either integrated into the motherboard or are an expansion card that fits into an expansion slot.

- Most laptop network interfaces are either integrated into the motherboard or fit into a PCI Card or PCI Express Bus expansion slot.

- USB network adapters plug into any available USB port and can be used with both desktops and laptops.

Before purchasing a NIC, you should research the speed, form factor, and capabilities that the card offers. Check the speed and capabilities of the hub or switch that will be connected to the computer.

Ethernet NICs may be backward-compatible:

- If you have a 10/100-Mbps NIC and a hub that is only 10 Mbps, the NIC operates at 10 Mbps.

- If you have a 10/100/1000-Mbps NIC and a switch that operates at only 100 Mbps, the NIC operates at 100 Mbps.

However, if you have a Gigabit Ethernet switch, you will most likely need to purchase a Gigabit Ethernet NIC to match speeds. If plans exist to upgrade the network to Gigabit Ethernet in the future, be sure to purchase NICs that can support the speed. Costs can vary greatly, so select NICs that match your customer's needs.

Wireless NICs are available in many formats with many capabilities. You should select wireless NICs based on the type of wireless network that is installed, as described in the following examples:

- 802.11b NICs can be used on 802.11g networks.

- 802.11b and 802.11g NICs can be used on 802.11n networks.

- 802.11a can be used only on a network that supports 802.11a.

Choose wireless cards that match your customer's needs. You should know what wireless equipment is in use and what will be installed on the network to ensure compatibility and usability. Figure 15-2 shows four types of wireless network interfaces.

Figure 15-2   Wireless Network Interfaces

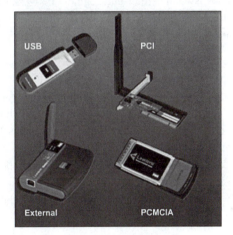

Select the Network Device

Several types of devices are available to connect components on a network, including hubs, switches, routers, and ISP equipment. Select network devices to meet your customer's needs.

Hubs

A hub is used to share data between multiple devices on a section of the network. The hub may connect to another networking device such as a switch or router that connects to other sections of the network. The maximum speed of the network is determined by the speed of the hub.

Hubs are used less often today because of the effectiveness and low cost of switches. Hubs do not segment network traffic, so they decrease the amount of available bandwidth to any device. In addition, because a hub cannot filter data, a lot of unnecessary traffic constantly moves between all the devices connected to it.

One advantage of a hub is that it regenerates the data that passes through it. This means that a hub can also function as a repeater. A hub can extend the reach of a network because rebuilding the signal pulses overcomes the effects of distance.

Switches

In modern networks, switches have replaced hubs as the central point of connectivity. As with a hub, the speed of the switch determines the maximum speed of the network. However, switches filter and segment network traffic by sending data only to the device to which it is supposed to be sent. This provides higher dedicated bandwidth to each device on the network.

Switches maintain a switching table. The switching table contains a list of all MAC addresses on the network and a list of which switch port can be used to reach a device with a given MAC address. The switching table records MAC addresses by inspecting the source MAC address of every incoming frame, as well as the port on which the frame arrives. The switch then creates a switching table that maps MAC addresses to outgoing ports. When a frame arrives that is destined for a particular MAC address, the switch uses the switching table to determine which port to use to reach the MAC address. The frame is forwarded from the port to the destination. When frames are sent from only one port to the destination, other ports are unaffected, and bandwidth on the entire network is unaffected.

Routers

Routers connect networks. On a corporate network, one router port connects to the WAN connection, and the other ports connect to the corporate LAN. The router becomes the gateway, or path to the outside, for the LAN. In a home network, the router connects the computers and network devices in the home to the Internet. In this case, the router is a home gateway. The wireless router, shown in Figure 15-3, serves as a firewall and provides wireless connectivity. When the home router provides multiple services, it may be called a multifunction device.

Figure 15-3   Home Networking Devices

ISP Equipment

When subscribing to an ISP, you should find out what type of equipment is available so that you can select the most appropriate device. Many ISPs offer a discount on equipment that is purchased at the time of installation.

Some ISPs may rent equipment on a month-to-month basis. This may be more attractive because the ISP supports the equipment if it fails or if the technology needs to be changed or upgraded. Home users may select to purchase equipment from the ISP because eventually the initial cost of the equipment will be less than the cost of renting the equipment.

Implement the Customer's Network

Installing and implementing a network can be a complicated task. Even a small home network installation can become difficult and time consuming. However, careful planning helps ensure an easier and faster installation.

Here is an installation checklist:

❑ All parts are in.

❑ Installation is scheduled.

❑ Backups are available.

❑ Access to needed passwords.

❑ Extra supplies are handy.

❑ Install components.

❑ Test components.

During the installation, the existing network may experience some downtime. For example, building modifications and network cable installation can cause disruption. The project is not complete until all devices have been installed, configured, and tested.

After completing this section, you will meet these objectives:

- Install and test the customer's network.

- Configure the customer's Internet and network resources.

Install and Test the Customer's Network

After you have determined the location of all network devices, you are ready to install the network cables. In some new or newly renovated buildings, network cables may have been installed during construction to avoid the problem of installing cables in finished walls later. If there is no preinstalled cable, you have to install it or have it installed.

If you plan to install the cable yourself, you need time to prepare. All the necessary materials should be available at the site at the time of installation, as well as the cable layout plan.

These steps outline the process of physically creating a network:

How To

Step 1. To install the cable in ceilings and behind walls, you perform a cable pull. One person pulls the cable, and the other feeds the cable through the walls. Be sure to label the ends of every cable. Follow a labeling scheme that is already in place, or follow the guidelines outlined in TIA/EIA 606-A.

Step 2. After the cables have been terminated on both ends, test them to make sure there are no shorts or interference.

Step 3. Make sure that network interfaces are properly installed in the desktops, laptops, and network printers. After the network interfaces have been installed, configure the client software and the IP address information on all the devices.

Step 4. Install switches and routers in a secured, centralized location. All the LAN connections terminate in this area. In a home network, you may need to install these devices in separate locations, or you may have only one device.

Step 5. Install an Ethernet patch cable from the wall connection to each network device. Check to see if you have a link light on all network interfaces. In a home network, make sure that each network device port that connects to a device is lit.

Step 6. When all devices are connected and all link lights are functioning, you should test the network for connectivity. Use the **ipconfig /all** command to view the IP configuration on each workstation. Use the **ping** command to test basic connectivity. You should be able to ping other computers on the network, including the default gateway and remote computers. After you have confirmed basic connectivity, you must configure and test network applications such as email and an Internet browser.

Configure the Customer's Internet and Network Resources

After the network has been set up and tested, you should configure a web browser, such as Microsoft Internet Explorer. You can configure browser settings and perform maintenance tasks in the Internet Options dialog box, as shown in Figure 15-4.

Internet Explorer includes settings for temporary Internet files and the default browser. The customer may also need you to configure network resources such as file and printer sharing. The next sections describe these topics.

Figure 15-4   Internet Explorer Options

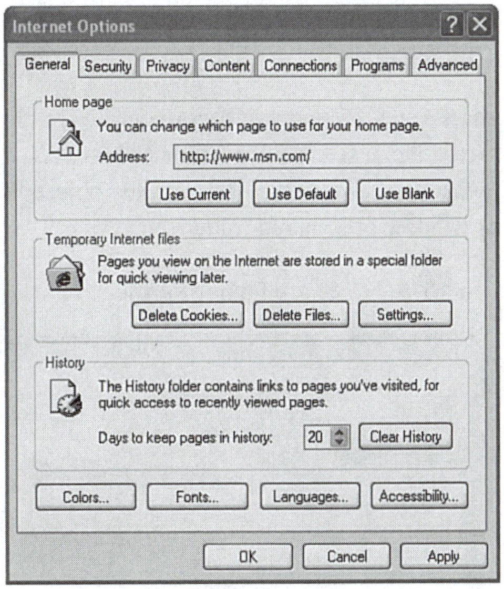

Temporary Internet Files

When an operating system such as Windows XP has been installed, Internet Explorer is also installed by default. With Internet Explorer, every time you visit a website, many files are downloaded to your computer in the Temporary Internet Files folder. Most of these files are image files that represent banners and other components of the website.

Temporary Internet files are stored on your computer so that the browser can load content faster the next time you visit a website you have been to before. Depending on the number of websites you visit, the Temporary Internet Files folder can fill up quickly. Although this may not be an urgent problem, you should delete the files occasionally. This is especially important after you have done online banking or have entered other personal information into the web browser.

Default Browser

You can confirm which browser Windows uses by default. In Windows XP, choose **Start > Run**, enter a website address, and click **OK**.

In Windows Vista, choose **Start > Start Search**, enter a website address, and click **OK**. The website opens in the browser that is currently set as the default.

If you want Internet Explorer to be your default browser, start by opening Internet Explorer. On the toolbar, choose **Tools > Internet Options**. On the Programs tab, you can check to see if Internet Explorer is your default browser, and select it if is not.

File Sharing

Users can share resources over the network. You can share a single file, specific folders, or an entire drive.

To share a file, first copy it to a folder. Right-click the folder and select **Sharing and Security**. Next, select **Share This Folder**. You can identify who has access to the folder and what permissions they have on the objects in the folder. Figure 15-5 shows the permissions window of a shared folder.

Figure 15-5   Share Folder Permissions

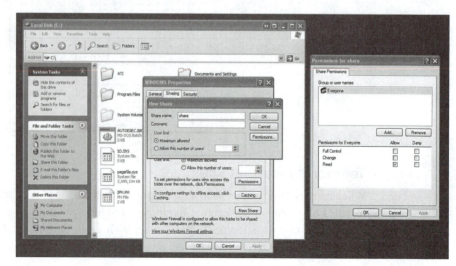

Permissions define the type of access a user has to a file or folder:

- **Read**: Allows the user to view the file and subfolder names, navigate to subfolders, view data in files, and run program files.

- **Change**: Has the same permissions as the Read permission and also allows the user to add files and subfolders, change the data in files, and delete subfolders and files.

- **Full Control**: Has the same permissions as Change and Read. If the file or folder is in an NTFS partition, Full Control allows you to change permissions on the file or folder and take ownership of the file or folder.

Windows XP Professional and Windows Vista Business are limited to a maximum of ten simultaneous file-sharing connections.

Printer Sharing

To share a printer in Windows XP, choose **Start > Control Panel > Printers and Faxes**. Right-click the printer icon and select **Sharing**. Click **Share This Printer** and then click **OK**. The printer is now available for other computers to access.

To access a printer shared by another computer in Windows XP, choose **Start > Control Panel > Printers and Faxes**. Click **File > Add Printer**. Use the Add Printers Wizard to find and install the shared network printer.

To share a printer in Windows Vista, choose **Start > Control Panel > Printers**. From the list of available printers, right-click the printer icon and choose **Sharing > Change Sharing Options > Continue**. Click **Share This Printer** and then click **OK**. The printer is now available for other computers to access.

To access a printer shared by another computer in Windows Vista, choose **Start > Control Panel > Printers**. Click **Add a Printer**. Use the Add Printers Wizard to find and install the shared network printer.

Lab 15.4.2: Configure Browser Settings in Windows XP

In this lab, you configure an Internet browser in Windows XP. Refer to the lab in *IT Essentials: PC Hardware and Software Lab Manual, Fourth Edition*. You may perform this lab now or wait until the end of the chapter.

Optional Lab 15.4.2: Configure Browser Settings in Windows Vista

In this lab, you configure an Internet browser in Windows Vista. Refer to the lab in *IT Essentials: PC Hardware and Software Lab Manual, Fourth Edition*. You may perform this lab now or wait until the end of the chapter.

Lab 15.4.2: Share a Folder, Share a Printer, and Set Share Permissions in Windows XP

In this lab, you share a folder, share a printer, and set permissions. Refer to the lab in *IT Essentials: PC Hardware and Software Lab Manual, Fourth Edition*. You may perform this lab now or wait until the end of the chapter.

Optional Lab 15.4.2: Share a Folder, Share a Printer, and Set Share Permissions in Windows Vista

In this lab, you share a folder, share a printer, and set share permissions in Windows Vista. Refer to the lab in *IT Essentials: PC Hardware and Software Lab Manual, Fourth Edition*. You may perform this lab now or wait until the end of the chapter.

Upgrade the Customer's Network

You must be able to upgrade, install, and configure components when a customer asks for increased speed or new functionality to be added to a network. Devices such as wireless access points, wireless network cards, and faster network equipment and cable can be integrated into a network to allow the customer to communicate wirelessly or more quickly.

If your customer is adding computers or wireless functionality, you should be able to recommend equipment based on their needs. The equipment that you suggest must work with the existing equipment and cabling, or the existing infrastructure must be upgraded.

Network upgrades include the following:

- Cable type
- Type of NIC
- Additional functionality (wireless, print server, and so on)

After completing this section, you will meet these objectives:

- Install and configure a wireless NIC.
- Install and configure wireless routers.
- Test the connection.

Install and Configure a Wireless NIC

To connect to a wireless network, your computer must have a wireless network interface. A wireless network interface is used to communicate with other wireless devices, such as computers, printers, and wireless access points.

Before purchasing a wireless adapter, you should make sure that it is compatible with other wireless equipment that is already installed on the network. Also, verify that the wireless adapter is the correct form factor to fit in a desktop or laptop. A wireless USB adapter can be used with any desktop or laptop computer that has an open USB port.

To install a wireless NIC on a desktop computer, you must remove the case cover. Install the wireless NIC into an available PCI slot or PCI Express slot. Some wireless NICs have an antenna connected to the back of the card. Some antennas are attached with a cable so that they can be moved around or away from objects that may cause a poor connection.

After the wireless adapter is installed, you must perform additional configuration steps. These include configuring device drivers and entering network address information. When this is complete, the computer should be able to detect and connect to the wireless LAN.

Wireless network adapters may use a wizard to connect to the wireless network. In this case, you would insert the CD-ROM that comes with the adapter and follow the directions to get connected.

Lab 15.5.1: Install a Wireless NIC in Windows XP

In this lab, you install a wireless NIC in Windows XP. Refer to the lab in *IT Essentials: PC Hardware and Software Lab Manual, Fourth Edition*. You may perform this lab now or wait until the end of the chapter.

Optional Lab 15.5.1: Install a Wireless NIC in Windows Vista

In this lab, you install a wireless NIC in Windows Vista. Refer to the lab in *IT Essentials: PC Hardware and Software Lab Manual, Fourth Edition*. You may perform this lab now or wait until the end of the chapter.

Packet Tracer Activity 15.5.1: Install a Wireless NIC

In this Packet Tracer activity, you install a wireless NIC and configure the PC to join a wireless network using Packet Tracer. Refer to the CD in this book to find the activity. You may perform this activity now or wait until the end of the chapter.

Install and Configure a Wireless Router

When installing a wireless network, you have to decide where you want to put access points, and then configure them. The following steps describe the installation of an access point:

How To 🔍

Step 1.   Use a floor plan to find locations for access points that allow maximum coverage. The best place for a wireless access point is at the center of the area you are covering, with a line of sight between the wireless devices and the access point.

Step 2.   Connect the access point to the existing network. On the back of the router are five ports. Connect a DSL or cable modem to the port labeled "Internet." The device's switching logic forwards all the packets through this port when communication exists to and from the Internet and other connected computers. Connect one computer to any of the remaining ports to access the configuration web pages.

Step 3.   Turn on the broadband modem and plug the power cord into the router. When the modem finishes establishing a connection to the ISP, the router automatically communicates with the modem to receive network information from the ISP that is necessary to gain access to the Internet: IP address, subnet mask, and DNS server addresses.

Step 4.   When the router has established communication with the modem, you must configure the router to communicate with the devices on the network. Turn on the computer that is connected to the router. Open a web browser. In the Address field, enter the web interface IP address of the router, for example 192.168.1.1. This is the default address for router configuration and management.

Step 5.   A security window prompts you for authentication to access the router configuration screens. Leave the User Name field empty. Enter **admin** as the default password. When you are logged in, the first setup screen appears.

Step 6.   Continue with the setup. The setup screen has tabs that have subtabs. You must click **Save Settings** at the bottom of each screen after making any changes.

When you use the configuration screens of the 300N router, you can click the Help tab to see additional information about a tab. For information beyond what is shown on the Help screen, consult the user manual.

After establishing the connection, there are several configurations that can help secure and increase the speed of a wireless network. Some of these configurations are listed here:

- 802.11 protocol selection
- Static IP address configuration
- Service set identifier (SSID) setting
- Firmware update

802.11 Protocol Selection

The 802.11 protocol can provide increased throughput based on the wireless network environment. If all wireless devices connect with the same 802.11 standard, maximum speeds can be obtained for that standard. If the access point is configured to accept only one 802.11 standard, devices that do not use that standard will not be able to connect to the access point.

A mixed-mode wireless network environment can include 802.11a, 802.11b, 802.11g, and 802.11n. This environment provides easy access for legacy devices that need a wireless connection.

Static IP Address Configuration

Static IP address assignments give better protection against network attacks than DHCP. For example, static IP address assignments allow firewalls to be configured to permit specific traffic or connections between specific devices. There are disadvantages to configuring static IP addresses on large networks. It is more time consuming to assign static IP addresses and more difficult to manage than using DHCP assignments.

SSID Setting

The SSID is the name of the wireless network. The SSID broadcast allows other devices to automatically discover the name of the wireless network. When the SSID broadcast is disabled, you must manually enter the SSID on wireless devices. This provides protection from automatic discovery of the wireless network name.

Firmware Update

Firmware updates can improve performance, fix bugs, or update security features. When updating the firmware, it is vital to follow the manufacturer's instructions. Firmware updates and instructions can be downloaded from the manufacturer's website. Always back up the wireless router configuration files and current firmware before updating.

Note

The access point can stop functioning if the update fails to complete.

Lab 15.5.2: Configure Wireless Router

In this lab, you install a wireless router. Refer to the lab in *IT Essentials: PC Hardware and Software Lab Manual, Fourth Edition*. You may perform this lab now or wait until the end of the chapter.

Test the Connection

It might be difficult to know if your wireless connection is working properly, even when Windows indicates that you are connected. You may be connected to a wireless access point or home gateway, but you may not be connected to the Internet. The easiest way to test for an Internet connection is to open a web browser and see if the Internet is available. To troubleshoot a wireless connection, you can use the Windows GUI or CLI.

Network Connections

To verify a wireless connection using the Windows XP GUI, choose **Start > Control Panel > Network Connections**, as shown in Figure 15-6. Double-click the wireless network connection to display the status.

Figure 15-6   Network Connections

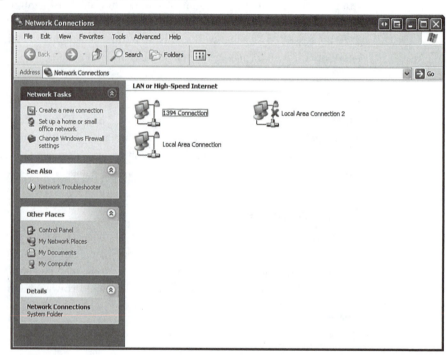

The Wireless Network Connection Status screen, shown in Figure 15-7, displays the number of packets that have been sent and received. The packets are the communication between the computer and the network device. The window shows whether the computer is connected, along with the connection's speed and duration.

To display the Address Type, as shown in Figure 15-8, choose the **Support** tab on the Wireless Network Connection Status screen. The Connection Status information includes either a static address, which is assigned manually, or a dynamic address, which is assigned by a DHCP server. The subnet mask and default gateway are also listed. To access the MAC address and other information about the IP address, click **Details**. If the connection is not functioning correctly, click **Repair** to reset the connection information and attempt to establish a new connection.

Figure 15-7   Wireless Network Connection Status

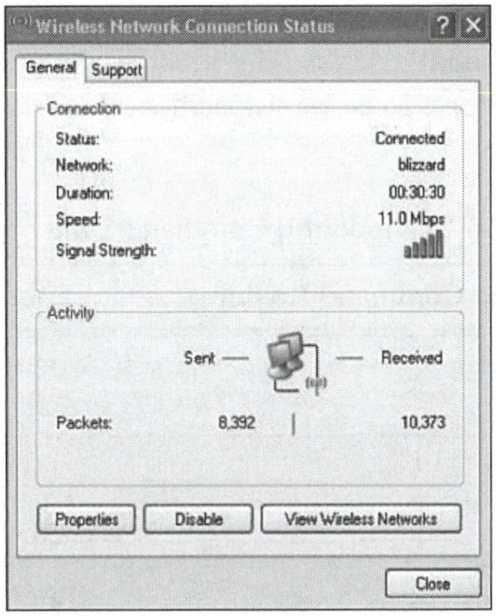

Figure 15-8   Address Type

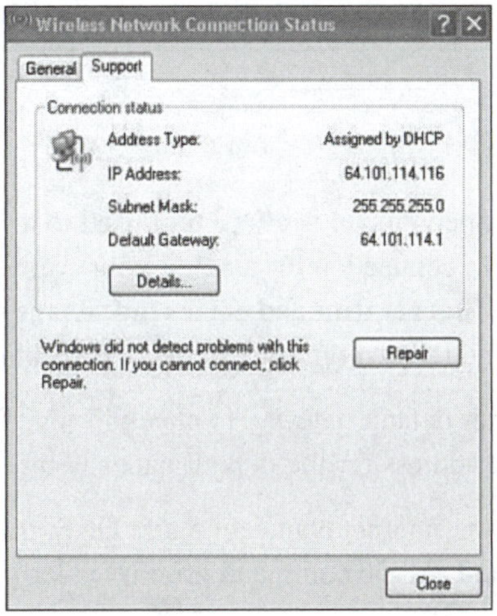

To verify a wireless connection using the Windows Vista GUI, select **Start > Control Panel > Network and Sharing Center > Manage Network Connections**. Double-click the wireless network connection to display the status.

Click the **Details** button on the Wireless Network Connection Status screen. The Connection Status information includes either a static address, which is assigned manually, or a dynamic address, which is assigned by a DHCP server. The subnet mask, default gateway, MAC address, and other information about the IP address are also listed. If the connection is not functioning correctly, click **Diagnose** to reset the connection information, and attempt to establish a new connection.

ipconfig

The **ipconfig** command is a command-line tool that is used to verify that the connection has a valid IP address. The window displays basic IP address information for network connections. To perform specific tasks, add switches to the **ipconfig** command, as shown in Table 15-3.

Table 15-3   ipconfig Command Switches

ipconfig Command Switch	Description
/all	Displays the full configuration of all network adapters
/release	Releases the IP address of a network adapter
/renew	Renews the IP address of a network adapter
/flushdns	Empties the cache that stores DNS information
/registerdns	Refreshes DHCP leases and reregisters the adapter with DNS
/displaydns	Shows DNS information in the cache

ping

The **ping** command is a CLI tool used to test connectivity between devices. You can test your own connection by pinging your computer. To test your computer, ping your NIC. Choose **Start > Run** and enter **cmd**. At the command prompt, enter **ping localhost**. This command tells you if your adapter is working properly.

Ping your default gateway to check if your WAN connection is working properly. You can find the address for the default gateway by using the **ipconfig** command.

To test the Internet connection and DNS, ping a popular website. Choose **Start > Run** and enter **cmd**. At the command prompt, enter **ping** *destination name*.

The response of the **ping** command displays the domain's IP address resolution. The response shows replies from the ping or shows that the request timed out because a problem occurred.

tracert

The **tracert** command is a CLI tool that traces the route that packets take from your computer to a destination address. Choose **Start > Run** and enter **cmd**. At the command prompt, enter **tracert**.

The first listing in the window for the tracert result is the default gateway. Each listing after that is the router that packets are traveling through to reach the destination. Tracert shows you where packets are stopping, indicating where the problem is occurring. If listings show problems after the default gateway, this might mean that the problems are with the ISP, the Internet, or the destination server.

net

The **net** command is used to manage network computers, servers, and resources like drives and printers. **net** commands use the NetBIOS protocol in Windows. These commands are used to start, stop, and configure networking services.

nslookup

nslookup is a CLI tool for testing and troubleshooting DNS servers. The nslookup command queries the DNS server to discover IP addresses or hostnames.

In Windows XP, select **Start > Run > cmd**. At the command prompt, enter **nslookup** *hostname*. **nslookup** returns the IP address for the hostname entered. A reverse **nslookup** command, **nslookup** *IP_address*, returns the corresponding hostname for the IP address entered.

Lab 15.5.3: Test the Wireless NIC in Windows XP

In this lab, you test the connection of the wireless NIC in Windows XP. Refer to the lab in *IT Essentials: PC Hardware and Software Lab Manual, Fourth Edition.* You may perform this lab now or wait until the end of the chapter.

Optional Lab 15.5.3: Test the Wireless NIC in Windows Vista

In this lab, you test the connection of the wireless NIC in Windows Vista. Refer to the lab in *IT Essentials: PC Hardware and Software Lab Manual, Fourth Edition.* You may perform this lab now or wait until the end of the chapter.

Packet Tracer Activity 15.5.3: Test a Wireless Connection

In this Packet Tracer activity you will install a wireless NIC, configure the PC to join a wireless network, and test the wireless connection using Packet Tracer. Refer to the CD in this book to find the activity. You may perform this activity now or wait until the end of the chapter.

Describe the Installation, Configuration, and Management of a Simple Mail Server

An email system uses email client software on the users' devices, and email server software on one or more email servers. This section describes the protocols and servers that enable email communication.

Clients read email from the email server using one of two protocols:

- POP

- IMAP

Clients send email to an email server, and email servers forward email to each other, using SMTP.

You need to know how to configure a client computer to accept the correct incoming mail format, and also understand the process for setting up a mail server. You can configure the email client software using connection wizards, such as the one shown in Figure 15-9.

Figure 15-9   Email Protocols in Internet Connection Wizard

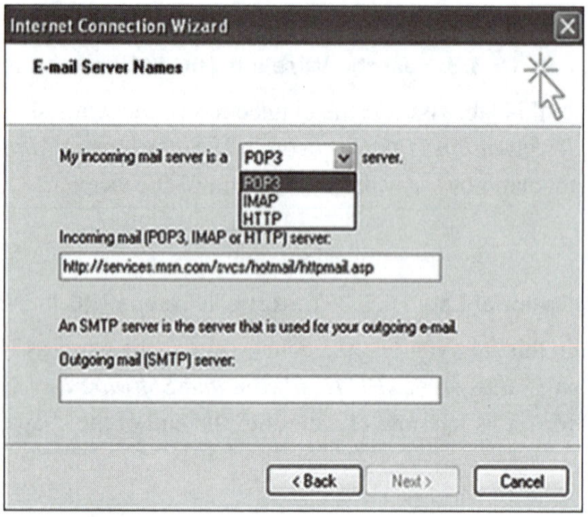

Table 15-4 lists the advantages and disadvantages of each email protocol.

Table 15-4   Email Protocol Comparison

Protocol	Advantages	Disadvantages	Port	Sends Mail?	Retrieves Mail?
SMTP	Delivers email from one server to another	Client upload only	25	Yes	No
	Can send mail directly to the destination				
POP	Simple				
	Supports intermittent connections	Download only Cannot manage the mail on the server	110	No	Yes
IMAP	Simple	Requires more disk space and CPU resources			
	More features than POP				
	Stores mail on the server				
	Faster than POP				
	Allows simultaneous access by multiple clients		143	No	Yes

SMTP

SMTP sends email from an email client to an email server, or from one email server to another. SMTP has these characteristics:

- Simple, text-based protocol
- Sent over TCP using port 25
- Must be implemented to send email
- Message is sent after recipients are identified and verified

POP

An email client uses POP to download email from an email server. The most recent version of POP is POP3. POP3 usually uses port 110.

POP3 supports end users who have intermittent connections, such as dialup. A POP3 user can connect to the server, download email from the server, delete the email, and then disconnect.

IMAP

IMAP is similar to POP3, but it has additional features. Like POP3, IMAP allows you to download email from an email server using an email client. The difference is that IMAP allows the user to organize email on the network email server. IMAP is faster than POP3 and requires more disk space on the server and more CPU resources. The most recent version of IMAP is IMAP4. IMAP4 is often used in large networks such as a university campus. IMAP usually uses port 143.

Email Server

An email server is a computer that can send and receive email on behalf of email clients. Common email servers include the following:

- Microsoft Exchange
- Sendmail
- Eudora Internet Mail Server (EIMS)

Note

Eudora is now known as Thunderbird. In 2006, Qualcomm stopped development of the commercial version and sponsored the creation of a new, open source version based on Mozilla Thunderbird, code-named Penelope.

As shown in Figure 15-10, wizards and tools often are available to guide you in setting up an email server. To install and set up an email server, such as Microsoft Exchange, you must first make sure that the network has all the proper qualifications in place and that it is properly configured. Be prepared with the proper equipment and information:

- Fully functional and reliable DNS deployment
- Active Directory domain
- At least one global catalog
- Windows 2000 or higher native domain functionality
- Exchange server software

- Windows Server 2003 or 2008 support tools

- Schema master server

- High-speed Internet connection

Figure 15-10   Exchange Server Installation Screen

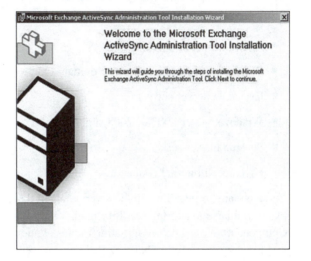

Active Directory servers, global catalog servers, and Domain Name System (DNS) servers must all be in place and functioning before Exchange can be installed and work properly. An Active Directory server is a computer that hosts a database that allows centralized administration over an enterprise network. A global catalog server is a centralized repository that contains information about every domain in an enterprise network.

The Active Directory database is organized in a pattern called a schema. One server running Windows Server 2003 is designated as the schema master. This is the only server that can change how the Active Directory user database is organized. When the network administrator needs to modify the Active Directory structure, the change is made on the schema master. Active Directory then automatically copies the update to the rest of the authentication servers.

Email Server Installation

You should test the environment before you install Exchange. To prevent the installation from affecting the daily operation of your network, set up the services required, and install

Exchange on a dedicated set of servers away from the main network. Keep the installation of Exchange separate from your production network until you are sure that it is functioning properly.

Before you install Exchange, be prepared with the proper equipment and information:

- Fully functional and reliable DNS deployment
- Active Directory domain
- At least one global catalog
- Windows 2000 or higher native domain functionality
- Exchange Server software
- Windows server 2003 or 2008 support tools
- Schema master server
- High-speed Internet connection

You are ready to install the mail server when all the qualifications of your network are in place. You have to add Internet Information Services (IIS) using the Add/Remove Windows Components Wizard before initiating the installation of the Exchange server. IIS is a server that has programs used to build and administer website services. After IIS has been installed, Exchange can be installed. Insert the installation CD-ROM and begin the New Exchange installation wizard.

The installation wizard takes you through a series of steps to verify that Exchange is ready to be installed. The wizard checks to make sure that IIS is installed, the domain servers are running properly, and the Windows support tools are installed. The setup program notifies you of any problems with the installation environment. Restart the setup program from the beginning after fixing any issues.

After Exchange is installed, the Microsoft Management Console plug-in for Exchange provides access to many settings in one convenient location. Be sure to install all updates so that the server will run properly. The Exchange System Manager, which is a console that controls the Exchange deployment, can be used to manage the server's options.

Use the Active Directory Users and Computer (ADUC) console to configure a user's mailbox. This is also known as making the user "mailbox enabled."

Open the ADUC console to create a new user. Fill out the username and password information according to the domain security policy. The Exchange server creates the user's mailbox when the user receives the first email.

Setting up Exchange takes careful planning, including ensuring that the servers, services, and technologies are in place and working correctly on the network. In some cases, during an installation, if a failure occurs, you may need to reinstall the operating system and start the Exchange installation from the beginning.

> **Note**
>
> Before planning an email server installation, consult with network professionals, experienced Windows networking experts, or experienced email technicians.

Describe Preventive Maintenance Procedures for Networks

Preventive maintenance is just as important for the network as it is for the computers on a network. You must check the condition of cables, network devices, servers, and computers to make sure that they are kept clean and are in good working order. You should develop a plan to perform scheduled maintenance and cleaning at regular intervals. This helps you prevent network downtime and equipment failures.

As part of a regularly scheduled maintenance program, inspect all cabling for breaks. Make sure that cables are labeled correctly and labels are not coming off. Replace any worn or unreadable labels. Check that cable supports are properly installed and that no attachment points are coming loose. Cabling can become damaged and worn. You should keep the cabling in good repair to maintain good network performance.

As a technician, you may notice if equipment is failing, damaged, or making unusual sounds. Inform the network administrator to prevent unnecessary network downtime.

Cables at workstations and printers should be checked carefully. Cables are often moved or kicked when they are under desks, and they can be bent. These conditions can result in loss of bandwidth or connectivity. You should also be proactive in the education of network users. Demonstrate to network users how to properly connect and disconnect cables, as well as how to move them if necessary.

Troubleshoot the Network

To begin troubleshooting a network problem, you should first try to locate the source of the problem. Check to see if a group of users or only one user has the problem. If the problem is with one user, begin troubleshooting the problem starting with that person's computer.

After completing this section, you will meet these objectives:

- Review the troubleshooting process.
- Identify common problems and solutions.
- Apply troubleshooting skills.

Review the Troubleshooting Process

Network problems can result from a combination of hardware, software, and connectivity issues. Computer technicians must be able to analyze the problem and determine the cause of the error to repair the network issue. This process is called troubleshooting.

Review the following troubleshooting process:

How To

Step 1.   Identify the problem.

Step 2.   Establish a theory or probably causes.

Step 3.   Determine an exact cause.

Step 4.   Implement a solution.

Step 5.   Verify solution and full system functionality.

Step 6.   Document findings.

Step 1: Identify the Problem

The first step in the troubleshooting process is to identify the problem.

Ask the customer open-ended questions about network errors. (The following list is *not* comprehensive.)

- When did the problem start?

- What problems are you experiencing?

- Is there anything else you can tell me about the problem?

- What other users are having the problem?

- What type of equipment is having the problem?

- What are the effects of the problem?

- Describe your work environment.

- When did you last back up your computer?

- What type of backup did you perform?

- What group are you a member of?

Ask the customer closed-ended questions about network errors. (The following list is *not* comprehensive.)

- Has any equipment changed?

- Have any peripherals been added?

- Have any other computers been added to the network?

- Have you rebooted the equipment?

Step 2: Establish a Theory of Probable Causes

After you talk to the customer, you should establish a theory of probable causes. These may include the following:

- Incorrect IP information

- Incorrect settings on the network equipment

- Examine the network equipment LEDs

- Is there activity on the wireless router?

- Incorrect wireless client configuration

- Disabled network connection

Step 3: Determine an Exact Cause

After you have established a theory of probable causes, determine an exact cause. Try the following solutions to network problems:

- Restart the network equipment.

- Examine the network equipment LEDs.

- Renew the IP address.

- Flush DNS.

- Roll back a driver.

- Return to the previous saved restore point.

- Reconnect all the network cables.

- Verify the wireless router configuration.

- Ping the local host.

- Ping the default gateway.

- Ping an external website.

- Verify the network equipment settings.

Step 4: Implement a Solution

After you have determined an exact cause, it is time to implement a solution. If no solution is achieved in the previous step, here are some different ways to gather information about the network problem:

- Problem-solving experience

- Other technicians

- Internet search

- Newsgroups

- Manufacturer FAQs

- Computer manuals

- Device manuals

- Online forums

- Technical websites

Step 5: Verify Solution and Full System Functionality

At this point, you should verify the solution and full system functionality. When performing this step, do the following tests:

- Reboot all the network equipment.

- Reboot any computer that experienced network problems.

- Validate all LEDs on the network equipment.

- Use the **ipconfig /all** command to display addressing information for all network adapters.

- Use the **ping** command to check network connectivity to an external website.

- Use the **nslookup** connectivity to query a DNS server.

- Use the **net view** command to show the available shared resources on a network.

- Print to both a shared and a local printer.

Step 6: Document Findings

After you have solved the problem, you close with the customer. Tasks required to complete this step include the following:

Step 1.   Discuss the solution implemented with the customer.

Step 2.   Have the customer verify that the problem has been solved.

Step 3. Provide the customer with all the paperwork.

Step 4. Document the steps taken to solve the problem in the work order and the technician's journal.

Step 5. Document any components used in the repair.

Step 6. Document the time spent to resolve the problem.

Identify Common Problems and Solutions

Network problems can be attributed to hardware, software, networks, or some combination of the three. You will resolve some types of problems more often than others. Table 15-5 is a chart of common network problems and solutions. Table 15-6 is a chart of email failures. Table 15-7 outlines FTP and secure Internet connection problems and possible solutions. Table 15-8 is a chart of general network troubleshooting techniques.

Table 15-5   Network Connection Problems

A computer can connect to a network device by the IP address but not by the hostname.	Incorrect hostname.	Reenter the hostname.
	Incorrect DNS setting.	Reenter the IP address of the DNS server.
	DNS server is not operational.	Reboot the DNS server.
The computer does not obtain or renew the IP address.	The computer is using a static IP address.	Enable the computer to obtain an IP address automatically.
	Loose network cable.	Check the cable connections.
	Firewall is blocking DHCP.	Change the firewall settings to allow DHCP traffic.
An IP address conflict message displays when a new computer joins a computer network.	The same IP address is assigned to two different devices on a network.	Configure each device with a unique IP address.
A computer has network access but does not have Internet access.	The gateway IP address is incorrect.	Reboot the router and reconfigure the settings.
	A router is not operational or is configured incorrectly.	Reboot the router and examine the settings.

continues

Table 15-5   Network Connection Problems   *continued*

The computer automatically obtained the IP address 169.254.x.x but cannot connect to a network.	The DHCP server is not on.	Turn on the DHCP server.
	The computer s not connected to the network.	Reconnect the cables.
A computer cannot **ping** the loopback address.	The TCP/IP suite is corrupted.	Uninstall and reinstall the TCP/IP suite.
	The NIC is damaged.	Replace the NIC.

Table 15-6   Email Failure

The computer cannot send or receive email.	The computer has incorrect email client settings.	Reconfigure the client settings.
	The email server is down.	Reboot the email server or notify your email service provider.
	There is a loose or disconnected network cable.	Reconnect the network cables.
The computer can send but not receive email.	The inbox is full.	Archive or delete emails to create space.
The computer cannot receive a certain email attachment.	The email attachment is too large.	Ask the sender to split the attachment into smaller parts and resend them in individual emails.
	The email attachment contains a virus and has been blocked by virus protection.	Ask the sender to scan the attachment before sending it.
The computer cannot authenticate the email server.	The username or password is not correct.	Enter the correct username and password.

Table 15-7   FTP and Security Internet Connection Problems

A user cannot access the FTP server.	Port forwarding is not enabled in the router.	Enable port forwarding on the router to forward port 21 to the IP address of the FTP server.
	The maximum number of users has been reached.	Increase the number of simultaneous FTP users on the FTP server.
The FTP client software cannot find the FTP server.	The FTP client has an incorrectaddress or port setting.	Enter the correct IP address and port settings in the FTP client.
	The FTP server is not running.	Reboot the FTP server.
The FTP server disconnects the client after a short period of inactivity.	The FTP server does not allow connected clients to remain connected when no commands are being sent to the FTP server.	Increase the amount of time an FTP client is allowed to remain connected without performing any actions.
A user cannot log on to the FTP server.	The username or password is incorrect.	Enter the correct username and password in the FTP client.
Unauthorized users discover authentication information during a telnet session.	Telnet connection is not secure.	Use SSH protocol to log on to a remote host.
A computer cannot access a specific HTTPS site.	The browser certificate SSL setting is incorrect.	Clear the SSL state.
		Add the trust root certificate.
		Select **Tools > Internet > Options > Advanced tab** and ensure the SSL checkbox is enabled.

Table 15-8   Troubleshooting Tools

The computer can ping an IP address but not a host name.	The hostname is incorrect.	Enter the correct hostname.
	The DNS settings of the computer are incorrect.	Enter the correct DNS settings.
	The DNS server is not operational.	Reboot the DNS server.
	NetBIOS over TCP/IP is not enabled.	Enable NetBIOS over TCP/IP.
A computer on one network cannot ping a computer on another network.	There is a bad connection or broken device between the two networks.	Use **tracert** to locate which link is down and fix the broken link.
	ICMP echo request is disabled.	Ensure that the ICMP echo request is enabled.
	The other computer has its firewall enabled.	Temporarily disable the firewall on the other computer.
Nslookup reports "Can't find server name for address 127.0.0.1: timed out."	The DNS IP address is not configured on the local computer.	Add the IP address of a valid DNS server to the TCP/IP properties of the LAN adapter.
A computer cannot connect to a shared network folder using the **net use** command.	A computer cannot connect to a shared network folder using the **net use** command.	Make sure the network folder is shared using he **netshare** command.
		Set the computer to the same workgroup as the computer with the shared network folder.
When attempting to use the **ipconfig /release** or **ipconfig /renew** command, you receive the message, "No operation can be performed on the adapter while its media is disconnected."	The network cable is unplugged.	Reconnect the network cable.
	No NIC is installed.	Install a NIC.
	The computer has been configured with static IP addresses.	Change the TCP/IP properties on the LAN adapter to use DHCP.

The computer cannot Telnet into a remote computer.	The Telnet service has stopped.	Start the Telnet service on the remote computer.
	The remote computer has not been configured to accept Telnet connections.	Configure the remote computer to accept Telnet connections.

Apply Troubleshooting Skills

Now that you understand the troubleshooting process, it is time to apply your listening and diagnostic skills.

Lab 15.8.3 is designed to reinforce your skills with networks. You troubleshoot and fix a computer that does not connect to the network.

Remote Technician 15.8.3 is designed to reinforce your communication and troubleshooting skills. In this lab, you follow these steps:

- Receive the work order.
- Take the customer through various steps to try and resolve the problem.
- Document the problem and the resolution.

Lab 15.8.3: Fix Network Problem

In this lab, you correct a network problem. Refer to the lab in *IT Essentials: PC Hardware and Software Lab Manual, Fourth Edition*. You may perform this lab now or wait until the end of the chapter.

Lab 15.8.3: Remote Technician: Fix Network Problem

In this lab, you instruct a customer on how to correct a network problem. Refer to the lab in *IT Essentials: PC Hardware and Software Lab Manual, Fourth Edition*. You may perform this lab now or wait until the end of the chapter.

Optional Lab 15.8.3: Troubleshooting Network Problems in Windows XP

In this lab, you troubleshoot a network problem in Windows XP. Refer to the lab in *IT Essentials: PC Hardware and Software Lab Manual, Fourth Edition*. You may perform this lab now or wait until the end of the chapter.

Lab 15.8.3: Troubleshooting Network Problems in Windows Vista

In this lab, you troubleshoot a network problem in Windows Vista. Refer to the lab in *IT Essentials: PC Hardware and Software Lab Manual, Fourth Edition*. You may perform this lab now or wait until the end of the chapter.

Summary

This chapter has discussed the planning, implementation, and upgrading of networks and network components. The following are some of the important concepts to remember from this chapter:

- Many safety hazards are associated with network environments, devices, and media. You should follow proper safety procedures at all times.

- Networks must be designed with the customer in mind. Make design decisions that meet your customer's needs and goals.

- Select network components that offer the services and capabilities necessary to implement a network based on the customer's needs.

- Plan network installations based on the services and equipment necessary to provide the network that is needed.

- Upgrading a network may involve additional equipment, advanced equipment, or cabling. Discuss how upgrading can help enhance the network's usability in the future.

- Plan for an email installation before deployment. Consult a specialist to make sure that the installation and configuration of an email server go smoothly.

- Prevent network problems by developing and implementing a solid preventive maintenance policy.

- Follow a logical methodology to troubleshoot advanced network problems.

Summary of Exercises

This is a summary of the Labs, Worksheets, Remote Technician exercises, Class Discussions, Virtual Desktop activities, and Virtual Laptop activities associated with this chapter.

Labs

The following labs cover material from this chapter. Refer to the labs in *IT Essentials: PC Hardware and Software Lab Manual, Fourth Edition*.

Lab 15.4.2: Configure Browser Settings in Windows XP

Optional Lab 15.4.2: Configure Browser Settings in Windows Vista

Lab 15.4.2: Share a Folder, Share a Printer, and Set Share Permissions in Windows XP

Optional Lab 15.4.2: Share a Folder, Share a Printer, and Set Share Permissions in Windows Vista

Lab 15.5.1: Install a Wireless NIC in Windows XP

Optional Lab 15.5.1: Install a Wireless NIC in Windows Vista

Lab 15.5.2: Configure Wireless Router

Lab 15.5.3: Test the Wireless NIC in Windows XP

Optional Lab 15.5.3: Test the Wireless NIC in Windows Vista

Lab 15.8.3: Fix Network Problem

Lab 15.8.3: Remote Technician: Fix Network Problem

Lab 15.8.3: Troubleshooting Network Problems in Windows XP

Optional Lab 15.8.3: Troubleshooting Network Problems in Windows Vista

Worksheets

The following worksheets cover material from this chapter. Refer to the worksheets in *IT Essentials: PC Hardware and Software Lab Manual, Fourth Edition.*

Worksheet 15.2.2: Protocols

Worksheet 15.3.2: ISP Connection Types

Packet Tracer Activities

This is a summary of the Labs, Worksheets, Remote Technician exercises, Class Discussions, Virtual Desktop activities, and Virtual Laptop activities associated with this chapter.

15.5.1 Packet Tracer Activity: Install a Wireless NIC

15.5.3 Packet Tracer Activity: Test a Wireless Connection

Check Your Understanding

You can find the answers to these questions in the appendix, "Answers to Check Your Understanding Questions."

1. Which protocol is fast and useful on small Windows-only networks with low security requirements?

    A. AppleTalk

    B. HTTP

    C. IPX/SPX

    D. NetBEUI

2. What is a hazard of working with copper cabling?

   A. Chemicals

   B. Copper strands

   C. Glass splinters

   D. Light

3. Which Internet technology offers a high-speed connection in rural areas but can be adversely affected by the weather?

   A. Cable

   B. DSL

   C. ISDN

   D. Satellite

4. Which network device can regenerate the data signal and segment the network using MAC addresses?

   A. Switch

   B. Modem

   C. Hub

   D. Router

5. A network technician has been asked to install cabling in a new building. Which important task must be completed as part of the installation?

   A. Label one end of every cable to identify the cable.

   B. Cordon off the area, and allow only two technicians in the area.

   C. Run all cabling, using only one person to avoid confusion.

   D. Label both ends of the cabling to identify each cable.

6. How do you access the wireless network connection using Windows XP?

   A. Choose **Start > Control Panel > Administrative Tools > Network Devices**.

   B. Choose **Start > Control Panel > Network Connections**.

   C. Choose **Start > Control Panel > Network Devices**.

   D. Choose **Start > Control Panel > Hardware > Network Connections**.

7. Which two protocols are used to receive email?

   A. DHCP

   B. SNMP

   C. IMAP

   D. POP3

   E. SSH

8. A company purchases several wireless NICs at a great price. After installing the NICs, it finds that the users cannot connect to the wireless 802.11n network. What is a likely cause of the problem?

   A. The NICs are designed for the 802.11a standard.

   B. The NICs are designed for the 802.11b standard.

   C. The NICs are designed for the 802.11g standard.

   D. The NICs are designed for the 802.11n standard via USB.

CHAPTER 16

Advanced Security

Objectives

Upon completion of this chapter, you should be able to answer the following questions:

- How do I outline security requirements based on customer needs?

- How can I select security components based on customer needs?

- What is the process to implement my customer's security plan?

- How do I perform preventive maintenance on security?

- What is the process to troubleshoot security?

Key Terms

This chapter uses the following key terms. You can find the definitions in the Glossary.

security policy   page 634

physical security   page 637

intrusion detection system (IDS)   page 639

hash encoding   page 641

symmetric encryption   page 641

asymmetric encryption   page 642

Virtual Private Network (VPN)   page 642

two-factor security   page 643

smart card   page 644

security key fob   page 644

biometric device   page 644

hardware firewall   page 645

software firewall   page 645

packet filter   page 645

proxy server   page 645

stateful packet inspection   page 646

Wired Equivalent Privacy (WEP)   page 648

Wi-Fi Protected Access (WPA)   page 648

MAC address filtering   page 648

Service Set Identifier (SSID)   page 648

Windows XP Firewall   page 650

zombie   page 654

guest account   page 656

This chapter reviews the types of attacks that threaten the security of computers and the data contained on them. A technician is responsible for the security of data and computer equipment in an organization. The chapter describes how you can work with customers to ensure that the best possible protection is in place.

Risks to computers and network equipment come from both internal and external sources. Risks include physical threats, such as theft or damage to equipment, and data threats, such as the loss or corruption of data.

After completing this chapter, you will meet these objectives:

- Outline security requirements based on customer needs.
- Select security components based on customer needs.
- Implement a customer's security plan.
- Perform preventive maintenance on security.
- Troubleshoot security.

Outline Security Requirements Based on Customer Needs

An organization should strive to achieve the best and most affordable security protection against data loss or damage to software and equipment. Network technicians and the organization's management should work together to develop a *security policy* to ensure that data and equipment have been protected against all security threats. A security policy includes a comprehensive statement about the level of security required and how this security will be achieved.

You might be involved in developing a security policy for a customer or organization. When creating a security policy, you should ask the following questions to determine security factors:

- Is the computer located at a home or a business?

  Home computers generally are more vulnerable to wireless intrusion than business computers. Business computers have a higher threat of network intrusion, because of users abusing their access privileges.

- Is there full-time Internet access?

  The more a computer is exposed to the Internet, the greater the chance of attacks from other infected computers. A computer accessing the Internet should include firewall and antivirus solutions.

- Is the computer a laptop?

  Physical security is an issue with laptop computers. There are measures to secure laptops, such as cable locks.

After completing the following sections, you will meet these objectives:

- Outline a local security policy.

- Explain when and how to use security hardware.

- Explain when and how to use security application software.

Figure 16-1 illustrates how the different approaches to security work together to ensure physical and data security.

Figure 16-1   Security Components

Outline a Local Security Policy

A security policy is a collection of rules, guidelines, and checklists. Network technicians and managers of an organization work together to develop the rules and guidelines for the security needs of computer equipment. A security policy includes the following elements:

- Defines an acceptable computer usage statement for an organization.

- Identifies the people permitted to use the computer equipment in an organization.

- Identifies devices that are permitted to be installed on a network, as well as the conditions of the installation. Modems and wireless access points are examples of hardware that could expose the network to attacks.

- Defines the requirements necessary for data to remain confidential on a network.

- Determines a process for employees to acquire access to equipment and data. This process can require the employee to sign an agreement regarding the company rules. It also lists the consequences for failure to comply.

The security policy should also provide detailed information about the following issues in case of an emergency:

- Steps to take after a breach in security

- Who to contact in an emergency

- Information to share with customers, vendors, and the media

- Secondary locations to use in an evacuation

- Steps to take after an emergency is over, including the priority of services to be restored

Caution

A security policy must be enforced and followed by all employees to be effective.

Here is an example of the types of security issues:

- Data loss caused by

  — Equipment theft

  — Wiretapping

  — Internal personnel

  — External personnel

  — Temporary personnel/contractors/vendors

- Power-related emergencies:

  — Building or floor power outage

  — Local power outage

  — Large or regional power outage

- Terrorist action:

  — Terrorist attacks leading to evacuation

  — Terrorist attacks leading to lockdown

- Physical theft of

  — Network device

  — Desktop computer

  — Laptop

Worksheet 16.1.1: Answer Security Policy Questions

In this worksheet, you answer security questions regarding the IT Essentials classroom. Refer to the worksheet in *IT Essentials: PC Hardware and Software Lab Manual, Fourth Edition*. You can complete this worksheet now or wait until the end of the chapter.

Explain When and How to Use Security Hardware

The security policy should identify hardware and equipment that can be used to prevent theft, vandalism, and data loss. There are four interrelated aspects to *physical security*, which are access, data, infrastructure, and computers, as illustrated in Figure 16-2.

Figure 16-2   Physical Security

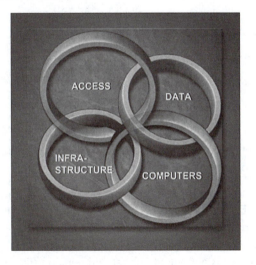

Restrict access to premises with the following:

- Fences

- Security hardware

Protect the network infrastructure, such as cabling, telecommunication equipment, and network devices, by implementing the following measures:

- Secured telecommunications rooms

- Wireless detection for unauthorized access points

- Hardware firewalls

- Network management system that detects changes in wiring and patch panels

Protect individual computers by using the following:

- Cable locks

- Laptop docking station locks

- Lockable cases

- Secured cages surrounding desktop cases

Protect data with hardware that prevents unauthorized access or theft of media through the use of the following:

- Lockable hard drive carriers

- Secure storage and transport of backup media

- USB security dongles

Factors that determine the most effective security equipment to use to secure equipment and data include the following:

- How the equipment will be used

- Computer equipment location

- User-required access to data

For example, a computer in a busy public place, such as a library, requires additional protection from theft and vandalism. In a busy call center, a server might need to be secured in a locked equipment room.

Where it is necessary to use a laptop computer in a public place, a security dongle, shown in Figure 16-3, ensures that the system locks if the user and laptop are separated. The user carries the dongle in a pocket. When the USB transceiver senses that the dongle is in range, it unlocks the laptop. Many car keys work on the same principal. If the chip embedded in the key is not sensed, the car will remain locked or will not start.

Figure 16-3   USB Security Dongle

Explain When and How to Use Security Application Software

Security applications protect the operating system and software application data.

The following products and software applications can be used to protect network devices:

- **Software firewall**: Filters incoming data and is built into Windows XP

- *Intrusion detection system (IDS)*: Monitors and reports on changes in program code and unusual network activity

- **Application and OS patches**: Update applications and the operating system to repair security weaknesses that are discovered

Several software applications are available to protect computers from unauthorized access by malicious computer code:

- Virus protection

- Spyware protection

- Adware protection

- Grayware protection

In small offices and homes, computers generally connect directly to the Internet rather than through a protected LAN that organizations use. This puts computers outside of a LAN at high risk for viruses and other attacks. At a minimum, these computers should use antivirus and antimalware protection programs. Application software and the operating system should be updated with the latest patches. A software firewall can also be part of the solution.

The security policy should determine the level of security applications put in place. Each step that increases protection costs money. In developing a policy, management should calculate the cost of data loss versus the expense of security protection and determine what trade-offs are acceptable.

Select Security Components Based on Customer Needs

The security policy helps customers to select the security components necessary to keep equipment and data safe. If there is no security policy, you should discuss security issues with the customer.

Use your past experience as a technician and research the current security products on the market when selecting security components for the customer. The goal is to provide the security system that best matches the customer's needs.

After completing the following sections, you will meet these objectives:

- Describe and compare security techniques.
- Describe and compare access control devices.
- Describe and compare firewall types.

Describe and Compare Security Techniques

A technician should determine the appropriate techniques to secure equipment and data for the customer. Depending on the situation, more than one technique might be required. The sections that follow describe the different techniques to secure equipment and data.

Passwords

Using secure, encrypted login information for computers with network access should be a minimum requirement in any organization. Malicious software monitors the network and can record plain-text passwords. If passwords are encrypted, attackers would have to decode the encryption to learn the passwords.

Tip

As covered in Chapter 9, "Fundamental Security," a strong password should contain a mixture of numbers, special characters, and uppercase and lowercase letters and have a minimum number of eight characters total.

Logging and Auditing

Event logging and auditing should be enabled to monitor activity on the network. The network administrator audits the log file of events to investigate network access by unauthorized users.

Wireless Configurations

Wireless connections are especially vulnerable to access by attackers. Wireless clients should be configured to encrypt data.

Security Technologies

Security technologies include hash encoding, symmetric encryption, asymmetric encryption, and Virtual Private Networks (VPN). Each technology is used for a specific purpose.

Hash encoding, or hashing, ensures that messages are not corrupted or tampered with during transmission. Hashing uses a mathematical function to create a numeric value that is unique to the data. If even one character is changed, the function output, called the message digest, will not be the same. However, the function is one-way. Knowing the message digest does not allow an attacker to re-create the message. This makes it difficult for someone to intercept and change messages. Figure 16-4 illustrates the hash-encoding process. The names of the most popular hashing algorithms are Secure Hash Algorithm (SHA) and Message Digest 5 (MD5).

Figure 16-4   Hash Encoding

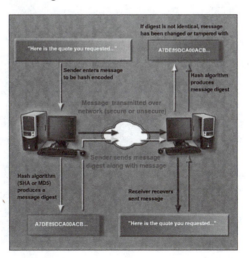

Symmetric encryption requires both sides of an encrypted conversation to use an encryption key to be able to encode and decode the data. The sender and receiver must use identical keys. Figure 16-5 illustrates the symmetric encryption process.

Figure 16-5   Symmetric Encryption

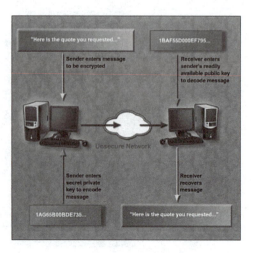

Asymmetric encryption requires two keys, a private key and a public key. A private key is required for writing a message, and a public key is needed to decode the message. The advantage of asymmetric encryption is that only the private key needs to be kept secret. Public keys can be distributed openly by email or by posting them on the web. Figure 16-6 illustrates the asymmetric encryption process.

Figure 16-6   Asymmetric Encryption

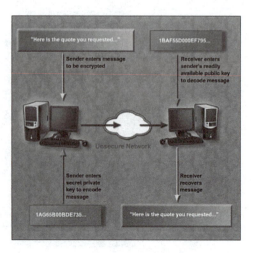

A *Virtual Private Network (VPN)* uses encryption to secure data as if it were traveling in a private, corporate LAN, even though the data actually travels over any network (for example, the Internet). The secured data pipelines between points in the VPN are called "secure tunnels." Figure 16-7 illustrates how a VPN is used to provide security.

Figure 16-7   Virtual Private Network

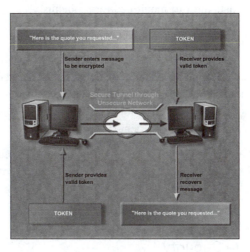

Describe and Compare Access Control Devices

Computer equipment and data can be secured using overlapping protection techniques to prevent unauthorized access to sensitive data. An example of overlapping protection is using two different techniques to protect an asset. This is known as *two-factor security*. When considering a security program, the cost of the implementation has to be balanced against the value of the data or equipment to be protected.

One example of a two-factor security technique is as follows:

Password (good protection) + biometrics or smart card (good protection) = two-factor security (much better protection)

Physical Security

Use security hardware to help prevent security breaches and loss of data or equipment. Physical security access control measures include the following:

- **Lock**: The most common device for securing physical areas. If a key is lost, all identically keyed locks must be changed.

- **Conduit**: A casing that protects the infrastructure media from damage and unauthorized access.

- **Card key**: A tool used to secure physical areas. If a card key is lost or stolen, only the missing card must be deactivated. The card key system is more expensive than security locks.

- **Video equipment**: Records images and sound for monitoring activity. The recorded data must be monitored for problems.

- **Security guard**: Controls access to the entrance of a facility and monitors the activity inside the facility.

Network equipment should be mounted in secured areas. All cabling should be enclosed in conduits or routed inside walls to prevent unauthorized access or tampering. Network outlets that are not in use should be disabled. If network equipment is damaged or stolen, some network users may be denied service.

The security policy should specify the level of security required for the organization. Biometric devices, which measure physical information about a user, are ideal for use in highly secure areas. However, for most small organizations, this type of solution would be too expensive.

Data Security

You can protect data by using data security devices to authenticate employee access. Two-factor identification is a method to increase security. Employees must use both a password and a data security device, similar to those listed here, to access data:

- *Smart card*: A device that can store data safely. The internal memory is an embedded integrated circuit chip (ICC) that connects to a reader either directly or through a wireless connection. Smart cards are used in many applications worldwide, like secure ID badges, online authentication devices, and secure credit card payments.

- *Security key fob*: A small device that resembles the ornament on a key ring. It has a small radio system that communicates with the computer over a short range. Fobs are small enough that many people attach them to their key rings. The computer must sense the signal from the key fob before it will accept a username and password.

- *Biometric device*: Measures a physical characteristic of the user, such as fingerprints or the patterns of the iris in the eye. The user is granted access if these characteristics match its database and the correct login information is supplied.

Hardware destruction is the process of removing sensitive data from hardware and software when data is no longer needed. Hardware destruction must be performed before recycling or discarding items that store data. Three methods are commonly used to either destroy or recycle data and hard drives:

- Data wiping

- Hard drive destruction

- Hard drive recycling

The level of security that the customer needs determines which devices are used to keep data and equipment secure, and how the data should be removed or destroyed.

Note

Do not forget to erase any hard drives or other memory storage devices on printers and photocopiers.

Describe and Compare Firewall Types

Hardware and software firewalls protect data and equipment on a network from unauthorized access. A firewall should be used in addition to security software.

A *hardware firewall* is a physical filtering component that inspects data packets from the network before they reach computers and other devices on a network. Hardware firewalls are often installed along with routers. A hardware firewall is a freestanding unit that does not use the resources of the computers it is protecting, so there is no impact on processing performance.

A *software firewall* is an application on a computer that inspects and filters data packets. Windows Firewall is an example of a software firewall that is included in the Windows operating system. A software firewall uses the resources of the computer, resulting in reduced performance for the user.

Consider the items listed in Table 16-1 when selecting a firewall.

Table 16-1   Hardware Versus Software Firewall

Hardware Firewall	Software Firewall
Freestanding and uses dedicated hardware.	Available as third-party software and cost varies.
Initial cost for hardware and software updates can be high.	Windows XP operating system provides a software firewall.
Multiple computers can be protected.	Typically protects only the computer it is installed on.
Little impact on computer performance.	Uses the CPU, potentially slowing the computer.

Hardware and software firewalls have several modes for filtering network data traffic:

- *Packet filter*: A set of rules that allows or denies traffic based on criteria such as IP addresses, protocols, or ports used.

- *Proxy server*: A firewall that inspects all traffic and allows or denies packets based on configured rules. A proxy acts as a gateway that protects computers inside the network.

- *Stateful packet inspection*: A firewall that keeps track of the state of network connections traveling through the firewall. Packets that are not part of a known connection are not allowed back through the firewall.

> **Note**
>
> On a secure network, if computer performance is not an issue, you should enable the internal operating system firewall for additional security. Some applications might not operate properly unless the firewall is configured correctly for them.

Worksheet 16.2.3: Research Firewalls

For this worksheet, you use the Internet, a newspaper, or a local store to gather information about hardware and software firewalls. Refer to the worksheet in *IT Essentials: PC Hardware and Software Lab Manual, Fourth Edition*. You can complete this worksheet now or wait until the end of the chapter.

Implement a Customer's Security Policy

Adding layers of security to a network can make the network more secure, but additional layers of security protection can be expensive. You must weigh the value of the data and equipment to be protected against the cost of protection when implementing the customer's security policy.

After completing the following sections, you will meet these objectives:

- Configure security settings.
- Describe configuring firewall types.
- Describe protection against malicious software.

Configure Security Settings

Two common security errors are incorrect permissions on folders and files and incorrect configuration of wireless security. The sections that follow examine appropriate permission settings and wireless security configuration.

Permission Levels for Folders and Files

Permission levels are configured to limit individual or group user access to specific data. Both FAT and NTFS allow folder sharing and folder-level permissions for users with network access. NTFS folder permissions are categorized as follows, allowing the user or group to perform the actions described:

- **Full Control**: Change permissions of the folder, take ownership of it, and perform all activities included in all other permissions

- **Modify**: Delete the folder plus perform actions permitted by the group policy

- **Read and Execute**: Move through folders to reach other files and folders, even if the users don't have permission for those folders, and perform actions permitted by the Read permission and List Folder Contents permission

- **List Folder Contents**: See the names of the files and subfolders in the folder

- **Read**: See files and subfolders in the folder and view folder ownership, permission, and attributes

- **Write**: Create new files and subfolders within the folder, change folder attributes, and view folder ownership and permissions

NTFS provides additional security of file-level permissions:

- **Full Control**: Change permissions and take ownership, plus perform the actions permitted by all other NTFS file permissions

- **Modify**: Modify and delete the file, plus perform the actions permitted by the Write permission and Read and Execute permission

- **Read and Execute**: Run applications, plus perform the actions permitted by the Read permission

- **Read**: Read the file and view file attributes, ownership, and permissions

- **Write**: Overwrite the file, change file attributes, and view file ownership and permissions

Wireless Antennae

The gain and signal pattern of the antenna connected to a wireless access point can influence where the signal can be received. Avoid transmitting signals outside of the network area by installing an antenna with a pattern that serves only your network users.

Network Device Access Permissions

Many wireless devices built by a specific manufacturer have the same default username and password for accessing the wireless configuration. If left unchanged, unauthorized users can easily log on to the access point and modify the settings. When you first connect to the network device, change the default username and password. Some devices allow you to change both the username and the password, while others only allow you to change the password.

To change the default password, use a web browser to navigate to the following path on the wireless router: **Administration > Management**. Type the new router password, reenter the password to confirm, and click **Save Settings**.

Wireless Security Modes

Most wireless access points support several different security modes. The most common ones are

- *Wired Equivalent Privacy (WEP)*: Encrypts the broadcast data between the wireless access point and the client using a 64-bit or 128-bit encryption key.

- *Wi-Fi Protected Access (WPA)*: Provides better encryption and authentication than WEP.

- *MAC address filtering*: Restricts computer access to a wireless access point to prevent the casual user from accessing the network. MAC address filtering is vulnerable when used alone and should be combined with other security filtering.

- *Service set identifier (SSID)*: By default, the wireless router broadcasts the SSID of the wireless network. Turning off the SSID makes the network seem to disappear, but this is an unreliable form of wireless network security.

- **Wireless antennas**: The gain and signal pattern of the antenna connected to a wireless access point can influence where the signal can be received. Avoid transmitting signals outside of the network area by installing an antenna with a pattern that serves only your network users.

To add wireless security, use a web browser to navigate to the following path on the wireless router: **Wireless > Wireless Security**. Select a Security Mode, select an Encryption Type, type the Pre-shared Key, set Key Renewal, and click **Save Settings > Continue**.

SSID

A wireless access point broadcasts the SSID by default so that wireless devices can detect the wireless network. You can disable SSID broadcasting on a wireless network to prevent the wireless access point or router from revealing the name of the wireless network.

To disable SSID broadcasting, use a web browser to navigate to the following path on the wireless router: **Wireless > Basic Wireless Setting**. Select **Disabled for SSID Broadcast** and click **Save Settings > Continue**.

Disabling SSID broadcasting can make it more difficult for legitimate clients to find the wireless network. Manually enter the SSID on wireless devices to connect to the wireless network when the SSID broadcast has been disabled on the wireless router or access point. Simply turning off the SSID broadcast is not sufficient to prevent unauthorized clients from connecting to the wireless network. Instead of turning off the SSID broadcast, use stronger encryption such as WPA or WPA2.

MAC Address Filtering

MAC address filtering is a technique used to deploy device-level security on a wireless LAN. Because every wireless client has a unique MAC address, wireless access points can prevent wireless clients from connecting to the wireless network if they do not have authorized MAC addresses. MAC address filtering is vulnerable to attack when used alone and should be combined with other security techniques.

To set up a MAC address filter, use a web browser to perform the following steps on the wireless router:

Step 1.   Choose Wireless > Wireless MAC Filter and select Enabled.

Step 2.   Select Prevent or Permit for the access restriction type.

Step 3.   Select Wireless Client List, select the client, and choose Save to MAC Address Filter List > Add > Save Settings > Continue.

Step 4.   Add a MAC address for each client that you wish to permit or deny access to the wireless client list.

The MAC address of a wireless NIC can be found by typing **ipconfig /all** at the command prompt. For devices other than computers, the MAC address can usually be found on the label of the device or within the manufacturer's instructions. On wireless networks with a large number of clients, MAC address filtering can become tedious because you must enter each MAC address in the filter.

MAC address filtering is not a strong layer of security. Instead of using MAC address filtering, use stronger encryption techniques such as WPA or WPA2.

Firewalls

A firewall is a device or application installed on a network to protect it from unauthorized users and malicious attacks. A software firewall is software installed on a computer to block specific incoming or outgoing traffic. For example, a firewall that is configured to block outgoing traffic on port 21 will not allow the computer to connect to a standard FTP server. The firewall can be configured to block multiple individual ports, a range of ports, or even traffic specific to an application.

A hardware firewall isolates your network from other networks. A hardware firewall will pass two different types of traffic into your network:

- Traffic that originates from inside your network

- Traffic destined for a port that you have intentionally left open

There are several types of hardware firewall configurations:

- **Packet filter**: This configuration does not allow packets to pass through the firewall unless they match the established rule set configured in the firewall. Traffic can be filtered based on many attributes, such as source IP address, source port or destination IP address or port, and destination services such as web or FTP.

- **Application layer**: This configuration intercepts all packets traveling to or from an application. It prevents all unwanted outside traffic from reaching protected devices.

- **Proxy**: This configuration intercepts all traffic between computers and different networks and uses established rules to determine if data requests should be allowed.

To configure hardware firewall settings on the Linksys WRT300N, choose **Security > Firewall** and select **Enable for SPI Firewall Protection**. Then select other Internet filters and web filters required to secure the network. Click **Save Settings > Continue**.

Figure 16-8 shows *Windows XP Firewall.*

Figure 16-8   Windows XP Firewall

Port Forwarding and Port Triggering

Hardware firewalls are mainly used to block ports to prevent unauthorized access in and out of a LAN. However, there are situations when specific ports must be opened so that certain programs and applications can function properly. Port forwarding is a rule-based method of directing traffic between devices on separate networks. When traffic reaches the router, the router determines if the traffic should be forwarded to a certain device based upon the port number found with the traffic. For example, port numbers are associated with specific services such as FTP, HTTP, HTTPS, and POP3. The rules determine which traffic will be sent onto the LAN. For example, a router might be configured to forward port 80, which is associated with HTTP. If the router then receives a packet with the destination port of 80, the router will forward this traffic to a web server inside the network.

To add port forwarding, choose **Applications & Gaming > Single Port Forwarding** and select or enter an application name. You may need to enter the external port number, Internet port number, and protocol type. Then enter the IP address of the computer that should receive the requests. Click **Enable > Save Settings > Continue**.

Port triggering allows the router to temporarily forward data through inbound ports to a specific device. You can use port triggering to forward data to a computer only when a designated port range is used to make an outbound request.

For example, a video game might use ports 27000 to 27100 for connecting with other players. These are the trigger ports. A chat client might use port 56 for connecting the same players so that they can interact with each other. An example of a port triggering rule is that when any gaming traffic uses an outbound port that is within the triggered port range, inbound chat traffic on port 56 will be forwarded to the computer that is being used to play the video game and chat with friends. When the game is over and the triggered ports are no longer in use, port 56 will no longer be allowed to send traffic of any type to this computer.

To add port triggering, choose **Applications & Gaming > Port Range Triggering** and type the application name. Enter the starting and ending port numbers of the triggered port range, and starting and ending port numbers of the forwarded port range. Click **Enable > Save Settings > Continue**.

Lab 16.3.1: Configure Wireless Security

In this lab, you configure and test the wireless settings on the Linksys WRT300N. Refer to the lab in *IT Essentials: PC Hardware and Software Lab Manual, Fourth Edition*. You can perform this lab now or wait until the end of the chapter.

Describe Configuring Firewall Types

A firewall selectively denies traffic to a computer or network segment. Firewalls generally work by opening and closing the ports used by various applications. By opening only the required ports on a firewall, you are implementing a restrictive security policy. Any packet not explicitly permitted is denied. In contrast, a permissive security policy permits access through all ports except those explicitly denied. In the past, software and hardware were shipped with permissive settings. Because users neglected to configure their equipment, the default permissive settings left many devices exposed to attackers. Most devices now ship with settings as restrictive as possible, while still allowing easy setup.

Software Firewalls

Software firewalls can be either an independent application or part of the operating system. There are several third-party software firewalls. There is also a software firewall built into Windows XP.

Configuring the Windows XP or Windows Vista firewall can be completed in two ways:

- **Automatically**: The user is prompted to Keep Blocking, Unblock, or Ask Me Later for any unsolicited requests. These requests may be from legitimate applications that have not been configured previously or may be from a virus or worm that has infected the system.

- **Manage Security Settings**: The user manually adds the program or ports that are required for the applications in use on the network.

Windows XP Firewalls

To add a program, choose **Start > Control Panel > Security Center > Windows Firewall > Exceptions > Add Program**.

To disable the firewall, choose **Start > Control Panel > Security Center > Windows Firewall**.

Windows Vista Firewalls

To add a program, choose **Start > Control Panel > Security Center > Windows Firewall > Change Settings > Continue > Exceptions > Add Program**.

To disable the firewall, choose **Start > Control Panel > Security Center > Windows Firewall > Turn Windows Firewall On or Off > Continue > select Off (Not Recommended) > OK**.

Windows Firewall blocks all incoming network connections except for specific programs and services. For example, the Windows Update service and Internet Explorer are allowed through the firewall by default. An exception is a rule that opens a blocked port in the firewall for a specific need. For instance, to allow an FTP connection, you must create an exception that will open up port 21. Each different type of connection requires a unique port number to pass data through the firewall.

To add a port exception to Windows Firewall, click the **Exceptions** tab, click **Add Port**, type a name, type a port number, and select a protocol. To specify that only certain computers will be affected by the exception, click **Change Scope**, specify the computers, and click **OK > OK > OK**.

Lab 16.3.2: Configure Windows XP Firewall

In this lab, you explore Windows XP Firewall and configure some advanced settings. Refer to the lab in *IT Essentials: PC Hardware and Software Lab Manual, Fourth Edition.* You can perform this lab now or wait until the end of the chapter.

Optional Lab 16.3.2: Configure Windows Vista Firewall

In this lab, you explore Windows Vista Firewall and configure some advanced settings. Refer to the lab in *IT Essentials: PC Hardware and Software Lab Manual, Fourth Edition.* You can perform this lab now or wait until the end of the chapter.

Describe Protection Against Malicious Software

Malware is malicious software that is installed on a computer without the knowledge or permission of the user. Certain types of malware, such as spyware and phishing attacks, collect data about the user that can be used by an attacker to gain confidential information.

You should run virus- and spyware-scanning programs to detect and clean unwanted software. Many browsers now come equipped with special tools and settings that prevent the operation of several forms of malicious software. It might take several different programs and multiple scans to completely remove all malicious software:

- **Virus protection**: Antivirus programs typically run automatically in the background and monitor for problems. When a virus is detected, the user is warned and the program attempts to quarantine or delete the virus.

- **Spyware protection**: Antispyware programs scan for keyloggers and other malware so that it can be removed from the computer.

- **Adware protection**: Anti-adware programs look for programs that display advertising on your computer.

- **Phishing protection**: Antiphishing programs block the IP addresses of known phishing websites and warn the user about suspicious websites.

A dangerous form of malicious software that incorporates elements of social engineering is the phishing attack. Figure 16-9 demonstrates a phishing attack website.

Figure 16-9   Phishing Attack Example

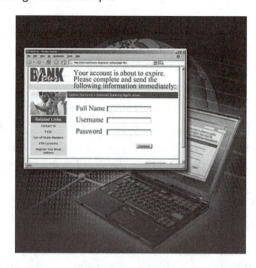

Note

Malicious software can become embedded in the operating system. Special removal tools are available from the operating system manufacturer to clean the operating system.

Perform Preventive Maintenance on Security

Several maintenance tasks are necessary to ensure that security is effective. The following sections cover how to maximize protection by performing updates, backups, and reconfiguration of the operating systems, user accounts, and data.

After completing the following sections, you will meet these objectives:

- Describe the configuration of operation system updates.

- Maintain accounts.

- Explain data backup procedures, access to backups, and secure physical backup media.

Describe the Configuration of Operating System Updates

An operating system is a likely target of attack because obtaining control of it can provide control of the computer. Then the compromised computer can be seized and put to work by the criminals. One popular use is to turn targeted computers into spam generators that launch attacking emails without the user being able to stop them. A computer compromised in this way is called a *zombie*.

Windows XP automatically downloads and installs updates to operating systems by default. However, this might not be the best way to update systems. The updates might conflict with the security policy of an organization or might conflict with other settings on a computer. Furthermore, a network administrator might want to test the updates before the updates are distributed to all the network computers. The following Windows XP options give users the ability to control when software is updated:

- **Automatic**: Downloads and installs updates automatically without user intervention

- **Only Download Updates**: Downloads the updates automatically, but the user is required to install them

- **Notify Me**: Notifies the user that updates are available and gives the option to download and install

- **Turn Off Automatic Updates**: Prevents any checking for updates

If the user is on a dialup network, the Windows Update setting should be configured to notify the user of available updates, or it should be turned off. The dialup user might want to control the update by selecting a time when the update does not interrupt other network activity or use the limited resources available.

Maintain Accounts

Employees in an organization may require different levels of access to data. For example, a manager and an accountant might be the only employees in an organization with access to the payroll files.

Employees can be grouped by job requirements and given access to files according to group permissions. This process helps manage employee access to the network. Temporary accounts can be set up for employees that need short-term access. Close management of network access can help to limit areas of vulnerability that allow a virus or malicious software to enter the network.

Terminating Employee Access

When an employee leaves an organization, access to data and hardware on the network should be terminated immediately. If the former employee has stored files in a personal space on a server, eliminate access by disabling the account. At a later time, if the employee's replacement requires access to the applications and storage space, reenable the account and change its name to the name of the new employee.

Guest Accounts

Temporary employees and guests might need access to the network. For example, many visitors require access to email, the Internet, and a printer on the network. These resources can all be made available to a special account called Guest. When guests are present, they can be assigned to the *guest account*. When no guests are present, the account can be suspended until the next guest arrives.

Some guest accounts can require extensive access to resources, as in the case of a consultant or a financial auditor. This type of access should be granted only for the period of time required to complete the work.

Explain Data Backup Procedures, Access to Backups, and Secure Physical Backup Media

A data backup stores a copy of the information on a computer to removable backup media that can be kept in a safe place. If the computer hardware fails, the data can be restored from the backup to functional hardware.

Data backups should be performed on a regular basis. The most current data backup is usually stored offsite to protect the backup media if anything happens to the main facility. Backup media is often reused to save on media costs. Always follow your organization's media-rotation guidelines.

Backup operations for Windows XP can be performed at the command line or from a batch file using the **ntbackup** command. The default parameters for **ntbackup** will be the ones set in the Windows XP backup utility. Any options you want to override must be included in the command line. You cannot restore files from the command line using the **ntbackup** command.

The Windows XP Backup or Restore Utility wizard files have the extension .bkf. A .bkf file can be saved to a hard drive, a DVD, or to any other recordable media. The source location and target drive can be either NTFS or FAT.

The Windows Vista backup files have the extension .zip. Backup data is automatically compressed, and each file has a maximum compressed size of 200 MB. A Windows Vista backup file can be saved to a hard drive, any recordable media, or another computer or server connected to your network. The backup can only be created from an NTFS partition. The target hard drive must be either NTFS or FAT formatted.

Note

You can manually exclude directories in the Windows XP Backup or Restore Utility wizard. This is not supported in the Windows Vista Backup Files wizard.

You can make a Windows backup manually or schedule how often the backup will take place automatically. To successfully back up and restore data in Windows, the appropriate user rights and permissions are required:

- All users can back up their own files and folders. They can also back up files for which they have the Read permission.

- All users can restore files and folders for which they have the Write permission.

- Members of the Administrators, Backup Operators, and Server Operators (if joined to a domain) can back up and restore all files (regardless of the assigned permissions). By default, members of these groups have the Backup Files and Directories and Restore Files and Directories user rights.

Table 16-2 shows the five backup types that the Windows XP Backup or Restore Utility wizard provides.

Table 16-2   Backup Types

Type of Backup	Description
Full or Normal	Archives all selected files and resets the archive bit
Incremental	Archives all selected files that have changed since the last incremental backup
Differential	Archives all selected files that have changed since the last full backup
Daily	Archives all selected files that have changed on the day of the backup
Copy	Archives all selected files but does not reset the archive bit

To start the Windows XP Backup or Restore Utility wizard, choose **Start > All Programs > Accessories > System Tools > Backup**. The Backup or Restore wizard starts. To change the backup setting, select **Advanced Mode > Tools > Options**.

To restore a backed up file in Windows XP, in the Backup or Restore wizard, choose **Next > Restore Files and Settings > Next**, select the backed up file, and click **Next > Finish**.

To start the Windows Vista Backup Files wizard, choose **Start > All Programs > Maintenance > Backup and Restore Center > Back Up Files**.

To change the backup settings, choose **Change Settings > Change Backup Settings > Continue**.

To restore a backed up file in Windows Vista, use the icon in the Control Panel or choose **Start > All Programs > Maintenance > Backup and Restore Center > Restore Files**.

Using a combination of backup types allows the data to be backed up efficiently. A full backup is a copy of all files on the drive. An incremental backup backs up only those files created or changed since the last normal or incremental backup. It marks files as having been backed up. A differential backup copies files created or changed since the last normal or incremental backup, but it does not mark files as having been backed up. Backing up data can take time, so it is preferable to do backups when the network traffic is low. Other types of backups include daily backup and copy backup, which do not mark the files as having been backed up.

The data backup media is just as important as the data on the computer. You should store the backup media in a climate-controlled offsite storage facility with good physical security. The backups should be readily available for access in case of an emergency.

Lab 16.4.3: Data Backup and Recovery in Windows XP

In this lab, you back up and recover data in Windows XP. Refer to the lab in *IT Essentials: PC Hardware and Software Lab Manual, Fourth Edition*. You can perform this lab now or wait until the end of the chapter.

Optional Lab 16.4.3: Data Backup and Recovery in Windows Vista

In this lab, you back up and recover data in Windows Vista. Refer to the lab in *IT Essentials: PC Hardware and Software Lab Manual, Fourth Edition*. You can perform this lab now or wait until the end of the chapter.

Troubleshoot Security

The troubleshooting process is used to help resolve security issues. These problems range from simple, such as creating a backup, to more complex, such as a firewall configuration. Follow the steps outlined in the following sections to accurately identify, repair, and document the problem:

Step 1. Identify the problem.

Step 2. Establish a theory of possible solutions.

Step 3. Determine an exact cause.

Step 4. Implement a solution.

Step 5. Verify the solution and verify full system functionality.

Step 6. Document your findings.

After completing the following sections, you will meet these objectives:

- Review the troubleshooting process.
- Identify common problems and solutions.
- Apply troubleshooting skills.

Review the Troubleshooting Process

Computer technicians must be able to analyze a security threat and determine the appropriate method to protect assets and repair damage. This process is called troubleshooting.

Step 1: Identify the Problem

The first step in the troubleshooting process is to identify the problem. Table 16-3 provides a list of open-ended and closed-ended questions to ask the customer about security threats. (This list is *not* comprehensive.)

Table 16-3   Security Threats: Open-Ended and Closed-Ended Questions to Ask

Open-Ended Questions	Closed-Ended Questions
Are there any network resources that you can access by wireless?	Do you have a firewall?
When did the problem start?	Does your company have a security policy?
What problems are you experiencing?	Has anyone else used your computer?
What security software is installed on your computer?	Is your security software up to date?
How are you connected to the Internet?	Have you scanned your computer recently for viruses?
What type of firewall are you using?	Have you ever had any problems like this before?
Describe your work environment?	Have you changed your password recently?
When did you last back up your computer?	Have you received any error messages on your computer?
What type of backup was performed?	Have you shared your password?
What group are you a member of?	Do you back up your computer?
	Do you have permissions for the resource?

Step 2: Establish a Theory of Probable Solutions

After you have identified the problem, you should establish a theory of probable causes. Common security-related problems include the following:

- The user account is disabled.
- The user is using an incorrect username or password.
- The user does not have the correct file or folder permissions.

- The firewall settings are incorrect.

- The user's computer has been infected by a virus.

- The wireless security configurations on the client are incorrect.

- The security configurations on the wireless access point are incorrect.

Step 3: Determine an Exact Cause

After you have established a theory of possible causes, determine an exact cause. The following steps are used to determine an exact cause:

- Verify the user's account settings.

- Reset the user's password.

- Verify the user's permissions for files and folders.

- Check the firewall settings.

- Scan and remove viruses from the computer.

- Verify the wireless security configuration of the client.

- Verify the security configuration on the wireless access point.

Step 4: Implement a Solution

After you have determined the exact cause, implement a solution. Some resources for possible solutions include the following:

- Problem-solving experience

- Other technicians

- Internet search

- Newsgroups

- Manufacturer FAQs

- Computer manuals

- Device manuals

- Online forums

- Technical websites

Step 5: Verify the Solution and Verify Full System Functionality

At this point, verify your solution and full system functionality. Some resources for possible solutions include the following:

- Reboot the computer.
- Log on to the computer.
- Connect to the network wirelessly.
- Verify file and folder access.
- Run a virus scan.

Step 6: Document Your Findings

After you have solved the problem, document your work. This usually includes the following:

How To

Step 1. Discuss the solution implemented with the customer.

Step 2. Have the customer verify that the problem has been solved.

Step 3. Provide the customer with all paperwork.

Step 4. Document the steps taken to solve the problem in the work order and the technician's journal.

Step 5. Document any components used in the repair.

Step 6. Document the time spent to resolve the problem.

Identify Common Problems and Solutions

Security problems can be attributed to hardware, software, networks, or some combination of the three. You will resolve some types of security problems more often than others.

Malware Settings

Virus and spyware protection problems are often related to incorrect software settings or configurations. As a result of these faulty settings, a computer may display one or more of the symptoms caused by malware and boot sector viruses.

User Accounts and Permissions

Unauthorized access or blocked access is often caused by incorrect user account settings and incorrect permissions.

Computer Security

Computer security problems can be caused by incorrect security settings in the BIOS or on the hard drive.

Firewall and Proxy Settings

Blocked connections to networked resources and the Internet are often related to incorrect firewall and proxy rules, and incorrect port settings.

Table 16-4 is a chart of common security problems and solutions. Table 16-5 is a list of common virus infection symptoms. Table 16-6 outlines what happens when the incorrect user account settings are used. Table 16-7 outlines what happens when the incorrect permissions are granted. Table 16-8 is a chart explaining common incorrect computer security settings. Table 16-9 explains incorrect firewall or proxy settings.

Table 16-4   Common Security Software Settings

Identify the Problem	Probable Causes	Plausible Solutions
Antivirus software has found infected files.	A virus has been downloaded to the computer from removable flash media, the Internet, or an email.	Repair, delete, or quarantine the infected files. Enable real-time scanning. Enable automatic updates for antivirus software.
The computer runs slowly at the same time every day.	Antivirus is set to scan the computer at the same time every day.	Configure the antivirus software to scan the computer when it is not in use.
The computer runs more slowly than normal, stops responding, or locks up often. Installed programs are corrupt or missing. The computer reports less memory than the amount of memory installed. The computer powers off by itself. The Windows Start button does not display.	The computer is infected with a virus.	Run antivirus software and repair, delete, or quarantine the infected files. Enable real-time scanning. Enable automatic updates for the antivirus software.

Identify the Problem	Probable Causes	Plausible Solutions
The Internet browser displays an incorrect home page.	The computer has been infected with spyware.	Run anti-spyware software and remove any infections.
Software firewall and antivirus programs are turned off automatically.		

Table 16-5   Malware or Virus Infection Symptoms

Identify the Problem	Probable Causes	Plausible Solutions
The message "MBR has been changed or modified" appears at bootup.	A boot sector virus has changed the master boot record.	Boot the computer with a bootable floppy or flash drive, and run antivirus software to remove the boot sector virus.
The Windows XP computer will not boot.	A virus has damaged the master boot record.	Boot the computer from the Vista installation media. At the install Windows screen, select R – Recovery Console. At the command prompt use the **fixmbr** command.
The Windows Vista computer starts with the error message, "Error Loading Operating System."	A virus has damaged the master boot record.	Boot the computer from the Vista installation media. At the Install Windows screen, select **Repair your computer**. At the command prompt, type **bootrec.exe /fixmbr**.
The Windows Vista computer starts with the error message, "Caution the hard disk may be infected by virus!"	A virus has damaged the boot sector.	Boot the computer from the Vista installation media. At the Install Windows screen, select **Repair your computer**. At the command prompt, type **bootrec.exe /fixboot**.

Table 16-6   Incorrect User Account Settings

Identify the Problem	Probable Causes	Plausible Solutions
The system administrator's assistant is not able to create and modify user accounts.	The system administrator's assistant does not have the correct permissions.	Add the administrator's assistant to the Power Users group.
A user working with Windows Vista is able to install unauthorized software.	The user knows the administrator login information.	Change the administrator login information.
	UAC is disabled on the computer.	Enable UAC on the computer.
A temporary user was able to log in last month but now is unable to log in.	The username or password has been spelled incorrectly.	Reenter the username and password correctly.
	The user's account is disabled.	Reenable the temporary account.
	The password has expired.	Change the password on the temporary user's account.

Table 16-7   Incorrect User Permissions

Identify the Problem	Probable Causes	Plausible Solutions
User can log on but cannot access some files and folders.	The user is not a member of the group that has access to the files and folders.	Add the user to the correct group.
		Add the correct user's permissions to the files and folders.
User can locate a file on the server but cannot download it.	The user permissions are not correct.	Change the user's permissions on the file to read and execute.
User is gaining access to a subfolder that should be inaccessible.	The subfolder inherited permissions from the upper-level folder.	Change the subfolder permission settings so it does not inherit the permissions from the parent folder. Set the proper permissions for the subfolder.

Identify the Problem	Probable Causes	Plausible Solutions
Users of a group cannot see one folder to which they are supposed to have access.	The folder permissions are set to deny.	Change the folder permissions to allow.
Encrypted files that are moved over the network to a new computer are no longer encrypted.	The new computer does not have an NTFS partition.	Convert the partition on the new computer to NTFS and reencrypt the file.

Table 16-8   Computer Security Settings

Identify the Problem	Probable Causes	Plausible Solutions
User complains that the computer BIOS settings keep changing.	The BIOS password is not set, allowing others to change the BIOS setting.	Set a password to protect access to the BIOS settings.
	BIOS battery might no longer hold a charge.	Replace the BIOS battery.
TPM does not show up in Device Manager.	The TPM is disabled.	Enable the TPM in the BIOS.

Table 16-9   Incorrect Firewall or Proxy Settings

Identify the Problem	Probable Causes	Plausible Solutions
Computer cannot ping another computer on the network.	The Windows firewall is blocking ping requests.	Configure the Windows firewall to allow ping requests.
	A router is blocking ping requests.	Configure the router to allow ping requests.
Laptop firewall exceptions are allowing unauthorized connections from rogue computers.	The Windows firewall settings are incorrect.	Set the Windows firewall to **Do not allow exceptions when using a public network**.
	The Windows firewall is disabled.	Enable Windows Firewall.

continues

Table 16-9   Incorrect Firewall or Proxy Settings   *continued*

Identify the Problem	Probable Causes	Plausible Solutions
Computer cannot telnet to another computer.	The Windows firewall blocks port 23 by default.	Configure the Windows firewall to open port 23.
	The router is blocking port 23.	Configure the router to allow port 23.
Email program is properly configured but cannot connect to the email server.	The email server is down.	Verify that the email server is operational.
	The Windows firewall is blocking the email software.	Create a Windows firewall exception for your email software.
Computer can ping outside the local network but cannot access the World Wide Web.	The Windows firewall is blocking port 80.	Configure Windows firewall to open port 80.
	The router is blocking port 80.	Configure the router to allow port 80.
	The default gateway setting on the computer might be incorrect.	Set the default gateway correctly on the computer.
Computer can ping the proxy server but cannot access web pages.	The browser proxy server settings are incorrect.	Reenter the proxy server settings, including the IP address and port of the proxy server and any exceptions that should be defined.
	The proxy server is offline.	
		Reboot the proxy server.

Apply Troubleshooting Skills

Now that you understand the troubleshooting process, it is time to apply your listening and diagnostic skills.

The first lab is designed to test your troubleshooting skills with security problems. You will troubleshoot and repair a computer with a security problem that is preventing it from connecting to the wireless network.

The second lab is designed to reinforce your communication and troubleshooting skills. In this lab, you will perform the following steps:

- Receive the work order.

- Talk the customer through various steps to try and resolve the problem.

- Document the problem and the resolution.

The third lab is designed to test your troubleshooting skills with security problems. You will troubleshoot and repair a network that has more than one security problem.

Lab 16.5.3: Fix a Security Problem

In this lab, you gather data from the customer and then instruct the customer on how to correct a security issue that is preventing connection to the wireless network. Refer to the lab in *IT Essentials: PC Hardware and Software Lab Manual, Fourth Edition*. You can perform this lab now or wait until the end of the chapter.

Lab 16.5.3: Remote Technician: Fix a Security Problem

In this lab, you gather data from the customer to begin the troubleshooting process and document the customer's problem in the work order provided in the lab. Refer to the lab in *IT Essentials: PC Hardware and Software Lab Manual, Fourth Edition*. You can perform this lab now or wait until the end of the chapter.

Lab 16.5.3: Troubleshooting Access Security with Windows XP

In this lab, you troubleshoot access security with Windows XP. Refer to the lab in *IT Essentials: PC Hardware and Software Lab Manual, Fourth Edition*. You can perform this lab now or wait until the end of the chapter.

Optional Lab 16.5.3: Troubleshooting Access Security with Windows Vista

In this lab, you troubleshoot access security with Windows Vista. Refer to the lab in *IT Essentials: PC Hardware and Software Lab Manual, Fourth Edition*. You can perform this lab now or wait until the end of the chapter.

Summary

This chapter discussed computer security and explained why it is important to protect computer equipment, networks, and data. Threats, procedures, and preventive maintenance relating to data and physical security were described to help you keep computer equipment and data safe. Security protects computers, network equipment, and data from loss and physical danger. The following are some of the important concepts to remember from this chapter:

- Security threats can come from inside or outside of an organization.

- Viruses and worms are common threats that attack data.

- Develop and maintain a security plan to protect both data and physical equipment from loss.

- Keep operating systems and applications up to date and secure with patches and service packs.

Follow these steps when setting up a security plan:

Step 1. Outline the customer's security requirements.

Step 2. Select security components.

Step 3. Implement a security plan.

Step 4. Perform preventive maintenance.

Step 5. Troubleshoot security.

Summary of Exercises

This is a summary of the Labs, Worksheets, Remote Technician exercises, Class Discussions, Virtual Desktop activities, and Virtual Laptop activities associated with this chapter.

Labs

The following labs cover material from this chapter. Refer to the labs in *IT Essentials: PC Hardware and Software Lab Manual, Fourth Edition*.

Lab 16.3.1: Configure Wireless Security

Lab 16.3.2: Configure Windows XP Firewall

Optional Lab 16.3.2: Configure Windows Vista Firewall

Lab 16.4.3: Data Backup and Recovery in Windows XP

Optional Lab 16.4.3: Data Backup and Recovery in Windows Vista

Lab 16.5.3: Fix a Security Problem

Lab 16.5.3: Remote Technician: Fix a Security Problem

Lab 16.5.3: Troubleshooting Access Security with Windows XP

Optional Lab 16.5.3: Troubleshooting Access Security with Windows Vista

 # Worksheets

The following worksheets cover material from this chapter. Refer to the worksheets in *IT Essentials: PC Hardware and Software Lab Manual, Fourth Edition.*

Worksheet 16.1.1: Answer Security Policy Questions

Worksheet 16.2.3: Research Firewalls

Check Your Understanding

You can find the answers to these questions in the appendix, "Answers to Check Your Understanding Questions."

1. Which aspect of security includes biometrics and door locks?

   A. Securing access to data files

   B. Securing login access

   C. Securing wireless access

   D. Securing access to facilities

2. Which practice is a minimum requirement for securing a network?

   A. Deploy a firewall.

   B. Create secure login information for all users.

   C. Encrypt all data.

   D. Log all activity on the network.

3. Which item physically protects networking media from damage and unauthorized access?

   A. Conduit

   B. Hub

   C. Security guard

   D. Video equipment

4. Which type of attack is launched by a hacker appearing to be a trusted organization and sending email to trick the user into providing confidential information?

   A. Denial of service

   B. Grayware

   C. Phishing

   D. Trojan

5. Where should a technician begin gathering data when troubleshooting a computer problem?

   A. Operating system knowledge base

   B. Operating system logs

   C. User

   D. Vendor of the computer

6. A security consultant is trying to find a hardware device that will allow only authorized users to access confidential data. Which device will ensure that the data will be accessible by authorized employees only?

   A. Cable lock

   B. Docking station lock

   C. Lockable case

   D. USB security dongle

7. On a Windows XP network, which task is necessary to ensure that any operating system vulnerabilities are removed and that identified errors are repaired?

   A. Audit both the system and user files on the computer system on a regular basis.

   B. Use a software-based firewall on a regular basis.

   C. Install a third-party spyware program to monitor traffic on a regular basis.

   D. Download and install operating system updates on a regular basis.

Answers to Check Your Understanding Questions

Chapter 1

1. E
2. A
3. B
4. B
5. D
6. B
7. C
8. B

Chapter 2

1. C
2. B
3. A
4. C
5. B
6. B, F
7. B
8. C
9. A, B, D
10. C

Chapter 3

1. C
2. D
3. D
4. B
5. B
6. A
7. D
8. D, E

Chapter 4

1. B, C, D
2. C, E
3. B
4. B
5. E

Chapter 5

1. A
2. C
3. B
4. E
5. C
6. A
7. E
8. A
9. B

Chapter 6

1. A
2. B
3. B
4. D
5. B
6. A, D
7. C
8. D
9. D
10. B
11. C
12. B, C
13. B

Chapter 7

1. E
2. C
3. C, D, E
4. E
5. A
6. D
7. B
8. B

Chapter 8

1. C
2. A
3. A
4. D
5. E
6. D
7. D
8. A
9. C
10. A

Chapter 9

1. A
2. D
3. D
4. B
5. C
6. A
7. A, D
8. D
9. B
10. A, D
11. C
12. B

Chapter 10

1. B
2. B, C
3. C
4. B
5. D
6. A, B
7. B
8. B
9. C
10. C
11. A
12. C

Chapter 11

1. A, D, E
2. B
3. D, E
4. B, E, F
5. B
6. A, C
7. C
8. B
9. B, C
10. B
11. C, D

Chapter 12

1. A
2. C, E
3. C
4. A
5. B
6. A
7. C

Chapter 13

1. F
2. D
3. D, E
4. D
5. E
6. A, C
7. A
8. B, F

Chapter 14

1. A, C
2. C
3. B, D
4. C
5. A, B
6. B, D, F
7. A, C
8. C

Chapter 15

1. D
2. B
3. D
4. A
5. D
6. B
7. C, D
8. A

Chapter 16

1. D
2. B
3. A
4. C
5. C
6. D
7. D

This Glossary defines many of the terms and abbreviations related to PC hardware and operating systems. It includes the key terms used throughout the book. As with any growing technical field, some terms evolve and take on several meanings. Where necessary, multiple definitions and abbreviation expansions are presented.

10BASE-T   A 10-Mbps baseband Ethernet specification that uses two pairs of Category 3, 4, or 5 twisted-pair cabling. One pair of wires is used to receive data, and the other pair is used to transmit data. 10BASE-T, which is part of the IEEE 802.3 specification, has a distance limit of approximately 328 feet (100 m) per segment.

100BASE-TX   A 100-Mbps baseband Fast Ethernet specification that uses two pairs of UTP or STP wiring. Based on the IEEE 802.3 standard.

100BASE-X   A 100-Mbps baseband Fast Ethernet specification that refers to the 100BASE-FX and 100BASE-TX standards for Fast Ethernet over fiber-optic and copper cabling. Based on the IEEE 802.3 standard.

1000BASE-T   A Gigabit Ethernet specification that uses UTP Category 5, 5e, or 6. Each network segment can have a maximum distance of 328 feet (100 m) without a repeater. Also known as 801.3ab.

A

AC power connector   A socket that is used to connect the AC power adapter to a computer or docking station.

AC power cord   A cable that transfers electricity from the AC power supply to the computer power supply.

Accelerated Graphics Port (AGP)   A high-speed, 32-bit bus technology designed to support the acceleration of 3D computer graphics.

Access Control List (ACL)   A list managed by a network administrator that itemizes what a user is permitted to access and the type of access granted. The network administrator uses ACLs to restrict packet access to the network.

access point   A device that connects wireless devices to form a wireless network. An access point usually connects to a wired network, and it can relay data between wired and wireless devices. Connectivity distances can range from several feet or meters to several miles or kilometers.

accidental threat   Accidental destruction or loss of data or equipment.

active partition   A partition on a hard disk drive that is set as the bootable partition. It usually contains the operating system to be used on the computer. Only one partition on a computer can be set as an active or bootable partition on a hard disk drive.

ActiveX   An applet or small program created by Microsoft to control interactivity on web pages that has to be downloaded to gain access to the full functionality.

adapter card   An expansion card that increases the number of controllers and ports available on a computer.

Address Resolution Protocol (ARP)   Discovers the local address (MAC address) of a station on the network when the IP address is known. End stations as well as routers use ARP to discover local addresses. The following switches are used with the **ARP** command:

-a displays the cache.
-d deletes an entry from the ARP cache.
-s adds a permanent IP-to-MAC address mapping.

administrator   Someone who queries the User Registrar to analyze individual subscriber status and to gather data.

Advanced Configuration and Power Interface (ACPI)   An interface that allows the operating system to control power management. Replaces Advanced Power Management (APM).

Advanced Power Management (APM)   An interface that allows the BIOS to control the settings for power management. This has been replaced by the Advanced Configuration and Power Interface (ACPI).

Advanced Technology Extended (ATX)   A standard computer case form factor for modern computers.

Advanced Technology Extended (ATX) power connector   A 20-pin or 24-pin internal power supply connector.

adware   A software program that displays advertising on a computer, usually distributed with downloaded software.

all-in-one type printer   A multifunctional device designed to provide services such as printing, fax, and copier functions.

alternating current (AC)   Current that changes direction at a uniformly repetitious rate. This type of electricity typically is provided by a utility company and is accessed by wall sockets.

American National Standards Institute (ANSI)   A private, nonprofit organization that administers and coordinates the U.S. voluntary standardization and conformity assessment system. ANSI identifies industrial and public requirements for national consensus standards. It also coordinates and manages their development, resolves national standards problems, and ensures effective participation in international standardization.

American Standard Code for Information Interchange (ASCII)   An 8-bit code for character representation (7 bits plus parity).

analog telephone   A telephone system that uses audio signals on copper wire.

analog transmission   Signal transmission over wires or through the air in which information is conveyed through the variation of some combination of signal amplitude, frequency, and phase.

answer file   A file that contains predefined settings and answers to the questions that are required by the operating system setup wizard.

antistatic bag   Packaging material that protects components from electrostatic discharge (ESD).

antistatic mat   A surface that provides a safe environment for computer components by dissipating ESD.

antistatic wrist strap   A device worn on the wrist to dissipate electrostatic discharge (ESD) between a person and electronic equipment.

antivirus application   A program that is installed on a system to prevent computer viruses from infecting the computer.

AppleTalk   A protocol suite to network Macintosh computers. It is composed of a comprehensive set of protocols that span the seven layers of the OSI reference model.

application layer   Layer 7 of the Open Systems Interconnection (OSI) reference model. This layer provides services to application processes such as e-mail, file transfer, and terminal emulation that are outside the OSI reference model. The application layer identifies and establishes the availability of intended communication partners and the resources required to connect with them. It also synchronizes cooperating applications and establishes agreement on procedures for error recovery and control of data integrity. It corresponds roughly with the transaction services layer in the Systems Network Architecture (SNA) model. The OSI reference model includes the application layer, presentation layer, session layer, transport layer, network layer, data link layer, and physical layer.

application layer protocols   Protocols that govern applications; for example, HTTP supports web browsers, and POP supports email clients.

application software   A program that performs a specific function by accepting input from the user and then manipulating it to achieve a result, known as the output.

arm (Acorn RISC Machine) architecture   A low-power RISC CPU.

Asymmetric DSL (ADSL)   Currently the most common DSL implementation. Speeds vary from 384 kbps to more than 6 Mbps downstream. The upstream speed typically is lower.

asymmetric encryption   A method of encrypting data on a network. Uses a private key to write messages and a public key to decode the messages. Only the private key needs to be kept secret. Public keys can be distributed openly.

attention (AT) command set   Issues dial, hang-up, reset, and other instructions to the modem. It is based on the Hayes command set.

attenuation   The distance a signal can travel before it is too weak to be read.

Automated System Recovery (ASR)   A backup utility that makes a copy of the operating system and installed applications but not the user data. It is used to recover from a hard drive crash.

Automatic Private IP Addressing (APIPA)   An operating system feature that enables a computer to assign itself an address if it is unable to contact a DHCP server. The Internet Assigned Numbers Authority (IANA) has reserved private IP addresses in the range of 169.254.0.0 to 169.254.255.255 for APIPA.

Automatic Update   A utility to schedule the Windows Update feature to check for critical updates.

auxiliary (AUX) power connector   A four-, six-, or eight-pin connector that supplies extra voltage to the motherboard from the power supply.

B

backplane   A physical connection between an interface processor or card, the data buses, and the power distribution buses inside a chassis.

backup   A copy of data saved to alternate media. Should be physically removed from the source data.

backward-compatible   Hardware or software systems that can use interfaces and data from earlier versions of the system or with other systems.

bandwidth   The amount of data that can be transmitted within a fixed amount of time.

base station   A device that attaches a laptop to AC power and to desktop peripherals.

Basic Input/Output System (BIOS)   A program stored in a ROM chip in the computer that provides the basic code to control the computer's hardware and to perform diagnostics on it. The BIOS prepares the computer to load the operating system.

Basic Rate Interface (BRI)   An ISDN interface composed of two B channels and one D channel for circuit-switched communication of voice, video, and data. Compare with PRI.

basic service set (BSS)   A basic wireless network with devices connecting to one wireless router or access point.

battery   An electrical device that converts chemical energy into electrical energy.

battery bay   The space were the battery is stored on a laptop.

battery latch   A tool used to insert, remove, and secure the laptop battery.

battery status indicator LED   A light that indicates the condition of the laptop battery.

beep code   An audible reporting system for errors that are found by the BIOS during the POST, represented by a series of beeps.

Berg power connector   A keyed connector that supplies power to a floppy drive.

biometric device   A tool that uses sensors, such as a fingerprint or retinal scanner, that identify the user's physical characteristics to allow access to a device or a network.

bit   The smallest unit of data in a computer. A bit can take the value of either 1 or 0. A bit is the binary format in which data is processed by computers.

bit rate   The speed at which bits are transmitted, usually expressed in bits per second (bps).

bits per second (bps)   The unit measurement of data transfer. Usually a multiplier such as kilo (k), mega (M), or giga (G) precedes bps.

blackout   A complete loss of AC power.

blue screen of death (BSoD)   A memory dump. There is no recovery from these errors, and the user is forced to restart the PC, losing any unsaved data as a result.

Bluetooth   A wireless industry standard that uses an unlicensed radio frequency for short-range communication, enabling portable devices to communicate over short distances.

boot   To start a computer.

boot.ini   The file that manages multiple OSs on a PC.

bootable disk   A troubleshooting tool that allows the computer to boot from a disk when the hard drive will not boot.

boot record   A 512-byte file containing a table that describes the partition, the number of bytes per sector, and the number of sectors per cluster.

Border Gateway Protocol (BGP)   Used to exchange routing information between autonomous systems on the Internet.

bridge   Segments network traffic by filtering and forwarding packets based on MAC addresses.

broadband   Multiple signals using multiple frequencies over one cable.

broadband optical telepoint   Infrared broadband transmission that can handle high-quality multimedia requirements.

broadband satellite   A network connection using a satellite dish.

brownout   A temporary drop in AC power.

buffer   A storage area used to handle data in transit. Buffers are used in internetworking to compensate for differences in processing speed between network devices. Bursts of data can be stored in buffers until they can be handled by slower processing devices. Sometimes called a packet buffer.

bus   A medium through which data is transferred from one part of a computer to another. The bus can be compared to a highway on which data travels within a computer.

bus topology   A network in which each computer connects on a common cable.

byte   A unit of measure that describes the size of a data file, the amount of space on a disk or other storage medium, or the amount of data being sent over a network. One byte consists of 8 bits of data.

C

C: drive   Generally the label for the first hard drive in a computer system. Drive A and Drive B are reserved for floppy drives. Drive B is rarely used on current computers.

cable   A set of conductors, bundled and sheathed, made of insulated copper or optical fiber, that transport signals and power between electrical devices.

cable modem   Acts like a LAN interface by connecting a computer to the Internet. The cable modem connects a computer to the cable company network through the same coaxial cabling that feeds cable TV (CATV) signals to a television set.

cable tie   A fastener used to bundle cables inside and outside a computer.

cache   A data storage area that provides high-speed access for the system.

cache memory   A separate RAM memory used to optimize performance by storing frequently accessed data.

caching   The local storage of data to expedite access time.

call center   An office in which technicians troubleshoot problems over the phone.

Caps Lock indicator LED   A light that shows the on/off status of the Caps Lock.

card key   An identity card with a chip that stores user data, including the level of access.

carrier sense multiple access collision detect (CSMA/CD)   An access control method that allows any end stations to send a message at any time, assuming it first listened and heard no other end station transmitting. If two end stations send at the same time and the collision is detected, a jam signal is sent and every host stops sending. Each end station must wait a number of milliseconds before it can transmit again. That wait time can be randomly assigned or based on the MAC address, depending on the specific protocols.

Category 3   A cable that is primarily used in telephone connections.

Category 5   A cable that contains four pairs of wires, with a maximum data rate of 1 Gbps.

Category 5e   A cable that provides more twists per foot than Category 5 at the same data rate of 1 Gbps.

Category 6   A cable that is enhanced with more twists than Category 5e cable. It contains a plastic divider that separates the pairs of wires to prevent crosstalk. It is capable of 10 Gbps.

cellular WAN   A wide-area network that has the technology for the use of a cell phone or laptop for voice and data communications.

central processing unit (CPU)   Interprets and processes software instructions and data. Located on the motherboard, the CPU is a chip contained on a single integrated circuit called the microprocessor. The CPU contains two basic components, a control unit and an Arithmetic/Logic Unit (ALU).

certification   A certificate that provides evidence of knowledge of or a specific skill set pertaining to an area of focus.

chip   A small slice of silicon or germanium processed to have electrical characteristics so that it can be developed into an electronic component. Also called a semiconductor.

chip set   Chips on a motherboard that enable the CPU to communicate and interact with the computer's other components.

CHKDSK   A command used to check the integrity of files and folders on a hard drive by scanning the disk surface for physical errors.

client/server network   A network in which services are located in a dedicated computer that responds to client (user) requests.

cluster   The smallest unit of space used to store data on a disk. Also called the file allocation unit.

Cmd   The command used to launch a command prompt.

CMOS battery   A battery that supplies power to maintain basic configuration information, including the real-time clock, when the computer is turned off.

CMYK   Display colors: cyan, magenta, yellow, and black.

coaxial cable   Copper-cored cable surrounded by a heavy shielding. Used to connect computers in a network.

cold boot   To power up a computer from the off position.

color ink jet printer   A type of printer that uses liquid-ink-filled cartridges that spray ink to form an image on the paper.

command-line interface (CLI)   An interface, such as a DOS prompt, that requires commands to be entered manually on the command line.

communication skills   A skill set that allows a technician to communicate information so that it is understood by the customer.

compact disc (CD) drive   An optical device that reads compact discs.

compact disc read-only memory (CD-ROM) An optical storage medium for audio and data.

compact disc recordable (CD-R)   An optical medium that allows data to be recorded but not modified.

compact disc rewritable (CD-RW)   An optical storage medium that allows data to be recorded and modified.

compatibility mode   Allows applications to run as if they were is an older operating system.

Complementary Metal Oxide Semiconductor (CMOS)   A type of semiconductor, or low-power memory firmware, that stores basic configuration information.

complex instruction set computer (CISC)   An architecture that uses a broad set of instructions, with several choices for almost every operation. The result is that a programmer can execute precisely the command needed, resulting in fewer instructions per operation.

compressed air   Air under pressure in a can that blows dust off of computer components without creating static. Also called canned air.

computer   An electrical machine that can execute a list of instructions and perform calculations based on those instructions.

computer-aided design (CAD)   An application used to create architectural, electrical, and mechani-

cal design. More complex forms of CAD include solid modeling and parametric modeling, which allow objects to be created with real-world characteristics.

Computer Management   A tool that allows administrators to access system tools that manage storage, services, and applications.

computer network   Two or more computers connected by a medium to share data and resources.

computer system   A combination of hardware and software components. Hardware is the physical equipment such as the case, floppy disk drives, keyboards, monitors, cables, speakers, and printers. Software describes the programs that operate the computer system.

conduit   A casing that protects the infrastructure media from damage and unauthorized access.

configuration tool   A service management tool or element management service tool with a GUI.

connector   A device used to terminate cable.

Control Panel applets   A collection of programs and utilities that can be used to configure the operating system.

conventional memory   All memory addresses from 0 to 640 KB.

cookie   A small text file that is stored on the hard disk that allows a website to track the user's association to that site.

copy backup   Backs up user-selected files to tape. This backup does not reset the archive bit.

CPU throttling   Manually setting the CPU to run slower, usually to reduce heat.

critical battery alarm   An alarm warning the user to connect the portable device to a power source very soon or risk a shutdown and potentially the loss of data.

crosstalk   Interfering energy, such as electromagnetic interference (EMI), that is transferred from one circuit to another.

current (I)   The flow of electrons in a conductor that is measured in amperes.

customer-replaceable unit (CRU)   A component that customers may install at their location.

cylinder   All the tracks on a hard disk with the same number. Collectively, the same track on all platters of a multiplatter hard drive.

D

daily backup   Backs up only the files that are modified on the day of the backup. This backup does not reset the archive bit.

data backup   Information on a computer stored on removable backup media that can be kept in a safe place. If the computer hardware fails, the data backup can be restored so that processing can continue.

data encryption   Scrambles data by applying an algorithm. An encryption key is used to rearrange the data to make it intelligible again.

data link layer   Layer 2 of the Open Systems Interconnection (OSI) reference model. This layer provides reliable transit of data across a physical link. The data link layer is concerned with physical addressing, network topology, line discipline, error notification, ordered delivery of frames, and flow control. The IEEE has divided this layer into two sublayers—the MAC sublayer and the LLC sublayer,

sometimes simply called link layer. Roughly corresponds to the data link control layer of the Systems Network Architecture (SNA) model. The OSI reference model includes the application layer, presentation layer, session layer, transport layer, network layer, data link layer, and physical layer.

database   An organized collection of data that can be easily accessed, managed, indexed, searched, and updated.

data transfer rate   Refers to how fast the computer can transfer information into memory.

default gateway   A node or router on a network that provides access to another network or the Internet.

default installation   An installation that requires minimal user interaction. Also called a typical installation.

default printer   The first option that an application uses when the user clicks the printer icon. The user can change the default printer.

DEFRAG   A command that rearranges the data and rewrites all the files on the hard drive to the beginning of the drive. This makes it easier and faster for the hard drive to retrieve data.

denial of service (DoS)   A form of attack that prevents users from accessing normal services, such as e-mail or a web server, because the system is busy responding to an abnormally large number of requests. DoS works by sending an abundance of requests for a resource. This causes the system to overload and stop operating.

desktop   A metaphor used to portray file systems. A desktop consists of pictures, called icons, that show files, folders, and any resource available to a user in a GUI operating system.

desktop computer   A type of computer designed to fit on top of or under a desk. Desktop computers are not mobile like laptop computers.

Device Manager   An application that displays a list of all the hardware that is installed on the system.

diagnostic software   Programs that assist in the troubleshooting process.

diagnostic tools   Utilities that monitor the network server.

dialup networking (DUN)   Using the public telephone system or network to communicate.

differential backup   Backs up all the files that have been created or modified since the last full backup. It does not reset the archive bit.

digital audio tape (DAT)   A tape standard that uses 4-mm digital audiotapes to store data in the digital data storage (DDS) format.

digital linear tape (DLT)   Technology that offers high capacity and relatively high-speed tape backup capabilities.

digital multimeter (DMM)   A tool that combines the functionality of a voltmeter, ohmmeter, and ammeter into one easy measuring device.

digital signals   Signals that are in a binary form.

digital subscriber line (DSL)   A public network technology that delivers high bandwidth over conventional copper wiring at limited distances. Always-on technology that allows users to connect to the Internet.

digital versatile disc (DVD)   A removable medium that is used primarily for movie and data storage.

Digital Visual Interface (DVI)   An interface that supplies uncompressed digital video to a digital monitor.

Digital Visual Interface (DVI) port   A digital video port that allows backward compatibility to analog video signals. It can transmit very large amounts of data and is often used for applications that require a large monitor resolution.

direct current (DC)   Current flowing in one direction, as used in a battery.

direct memory access (DMA)   A method of bypassing the CPU when transferring data from the main memory directly to a device.

directory   1) A type of file that organizes other files in a hierarchical structure. 2) Related program and data files organized and grouped in the DOS file system. 3) A place to store data in the Windows file-management system.

disk cleanup   Disk-management software that is used to clear space on a hard drive by searching for files that can be safely deleted, such as temporary Internet files.

disk cloning   Copying the contents of an entire hard drive to another hard drive, thereby decreasing the time it takes to install drivers, applications, updates, and so forth on the second drive.

disk management   A system utility used to manage hard drives and partitions, such as initializing disks, creating partitions, and formatting partitions.

disk operating system (DOS)   A collection of programs and commands that control overall computer operations in a disk-based system.

display   A computer output surface and projecting mechanism that shows text and graphic images.

distributed DoS (DDoS)   A denial of service attack launched from multiple sources called zombies, which amplifies the effect and makes it more difficult to trace back to the source.

DNS poisoning   Changing the DNS records on a system to point to false servers where the data is recorded.

docking connector   A socket used to attach a docking station to the laptop.

docking station   A device that attaches a laptop to AC power and desktop peripherals.

docking station connector   The port through which a laptop connects to a docking station. Details regarding the shape and design of docking station connectors vary widely among manufactures.

domain   A logical group of computers and electronic devices with a common set of rules and procedures administered as a unit.

Domain Name System (DNS)   A system that provides a way to map friendly hostnames, or URLs, to IP addresses.

dot-matrix printer   A printer that operates by impacting the ribbon to place an image on the paper.

dots per inch (dpi)   A measurement of print quality on a dot-matrix printer. The higher the dpi, the higher the print's quality.

Double Data Rate (DDR)   RAM that reads on the rising and on the falling side of the clock cycle, thereby doubling the access speed. Normal SDRAM is read once per clock cycle.

Double Data Rate 2 (DDR2)   DDR RAM with a modified bus speed that allows RAM to be read four times every clock cycle.

drive bay   A standard-sized area for adding hardware to a computer case. The two most common drive bays are used to house a CD/DVD drive and a floppy drive.

drive letter   A designation that distinguishes the physical or logical drives in Windows.

drive mapping   The process of assigning a letter to a physical or logical drive.

dual-core CPU   Two cores inside a single CPU chip. The cores can be used together to increase speed, or they can be used in two locations at the same time.

dual inline memory module (DIMM)   A circuit board with a 64-bit data bus that holds memory chips. A memory module with 168 pins. Supports 64-bit data transfers. A RAM chip with contacts on both sides.

dual inline package (DIP)   A rectangular micro chip with metal contacts on two sides.

dual ring   All the devices on the network connect to two cables, and the data travels in both directions. Only one cable is used at a time. If one ring fails, data is transmitted on the other ring.

DVD drive   An optical device that reads DVDs. A DVD-rewritable (DVD-RW) drive can write to DVD-RWs.

DVD-R   A DVD recordable format.

DVD+R   A DVD that is a once-writable optical disc with 4.7 GB of storage.

DVD-ROM   A DVD format that is designed to store computer files.

DVD-RW   Technology that allows the medium to be recorded multiple times.

DVD+RW   The name of a standard for optical discs. It is one of several types of DVD that hold up to 4.7 GB.

DVD-Video   A DVD format that is used by stand-alone DVD players for movies and extras.

Dxdiag   A tool used to test video and sound cards as well as the functionality of DirectX.

dye-sublimation printer   A printer that uses solid sheets of ink that change from solid to gas in a process called sublimating. The gas then passes through the paper, where it turns back to a solid. The print head passes over a sheet of cyan, magenta, yellow, and a clear overcoat (CMYO). Also called a thermal dye printer.

Dynamic Host Configuration Protocol (DHCP) A software utility that automatically assigns IP addresses to client devices in a large network.

dynamic RAM (DRAM)   RAM that stores information in capacitors that must be periodically refreshed. Delays can occur because DRAMs are inaccessible to the processor when refreshing their contents. However, DRAMs are less complex and have greater capacity than SRAMs.

dynamic routing   Routing that adjusts automatically to network topology or traffic changes. Also called adaptive routing.

E

eject button   The lever that releases an object, such as the button on a floppy drive.

Electronic Industries Association (EIA)   A group that specifies electrical transmission standards. The EIA and the Telecommunications Industry Association (TIA) have developed numerous well-known communications standards, including EIA/TIA-232 and EIA/TIA-449.

electronic mail (e-mail)   Users' ability to communicate over a computer network. The exchange of computer-stored messages by network communication.

electronically erasable programmable read-only memory (EEPROM)   The standard memory that allows for rewriting the fundamental instruction set called the basic input/output system (BIOS).

electrophotographic drum   A central part of the laser printer that acquires the toner to be printed on paper.

electrostatic discharge (ESD)   The discharge of static electricity from one conductor to another conductor of a different potential.

email bomb   A denial of service attack on an email server or an individual email account carried out by flooding it with countless junk emails.

emergency repair disk (ERD)   A backup utility that makes a copy of the hard drive in case it crashes.

encryption   A security feature that applies coding to a file so that only authorized users can view the file.

Encryption File System (EFS)   A Microsoft-specific file system for encryption.

Enhanced Data Rates for GSM Evolution (EDGE)
A protocol that achieves near broadband data transfers over existing GSM technology. It is found in 3G and 4G phones.

Enhanced Integrated Drive Electronics (EIDE)
An enhanced version of the standard IDE interface that connects hard disks, CD-ROM drives, and tape drives to a PC.

error-correcting code (ECC)   A technology that increases the reliability of data.

Ethernet   A baseband LAN specification invented by Xerox Corporation and developed jointly by Xerox, Intel, and Digital Equipment Corporation. Ethernet networks use CSMA/CD and run on a variety of cable types at 10 Mbps or more. Ethernet is similar to the IEEE 802.3 series of standards.

Ethernet port   An RJ-45 socket that is used to connect a computer to a cabled LAN.

event   A network message indicating operational irregularities in physical elements of a network or a response to the occurrence of a significant task, typically the completion of a request for information.

Event Viewer   An application that monitors system events, application events, and security events.

Evolution-Data Optimized (EV-DO)   A data protocol that provides fast download rates and is found on many 3G phones.

exhaust vent   An outlet that expels hot air from the interior of a device or room.

expansion card modem   A modem that is inserted into a motherboard expansion slot (ISA or PCI). Also called an internal modem.

expansion slot   An opening in a computer where a PC card can be inserted to add capabilities to the computer.

ExpressCard   A high-throughput laptop expansion card standard that was developed by the PCMCIA. The ExpressCard expansion slot uses the built-in PCI Express (x1) and/or USB bus of a laptop. ExpressCards have a 26-pin connector and are hot-swappable.

Extended Data Out (EDO)   DRAM that uses a small SRAM chip as a cache.

extended memory   Memory above 1 MB.

extended partition   The second partition on the hard drive.

extended service set (ESS)   A combination of two or more access points that usually overlap and share the same SSID but use different channels so users can roam from one to the other without losing network connectivity.

extended-star topology   A star topology that is expanded to include additional networking devices.

external diskette drive connector   A port that connects older laptops to floppy disk drives.

external hard drive   A device that connects to the computer to provide additional data storage.

external modem   A modem that connects to the serial port (COM1 or COM2) of most computers. An external modem, such as a cable modem, typically is used for high-speed connections.

F

Fast Ethernet   Any of a number of 100-Mbps Ethernet specifications. Fast Ethernet offers a speed increase ten times that of the 10BASE-T Ethernet specification while preserving such qualities as frame format, MAC mechanisms, and MTU. Such similarities allow the use of existing 10BASE-T applications and network management tools on Fast Ethernet networks. Based on an extension to the IEEE 802.3 specification. Compare with Ethernet.

Fast Page Mode (FPM)   An older type of RAM that improved the access time of page mode RAM.

FDISK   A command used to delete and create partitions on the hard drive. The **:\ STATUS** switch displays partition information when used with the **FDISK** command.

Fiber Distributed Data Interface (FDDI)   A type of Token Ring network that is used in larger LANs.

fiber-optic cable   A physical medium that can conduct modulated light transmission. Compared with other transmission media, fiber-optic cable is more expensive, but it is not susceptible to electromagnetic interference, and it is capable of higher data rates. Sometimes called optical fiber. Uses glass or plastic wire, also called fiber, to carry information as light pulses. Conducts modulated light to transmit data.

field-replaceable unit (FRU)   A component that a trained service technician may install at a remote location.

file   A block of logically related data that is given a single name and is treated as a single unit.

file allocation table (FAT)   A table that the operating system uses to store information about the location of the files stored on a disk. This file is stored in track 0 on the disk.

file extension   A designation that describes the file format or the type of application that created a file.

file management   A hierarchical structure of files, folders, and drives in Windows.

file system   The two file systems available in Windows XP and Windows Vista are FAT32 and NTFS. NTFS has greater stability and security features.

file system security   Enables administrators to encrypt entire partitions for increased security.

File Transfer Protocol (FTP)   A set of rules governing how files are transferred. FTP allows multiple simultaneous connections to remote file systems.

fingerprint reader   An input device that scans fingerprints to authenticate login using biometric identification.

firewall   A router or access server, or several routers or access servers, designated as a buffer between any connected public networks and a private network. A firewall router uses access lists and other methods to ensure the security of the private network.

Firewire   A high-speed, platform-independent communication bus. Firewire interconnects digital devices such as digital video cameras, printers, scanners, digital cameras, and hard drives. Firewire is also known as IEEE 1394, i.Link (Sony-proprietary), and linear heat-detecting cable (LHDC) in the U.K.

firmware   A program that is embedded in a silicon chip rather than stored on a floppy disk.

flash memory   A rewritable memory chip that retains data after the power is turned off.

flat-head screwdriver   A tool used to loosen or tighten slotted screws.

floppy data cable   An external cable that transfers data between the computer and the floppy drive.

floppy disk drive (FDD)   A device that spins a magnetically coated floppy disk to read data from it and write data to it.

floppy drive cable   An external cable that connects the computer and the floppy drive.

format   To prepare a file system in a partition to store files.

form factor   The physical size and shape of computer components. Components that share the same form factor are physically interchangeable.

full backup   Backs up all files on a disk. Also called a normal backup.

full-duplex transmission   Data transmission that can go two ways at the same time. An Internet connection using DSL service is an example.

function key (Fn key)   A modifier key usually found on laptop computers. It is used in combination with other keys to perform specific functions.

G

gamepad   An external controller used as an input device, primarily for gaming.

General Packet Radio Service (GPRS)   Found mainly in 2G and 3G cell phones, a method of sending data to and from portable devices.

gigabits per second (Gbps)   Describes data transferred at a rate of 1 billion bits per second.

gigahertz (GHz)   A common measurement of a processor equal to one billion cycles per second.

Global System for Mobile Communications (GSM)   A worldwide cellular network.

graphical user interface (GUI)   An interface that allows the user to navigate through the operating system using icons and menus.

graphics application   Creates or modifies graphical images. The two types of graphical images include object- or vector-based images, and bitmaps or raster images.

Graphics Device Interface (GDI)   A Windows component to manage how graphical images are transmitted to output devices. GDI works by converting images to a bitmap that uses the computer instead of the printer to transfer the images.

grayware   Spyware that installs on a computer without being prompted and downloads additional applications without permission from the user.

guest account   A default user account that is intended to provide limited access to unauthorized users. It has since become a serious security risk and should be disabled on all Windows XP computers.

H

half-duplex transmission   Data transmission that can go two ways, but not at the same time. A two-way radio is an example.

hand tools   Tools that are powered or controlled by a person. They are normally small and have dedicated functions. Examples include a screwdriver, pliers, and drill.

handshaking sequence   A series of short communications that occur between two modems. This establishes the readiness of the two modems and computers to engage in data exchange.

handwriting recognition   The ability of computers, especially mobile devices, to recognize letters and numbers written by hand and convert them to ASCII text.

hard disk drive (HDD)   A device that stores and retrieves data from magnetic-coated platters that rotate at high speeds. The HDD is the primary storage medium on a computer.

hard drive access panel   The panel that allows access to a hard drive in a laptop.

hardware   Physical electronic components that make up a computer system.

Hardware Abstraction Layer (HAL)   A library of hardware drivers that communicate between the operating system and the hardware that is installed.

Hardware Compatibility List (HCL)   A utility that verifies that existing hardware is compatible with an operating system.

hardware firewall   A hardware device that filters data packets from the network before reaching computers and other devices on a network.

hash encoding   Data that has had an algorithm applied to it to make it unintelligible if it is intercepted during transmission.

Hayes-compatible command set   A set of AT commands that most modem software uses. This command set is named after the Hayes Microcomputer Products Company, which first defined it.

header   The first part of a packet that contains source and destination IP and MAC addresses.

headphone jack   A socket that is used to attach an audio output device.

heat sink and fan assembly   A device that dissipates heat from electronic components into the surrounding air.

hex driver   A driver used to tighten nuts. Sometimes called a nut driver.

Hibernate   A power level in which the computer is essentially off. RAM is copied to the hard drive so the computer does not need to power even the RAM. It is very efficient but takes longer to recover from hibernate than from standby.

hibernate/standby indicator LED   A light that shows if the computer is in standby or hibernate mode.

hierarchical   Organized groupings within a collection. In networking, IP addressing is considered hierarchical because the addresses are grouped by network names.

hierarchical star topology   An extended star topology in which a central hub is connected by vertical cabling to other hubs that are dependent on it.

High Data Rate DSL (HDSL)   Provides bandwidth of 768 kbps in both directions.

High-Definition Multimedia Interface (HDMI) A video, plasma, LCD, or DLP projector.

High Speed Downlink Packet Access (HSDPA)   A data protocol found on 3G phones that provides enhanced access speed.

HKEY_   The designation at the beginning of Windows Registry boot filenames.

host   A computer system on a network. Similar to the term node, except that host usually implies a computer system. Node generally applies to any networked system, including access servers and routers.

hot-swappable interface   Allows peripherals to be changed while the system is running. USB is an example.

hub   1) Generally, a term used to describe a Layer 1 device at the center of a star topology network. 2) A hardware or software device that contains multiple independent but connected modules of network and internetwork equipment. Hubs can be active (where they repeat signals sent through them) or passive (where they do not repeat, but merely split, signals sent through them). 3) In Ethernet and IEEE 802.3, an Ethernet multiport repeater, sometimes called a concentrator.

Hypertext Markup Language (HTML)   A page-description language used by browser applications such as Windows Internet Explorer and Mozilla Firefox.

Hypertext Transfer Protocol (HTTP)   Governs how files are exchanged on the Internet.

I

icon   An image that represents an application or a capability.

IEEE 802.1   An IEEE specification that describes an algorithm that prevents bridging loops by creating a spanning tree. This algorithm was invented by Digital Equipment Corporation. The Digital algorithm and the IEEE 802.1 algorithm are not exactly the same, nor are they compatible.

IEEE 802.11   An IEEE standard that specifies carrier sense media access control and physical layer specifications for 1- and 2-Mbps wireless LANs.

IEEE 802.11a   An IEEE standard for wireless LANs that operates in the 5-GHz band. Uses 52-subcarrier orthogonal frequency-division multiplexing (OFDM) with a maximum raw data rate of 54 Mbps.

IEEE 802.11b   The first widely accepted wireless networking standard. Because it operates in the 2.4-GHz band, other devices that operate in the same band can cause interference.

IEEE 802.11g   An extension of the 802.11 standard. 802.11g applies to wireless LANs and provides up to 54 Mbps. Because it operates in the 2.4-GHz band, other devices that operate in the same band can cause interference.

IEEE 802.11n   A proposed new extension to the 802.11 standard. 802.11n applies to wireless LANs and provides up to 540 Mbps in the 2.4- or 5-GHz band.

IEEE 802.12   An IEEE LAN standard that specifies the physical layer and the MAC sublayer of the data link layer. IEEE 802.12 uses the demand priority media access scheme at 100 Mbps over a variety of physical media.

IEEE 802.2   An IEEE LAN protocol that specifies an implementation of the LLC sublayer of the data link layer. IEEE 802.2 handles errors, framing, flow control, and the network layer (Layer 3) service interface. Used in IEEE 802.3 and IEEE 802.5 LANs.

IEEE 802.3   An IEEE LAN protocol that specifies an implementation of the physical layer and the MAC sublayer of the data link layer. IEEE 802.3 uses CSMA/CD access at a variety of speeds over a variety of physical media. Extensions to the IEEE 802.3 standard specify implementations for Fast Ethernet. Physical variations on the original IEEE 802.3 specification include 10BASE2, 10BASE5, 10BASE-F, 10BASE-T, and 10Broad36. Physical variations for Fast Ethernet include 100BASE-T, 100BASE-T4, and 100BASE-X.

IEEE 802.3i   A physical variation on the original IEEE 802.3 specification that calls for using

Ethernet-type signaling over twisted-pair networking media. The standard sets the signaling speed at 10 Mbps using a baseband signaling scheme transmitted over twisted-pair cable employing a star or extended star topology.

IEEE 802.4   An IEEE LAN protocol that specifies an implementation of the physical layer and the MAC sublayer of the data link layer. IEEE 802.4 uses token-passing access over a bus topology and is based on the token bus LAN architecture.

IEEE 802.5   An IEEE LAN protocol that specifies an implementation of the physical layer and MAC sublayer of the data link layer. IEEE 802.5 uses token passing access at 4 or 16 Mbps over shielded twisted-pair (STP) cabling and is similar to IBM Token Ring.

IEEE 802.6   An IEEE MAN specification based on Distributed Queue Dual Bus (DQDB) technology. IEEE 802.6 supports data rates of 1.5 to 155 Mbps.

impact printer   A class of printer that includes dot matrix and daisy wheel.

incremental backup   A procedure to back up all the files and folders that have been created or modified since the last full or normal backup.

information technology (IT)   The field of study or business that concerns itself with the design, development, implementation, support, and management of computer hardware and software applications.

infrared (IR)   Electromagnetic waves whose frequency range is above that of microwaves but below that of the visible spectrum. LAN systems based on this technology represent an emerging technology.

infrared port   A line-of-sight wireless transceiver that is used for data transmission.

infrared scatter   An infrared signal that is bounced off ceilings and walls. Devices can connect without line of sight, but data transfer rates are lower, and distances are shorter.

inkjet printer   A type of printer that uses liquid-ink-filled cartridges that spray ink to form an image on the paper.

input device   Any device that takes information from outside the PC, translates it into binary, and sends it inside the PC.

input/output (I/O)   Any operation, program, or device that transfers data to or from a computer.

input/output (I/O) address   A unique hexadecimal memory address that is associated with a specific device on a computer.

installation CD   A compact disc that includes new software with drivers and manuals. Additionally, may include diagnostic tools and trial software.

instant messaging (IM)   A real-time text-based method of communication conducted over a network between two or more users.

Institute of Electrical and Electronics Engineers (IEEE)   An organization that oversees the development of communication and network standards.

insulation   A high-resistance material that inhibits the flow of current between conductors in a cable.

Integrated Services Digital Network (ISDN)   A communication protocol, offered by telephone companies, that permits telephone networks to carry data, voice, and other source traffic.

Integrated Services Digital Network DSL (IDSL)   An early digital network that ran over analog telephone lines.

interface   1) A connection between two systems or devices. 2) In routing terminology, a network connection. 3) In telephony, a shared boundary defined by common physical interconnection characteristics, signal characteristics, and meanings of interchanged signals. 4) The boundary between adjacent layers of the OSI reference model.

Internet Explorer (IE)   Microsoft's main Web browser.

Interior Gateway Protocol (IGP)   An Internet protocol that is used to exchange routing information within an autonomous system. Examples of common Internet IGPs include EIGRP, OSPF, and RIP.

International Electrotechnical Commission (IEC)   An industry group that writes and distributes standards for electrical products and components.

International Organization for Standardization (ISO)   An international organization that sets standards for networking. ISO developed the OSI reference model, a popular networking reference model.

Internet   The largest global internetwork. Connects tens of thousands of networks worldwide.

Internet Architecture Board (IAB)   The board of internetwork researchers who discuss issues pertinent to Internet architecture. Responsible for appointing a variety of Internet-related groups, such as the IANA, IESG, and IRSG. The IAB is appointed by the trustees of the ISOC.

Internet Control Message Protocol (ICMP)   Used for network testing and troubleshooting, ICMP enables diagnostic and error messages. The ping utility uses ICMP echo messages to determine whether a remote device can be reached.

Internet Message Access Protocol (IMAP)   Used by local e-mail clients to synchronize and retrieve e-mail from a server and leave e-mail on the server.

Internet Protocol (IP)   A network layer protocol in the TCP/IP stack that offers a connectionless internetwork service. IP provides features for addressing, type-of-service specification, fragmentation and reassembly, and security. Documented in RFC 791.

Internet service provider (ISP)   A company that provides Internet and e-mail services to consumers and businesses.

Internetwork Packet Exchange/Sequenced Packet Exchange (IPX/SPX)   Used by Novell Netware. IPX is a connectionless communication. SPX is the transport layer (Layer 4 of the OSI reference model).

interrupt request (IRQ)   A request from a device for communication with the CPU.

intrusion detection system (IDS)   Looks for and reports suspicious traffic on a network and possible threats to a management station.

I/O shield   A grounded metal plate installed in the rear of the case that enables the motherboard connectors to be accessed from the outside of the case.

IP address   The Layer 3, logical address that has been assigned to a networked computer or device.

isopropyl alcohol   A colorless flammable chemical compound with a strong odor used to clean the contacts on computer components.

J

Java   A programming language for applets to run within a web browser. Examples of applets include a calculator and a counter.

JavaScript   A programming language developed to interact with HTML source code for interactive websites. Examples include a rotating banner and a popup window.

jumper   An electrical contact point used to set a hard drive as master or slave.

K

keyboard   An input device with multifunctional keys.

keyboard port   A PS/2 socket used to attach an external keyboard.

kilobytes per second (KBps)   A measurement of the amount of data that is transferred over a connection, such as a network connection. A data transfer rate of 1 KBps is a rate of approximately 1000 bytes per second.

L

LAN architecture   Comprises all the components—including hardware, software, protocols, and sequence of operations—that make up the structure of a communications system.

laptop   A small form factor computer designed to be mobile. Operates much the same as a desktop computer. Laptop hardware is proprietary and usually is more expensive than desktop hardware.

laptop battery   A rechargeable battery that powers the laptop.

laptop connector   A socket that is used to attach the laptop to a docking station.

laptop keyboard   An input device that includes alphanumeric, punctuation, and special function keys.

laptop latch   A lever used to open the laptop lid.

laser printer   A type of printer that uses static electricity and a laser to form the image on the paper.

latent image   In laser printers, the undeveloped image.

LCD monitor   An output device that passes polarized light through liquid crystals to produce images on the screen.

level-one technician   A front-line technician whose goal is to handle most of the troubleshooting. Level-one technicians serve as screeners, allowing the level-two technicians to focus on the more challenging problems.

level-two technician   A more experienced and skillful technician than a level-one technician. Level-two technicians receive escalated calls that a level-one technician is incapable of solving.

light-emitting diode (LED)   A type of semiconductor that emits light when current is passed through it. The LED indicates whether components inside the computer are on.

Lightweight Extensible Authentication Protocol (LEAP)   A Cisco proprietary wireless encryption protocol that frequently reauthenticates with new keys.

line conditioner   An electrical device that provides clean AC power to sensitive electrical equipment.

line-in connector   A socket that is used to attach an audio source.

line of sight   A characteristic of certain transmission systems such as laser, microwave, and infrared systems in which no obstructions in a direct path between transmitter and receiver can exist.

Linux   A popular version of UNIX that offers a much more user-friendly GUI than previous versions of UNIX offered.

liquid crystal display (LCD)   A type of light-weight, high-resolution display that works by blocking light rather than creating it.

local-area network (LAN)   A communication network that covers a small geographic area and is under the control of a single administrator.

local security policy   A combination of security settings that define the security of the computer on which the settings reside.

logical drive   A section that a partition is divided into.

logical topology   The method (ring or bus) by which different computers and other equipment in a network communicate with one another. Contrast with physical topology.

loopback plug   A diagnostic tool that redirects signals to the transmitting port to troubleshoot connectivity.

low battery alarm   An alarm warning the user to connect the portable device to a power source.

M

MAC address   A standardized data link layer address that is required for every port or device that connects to a LAN. Other devices in the network use these addresses to locate specific ports in the network and to create and update routing tables and data structures. MAC addresses are 6 bytes long and are controlled by the Institute of Electrical and Electronics Engineers (IEEE). Also known as a hardware address, MAC layer address, burned-in address, or physical address.

MAC address filtering   A filter that permits or denies network traffic based exclusively on the hosts' MAC address.

main distribution facility (MDF)   A building's primary communications room. Also, the central point of a star networking topology, where patch panels, hubs, and routers are located.

malicious threat   An intentional attack or other threat with the aim of theft or destruction of software or personal data.

malware   A term taken from the phrase malicious software. Malware is designed to infiltrate or damage a computer system without the user's knowledge.

Master Boot Record (MBR)   A program on the first sector of a hard disk that starts the boot process. The MBR determines which partition is used to boot the system and then transfers control to the boot sector of that partition, which continues the boot process. The MBR allows programs such as DOS to load into RAM.

Material Safety and Data Sheet (MSDS)   A fact sheet that identifies hazardous materials.

mean time between failures (MTBF)   The average length of time that the device will work without failing. This information can be found in the manual or on the manufacturer's website.

media   The plural form of medium. The various physical environments through which transmission signals pass. Common network media include twisted-pair, coaxial, and fiber-optic cable, and the atmosphere (through which microwave, laser, and infrared transmission occurs).

Media Access Control (MAC)   The lower of the two sublayers of the data link layer defined by the Institute of Electrical and Electronics Engineers

(IEEE). The MAC sublayer handles access to shared media, such as whether token passing or contention will be used. Also, the rules for coordinating the use of the medium on a LAN.

media-handling options   Options by which a printer handles media, including the paper's orientation, size, and weight.

megabit   1,048,576 bits (approximately 1 million bits).

megabits per second (Mbps)   A common measurement of the amount of data that is transferred over a connection in one second. A data transfer rate of 1 Mbps is a rate of approximately 1 million bits or 1000 kilobits per second.

megabyte (MB)   1,048,576 bytes (or approximately 1 million bytes).

mesh grip   A tool attached to the end of a cable to help pull cable.

mesh topology   A method of connecting users that provides alternative paths for data. If one path is severed or unusable, the data can take an alternative path to its destination.

microphone   An audio input device.

microphone jack   A socket used to connect a microphone used for audio input.

Microsoft Windows   The family of Microsoft operating systems that includes Windows XP, Windows Vista, and Windows 7. It also includes operating systems for network servers and for portable devices. Legacy Windows OSs include Windows 3.1, NT, 95, 98, Me, and 2000.

microwave   An electromagnetic wave that ranges from 1 to 30 GHz. Microwave-based networks are an evolving technology gaining popularity because of their high bandwidth and relatively low cost.

mobile processor   A CPU that is optimized to use less power, allowing laptop batteries to last longer.

modem port   An RJ-11 jack that connects a computer to a standard telephone line. The modem port can be used to connect the computer to the Internet, to send and receive fax documents, and to answer incoming calls.

modulator/demodulator (modem)   A device that converts digital computer signals into a format that is sent and received over an analog telephone line.

Molex power connector   A four-wire computer power connector used to connect many devices, such as optical drives and hard drives.

monitor   A display device that works with the installed video card to present output from a computer. The clarity of a CRT monitor is based on video bandwidth, dot pitch, refresh rate, and convergence.

motherboard   The main printed circuit board. Connects all the computer's components, such as the CPU, BIOS, memory, mass storage interfaces, serial and parallel ports, expansion slots, and controllers required for standard peripheral devices.

mouse port   A PS/2 socket that is used to attach an external mouse.

Mozilla Firefox   Mozilla's Web browser.

MSCONFIG   A Windows utility designed to aid in troubleshooting the operating system. Allows the user to edit start-up applications and access the BOOT.INI, SYSTEM.INI, and WIN.INI files.

Msinfo32   The filename of System Information utility. It provides very detailed information about the hardware, OS, and key applications.

Multimedia Messaging Service (MMS)   The protocol used in picture or video text messaging.

multimeter   A troubleshooting tool that measures electrical voltage, resistance, and current.

multimode   Optical fiber that has a thicker core than single-mode. It is easier to make, can use simpler light sources (such as LEDs), and works well over short distances. This type of fiber allows light waves to be dispersed into many paths as they travel through the fiber.

multiprocessing   To enable programs to share two or more CPUs.

Multipurpose Internet Mail Extensions (MIME) A standard that extends the e-mail format to include text in ASCII standard format, as well as other formats, such as pictures and word processor documents. Normally used in conjunction with SMTP.

multitask   To run two or more applications at the same time.

multithread   To divide a program into smaller parts that can be loaded as needed by the operating system. Multithreading allows individual programs to be multitasked.

multiuser   Two or more users running programs and sharing peripheral devices, such as a printer, at the same time.

My Computer icon   A desktop icon that provides access to the installed drives and other computer properties.

N

native resolution   The best quality resolution setting for an LCD monitor.

near-letter quality (NLQ)   A quality of print that is better than draft quality, but not as good as letter quality.

needle-nose pliers   A tool with long and slender jaws that can be used to grasp small objects.

netbook   A small, lightweight, energy-efficient laptop. Netbooks are often less robust and have limited processing capability but are very portable and durable.

Netiquette   Being polite in email, text, forums, and all Internet-based interactions.

NetView   An IBM network management architecture and related applications. NetView is a virtual telecommunications access method (VTAM) application used to manage mainframes in Systems Network Architecture (SNA) networks.

network   A group of two or more electronic devices, such as computers, PDAs, and smartphones, that communicate with each other to share data and resources.

network access layer protocol · Determines how data is physically transmitted; for example, over copper wire, over fiber-optic cable, or wirelessly.

Network Access Point (NAP)   The point at which access providers are interconnected.

network administration   The task of maintaining and upgrading a private network that is done by network administrators.

Network Basic Input/Output System (NetBIOS) An application programming interface (API) used by applications on an IBM LAN to request services from lower-level network processes. These services might include session establishment and termination, and information transfer.

network cable   The physical medium used to connect devices for communication.

network file service   Allows documents to be shared over a network to facilitate the development of a project.

network LED   A light that shows the status of the network connection. The green link light indicates network connectivity. The other LED indicates traffic.

networking medium   Material (either cable or air) by which signals are sent from one network device to another.

network interface card (NIC)   A computer interface with the LAN. This card typically is inserted into an expansion slot in a computer and connects to the network medium.

network layer   Layer 3 of the Open Systems Interconnection (OSI) reference model. This layer provides connectivity and path selection between two end systems. The network layer is the layer at which routing occurs. Corresponds roughly with the path control layer of the Systems Network Architecture (SNA) model. The OSI reference model includes the application layer, presentation layer, session layer, transport layer, network layer, data link layer, and physical layer.

network operating system (NOS)   An operating system designed specifically to provide additional network features.

network printer   A printer connected to the computer network that is set up to be shared by multiple users.

network server   A computer that provides some network services, such as file sharing, and that can handle multiple users and multiple jobs.

network topology   The way in which computers, printers, and other devices are connected.

networking   Connecting to and sharing resources, devices, storage, and applications between computers.

New Technology File System (NTFS)   A type of file system that provides improved fault tolerance over traditional file systems, and also provides file-level security.

nibble   Half a byte, or 4 bits.

node   1) The endpoint of a network connection or a junction common to two or more lines in a network. Nodes can be processors, controllers, or workstations. Nodes, which vary in routing and other functional capabilities, can be interconnected by links, and they serve as control points in the network. The term node is sometimes used generically to refer to any entity that can access a network, and it is frequently used interchangeably with device. 2) In Systems Network Architecture (SNA), the basic component of a network, and the point at which one or more functional units connect channels or data circuits.

noise   Interference, such as EMI or RFI, that causes unclean power and may cause errors in a computer system.

nonbootable disk   A damaged or missing disk, or a disk that does not contain one or more system boot files.

northbridge   One of the two chips in the core logic chipset of a PC motherboard. It typically handles communications between the CPU, RAM, AGP, PCIe, and the southbridge core chip. Also called a Memory Controller Hub (MCH).

notebook   Another name for a laptop. In general, notebooks are smaller than laptops but larger than netbooks.

Novell NetWare   A network OS that was very popular in the late 1980s and throughout the 1990s. It has largely been replaced by Microsoft and Linux network OSs.

NSLOOKUP   A command that returns the IP address of a given hostname. This command can also do the reverse and find the hostname for a specified IP address.

NT Loader (NTLDR)   A boot file that loads Windows-based operating systems.

NTDETECT   A program used by Intel-based systems to detect installed hardware.

Num Lock indicator LED   A light that shows the on/off status of the ten-key number pad.

O

Ohm's Law   The mathematical relationship between current, resistance, and voltage, in which voltage is equal to the current multiplied by the resistance.

operating system   A software program that performs general system tasks, such as controlling RAM, prioritizing the processing, controlling input and output devices, and managing files.

optical drive   A disk drive that uses a laser to read and/or write CDs and DVDs.

optical drive status indicator   A light that shows drive activity.

Outlook Express   The default email client bundled in Windows XP and Vista.

overclocking   The act of using jumpers or BIOS settings to increase the speed of a CPU.

P

packet   A logical grouping of information that includes a header that contains control information and usually user data. The term packet is most often used to refer to network layer units of data. The terms datagram, frame, message, and segment are also used to describe logical information groupings at various layers of the OSI reference model and in various technology circles.

packet filter   A network filter that uses IP addresses, protocols, or ports to allow or deny packets through.

packet switching   An Internet standard that sends messages as packets instead of dedicated circuits. The advantage is that the shared medium can accommodate more users.

Page Description Language (PDL)   Code that describes the contents of a document in a language that the printer can understand.

page file   Another name for a swap file. It is the data that is transferred between the RAM and the hard drive when the OS uses virtual memory.

pages per minute (ppm)   The measure of a printer's speed.

Parallel Advanced Technology Attachment (PATA)   The standard for connecting hard drives and optical drives into computer systems. Uses a parallel signaling technology.

Parallel Advanced Technology Attachment (PATA) data cable   An internal cable that transfers data between the motherboard and an ATA drive.

parallel cable   An external cable that connects the computer's parallel port to a printer or another parallel communications device. Also called a printer cable.

parallel port   A socket used to connect a device such as a printer or scanner.

partition   To divide memory or mass storage into isolated or logical sections. After a disk is partitioned, each partition behaves like a separate disk drive.

password protection   Protecting a file, computer, account, or other resource by requiring that a password be entered to gain access.

PC Card   An expansion card used in laptops to conform to PCMCIA standards.

PC Card/ExpressCard slot   Two legacy laptop expansion slots that allowed early laptops to install wireless NICs, external hard drives, and other devices that typically connect through USB ports today.

peer-to-peer computing   Each network device runs both client and server portions of an application. Also describes communication between implementations of the same OSI reference model layer in two different network devices.

peer-to-peer network   See *peer-to-peer computing*.

Performance Monitor   A tool that shows the real-time levels of CPU and RAM usage.

Personal Computer Memory Card International Association (PCMCIA)   An industry trade association that defines laptop expansion card standards.

personal digital assistant (PDA)   A standalone, handheld device with computing and communicating abilities.

Phillips-head screwdriver   A tool used to tighten or loosen crosshead screws.

phishing   A type of spam intended to persuade the recipient to provide the sender with information that will enable the sender to access the recipient's personal information.

physical layer   Layer 1 of the Open Systems Interconnection (OSI) reference model. The physical layer defines the electrical, mechanical, procedural, and functional specifications to activate, maintain, and deactivate the physical link between end systems. Corresponds with the physical control layer in the Systems Network Architecture (SNA) model. The OSI reference model includes the application layer, presentation layer, session layer, transport layer, network layer, data link layer, and physical layer.

physical security   Includes security measures like door locks that prevent physical access to network equipment and servers.

physical topology   The physical layout of the components on the network.

piezoelectric   For printers, an electrically charged plate changes the nozzle's size and shape. This change in size causes the nozzle to act like a pump. The pumping action forces ink out through the nozzle and onto the paper.

ping   A simple but highly useful command-line utility that is included in most implementations of TCP/IP. Ping can be used with either the hostname or the IP address to test IP connectivity. Determines whether a specific IP address is accessible by sending an ICMP echo request to a destination computer or other network device. The receiving device then sends back an ICMP echo reply message.

ping of death   An attack that uses repetitive, larger-than-normal pings to slow or crash the receiving computer.

plain old telephone service (POTS)   The regular phone system, which typically uses analog signals to transmit voice and data. Sometimes called the Public Switched Telephone Network (PSTN).

platen   A large roller in a dot-matrix printer that applies pressure to keep the paper from slipping. If multiple-copy paper is used, the platen gap can be adjusted to the paper's thickness.

plug-and-play   Technology that allows a computer to automatically configure the devices that connect to it.

point of presence (POP)   The point of interconnection between the communication facilities provided by the telephone company and the building's main distribution facility.

popup   An online advertisement that suddenly appears, blocking what you intended to see on the web page.

port protection   Using a firewall to close ports that are not in use to prevent others from gaining access through those unused ports.

port replicator   A fixed base unit in which a laptop is inserted and can connect to peripheral devices.

Post Office Protocol (POP)   An application layer protocol used to allow clients to communicate with email servers.

power adaptor   A device that transforms AC to DC to provide electricity to the computer and charge the battery.

power button   A control that turns a device on and off.

power cable   An external cable consisting of color-coded conductors that transfer electricity to a computer and attached electrical devices.

power line communication (PLC)   A communication method that uses power distribution wires (local electric grid) to send and receive data.

power on indicator LED   A light that shows the laptop's on/off status.

power-on self-test (POST)   A diagnostic test of memory and hardware when the system is powered up.

power supply   Converts AC (alternating current) into the lower voltages of DC (direct current), which powers all the computer's components. Power supplies are rated in watts.

presentation layer   Layer 6 of the Open Systems Interconnection (OSI) reference model. This layer ensures that information sent by the application layer of one system can be read by the application layer of another. The presentation layer is also concerned with the data structures used by programs and therefore negotiates data transfer syntax for the application layer. Corresponds roughly with the presentation services layer of the Systems Network Architecture (SNA) model. The OSI reference model includes the application layer, presentation layer, session layer, transport layer, network layer, data link layer, and physical layer.

preventive maintenance   Regular and systematic inspection, cleaning, and replacement of worn parts, materials, and systems.

preventive maintenance policy   A detailed program that determines maintenance timing, the type of maintenance performed, and the specifics of how the maintenance plan is carried out.

primary corona wire   A voltage device that erases the charge on the printing drum. Also called the grid or conditioning roller.

primary partition   The first partition on a hard drive. A primary partition cannot be subdivided into smaller sections.

Primary Rate Interface (PRI)   An ISDN interface to primary rate access. Primary rate access consists of a single 64-Kbps D channel plus 23 (T1) or 30 (E1) B channels for voice or data. Compare to BRI.

Printer Control Language (PCL)   Developed by Hewlett-Packard to allow software applications to communicate with HP and HP-compatible laser printers. PCL is now an industry standard for most printer types.

printer driver   Software that must be installed on a PC so that the printer can communicate and coordinate the printing process.

printer network interface card (NIC)   An adapter that the printer uses to access the network media.

printer-output option   Determines how the ink or toner is transferred to the paper. Includes color management, print quality, and speed.

printer queue   A temporary holding area for print jobs. The jobs in the queue are fed to the printer when it is ready for the next job.

print resolution   The number of tiny dots that the print head places per inch on the paper when forming an image.

professionalism   Acting in a manor that reflects well on the company and yourself.

protected mode   Allows programs to access more than 1 MB of physical memory. Also protects against misuse of memory, such as programs that cannot execute a data segment or write into a code segment.

protocol   1) A formal description of a set of rules and conventions that govern how devices on a network exchange information. 2) A field within an IP datagram that indicates the upper-layer (Layer 4) protocol that sent the datagram.

protocol data unit (PDU)   A unit of data that is specified in a protocol of a layer of the OSI reference model. For example, the PDU for Layer 1 is bits or the data stream, Layer 2 is framing, Layer 3 is the packet, and Layer 4 is the segment.

proxy   An entity that, in the interest of efficiency, acts on behalf of another entity.

proxy server   A filter that inspects all traffic and is designed to protect computers and resources on a network.

Public Switched Telephone Network (PSTN)   A general term that refers to the variety of telephone networks and services in place worldwide. Sometimes called plain old telephone service (POTS).

Q

Quad-band   Transmits and receives data and voice on four different GSM frequencies.

R

radio frequency (RF)   A generic term that refers to frequencies that correspond to radio transmissions. Cable TV and broadband networks use RF technology.

radio frequency interference (RFI)   Radio frequencies that create noise that interferes with information being transmitted across unshielded copper cabling.

RAM access panel　The panel that grants easy access to RAM on a laptop.

Rambus DRAM (RDRAM)　A proprietary RAM found in some gaming systems and video cards.

Rambus in-line memory module (RIMM) Proprietary RAM chips that are made by the RAM-BUS corporation which provide very high-speed data access found in high-end game systems and in game consoles such as Nintendo 64 and Sony PlayStation 2 and 3.

random-access memory (RAM)　Memory that temporarily stores data for processing by the CPU. Also called physical memory.

read-only memory (ROM)　Memory that permanently stores prerecorded configuration settings and data on a chip that can only be read. This type of memory retains its contents when power is not being supplied to the chip.

real mode　Gives applications direct access to RAM.

reduced instruction set computer (RISC)　An architecture that uses a relatively small set of instructions. RISC chips are designed to execute these instructions very rapidly.

Redundant Array of Independent Disks (RAID) Provides fault tolerance to prevent loss of data in the event of disk drive failure on a network server. Also known as Redundant Array of Inexpensive Disks.

Regedit　A Windows application that allows users to edit the registry.

registry　A system-wide database used by the Windows operating system to store information and settings for hardware, software, users, and preferences on a system.

remote-access server (RAS)　A server that is dedicated to users who need to gain access to files and print services on the LAN from a remote location.

Remote Desktop　A utility that can be used to remotely control one networked computer from another networked computer via a graphical interface.

remote installation services (RIS)　The ability to download a Windows operating system installation across the network. This installation can be requested by the user or forced onto the computer by the administrator.

removable drive　A drive that can be removed from a computer to transport data.

replay　Analyses network traffic and captures usernames and passwords that the hacker can use to later gain access to network resources.

resistance (r)　The measurement, expressed in ohms, of the opposition of a material to the flow of current.

resolution　The number of distinct pixels in each dimension that can be displayed on a computer screen. The higher the resolution, the better quality the screen display is. Also called display resolution.

restore point　A utility in Microsoft's Windows Me, XP, and Vista operating systems. It allows the rolling back of system files, registry keys, and installed programs to a previous state in the event of system failure. User data is unaffected by performing a restore point.

ring topology　A network topology that consists of a series of repeaters connected to one another by unidirectional transmission links to form a single closed loop. Each station on the network connects to the network at a repeater. Although logically they are a ring, ring topologies are most often organized in a closed-loop star.

router   A network layer device that uses one or more metrics to determine the optimal path along which network traffic should be forwarded. Routers forward packets from one network to another based on network layer information. Occasionally called a gateway, although this definition of gateway is becoming increasingly outdated.

Routing Information Protocol (RIP)   An Interior Gateway Protocol (IGP) supplied with UNIX Berkeley Standard Distribution (BSD) systems. The most common IGP on the Internet. RIP uses hop count as a routing metric.

S

safe mode   An option when booting the system that loads only the basic devices that Windows needs to run. It is used for troubleshooting.

satellite communication   The use of orbiting satellites to relay data between multiple Earth-based stations. Satellite communications offer high bandwidth and broadcast capability at a cost that is unrelated to the distance between Earth stations. Because of the satellite's altitude, satellite communications can be subject to long propagation delays.

SCANDISK   A Windows utility used to examine all files on a drive.

Scheduled Tasks utility   Enables users to schedule events such as backups or updates.

sector   A hard drive area that contains a fixed number of bytes, generally at least 512.

Secure Shell   A network protocol that allows data to be exchanged over a secure channel between two computers.

security key fob   A small radio system that communicates with the computer over a short range. The computer must sense the signal from the key fob before it accepts the user login name and password.

security keyhole   A hard point in the case that is used to attach a security cable.

security policy   A document that outlines procedures regarding physical security, and the protection of data, research and development, and customer information.

segment   A portion of a computer network in which every device communicates using the physical layer of the OSI reference model. Hubs and repeaters extend and become part of a network segment, whereas switches and routers define and separate network segments.

semiconductor   Material used to make computer chips that can be either a conductor or an insulator, depending on the control signals applied to it. The most common semiconductor materials are silicon and germanium. These materials then have other materials added to them to increase conductivity.

serial advanced technology attachment   A computer bus primarily designed to transfer data between a computer and storage devices.

Serial Advanced Technology Attachment (SATA) data cable   The cable that connects the motherboard and the SATA drive. Most commonly they have 7 pins. Some cables can also provide power to the drive as well as data.

Serial Advanced Technology Attachment (SATA) power connector   An adapter specifically designed to provide power to SATA drives. The 6-pin and 15-pin versions provide 3.3 volts in addition to the standard 5 and 12 volts. The 9-pin version does not provide the 3.3 volts.

serial cable   An external cable that connects the serial port on the computer to a peripheral device.

serial data transfer   The movement of single bits of information in a single cycle.

serial port   A socket that is used to connect a device such as a mouse or trackball.

serial transmission   A method of data transmission in which the bits of a data character are transmitted sequentially over a single channel.

server   A repository for files, or other resources, that can be accessed and shared across a network by many users.

service level agreement (SLA)   A contract that defines expectations between an organization and the service vendor to provide an agreed-upon level of support.

Service Set Identifier (SSID)   The broadcast name of a wireless network.

Services   The Windows Services utility is a program that lets you manage services.

session layer   Layer 5 of the Open Systems Interconnection (OSI) reference model. This layer establishes, manages, and terminates sessions between applications and manages data exchange between presentation layer entities. The OSI reference model includes the application layer, presentation layer, session layer, transport layer, network layer, data link layer, and physical layer.

shielded twisted pair (STP)   A two-pair wiring medium used primarily with Token Ring networks. STP cabling has a layer of shielded insulation to reduce electromagnetic interference (EMI). Compare with UTP.

Short Message Service (SMS)   The protocol used in text messaging.

shortcut   A key combination that activates a command.

signature file   The list of known viruses to which antivirus software compares files to determine if the file is infected with a virus.

Simple Mail Transfer Protocol (SMTP)   An e-mail protocol servers use to send ASCII text messages. When augmented by the MIME protocol, SMTP can carry e-mail with pictures and documents. E-mail clients sometimes use SMTP to retrieve messages from an e-mail server. However, because of the limited capability to queue messages at the receiving end, other protocols such as POP or IMAP typically are used to receive e-mail.

simplex   The capability for data transmission in only one direction between a sending station and a receiving station.

single inline memory module (SIMM)   A RAM chip with contacts on one side only and that must be installed in pairs.

single-mode   A fiber cable that has a very thin core. Uses a high-energy laser as a light source. Can transmit signals over longer distances than multi-mode fiber-optic cable.

site survey   Physically inspecting a building to help determine a basic network topology.

Small Computer System Interface (SCSI)   A parallel interface standard that supports multiple devices on the same cable and achieves faster data transmission rates than standard buses.

Small Computer System Interface (SCSI) cable
An external or internal cable that connects the SCSI controller to SCSI ports of multiple internal and external devices.

small outline dual in-line memory module (SODIMM)   The RAM form factor found in most laptops.

smart card   A credit-card-sized device that includes a processor and memory. Used to store information and authenticate network users. Smart cards provide two-factor identification because the user must have both the card and a password to access the network.

smartphone   A portable electronic device that through the use of applications does more than make phone calls. Common applications include personal calendars, email clients, and web browsers.

social engineering   Manipulating people so they perform security-compromising actions or give out sensitive information.

software firewall   An application on a computer that inspects and filters data packets.

solenoid   A coil of wires that forms electromagnets that fire the pins in a dot-matrix printer.

solid-ink printer   A printer that uses solid sticks of ink rather than toner or ink cartridges. Solid-ink printers produce high-quality images. The ink sticks are nontoxic and can be handled safely.

sound card   An integrated circuit board that enhances a computer's audio capabilities.

southbridge   A chip that implements the slower capabilities of the motherboard. It is connected to the CPU through the northbridge chip. Also called the Input/Output (I/O) Controller Hub (ICH).

spam   Unsolicited e-mail.

speaker   An audio output device.

spike   A sudden increase in voltage that is usually caused by a lightning strike.

spoof   To gain access to resources on devices by pretending to be a trusted computer.

spooling   The process of loading documents into a buffer (usually an area on a hard drive) until the printer is ready to print the documents.

spyware   Malware that monitors activity on the computer. The spyware then sends this information to the organization responsible for launching the spyware.

standby   A power level that leaves data in RAM and reduces power or turns off peripheral devices. Recovering from Standby is quicker than recovering from Hibernate but consumes more power.

standby power supply (SPS)   Battery backup that is enabled when voltage levels fall below normal.

standoff   A barrier/screw used to physically separate parts—in particular, the system board—from the case.

star topology   A LAN topology in which endpoints on a network are connected to a common central switch by point-to-point links. A ring topology that is organized as a star and implements a unidirectional closed-loop star instead of point-to-point links.

stateful packet inspection   A more sophisticated filter than a standard packet filter. Stateful packet inspection keeps track of strings of packets, so it is not as vulnerable to spoofing attacks.

static RAM (SRAM)   A type of RAM that retains its contents for as long as power is supplied. SRAM does not require constant refreshing, like dynamic RAM (DRAM).

static random-access memory (SRAM)   Memory that holds data as long as voltage is applied. Used mainly as cache memory for the CPU.

stereo headphone jack   A small round plug that uses cylindrical bands as contacts. Two audio signal wires (right and left) transmit analog audio signal.

stress management   Techniques or activities used to reduce stress.

stylus   A writing utensil. Typically used as an input method for the touch-sensitive screens of PDAs and graphics tablets.

subnet mask   The second group of numbers used when configuring an IP address on a device. End devices use the subnet mask to determine the network portion of an IP address.

subnetting   A logical division of a network. It provides the means to divide a network, and the subnet mask specifies how it is subdivided.

surge   Any voltage increase above 110 percent of the normal voltage carried by a power line.

surge protector   A suppressor that regulates the voltage going to a device.

surge suppressor   A device that ensures that the voltage going to another device stays below a certain level.

S-video connector   A four-pin mini-DIN connector that is used to output video signals to a compatible device. S-video separates the brightness and color portions of a video signal.

switch   1) An operation that is added to a DOS command to modify the command's output. 2) A Layer 2 network device also known as a multiport bridge.

Symmetric DSL (SDSL)   A version of a DSL service that provides the same speed for uploads and downloads.

symmetric encryption   Encryption that requires both sides of an encrypted conversation to use an encryption key to be able to encode and decode the data. The sender and receiver must use the same key at the same time.

SYN flood   Randomly opens TCP ports, tying up network equipment or computer resources with a large number of false requests, causing sessions to be denied to others. See also *denial of service (DoS)*.

Synchronous DRAM (SDRAM)   RAM that is tied to the system clock.

System File Checker (SFC)   Enables you to check all the protected system files, such as krnl386.exe, and replace them with known good versions if they have become corrupted or deleted.

System Restore   A Windows XP service that runs in the background and allows the user to restore the operating system to a predefined point in time.

system utilities   Small programs that configure the operating system.

T

tablet   A portable PC that can be folded back on the keyboard or, more commonly, has no moving parts and is read and handled like a piece of paper. They often use touch screen technology in place of a mouse and keyboard.

tape drive   A device used to back up data on a network server drive.

Taskbar   A utility within Microsoft Windows that graphically represents open applications, computer contents, and other information. Also provides a way to quickly access these resources.

Task Manager   Displays active applications and identifies those that are not responding so that they can be shut down.

Telecommunications Industry Association (TIA) An organization that develops standards that relate to telecommunications technologies. Together, the TIA and the Electronic Industries Association (EIA) have formalized standards, such as EIA/TIA-232, for the electrical characteristics of data transmission.

Telnet   A remote-access application that provides remote terminal access between hosts on a network. As a troubleshooting tool, Telnet can verify the application layer software between source and destination stations. This is the most complete test mechanism available for the OSI reference model.

thermal compound   A substance that increases thermal conductivity between the surface of two of more objects.

thermal paper   Chemically treated paper with a waxy quality. It becomes black when heated. Most thermal printer print heads are the width of the paper. The paper is supplied in the form of a roll.

thermal printer   A printer that marks special thermal paper by applying heat to areas of the paper that are to be darkened to represent characters.

thicknet   Coaxial cable that was used in older networks and operated at 10 Mbps with a maximum length of 500 meters. Also called 10BASE5.

thinnet   Coaxial cable that was used in older networks and operated at 10 Mbps with a maximum length of 185 meters. Also called 10BASE2.

three-claw part retriever   A tool used to retrieve and manipulate small parts.

time management   The act of organizing time efficiently in order to increase productivity.

Token Ring network   Uses a ring topology and a token-passing methodology to create collision-free data transmission.

toner   Powder-type ink used in laser printers and photocopiers to form text and images on printer paper.

topology   The actual physical layout of a network. Or, in the case of a logical topology, the signal or data flows in a network.

torx screwdriver   A tool used to tighten or loosen screws that have a star-shaped depression on the top, a feature that is mainly found on laptop screws.

touchpad   A pressure-sensitive input pad that controls the cursor.

touch screen   An interactive LCD or CRT monitor that detects when something is pressed on it.

tracert   A Windows utility that traces the route that a packet takes from source computer to destination host.

track   A complete circle around a hard-drive platter made up of groups of 512-byte sectors.

trackball   A ball that is rotated to control the cursor.

trackpoint   An input stick that controls the cursor.

Transmission Control Protocol (TCP)   The primary Internet protocol for delivering data. TCP includes facilities for end-to-end connection establishment, error detection and recovery, and metering the rate of data flow into the network. Many standard applications, such as e-mail, web browsers, file transfer, and Telnet, depend on the services of TCP.

Transmission Control Protocol/Internet Protocol (TCP/IP)   The common name for the suite of protocols developed by the U.S. Department of Defense (DoD) in the 1970s to support the construction of worldwide internetworks. TCP and IP are the two best-known protocols in the suite.

transport layer   Layer 4 of the Open Systems Interconnection (OSI) reference model. This layer is responsible for reliable network communication between end nodes. The transport layer provides mechanisms for the establishment, maintenance, and termination of virtual circuits; transport fault detection and recovery; and information flow control. Corresponds to the transmission control layer of the Systems Network Architecture (SNA) model. The OSI reference model includes the application layer, presentation layer, session layer, transport layer, network layer, data link layer, and physical layer.

transport layer protocols   Manage the flow of data and perform error checking and correction functions.

Trojan horse   A program that appears harmless but actually contains malicious software.

troubleshooting   A systematic approach to locating the cause of a fault in a computer system.

tweezers   A tool used to retrieve and manipulate small parts.

twisted pair   A pair of insulated wires wrapped together in a regular spiral pattern to control the effects of electrical noise. The pairs can be shielded or unshielded. Twisted pair is common in telephony applications and data networks. Category 3, Category 5, Category 5e, and Category 6 twisted-pair cables all contain four twisted pairs in a common jacket.

two-factor security   Access is granted only after two forms of identification have been authenticated. One is usually a PIN or password, and the other is usually a physical object such as a fingerprint, ATM card, or smart card.

U

unattended installation   A custom installation of an operating system with minimal user intervention. Windows performs unattended installations by using an answer file called unattend.txt.

Uninterruptible Power Supply (UPS)   A device that maintains a continuous supply of electric power to connected equipment by supplying power from a separate source when utility power is unavailable.

universal bay status indicator LED   A light that shows that a device is installed in the laptop bay.

Universal Serial Bus (USB)   An external serial bus interface standard for the connection of multiple peripheral devices. USB can connect up to 127 USB devices at transfer rates of up to 480 Mbps and can provide DC power to connected devices.

Universal Serial Bus (USB) cable   An external cable that connects the USB port on the computer to a peripheral device.

Universal Serial Bus (USB) port   An external, hot-swappable, bidirectional connection for USB cables connecting to peripheral devices.

UNIX   An operating system that is used primarily to run and maintain computer networks.

unshielded twisted pair (UTP) A four-pair wire medium used in a variety of networks. UTP is rated in categories, with higher categories providing the best performance and highest bandwidth. The most popular categories are Category 3, Category 5, Category 5e, Category 6, and Category 6A.

Upgrade Advisor Microsoft's tool to advise customers on what hardware is compatible with an OS. It is used to determine whether an OS upgrade will be successful.

User Datagram Protocol (UDP) A connectionless service for delivery of data with less overhead than TCP and designed for speed. Network management applications, network file systems, and simple file transport use UDP.

user interface The part of the operating system that allows the user to communicate with the computer. User interfaces can provide a command-line interface (text) or graphical user interface (GUI).

user profile A specific setting for the user who is logged in to the computer.

V

ventilation A series of vents that allow hot air to be expelled from the interior of the device.

very high data rate DSL (VDSL) Broadband data transfer capable of bandwidths of 13 Mbps to 52 Mbps.

video accelerator card An integrated circuit board that contains a processor and memory to increase the speed of video graphics. Video accelerator cards are primarily used for 3D and gaming applications.

video adapter card An integrated circuit board that stores digital data in VRAM and converts it to analog data.

video graphics array (VGA) Supplies analog video to an analog monitor. The connector is a 15-pin D-subtype connector.

video memory Dedicated random-access memory on a video graphics adapter (video RAM or VRAM). Also, an area of the system RAM shared with the CPU.

video surveillance equipment Used to record images and sound to monitor activity.

virtual Something that is conceptual rather than physical.

virtual memory Memory created and controlled by the operating system by manipulating free hard-disk space to mimic more RAM than is actually installed in the system.

virtual private network (VPN) An encryption system that protects data as it travels, or tunnels, over the Internet or another unsecured public network.

virtual real mode Creates a virtual copy of RAM that gives applications the impression that they have direct access to RAM.

virus In computer terms, a malicious piece of software or code that can copy itself and infect a computer without the user's knowledge or permission. Some viruses are benign and do not adversely affect a computer, whereas others can damage or delete operating system and data files.

virus protection software Compares files on a computer to known viruses and watches the behavior of software to stop virus-like actions.

virus scan A utility that checks all hard drives and memory for viruses.

Voice over IP (VoIP) A method to transmit telephone calls over the Internet using packet-switched technology.

volatile memory   Computer memory that requires power to maintain the stored information.

voltage (V)   A force that creates a current by moving electrons. Electromotive force or potential difference expressed in volts.

volume control   A button that adjusts audio output.

W

warm boot   Restarting a computer that is already turned on without first turning it off.

What You See Is What You Get (WYSIWYG)   Printer output that matches what the user sees onscreen.

wide-area network (WAN)   A data communications network that serves users across a broad geographic area and often uses transmission devices provided by common carriers. Frame Relay, SMDS, and X.25 are examples of WANs.

Wi-Fi   A brand originally licensed by the Wi-Fi Alliance to define the embedded technology of a wireless network. Based on the IEEE 802.11 specifications.

Wi-Fi Protected Access (WPA)   A security standard for Wi-Fi wireless technology. Provides better encryption and authentication than the earlier WEP system.

Wi-Fi Protected Access 2 (WPA2)   Wireless encryption that uses 128-bit AES block ciphering to encrypt data. WPA2 can be enabled in two versions: Personal (password authentication) and Enterprise (server authentication). It is not backward compatible with WEP.

Windows Explorer   A Windows utility that graphically represents the file-management structure.

Windows XP Firewall   A local firewall integrated into Windows XP, Windows Vista, and Windows 7. It inspects packets entering the PC.

wire cutters   A tool used to strip and cut wires.

Wired Equivalent Privacy (WEP)   A first-generation security standard for wireless technology.

wireless access point (AP)   See *access point*.

wireless connection   A connection to a network using radio signals, infrared technology (laser), or satellite transmissions.

wireless indicator LED   A light that shows activity of the wireless network connection.

wireless LAN (WLAN)   A network that uses radio signals instead of cables to connect computers to access points and wireless routers.

wireless NIC   An expansion card that enables a computer to connect to a wireless modem using RF signals.

Wireless Transport Layer Security (WTLS)   A layer that provides security for mobile devices that use Wireless Application Protocol (WAP).

workgroup   A collection of workstations and servers on a LAN that are designed to communicate and exchange data with one another.

workstation ergonomics   Efficient arrangement of equipment and supplies to increase productivity and reduce the risk of injury.

worm   A program that copies itself and spreads exponentially, consuming bandwidth and filling hard drives.

Z

zero insertion force (ZIF) socket   A chip socket that permits the insertion and removal of a chip without using tools or force. This is common for delicate chips such as a CPU.

zombie   A computer that has been commandeered by hackers and unwillingly launches attacks against networks and servers.

Index

J-K

X-Y-Z